AMERICAN FILM CYCLES

**Recent Titles in
Bibliographies and Indexes in the Performing Arts**

Lighting Design on Broadway: Designers and Their Credits, 1915–1990
Bobbi Owen

Scenic Design on Broadway: Designers and Their Credits, 1915–1990
Bobbi Owen

The Hispanic Image on the Silver Screen: An Interpretive Filmography from Silents into Sound, 1898–1935
Alfred Charles Richard, Jr.

A Guide to Silent Westerns
Larry Langman

Censorship and Hollywood's Hispanic Image: An Interpretive Filmography, 1936–1955
Alfred Charles Richard, Jr.

A Guide to American Silent Crime Films
Larry Langman and Daniel Finn

Contemporary Hollywood's Negative Hispanic Image: An Interpretive Filmography, 1956–1993
Alfred Charles Richard, Jr.

Theatre at Stratford-upon-Avon, First Supplement: A Catalogue-Index to Productions of the Royal Shakespeare Company, 1979–1993
Michael Mullin

A Guide to American Crime Films of the Thirties
Larry Langman and Daniel Finn

An Index to Short and Feature Film Reviews in the Moving Picture World: The Early Years, 1907–1915
Annette M. D'Agostino, compiler

A Guide to American Crime Films of the Forties and Fifties
Larry Langman and Daniel Finn

Theatrical Design in the Twentieth Century: An Index to Photographic Reproductions of Scenic Designs
W. Patrick Atkinson

AMERICAN FILM CYCLES
The Silent Era

ଓ

LARRY LANGMAN

Bibliographies and Indexes in the Performing Arts, Number 22

Greenwood Press
Westport, Connecticut • London

Library of Congress Cataloging-in-Publication Data

Langman, Larry.
    American film cycles : the silent era / Larry Langman.
      p. cm.—(Bibliographies and indexes in the performing arts,
  ISSN 0742–6933 ; no. 22)
    Includes bibliographical references and index.
    ISBN 0–313–30657–5 (alk. paper)
    1. Silent films—Catalogs. I. Title. II. Series.
PN1995.75.L37   1998
016.79143'75—dc21   97–53128

British Library Cataloguing in Publication Data is available.

Copyright © 1998 by Larry Langman

All rights reserved. No portion of this book may be
reproduced, by any process or technique, without the
express written consent of the publisher.

Library of Congress Catalog Card Number: 97–53128
ISBN: 0–313–30657–5
ISSN: 0742–6933

First published in 1998

Greenwood Press, 88 Post Road West, Westport, CT 06881
An imprint of Greenwood Publishing Group, Inc.

Printed in the United States of America

The paper used in this book complies with the
Permanent Paper Standard issued by the National
Information Standards Organization (Z39.48–1984).

10 9 8 7 6 5 4 3 2 1

The motion picture, although quite an art in its present state, is still in its infancy. . . . Fearing that an adult type of photoplay might be 'over the heads' of the average audience, too many producers have made pictures so silly, so puerile that a good percentage of the public is cynical in its attitude toward the screen.

                      Milton Sills in *The Truth About Movies* (1926)

Contents

Preface xi

Introduction xiii

CYCLES

Abandoned Spouse 1

Alcoholism 11

Amnesia 23

Avenging Spouse 33

Backstage 43

Battered Women 53

Biographies 63

Black Hand 73

Burglary 81

Capital Punishment 91

Capital vs. Labor 101

Childbirth 113

Circumstantial Evidence	121
Circus	129
City vs. Country	139
Class Distinction	149
Courtroom	159
Cross Dressing	169
Detectives	179
Divorce	189
Drugs	199
Eugenics	211
Gangs and Gangsters	219
Greenwich Village	231
Jungle	241
Mythical Kingdoms	251
Patriotism	263
Political Corruption	275
Prejudice	285
Prostitution	297
Red Scare	307
Seduction and Abandonment	319
Slums	333
Vampires	345

White Slavery	355
Women's Rights	363
Bibliography	371
Name Index	373
Title Index	387

Preface

American Film Cycles: The Silent Era discusses more than one thousand silent dramas and comedies released from before 1900 through 1929, all of which help to develop the dozens of cycles that have dominated the silent screen for three decades.

The book focuses on both short works and feature-length films, all of which are generally arranged chronologically under specific chapters. Each entry lists the title, year of release, director and original source, if provided by the film. The major players are often included within the plot summary and analysis. Remakes and films with alternate titles are noted as such. If the plot of a remake is similar to that of the original, the remake is given less space.

Historical sources sometimes fail to list the director or cast members. Where more recent published references have corrected these omissions, the corrections have been added to the text. On occasion, a player's name is spelled differently from one film to another. As a general rule, we have kept the spelling of names uniform so that readers will not falsely assume that a different spelling implies another player.

The length of a film entry does not necessarily reflect upon the work's artistic quality. A particular aspect of a low-budget, routine drama may have a special interest that lends itself to greater analysis and discussion. Also, the circumstances under which a film was made or how it was accepted upon its release may be of particular concern. These points were taken into account in presenting the entries.

Unfortunately, because of limitations of space and the general scope of the work, certain genres have been omitted. Serials, series and documentaries, many of each category no doubt of particular interest to the general reader, will have to be sought elsewhere. Several detailed and comprehensive studies of these genres are readily available. In addition, the Name Index includes the major players and all the directors, but not the original authors.

The author hopes that the reader will find the individual introductions to each chapter helpful, informative and entertaining.

Several persons have contributed to the final manuscript and deserve recognition. The author wishes to thank Shoshana Kaufman, Coordinator of Information Services at Queens College, Flushing, New York, and Lisa Flanzraich of the Reference Department at Queens College Library, for the use of various library materials; and David and Spencer Fisher for their editorial suggestions.

Larry Langman

Introduction

Early American silent films reflected the beginning of American civilization. Hollywood later, during its golden silent period of the twenties, produced works of beauty, irony, affirmation, and despair. The films were also able to capture the violence and turmoil of the twentieth century in a similar way that American literature did. The parallels between American films and literature are reminiscent of the similarities between American films and American history.

American Film Cycles: The Silent Era examines forty cycles and more than one thousand silent films to discern how the screen reflected contemporary social, political and national trends during the silent years. The period has been arbitrarily divided into the early silent years (1900-1919), with films of one or two reels dominating for the first fifteen years, and the later silent period (1920-1929), known as the Golden Age of the Silents, in which "feature length" films dominated. The twenties witnessed a revolution in communications, the telephone, radio, and especially film. The decade all but unseated camp meetings and political rallies as the primary mass entertainment for Americans. By the mid-twenties, every major city in the country had large movie houses which could seat thousands of moviegoers. And by the end of the decade, weekly attendance soared to 90 million.

Many early dramas, like *The Christmas Burglars* (1908), *The Sealed Door* (1909) and *His Last Burglary* (1910), from the fecund imagination of pioneering director David Wark Griffith, were both sentimental and overly romantic; his characters and bucolic settings often resembled Norman Rockwell's mythic paintings of an ideal America. Griffith's piercing and memorable visual images come to us like long-buried artifacts of the everyday. The more we study his best work – especially his films about America – the more we tend to overlook their shortcomings, even delight in them, because they tell us about a time of which we lack clear knowledge.

The slum cycle depicted the wretched of urban slum life in such dramas as *A Prince in a Pawnshop* (1916) and *The Little Liar* (1916). Meanwhile, films like *Conscience* (1913) and *Prohibition* (1915) explored the problems of drug and alcohol addiction. The former took us into haunts where opium, cocaine and morphine (the drugs of choice during these years) dominated the lives of some New York City inhabitants, and the latter served as a rallying cry for contemporary anti-drinking organizations. *The High Road* (1915) reminded us of the real-life Triangle shirtwaist factory fire that occurred in New York City in 1911, resulting in the deaths of many workers, and *Those Who Toil* (1916) examined the conflicts between capital and labor. Some dramas portrayed impoverished immigrants undergoing experiences of unrelenting heartache and disappointment. They only intensified the disparity between the opportunity these newcomers expected to find and the exploitation and poverty they actually encountered. Many of these dramas were acerbic critiques of contemporary society, politics and manners that subverted the conventions of mainstream "feel-good" movies.

The cycles about divorce, the courtroom and political corruption often depended on newspaper headlines and stories, with sensational trials a particularly favorite topic which motivated audiences to flock to their local theaters. *The Governor's Boss* (1915) concerned the real-life impeachment of ex-Governor Sulzer of New York State. *The People vs. John Doe* (1916), an attack on capital punishment in cases of circumstantial evidence, was based chiefly on the celebrated Stielow case of the period. *Should She Obey?* (1917) showed important political figures and state officials from Nevada and Illinois commenting upon such issues as the rising divorce rate and "poisoned marriages." *The Caillaux Case* (1918), set during World War I, was based on an actual contemporary trial. Films dealing with political corruption exposed various social and political ills – child labor abuse in *The White Terror* (1915), corrupt lobbyists in *The Man From Oregon* (1915), voting fraud in *The Human Orchid* (1916) and police corruption in *A Son of Erin* (1916). In addition, several features reminded the public about the close ties between politics and the underworld. If we are a country of cynics, as some social critics have assumed, then the above films certainly reflected society's bedrock assumptions – money is everything, cops are crooked, and politicians cannot be trusted.

The mythical kingdom cycle, which offered such films as *A Son of the Immortals* (1916) and *The Gilded Cage* (1916), hinted at the promise of democracy, and *His Majesty, the American* (1919), starring Douglas Fairbanks, carved out its own niche with the public, as did such South Sea island adventures as *Aloha Oe* (1915) and *The Island of Desire* (1917). Western screen heroes like William S. Hart, Tom Mix and Buck Jones occasionally abandoned the prairie and set their escapist tales in mythical lands. Novels, stories and stage plays supplied the film studios with plenty of scripts and built-in audiences eager to see how the movie world treated their favorite narratives. Specific political and social problems received equal and often sensational treatment. The capital punishment cycle featured *Capital Punishment* (1915) and *The Public Defender* (1917). True to the naïve idealism of the early silents, these dramas usually cast their lot with those who were opposed to the death sentence. *The Wall Between* (1916) and *A Daughter of the Poor* (1917), films about class distinction, usually sided with the working class. Prejudice against the Native American and the Mexican was explored in such early social dramas as *The Justice of the Redskin*

(1908) and *The Mexican* (1914), respectively. Several dramas like *The Supreme Sacrifice* (1916) treated prostitutes as evil characters almost beyond redemption, while other films, like *The Scarlet Woman* (1916), tended to regard them sympathetically, often suggesting external causes, such as economic, social or political failings, for their fall from grace.

American film studios exploited the Red Scare of 1919-1920 for various plots, ranging from drama to comedy. Although most of these films were based on fiction, they served to reinforce in the moviegoer his or her own perceptions of the Communists, Bolsheviks and general radicals. Incidents of bomb throwing appeared on screen even earlier than the years of the Red Scare, thereby setting the tone for the cycle. In *The Bomb Throwers* (1915), for example, local Communists threaten the life and family of an honest district attorney. *Bolshevism on Trial* (1919), based on Thomas Dixon's 1909 novel, *Comrades*, satirized Upton Sinclair's real-life social experiment in New Jersey. Several dramas, such as the influential *Traffic in Souls* (1913) and *White Slaver* (1914), exposed the horrifying practice of white slavery in the nation, while others, such as *The Inside of the White Slave Traffic* (1913), bordered on blatant sensationalism. The difficult struggle for women's rights was captured in a host of early silent dramas. A daughter who inherits control of her father's bank battles against male opposition and prejudice when she decides to run for mayor in *The Fight* (1915). *One Law for Both* (1917) examined the discrepancy in treatment between men and women. In *A Doll's House* (1917), an otherwise submissive wife, finally aware of her husband's selfishness, walks out on him and her family. Many of these films were designed to stir their audiences into discussing the controversies as they left the theater.

A handful of cycles presented a dilemma for the movie studios. For example, films about mythical kingdoms forced the studios to side with either royalty or the rebellious rabble struggling to lift the yoke of oppression from their class. The movie companies solved the problem by overthrowing those who proved cruel and despotic (in the style of the American Revolution) and installing in their place democratic leaders chosen by the people (again in emulation of the United States). The uprising and revolution cycle was also troubling for the moguls, who generally believed in and supported the status quo and did not look with favor upon the unions. They resolved this conflict by again seeing to it that dictators, and especially Bolsheviks, were deposed and the masses took control of their own destiny – with the help of an American adventurer, as in *The Americano* (1917). Caught in the middle of a revolution in a fictitious South American country, American mining engineer Douglas Fairbanks, after being arrested, rescues the deposed leader from prison and restores him to his former executive position. In the comedy, *Bullin' the Bullsheviki* (1919), a young American woman journeys to Russia to wipe out Bolshevism.

In addition, these early cycles of films often conjured up both true and fanciful tales of quintessential American heroes and heroines who embodied a firm moral code, along with deeply vibrant ideas about good and evil. Unfortunately, the world that molded and valued that code has virtually vanished. Perhaps this survey of films and the times in which they were released may inspire us to pay tribute to those who bestowed upon us so rich a heritage.

Other films are closer akin to genres than cycles. The Civil War film during the early silent years tended to focus on particular famous battles, locales and important figures of the period – *In the Shenandoah Valley* (1908), *Sheridan's Ride*, *Escape From Andersonville* (1909). In addition, several films were adapted from well-known stage dramas, as were *The Heart of Maryland* (1915) and *Secret Service* (1919). Various studios produced these features, with the major companies, Biograph and Selig, dominating. Both had been making historical dramas for several years. Those released from about 1908 through 1913, however, were chiefly one- or two-reelers, especially D. W. Griffith's Civil War cycle. The pioneer director turned out eleven one- and two-reel dramas that used the war as background during his tenure with the Biograph studio. For the first time since the American Revolution, the loyalties of the country's citizens were tested during the war and were depicted in such dramas as *The Southerners* (1914) and *The Last Rebel* (1918). These films depicted troubled lovers who were separated by the Mason-Dixon Line. Proud Southern fathers disowned their daughters who married Northerners, as in *The Pride of the South* (1913). The Civil War cycle was not without its romantic dramas, as represented by *May Blossom* (1915) and *The Little Yank* (1917).

By the 1920s, the Civil War film fell out of favor – as did films about World War I. The pain, suffering and staggering casualties of The Great War shocked the nation – as well as the world. Releases concerning the War Between the States faced cuts in production values and fell to a trickle. Some films, like *Barbara Frietchie* (1924), were remakes of earlier versions. Others repeated the earlier practice of adapting popular stage plays, as with *The Heart of Maryland* (1927), another remake of an earlier drama. Others, like *Court Martial* (1928), were strictly action dramas that had very little to do with the burning issues of the war itself. The portrayal of President Abraham Lincoln returned in *The Highest Law* (1921), this time as hero as well as mythical figure with a heart, when he helps commute a young soldier's sentence of death in Griffith's *Abraham Lincoln* (1925). *Morgan's Last Raid* (1929), starring cowboy star Tim McCoy, returned to the earlier concept of recounting actual incidents and persons, although these films were more generous with their fictional elements than with their facts. Finally, several entertaining Civil War comedies were released during the second half of the decade, one with Raymond Griffith titled *Hands Up* (1926), and another with screen comic Buster Keaton, who came out with a surprising hit comedy, *The General* (1927), based on a true incident, and which has become a classic of the silent screen.

Films about the Canadian Northwest were also popular. Originally called the Royal Canadian Mounted Police, the organization was founded in 1873 to establish law and order to the Canadian West and to keep the peace among the various tribes. Its present name, the Northwest Mounted Police, was established in 1920. The constabulary earned its more romantic reputation following its daring exploits as it pursued its lawbreakers across the vast country. Its members are popularly known as Mounties. Like the frontier in many westerns, the Canadian Northwest often served as metaphor. The rugged land, which reflected the character of its people, promised its inhabitants a chance to start a new life, regardless of their questionable past, as in *Thou Shalt Not* (1914). Another similarity to the traditional western was the introduction of violence into the plots, especially murder. *In Defiance of the Law* (1914) focused on intrigue and murder. The cycle offered several interesting and entertaining entries, although most of the films, like films in general, suffered from familiar plot gimmicks, stereotyped characters and predictable endings. The stalwart Mountie's attributes were so similar to that of the cowboy hero that often the same actors were used in both settings. Tom Mix, William S. Hart and Will Jeffries were some popular western heroes who portrayed Mounties. The treacherous half-breed became a staple of Canadian Northwest films as early as 1909 in *The Cattle Thieves* and other dramas, including *From Out of the Big Snows* (1915). However, W. S. Hart in *The Dawn Maker* (1916) reversed this perception and made his half-breed hero sympathetic, somewhat controversial for the period.

American films about Canada's Northwest grew in popularity and increased in number during the twenties. Evidently, the studios that were turning out these outdoor action dramas tapped into a deep-seated interest among movie audiences. Most of the films were of low-budget quality and featured either unknown, young players or once-famous stars now suffering from a fading career. The hackneyed plots were similar to those used by conventional westerns. Other similarities extended to the minor players, the screenwriters, the heroines and many of the other main players. Films like *Bring Him In* (1921) continued to portray the half-breed as a villainous character. Popular cowboy players Ken Maynard, William Russell, Leo Maloney and William Desmond often portrayed Mounties who had to battle smugglers, bank robbers, rum runners and the harsh elements. James Oliver Curwood, one of the most popular writers of these outdoor action tales, had many of his stories adapted for the screen, including *The Broken Silence* (1922), *God's Country and the Law* (1922) and *The Flaming Forest* (1926). As these films grew in number and popularity, they also broadened in plots, often including stories without the presence of the otherwise ubiquitous Mountie. Despite their conventional plots and characters and other shortcomings, they at least offered a different environment to their audiences. When filmed with some imagination, they captured the ruggedness of the northern wilderness and the overall splendor of nature.

Fighting journalists made their screen appearance early during the silent era. They usually emerged from society as spoiled, bored sons and daughters of parents who strongly disapproved of their offsprings' embarrassing and pointless escapades. These misadventures occasionally led to the parents' disowning their wayward children, forcing them to fend for themselves. Some entered the world of journalism for a lark, others to flirt with a member of the opposite sex who has caught their fancy, and still others for purely idealistic reasons, as in the case of Hobart Henley in *The White Terror* (1915). Some amateur journalists took their crusading seriously, delving into social ills, corrupt politicians, or greedy businessmen bilking the public. George Larkin in *The Fringe of Society* (1917), for example, exposed crooked politicians. Occasionally, their investigations exposed corrupt members of their own class, or, more startlingly, members of their own family, as Carlyle Blackwell did in *The Clarion* (1916). A reporter was forced to protect the rights of an Italian immigrant in *One More American* (1918). Some of these dramas tell more about the social and political ills of society than they reveal about the world of journalism. And perhaps that was the general purpose of those who wrote, directed and produced these early silent films.

Crusading journalists in films of the twenties continued to fight injustice, corruption and all the conditions their predecessors attacked a decade earlier. One interesting twist concerned several westerns, which had their heroes defending the freedom of the press – either peripherally or directly, as they became involved in taking over the town press. Some studios tried blending journalism and politics in their films as early as 1913, with such comedy dramas as *A Campaign Manageress* – with mixed results, and again in the twenties, with the social drama, *The Passionate Pilgrim* (1921), which attacked corrupt elected officials. George Larkin in *Midnight Secrets* (1924) exposed other examples of political corruption. Several newspaper dramas, such as *The Passionate Pilgrim* and *Freedom of the Press* (1928) and *Protection* (1929), depicted actual incidents in which bootleggers and gang leaders either manipulated the press or physically took over the operations of the paper. Most newspaper films had urban settings – probably to take advantage of nightclub backgrounds, plots about large-scale corruption and a variety of criminal types. However, popular cowboy stars made their contributions to the field of journalism by way of their horse, fists and six-shooters. Hoot Gibson, in *Red Courage* (1921), for example, bought a newspaper to fight local corruption. Jack Hoxie in *Grinning Guns* (1927) used the press to intimidate local lawbreakers to leave town. Tim McCoy, as Texas Ranger in *Riders of the Dark* (1928), protected the freedom of the press in a frontier town. Perhaps the plots and themes were not as sophisticated as those of their urban cousins, but at least their films guaranteed more action.

Historical films were always a popular genre for American audiences. The filmmakers gave us a sweep of a segment of history. Early silent films about historical events and people drew from world history. *The Bugler of Algiers* (1914) was set in the Algerian-French Wars of 1830-1847; *The Dawn of Freedom* (1910) during the Cuban War of Independence; *The Standard Bearer* (1908) during the Franco-Prussian War (1870-1871); and *Foreign Devils* (1928) during the Boxer Rebellion. However, American film studios focused chiefly on American history and American heroes. The most popular subject was the American Civil War, followed by the nation's War of Independence. Many of these works were short, usually one- or two-reelers, ranging in time from fifteen to thirty minutes. But what they lacked in depth or details they made up for in passion and action. George Washington (*Washington at Valley Forge*), Nathan Hale, Paul Revere, Abraham Lincoln, Generals Grant and Lee, all come alive on the big screen as they grapple with the country's problems of peace and war. Contemporary critics often were amazed at the accuracy of the reenactments of incidents, battles, costume and settings. Later critics were quick to attack the excessive patriotism, intolerance and insensitivity of the early filmmakers. Whatever the final assessment of these early films, they were sure to prove interesting and informative as social and political documents of the time in which they were made.

Historical films during the twenties took three different paths. One led to the release of similarly plotted and thematically familiar works as those of the previous decade, such as American-oriented subjects (*The Last of the Mohicans*) and foreign topics (*Stranger Than Death*, about India's savage nineteenth-century mutiny). The second path, least traveled, led to more innovative works, built around complex characters and plots, such as D. W. Griffith's *Orphans of the Storm*, which balanced its sympathetic portrayal of the masses in one scene with their condemnation in another when they act as a mob. He then treated the aristocrats in the same manner, both as brutal and vicious in some scenes and as kind and generous in others. The third path led to many releases that reverted to the conventional patriotism and glorification of early America, in such films as *Cardigan* (1922) and *The Covered Wagon* (1923). Meanwhile, other films like *The Rough Riders* (1927) and *Foreign Devils* (1928) almost unabashedly promoted a pro-imperialistic stance. They virtually foreshadowed the dark course of world history and human suffering that shaped the next two decades.

The romance and adventure of the South Sea islands came early to the history of motion pictures. And like the castaway in its many tales, the genre struggled to survive many changes. The island cycle can be traced to various literary sources and proved to be more than resilient. It borrowed from other movie types like the spy, war and western dramas while tossing in a dash of its own original ingredients. The South Sea island film had its catalog of unique characteristics. Plot contrivances – threatening volcanoes, shipwrecks, savage attacks by hostile tribes and dramatic rescues – played a significant role in early island films, portraying conflicts between primitive and Western cultures. One of the earliest films to include a volcano sequence was *Volcanoes of Java*, a one-reel documentary released in 1909. Other films depicted clashes between American troops and Spanish soldiers or Filipinos during the Spanish-American War or the Philippine Insurrection. Other elements in the genre soon followed. Scheming South Sea traders, pirates, hidden maps and buried treasure all played roles. But the greatest threat to the islands came from greedy and depraved white opportunists who schemed to take advantage of the innocent and gullible natives. Island films, with their lazy lagoons, balmy climate and scantily clad natives, were natural receptacles for introducing suggestions of nudity.

Interest in the South Seas region grew during the 1920s, especially in song and story. While some Americans read tales of faraway islands and others plucked at ukuleles, Hollywood surged forward with its production of island films. Gone were most of the plots set in the Philippines, only to be replaced with other similarly romantic places and adventures. Many of these films suggested a common thread – a search for paradise – whether it was a greedy trader pursuing riches, and embittered captain seeking to escape his past, or a disillusioned soul groping for love or happiness. The films retained most of the conventions of the genre while exploring others. Characters became more complex, atmospheric settings improved and more mature themes emerged. Shipwrecks continued to propel main characters into perilous and romantic situations, as in *The Isle of Destiny* (1920). Frank Mayo in *The Shark Master* (1921) learned about the exotic powers of the South Sea islands and their effects on those who came from more "civilized" societies. The cannibal continued to pose a threat in the island films of the 1920s. The volcano continued to imperil natives and visitors alike in a string of action dramas, including *A Virgin Paradise* (1921). Films about lost or buried treasure played a lesser role in island films during the twenties. Various forms of violence periodically invaded the placid island life. Provocative suggestions of nudity continued to show up in several films, including *God's Gold* (1921), which suggested that heroine Audrey Chapman was swimming nude; *Lost and Found on a South Sea Island* (1923), in which a young woman was apparently bathing nude in a picturesque pond; and a sequence in *Hula* (1927) that suggested Clara Bow was swimming with very little covering her upper body.

The climate of the tropical islands was not the only element that helped to raise temperatures in movie theaters. Aside from these conventions, the island films of the twenties introduced or fine-tuned other devices. Underwater sequences began to appear regularly. Generally superior camera work, exotic settings and effective atmosphere lifted the island films of the twenties to a higher artistic level. *Lost and Found on a South Sea Island*, directed by Raoul Walsh, excelled in its atmospheric setting. *Where the Pavement Ends* (1923), directed by Rex Ingram, provided picturesque settings and poetic photography. *Aloma of the South Seas* (1926), directed by Maurice Tourneur, was singled out for its visual beauty. *Black Paradise* (1926) offered an unusually exotic setting. *White Shadows in the South Seas* (1928), directed by W. S. Van Dyke, took full advantage of its visual settings, offering many striking and unforgettable island vistas. Van Dyke's film depicted the exploitation of natives. His drama, *The Pagan* (1929), continued to underscore the contrast between the simple and kindly native and the hypocritical brutality of a white trader, suggested that civilized man's main purpose in the South Seas was to corrupt and exploit unsophisticated islanders. The Pacific Ocean not only lapped the island beaches with its gentle waves, it washed ashore some of the worst reprobates to ever sail the South Seas.

One of the more significant and controversial themes, introduced a decade earlier and continued into the 1920s, dealt with relationships between different races. In Julia Crawford Ivers's *The White Flower* (1923), Edmund Lowe, a young American, fell in love with Betty Compson, the product of an American father and a native mother. In Rex Ingram's *Where the Pavement Ends* (1923) the love between Ramön Navarro, a dark-skinned islander, and Alice Terry, the daughter of a European missionary, resulted in tragedy. Although these films were rare, they tore down, if only temporarily, some of these social taboos. Many of the entries may have depicted affairs between whites and natives, but they almost never ended in marriage. Just as the desire for treasure often echoed the illusory nature of the search for paradise, these films, reflecting a longing for love and romance, touched upon another search for paradise – and also suggested the fragile and elusive nature of the quest.

During the early silent period, American studios released numerous mountain dramas whose subjects dealt with feuds, moonshining, the fierce independence of mountain people, their general resistance to change, and a suspicion of strangers – especially city folks, revenue agents, and other government officers. The American mountain films, with these distinct characteristics, differed greatly from the German mountain film, a distinctly national genre, which became popular in that country during the twenties. The German films, with their inflated plots and often phony sentiment, glorified the beauties of nature, depicted the struggle of devoted climbers to triumph over the near inaccessibility of the mountains, and suggested a sense of heroic idealism. American films, on the other hand, depicted the austere and rugged mountains as a metaphor for the harsh, backward and violent lives of those who lived there.

Rural silent films usually embraced the conventional images of lives whose purity and simplicity contrasted sharply with the corrupt and artificial lifestyles of the city. The people are simple but not stupid, chiefly uneducated but not unintelligent, poor but not wanting of most necessities. Country surroundings symbolized cleanliness and purity. Audiences, it seemed, preferred to believe that the pastoral life generated and retained purity even if these backgrounds proved to have as much crime and immorality as urban areas. Young people in rural films frequently plan on leaving their towns and head for the big city, where they hope to realize their dreams but often meet with disappointment.

Films of resistance and revolution date back to the early silent period when movies were a fledgling entertainment industry. Sympathy often lay with the oppressed underdogs and their noble struggle for democratic ideals. Peasants at times wore quaint native costumes, while fearless guerrilla leaders fought the good cause against one-dimensional sadistic and brutal villains. The better films presented an image of ordinary people engaged in a heroic struggle against overwhelming odds. In today's more complex world we often look back with some regret at the passing of their simple, optimistic spirit and courage and moral sense of right and wrong.

Silent films occasionally depicted the women's rights movement, a subject worthy of a separate volume. The movement arose in Europe in the late 18th century. In England, Mary Wollstonecraft wrote *A Vindication of the Rights of Woman* (1792), the first major modern feminist work. In 1848 more than 100 persons held the first women's rights convention at Seneca Falls, N.Y. Led by the abolitionist Lucretia Mott and the feminist Elizabeth Cady Stanton, they demanded equal rights, including the vote and an end to the double standard. Suffrage, which became a major goal of American feminists, encountered substantial resistance, despite massive and sometimes violent campaigns. The right to vote was only granted after World War I, partly in recognition of women's contributions to the war effort. Hal Reid's drama, *Votes for Women* (1912), was the first significant film about women's suffrage. The film was quite successful and was used extensively as a propaganda vehicle by various organizations. Unfortunately, this historically important film has disappeared. Early silent films about suffragettes reflected a similar hard line, and they were treated comically, as in *Suffrage and the Man* (1912), *A Suffragette in Spite of Himself* (1912), *The Suffragette* (1913), *The Suffragette Minstrels* (1913) and *The Suffragette Battle of Nuttyville* (1914). Complete political, economic, and social equality with men remained to be achieved. American films during the twenties began to reflect those freedoms that women had fought for. Mary Alden in *A Woman's Woman* (1922) finally attains her own independence after she learns about her philandering husband's activities. Fiercely independent Claire Windsor in *Grand Larceny* (1922) rejects two husbands who try to change her. On the other hand, audiences during later silent films occasionally displayed a general resentment toward the feminist movement. For example, in dramas like *The Temptress* (26), when a subtitle, meant to express a deep philosophical thought about women being the noblest work of God, the audience response came in the form of giggles.

One of the author's goals was to illustrate the success, and sometimes the failure, of these films to capture the social and political times of their release. Hollywood inadvertently helped through its efficacy in exploiting the direct, vivid and raw. The studios succeeded in capturing many of the social and political problems of the first two decades of the century, but the later silent films often failed to address the significance of Prohibition and the rise of the gangster and the racketeer, three problems that arose during the twenties, remained unsolvable, and tore at the social fabric of many cities and the nation in general.

Abandoned Spouse

I. Husbands and Wives in Quiet Desperation

Films concerning an abandoned spouse became popular. Several appeared during the first decade and grew in numbers between the years 1915 and 1917. Whichever spouse did the fleeing and whatever the reason, these early films almost invariably came to either one of two major conclusions – the guilty party received his/her just deserts, or both parties came to a reconciliation. In *The Planter's Wife* (1908), for example, farm life proved too tedious for Claire McDowell. The wife in *An Eye for an Eye* (1909) preferred a younger lover. And a husband's excessive gambling drove his wife into the arms of another man in *The Blight of Sin* (1909). These films hinted at the disparity in men's and women's roles at home and in the workplace. Gloria Swanson in *The Prodigal Wife* (1918) abandons her family in a remote town to achieve success on stage before returning home. To some degree, these early films anticipated, if not advocated, social changes. A few plots skirted around issues like social tolerance of divorce, birth control, abortion, premarital and extramarital sex – all part of the future sexual revolution. But films like *Old Wives for New* (1918) and *Modern Husbands* (1919) that dealt with sexual freedom were often condemned by critics and civic groups. Meanwhile, audiences had to wait on the platform for the arrival of the train to transport them to women's liberation.

Sometimes the woman, driven by anger or passion, or simply a husband's neglect, financial failure or a weakness such as excessive drinking or gambling, ran off with her former lover or a lecherous stranger. In D. W. Griffith's *The Planter's Wife* (1908), for example, Claire McDowell, as the title character, grows bored with her tedious life on the farm and decides to run off with her lover, who convinces her to leave her husband and baby. Meanwhile, her more practical sister discovers the wife's intention and resolves to follow the fleeing couple. When she catches up with them, the sister, now masked and brandishing a revolver, forces the fleeing wife and mother to return home. The lover struggles with the intruder while the wife grabs the pistol. During the encounter the wife shoots her lover, who then runs off. McDowell returns to her family and is greeted by her loving husband, who is unaware of the entire escapade.

A wife is not so fortunate in the farfetched drama, *An Eye for an Eye* (1909). After marrying an older man in Italy, she agrees to elope with a young cad, who has won her love. They leave for America, with the abandoned husband swearing vengeance and following them. Once the lovers arrive in the United States, the young man grows tired of his mistress and leaves her. Meanwhile, the husband arrives and coincidentally enters a café where the male lover is seen flirting with a waitress. The couple retire to a back room, where his first love has followed him. She begins to physically attack the waitress. The lover separates them and strangles the wife. The husband and others, hearing the commotion, rush to the back room, where the husband, upon observing the tragedy, kills the male lover. He then takes his wife back to her apartment where she dies.

A husband's excessive gambling drives his already unfaithful wife further into the arms of another in *The Blight of Sin* (1909). Her lover in a letter proposes they both elope. The woman's husband has lost heavily at gambling while she remains alone with their little daughter. When he returns in the morning, he finds his wife is gone. He reads a note she left for him. Suspecting the route of the lovers, the husband and a good friend pursue the couple and find the runaways aboard a steamer. The lover-gambler, to cause a diversion, sets fire to the cargo and jumps overboard to save himself. The husband dives after his wife whom her cowardly lover has thrown into the river. The couple are rescued by a rowboat. Later, the husband begs to be forgiven for his gambling and neglect.

The second wave of the abandoned spouse cycle began in 1915. *The Sacrifice of Jonathan Gray* (1915), with Murdock MacQuarrie in the title role, proved to be a popular tearjerker. He portrays a kind-hearted country husband whose city-bred wife, Lydia Landowska, deserts him. She runs off with her little daughter to join her former lover, now a drug addict, who convinces the mother to abandon her daughter for the child's sake. Years later, MacQuarrie, now a humble cobbler, fits the wedding slippers for his daughter, who has been raised by a wealthy family. But he never tells her that he is her real father.

Burton King's drama, *The Reapers* (1916), injected religion into his abandoned spouse theme by touching upon the powers of Christian Science. John Mason, a publishing house clerk, suddenly loses the use of his legs, following a motor accident. When he is forced to earn a living by operating a newspaper stand, Clara Whipple, his frustrated and disappointed wife, abandons him and Edna, their six-year-old daughter. The wife joins her former lover, a dissolute gambler. A science healer takes an interest in Mason's misfortune and introduces him to the work of his church. The father eventually regains the use of his limbs, returns to the world of business and becomes a success. Years later, his daughter, who believes her mother is dead, marries an assistant district attorney. In the meantime, her mother's life has deteriorated physically and morally. Her lover now owns a seedy dance hall that the assistant district attorney, Edna's husband, has sworn to shut down. One evening, Mason and the district attorney visit one of the clubs and meet Mason's wife. The couple reconcile their differences, and she agrees to attend a convent to reform – after seeing her daughter for the last time.

Allen Holubar's domestic drama, *Heart Strings* (1916), is just another in the long line of familiar films about wives and mothers who abandon their families to join their lovers. In this entry, a mother competes with her own daughter for the love of a young medical student. The mother had abandoned her husband and little daughter to run off with her lover. A doctor (portrayed by director Holubar) adopted the child who, years later, is betrothed to the medical student. The youth falls temporarily into the web of the sexually attractive mother, who is unaware of her daughter's identity.

The bright lights of the romantic city lure a young wife in Ivan Abramson's trite drama, *The City of Illusion* (1916). Carleton Macy, a wealthy Southerner, marries his caretaker's daughter, Mignon Anderson. But the young bride proves unsophisticated and out of place in her husband's family home. She meets a New York lawyer, Macy's cousin, who paints a rosy picture of city life – which immediately influences Anderson. She then insists on a divorce, stating she has been unfaithful. Macy reluctantly grants her her wish, and she heads for the city, expecting the lawyer to marry her. Instead, he has married a rich woman and plans to run for district attorney. Anderson demands that he divorce his wife or she will expose him. His wife, upon hearing the entire story, offers Anderson money to leave. Meanwhile, Macy arrives at one of his cousin's political rallies and also threatens to expose the lawyer. But when all participants gather at the lawyer's home, everything is straightened out and both couples reconcile their differences.

Occasionally, the tale of abandonment uses the flashback device, as in Julius Steger's *The Law of Compensation* (1917). In this didactic drama, based on the play by Wilson Mizner, Norma Talmadge enacts a dual role – that of a daughter who desires a career as a singer and, in a long flashback, that of her own mother. The father, upon learning that his impatient, married daughter is about to leave her husband, decides to intervene. He relates a tragic story of his own failed marriage – how her mother met an unhappy end after running off with her lover, the family lawyer. Meanwhile, the father had earlier forced a signed confession from Edmund Stanley, an unscrupulous song plugger who has influenced young Talmadge to run away with him. When the father shows the confession to his daughter, she realizes how close she had come to ruining her own life. Her husband returns from a business trip, and she greets him warmly.

A hatred of small-town isolation drives Gloria Swanson to leave her husband in Arthur Hoyt's railroad drama, *The Prodigal Wife* (1918). Railway station attendant Lee Hill and Swanson, his devoted wife, live in a remote area. When their baby dies because a doctor could not reach them in time to save the child, Swanson begins to hate their lonely existence. A theatrical manager offers her a position in a show, and she seizes the opportunity. Later, after achieving success, circumstances lead her back to the railroad where, during a torrential downpour, she prevents a horrendous train wreck. Realizing how vital their work is, she rejoins her husband.

Other films show the husband doing the abandoning, often taking up with a former lover, a secretary or someone in the theater, at times used in films as a symbol for vice and immorality. In Paul Powell's backstage drama, *Bred in the Bone* (1915), for instance, an actor deserts his wife, who has recently become a mother. The couple have worked for the same traveling show. The wife, seeking her own freedom, then reluctantly leaves her little daughter on the doorstep of a Quaker family. That same year, Theda Bara, in J. Gordon Edwards's *The Galley Slave*, finds herself abandoned by her artist husband, played by Stuart Holmes.

Again in 1915, Gladys Hanson appeared as a self-sacrificing wife in a more complex drama, Theodore Marston's *The Primrose Path,* based on the 1907 play by Bayard Veiller. Hanson, as a young wife, sacrifices herself to restore to health Hal Forde, her artist husband. While in Paris for their honeymoon, Forde grows ill. Impoverished and unable to sell his paintings, the couple have no money to buy medicine. His wife gives herself to an unscrupulous art dealer to raise funds for the proper medicine. The ailing husband believes her family sent her the money. They return to the United States, where he finally achieves success. He meets an attractive young woman who is unaware of his marital status. After she meets his wife, she decides to leave her lover. The couple are finally reunited.

Francis X. Bushman learns too late about the duplicity of his wife's family in the drama, *The Great Silence* (1915). Bushman, a young mine owner, meets and falls in love with a young woman whom he marries. He then discovers that her father and brother had arranged the entire affair for the purposes of gaining control of his money. Disillusioned, he abandons his wife and returns to his more faithful mine. His wife, now all alone, realizes that she really loves Bushman. She makes the arduous journey to join him at his mine, where the couple reconcile their differences and live together in happiness.

Discontent sets into the husband of an otherwise happy Chicago couple who remain childless after several years of trying to increase their family in Harry Chandlee's drama, *The Blessed Miracle* (1915). The husband, who desperately wants a child, begins staying out late. The wife stays at home attending to her chores. A former school friend who is looking for a husband visits her and sets her goal on the husband. When he leaves suddenly for New York, the friend follows and joins him, and the two have an affair. He decides to visit Europe, but before he does, he writes to his wife, asking for a divorce. She, in turn, writes to him that she is pregnant, but he never gets the letter. He sails for Europe, while his lover returns the unopened letter to the wife. Months later, after agreeing to the divorce, the wife decides to come to New York to greet her husband upon his return. All three are staying at the same hotel, where a clerk informs the husband that his wife is very ill and is calling for him. As he leaves for her room, he meets the other woman who lures him into her room where she tries to engage him in some lovemaking. But his conscience will not let him, and he finally joins his wife who informs him of the good news. The film ends with a scene of the happy couple enjoying their life together with their three children.

Harry T. Morey portrays a family man who strays during a business trip to England in William P. S. Earle's domestic drama, *The Courage of Silence* (1917). Morey meets and falls in love with Alice Joyce, a Spanish ambassador's wife, who is unaware that he is married. Following several complications, he returns to England and elopes with Joyce. During their journey to France he finally reveals that he has a family in the United States. Disturbed by this disclosure, she leaves him and enters a convent. When his family arrives in France to find him, his two children become ill and their mother asks for a local nun to care for them. Joyce arrives and meets the family for the first time. She then sets up a reconciliation between the father and his family, without Morey's ever learning that his former lover arranged matters.

Darrel Foss leaves his provincial wife and cold-hearted deacon father in E. Mason Hopper's *Without Honor* (1917), a tale of abandonment, bigamy and desertion. He gets a job with a hardware firm through Arthur Moon, his drinking companion. Moon is a sales representative with the company. Foss soon rises to assistant manager, falls in love with Margery Wilson, the company stenographer, and marries her without telling her he is already married. A baby is born to the happy couple. Suddenly, Foss's father arrives with a law officer, charging his own son with bigamy. When Foss beseeches his wife to say they were never legally married, she agrees. He then leaves with his father. Foss is killed when he falls from a cliff. Meanwhile his second wife, carrying her child, arrives in his town and shows up at the deacon's church. The heartless father assembles a committee who seek to drive her out of the community. Moon, the salesman, makes an appearance and rescues the widow and child. Moon has always loved her, but never revealed his feelings to her.

Cecil B. DeMille's domestic drama, *Old Wives for New* (1918), tells about successful businessman Elliott Dexter, who tires of his wife of twenty years. He finds she has grown sloppy and pudgy and has lost her charm. In the north woods he meets the young and pretty Florence Vidor and falls in love with her. When he tells her he is married, she avoids his presence. Following several complications, he follows her to Europe. His wife divorces him, thereby leaving him free to seek out his new love whom he then marries. The film, based on the once-popular novel by David Graham Phillips, was considered immoral by some contemporary critics and moviegoers.

When David Butler marries Mary MacLaren, a young Swedish hired woman, his aristocratic family frowns upon his decision, in Tod Browning's simple but effective domestic drama, *The Unpainted Woman* (1919), based on a story by Sinclair Lewis. After one year, Butler, who still faces disapproval from his family and many townspeople about his marriage, starts to drink heavily. He finds small comfort in whiskey, but at least some escape. After five years and one child born to the hapless couple, relations between them grow more intolerable, with his wife finding escape only in the child, while the husband continues his drinking. After a loud confrontation between them, Butler decides to abandon his family. Meanwhile, his wife scrapes together enough money to buy a farm, which she runs successfully. Butler, reduced to poverty after wandering aimlessly, returns as a worker on the farm, where he finally fights off his addiction to drink. The pair eventually embrace after reconciling their differences.

Hard-working and faithful husband Henry B. Walthall, in Francis J. Grandon's *Modern Husbands* (1919), arrives home one evening and finds his wife (Ethel Fleming) with her lover (Neil Hardin). An altercation ensues and Walthall orders the interloper to leave. Later, when Walthall faces financial ruin, he leaves his wife. He eventually recovers financially and effects a reconciliation with his wife.

II. Marriage and the New Freedoms

The abandoned spouse cycle during the next decade varied little in plot and theme – although a drastic social upheaval was occurring in the nation. These changes were slowly incorporated into the characters' actions and dialogue (printed titles), if not directly into the plot. Outspoken advocates like Elizabeth Cady Stanton and Susan B. Anthony fought for and achieved full legal and economic equality for women, who also won the right to own property and enter the professions. By 1920, the nineteenth amendment to the Constitution granted nationwide women's suffrage. Although the bored wife in *Out of the Dust* (1920) eventually finds independence and a kind of self-fulfillment as a dance hall entertainer before returning to her husband and child, one may well ask whether she was morally right to leave them in the first place. Other films of the twenties raised similar moral questions. Was the insensitive Jack Mulhall justified in abandoning his wife in *Should a Woman Tell?* (1920) after she confesses she had been raped before their marriage? Tired married businessman Lewis Stone finds a private paradise with another woman in *Cytherea* (1924) – until her death. Only then does he return home and beg for forgiveness. Mae Busch, who thinks her marriage is failing, has an affair with another man in *The Truthful Sex* (1927), and then reconsiders returning to her husband and child. Irene Rich, the long-suffering wife in *The Honeymoon Express* (1926), finally walks out on her philandering, heavy-drinking husband and three grown children, and returns to her children with a new husband. These films of the twenties reflected the decade's extended social tolerance of premarital and extramarital sex, and emphasized that these new freedoms brought additional responsibilities.

This greater freedom of choice manifested itself – justly or unjustly – in several films. In John P. McCarthy's *Out of the Dust* (1920), for instance, the bored wife of an army captain at a frontier outpost in the Southwest decides to elope with a handsome young trapper. This occurs while her spouse is out on patrol. Leaving him and their little son behind, she takes off with her lover, whose excessive drinking soon repulses her. She leaves and decides to become an entertainer at a dance hall. Realizing how much she misses her boy, she returns to her husband and child.

When Enid Bennett, the daughter of socially prominent parents in Fred Niblo's drama, *Woman in the Suitcase* (1920), learns that her father is carrying on an affair with another woman, she determines to break up the relationship. She discovers a photo of "the other woman" in her father's luggage one day. So Bennett decides to meet the former Follies showgirl and befriend her. The two females begin going to parties and nightclubs together until Bennett schemes to be present at the apartment that her father has set up for his mistress. She puts on a drunk act for her father, who is startled by the bizarre scene. The shocked wayward husband and father finally is made aware of his responsibilities and returns to his faithful wife.

Helen Holmes Eddy suspects her husband, Hallam Cooley, is having an affair with seductress Claire Du Brey, in George L. Cox's domestic drama, *A Light Woman* (1920), based on the 1855 short story by Robert Browning. Cooley's father, disappointed in his son's romantic affair, is determined to end that relationship. He offers Du Brey ten thousand dollars to break off her relations with his son, then arranges for his son to learn the greedy nature of the woman he thinks he loves. Realizing the truth, Cooley returns to his wife and the couple are reunited. Du Brey ends up alone and without the money.

Confessing an earlier indiscretion, one that was not particularly the young woman's fault, does not always evoke sympathy. In John E. Ince's drama, *Should a Woman Tell?* (1920), Alice Lake is assaulted by John Gilbert, the nephew of her benefactress. The young woman, before she is to marry Jack Mulhall, writes him a letter telling him of her earlier experience. Somehow, he doesn't get the letter and the marriage proceeds on schedule. When she later tells him personally of the terrible incident, Mulhall walks out on her. Still later, thinking he is dead, she marries Gilbert, her seducer. Then Mulhall returns and, following a bitter fight between the two men, Gilbert is killed, leaving Mulhall and his wife to repair their marriage.

The perfidious sham wedding, employed in earlier films, is used here by the title character. Pauline Frederick portrays the daughter of a destitute musician in William Parke's drama, *The Paliser Case* (1920), based on the novel by Edgar Saltus. Albert Roscoe enters the young woman's life, resulting in his wealthy fiancée's breaking her engagement to him. Monty Paliser (Warburton Gamble), another of Frederick's admirers, engineers a phony ceremony and marries Frederick. The father, Roscoe and the bride, upon learning of the treachery, plot to kill Paliser. In an opera house, he is stabbed by an unknown assailant. Roscoe, who had earlier threatened the dead man, is quickly arrested. Frederick enters the district attorney's office and, in the presence of Roscoe, confesses to the murder. Later, the father confesses to the police that he committed the crime by using a cane sword. The father's death then exonerates his daughter and Roscoe.

William P. S. Earle's *Whispers* (1920) concerns the terrible results of scandalous rumors, especially as practiced by scandal sheets. One such sheet almost ruins the reputation of innocent young Elaine Hammerstein, who is living with her aunt. When she accepts the affections of a married man, her aunt (Ida Darling) warns her about not becoming involved with him. The niece ignores the advice, aware that her aunt wants her to marry an unattractive local dolt. The married man takes her to the opera, where his wife unexpectedly arrives with some friends. A row occurs and Hammertein goes home alone. The incident appears in a scandal sheet the following day, but without Hammerstein's name. To avoid further arguments with her aunt, she takes a train to another town, where her father runs a small newspaper. Meanwhile, the married man, who has decided to leave town to escape the fallout from the embarrassing article, takes the same train as the young woman. Following several complications, Hammerstein arrives in her father's town and meets Matt Moore, a reporter for the scandal sheet. He has been assigned to write a follow-up on his story. She convinces him of her innocence, and Moore, unhappy with his present job, accepts an offer to work on her father's paper.

Rudolph Valentino, as a famous matador, has to battle more than the bulls in this lavish but dated 1922 production of Fred Niblo's *Blood and Sand*, based on the novel by Blasco Ibanez. The "great lover," as Valentino was later called, must come to grips with deciding between his obligations to Lila Lee, his faithful wife, and his passionate desire for the seductive Nita Naldi. The film concludes with an attack on the spectacle of bullfighting. A Greek chorus-like character declares: "Poor matador, poor beast." He then points to the spectators. "But the real bull is out there," he charges. "There is the beast with ten thousand heads." Rouben Mamoulian turned out a remake in 1941, with Tyrone Power, Linda Darnell and Rita Hayworth in the leading roles.

In Wesley Ruggles' drama, *The Age of Innocence* (1924), based on the 1920 novel by Edith Wharton, Countess Ellen Olenska (Edith Roberts) leaves her bestial husband in Poland and returns to her family in New York. She learns that her cousin is about to become engaged to Elliott Dexter. A love affair soon develops between the countess and Dexter, who reluctantly marries her cousin, hoping to forget the countess. Later, the lovers meet and Dexter proposes that they run off together, but the countess, learning that Dexter's wife, her cousin, is pregnant, rejects the offer. Instead, she returns to her husband. Dexter then promises his wife that he will reform.

Lewis Stone, a tired businessman bored with his routine family existence, seeks a more idyllic life with Alma Rubens in George Fitzmaurice's romantic drama, *Cytherea* (1924), based on the 1922 novel, *Cytherea, Goddess of Love*, by Joseph Hergesheimer. Stone meets Rubens, who reminds him of the woman of his dreams – and a doll he has named Cytherea, who promises a world of escape and romance. Leaving his wife and children, he engages in a torrid affair with Rubens. They plan for an ideal life together in Cuba, that they label their personal paradise – until her sudden death. Stone returns to his family and asks for their forgiveness.

George Babbitt (Willard Louis), a foolish middle-aged, fairly successful businessman, tires of his wife and home life, in Harry Beaumont's disappointing drama of small-town life, *Babbitt* (1924), based on the successful novel by Sinclair Lewis. Babbitt falls for Carmel Myers, the first seductress he meets. She walks into his real-estate office in search of a studio apartment. He personally caters to her wants, including handing over several hundred dollars when she confides she is short of money. He then suggests to his wife, Mary Alden, that she take a vacation. After she leaves, Myers increases her demands on Babbitt, proposing that they begin a new life together. Finally, his level-headed son talks him out of continuing his affair with Myers and persuades him to return home to his family. The film digresses from Lewis's original work. A moderately more accurate remake appeared in 1934 with Guy Kibbee in the title role.

In Herbert Brenon's drama, *Dancing Mothers* (1926), Alice Joyce as a caring mother is burdened with a selfish husband (Norman Trevor) and equally selfish daughter (Clara Bow). Learning that her flapper daughter has become involved with the lecherous Conway Tearle, she decides to save her sibling by eloping with Tearle on an ocean voyage. However, the mother unconsciously has fallen in love with Tearle. When her husband discovers her new infatuation, he tries to discourage it and begs her to return home. Instead, she sails for Paris, where she intends to begin a new life for herself.

Overburdened Irene Rich is cursed with a philandering husband whose heavy drinking and infidelities take a heavy toll on his wife and three children in James Flood's domestic drama, *The Honeymoon Express* (1926), based on a play by Ethel Clifton and Brenda Fowler. The middle-aged husband thinks he is some kind of sheik and frequents the nightclub circuit, while his wife, disregarding his affairs, remains at home attending to her family's needs. One daughter (Helene Costello) is serious, another (Virginia Lee Corbin) travels in potentially dangerous circles, and a son (Harold Goodwin) follows in his father's footsteps with his interest in nightclubs and carousing. It is not long before the abused wife walks out on the neglectful husband, who temporarily returns to the fold. The wild son promises to reform, and the mother brings back the remaining daughter. She then introduces her clan to their new father. The film was plagued by two major mishaps. Ernst Lubitsch, who was originally scheduled to direct, became ill and was replaced. Willard Louis, who was to play the role of the philandering husband, died halfway through the production, and he had to be written out of the script.

Greta Garbo portrays a temptress who comes between two longtime friends in Clarence Brown's romantic drama, *Flesh and the Devil* (1927). John Gilbert, who had earlier killed Garbo's husband in a duel, is forced to leave the country. He leaves his friend, Lars Hanson, to care for her. He returns in three years, intending to marry the widow, but learns she has married Hanson. Garbo plans to keep both men, her husband for his money and Gilbert for his lovemaking, but the latter balks at this. He arranges a duel at the same site where he had fought before. He then realizes the irony of the situation. Meanwhile, Garbo, rushing across the ice to prevent the duel, falls into the icy water and drowns. Her death, ironically, saves the friendship of the two men in her life.

John Gilbert and Greta reappeared as lovers in Edmund Goulding's romantic tragedy, *Love* (1927), a contemporary adaptation of Leo Tolstoy's novel, *Anna Karenina*. Garbo, married and with a son, falls in love with attractive Gilbert, a military guard who strikes an imposing figure in his various uniforms. The love scenes are not as torrid as those in *Flesh and the Devil*. Garbo appeared with Fredric March in a sound remake of Tolstoy's work in 1935, titled *Anna Karenina*, again directed by Clarence Brown.

In Richard Thomas's comedy drama, *The Truthful Sex* (1927), based on the story, "Husband's Preferred," by Albert Shelby Le Vino, Mae Busch realizes that her marriage to Huntly Gordon is coming apart. Gordon senses this even more, when he notices his wife takes a greater interest in their newly born son than in her husband. Busch has an affair with Paul Gregg and plans to leave with him. She is deterred, however, when a thief, a friend of the family governess, steals her jewels. Meanwhile, Busch has a chance to think over her actions. She returns to her husband and child, determined to make the marriage a success.

A sea captain explains his hatred of the opposite sex by way of flashbacks in George B. Seitz's minor action drama, *After the Storm* (1928). Following his description of how the first woman he ever loved betrayed him and his smuggling activities to the proper authorities, he next goes on to tell how his wife, a young Singapore coquette, deserted him when he was captured and imprisoned.

Belle Bennett in Erle Kenton's slow drama, *The Sporting Age* (1928), has an affair with her husband's male secretary before and after her spouse loses his eyesight in a train accident. Earlier, Bennett believed that Holmes Herbert, her spouse, was more interested in his horses than in her. Herbert discovers her infidelity with Carroll Nye when he recovers his sight. His wife and Nye are not aware of her husband's good fortune until it is too late. They soon learn that he is watching them. Herbert, now more optimistic than ever, purposely invites his niece to visit, hoping her youth and charm will attract Nye. His scheme works, and the married couple are reunited.

Alcoholism

I. Carry A. Nation and the Silent Battle

Early silent films dealing with alcohol began appearing around 1901, one year after Carry A. Nation (1846-1911) attacked her first saloon in Wichita, Kansas, in December 1900. Such titles as *The Kansas Saloon Smashers, Why Mr. Nation Wants a Divorce, Carry Nation Smashing a Saloon*, and *Mrs. Nation and Her Hatchet Brigade* attest to her national notoriety and influence upon the early movie studios. Other early films about alcohol addiction often considered the problem a curse that affected both the highest echelons of society and the most impoverished members of the community. Neither does the problem discriminate as to one's age or sex, although the problem of alcoholism among women has not appeared frequently as subject matter on the early silent screen. In all these examples, the films illustrate that not only the addicted drinker suffers. His habit more often than not touches his family, his community and his friends. In *Buddy, the Little Guardian* (1911), for example, the father's alcoholism leads to his little son's being struck by a car. Films like *The Iconoclast* (1910) suggest that one of the first setbacks the tippler faces is the loss of his job. This is usually followed by condemnation from family members, friends and neighbors, as in *The Message of the Violin* (1910). Loss of self-respect is not far behind as the boozer seeks ways to pay for his habit. Embarrassment, degradation and depression all take their toll – before any rehabilitation or reformation emerges. To prepare audiences for a happy ending, a handful of dramas conjure up an angelic or allegorical figure, usually a young woman, who steps forward to help the alcoholic battle his affliction. To make the plot even more unrealistic, writers and directors add a scene showing the derelict either getting his old job back, or, if the subject is a creative sort, achieving success in selling a painting, publishing a work or scoring big-time on the stage. Some early films, such as *Prohibition* (1915) and *The Silent Battle* (1916), suggested that drinking is hereditary. This thesis continued for several years in such dramas as *Once to Every Man* (1918).

Films about alcoholics were, for the most part, crude and devoid of subtlety. *Ten Nights in a Bar Room* (1909), based on the original play by William W. Pratt, tells the story of an honest workman who falls under the spell of drink. His struggles to kick the habit often fail. Numerous versions of Pratt's play appeared on film, the earliest was released in 1897.

The Drunkard's Fate (1909), released the same year as *Ten Nights*, depicts a young man who is addicted to alcohol, marries, and, on his wedding night, has an altercation with another groom whom he and his bride meet. The remainder of this cautionary tale deals with his drinking problem. The film stresses the young man's temptations and weaknesses, demonstrating his inability to cope with his addiction. Several similar films appeared during this period, including, among others, *The Drunken Acrobat* (1896), *Drunken Scene* (1903), *Drunkard's Child* (1909), *The Drunkard's Christmas* (1909), *A Drunkard's Son* (1909) and *A Drunkard's Reformation* (1909).

The captious and didactic approach continued in such moralistic dramas as D. W. Griffith's *The Iconoclast* (1910), a tale that unfolds simplistically in its portrayal of how an impoverished worker almost ruins his life because of his dependence on whiskey. His drinking problem results in the loss of his job. An otherwise honest worker and devoted family man, he grows so depressed over losing his position that he plots to murder his former employer. He goes to the man's house intending to shoot him, but when he observes the father's strong love for his crippled daughter, the former employee cannot bring himself to harm the already burdened family. Ironically, Griffith, who had directed more than a dozen anti-drinking dramas, was himself a confirmed alcoholic.

A family drunk is unfortunate enough, but when he is an abusive parent, the situation borders on tragedy. A young violinist in D. W. Griffith's slight tale, *The Message of the Violin* (1910), is burdened with an alcoholic father. The impoverished family undergoes abuse from the drunken father, who belittles both his patient wife and his tender and affectionate son, while he guzzles down one draught of beer after another. Later, the film portrays the dying father in a deranged state. The film ends when the son wins back his girlfriend by playing her favorite tune on his violin.

Another cautionary tale about the evils of devil rum, *Buddy, the Little Guardian* (1911) opens with a happy and cheerful family and ends in tragedy. The family joy is disturbed by the father's addiction to drink. His wife, refusing to contend with this condition, forces him to leave. He takes young Buddy with him for support, but his addiction grows worse. He collapses and ends up in a hospital. To help out, Buddy gets a job as a messenger and is run over by a car. He is sent to the same hospital as his father. Ironically, the mother is a nurse there. But the father dies before she learns where he is.

John Barleycorn (1914), an anti-saloon tract directed by Hobart Bosworth and based on the story by Jack London, reportedly is an account of part of the author's life. The film covers three stages. The first depicts London as a young boy who, while delivering beer to his father, drinks most of it and gets drunk. The second part shows the young author, an employee on a ranch, being encouraged by his fellow workers to get drunk on red wine. The last stage portrays him as a young man who falls in love, marries, and is helped by his wife to lick his drinking problem. Three different actors portray London. The third, Elmer Clifton, continued in films for decades, directing numerous action features, especially westerns.

Walter Fischter, as a young husband with a drinking problem, resorts to kidnapping his own child to raise money for his habit, in Frank Crane's drama, *As Ye Sow* (1914). Fischter, raised in New England, comes to the big city and marries Alice Brady, his boss's daughter. When her father dies, the couple move into the family mansion. After their child is born, his wife becomes aware of her husband's excessive drinking and refuses to provide him with money to feed his habit. He leaves, kidnapping their son, whom he then abandons on his mother's doorstep in Cape Cod. Fischter then ships out on a fishing vessel. Meanwhile, his wife meets and falls in love with her husband's brother, a reverend. Thinking Fischter dead, she agrees to marry the reverend. But her husband returns, the survivor of a shipwreck. The estranged couple reconcile their differences and their married life resumes. But Fischter returns to his heavy drinking, much to the disgust of his wife. He is later killed during a fight with a companion. The widow and the dead man's brother mourn over Fischter's body.

Margarita Fischer, the daughter of a railroad president, foolishly becomes infatuated with minor actor Joseph E. Singleton, a performer in a road show, in Harry Pollard's drama, *Infatuation* (1915), based on the novel by Lloyd Osbourne. The young woman elopes with her lover, a move that angers her father to the point that he ends up disowning her. Shortly after, Singleton's continuous drinking leads to his being dismissed from the company. Hoping to re-establish his reputation, he returns to New York, seeking a decent role. Meanwhile, his influential father-in-law, who wants Singleton to divorce his wife, pulls enough strings to keep the actor from obtaining work. But the ploy fails, and the actor, now cured of his affliction, is accepted as one of the family.

Some films suggested that the addiction to drink is inherited. One such work, Hal Reid's social drama, *Prohibition* (1915), also served as a rallying cry for contemporary anti-drinking organizations interested in influencing both state and national politics. Famous personalities of the period, among them William Jennings Bryan, the eminent American lawyer and politician; Josephus Daniels, an American journalist who served as secretary of the navy (1913-1921) and as ambassador to Mexico (1931-1941); and Richmond Pearson Hobson, Senator from Alabama; introduced this polemical drama, giving the unsentimental production an authoritative and dignified tone. The plot suggests that addiction to liquor may be an inherited disease. When one brother is rejected by a young woman, who selects his brother as her mate, the former plots revenge. He injects the innocent's food and drink with alcohol, knowing the family's weakness for drink. All this brings misery and suffering to the wife and husband – until the decent brother, in self-defense, is forced into a case of justifiable murder.

This was followed by a similar film, Jack Conway's *The Silent Battle* (1916), based on the 1913 novel by George Fort Gibbs. Like *Prohibition*, released one year earlier, it also suggested drinking is hereditary. The drama begins in 1855 and shows a father imbibing heavily, a scene that is repeated in the next generation by his son, a brilliant young lawyer (J. Warren Kerrigan). The attorney, aware of his problem, vacations in the woods, seeking a cure. Here he meets Lois Wilson, a wealthy young woman. During a hike, the couple lose their way. Exhausted and thirsty, they rest for a moment and she offers him a drink from her flask. The sip of alcohol proves too much for Kerrigan, and he consumes the entire contents. He then tries to take advantage of his companion. This leads to their splitting up. By the end of the film, he conquers his addiction and the couple renew their relationship.

T. Hayes Hunter's *Once to Every Man* (1918), based on the novel by Larry Evans, continues the premise that alcoholism is an inherited trait. Jack Sherrill portrays a likable young man raised in the country and who struggles with his dependence on liquor. A disagreement with his girlfriend, Mabel Withee, sends him to the big city where he tries his hand at prizefighting. Because he is physically capable of withstanding a brutal pounding, he proves to be a formidable opponent in the ring. He wins the lightweight championship, returns home a hero, and rekindles his relationship with his sweetheart.

The effects of liquor take their toll on two principal characters in George E. Middleton's *Salvation Nell* (1915), based on the 1908 play by Edward Sheldon. The forceful drama centers on the trials and tribulations of the title character, played intelligently by Beatriz Michelena. Her drunken father murders Nell's mother and he is himself killed in a saloon brawl. Nell then becomes the mistress of William Pike, a thief, who is soon caught and imprisoned. Following a string of complications, little Nell reforms into a God-fearing young woman. When Pike, her lover, is released from prison, he marries Nell and joins the army. A sub-plot tells the tragic story of Nell's girlfriend, who slid from mistress to alcoholic, followed by a life of complete degradation, disease and death.

In E. H. Calvert's *The Outer Edge* (1915), a drama of rehabilitation and redemption that is hampered by too many coincidences, Henry B. Walthall portrays a highly respected surgeon who is cursed by his obsession with liquor. His heavy drinking results in his loss of prestige and in his ending up as a hardened drunkard. He pawns all of his possessions, except for a gun, which he intends to use on himself when his condition grows unbearable. One day, he accidentally enters the wrong apartment and finds a mother and child suffering from starvation. When Walthall sees that the child is very ill, he rushes out, pawns his gun and returns with food for them. He calls for an ambulance and learns that the child's condition is hopeless, that only a gifted surgeon can save the child. Walthall decides to operate. He saves the child's life and, later, rekindles his relationship with his former girlfriend.

A popular matinee idol, E. Forrest Taylor loses his standing in the world of the theater because of his addiction to alcohol in William Bertram's *The Idol* (1915). The once-famous thespian is now a pathetic derelict. He is finally rescued by Helene Rosson, an actress who has joined the ranks of the Salvation Army as a means of enhancing her experience for a similar stage role. Taylor joins the Army and is on the road to rehabilitation when Rosson leaves for the stage. The despondent Taylor reverts to his heavy drinking. He struggles to fight his affliction and, when sober, goes to the theater to see Rosson's performance. Before the curtain rises, the leading man is taken ill. When members of the production recognize Taylor, they persuade him to fill in. He reluctantly agrees and gives an exceptional performance, thereby re-establishing himself as a major actor and regaining his self-esteem.

A similar plot occurs in Otis Turner's *A Little Brother of the Rich* (1915), based on the novel by Joseph Medill Patterson, in which Hobart Bosworth, as an alcoholic actor, reforms because of his love for Jane Novak. The young woman, rejected by Hobart Henley, her hometown fiancé, struggles to find work in the city. Hired to work in a stock company, she depends on Bosworth's tutoring to learn about acting. He eventually falls in love with her and gives up his addiction to liquor. Meanwhile, Henley has left his unfaithful wife, who then dies in an automobile accident. He renews his relationship with Novak and suggests that she become his mistress. She rejects the offer and turns to Bosworth, who has just given a successful performance. A remake was released in 1919, directed by Lynn Reynolds, with J. Barney Sherry and Kathryn Adams in the leading roles.

Addiction to alcohol almost results in ending a man's life in Barry O'Neil's improbable drama, *The Unpardonable Sin* (1916). Holbrook Blinn portrays an otherwise decent young man whose addiction to the bottle almost costs him his life. As a heavy drinker, he loses two girlfriends to rivals. After his first love rejects him, a friend helps him to fight off his drinking problem. Once cured, he returns to his former active social life where he meets and falls in love with Julia Landis, who abhors drinking and drunks. Another rival, jealous of Blinn and aware of his past battle with the bottle, purposely gets Blinn soused and marches him before the young woman. She walks out on Blinn and decides to marry the duplicitous rival. Blinn returns to his drinking habit. When he finally learns how his rival had tricked him, he vows revenge. He stops drinking, becomes a successful investor, and financially breaks his former rival. The man is murdered by another, and Blinn is accused. At the last moment, before he is to be executed, the truth comes out and Blinn is exonerated. He returns to Julia, who is now a widow, and renews his love for her.

Emile Chautard's social drama, *The Man Who Forgot* (1917), based on the 1915 novel by John Hay Jr., is a sententious work designed to promote Prohibition. Robert Warwick, who suffers from alcohol addiction, finally realizes the evils of liquor. He gives up drinking and becomes an ardent supporter of Prohibition. He meets Doris Kenyon, the daughter of a senator who is in league with the liquor cartel. Following several complications, including an attempt by the whiskey interests to frame Warwick, he is later exonerated. After the Prohibition bill passes and Warwick regains his memory, he proposes to Kenyon, who has been faithful all along.

William Desmond portrays the title character in Walter Edwards's *The Last of the Ingrahams* (1917), a decent New England inhabitant whose obsession with liquor is leading him to an early demise. One day, he helps Margery Wilson, a young woman treated locally as a disreputable character. He helps her carry a heavy bundle. When he is evicted from his home after spending all his inheritance on liquor, Wilson provides him with lodgings and helps him to conquer his drinking problem. When he recovers, he learns that certain properties he owns in the West contain oil. Once financially secure, he marries the young woman who has helped him.

A similar fate awaits Henry Kolker, a friendly supervisor and family man, in Edmund Lawrence's cautionary drama, *The Warning* (1915), that is hampered by a familiar twist ending. Kolker, a disappointment to his boss, his wife and family and his best friend, fails to heed his employer's warning. One evening, while watching his little son asleep, he himself dozes off. He later finds himself celebrating with a strange woman, who becomes his mistress. He is caught stealing from his boss and is discharged. He pushes his little son, Bobbie, away from him and the boy is hit by a car. The accident cripples the boy for life, and his wife divorces him. In Hell, he sees the boy above, but is prevented from joining his son. He then awakens, with his son still asleep next to him. Giving thanks for the warning, he graciously embraces his wife and child.

Joseph De Grasse's *Hell Morgan's Girl* (1917) retells the story of a wealthy man who disowns his son when the latter chooses a career in art over business. William Stowell, as the son, drifts into a wasted life of drunkenness. Dorothy Phillips, the daughter of a Barbary Coast dive owner, rescues Stowell. The film has been singled out for its realistic settings.

Harry Beaumont's drama, *Burning the Candle* (1917), illustrates another example of how a young man, after sinking to the depths of despair because of his weakness for liquor, eventually recovers. Henry B. Walthall, after marrying Southern belle Mary Charleson, takes her to live in New York, where he gains employment with a cotton broker. But he soon becomes addicted to drink and loses his position, his wife and his self-respect. His wife leaves for the South and her family. When he learns she is demanding a divorce, Walthall struggles to fight off his addiction, regains his job and wins back the love of his wife.

Lois Weber, in her allegorical drama, *Even As You and I* (1917), took the anti-drinking drama in a different direction. The plot has the Devil sending several of his messengers to bring about the downfall of Carrillo and Selma, two innocent youthful lovers. But the couriers from the lower depths fail, for the young pair are protected by Love, Youth and Honor. When the lovers, thus armed, resist Poverty, Lust and Suspicion, the Devil introduced them to Drink, which the pair cannot resist. Wisdom and Experience enter, but to no avail. The lure of Drink proves too strong for these forces. But the couple find salvation only through Loyalty. They begin their lives again, *sans* Love, Youth and Honor. Several earlier films had used allegory effectively, including *The Warning*, in which Henry Kolker, an alcoholic, envisions his life in Hell, and returns to earth a more prudent person.

Winifred Allen, a young woman with no life of her own, must share the burden of a no-account, drunken father in Albert Parker's drama, *The Man Hater* (1917), based on the story by Mary Brecht Pulver. Head of a squalid family of several young children after her mother dies in childbirth, Allen must care for all and take care of the house while her drunken father wiles away his time indulging himself in his only interest. Finally fed up with her dreary life and her father's indifferent attitude, she leaves the nest and marries her beau, the village blacksmith, hoping that neighbors will care for her little sisters and brothers.

Allan Dwan's approach to the drinking issue in *A Case at Law* (1917), a pre-Prohibition anti-liquor drama, differs from other similar films. It does not advocate the outright banning of liquor, but rather its regulation – so that alcohol does not reach the hands of the young and others who are incapable of handling it. Dick Rosson portrays a young alcoholic reporter. An Easterner with a weakness for booze, Rosson journeys to a small town in the West with Pauline Curley, his fiancée, both hoping he will recover there from his problem. But during his first day on the job, he celebrates with his fellow reporters and staggers home drunk. His wife calls upon Riley Hatch, the local doctor and a staunch enemy of alcohol, who takes the young man to his home to cure him. Hatch himself is a former alcoholic. After recovering sufficiently, Rosson is assigned to interview local saloon keeper Jack Dillon about the national drinking problem. Dillon, an enemy of the doctor, decides to take his revenge out on the reporter, who again returns home drunk. The irate Hatch storms into the saloon and shoots up the place, an act that results in his wounding Dillon in the arms and legs. At his trial, the jury acquits the doctor, dismissing the shooting as "justifiable self-defense."

Emily Stevens has grown impatient and frustrated with her alcohol-addicted husband, and the couple split up, in Albert Capellani's *Daybreak* (1918), based on the play by Jane Cowl and Jane Murfin. The break comes only after the wife, who is now pregnant, reads in a newspaper that her husband, while drunk one night, has pushed a newsboy under a car. She tells him she will only return to him when he has stopped drinking permanently. A reconciliation occurs several years later, only after the husband accidentally learns that he is a father. His wife has kept this fact a secret for four years. She has been employing a nurse to care for their child in a private apartment.

Harry Morey portrays a doctor who begins drinking heavily when he learns that his wife is unfaithful in Paul Scardon's drama, *The Other Man* (1918). His dependency on the bottle results in his landing in the gutter, where some shady politicians hire him and install him in a boarding house, where he patches up wounded gangsters. He meets Grace Darmond, a socialite who, on a bet, wagers she can live on very little in a slum for one month. Unaware of each other's social background, they develop a friendship that soon turns to love. When she wins her bet, she turns over the money to her lawyers to help rehabilitate the fallen surgeon. He overcomes his drinking problem and returns to his work as a major surgeon. He then accidentally meets the young woman he has grown to love and they continue their romance.

An occasional comedy used the drinking theme as the basis of its plot, as in Marshall Neilan's *Hit-the-Trail Holliday* (1918), based on George M. Cohan's 1915 stage play. Employing satire and farce, the film pokes fun at such diverse topics as the New York subway system and the Germans (the film was made and released during the Great War). Cohan portrays Bill Holliday, allegedly a take-off on Billy Sunday, the popular evangelist. Cohan, a bartender, is discharged for refusing to sell liquor to minors. He later joins a temperance movement and speaks out adamantly against drinking. When he begins to promote a non-alcoholic beverage, workers at a nearby brewery try to attack him. But he repels them by offering them jobs if they join the cause of Prohibition. The production is basically all comedy as it presents its case for Prohibition.

Henry B. Walthall portrays a successful lawyer whose craving for drink almost ruins his career and life in L. V. Chandler's fast-paced drama, *The Long Lane's Turning* (1919). Walthall's excessive imbibing causes him to lose a case. This results in an innocent man's incarceration. Determined to regain his reputation, the disgraced lawyer shakes his affliction and prevents heroine Mary Charleson from being forced into an unwanted marriage with a villain. Walthall soon wins the governor's seat.

Virginia Pearson, as a young woman from a poor background, leaps at the opportunity to marry wealthy Hugh Thompson, who turns out to be an alcoholic, in Edmund Lawrence's drama, *The Love Auction* (1919). Pearson is not aware of her husband's drinking problem till he comes staggering home intoxicated one evening. Her disgust quickly turns to grief when she realizes she had made a mistake to marry only for money. The film is hampered by too many familiar stereotyped characters: the poor girl marrying for money, the drunken husband, a former sweetheart, and a fanatical cult leader.

A young alcoholic officer in the U.S. Navy (Monroe Salisbury) is entrusted with important documents in William Wolbert's World War I spy drama, *The Light of Victory* (1919). He goes to a sleazy bar, get soused and loses the papers to German spies. His fellow officers find him and return him for a court-martial. The officers, his former friends, suggest that he take his own life. When he refuses, they abandon him on a Pacific island. He soon finds work with the Germans, supplying information to those aboard an enemy submarine. The sub then plans to sink Salisbury's former ship, The U.S.S. *Victory*. The exiled lieutenant warns those on board and the sub is destroyed. He then struggles with a German officer and is mortally wounded. The young American's repentance – a final salute to his country's colors before he dies – comes too late. He is honored posthumously aboard his old vessel.

David O. Fischer's routine drama, *The Law of Nature* (1919), tells the overly familiar story of a young man who finds himself trapped by his obsession with booze. Fischer, who also directed and wrote the screenplay, portrays the principal character. He becomes involved with road houses, the police, forgery and murder.

The Moonshine Trail (1919), directed by J. Stuart Blackton, was one of the last dramas of the decade to champion the cause of Prohibition. However, the film was released too late – Prohibition had already become the law of the land and was to go into effect in January 1920. The film also touches upon the issue that alcohol is an inherited vice. Louis Dean plots to seduce Sylvia Breamer by first getting her boyfriend, Robert Gordon, drunk. Dean is aware that Gordon's father is an alcoholic. But Dean later reforms when his own daughter dies, the result of her nurse's addiction to the bottle. Gordon promises Breamer he will abstain if she will marry him.

II. Prohibition and the Long Binge

By the end of the decade, a Variety movie critic commented on October 3, 1919, "It is about time someone stepped in and called a halt on the anti-booze propaganda film." The Volstead Act of 1919, which went into effect the following year, prohibited the sale and manufacture of alcoholic beverages. But the film critic's plea and the law could not stop the flow of illegal alcohol pouring into the nation's homes and speakeasies. Neither could they prevent the numerous Hollywood dramas and comedies released during the twenties from their assaults on drinking or drunks. The major cause of drinking, they generally suggested, was weakness of character. Some films, like *Fighting Chance* (1920), continued to insist that drinking was hereditary. One possible cure, the studios concluded, was the love of a good woman, as in *The Bonded Woman* (1922), in which Betty Compson has to travel to the South Seas to help cure her alcoholic husband. This simplistic approach to the cause and cure, unfortunately, offered limited insight and even fewer possible solutions. Professionals were not immune, as Hollywood was quick to point out in such films as *Water, Water, Everywhere* (1920) and *White Shadows in the South Seas* (1928), both depicting an alcoholic doctor, and *The Drag Net* (1928), with tough city detective George Bancroft hitting the bottle. But he sobers up in time to smash a gang of criminals. His rehabilitation anticipates the end of the nation's long binge as it prepares itself for the decade of the thirties, with the repeal of the Volstead Law, the end of the flappers and the beginning of the Depression. Meanwhile, Prohibition in part contributed to the rise of organized crime, gang wars and notorious crime czars like Al "Scarface" Capone, who controlled Chicago vice during the twenties. Ironically, his brother Vincenzo, who changed his name to Hart, served as a federal liquor agent in the West, where, as "Two Gun" Hart, he fought to keep the area alcohol-free.

Charles Maigne's *Fighting Chance* (1920), based on the novel by Robert Chambers, reverts to the familiar theme that drinking is a hereditary trait. Conrad Nagel, as the weak son of a family well entrenched in society, has been ostracized from his conservative private club for disregarding some of its principles (he sneaks a girl onto the premises) and because of his heavy drinking. Socialite Anna Q. Nilsson, who loves Nagel but abhors his drinking, shuns him. He eventually recovers the lost family fortune and gives up his drinking habit.

Several films attacked the problem head on by coming out in favor of Prohibition. Harry Beaumont's *The Great Accident* (1920), based on a story by Ben Ames Williams, advocates Prohibition, although it was released after Prohibition had been enacted. Tom Moore, as the son of a mayoralty candidate, has a reputation for indulges too often in drinking. As a lark, the politicians place his name on the ballot and he wins the election. Surprising all, he decides to end his drinking habit and cracks down on the local bars. His enemies then frame him, using Jane Novak, whom they hire to claim he is the father of her child. Following some minor complications, he is exonerated of these false charges and ends up marrying his accuser.

As with many films about alcoholics of the previous decade, several released in the twenties also focused on employees faced with a drinking problem. John Lowell, a logger in a Northern camp, finds himself addicted to alcohol, in Oscar Apfel's familiar drama, *Ten Nights in a Bar Room* (1921), based on the 1890 play by William S. Pratt. His heavy drinking affects his work and results in his neglecting his wife and little daughter. The child is sent to the saloon to fetch him home. Suddenly, a flung beer glass strikes her, an unfortunate incident that leads to her death. The father, out for revenge, goes on a rampage, resulting in a tremendous fire. Lowell, who has given up drinking, ends his search for revenge and rejoins his wife. Several other versions of Pratt's work appeared on screen, including a 1926 film which featured an all African-American cast, led by Charles Gilpin and Bessie Smith.

Railroad engineer Harry T. Morey's drinking problem has earned him the epithet of village drunk in Harry O. Hoyt's drama, *The Curse of Drink* (1922), based on the 1904 play by Charles E. Blaney. Local bootleggers have been able to affect Morey's dependence on the bottle to the point that he endangers his daughter's happiness. During a party celebrating his daughter's proposed marriage to Edmund Breese, the son of her boss, Breese's father only agrees to the union after Morey promises to give up drinking. But the bootleggers get to Morey, who then, in a drunken state, breaks up a party. After Morey is fired, he plots to destroy a train as revenge. But his daughter and her fiancé stop him in time.

In another cautionary drama, Phil Rosen's *The Bonded Woman* (1922), adapted from the story, "The Salvaging of John Somers" by John Fleming

Wilson, Betty Compson journeys to the South Seas to rescue John Bowers, her alcoholic husband, a former ship captain. Bowers had earlier rescued Compson's father from drowning, and she is determined to repay him by saving him from himself. She had married him and mortgaged her home to purchase a ship captain's position for him. They meet and he continues his drinking. Compson runs his ship onto an uninhabited island. "I'll talk to you when you have emptied those bottles," she declares, pointing to his cases of whiskey. He finally realizes this is his last chance to reform and proceeds to smash all the bottles. A ship then conveniently arrives to take the reformed husband and his persistent wife off the island.

Several films focused on chorus girls. In James Cruze's comedy drama, *The Enemy Sex* (1924), based on the novel, *The Salamander* (1914), by Owen Johnson, chorus girl Betty Compson fends off an array of tempting propositions offered by several wealthy men she meets at a party. It seems they each want to add her to their conquests by offering her either a successful career, wealth or social position. She turns them all down, explaining she will spend her time reforming Percy Marmont, a confirmed alcoholic.

Evelyn Brent, another chorus girl, faces a different problem in Wesley Ruggles's society drama, *Broadway Lady* (1925), when she reluctantly marries wealthy Theodore von Eltz. At first, she refuses his proposal of marriage because of his excessive drinking, but when she learns that his snobbish family has rejected her, she accepts his offer. The marriage, she feels, will teach his family a lesson in their aristocratic shortsightedness. Meanwhile, she discovers that her husband's impetuous sister plans to elope with her disreputable lover. When she goes to her sister-in-law's apartment to talk her out of eloping, the man is gunned down. Brent accepts the blame, hoping to protect the girl. Later, the girl confesses, explaining the shooting was an accident, and both women are set free.

As in earlier films, some releases in the twenties dealt with professionals who became addicted to the bottle. Clarence Badger's mild pre-Prohibition comedy, *Water, Water, Everywhere* (1920), based on the novel by William R. Lighton, fortunately has the popular humorist Will Rogers as a friend to Irene Rich, a young woman in love with Rowland Lee, a tippling young doctor. She fears his affection for the bottle will only grow worse. A mine accident brings out the best in the young doctor. After he sobers up and performs some remarkable surgery, he and Rich marry. The scenes involving drinking and drunkenness are dull as well as dated.

Alcoholic physician and South Sea island recluse Monte Blue's sympathetic stand against the exploitation of natives creates numerous problems for him in W. S. Van Dyke's picturesque drama, *White Shadows in the South Seas* (1928), loosely based on the book by Frederick O'Brien. Blue has drifted to an island untouched by civilization, after being driven off another controlled by Robert Anderson, an unscrupulous and greedy store owner. Here the doctor is amazed at the simple and happy life of the islanders, who enjoy their unspoiled environment. Blue meets and falls in love with Raquel Torres, the daughter of the tribal chief. Suddenly, Anderson and several of his toughs invade the island and establish a trading post that allows them to swindle the unsophisticated islanders, whom the whites dupe into diving for pearls. In a downbeat ending, Blue is killed by one of the whites, leaving Anderson free to continue his exploitation unencumbered. The production takes advantage of the visual settings, including depictions of local customs and inherent dangers to the natives. One sequence, for example, shows a giant clam closing on the foot of a diver. Basically a silent feature, it is one of the earliest to include synchronized sound segments.

George Bancroft, as a tough city detective, begins hitting the bottle after he is convinced he has killed one of his own men in Joseph von Sternberg's crime drama, *The Drag Net* (1928). Bancroft earlier realizes he and his men represent the only bastion between law and disorder in a city where crime and murder run rampant. Witnesses are murdered while testifying in courtrooms. Debonair gang leader William Powell, to stop Bancroft's crusade against crime, plants the seed in the detective's thoughts that he killed a fellow officer. Bancroft, driven by guilt, resigns and becomes a heavy drinker. Evelyn Brent, Powell's girlfriend, falls in love with Bancroft and tells him the truth about the crime. The detective sobers up and brings Powell and his gang to justice.

Amnesia

I. Amnesia's Sweet Song of Coincidence

Film plots and settings about amnesia victims range widely, the disparity encompassing such backgrounds as society, crime and war. One of the shortcomings of the amnesia drama is its heavy reliance on the long arm of coincidence. Another is the often facile way the victim or patient regains his memory. Some of the more familiar ploys include a sudden shock, a repeated blow to the head, a song from a loved one or a photograph. Writers never seem to run out of devices. The amnesiac as victim (almost invariably a man) often returns to find his life in a shambles and his world turned upside down. Either his wife has remarried, as in *The Right of Way* (1915), or is on the verge of doing so. Although most of these dramas end happily for most of the principals, with the sympathetic victim regaining his memory and reunited with his loved ones, occasionally he sacrifices himself for the happiness of others, who have come to believe he has died or has been killed. In *A Million Bid* (1914), a new twist is introduced. An amnesiac who returns to his wife who has remarried, dies accidentally on the operating table at the hands of the second husband. Another variation found in several films about amnesiacs is the use of crime elements, such as in the comedy drama *The Lost Bridegroom* (1916) and *The Scarlet Car* (1917), the latter concerning a bank robbery. However hackneyed and sentimental the entries in this cycle seem, the amnesia film still appears from time to time – attesting to audience interest in the subject.

Several early domestic dramas have characterized the amnesia victim as a woman, but these were rare occasions. Beulah Poynter portrays a young wife who, after being hit on the head by her drunken husband, loses her memory in the weak drama, *Born Again* (1914). She had earlier run away from a cruel stepmother, achieved success on the stage, and gave up her career to marry a wealthy man. After the blow on her head, she leaves her spouse, unaware of anything that had occurred earlier in her life. After being taken in by a kindly widow and her son, Poynter recovers her health, but still cannot remember anything of her past. When the widow's son proposes marriage to her, she accepts. After one year, a baby is born to the happy couple. Suddenly her memory returns and the anxious wife and mother realizes she now has two husbands. Forced to reveal this to someone, she tells the doctor who had earlier attended to her. He informs her that her first husband had died in a car accident.

A young woman goes into a state of shock when she witnesses the murder of her brother in Otis Turner's drama, *Called Back* (1915), based on the 1884 novel by Hugh Conway. Following the killing, she loses her memory. Present in the room are two Russian Nihilists, one the killer and the other, his accomplice, is the uncle of the victim and the woman. When a blind man stumbles onto the scene, the two men at first plan to kill him, but when they realize he is blind they drug him and return him to his own rooms. Following several complications and the passing of a few years, the blind man regains his sight, incidentally meets the woman whose memory has still not returned and falls in love with her. He later marries her and, during his journey to Siberia, he meets the uncle who has been arrested after a failed assassination attempt and sentenced to the wastes of Siberia. The husband learns the truth about his wife's memory loss from the prisoner.

Harry Handworth's *When Fate Leads Trump* (1915), based on the novel by Alice M. Roberts, relates another strange tale about an unfortunate young woman who marries the son of a smuggler. A child is born, and the man is called back by the father, who wants his son to lead the gang of smugglers. The couple arrive at the cave hideout, where the wife is held prisoner and the child disappears. The son consents to join the band, but the police raid the smugglers' cave and arrest the gang. Meanwhile, the wife escapes into the woods and passes out from exhaustion. A woodsman finds her and takes her to his hut, where he nurses her back to health. The wife, who has lost her memory, subsequently agrees to marry her savior. Later, a child is born. Allowing for coincidence, her first husband, released from prison, meets his wife, who then has a flash of recognition as her past life returns to her. She introduces him to her present husband and child. The two confused husbands agree to a duel to decide who shall claim the woman. The ex-convict, witnessing the family's life of peace and contentment, furtively removes the lead from his bullet, thereby sacrificing himself so that the woman he loves can continue to find happiness in her new life.

Victims of memory loss may have diverse professional backgrounds, ranging from art to law. Robert A. Dillon's *The Key to Yesterday* (1914), based on the novel by Charles Neville, stars Carlyle Blackwell in a dual role. The drama begins with his escape from Mexicans who mistake him for a spy during a revolution. He is next seen as an artist who has lost his memory. The only link to his past is his key to his Paris apartment. Blackwell travels around the world, and, because he has shaven off his beard, he is mistaken as the spy who had escaped the Mexicans. Following several complications, he finds the lock for his key, which also helps to unlock his past. He learns that his wife has died. So he returns to the United States to a girlfriend whom he had met while he suffered from memory loss.

William Faversham portrays a brilliant young lawyer who, during a barroom brawl, loses his memory, in John W. Noble's drama, *The Right of Way* (1915), based on the novel by Sir Gilbert Parker. The confused attorney heads for Canada, where some of the folks there nurse him back to health. About a year later, sporting a dark beard and regaining his memory, he chooses not to return home. He had learned earlier that his wife, thinking him dead, has remarried. Instead, he takes an interest in religion. But an assassin's bullet mortally wounds Faversham. Jack Dillon directed a remake in 1920.

The amnesia film sometimes suggested man's capacity for both good and evil. Thomas Santschi's short drama, *The Two Natures Within Him* (1915), tells the strange tale of a minister who is hit over the head by a burglar. Not only does he lose his memory, but he befriends his attacker and joins in the criminal's escapades. Months later, when the minister returns home, his girlfriend, who has taken up residence in his home to care for his affairs, enters with a revolver. Recognizing him, she drops the gun and embraces her lost lover. But the minister, still suffering from memory loss, does not know who she is and begins strangling her. A policeman who has heard the disturbance enters and arrests him. The young woman's father, a doctor, is also living at the minister's home. He appears at the trial and proves that a serious blow to the head is the cause for the defendant's radical behavior. He later operates on the minister and helps to restore his memory.

At other times, the afflicted victim may fall prey to the forces of evil. Edwin Stevens personifies the devil in Harley Knoles's drama, *The Devil's Toy* (1916), an adaptation of Edward Madden's poem, "The Mills of the Gods." Adele Blood, a blonde beauty, is loved by two men. Both are artists, but one displays real genius in his painting while the other is bereft of talent. The genius, Jack Halliday, is loved by his model, the blonde woman. Despite his talent, he can barely survive through his painting. Meanwhile, his model follows a stage career. Stevens, the less-talented artist, murders his uncle for his wealth. Money, however, is not enough to satisfy him and, on learning of his old friend's situation, visits him and finds him seriously ill. Stevens sends him to a sanitarium where he recovers his health, but not his memory. Thereupon, Stevens seizes his friend's best paintings and displays them as his own. But the model instantly recognizes the work as that of her former lover. In seeking to obtain her love, Stevens squanders all the money he had so ignobly acquired. On the other hand, the former model finds her true lover, who recognizes her and regains his memory. The film ends with Stevens accidentally locked in the same vault with his murdered uncle.

The villain can sometimes be the very husband of a wife who loves, perhaps, too well. A persistent reporter, investigating an apparently simple shooting of an intruder, virtually forces a woman to talk about a previous murder and an unusual cover-up, in Lawrence McGill's farfetched drama, *The Woman's Law* (1916), based on the 1914 novel by Maravene Thompson. Duncan McRae, in a dual role, portrays Florence Reed's husband, the millionaire murderer of an artist. Before he is arrested, Reed meets a disoriented stranger who is her husband's double. Thinking more of protecting her child than covering up her unfaithful husband's crime, she takes the man home. The police arrest the stranger instead of her husband, who has fled. The innocent man is institutionalized and, still suffering a loss of memory, is finally released. Reed takes the amnesiac home as her husband. When her real husband returns in an attempt to extract money from her, the butler mistakes him for a burglar and shoots him. The amnesiac, hearing the wife's confession, soon establishes his own identity and decides to marry the widow.

The most familiar plot involving amnesia is the returning husband, who now poses a threat to the harmony of a newly established family. In Ralph W. Ince's *A Million Bid* (1914), based on the 1908 play, *Agnes*, by George Cameron, Anita Stewart experiences just such a problem. She is forced by her mother to reject a struggling doctor and instead marry a wealthy Australian. Both her mother and husband drown when their yacht capsizes, and Stewart returns to the States. She rekindles her romance with her true love, E. K. Lincoln. Now happily married and raising a son, she and her family face a problem. One of the doctor's patients, an amnesiac, turns out to be the wife's former husband. She begs her husband not to operate, but he refuses her request. His brain operation fails, and his patient dies.

Many amnesia films, whether comedies, dramas or a combination of both, depended heavily on crime plots. John Barrymore portrays a bridegroom who is hit on the head by hoodlums on the night before his wedding day in James Kirkwood's trifling comedy drama, *The Lost Bridegroom* (1916). The blow causes him to lose his memory. By coincidence, the crooks who had struck him take him to help rob the house of his fiancée. It is here, by sheer recognition of the familiar surroundings, that he recovers his memory. The film was originally titled *His Lost Self.*

A middle-aged bank cashier in Joseph De Grasse's farfetched drama, *The Scarlet Car* (1917), based on the novel by Richard Harding Davis, discovers that the bank president and his son have embezzled a large sum of money from the bank. When he threatens to expose the pair, they strike him on the head. Thinking they have killed the cashier, they then direct the broker, who is handling the stolen funds, to dump the body off near a deserted road. The car crashes and the broker is killed. The cashier escapes and, while suffering a loss of memory, wanders off. The bank president, hearing of the accident, announces the loss of funds and accuses the missing cashier of the theft. Later, the victim's daughter and her boyfriend, Franklyn Farnum, discover her father's hat in the wrecked car. They conclude that he is still alive and that the president and his son are the embezzlers. They find the missing father, who slowly begins to recall the entire series of events. He had hidden away a missing page of the bank ledger – proof that the president had taken the missing money.

War stories, with their plots about lost love, long separations, various dangers and unimaginable suffering, lend themselves to tales of amnesia. In the drama *The Girl of the Sunny South* (1913), based on the play by Travers Vale, a soldier during the Civil War is betrayed by a rival suitor and accused of desertion. He is shot, but survives the wound, with a case of amnesia. Now a tramp, he wanders back to his home town after the war, where his rival, hoping to win the amnesiac's estate and wife for himself, kills the woman's father. Following a series of further complications, the husband is exonerated. With his memory restored, he is reunited with his wife, Louise Vale.

Several films about amnesia victims were made during World War I and incorporated war elements into their plots. Similar in theme to *The Two Natures Within Him* (1915), John Ince's drama, *The Struggle* (1916), also touches upon the dual nature of man. The film depicts how a reprobate who, after receiving a blow to the head, turns into a selfless and altruistic human being. However, following an operation whereby his memory is restored, he reverts to his former miscreant nature. Set during World War I, the film begins with Arthur Ashley, a lieutenant in the U.S. Army, marrying Ethel Grey Terry, the commandant's daughter, whom Frank Sheridan, a middle-aged major, loves. When the major discovers his junior officer is having an affair with another officer's wife, he requests a transfer to the Philippines and arranges to have Ashley join him. Both men, accompanied by Ashley's wife, sail for the South Pacific, but their steamer is sunk by a German submarine. Sheridan and Terry are washed ashore on one island, while her husband reaches another island, a leper colony, run by Dominican fathers. Ashley, in his struggle to save himself, receives a blow to his head and loses his memory. At his new home he devotes himself entirely to caring for the unfortunate, afflicted souls. After the couple are rescued, the major, a physician by profession, is assigned to inspect the leper colony. He finds Ashley there and brings him home. The lieutenant is successfully operated on and upon recovery accuses his wife and the major of having an affair behind his back. Discovering he has contracted leprosy, he takes his own life.

The crime element is best exemplified by films adapted from novels. Cleveland Moffat's 1909 detective novel about master sleuth Coquenil (the thinking man's detective) finds him on the trail of an arch-criminal in Rollin Sturgeon's drama, *Through the Wall* (1916). The villain, George Holt, a master of disguise, poses as the father of amnesia victim Nell Shipman. To protect his identity, he shoots the young woman's uncle and frames her brother. However, William Duncan, as the detective, unmasks the impostor. Contemporary critics praised the exterior shots, especially those that depict an ocean liner being torpedoed and the resultant panic and confusion of the passengers struggling in the icy waters.

In George Archainbaud's World War I drama, *A Maid of Belgium* (1917), a young Belgian wife loses her memory as the result of German atrocities. An

American couple, driving through a Belgian village that has been bombarded by the Germans, find Alice Brady, a lonely survivor, who has lost her memory. Because the war is still raging, and the couple are childless, they decide to adopt the girl and take her to America. Once they are home, the wife learns that their ward is pregnant. Following several complications, including the birth of the child, the young mother regains her memory when she is shocked by a nearby explosion. It seems that she had been married to a Belgian viscount who went to war and is now visiting the United States. The American husband sends for the viscount, and the separated pair are brought together.

Robert Gordon portrays a lieutenant who loses him memory on the battlefields of France in James Young's *Missing* (1918), a World War I drama set chiefly in England and based on the novel by Mrs. Humphrey Ward. Gordon, recuperating in a hospital in France, has a wife, Sylvia Breamer, back home, but remembers little of his past life. Her older sister, who had wanted Breamer to marry wealthy Thomas Meighan, intercepts a telegram stating a wounded soldier's claims he is married to Breamer. The sister destroys the message, hoping that the grieving wife, believing her husband is dead, will now marry Meighan. A second telegram arrives, and this time Breamer reads it and is overjoyed to learn that Gordon is alive. She rushes to greet him, and when she sings his favorite tune, he regains his memory.

Peggy Hyland, a Scotch lass betrothed to William Bailey, watches him march off to war in Harry Millarde's *Bonnie Annie Laurie* (1918), a minor World War I drama set in a peaceful village in Scotland. When a stranger, ill of health who is suffering a memory loss, enters the village, Hyland takes it upon herself to nurse him back to health. Their fondness for each other grows to love, and she agrees to elope with him. But a storm upsets their plans. The storm also helps him to recover his memory. He recalls that he is an American officer (Sidney Mason), and reports back to his post, forgetting all about his Scotch love. Once again in the trenches, he accidentally meets Bailey, the girl's fiancé, who soon loses his eyesight. Hyland, now a war nurse, meets the two friends later, and the love between her and the American is revived. When Bailey's sight returns to him, he and his betrothed return to Scotland. The American, realizing he is an interloper, returns to his homeland.

II. Crime and the Closed Gates of Memory

Films using the ploy of memory loss continued to be produced throughout the next decade – with varying degrees of success. They often relied on the familiar devices employed so successfully in the earlier entries, including even a handful of World War I tales. In *His Forgotten Wife* (1924), wounded soldier Warner Baxter, suffering from loss of memory, forgets about his fiancée and marries a nurse. In *Wandering Fires* (1925) the wounded soldier suffering from memory loss is restored to his old self when he hears a familiar tune from his past. And in *The Closed Gate* (1927), Amnesia victim Robert Harron, who had earlier been rejected by his widowed father, returns from France with his wife and reconciles his differences with his stern father. Crime seemed to dominate the amnesia-oriented films of the twenties, opening with *Nobody* (1921), a drama about a murder trial. Perhaps the emphasis on crime and other elements of violence was the result of World War I, with its devastating and unexpected slaughter of so many and its vast destruction. The new string of amnesia films contained elements of rape (*Nobody*), gangs and gangsters (*Souls in Bondage*), kidnappings (*The Highbinders*), cop killings (*Blindfold*) and brothers killing brothers (*A Modern Cain*). The topic of amnesia encompassed darker meanings after World War II. For example, West German author Heinrich Boell (1917-1985), who won the Nobel prize for literature in 1972, was critical of postwar West German materialism, consumerism and collective amnesia about Nazism.

Rape, loss of memory and a melodramatic trial are only some of the elements in Roland West's drama, *Nobody* (1921), about a woman accused of murdering a millionaire. After a rich man rapes Jewel Carmen, she loses her memory. She goes to his residence, shoots him, and returns to her own home where she remembers nothing. At the trial where the jury is deliberating her fate, its members are shocked to learn that William Davidson, one of the jurors, is the defendant's husband. After he tells them the entire story, they pledge to keep his secret and find his wife not guilty. An earlier film about another jury member playing an important role in a courtroom drama appeared in 1909 in D. W. Griffith's *Was Justice Served?* In Griffith's film, a juror turns out to be the actual thief in the case.

Bert Lytell, a cynical, alcoholic lawyer in Jack Dillon's *The Right of Way* (1920), based on Sir Gilbert Parker's 1901 novel, is rescued from a drunken brawl by a man he has earlier condemned. He is taken to a village while suffering from amnesia and meets Leatrice Joy. She helps Lytell, who rejects the power of God, to reform. He is mortally wounded trying to protect the church funds from a pair of thieves. Seeking redemption, he dies in Joy's arms. An earlier screen version of Parker's novel appeared in 1915.

Family man Jerome Patrick, suffering from amnesia, has no memory of his wife, child or profession in Edward Sloman's drama, *The Other Woman* (1921), based on the 1920 novel by Norah Davis. Five years after assuming another identity, he is recognized by his best friend, William Conklin, who thinks the man is someone else. He offers Patrick a job in another city. Years later, When Patrick falls in love with and becomes engages to Conklin's cousin, the latter exposes him as an ex-convict and a married man. The news shocks Patrick into recalling his former life, and he returns to his wife and family. But he again assumes his second life and marries Jane Novak, his friend's cousin. After the couple have a child, his first wife understands his problem and allows him to stay with Novak.

When her husband finds her in the company of another man and rushes way, Alice Lake, his wife, follows him to explain. But she loses her memory when she is struck by an automobile, in Edward Le Saint's drama, *More to Be Pitied*

Than Scorned (1922), based on the 1903 play by Charles E. Blaney. Several years later, J. Frank Glendon, her actor husband, marries Rosemary Theby, a fellow player, who has been raising his daughter. His first wife recovers her memory and gains custody of her daughter. Philo McCullough, the man she was with that fateful night of the accident, threatens to hurt the girl if the mother refuses to marry him. Lake then takes the daughter back to Glendon. During a play, McCullough accidentally shoots Theby and is himself killed. This paves the way for Glendon and his first wife to reconcile their differences.

Raymond Bloomer, a gambler and alcoholic, argues with his wife's cousin and kills him in J. Gordon Edwards's drama, *The Net* (1923), based on the novel, *The Woman's Law*, by Maravene Thompson. He flees, after he exchanges identities with a stranger (Albert Roscoe), who suffers from amnesia. Bloomer then persuades his wife (Barbara Castleton) to tell the police that Roscoe committed the murder. To protect her son, she reluctantly agrees. Bloomer eventually is killed, and Roscoe, regaining his memory, establishes his innocence. He then marries Castleton. The film is a remake of *The Woman's Law*, released in 1916.

A wealthy member of a gang of thieves suffers a loss of memory, which finally leads to his reformation, in William H. Clifford's drama, *Souls in Bondage* (1923). Pat O'Malley, as the young, adventurous thief, receives a blow to the head by a policeman and loses his memory. Later, he takes an interest in a young and pretty socialite and returns her stolen jewels to her. His jealous girlfriend, fellow gang member Cleo Madison, informs the gang leader. But before any harm can come to O'Malley, the police arrive. The socialite arranges that all charges be dropped, leading to O'Malley's reconciliation with Madison and the reformation of the entire gang.

A writer, after losing his memory, gets involved in a kidnapping and regains his memory, in George W. Terwilliger's predictable drama, *The Highbinders* (1926). William T. Tilden, as the author, is hit on the head during a robbery and loses his memory. A friend helps him out, hoping that Tilden will regain his identity. The unfortunate writer meets a young woman with whom he falls in love, but she is kidnapped by a gangster. Tilden rescues her and is again hit on the head – a blow that helps him to regain his memory.

A police officer out to get those who killed a fellow cop is the focus of Charles Klein's revenge drama, *Blindfold* (1928), a film offering little that is fresh. George O'Brien is the avenging officer who is determined to bring several powerful individuals to justice. However, he is thrown off the force for his rash arrests of prominent citizens. Meanwhile, Lois Moran, his girlfriend, develops a case of amnesia, and ends up as part of the gang responsible for his buddy's death. O'Brien rescues her and in turn she calls in the police to help her beau capture the gang – this time with enough evidence to convict its members.

Although the war film became box office poison by the early twenties, studios occasionally approached the genre obliquely as they blended the amnesia film with the war story. Emphasis shifted from the violent and bloody to the romantic or comical aspects – with ambiguous success. In William A. Seiter's trite drama, *His Forgotten Wife* (1924), wounded World War I soldier Warner Baxter, who has lost any memory of his fiancée back home, falls in love and marries his nurse, Madge Bellamy, while recuperating. Back in the States, the couple are forced to seek employment as domestics in a Long Island home. By coincidence, Baxter happens to be the former master of the estate. He had assigned his property and investments to his amoral fiancée. Believing she is being ignored, she flees with his bonds. His wife gives chase and, at gunpoint, retrieves her husband's valuable investments.

Matt Moore, a doctor who believes he has killed his lover's husband, flees to a remote cabin, in Herbert Brenon's mystery drama, *The Breaking Point* (1924), based on the 1922 novel by Mary Roberts Rinehart. The journey proves too exhausting for Moore, who almost perishes during a blizzard. Recovering shortly after, he suffers from amnesia. At home, others think he is dead. An actress finally recognizes him. When the real murderer confesses, the young doctor regains his memory and is reunited with his lover.

Soldier George Hackathorne, considered killed in action, returns to the surprise of many, in Maurice Campbell's weak, post-World War I drama, *Wandering Fires* (1925), based on a story by Warner Fabian. He arrives home as a shell-shocked figure who has suffered loss of memory. However, a familiar piano tune helps him to recall his past. Married couple Wallace MacDonald and Constance Bennett are directly affected by the warrior's sudden return, since the latter had had an affair with him before he left for France. But she assures her husband that Hackathorne's presence will not influence their marriage.

Norman Ward and Ted Williams, African-American twin brothers who were orphaned at an early age, later fall in love with the same young woman in the domestic drama, *A Modern Cain* (1925). Williams, jealous over his brother, pushes his rival off a cliff and later reports his brother, who is also his business partner, as missing. Ward, however, survives the fall, but loses his memory. A physician is able to cure him. Ward returns home, only to learn that his brother, a drug addict, has died as a result of his addiction. He marries the woman whom he and his brother had loved.

Another tale about a World War I soldier suffering from shell-shock and amnesia, Phil Rosen's domestic drama, *The Closed Gate* (1927), adds a family conflict involving a strong-willed, unforgiving father and his fun-loving, adolescent son, John Harron. Early in the film Harron hops on the running board of a car driven by a female companion. The vehicle goes over a cliff and the woman is killed. When Harron's mother learns of the incident, she collapses and dies. His father, holding his son's behavior partially responsible, disowns Harron, who then volunteers to serve in France. His father believes his son has been killed in action. In reality, Harron has lost his memory. His nurse, Jane Novak, after falling in love with him, marries him and accompanies the young man back to the States. Following a string of complications, Harron and his formerly stern father reconcile their differences.

Avenging Spouse

I. The Unfaithful and the Vindictive

The avenging spouse cycle, like the cycles dealing with battered women and divorce, often says more about contemporary society than the plot or characters of an individual film. Some of the earliest revenge entries, from *Justified* (1909) to *The Unfaithful Wife* (1915), focused on the confinement or concealment of morally suspected spouses or lovers. The use of this image, perhaps as a metaphor for hiding or covering up guilt on the part of transgressors or denial by the offended spouse, suggests questions about the social and moral codes of the period. How prevalent was the need for vengeance on the part of a spouse during this period? One strange ploy witnessed in some of these plots depicts a vindictive woman who, as part of her strategy, purposely marries her intended target, as in *The Barricade* (1917). Since infidelity seems to be the major cause of the spouse's retaliation, as exemplified in such films as *Justified* (1909), *The Sealed Door* (1909) and *The Light Within* (1918), just how widespread was this problem in society during the early decades of this century? Was this a major social issue or problem at that time? Did movie audiences generally condone or condemn the obsessed or consumed perpetrator for his or her actions? What was the general attitude of the directors and screenwriters toward their characters? Did the moral tone in these dramas change over the years? Many of these questions are worth considering in retrospect.

A wife's secret lover hides in a trunk when the pair learns her husband is returning in Thomas Ricketts's *Justified* (1909), a short, intelligently developed drama. When the husband, J. H. Gilmour, enters, he observes his wife's (Ethel Clayton) nervousness. His suspicions are confirmed when he sees a smoldering cigar stump. He then takes a revolver and acts as though he is about to do some target practicing. He then forces his wife to attach a paper target to the trunk containing her lover. He then fires once into the trunk. When a porter arrives, the husband directs him to remove the labeled trunk.

A king, suspicious of his wife, builds a sealed room in D. W. Griffith's revenge drama, *The Sealed Door* (1909). To confirm his suspicions, he then closely observes the woman and her lover. He then announces that he must leave on a long trip concerning matters of state. Following his departure, the lovers immediately enter the newly built room. The king returns and, in a scheme to smother the lovers, orders workers to seal the door, the only access to the room. The couple, after realizing they are trapped, are seen suffocating to death. The film is sometimes listed under its alternate title: *The Sealed Room*.

A similar tale unfolds in the crudely produced drama, *Buried Alive*, also released in 1909, about two months after Griffith's work. When a miser offers to cancel a neighbor's debt if he can have the debtor's daughter for his wife, the father refuses. But the young woman, to help her father, agrees. Once married, she displays only contempt toward her spouse. When the senile miser leaves for business, she meets secretly with her young boyfriend. The youth quickly hides in a closet before the husband returns. The miser, noticing two glasses on the table, grows suspicious. Seeking revenge, he hires masons to seal the closet door, which he has deduced is the hiding place of the intruder. The youth is then seen suffocating in the sealed closet. He eventually forces open the sealed door. When the elderly miser sees his victim freed from his intended tomb, he succumbs to a heart attack.

A struggling couple undergo a string of adversities in *The Price of Fame* (1910). The husband, a poor musician, has difficulties selling his composition. His wife is forced to take in sewing just to put some scraps of food on the table. When he, in disgust, throws his composition into the fire, his spouse saves it and submits it to a contest. One day, a neighbor enters the apartment and tries to make love to the wife, who rejects him. As he embraces her, the husband enters. In anger, he misconstrues the incident and forces her to leave. He then learns his piece has won ten thousand dollars in the contest. Later, the neighbor explains to the musician exactly what had occurred between him and the man's wife. The husband then finds his wife, who is living in squalor. He begs her forgiveness, and the couple return to their home to enjoy his newfound fame.

Genevieve Hamper portrays the title character in J. Gordon Edwards's *The Unfaithful Wife* (1915), a gruesome revenge drama set in Italy during a cholera plague. Hamper, who is married to a count (Robert Mantell), is having an affair with Stuart Holmes, an artist. When the count falls ill from sunstroke, his wife and lover bury him, thinking he has died. He returns, however, and, following a series of complications, he leads his unfaithful wife, now blindfolded, to a tomb and locks her in to suffer a slow death.

One popular theme was the lure of the city. Even this motif had its variations. The innocent woman either was fascinated with the stage, wanted to study art, or simply chose to leave her dull village or town for the bright lights of the city. A young, innocent country girl meets a handsome man vacationing in the vicinity, and the two soon become lovers, despite her father's warnings, in John H. Collins's drama, *Gladiola* (1915). When he asks her to accompany him to the city, she agrees. He sets her up in her own apartment and furnishes her with a fashionable wardrobe. Suddenly, her beau's wife arrives and introduces herself. This is enough to send the country girl back home, where gossip spreads quickly. A child is born. Meanwhile, the man, vacationing on his yacht, learns that his wife has died and is relieved. He goes to the country girl, who rejects him. Their child enters the room, but this does not influence her. She remains adamant about not rekindling the old romance.

William Farnum suspects his wife of infidelity in Oscar C. Apfel's drama, *A Man of Sorrow* (1916), based on the 1885 play, *Hoodman Blind*, by Henry Arthur Jones and Wilson Barrett. When he sees his wife, Dorothy Bernard, with another man, he leaves her in disgust and despair. He later meets a woman who strongly resembles his wife. She confesses that a man who has fallen in love with her hired her to impersonate Bernard. He wanted the stranger to flirt with a man so that Farnum would suspect the worst. Farnum then seeks out the culprit, beats him and turns him over to the law. It seems the villain is wanted for murder. Farnum then returns to his wife, and the couple reconcile their differences.

Mabel Taliaferro, a young woman who thinks Frank Currier is responsible for her father's financial ruin, agrees to marry him as a means of revenge in Edwin Carewe's unconvincing drama, *The Barricade* (1917). In reality, Currier has paid off her father's debt, a sum that the father had embezzled from his corporation. On their wedding night, the bride rejects his amorous advances and reveals her reason for the marriage. She then takes a large sum of money he has given her and invests it in Wall Street. After breaking her husband financially, she learns the truth from her father, who has just returned from a vacation. She rushes to her husband to beg his forgiveness.

Madame Petrova portrays a bacteriologist in Larry Trimble's *The Light Within* (1918), who, although married to Lumsden Hare, is in love with Thomas Holding, a fellow doctor. She originally married the wealthy Hare as a means of funding her research in discovering cures for various diseases. When she thinks she has a cure for meningitis, Holding volunteers to test her serum. She injects him with the deadly disease. But her jealous husband has secretly destroyed her new serum. When she discovers the loss, she furiously works to make a new batch. She succeeds and injects the dying doctor with the serum. Meanwhile, her husband, who has cut himself when he smashed the test-tube, has inoculated himself with the dreaded disease and dies a slow and agonizing death.

Jane Novak, the daughter of a deceased missionary, has been brought up in Japan in the home of Sessue Hayakawa in James Young's sentimental drama, *The Temple of Dusk* (1918). Her ward loves her, and she reciprocates his affection – until she meets a fellow American, Lewis Willoughby, whom she marries. Several years later, alone and about to die, she begs Hayakawa to take care of her young daughter. The father remarries and takes his family to the States, with Hayakawa hired to look after the child. The second wife renews an affair with a former lover, a situation that Hayakawa tries to conceal. Willoughby discovers the deception and stabs the lover. To protect the child, her caretaker confesses and goes to prison. During a storm, he senses the child is in danger. So he escapes, although he is wounded by a guard's bullet. He arrives at the house to find the child's bed empty. He then discovers her in the rain, soaking wet. She had been trying to go to him. He takes her back to her bed, all the while growing weaker. The guards arrive and discover he has died. The child, unaware of this, thinks he is asleep and has been stroking her hair.

Frank Mills, too busy accumulating wealth, assigns his best friend to entertain his wife in the hackneyed drama, *Her Husband's Friend* (1918). One night, J. Frank Glendon, the friend, takes out Lillian Kemble, his pal's wife, and both have too much to drink. After he brings her home, he enters her boudoir and hovers over her. Mills enters unexpectedly and, assuming the worst, turns her out, with their daughter, while he keeps the son. Years later, Kemble ends up impoverished, having gone through the settlement money. Using a pseudonym, she takes a position as supervisor of a fashionable restaurant, where her son, and the son of the man who had wronged her, are frequent patrons. They befriend Kemble's daughter. Following several complications, Glendon confesses all, and the family is reunited.

In George D. Baker's *The Cinema Murder* (1919), based on the novel by E. Phillips Oppenheim, married Wall Street backer Anders Randolf has a play director fire actress Marion Davies. He has devised a convoluted plot to make her his mistress. Davies falls for his line about promising her a trip abroad to study acting and a theater of her own upon her return. Later, she returns from abroad with a boyfriend, evoking jealousy in Randolf. When she rejects his proposition, he seeks revenge by checking the background of her beau. But he finally accepts his defeat and gives her his blessing. The drama uses an interesting trick opening that has been repeated in several films since. Marion Davies portrays a spurned mistress who shoots her lover after he refuses to marry her. She points to a baby in a crib, and then proceeds to fling the infant across the room. Suddenly, the screen reveals that the entire scene is actually part of a movie studio set with a movie camera filming the action.

II. The Silken Shackles of Love, Marriage and Betrayal

The next decade of films concerning the avenging spouse brought subtle changes to these dramas. The characters were more astutely drawn, given better motivation in general and, overall, were more interesting. Many of these films emphasized the inner strengths of their women. In *Hush* (1921), for example, a strong-willed wife who has suffered an indiscretion before her marriage refuses to tell her husband the man's name, even when he threatens to leave her. In *The Innocent Cheat* (1921), the wife of a reprobate husband who wants custody of their child in a lawsuit surprises him by admitting that the child was conceived by a former lover before the marriage. She wins the custody case. Characters were more responsive to their consciences, if not to their mates or other family members. In *Bitter Apples* (1927), for instance, Myrna Loy, who is determined to ruin Monte Blue, whom she blames for her father's death, deliberately marries him. However, she soon falls in love with him. And in *Conquest* (1929), Monte Blue intends to cause the death of H. B. Warner, who stole Blue's fiancée; instead, he ends up trying to save his life. Directors and writers spent more time exploring the ramifications of hate and the search for vengeance within characters. Revenge, infidelity, lust and greed still tended to dominate the plots, but these themes were handled more delicately in exposition – except where the films were blatantly sensational. A mine owner's obsession with vengeance in *Dawn of Revenge* (1922) costs him his own life as well as that of the man who wronged him. Even westerns exploited the revenge theme. In *The Crimson Challenge* (1922), for example, Dorothy Dalton avenges the murder of her father by eventually gunning down the man responsible, sinister saloonkeeper Frank Campeau.

H. B. Warner, as the title character in Robert Thornby's drama, *Felix O'Day* (1920), based on the 1915 novel by F. Hopkinson Smith, vows vengeance upon Ray Ripley, who stole Warner's wife and caused his father's death. He tracks Ripley to New York, where he learns that Ripley has attacked and robbed an antique shop owner. Warner is hired to help in the store, where he soon falls in love with the owner's daughter. One day he sees his wife pass the store and follows her to Ripley. But before he can catch him, the man falls to his death. Warner notices how wretched his wife looks, after living an impoverished life with Ripley. He joins her and starts to care for her. But it is too late. The sickly woman dies after she encourages her husband to marry the shop owner's daughter and build a new life with her.

Japanese architect Sessue Hayakawa, working as a gardener for a retired criminal, is framed for his employer's murder, in Colin Campbell's drama, *Black Roses* (1921). In addition, the former gang members of the victim have kidnapped Hayakawa's wife. Once in prison, Hayakawa meets a former member of the gang who has been betrayed by Myrtle Stedman, one of the gang leaders. He helps the architect to escape. Hayakawa then poses as a wealthy Japanese who lets it be known that he is looking to hire a young Japanese woman to impersonate a wealthy merchant's daughter. The gang, interested in his offer, leads him to where his wife is being held captive. He traps the gang, rescues his wife and provides evidence that convicts the gang of killing his former employer.

Clara Kimball Young, in Harry Garson's drama, *Hush* (1921), is troubled by an earlier indiscretion that she has never confessed to J. Frank Glendon, her husband. However, when her former lover and his wife show up at the same resort where Young and her husband are vacationing, she decides to reveal all – except the name of the man. Glendon suspects the wrong man and grows jealous. When he insists on knowing who the man is and she refuses to tell him, he elects to separate from her. However, a woman friend of the couple fortunately arranges reconciliation.

Charles Graham, who has discovered a silver mine in Richard Travers's weak drama, *Dawn of Revenge* (1922), is then cheated in love. Vowing vengeance upon the man who stole his love from him, Graham spends the next several years seeking his personal justice. Following a string of complications, he eventually arranges a scheme involving a marriage of two youths. But he learns that his plot was wrong-headed and ill conceived. His final act of revenge concerns his setting off a dynamite blast, in which both he and the villain perish. The convoluted plot works against the film.

Sinister saloon owner and political boss of a small cattle town Frank Campeau desires Dorothy Dalton, the daughter of a rancher, in Paul Powell's western drama, *The Crimson Challenge* (1922), based on the 1919 novel, *Tharon of Lost Valley*, by Vingie E. Roe. When she rejects him, Campeau has her father murdered. She swears to avenge her father's death. Meanwhile, Campeau learns that she loves cowboy Jack Mower, so he kidnaps the cowboy and threatens to kill him unless Dalton marries the saloon owner, who plans to divorce his wife, Irene Hunt. His wife, refusing to tolerate her husband's slighting her, informs Dalton of the place where Campeau is holding Mower. Dalton and the townspeople free the captive and attack Campeau and his gang. Dalton pursues the leader and kills him. The young couple then plan their wedding.

Lawson Butt portrays a husband who vows to avenge his wife in Lloyd Carleton's mild drama, *Beyond the Crossroads* (1922). When Butt returns home after being away for six months, he discovers his wife has left him for someone else. She then returns and asks him to forgive her. She dies a short time later, leaving the lamenting husband to swear vengeance upon the man who has wronged her. Butt sets out to find his target, and meets Ora Carew, a young woman with whom he begins to fall in love. He then learns she is engaged to the reprobate he is looking for. He gets his satisfaction by proving to Carew that her fiancé is involved in illegal business schemes.

Kathleen Kirkham's elderly and disreputable husband plots against her so that he can achieve a divorce and custody of their child in Ben Wilson's interesting domestic drama, *The Innocent Cheat* (1921). The husband prefers being surrounded by a bevy of thinly clad chorus girls aboard his yacht – rather than raise a family, a concern of his wife. In frustration, he hires a man to compromise his own wife. Although the plot fails, the husband nevertheless goes through with the divorce proceedings and wins custody of the child. At this point, Kirkham claims the child is not his. She explains that while separated from him, she met engineer Roy Stewart in her mountain retreat and the pair fell in love. When Stewart, who anticipated marrying Kirkham, learned she was already married, he began to drink heavily. The judge's decision is then reversed, and she regains custody of her little girl. Stewart, meanwhile, has stopped his drinking.

Henry King's *Fury* (1923) concerns a son's duty to carry out his father's dying wish. Richard Barthelmess is the young man burdened with the thought of avenging his father by finding the man who stole the latter's wife from him. The dying man, an embittered ship captain, has carried this hatred for years. His son, a sailor aboard his father's vessel, promises his father he will seek out the man and exact the proper punishment upon him. Once on shore, Barthelmess finds his mother and the man. A furious battle between the two ensues, with the son getting the worst of it. Back on board the ship, the disheartened youth faces another conflict with the newly appointed captain, his rival for the love of waterfront waif Dorothy Gish. The adversaries engage in a violent fight, with the captain slipping overboard into the sea.

An innocent wife's confession fails to help Blanche Sweet, as the poor, vulnerable title character in Marshall Neilan's *Tess of the d'Urbervilles* (1924), based on Thomas Hardy's popular novel. She is forced to work as a servant for the ruthless and unscrupulous Alec D'Urberville. Her shiftless father, believing he is the descendant of royal blood, compels his daughter to take the position. Meanwhile, Tess has a difficult time repelling the lustful master's advances – until he finally violates her. She leaves his house and gives birth to his child that soon dies. Tess is now a marked woman. Later, ashamed of her past, she reluctantly marries gentle Angel Clare (Conrad Nagel), who does not want to know about her past. In Hardy's book, she finally tells him, and he abandons her. Out of desperation, she renews her relationship with her former master, eventually killing him for ruining her life. She is caught and hanged as a murderess. This was the original film ending that was soon changed to a happier outcome for box-office purposes, much to the disappointment of both the director and Thomas Hardy.

An Italian immigrant couple, recently married and living in New York City, undergoes a series of adversities in Chester Bennett's implausible and somber domestic drama, *The Lullaby* (1924). The happy couple, expecting a child, suddenly suffers a horrible experience when Robert Anderson, the husband, witnesses his best friend in the midst of sexually attacking his wife, Jane Novak. A fight rages between the two men, after which the friend is gunned down in defense of the woman's honor. Both the husband and wife are arrested, the husband convicted of murder and his wife sentenced to twenty years. Anderson is eventually hanged. Novak's baby is born in prison and adopted by the kindly judge, who has advanced to governor. Seventeen years later, a gaunt, pale, broken woman emerges from prison, seeking her daughter, who is about to have her coming-out party. Novak interrupts the affair, and the mother and her daughter are reunited.

A Spanish army officer turns to banditry after his wife is killed by his own commanding officer in Tom Terriss's romantic drama, *The Bandolero* (1924), based on the 1904 novel by Paul Gwynne. Pedro de Cordoba, known as The Bandolero, the notorious bandit leader, avenges his dead wife by kidnapping

Manuel Granado, the son of the commander. Years later, Granado falls in love with The Bandolero's daughter, Renée Adorée, a romance condemned by the bandit leader. Granado leaves in frustration and becomes a famous matador. A bull gorges him as the result of a young vamp who is jealous of the matador's love for another. The commander discovers that Granado is his long-lost son and finally makes peace with The Bandolero. Both fathers consent to the marriage of their children.

Arthur Hohl portrays several roles in J. Gordon Edwards's disarming drama, *It Is the Law* (1924), based on the 1922 play by Elmer Rice and Hayden Talbot. Hohl and his friend, Herbert Heyes, both love Mimi Palmeri, who chooses Heyes for her husband. Hohl plots his revenge by assigning a tramp, who strongly resembles him, as his replacement when he calls the bridegroom to meet with him. As Heyes approaches, Hohl kills the tramp and arranges matters so that Heyes is accused of murdering Hohl, who then flees. His friend receives a life sentence. Five years later, Hohl, now sporting a beard, returns, hoping to win Palmeri's love. When she discovers the stranger is Hohl, she arranges for her husband's release. Heyes returns, finds Hohl, and shoots him, with the knowledge that no person can be prosecuted twice for the same crime. Hohl played the same role in the stage version several years earlier.

Tom Mix, married to Rose Bronson, is shot by gambler Ed Brady, who then runs off with Mix's wife, in Mix's action drama, *A Child of the Prairie* (1925). The couple's little daughter wanders off and is found on the prairie by two hunters who adopt her. Fifteen years later, she has grown into womanhood and the joy of a ranch. Mix returns, very much alive, and shoots the man who had stolen his wife. He then finds his lost daughter and the two renew their relationship. The film is an expansion of an older, two-reel western first released in 1915.

Conniving Ruth Stonehouse, who wants to hold on to Niles Welch, her wealthy fiancé, plots to eliminate her rival in Burton King's mediocre drama, *Ermine and Rhinestones* (1926). She visits her competition and tries to buy her off. Suddenly, someone comes to the door, and the visitor hides in another room. A villainous figure enters and gags Stonehouse's rival. He then turns on the gas and flees. Stonehouse reappears and, instead of reviving the victim of the brutal attack, she escapes through a window, leaving the unconscious woman exposed to the deadly gas. Fortunately, Welch arrives in time to save the woman he loves, explaining that he prefers her to his fiancée. The title obviously suggests that riches have little to do with character.

Huntly Gordon decided to teach Irene Rich, his flirtatious wife, a lesson or two, in Walter Morosco's sophisticated comedy, *Silken Shackles* (1926), based on a play by Charles K. Harris. Rich is attracted to a violinist in Hungary, who confides to her that he is of the aristocratic class, but the war has caused him to lose his fortune. Gordon, fed up with her flirtations, hires the musician (Victor Varconi) to romance the willing wife and then disillusion her by showing a loss of interest in her and rejecting her affections. However, the husband's scheme backfires when the musician begins to fall in love with Rich. Varconi's parents turn out to be ill-mannered peasants, whose boorishness quickly cures the wife's flirtatious way and sends her rushing back to her husband's arms.

Hobart Bosworth seeks vengeance upon the man who double-crossed him, stole his wife and child and framed him on a false murder charge, in George B. Seitz's action drama, *The Blood Ship* (1927). The embittered Bosworth is a sailor aboard a ship known as a hell hole because of its cruel captain (Walter James), who is not above killing disobedient crew members. Before he can fulfill his avowed revenge, he must first deal with James, who has earlier physically beaten Bosworth with a leather strap after hanging him by his wrists. In the final clash, Bosworth uses the same strap on James, beats him to death and throws his body to the sharks.

In Harry D'Arrast's light comedy, *A Gentleman of Paris* (1927), Adolphe Menjou portrays the title character, a womanizer who has even dallied with his valet's wife. When his valet learns about this betrayal of trust, he seeks revenge by planting a card up his master's sleeve. He then accuses Menjou of cheating. The nobleman is humiliated and disgraced. But when Menjou feigns suicide, he rekindles his valet's loyalty, and the latter publicly confesses to the frame-up.

Villainy is afoot against Gypsy leader Ronald Colman on his wedding night in George Fitzmaurice's romantic costume drama, *The Night of Love* (1927). Montagu Love, a vicious duke, kidnaps Colman's wife and, when he threatens what he will do to her, she takes her own life. The grieving widow, a Robin Hood-like Gypsy chief, seeks vengeance, and in time, the opportunity arises. When the duke marries Vilma Banky, a princess, the Gypsy leader kidnaps her, much to the chagrin of Love. But Colman, more human and sophisticated than his foe, turns his captive over to the Gypsy women to guard. Eventually, Banky falls in love with her captor. Instead of returning to her husband, she elects the Church for her future. The duke disguises himself as a priest, but his wife discovers his ploy and sends a message to Colman. The Gypsy leader responds immediately, but he is captured and ordered to be burned at the stake. Banky frees him, and in the fracas that follows, the treacherous duke is killed.

After his father dies, Monte Blue finds himself left with a bankrupt business that creates personal problems for him, in Harry O. Hoyt's drama, *Bitter Apples* (1927), based on the story by Harold McGrath. Although he sells his father's business, other investors' relatives hold him responsible. When one such investor takes his own life, his son, Paul Ellis, and his sister, Myrna Loy, take the Sicilian oath to avenge their father. The sister changes her name, makes Blue fall in love with her and marries him. Aboard an ocean liner on their honeymoon, she condemns her surprised husband for what his father did to her father. The ship then strikes a reef, and a band of rumrunners overpowers the crew. Blue rescues his wife from the drunken captain while a U.S. warship saves the passengers. The young married couple then reconcile their differences.

Monte Blue and H. B. Warner, while trying to fly their airplane to the South Pole, crash in a remote section of the Antarctic, in Roy Del Ruth's contrived drama, *Conquest* (1929), based on the story by Mary Imlay Taylor. When both men discover that Blue's leg is broken, Warner leaves him to die in the frozen wasteland and returns home to marry Blue's fiancée, Lois Wilson. She accepts his proposal out of pity for him and believing Blue has perished. Meanwhile, Blue is rescued by a whaling ship and, although he is partially scarred and half-crazed, he vows revenge. Once back home, he persuades Wilson's father to finance another flight. He takes Warner with him, and this time the latter's leg is fractured in a crash. Although planning to abandon Warner, Blue finds that he cannot carry out the horrible act. Instead, he helps him struggle toward safety. During the arduous journey, Warner begs his companion to forgive him and then proceeds to take his own life. This permits Blue to renew his romance with his former fiancée. Made during the transitional period in Hollywood, the film was also released in a sound version one month earlier.

Backstage

I. The Lure of the Footlights

Early films about life backstage included comedies, travesties and dramas, with some resorting to cross-dressing to get laughs. Travesties of the stage and screen soon began to appear. *The Fate of Flora Fourflush* (1914), a crude and frenetic spoof of movie melodramas, featured Clara Kimball Young as the title character. Early silent backstage dramas varied greatly in themes and plots, with some more popular than others. One favorite scenario centered on the lure of the footlights to the young from rural communities – along with the accompanying dangers, as Dorothy Gish faced in *Stagestruck* (1917). Another, such as *Behind the Scenes* (1914) and *The Final Curtain* (1916), concerned the chorus girl or performer who finds life away from these same footlights too difficult to bear. The villain in these films, if there was any, was usually the jealous or lecherous producer or manager, as in *Underneath the Paint* (1915), *The Destroying Angel* (1915) and *Stranded* (1916). Films like *The Reward* (1915) explored the morality of the world of the theater. These early films suggested the difficulties the main characters faced were of their own making. Perhaps not so surprising – chiefly because of their vulnerability – was the fact that virtually all the major characters were female.

Mary Pickford, as a former chorus girl in James Kirkwood's *Behind the Scenes* (1914), marries farmer James Kirkwood and prepares to settle down on his farm. But the humdrum existence of farm life and its solitude prove too much for the child of the Great White Way and she leaves when she is offered a starring role in a musical comedy. She is a smash hit on opening night and all the cast congratulate her. The heavy-set manager enters her dressing room to offer his accolades and begins to make love to her. Her husband, who has come to see her performance, arrives in time to witness his wife trying to fend off the repulsive manager's advances. Pickford, delighted to see him, resigns from the show and returns with her husband to their farm.

Alma Hanlon in *The Final Curtain* (1916) portrays a minor actress in a small-town repertory company who is "discovered" by a New York actor. She is hired for a Broadway musical and is a success. She then marries an admirer, woolen manufacturer Arthur Hoops, and retires from the stage. But when her husband places his business interests above those of his wife, she returns to the footlights. Hoops, in disgust, loses further interest in her. Later, when his business suffers and others are plotting against him, his wife, now a telephone operator, learns of the scheme and sends him an anonymous tip. His business secured, Hoops finds his wife and the couple are reunited.

Lillian Gish, as the title character in William Christy Cabanne's *Diana of the Follies* (1916), is plucked from the chorus by an eccentric millionaire (Sam De Grasse), who believes he can make her forget her past lifestyle. His scholarly background convinces him that he can replace her artificial stage life with that of culture and taste. They marry and, even after a child is born, she still yearns for the excitement and the applause of the stage. When she regales some of her former theater friends at home, her husband in disgust leaves her. Diana returns to the stage and becomes the star of the Follies. When she learns that her child is fatally ill, she rushes home, but it is too late. She then returns to her life on the stage.

These backstage dramas provided little opportunity for the writer to introduce a wide variety of villains. As a result, the most common rogue was the manager or the producer. Charles L. Gaskill's *Underneath the Paint* (1915), a bland, tasteless and disappointing drama, concerns a theatrical producer's efforts to besmirch an innocent actress's reputation to protect his son. When the father learns his son is falling in love with the actress, he contrives matters to make it appear that the young woman has been a mistress to the father. The disillusioned son leaves home and begins leading a dissolute life. The conscience-driven father, realizing his actions have led to his son's downfall, takes his own life. The young woman, finally achieving success on the stage, sends a note to her former lover, and the couple reconcile their differences.

Another villainous theatrical manager proves to be a murderer as well as a despoiler of women in Richard Ridgely's overly dramatic *The Destroying Angel* (1915), based on the novel by Louis Joseph Vance. Mabel Trunnelle portrays an actress who is one of the manager's potential victims. Following several murders, he is finally killed by the husband of one of the women he has been stalking.

In Cecil B. DeMille's drama, *Temptation* (1915), the villain is an impresario. The film retells the overworked tale of a lecherous impresario (Theodore Roberts) who discharges a qualified opera singer when she rejects his immoral requests. The singer, Geraldine Farrar, is in love with composer Pedro De Cordoba, who also is suffering because of the impresario. The latter refuses to buy the composer's work. Eventually, the couple overcome these adversities. Farrar gets to sing the starring role, and De Cordoba sells his opera. The lustful Roberts, on the other hand, succumbs to stab wounds from his jealous mistress.

Many backstage films explored the moral, and sometimes amoral, world of the theater. Reginald Barker's drama, *The Reward* (1915), suggests the commonly held belief that a young woman cannot rise in the world of the stage without making moral compromises. Bessie Barriscale portrays a chorus girl known as "The Iceberg" by her colleagues because she refuses to participate in their wild parties. Arthur Maude, a friend of the frolickers, doubts that a young woman, when offered the choice of taking "the easiest way," would refuse. To prove it, he bets he can break down Barriscale's resistance. The pair meet, and Maude fails in his attempts. But when she is fined for arriving at the theater late while two other dancers escape reprimand because they have contacts with some of the owners, she begins to believe her values may be all wrong. She goes to Maude's apartment, a move that disillusions the young man, who has been thinking of proposing to her. He tries to convince her to hold on to her standards. Just then a doctor in the hotel calls upon her to help him deliver a baby. After the pair witness the birth, Maude proposes to the woman he has grown to love.

Other films were more outspoken about the perils young women faced along the Gay White Way. In Frank Reicher's backstage drama, *The Chorus Lady* (1915), based on the 1906 play by James Forbes, Cleo Ridgely portrays a streetwise chorus girl who is engaged to detective Wallace Reid. She is forced to protect Margery Daw, her young, naïve sister. Daw, also a chorus girl, falls under the spell of Richard Grey, a theatrical backer who is seeking to take advantage of the inexperienced sister. Ridgely, in an attempt to distract him from his sister, decides to make a play for Grey. But her boyfriend, Reid, sees them embracing and breaks up with her. Later, Daw explains the situation and the couple are reunited. They move to the country to escape urban life. Daw and her new boyfriend, an assistant stage manager, join the married couple.

William Humphrey's episodic drama, *The Footlights of Fate* (1916), based on the 1913 novel, *Joan Thursday*, by Louis Joseph Vance, traces the trials and tribulations of Naomi Childers, a young woman determined to carve out a career for herself on the stage. But she is continually hampered by thoughtless and lust-driven men interested only in seducing her. As a young clerk and innocent, she is forced to slap an overly friendly boss. Later, when she and her vaudeville partner become successful, she rejects his amorous advances and he leaves the team. Another actor then lures her to his rooms. But his rejected and jealous mistress shoots him. In disgust, the aspiring actress finally returns home to her shiftless father.

Edward Morrisey's *Stagestruck* (1917) is just another cautionary tale about the perils that face a naïve young woman who pines for the world of the stage. Dorothy Gish, a star-struck youngster, leaves home, armed only with her hopes and dreams and a few dollars. She meets an unscrupulous theatrical promoter who takes her money and that of other members of a troupe of aspiring actors. He takes them out of town and then leaves them stranded. When she returns to her decrepit boarding house, she discovers that her husband, Frank Bennet, has abandoned her. Following several complications, she meets him and persuades him to reform from his dissolute ways – much to the satisfaction of his wealthy mother.

Joseph De Grasse's *Triumph* (1917), based on the story by Samuel Hopkins Adams, is another cautionary drama about the pitfalls that await young women who dream about a theatrical career. Stage-struck Dorothy Phillips meets a young actor of a repertory company at the railway station, and the two become friends. She arrives dreamy-eyed in New York, where a lascivious manager gives her a major role, in the hopes of eventually seducing her. When problems arise and the manager says the play will not be presented, the aspiring actress goes to his apartment to plead with him to reconsider. He then offers her his proposition – that she give herself to him or face the closing of the play. She accepts, if he calls the theater and announces that the show will be performed. She then stabs him and flees to the playwright who loves her. He sends her back to the theater, calls the police and confesses to the murder. He then takes his own life. When she learns what has occurred, she substitutes a real knife for the final act and kills herself on stage. The film then shifts back to the railway station and the actor, who announces to his fellow thespians that he has just concocted a story to cure an aspiring actress from going on the stage. The final scene shows Phillips returning to her boyfriend, whom she embraces.

An unscrupulous manager absconds with the evening's receipts, leaving his company of actors stranded in a small town in Lloyd Ingraham's entertaining drama, *Stranded* (1916). De Wolfe Hopper portrays a has-been Shakespearean actor who joins the fly-by-night troupe. When Bessie Love, as a trapeze artist with a broken arm, is left behind, the old actor remains with her. Hopper, posing as an acting teacher and Shakespeare scholar, is hired to coach a group of players in a nearby town, with Love pretend to be his daughter. She falls in love with the son of a hotel owner. As they are about to be married, Carl Stockdale, the crooked manager, shows up in town and threatens to expose the pair. A struggle ensues and Hopper is mortally shot. But he holds out long enough to recite the death scene from *Julius Caesar* for the wedding guests and give away the bride before he succumbs.

The stage holds out too strong a temptation for Julia Dean, a wife and mother, who is lured away by a silver-tongued scoundrel, in Edmund Lawrence's drama, *The Ransom* (1916), based on *The Marionettes* by Eve Unsell. But the romance and glamour, she soon discovers, are all illusory. As she sinks into the depths of despair, she ends up as a backstage maid to Louise Huff, her own daughter. Without revealing her true identity, she protects her daughter from the man who had led her astray by killing him. She then dies without revealing her real identity to her daughter.

Dorothy Phillips, a young woman from a small town, comes to New York and gets a job on Broadway as a chorus girl in Ida May Park's familiar romantic drama, *Broadway Love* (1917), based on the story by W. Carey Wonderly. Juanita Hansen, a fellow dancer, invites her to a party in her apartment, where Phillips meets William Stowell, a young millionaire who takes an interest in her. When the party gets a little too wild for Phillips, she asks Stowell to take her home. In the taxi, he mistakes her offer to mean she wants to be alone with him, so he becomes amorously aggressive. She dashes out of the taxi and hurts her leg. After the show closes and she runs out of money, Stowell offers to take care of her, but she refuses and moves away. He eventually finds her and the two reconcile their differences. Lon Chaney had a minor role as Phillips's crude and offensive small-town suitor.

Bessie Love portrays a young woman who aspires to become a major stage actress in Alice Blaché's *The Great Adventure* (1918), a minor drama based on the short story, "The Painted Scene," by Henry Kitchell. After appearing in school productions, the budding actress is encouraged to go to New York, where she will be an instant success. She and her aunt arrive in New York, where Love obtains a part in a play. A fellow actor, Chester Barnett, lives in the same boarding house, and the two become good friends. When the leading lady of the show leaves, Love is given the role and delights the audience with her performance. Donald Hall, the leading man, although married, makes a play for the aspiring actress, but following several complications, including Love's having to rescue the star who almost drowns, she chooses Barnett.

Perry N. Vekroff's *What Love Forgives* (1919) is an overly sentimental drama about sin and sinners. Barbara Castleton, a young woman and essentially the only character who keeps her virtue, ends up being sinned against by others. Muriel Ostriche, the star player in a road company, gets college song writer John Bowers drunk during a party and takes him to her room. The next morning, he displays disgust toward her and leaves. She in turn charges that he has ruined her life. She then marries well-to-do Joseph Smiley. Feeling guilty, Bowers returns, with plans to marry her. He meets Barbara Castleton, Smiley's daughter, and soon falls in love with her. Ostriche leaves her husband and, learning about Bowers' marriage, plans to blackmail him. But Castleton overhears the threat and forgives her husband.

Occasionally, the background may shift from the stage to film making. But the dangers remain the same. A film star, learning that a naïve young country girl is in love with him, plots to seduce her, in Maurice Tourneur's *A Girl's Folly* (1917). Inexperienced Doris Kenyon pines for a movie career and all the luxuries that accompany the life of a screen star. However, she is a dismal failure in Hollywood. Robert Warwick, as the actor she most admires and loves, proposes that if she lives with him, she will fulfill most of her dreams. She agrees, and he arranges a large party to celebrate their agreement. But after some second thoughts, she turns down the offer. Meanwhile, her mother arrives on the scene. Her appearance makes Warwick acutely aware of his actions, and he ends up persuading Kenyon to return home with her mother.

Backstage films explored other problems of actors and actresses in an assortment of plots. A popular actor in Phillips Smalley's *False Colors* (1914) loses his wife during childbirth on the same evening that he scores a major success on stage. Disliking the child, whom the actor (Phillips Smalley) blames for his wife's death, he leaves his daughter with his housekeeping couple and retires to an island. He sends enough funds to the couple to care for the girl's needs and education. Eighteen years later, he decides to return to the States. The couple, meanwhile, have squandered most of the money the father has sent on their own unworthy son. His daughter (Lois Weber) has left the housekeepers' quarters and has achieved some success on the stage. Her father greets her and tries to apologize for his neglect over the years, but she rejects him. Later, a reconciliation brings the pair together.

Gertrude McCoy portrays a stage actress wrongly accused of murdering her male lead in Duncan McRae's drama, *Through Turbulent Waters* (1915), based on the story by Gertrude Lyon. A maid had overheard the pair quarrel before their final appearance on stage. It seems that McCoy has learned that the their marriage was a fake, planned by the actor, who had made her into a star and had hoped to control her and her salary by marrying her. McCoy is arrested. Her lawyer receives an anonymous phone call from a father who confesses that he had substituted real bullets for the blanks. He was seeking revenge upon the actor, who had earlier ruined the caller's daughter. The man then commits suicide. All charges against the actress are dropped.

In William A. Brady's drama, *The Ballet Girl* (1916), based on the 1912 novel, *Carnival*, by Compton Mackenzie, Alice Brady portrays a dancer who achieves fame and fortune perhaps too quickly. She soon joins in the hectic night life of the big city. Her cousin, Holbrook Blinn, arrives from the country and sharply disapproves of her lifestyle. She laughs off his criticism and continues to party. But a ruinous romance with a playboy sours her on her social life. Realizing that her cousin was right, she changes her ways and marries Blinn.

Stage actress Mae Murray and fellow performer Philo McCullough, while playing a series of one-night stands, both miss the train and the rest of their troupe in Robert Z. Leonard's hackneyed drama, *Modern Love* (1918). The actor signs a hotel register as Mr. and Mrs., without Murray's knowledge. Later that evening, a fight breaks out as she tries to prevent him from molesting her. A hotel manager enters and evicts the actor. Memories of the incident continually interfere in the actress's romantic life.

Sometimes an actor can be as mean-spirited as critics, managers and others who haunt the world of the theater. For example, Bessie Barriscale, as a successful actress, is determined to make life miserable for Jack Livingston, who is separated from his wife, in Raymond B. West's trite drama, *The Cast-Off* (1918). When Howard Hickman, a doctor who loves her, asks why she wants to hurt Livingston, she tells him her story, which is unfolded in flashback. Years earlier, Livingston promised to take her to a local theater. She dresses up for the occasion and prepared to meet him at the theater. She then saw him in the company of another young woman. In disgust, she prepared to leave. But the theater manager offered her a job in a minor role. From that moment, she swore revenge. But she also grew in stature as an actress. The doctor then takes her to visit Livingston's home, where she sees a young child. Barriscale then realizes how wrong she has been in trying to hurt this family. Instead, she works out a reconciliation between the estranged couple and then marries the doctor.

Studios occasionally explored the lighter side of the stage world. Dorothy Dalton, in Raymond B. West's romantic comedy, *Chicken Casey* (1917), portrays an actress who tries to persuade a novelist to dramatize his latest work, with her in the lead role. When he objects, claiming she is not the right type, Dalton decides to pose as that character. Her portrayal is so realistic, that the author agrees to her request. The play is a success, and the pair fall in love.

II. The Street of Illusions

The decade of the twenties continued to offer backstage dramas, several avoiding the usual clichés associated with this category. More important, a handful expanded the themes and characters' motivations. Some of these films, like the comedy *Merton of the Movies* (1924) and the horror film *The Phantom of the Opera* (1925), became classics within their genres. Others gave burgeoning directors a chance to develop their innate talents. Frank Capra, for instance, honed his remarkable skills with romantic comedy in *The Matinee Idol* (1928). Film studios, with the releases of such features as *Souls for Sale* (1923) and *Merton*, proved they were not afraid to turn their cameras inwards for a close examination of various aspects of the industry. Above all, the legendary Broadway served as the goal and dream of many. By the end of the decade, most backstage silent films leaned toward comedy or romantic comedy. The curtain was slowly descending on the genre, foreshadowed by *The Jazz Singer* (1927) and other earlier sound films. They replaced forever the silent backstage features with a surge of singing, dancing, wisecracking Hollywood musicals of the sound era of the thirties.

A veteran vaudeville actress learns a lesson about men in Edward Griffith's human tale, *The Garter Girl* (1920), based on O. Henry's story, "The Memento." Corinne Griffith, as the actress, grows disenchanted with the men she meets among her fellow actors as well as those who loiter about the stage door after the show. So she quits her stage career and retires to a small town, hoping to find "real men" there. Following several complications, she realizes that actors can be human, too. Especially important to her discovery is Earl Metcalfe, another actor.

Marion Davies, who spends too much time dancing and dining with a group of college students, raises concern in her wealthy parents, in Robert G. Vignola's comedy drama, *Enchantment* (1921), based on the story, "Manhandling Ethel," by Frank Ramsay Adams. Her father, during a theater performance of Shakespeare's *Taming of the Shrew,* starring Forrest Stanley, gets the idea that Stanley would be the right person to curb his daughter's wild behavior. He arranges for the couple to meet, after which a friend of the actor suggests that Davies star in his production of *The Sleeping Beauty*. She is delighted with the offer and accepts. But during rehearsals she insists that her college pals be allowed to attend. Stanley reluctantly relents, and during the play he kisses her vigorously. At first she is indignant, but when he begins to leave, she admits she loves him.

Mary Carr, a retired theatrical star, has financial problems in J. Searle Dawley's sentimental drama, *Broadway Broke* (1923), based on the 1922 story by Earl Derr Biggers. At present, her only means of support depends on her aging vaudeville dog, "Chum." Finally, she is able to sell her plays to film executive Dore Davidson. In addition, motion picture studios suddenly rediscover her talents and she once again gains fame as an actress, this time in motion pictures.

Rupert Hughes's extravagantly produced *Souls for Sale* (1923) serves as a fascinating look into the inner workings of a Hollywood studio and its hardworking people. The film also presents a subtle piece of propaganda, offering a positive image of the movie industry, still reeling from a series of scandals. Eleanor Boardman portrays a minister's daughter who runs out on her husband during their honeymoon, sensing something is amiss. She hops off the train and ends up in a desert somewhere in the Southwest, where members of a movie crew find her and care for her. Later, she journeys to Los Angeles and finds work with a film studio. She eventually becomes a major actress, with her leading man and her director both in love with her. But she rejects them because of her marital status. Her husband, wanted by the police as a modern day bluebeard, shows up to make trouble for the fledgling star, but he is accidentally killed when he backs up into a wind machine. This leaves her free to choose the director for her mate.

Harry Beaumont's *The Gold Diggers* (1923), based on the play by Avery Hopwood, depicts the everyday life of chorus girls, generally showing them as hardworking and concerned about their future. The plot focuses on two sisters (Hope Hampton, Louise Fazenda), with one willing to sacrifice almost everything to make certain that her sister marry the man of her choice. This was the first in a series of "Gold Digger" films turned out by Warner Bros.

Hoot Gibson, as a small-town boob, becomes infatuated with Annie Cornwall, the leading actress in a one-night performance of a traveling theatrical group, in Edward Sedgwick's inane comedy, *Forty-Horse Hawkins* (1924). When the show leaves town, Gibson follows it to the city, where he searches for the young woman of his dreams. Cornwall has become a major Broadway star, and Gibson gets a job with the same production. But neither is aware of the other's presence. Before he can succeed in winning over her love, he has the hurdle of Richard Tucker, who stands in his way. But the boob triumphs in the end.

James Cruze's satirical comedy, *Merton of the Movies* (1924), based on the 1922 hit play by George S. Kaufman and Marc Connelly and the novel by

Harry Leon Wilson, tells about a movie fan who tries his luck at a film studio. Glenn Hunter, as the title character, after being fired from his job in a village store, heads for Los Angeles. He meets comic Viola Dana, who helps him get a job at her studio. When others laugh at his acting, he thinks he is a failure, but he is soon recognized as a bright new comedy personality. The film hurls a battery of barbs at Tinseltown and its numerous fans, including Merton, whose worship of his screen hero idol and his dreams drive him to California. Two remakes followed, one in 1932 under the title *Make Me a Star*, and the other in 1947, which retained its original title.

Former actor Charles Ogle, now a stage-door keeper, grows overprotective of struggling young chorus girl Lila Lee, in William de Mille's drama, *After the Show* (1925), based on the story, "The Stage Door," by Rita Weiman. Ogle's paternal interest in Lee leads him to invite her to his home, where she meets millionaire Jack Holt, who is the backer of the show. Holt becomes interested in the chorus girl and later invites her to a party at his summer home. Meanwhile, she is beginning to fall in love with Holt. Ogle tries to warn her against becoming too involved with Holt, but she ignores his advice. The old man decides to follow her to the summer home, where he pleads with her to return home with him. When she refuses, Ogle deliberately slashes his wrist with a broken bottle. Holt, to save the old man's life, offers his own blood for the necessary transfusion. When Ogle recovers, he learns that Holt intends to marry Lee, so he rests happily.

Backstage dramas rarely ever approached the impact of Rupert Julian's horror masterpiece, *The Phantom of the Opera* (1925), adapted from Gaston Leroux's 1910 novel. The talented Lon Chaney portrays Erik, the title character, a vengeful composer who lurks in the catacombs beneath the Paris Opera House. He kidnaps understudy Mary Philbin as his singing protégée, who eventually rips off his mask to reveal a hideous sight. Norman Kerry, as Philbin's fiancé, and Arthur Edmund Carewe, as Ledoux of the secret police, finally rescue the prisoner. The Phantom is beaten to death on a wharf by an angry mob. Several remakes include a color version in 1942, with Claude Rains as the Phantom, and a British production in 1962, with Herbert Lom in the title role.

Beatrice Lillie portrays a simple servant to a traveling stock company in Sam Taylor's poignant tale, *Exit Smiling* (1926). She cares for all the little matters that concern the company, but most of all, she takes special care of Jack Pickford, a young actor whom she helps find work with the troupe. From then on Lillie, who secretly loves him, protects him from harm and serves most of his other needs. Pickford, unaware of her feelings toward him, finally returns to his family and community, where he marries the banker's daughter – much to the regret of the young woman who has cared for him during his entire stay with the troupe.

Misunderstandings among show folks provide the plot for Phil Stone's comedy drama, *Backstage* (1927). Chorus girl Barbara Bedford and two of her fellow entertainers are stranded after weeks of rehearsing when the manager runs out of funds. The three young women are evicted from their lodging when they fail to pay their rent. Bedford meets Gayne Whitman, the manager, who lets her use his apartment. William Collier Jr., her boyfriend, misunderstands the arrangement and breaks off their relationship. Following a series of similar complications, the backer of the show explains it is his apartment and not the manager's. This satisfies Collier and the young couple are reunited.

Struggling fashion designer Gladys Hulette barely escapes the lascivious designs of well-known philanderer and wealthy theatrical backer Ernest Hilliard in Burton King's drama, *A Bowery Cinderella* (1927). Residing on New York's Bowery with her sick mother, Hulette and her boyfriend, Pat O'Malley, a reporter, plan to move her mother to the country. Hilliard meets Hulette and offers her a position to work on the costumes of his present production. She accepts the job and eventually joins one of his wild parties, where she is detained. Hilliard's wife sends O'Malley to check on her husband. He finds his girlfriend in Hilliard's apartment in a compromising position and becomes disillusioned. Although she rejects Hilliard's earlier offers, she accepts his present of a new apartment for her and her mother. She and O'Malley then get back together, much to the philanderer's chagrin. He plots to get her back, but Hulette foils all his plans. O'Malley, who has earlier written a play, finally gets it produced. His success allows him to marry Hulette.

Ian Keith plays an envious ham actor in Erle C. Kenton's shallow and hackneyed drama, *The Street of Illusion* (1928), based on the story by Channing Pollock. The embittered Keith, appearing in a play, finds work for Virginia Valli, a young acquaintance. But when she begins to fall in love with Kenneth Thomson, the leading man, Keith's jealousy is aroused. He fails to recognize his own lack of talent. He replaces real bullets for the blanks in the pistol designed to shoot Thomson. When the lead is injured, Keith is called upon to fill in for him. Mortally wounded by his own treachery, Keith confesses all while listening to the applause of the audience. The final death scene on stage does little to enhance this generally dull production.

Frank Capra's romantic comedy, *The Matinee Idol* (1928), featured Johnny Walker and Bessie Love as two actors in a minor group of players. Walker, while having his car repaired in a small town in New York State, for a lark tries out for a part in a local playhouse. Hired as an extra, the overly dramatic Civil War play the thespians perform is more funny than serious. A producer in the audience hires the troupe to perform on Broadway. Walker befriends fellow actor Bessie Love, both of whom, unaware they are being exploited by the producer, are overjoyed to be appearing on Broadway. They finally realize the truth by the audience's ridiculing laughter. Love quits the show in disgust and leaves for home. Walker, who has fallen in love with her, follows her. A remake titled *The Music Goes Round* was released in 1936.

Battered Women

I. Abused in Body and Soul

Screen dramas about battered women began to appear rather early in the history of the media. But the subject was not exactly new to the nation. Socially aware writers like Jacob Riis uncovered the problem near the close of the nineteenth century. Riis, a pioneering journalist (1849-1914), was an early muckraker who wrote about city slums and abuses that occurred in lower-class urban life at the turn of the century. The movement for women's political, social and educational equality with men had many leaders, including Mary Wollstonecraft in England and Elizabeth Cady Stanton (who helped to guarantee women's rights over their children) and Susan B. Anthony (who organized the first women's temperance organization) in the United States. They insisted on full legal and economic equality for women. Early silent movies were rather crude in their presentations of the subject, while simultaneously remaining visually discreet. The writers and directors made it clear as to what was happening to the girlfriends or wives, but shied away from graphically exploiting the physical abuse on screen. Early films in this cycle established at least two distinct conventions. Audiences particularly enjoyed the first, in which the aggressor, often the brutal husband, eventually gets his just desert.

Gratitude (1909) was one of the earliest films to touch upon the subject, albeit in a crude and lighthearted way. This brief farce tells the story of an eccentric burglar who, breaking into a home and about to rob the owners of their jewels, concludes by lecturing the abusive husband about his drinking problem and, worse, his wife-beating. He finally returns the jewels after extracting a promise from the husband to stop hitting the bottle and his wife, and to offer her more love and affection. The two men conclude their business by shaking hands on the pledge.

Sometimes, the abuse occurs to a minor character. Theda Bara portrays a temptress who plots the death of her wealthy husband in Will S. Davis's social drama, *Destruction* (1915), adapted from Emile Zola's novel, *Labor*. She instigates a strike at her husband's mill, resulting in her spouse's aggravated heart condition. When her son-in-law, Gaston Bell, tries to bring his father and the workers together, Bara accused Bell of trying to rape her. The father evicts his son and plans to change his will to favor his treacherous wife. Following a series of further complications, Bara is burned to death, along with an equally evil and wicked spouse, J. Herbert Frank, a husband who has abused his wife. Bell's father dies, and the son marries the young abused widow of Frank.

The abused woman is more starkly exemplified in George Irving's powerful drama, *Body and Soul* (1915), set chiefly in Great Neck, Long Island. Florence Rockwell, while suffering from amnesia, wanders into the woods and into the cabin of sportsman Robert Whitworth. After one week, his desires toward her get the best of him and he sexually attacks her. He then brands her breast with a knife and burns down the cabin. She escapes, recovers her memory and returns home, where she becomes engaged to Kenneth Hunter, an editor. Whitworth finds her and lures her to his houseboat, where he explains that the scar on her breast means she belongs to him. He then tries to rape her, but she stabs him to death. Her fiancé and her doctor believe she is innocent because of the state of her mind. Her memory returns as the result of Hunter's tender care, and the couple soon marry. A remake appeared in 1920, directed by Charles Swickard and featuring Alice Lake, William Lawrence and Stuart Holmes.

June Daye, attracted to Francis Joyner's promise of money and security, rushes into a marriage with him, in Joseph Kaufman's domestic drama, *Heartaches* (1915). Little did Daye realize the physical abuse her husband was capable of, especially after he has engaged in one of his heavy drinking sessions. She deserts him and begins a job in a department store, where she meets wealthy Helen Greene. They both share the same apartment, and Daye meets her friend's brother, Arthur Forbes, who soon falls in love with her. Joyner, now divorced, re-enters the scene and wins Greene's love. He sours Greene on her roommate, who tries to warn her friend about his abusiveness. Although the two friends separate, Daye is determined to rescue Greene from Joyner. She persuades her friend to hide in another room while she, Daye, carries on with her ex-husband. Forbes walks in and, not understanding the situation, condemns Daye for her actions. But his sister, exposed to Joyner's real character, later explains everything to her brother and the lovers are reunited.

Fannie Ward, whose husband will not indulge her obsession with expensive clothes, invests $10,000 of charity funds entrusted to her, in the stock market and loses the money, in Cecil B. DeMille's drama, *The Cheat* (1915). To repay the stolen money, she borrows the sum from Sessue Hayakawa, a wealthy curio dealer – on one condition – that she come to him the next evening. However, when she gets the money from her husband, Hayakawa refuses to accept it. He prefers their original agreement, which she rejects. In anger, he brands her with a hot iron on her shoulder. Suffering from the pain, she shoots him. At her trial, she ends her testimony by exposing the brand on her shoulder. The angry crowd almost lynches Hayakawa. The film was remade in 1923 and was directed by George Fitzmaurice, starring Pola Negri and Jack Holt, and again in 1931, this time directed by George Abbott, starring Tallulah Bankhead, who was branded by Irving Pichel.

At times, the film studio would set their stories about battered women in foreign countries, thereby imbuing the dramas with an exotic atmosphere. William Garwood plays the title character, an Arab trader's slave, in the drama, *Imar the Servitor* (1914). He rescues an American tourist who has lost his way in the desert, and the two men become friends. Before he leaves, the American gives his friend a photograph of his fiancée. When the tourist returns home, he discovers that his girlfriend has married a horseman, both of whom have journeyed to the Arabian desert. Imar's master attacks the trader's wife. Her husband then accuses her of infidelity and starts to beat her. Imar recognizes her from the picture given to him by his American friend and rescues her. They both traverse the desert and meet her former fiancé, who has been sent for. Her husband and Imar's master are slain, leaving the three friends free of any retribution.

Marie Doro, a young woman, objects to her parents' request that she marry a native of a little fishing village in James Young's drama, *The Lash* (1916). Instead, she prefers a handsome young man who just happens to be visiting the village. Because of her recalcitrance, she is sentenced to the customary lash. But the young man returns in time to rescue Doro. He takes her to a city where they are married. The young wife later finds her husband under very suspicious circumstance with another woman, and decides to apply the lash to the intruder. Fed up with city life and all of its social demands, the young wife returns to her village, where the former sentence is renewed. But just as the lash is about to be applied, her husband again intervenes, claiming the practice is illegal.

Much of the ironically titled drama, *The Island of Happiness* (1916), is set on an exotic island. Lucille Ronald, to please her millionaire father, agrees to marry Jack Maitland, but she soon falls in love with pilot Neil Boyd. She elopes with Boyd to a deserted island, where she soon discovers her husband is an alcoholic only interested in her money. On a trip to the mainland, Boyd learns that his wife's father is offering a million dollar reward for her safe return. He telegraphs the father, asking him to reply by way of an announcement in a personal column. The father refuses and contacts the police. Boyd, now both angered and inebriated, returns and begins abusing his wife, who hides in a tree. Maitland, while searching for her, arrives at the island in his motorboat and hears her screams. He overpowers Boyd in a fight and rescues his former fiancée, who gratefully agrees to marry him.

George Beban, as the title character, an Italian immigrant living in New York, in William D. Taylor's drama, *Pasquale* (1916), loses Helen Jerome Eddy to Jack Nelson and is then drafted into the Italian army. Before leaving, he turns over his grocery business to Nelson so that he can support his bride. Beban is discharged after being wounded in action and returns to the States. Nelson has become a drunkard, the grocery business is in ruins, and the husband has been beating his wife. After Nelson, who has been involved in a blackmail plot, dies in a car accident, Beban, who never stopped loving the young woman, proposes to the widow and she accepts him.

Some of these entries were period dramas, offering their stars a chance to be seen in elaborate costumes against lavish settings. Ethel Barrymore portrays the title character, a young wife, in John W. Noble's poignant eighteenth-century drama, *Helena Ritchie* (1916), based on the novel by Margaret Deland. The wife's drunken and brutish husband drives her from their home, especially since he was responsible for the death of their child. In another city, she poses as the sister of her lover, Robert Cummings, and adopts an orphan boy. When William Williams, an otherwise friendly minister, discovers her marital status, he considers her unfit to serve as mother. Deciding to surrender the child, she prepares to leave the city. The minister, realizing her devotion and kindness to the orphan, places the child in her arms.

Vola Vale journeys to California to learn about her grandfather, a gold prospector, in Otto Hoffman's western drama, *The Secret of Black Mountain* (1917), based on the short story by Jackson Gregory. She learns that her grandfather has been robbed and killed by bandits. Just as she is about to return to Vermont, a strange man orders her to accompany him to his cabin, where she finds a dying woman. The woman reveals that she has been beaten by her husband, Charles Dudley, and directs Vale to look under a stone in the fireplace. The man who had taken her to the cabin is Philo McCullough, Dudley's cousin. When Dudley returns and orders McCullough to leave, a fight ensues and Dudley is seriously wounded. Vale then learns that her grandfather's treasure map has disappeared. She produces the map from the stone in the fireplace, and both she and McCullough set out to retrieve her grandfather's gold.

Some films about battered women were quite frank in their treatment of the theme. Unfortunately, Jack Gorman's unintentionally funny drama, *Corruption* (1917), opens with an abortionist and his wife, a reluctant participant in his illegitimate practice. A mother and her daughter enter. While the young woman confides to the doctor in his office that she is pregnant, the mother, who has remained outside, reveals to the doctor's wife (by way of a flashback) that she is not the mother. The young woman's real mother abandoned her because the father was too brutal. The doctor's wife turns out to be the patient's real mother. Another flashback reveals that the son of a Wall Street broker has sexually attacked the young woman. The doctor announces to the mother that his patient will have to remain with him for several days. He then phones the young man, demands a visit from him and a check for $5,000. The physician's wife refuses to have him perform the abortion. The young man begs the patient to marry him and sail with him to Europe. Following several complications, the boy's father forces the pair to marry and then evicts his son. When the doctor refuses to return the man's money, the bridegroom reports him to the police. The law officers arrive, only to find that the abortionist has committed suicide.

Although there are many plot variations concerning the battered woman theme, early silent dramas focused chiefly on bestial husbands. These brutish characters were often cruel to their children and employees as well. William P. S. Earle's drama, *I Will Repay* (1917), adapted from O. Henry's story, "A Municipal Report," concerns the ill and abusive treatment of a dissolute old Southern major toward his frail wife, who writes stories under a pseudonym. An Eastern magazine publisher assigns an editor to sign a contract with the wife. He later learns that her husband takes all her earnings for his drinking habit. When the editor gets his contract and gives the author an advance of fifty dollars, her husband violently takes the money from her for his own needs. An elderly African American servant, loyal to the wife, observes this scene and strangles the major. But in so doing, he leaves behind a button from his jacket. The sympathetic editor finds the button at the scene and secretly returns it to the servant.

Wyndham Standing portrayed another such husband in Maurice Tourneur's gripping drama, *The Law of the Land* (1917), based on the play by George Broadhurst. Olga Petrova, his distraught wife, suffers through a loveless marriage with the brutal Standing. Her husband is prone to beating both his wife and their child. Driven to despair, his wife eventually kills him. Riley Hatch, a local police inspector familiar with her horrific married life and thereby sympathetic to her and her child, lists Standing's death as an accident. This gives the widow a chance to remarry and start a new and happier life.

Again, a brutal, abusive husband strikes fear in his vulnerable wife in Travers Vale's strong drama, *The Dormant Power* (1917). Montagu Love, an unscrupulous New York businessman, woos Ethel Clayton, who lives with her father in a Texas town. Clayton likes Edward T. Langford, whom she has met accidentally and helps out of a scrape. When her father is hurt, she agrees to marry Love, hoping to provide comfort for her father. Her father, depressed by his condition, takes his own life. Love and his wife then move to New York, where Clayton begins to suffer abuse from her badgering husband. Love hires Langford, a successful lawyer. Clayton feels the rekindling of an old flame within her. Meanwhile, her ruthless husband cheats an inventor out of his design and then murders him. The victim's wife suspects Love and finally proves his guilt. But in a moment of rage, she kills him. A sympathetic jury acquits her, and Clayton, freed of her horrible, abusive life, is reunited with her young lover.

Olga Petrova practically repeated her role in *The Law of the Land* in another Maurice Tourneur drama titled *Exile* (1917), released the same year and set in a Portuguese colony. Once again she is the abused wife to a cruel and brutish husband, again played by Wyndham Standing. Petrova is an idealistic worker among the poor peasants, while her husband is a corrupt and much-hated chief magistrate. Attempting to gain control of the silk trade, he plots to involve Mahlon Hamilton in his scheme to sentence a man to death. But the latter, who likes Petrova, threatens to expose Standing's villainous machinations. The husband, who wants his wife to persuade Hamilton to become Standing's accomplice, invites him to dinner. That evening, Petrova and Hamilton discover that they love each other. Later, the peasants rise up against Standing and lynch him. Hamilton rescues the widow, and the lovers are permanently united.

Seena Owen makes a catastrophic mistake by marrying the brutal and cruel Charles Gerrard in Chester Withey's familiar drama, *A Woman's Awakening* (1917). However, she was not aware of his shortcomings, or of his desiring her only for her money. She was emotionally attracted only to the good times he promised her. Once married, he turns callous and selfish, even resenting his wife's paralytic mother, who is living with them. After he depletes her fortune, Gerrard contemplates deserting her. Meanwhile, A. D. Sears, a gentleman who secretly loves Owen, helps her out financially. Gerrard is finally killed by the elderly mother. Sears and the widow, each at first suspecting the other of the murder, eventually find happiness together.

Norma Talmadge falls into a similar trap after a hasty marriage in Edward José's drama, *The Moth* (1917), based on the 1912 novel by William Dana Orcutt. A spoiled young heiress who has indulged in a string of wild parties and light affairs, foolishly marries Hassard Short, who cares more for her money than for her. After the birth of their child, he starts demanding more money from her to support his mistress. Abusive to both women, he abandons his mistress, who then takes her own life. Short is then blamed for her death. Following several complications, Talmadge finally frees herself of her fortune-hunting spouse.

June Elvidge's hasty marriage proves disastrous for several persons in Arthur Ashley's drama, *The Marriage Market* (1917). To save her father who is facing financial ruin, Elvidge sells herself to Arthur Ashley. But by the time she arrives with the money to help her father, she finds he has already taken his life. She returns to her husband, who now treats her simply as his property. To gain some semblance of financial independence, she decides to sell her prize horse to Frederick Truesdell. But he has more lascivious thoughts on his mind. As he tries to rape Elvidge, she shoots him during the struggle, and then faints. Ashley, her husband who has followed her, enters and kills the wounded Truesdell and then flees. Carlyle Blackwell, Elvidge's former boyfriend, discovers the body and, assuming she killed him, pleads guilty to the murder. When she recovers, Elvidge realizes Blackwell's sacrifice and rushes to the courtroom to testify that she shot the victim. However, the deceased's butler testifies that he saw Ashley kill Truesdell. Ashley then commits suicide before the police can arrest him. .

Widow Gretchen Lederer portrays another wife who was unaware before marriage that the man she thought she loved would turn out to be so brutal and mean-spirited in Charles Swickard's domestic drama, *The Lair of the Wolf*

(1917). Joseph Girard, her husband, has indulged in several cruelties, including the ruination of another family. His dishonest business practices have caused the death of the wife and the downfall of the husband, who has become an alcoholic. The son swears vengeance against Girard. Lederer's son, Chester Bennett, abhors his stepfather and forces his mother to choose between her husband and her son. She reluctantly chooses Girard and goes to his country estate, where she learns more of his unsavory acts. She sends for her son to come and take her away. Girard is murdered, and his maid claims Bennett was in the house. The son is arrested, but following several complications, the dead man's gardener confesses to killing Girard when he caught his master struggling with the gardener's daughter. The suspect is freed, and the gardener is acquitted after pleading temporary insanity.

Ethel Clayton finds herself in a similar situation as that experienced by Seena Owen in the earlier *A Woman's Awakening*. As the recent bride of Noah Beery, Clayton serves only as a woman who could give him an heir, in Robert Vignola's drama, *The Woman Next Door* (1919), based on the novel, *Vicky Van*, by Carolyn Wells. After their honeymoon, which consisted of a motoring tour during which Clayton meets handsome Emory Johnson, Beery places his wife in the hands of his two sisters, who begin to teach her what their family expects of her. Clayton rebels and buys the house adjacent to her husband's and builds a hidden passage between both. When Beery discovers she is secretly seeing Johnson, he begins to physically beat her. He is later found dead, the victim of his wife's sympathetic maid.

Theodore Roberts, as the miserly old husband of Louise Huff, discovers that his young wife has fallen in love with a neighbor, in George H. Melford's domestic drama, *Wild Youth* (1918), based on the novel by Sir Gilbert Parker. Roberts owns a ranch in the picturesque California hills, where the young and handsome Jack Mulhall, a fellow rancher, resides. The crazed and jealous husband begins to strike his wife with a whip. Their Chinese servant (James Cruze), more loyal to his kindly mistress than to his cruel master, intervenes and strangles Roberts. The lovers are then united.

A child witnessing her father beating the mother can be a traumatic experience, a situation Baby Marie Osborne faces in William Bertram's domestic drama, *Tears and Smiles* (1917). Baby Marie sees her drunken father, Melvin Mayo, attack her mother, Marian Warner, and flees from the house. All alone now that her father has been arrested and her mother hospitalized, Marie befriends a dog in a park. The maid brings the child home to Philo McCullough's mansion, where the master becomes enchanted by the child's charms and wants to adopt her. His wife, too busy with her social life, doesn't mind. When Marie's mother leaves the hospital, she becomes aware of the good life her daughter has in her new home. Rather than deprive her of all these advantages, she becomes the child's governess so that she can be close to Marie. Later, Marie's father is killed while escaping from jail, and McCullough's wife commits suicide. This leaves the widow and widower free to start a new life.

In Arthur Ashley's *Shall We Forgive Her?* (1917), the director portrays Neil, a steady drinker, who strikes it rich in a Western gold field. A problem drinker when he lived in the East, he now invites his girlfriend, June Elvidge, to join him in the gold fields and share his success. His love for the bottle has now turned him into a depraved figure. When Elvidge arrives and he takes her into his cabin, she realizes his intentions are far from honorable. She flees, asking for help in a local miners' saloon. Two rough inhabitants pursue her back to the cabin, where she is forced to surrender to Ashley's lechery. With the help of a kind prospector, she eventually leaves him and returns to New York. Following many complications and a failed attempt on Ashley's part to blackmail her, Elvidge finally finds happiness with a jeweler, whom she marries.

Some films about battered women turned to other genres, such as the mystery and the western, as a receptacle for their plots. Arthur Ashley portrays June Elvidge's brutal husband and the conniving and false lover of several women in Harley Knoles's drama, *The Page Mystery* (1917). With such an unsavory background and reputation, it is no wonder that he is found murdered in his lodge. Ashley, as Colonel Page, has virtually "bought" his wife by canceling out her bankrupt father's debts in exchange for the elderly man's daughter. Another enemy and possible suspect is the housekeeper, whose home the colonel had destroyed by having an affair with the married woman. Still another suspect is his jealous mistress, who caught him flirting with an opera singer. The crime is solved only after the mistress, before taking poison, confesses to the shooting.

Madlaine Traverse, as the unhappy wife of William Conklin in Harry Millarde's mystery, *When Fate Decides* (1919), bears the blows, both psychological and physical, of her brutish husband out of respect to her marriage vows. When Clyde Fillmore, her former beau, learns how she is suffering, he begs her to leave Conklin, but she refuses. When her husband is found murdered, both his wife and her former lover become suspects. But they are finally vindicated.

II. Brutal Men and Submissive Women

Battered women continued to play a role – although a minor one – in films throughout the next decade. But there were changes, both subtle and major, in the films of the twenties. Americans were constantly bombarded by a variety of violent activity, including shootings, knifings and scenes of mass destruction as a result of the World War. Newspaper headlines reported the more lurid stories, such as that of David Stephenson, the Grand Dragon of the Indiana Ku Klux Klan. Stephenson in 1925 kidnapped and assaulted his secretary on a train. Her suicide by poison led to his sentence of life in prison. Movie audiences were bound to become hardened to the exposure of any further brutality in domestic and social dramas. Therefore, shocking sequences, which earlier would have been condemned by critics, organizations and large segments of the public, became more or less accepted and conventional as they worked their way into a variety of plots. Generally, however, the decade of the twenties continued to release films about battered women with little or no condemnation or discussion. Perhaps worst of all, scenes depicting women as overly submissive and subjected to debasement come across as particularly offensive to audiences today. Arguably, Geraldine Farrar epitomizes this submissiveness early in the decade in *The Woman and the Puppet* (1920). Although the proud Lou Tellegen has had many mistresses, he cannot accept Farrar's fierce display of pride. Two conventions of the cycle found in earlier films, the brutal villain getting his comeuppance and women marrying foolishly, continued to appear in dramas during the twenties, but with less frequency. In the first instance, the sadistic Sessue Hayakawa, who liked to brand his women in *The Brand of Lopez* (1920), is finally killed when he turns bandit. Noah Beery, the bestial husband in *Old Shoes* (1925), is trampled to death by a horse he has beaten. The foolish and spoiled Clara Bow in *The Adventurous Sex* (1925), offers an example of the second convention. She becomes too friendly with a lecherous ladies' man and pays the price for her wanton behavior. Finally, June Collyer in *Hangman's House* (1928) rushes into marrying Earle Foxe, an alcoholic and a profligate, to please her mother, although she loves another.

Sessue Hayakawa, as Vasco Lopez, matador and hero of Saville, in Joseph De Grasse's overly dramatic *The Brand of Lopez* (1920), is secretly betrothed to a flirtatious member of an opera company. Her mother rejects the matador, considering him a common bull fighter. When Hayakawa discovers her unfaithfulness with her childhood sweetheart, he marries her and brands her by burning her back with his cigarette to mark her as his personal property. Fortune in the ring turns against him, and he becomes an outlaw. Following several complications, including his rape of his wife's sister, Lopez is finally killed.

Geraldine Farrar, a cigarette maker in Seville, is admired by Lou Tellegen, a gentleman well known in the city, in Reginald Barker's romantic drama, *The Woman and the Puppet* (1920). Although he has had many mistresses, including a young woman he is presently seeing, he desires Farrar, who discourages him. Finally, when he offers to set her up in her own villa, she accepts. When he comes to claim her, she sees him give her mother some money. She had earlier boasted to him that no man can buy her, so upon witnessing this, she says she will join him the next day. But she flees to Cadiz, where she works as an entertainer in a waterfront dive. Tellegen finds her and furnishes her with a home. When he arrives at night, the gate is locked to him. Farrar shows up, teases him and sends him away. Brooding over the incident all night, he says to himself, "To think that I would have made her my wife." In the morning she comes to him, but he slaps her across the face several times. "I will be your wife this morning," she cries, kneeling before him. "You will help me never to be mean and cruel again."

Little Jackie Coogan, an orphan in a home that is running out of funds, is the last boy to be adopted, in Albert Austin's refreshing comedy drama, *Trouble*

(1922). A married couple, brutish plumber Wallace Beery and his servile wife, Gloria Hope, take the boy to their home. But all is not pleasant for the lad, who witnesses the bullying husband's beating his wife for apparently no reason. Beery is finally sentenced to a year in prison for his violent behavior after a trial in which Coogan performs touchingly and valiantly as a witness. One highlight of the film is the scene in which Beery is furiously battling a policeman, while little Coogan heaves flower pots at the villainous Beery. After the courtroom sequence, the wife takes the adopted boy back to the farm of her parents, where they will live in relative tranquility after their ordeal. Coogan, who scored a hit in Charlie Chaplin's sentimental classic, *The Kid* (1921), was again praised for his performance in the present film.

Noah Beery portrays a vengeful, brutal husband and stepfather in Frederick Stowell's heavy-handed drama of persecution, *Old Shoes* (1925). When Beery and his brother were young, they both loved the same woman, but she chose to marry his brother. Years later, her husband dies, and his widow, burdened with a son, agrees to marry Beery, whom she believes she had hurt by rejecting him. However, he turns out to be vindictive toward her and his brother's young son, John Harron. He enjoys inflicting physical and mental pain on both his wife and the boy every chance he gets — especially when he learns his wife still loves her dead husband. Two violent fights occur between Beery and his otherwise timid and weak stepson. In the second conflict, Harron knocks the older man unconscious with a statuette, but Beery regains consciousness and goes after the youth, brandishing a saber. While crossing a street, he strikes a horse that has gotten in his way. The animal retaliates by trampling Beery to death.

Lewis Stone, wounded during World War I, returns to his home in England to find that his baby son has died and his wife has run off with Walter Pidgeon, in Maurice Tourneur's domestic drama, *Old Loves and New* (1926), based on the novel, *The Desert Healer,* by E. M. Hull. Pidgeon, who is a heavy drinker and woman chaser, abandons Katherine McDonald, Stone's wife, to marry Barbara Bedford. Stone, disillusioned, journeys to the desert, where he serves as a patriarch to the Arabs. Years pass, and Pidgeon, still a heavy drinker, visits the desert with his wife. Stone meets her and later rescues her from horse thieves. The drunken and jealous Pidgeon begins to horsewhip his wife. Stone, horrified, intervenes. An elephant previously ill-treated by Pidgeon's brutality kills the drunk. Stone and Bedford are now free to continue their relationship.

Irish lass June Collyer, to please her dying mother, marries Earle Foxe, although she loves Larry Kent, in John Ford's Irish drama, *Hangman's House* (1928), based on the 1926 novel by Brian Oswald Donn-Byrne. Foxe, an alcoholic and a profligate, treats his wife and others badly. Finally, he dies in a duel with a soldier of fortune whose sister Foxe had wronged earlier. The widow is now free to renew her romance with Kent.

Biographies

I. Heroes and Myths

Not surprisingly, early silent films were quick to seize upon the advantages of retelling the lives of famous Americans, especially of those whose lives were colorful enough to offer dramatic impact, romance and action. Not only were they readily accessible, the stories were often highly embellished and retold multiple times – in features, serials and series. In addition, the studios quickly discovered, the sources were unlimited. Besides American heroes, there was always world history and mythology. Before them lay a wealth of material to provide enough entertaining features to span both the silent and sound eras. Meanwhile, the studios were kept busy with the early American icons, including such figures as Kit Carson, Daniel Boone, Davy Crockett, Buffalo Bill Cody and Wild Bill Hickok – to mention a few. Almost invariably, these early film biographies retained the mythological perceptions and numerous fictional accounts of the nation's heroes, while overlooking their faults and shortcomings – a bias that held fast until the post-Vietnam War period, with such films as Robert Altman's *Buffalo Bill and the Indians* (1976).

Other silent films focused on these legendary figures, including *Kit Carson* (1910), a one-reeler about the rescue of settlers who come under attack from hostile Indians. The film offers little insight into the life of the famous frontiersman or frontier life in general. The highlight is an Indian assault, replete with a hail of arrows, upon a stockade.

Hobart Bosworth's outdoor action drama, *Kit Carson's Wooing* (1911), also used the Carson name to tell a routine story. Director Bosworth, who also provided the screenplay, portrayed the title character. The daughter of an Indian chief saves Carson's life, but soon loses him, in this romantic drama about lovers who cross racial barrier. Carson, fascinated by her beauty, marries the young Indian maiden. He soon leaves her, explaining that his own people need him. He returns to a white settlement, where he is greeted by a pretty white woman. Several other films have exploited the name of Carson, including *Kit Carson* (1940). Of these, few adhered to historical incidents.

Wallace McCutcheon's short drama, *Daniel Boone* (1907), was probably the earliest depiction of this other famed trailblazer on film. It describes how a band of hostile Indians, stereotyped as bloodthirsty savages, kidnaps Boone's daughters and eventually captures the pioneer himself. Boone escapes, following some brutal torture scenes, frees his daughters and kills the leader of the raid. He is helped by a young Indian woman whom he had earlier befriended. The last-minute aid by an Indian became a staple of numerous silent films. The Indian in these early melodramas was almost invariably motivated by a past act of kindness on the part of a white person. Other silent films about the frontiersman include *Daniel Boone's Bravery* (1911) and Frank S. Mattison and Robert N. Bradbury's *Daniel Boone Thru the Wilderness* (1926).

Frank Boggs's *Davy Crockett* (1910) unabashedly exploits the famous frontiersman's name in this chiefly fictitious drama that presents a Lochinvar ending. The film is divided into two parts, the first dealing with Crockett (Hobart Bosworth) trapped in a cabin with his sweetheart and holding off a pack of wild wolves in the dead of night. In the second half the girl is forced to marry Crockett's rival. During the ceremony, held outdoors, the frontiersman rides up, grasps the reluctant girl and rides off with her as his friends hold the wedding party at bay. Other films of the period based on historical personalities, such as *James Boys in Missouri* and *The Younger Brothers*, both released in 1908, adhered more closely to actual incidents. Other silent films about the pioneer include *Davy Crockett in Hearts United* (1909), with Charles K. French; *Davy Crockett* (1916) with Dustin Farnum; and *Davy Crockett at the Fall of the Alamo* (1926), starring Cullen Landis.

William "Buffalo Bill" Cody portrays himself in Theodore Wharton's early epic, *The Adventures of Buffalo Bill* (1914), that deals with the Indian wars. The drama covers several historical battles, including those at Warbonnet Creek, Summit Springs and Wounded Knee, the last being the climactic highlight. Cody, who acted as producer, was determined to give an accurate account of the events while making a permanent record of the resistance of the Sioux. General Miles, a Civil War veteran who later captured Geronimo and subdued several tribes, acted as technical adviser. The U.S. government supported the project and lent cavalry troops to Cody. The final production caused some controversy. Indian spokesmen attacked the depiction of the battle at Wounded Knee as inaccurate. They claimed the cavalry killed innocent women and children while their men were away. The film shows the braves present and ready to turn in their arms to the soldiers when a shot is fired accidentally. Suddenly, the soldiers, fearing an uprising, begin shooting wildly. As a result, many braves, women and children lay dead. Criticism also came from historians who disputed the accuracy of different events. Unfortunately, much of the film has been lost. The drama was exhibited under a variety of titles, including, among others, *Buffalo Bill's Indian Wars, The Indian Wars,* and *The Indian Wars Refought.*

A reenactment of George Armstrong Custer's battle with the Sioux at Little Big Horn, Thomas H. Ince's historical drama, *Custer's Last Fight* (1912), focuses more on action than on motivations. Francis Ford portrays the doomed colonel in a tale that was to be repeated on screen numerous times. The film has much in common with D. W. Griffith's drama, *The Massacre*, made and completed at the same time as Ince's western, and remains a tribute to Griffith, whose strong influence is reflected in Ince's work. However, some film historians today believe Ince's westerns were superior to Griffith's. The film was reissued in 1925. Other early silent films centering on Custer include *Custer's Last Stand* (1910) and *Custer's Last Scout* (1915), both films only two reels each in length.

Indian chiefs occasionally became the subjects of several early silent films. *Sitting Bull - the Hostile Sioux Indian Chief* (1914), is representative. Little is known about this plains drama, which dealt more with the adventures of the Randall family and their clashes with Indians, than with Sitting Bull. Early in the film Frank Randall and his family, traveling in a covered wagon, are attacked by Chief Crazy Horse and his warriors. However, an Indian scout helps the family to escape. Years later the Randalls are again raided by Indians. Lieutenant Scott, young Ruth Randall's fiancé, rides to their aid. Still later, all the Randalls are killed, except for Ruth and her younger sister, both of whom are saved by the officer.

The rousing action drama. *Francis Marion, the Swamp Fox* (1914), tells the story of Francis Marion, known as the Swamp Fox, and how he routed the British and rescued General Gates during the American Revolution. The film, which includes several good battle sequences, adheres very closely to the actual incidents in Marion's life. Some melodramatics have been added for dramatic effect, such as the rescue of a heroine from a burning house.

Other personalities besides the rugged pioneers early became subjects for these silent biographical films, including presidents. The subjects were drawn not only from history but from contemporary life as well, such as songwriters and baseball players. *Life of Abraham Lincoln* (1908), produced by the Essanay studio, was one of the earliest attempts by a movie studio to present a dramatized biography of an American president. This short film covers Lincoln's boyhood, his parents and other important persons of the period. In addition, scenes show him as an attorney and judge. The drama also depicts his assassination and the fleeing of John Wilkes Booth, his assassin.

David W. Griffith's drama, *Home, Sweet, Home* (1914) depicts the life and death of John Howard Payne, the author of the immortalized title song. The film shows Payne writing the song in a foreign country and shortly after, dying, leaving behind a loving family to grieve for him. The next sequence is set in a Western mining camp, where a young man from the East falls in love with the waitress in a makeshift lunchroom. After they are engaged, he is called home. During his trip, he hears an organ grinder playing "Home, Sweet, Home" and is reminded of his fiancée. He rushes back to her and they are married. The remainder of the drama continues in this vein – demonstrating how the song helps various people cope with their problems.

Joe Sullivan portrays the title character in the biographical drama, *The Life of Big Tim Sullivan* (1914). Timothy D. Sullivan, a product of New York's Lower East Side, began life as a newsboy and eventually rose to serve as a United States Senator. Affectionately known as the "Bowery Senator," he never forgot his roots in the slums of the big city. He instituted an annual Christmas dinner for those citizens whom he served. Loved by his constituents, they prayed for the repose of his soul after his death.

The life of major league baseball player Mike Donlin is adequately captured on screen in Hugh Reticker's interesting feature titled *Right Off the Bat* (1915). The opening scenes portray Mike as a boy and southpaw pitcher, played capably by young Roy Hauck. For the remainder of the film, the popular baseball star plays himself. He rescues his childhood sweetheart from drowning and becomes the star pitcher for his plant, where he works as a machinist. After playing semi-pro for the Winsted, Connecticut team, he is spotted by a Giant's scout and signed up. John McGraw hires him, and Donlin finds himself playing major baseball. Much of the film was shot in Winsted.

Henry B. Walthall portrays the famous poet, Edgar Allan Poe, in Charles J. Brabin's bland biographical romance, *The Raven* (1915), based on the novel and play by George C. Hazleton. Reportedly covering the romance in his life, the film depicts his marriage to Virginia Clemm, her early death and his constant brooding over his loss. Earlier, scenes show him as an orphan and his foster father's disowning him when he is a youth. An artistic sequence shows him being visited by the spirit, Lost Lenore.

Dustin Farnum portrays the famous stage actor in Frank Lloyd's biographical drama, *David Garrick* (1916), based on the 1864 play by T. W. Robertson. The film studio assembled a highly professional group of players for the production, including Winifred Kingston as Ada Ingot, and Herbert Standing as Simon Ingot. Contemporary critics also commented on the historical correctness of the sets and costumes. The film covers his successful attempts to have the aristocracy of London accept the stage, his love life with Kingston and his eventual marriage to the tradesman's daughter. Other films about the actor's life include several British silent versions, one released in 1912, two in 1913 and one in 1928.

Near the end of the decade, and during World War I, some studios returned to the outdoor and patriotic heroes and heroines. Dustin Farnum, who impersonated the famous actor David Garrick, in a film of the same name, also portrayed another famous American, but of a very different background, that same year. *Davy Crockett* (1916), directed by William D. Taylor and adapted from the play by Frank Murdock, focusing chiefly on Crockett's exploits. The film has him rescuing a heroine from an unscrupulous gambler, and later, his Lochinvar-type of rescue. The latter incident appeared in an earlier film, also titled *Davy Crockett* (1910). He is the main character in several films, both silent and sound, including *Davy Crockett at the Fall of the Alamo* (1926), *Heroes of the Alamo* (1938) and *The Alamo* (1960).

Emile Chautard's historical drama, *The Heart of a Hero* (1916), set just before and during the American Revolution, tells part of the story of Nathan Hale. Robert Warwick portrays Hale, who organizes a company of volunteers and joins the Minute Men, after hearing news about Concord. When someone is called upon to learn the British plans, Hale volunteers. He almost succeeds in his mission, but he is recognized by a Tory, a relative of Hale's sweetheart, Alice Adams (Gail Kane). To prove he is a spy, the Tory invites Adams to a tavern frequented by British officers. At first, the cautious girlfriend pretends not to know Hale, but when she thinks it is safe, the lovers embrace – proving to the British that Hale is a spy. He is arrested and sentenced to hang at sunrise.

Benjamin Chapin's biographical feature, *The Lincoln Cycle* (1917), covers the life of Abraham Lincoln from his boyhood until he reaches the presidency and issues the first "Call to arms" in anticipation of hostilities between the North and the South. Scenes show Lincoln as a boy overpowering a local bully, others of his conflicts with his father, and still others of the firing on Fort Sumter. He has been portrayed numerous times in both silent and sound films, including *With Lee in Virginia* (1913), *The Heart of Lincoln* (1915), D. W. Griffith's Civil War epic, *The Birth of a Nation* (1915), *Defense or Tribute?* (1916), *The Crisis* (1916), *My Own United States* (1918), *Abraham Lincoln* (1924), and *The Heart of Maryland* (1927).

Betsy Ross (1917), directed by Travers Vale and George Cowl, tells the story of Betsy and her sister, Clarissa, both Quakers living in Philadelphia at the time of the Revolution. Thinking her boyfriend is dead, Betsy (Alice Brady) marries John Ross upon her father's insistence. Ross is soon killed in battle. The widow opens an upholstery store which is visited by General George Washington, who is looking for a flag to represent the fledgling colonies. At one point, she rescues her sister's lover, who is accused of spying for the British. She rushes to Washington's quarters with evidence to prove the man's innocence and returns in time to prevent the hanging.

William Farnum gives a robust impersonation of Sam Houston in R. A. Walsh's idealized filmed biography of the famous general in *The Conqueror* (1917). Portrayed as a poor youth who had spent years living among the Indians in Tennessee, Houston comes off too crude for Jewel Carmen, the woman he loves. She promises him marriage only after he achieves some degree of greatness. When he achieves the governorship, she marries him, but he now realizes she loves his title and not him. So he returns to his Cherokee companions and then sets out for Texas. Later, his wife seeks him out and, following his rescue of her from some villains, she asks his forgiveness. The film, which plays loosely with history, presents a number of big action scenes.

World War I opened the genre to venture outside the United States and still touch upon patriotic themes, albeit relating to other countries. Cecil B.

DeMille's intelligent drama, *Joan the Woman* (1916), offers an idealized version of the story of Joan of Arc, the young woman patriot of France. An all-star cast includes Geraldine Farrar as Joan, Raymond Hatton as Charles VII, Hobart Bosworth as General La Hire, Theodore Roberts as Cauchon and Wallace Reid as Eric Trent. The plot wisely develops a love story along with its thrilling battle sequences. Paralleling the main story with episodes of contemporary trench warfare (World War I) suggests that one of the major themes of the work included pro-French propaganda. Geraldine Farrar (1882-1967), a major star of the Metropolitan Opera, made about a dozen films, with *Carmen* (1915) and *Joan* two of her most memorable. Other silent films about Joan of Arc include several French releases – 1908, 1928 and 1929, and two Italian films, one released in 1909 and another in 1913.

Russia's most notorious holy man and courtier, Rasputin, who rose from his semiliterate, peasant background to a favorite of the Czar and Czarina, blended religious fervor with sexual indulgence. Such a mysterious and romantic figure was destined for the subject for a film biography. Arthur Ashley's provocative production, *Rasputin* (1917), featured Montagu Love in the title role. After he checked the bleeding of the couple's hemophiliac son, Rasputin demonstrated an unusual ability to influence the royal couple. This hypnotic hold reeked of evil. Several noblemen, suspecting him of plotting to make peace with Germany during World War I, murdered him.

Based on Ambassador James W. Gerard's book of the same name, William Nigh's feature film version, *My Four Years in Germany* (1918), purportedly gives a factual picture of the Kaiser and the German leaders prior to America's involvement in World War I. Halbert Brown portrays Ambassador Gerard and emphasizes how the German leaders deceived the United States as well as other countries with whom they were supposed to have had friendly relations. Interspersed with dramatic scenes, some of which show atrocities committed at German prison camps, are segments from newsreels and documentaries, all of which are designed to substantiate the conclusions drawn by the ambassador. The studio insisted that much of the film was compiled from actual newsreel footage. In truth, it was produced in a New Jersey studio. It cost about $50,000 to make and earned more than $400,000.

Virtually an *auteur* film (Rupert Julian directed, co-wrote the screen play and portrayed the title role), *The Kaiser, the Beast of Berlin* (1918), a blatant propaganda feature, emphasizes the weaknesses in the character of Kaiser Wilhelm. According to the plot, he is a self-deluded, vain figure who considers himself larger than life and seems obsessed with a desire for conquest. The film also suggests that his lust was not confined entirely to politics. In one scene he is shown fondling a young woman's hand. Some of the highlights of the work include the emperor's conspiring with his military leaders; his conference with the American ambassador, James Gerard, concerning the sinking of the *Lusitania*; his meeting with von Nagel, the U-boat captain responsible for the atrocity; and scenes of the invasion of Belgium. The film also underscores the atrocities allegedly committed by the Germans against the Belgian people. Since a steady stream of news releases reported these outrages – real or imagined – during the course of the war, audiences rarely doubted their accuracy. The film, which drew upon information from a book titled *Wilhelm II and His Consort*, added to the enmity hurled at the Kaiser not only on screen but in its advertising. "Warning," an ad for the film read. "Any person throwing mud at the poster will not be prosecuted."

Edith Cavell, a British nurse during World War I who remained in Brussels after the German occupation in 1915 to help smuggle Allied troops to the Dutch border, was caught by the Germans and executed in 1915. John G. Adolfi's eloquent biographical drama, *The Woman the Germans Shot* (1918) ,tells her courageous story. The film depicts her life from early childhood until her capture and execution. Nurse Cavell aided wounded Allied and German soldiers in Belgium, remaining at her post even as the enemy advanced and overran the dressing station where she worked. American stage actress Julia Arthur portrays the English heroine.

Based on Lieutenant Bert Hall's book, *In the Air*, Harry Revier's drama, *A Romance of the Air* (1918), recounts Hall's experiences in the Lafayette Escadrille during World War I. A flier with the famous air group, Hall is shot down over Germany, dons a fallen enemy's uniform and convalesces in a German hospital. He meets his American sweetheart in Germany, who has been trapped there since the war began. Together with a female German spy, they fly to freedom. Hall received several medals from the French, including the Croix de Guerre. He and Major Thaw allegedly were the only survivors of the original group of Americans who joined the celebrated Escadrille. The love story was added to the film version of the book. It was one of the few air war movies made by an American company during or immediately after the conflict. Another was *The Zeppelin's Last Raid* (1917). Interest in this genre did not develop until William Wellman's epic, *Wings,* appeared in 1927.

George Foster Platt's inspiring drama, *Deliverance* (1919), presents an emotionally uplifting tale about the deaf, dumb and blind Helen Keller and her struggle against adversities. Many memorable moments occur in the film, including an early sequence in which Edythe Lyle, as Anne Sullivan, Keller's famous teacher, reaches out her fingers to touch little Helen's hand, as the child begins to understand. Miss Keller later appears in person on the screen to show the audience how well, despite her handicaps, she has adjusted to the world around her.

II. Revered Heroes and Beloved Rogues

Biographical films of the next decade did not deviate much from the preceding years. American and foreign personalities – with emphasis on the latter – were still popular with the studios and audiences. There were films about an English statesman in *Disraeli* (1921), the French poet Francois Villon in *If I Were King* (1920), and England's King Richard in *Richard, the Lion-Hearted* (1923). With the First World War over and a population of moviegoers weary of propaganda films, studios concentrated on such genres as comedy, romance, adventure and crime for their escapism during the twenties – but they never quite forgot the nation's most venerable heroes and notorious outlaws and Indian chiefs. Such personalities as Wild Bill Hickok, Kit Carson and Buffalo Bill, as well as Jesse James and Sitting Bull, were to occupy the screens throughout the decade – a constant reminder of America's colorful past. Unfortunately, with these large-than-life figures, whether American or foreign, came all the falsehoods and historical inaccuracies that the studios could muster in their idealized and romanticized representations.

William Farnum portrays the roguish poet Francois Villon in J. Gordon Edwards's witty biographical drama, *If I Were King* (1920), the first screen adaptation of Justin Huntly McCarthy's popular novel and stage production. Villon, living a life of reckless abandon as a vagabond and thief who incidentally writes poems, gets an opportunity to act as the ruler of France for one week. Fritz Leiber plays the eccentric King Louis XI, who exhibits more than a trace of villainy. As a lark, and intrigued by the roguish poet, Louis gives Villon temporary free reign of the court. Betsy Ross Clarke, as the high-born Katherine, provides the romantic interest for the visitor, and Walter Law plays a traitor. McCarthy's play served as source material for several films, including another silent entry, *Beloved Rogue* (1927), starring John Barrymore as Villon.

George Arliss had performed the role of Disraeli on stage in his native England and in the United States for many years before performing it on film in Henry Kolker's unimaginative screen biography, *Disraeli* (1921), based on the play by Louis N. Parker. The main interest of this feature is Arliss's interpretation of England's prime minister, as he tries to gain possession of the Suez Canal for Queen Victoria by outsmarting the Russians and outguessing the governors of the Bank of England. He also plays Cupid to a young couple (Reginald Denny and Louise Huff). Arliss contributes to the humor and wit of the original play as well as to the dramatic strength of the production. His wife is played by the real-life Mrs. Arliss.

Wallace Beery, who had played King Richard in Douglas Fairbanks's production, *Robin Hood,* one year early, returned to the royal role in Chet Webey's *Richard, the Lion-Hearted* (1923). Adapted from Sir Walter Scott's novel, *The Talisman,* the story, set in the days of the Crusades, focuses on the adventures of the Lion-Hearted while Robin Hood goes about protecting the king's interests in England. The plot is not without its interesting moments. In one scene, for example, where Richard is ill, Saladin (Charles Gerrard), the king's mortal enemy, who prefers to see his foe die at his hands in battle and not in bed, masquerades as a physician and comes to his aid. When Richard recovers and learns the true identity of the doctor, he gives Saladin safe passage to his own lines. In another sequence, Saladin raids Richard's camp while the king is away and encounters Lady Edith (Marguerite De La Motte), whom he immediately desires. Upon Richard's return, the sultan is willing to promise anything as long as Richard gives him permission to marry the woman. The angry king objects strongly to the proposal. The film includes plenty of sword fights and battles.

A fictionalized biography of one of the great personalities of the Old West, Clifford Smith's historical drama, *Wild Bill Hickok* (1923), with William S. Hart as Hickok, centers on the American frontier scout and marshal James Butler Hickok's role in ridding Dodge City of its corruption and lawlessness. The action takes place after the Civil War when Kansas cow towns became gathering places of drifters, gamblers and ambitious men seeking a quick way to make their fortunes, the last represented by Jack McQueen. Hickok's confrontations with McQueen's outlaw gang end with his killing McQueen, thereby marking the restoration of law and order. The plot allows for the portrayals of several other historical persons, including Abraham Lincoln, George A. Custer, General Sheridan, Bat Masterson and Calamity Jane. Jane provides part of the romantic interest, as does the fictitious Elaine Hamilton, played by Kathleen O'Connor, with whom Hickok falls in love. When he learns that she is already married, he grows disillusioned with women and vows never to marry. Alone and embittered, he rides out of town. This was not first screen dramatization of Hickok although it was the most rounded depiction. *The Pioneer Peacemaker* appeared in 1913.

Frank S. Mattison returned to two familiar national heroes for his action drama, *Kit Carson Over the Great Divide* (1925). Jack Mower plays Kit Carson, and Arthur Hotaling portrays Lieutenant John C. Fremont, in this chiefly fictitious tale based loosely on incidents in the lives of these two historic figures. Carson and Fremont were again depicted together as major characters in George B. Seitz's 1940 highly fictionalized historical western, *Kit Carson*, with Jon Hall as the colorful title character, and Dana Andrews portraying the more straitlaced Fremont.

Buffalo Bill and the Union Pacific Trail serve as subjects for Frank S. Mattison's weak historical drama, *Buffalo Bill on the U. P. Trail* (1926). The film depends more heavily on trite fiction than on the exciting facts. Cullen Landis portrays a frontier scout in charge of a pioneer wagon train. Roy Stewart, as Buffalo Bill, does nothing for the famous hero who is seen here as a shrewd negotiator in real estate. Anticipating the needs of the railroad, Bill Cody and a partner construct an entire town on a strategic site necessary for the laying of track. Plenty of gun battles and fist fights and a stampede are interspersed to keep the plot moving. Several other action features about the title hero include *Buffalo Bill's Indian Wars* (1914) and *Buffalo Bill's Last Fight* (1927).

Robert N. Bradbury's low-budget action drama, *Sitting Bull at the Spirit Lake Massacre* (1927), recounts Sitting Bull's revengeful exploits against the whites. The film includes plenty of excitement in the battle sequences and some romance in a subplot involving Bryant Washburn as a brave army scout and

Anne Schaefer as a minister's daughter. Chief Yowlache portrays Sitting Bull. The drama relies little on historical facts concerning the Sioux chief.

A highly fictitious account of the famous bandit's exploits during and after the Civil War, Lloyd Ingraham's action drama, *Jesse James* (1927) opens with Jesse as a member of Quantrill's raiders during the conflict. At one point he is almost caught as a spy but manages to escape. When the war ends, he learns that his mother has been hurt by Union sympathizers and is about to be evicted from the town. He returns to seek revenge on those who have mistreated his mother, but ends up as an outlaw. Although the film includes the characters of Frank, Jesse's brother, and Bob Ford, the man who betrayed the bandits, the plot has little historical accuracy.

Several years after *If I Were King* (1920) was released, Francois Villon reappeared as the subject of Alan Crosland's *Beloved Rogue* (1927), again based on Justin Huntly McCarthy's play, and starring John Barrymore as the beggar poet. He rescues Marceline Day, King Louis XI's ward, from marrying the scheming Duke of Burgundy (Lawson Butt), by surrounding the duke's castle with his private vagabond army. The German actor Conrad Veidt portrayed the crafty king. The film had an abundance of comedy, with Slim Summerville and Mack Swain assisting Barrymore. Besides the earlier 1920 silent film, Villon was also the subject of several sound films, including two musicals or operettas, *The Vagabond King* (1930) and a color remake released in 1956.

With more fiction than fact, Alfred L. Werker's action drama, *Kit Carson* (1928), simply uses the name of the famous Indian scout for a conventional western feature about a hero besting a villain while preventing an Indian uprising against the whites. Fred Thomson portrays Carson, who, as a U.S. government agent, is assigned to make peace between Indian tribes about to take to the warpath. Meanwhile, our hero is plagued by the proverbial lascivious villain who tries to seduce every young woman Carson comes into contact with, including the daughter of an Indian chief. However, Carson finally defeats the villain, who falls to his death from a cliff after a hand-to-hand struggle. Carson then wins the confidence of the Indians, who depart in peace. Although it has very little to do with Kit Carson's life, the film offers the conventional action and thrills of the western genre.

Black Hand

I. "We Are Desperut"

At least one encyclopedia describes the Black Hand as a secret society organized to perform acts of terrorism and blackmail. The society had its roots in Europe and was known and feared in several countries. For example, Dragutin Dimitrijevic (1876-1917), a Serbian soldier and shadowy figure, was one of the plotters who assassinated King Alexander Obrenovic in 1903. He was also a founder of the secret society known as the Black Hand, which strove for union of all southern Slavs. Known as "The Bee," he engaged in irregular warfare in Macedonia and in an anti-Austrian movement in Bosnia. He served as chief of intelligence on the Serbian general staff in 1913. Also, he was suspected of helping to plan the murder of Archduke Francis Ferdinand at Sarajevo in 1914. He was later arrested, condemned, and shot. The Black Hand was active in the United States during the early years of the twentieth century – before World War I. Some films in this cycle include *Trailing the Black Hand* (1910); *The Black Hand* (1912), with Julia Stuart, F. Jamison and A. Ellery; *Binks, the Black Hand* (1913); *The Black Hand* (1913), with John Brennan, Marshall Neilan and Ruth Roland; Frank Powell's *In the Hands of the Black Hands* (1913), with Wilfred Lucas and Marion Leonard; *Rua and the Black Hand* (1913); and *Black Hand Conspiracy* (1914), with Fred Mace. Little is known about these films, since most of them have either disintegrated or are lost. Some of the players mentioned had long careers in films during the silent era, such as Wilfred Lucas and Fred Mace, the latter specializing in comedy. Marshall Neilan was a popular actor and director, and Ruth Roland became famous portraying the heroine in a string of early serials. The Black Hand was considered a loosely organized band of immigrant criminals who dealt chiefly in such crimes as kidnapping and extortion. Early silent films depicted these activities fairly accurately – if melodramatically. The growth of the Black Hand as a more ominous threat was not evident until the introduction of Prohibition in 1920, which ironically helped to contribute to the formation of organized crime in America and the rise of lawlessness and violence that followed in its wake.

Biograph was one of the earliest studios to depict films about the dreaded Black Hand society. The company's one-reeler, *The Black Hand* (1906), was directed by Wallace McCutcheon, with actors Robert Vignola and Tony O'Sullivan. This short drama is historically important for two reasons. It is an early example of a film based on an actual incident, and it was shot on the same New York streets where the real crime occurred. The Mafia plots a kidnapping by first mailing a threatening letter. "Bewar!" the crudely written letter states. "We are desperut ... We must have $1,000.00, give it to us or we will take your Maria and Blow up your Shop. BLACK HAND." They then proceed to kidnap their victim – a little girl. The police eventually capture the gang when they return to collect the ransom. The early use of location filming on the actual site of the incident added a note of authenticity to the work.

Kalem turned out *The Organ Grinder* (1909), which told a simple tale about a hardworking Italian immigrant who decided to leave his ethnic settlement and try his luck in a big city, where he could grind out his music and earn some money. Near the house of a wealthy banker, he plays his tunes, which attract the interest of the banker's ten-year-old daughter. When her parents notice how much she enjoys the music, the father rewards the musician with a bank note. He returns happily to his settlement to tell about his good fortune. Some unsavory riff-raff, associated with a Black Hand group, overhear his description of the rich parents and their home. Tempted by the possibilities of a fat ransom, they kidnap the child and take her back to a crude cabin in the settlement. The organ grinder recognizes her and notifies the parents. The police recover the child and return her to the banker and his wife, after which the musician receives a substantial reward.

The Detectives of the Italian Bureau (1909), another Kalem release, tells how little nine-year-old Rosa is kidnapped by a band of Black Hand hoodlums following the explosion of a bomb. The girl escapes and informs detectives of the Italian Bureau, who proceed to capture the gang and return the little heroine to her parents. Several cities established a special section of their police departments to deal with the infiltration of members of the Black Hand and other criminal elements who are identified as they arrive from Europe and are quickly deported. Lieutenant Joseph Petrosino, who led such a unit in New York City, known as the "Italian Squad," had carried out a successful campaign single-handed. The police commissioner eventually sent him to Italy in 1909 as a liaison officer to work with the Italian police. Unfortunately, Petrosino was gunned down in Palermo in March 1909. The studio, in conjunction with the release of the drama, boasted of the success of these Italian detective groups, and prematurely concluded that "Black Hand crimes have been practically blotted out in all of our large centers."

In the tragic drama, *The Criminals* (1913), members of the Black Hand kidnap a little Italian girl whom they end up killing when her father refuses to pay the ransom demanded by the gang. The police ironically arrest the father whom they mistake for one of the kidnappers and send the unfortunate man to prison. At least one trade film journal, the *Moving Picture World*, complimented the sets, the performances of the players and the camera work.

An Italian-American banker who rescues a young woman in the drama, *The Padrone's Ward* (1914), soon becomes the target of the Black Hand. The *padrone*, who heads an East Side gang of crooks and blackmailers, is the guardian of the rescued woman. Meanwhile, when the banker refuses to comply with the demands of the Black Hand, the gang assigns one of its members to kill him. The assassin, who happens to be the young woman's boyfriend, instead warns her about the threat to the banker, who escapes in time. The police then capture the entire gang.

Another Italian organ grinder in a New York ghetto is murdered by the Black Hand in *The Nightingale* (1914), a drama written by popular playwright Augustus Thomas. The victim's daughter (Ethel Barrymore) begins voice lessons, sponsored by Conway Tearle, the son of a wealthy banker. On the evening of her debut at the Paris Opera, Tearle tries to seduce the youthful star, informing her for the first time about his financial investment in her. She escapes from him and later stars at New York's Metropolitan Opera. This time the apologetic Tearle proposes to her and they are married. Her brother, Frank Andrews, a member of the Black Hand, robs Tearle's father's house and kills the banker. Barrymore dresses her brother's wounds, unaware of what he has done. Meanwhile, her husband suspects the brother of being his wife's secret lover. His suspicions are enough to drive her away from him – and she takes their small son with her. Later, after her brother dies, Tearle learns the brother's real identity and returns to his wife, asking her to forgive him.

This was later followed by *Under the Black Robe* (1914), a weak drama about the Black Hand. It offers little that is either fresh or original. Mindless action and improbable, hackneyed plot twists abound.

George Beban portrays a grieving Italian immigrant father in Raymond West's poignant drama, *The Alien* (1915), based on a popular theatrical sketch which Beban had made famous on the stage. Wealthy Jack Nelson, who desperately needs money, asks his older brother (Hayward Ginn), but is refused. He then kidnaps the daughter (Thelma Salter) and concocts a "Black Hand" ransom note demanding a large sum of money. He drives off, running down Beban's little daughter, Rosa. He takes the child home and barely escapes with his life from an angry mob. The kidnapped child's mother receives the ransom note demanding $10,000, which is to be delivered to a flower shop. The father informs the police, who set a trap for the kidnapper. Beban arrives and innocently buys a rose for his dead daughter Rosa's grave. The police assume he is one of the gang and arrest him. Beban made several films successfully portraying hardworking Italians – often stripped of the stereotyped mustache, bandana handkerchief and stiletto.

New York's Little Italy is the setting for Hobart Henley's Black Hand kidnapping drama, *A Child of Mystery* (1916). Gang members abduct the granddaughter of a judge. The captive, Gertrude Selby, is a pawn in a ransom game played by the Black Hand. She manages to escape at one point, only to be recaptured by her abductors. Her boyfriend and the judge give chase this time and kill the gang leaders, opening the door for a reconciliation among Selby, her boyfriend and the judge.

In *Poor Little Peppina* (1916), a Mafia gangster commits a murder and kidnaps Mary Pickford, who is then raised in Italy. Escaping the clutches of a lecherous *padrone* who desires her, she stows away aboard a vessel that takes her to New York. She then becomes entangled with a counterfeit ring that is headed by the same Mafia killer who had earlier kidnapped her.

Burton George's drama, *The Telltale Step* (1917), concerns a father and his blind daughter escaping from a vendetta. The father is hunted down and killed. The daughter's participation in the capture of the killer and the introduction of a love interest help to redeem this otherwise weak film, which was released near the end of the cycle of Black Hand and Mafia dramas. The film relied on the popular appeal of Mafia-type and other crime films during this period. The drama features Guido Colucci, Shirley Mason, Pat O'Malley, Charles Sutton, Bob Huggins and Nellie Grant.

Director Raymond Wells's *The Hand at the Window* (1918) features Joe King and Margery Wilson, the latter portraying a government agent in this counterfeiting drama. The heroine, whose true role is hidden for most of the story, is able to capture The Calabrian Kid, counterfeiter and thug, much to the surprise of her husband, police captain Roddy Moran. Acting, direction, and cinematography were all above average. The choice of Tony, The Calabrian Kid, as the gangster suggests that this film was designed to exploit the popularity of the Black Hand and Mafia film cycle prevalent during this period.

Racism defeats the romantic dreams of scientist Sessue Hayakawa, a Hindu educated in England, in William Worthington's *The Man Beneath* (1919). He falls in love with Scottish Helen Jerome Eddy and professes his true feelings to her. Although she loves him in return, she rejects him because of their racial differences. Meanwhile, Jack Gilbert, the boyfriend of Eddy's sister, Pauline Curley, becomes entangled in an intrigue involving members of the Black Hand, and they begin to hunt him down. He hides out with Hayakawa, asking the scientist his help. Hayakawa foils the gang members and, following several complications, Gilbert is reunited with his girlfriend, while his friend repeats his feelings of love for the sister.

II. The Forerunners of Organized Crime

By the 1920s, the Black Hand films all but disappeared from the American screen. They were replaced by more general crime films concerned with counterfeiting, smuggling, kidnapping and, perhaps the most important to affect organized crime, bootlegging – with its enormous profits and social and political ramifications. Film studios found new sources of menace that threatened the fabric of American society. They had to look no further than the headlines, which reported stories about the Red Scare and anarchists. An occasional drama referred, although peripherally, to the old Black Hand society, sometimes via a hero's fantasy, as in *Children of the Night* (1921), or by way of other cultures, as in *Chinatown Charlie* (1928), which refers to a secret Chinese society. Meanwhile, gangsters ran the speakeasies, the extortion racket and other criminal activities. New York City Mayor Rudolph Giuliani, in a 1997 television documentary about the rise of the Mafia, narrates how a relative was pressured to pay protection money to a group of immigrants known as the Black Hand, which was the forerunner of the Mafia. Before World War I, local gangs controlled such activities as burglary rings, prostitution houses and gambling operations. Sicilian gangs thrived on these rackets, but with the advent of Prohibition in 1920, the gangs flourished and emerged as today's American mob. The bootlegging business became the glue that cemented the New York crime groups together. To sell their illegal liquor, gangsters opened respectable nightclubs, such as the Embassy Club and the Copacabana. By the end of the twenties, the mob split into five competitive gang families, known as the Mafia. Their rituals and codes of honor gave them a sense of cohesion, discipline and organization – controls sorely lacking in other ethnic gangs.

Maurice Tourneur's drama, *The White Circle* (1920), is set in Scotland in the 1860s. The film is an adaptation of Robert Louis Stevenson's *The Pavilion on the Links*. The title refers to an Italian secret society (not unlike the Black Hand or Mafia) which has been embezzled by its treasurer Huddlestone (Spottiswoode Aitken). Fleeing from London to Scotland with his accomplice, Northmour (Harry Northrup), and his daughter Clara (Janice Wilson), the group meets Frank Cassilis (Jack Gilbert). An encounter occurs between Cassilis and Northmour and in the ensuing duel, Northmour gains the upper hand by holding his fire and reserving the right to use his shot at a later date. Eventually, the gangsters of the White Circle murder Huddlestone, and when the time comes for Northmour to exercise his shot at Cassilis, a totally unrealistic climax occurs.

In the routine drama, *Diane of Star Hollow* (1921), Bernard Durning plays a law officer who is torn between love and duty. He loves a young woman whose father is suspected of being the head of the Black Hand. Following a hectic gun fight, Durning is wounded and most of the gang killed. The father, suffering the rejection of his daughter and the demise of his gang, takes his own life. Other cast members include Evelyn Greeley, George Majeroni and Fuller Mellish.

William Russell portrays a stock clerk who fantasizes a more romantic life for himself in John Dillon's drama, *Children of the Night* (1921). He imagines he is a wealthy man set upon by a sinister gang of blackmailers who are holding his girlfriend captive. While trying to rescue her, he is drugged, captured and locked up. But he manages to escape and, following a slam-bang battle with the gang, rescues the heroine. Popular pulp fiction writer Max Brand wrote the original story.

An early tale about the Black Hand, Kenneth Webb's drama, *Fair Lady* (1922), uses the familiar ploy about a law officer penetrating a gang of criminals. The film deals with an Italian banker, played by Thurston Hall. In reality, Hall is the leader of a Mafia gang. Fortunately, Robert Elliott, a member of the U.S. Secret Service, has managed to penetrate the illegal organization and eventually gathers enough evidence to expose the banker and his cohorts. The film contains the conventional melodramatics of the period.

A schoolhouse becomes the center of operations for a gang of bootleggers in John Adolfi's slight drama, *The Little Red Schoolhouse* (1923), based on the play by Hal Reid. Martha Mansfield, a teacher at the school, is unaware of the activities going on in the basement until Harlan Knight, her boy friend, and several revenue officers smash the ring of mobsters.

A government agent trying to smash a gang of bootleggers, finds that his wife is friendly with its leader, in Russell Allen's drama, *Robes of Sin* (1924). Jack Mower, as the agent and neglectful husband, finally gets a lead concerning the leader of a bootlegging gang operating in New York's Times Square area. Meanwhile, his bored wife befriends the mastermind, played by Bruce Gordon, and her husband discovers them together at a nightclub. Mower realizes that he has been neglecting her and the couple are reconciled.

Charles Hutchison, as a man-about-town and amateur sleuth, is enlisted to help smash a gang of bootleggers in James Chapin's action drama, *Poison* (1924), set in San Francisco. Dan O'Brien, the real-life chief of police of that city, makes a cameo appearance in the film when he asks Hutchison to go after the gang that is passing bad hooch to its customers. This gives the sleuth a chance to get into and out of several fights, chases and other escapades until he rounds up the culprits and their leader – who just happens to be his rival for the hand of Edith Thornton, the heroine.

Considered as the most important film about bootlegging released during the Roaring Twenties, Lambert Hillyer's drama, *Those Who Dance* (1924), was adapted from the 1923 non-fiction work, *Prohibition Inside Out*, by Roy A. Haynes and William Pickett Helm Jr. An automobile wreck, the result of bootleg liquor, blinds young driver Warner Baxter and takes the life of his sister. He now declares war on all moonshiners. Baxter helps Ruth Jordan save her brother, Robert Agnew, who is employed by a bootlegger. The young man is framed for the killing of a revenue officer. The film was remade in 1930 in two versions, one sound and the other silent, under the same title, with Monte Blue and Lila Lee playing the leads.

Milton Sills, a proficient police officer, sacrifices his honor and job for the woman he loves in Lambert Hillyer's drama, *The Making of O'Malley* (1925), based on the 1924 story by Gerald Beaumont. Sills proves too effective when he cites average citizens for minor and petty infractions, forcing his supervisor to transfer him to an assignment where he will be rendered harmless. His superior complains that Sills is too technical and not sensitive enough. At his new post, Sills falls in love with local schoolteacher Helen Rowland, whose fiancé is a bootlegger. When Sills, now imbued with more feeling, learns this, he lets the crook go and is dismissed from the force. However, he gets his job back and wins Rowland's love after her father, who is released from prison, exposes the bootlegger.

The female member of a gang of bootleggers has problems trying to go straight in J. P. McGowan's stark drama, *Barriers of the Law* (1925). Helen Holmes, as the troubled heroine, is taken to the gang leader's dive where she is forced to strip and don a kimono. She escapes and ends up in the apartment of the district attorney, William Desmond, who is trying to smash the smuggling operation. The couple fall in love and marry, but later they are threatened by the gang leader. A fight ensues between the two rivals, with the hero-husband emerging victorious. Helen Holmes was the star of many silent serials before she made this minor action film.

Lois Wilson, an impoverished young woman, inherits a small-town newspaper in Alan Crosland's routine drama, *Contraband* (1925), based on the 1923 novel by Clarence B. Kelland. When she arrives in town she discovers that a gang of bootleggers is operating a flourishing business. She helps to capture the gang who, in the course of its operations, has killed the local sheriff. She then exposes the leader of the bootleggers.

Ricardo, a grocer who loves Lolita Lee but loses her to a poolroom loafer, next finds himself forced to work as a cook for a gang of bootleggers, in George Beban's drama, *The Loves of Ricardo* (1926). Beban, who portrays Ricardo, has bought some land that the bootleggers find convenient for docking and unloading their illegal booze. They then kidnap Ricardo and force him to work on their yacht as their cook. He cleverly sends out a parrot with a message that informs the revenue agents about the activities and location of the gang. After he is rescued, he proceeds to battle his rival, Steve Randall, for the woman he loves. Beban was best known for his portrayal of leading Italian characters in several dramas.

With the advent of Prohibition in 1920, organized crime and its lucrative bootlegging racket became popular subjects for several film genres, including the western. A young woman clashes with a gang of bootleggers as she and her father search for a hidden vein of silver in William Bertram's minor drama, *Ghost City* (1921). Helen Holmes plays the daring young daughter who bravely defies the dangers of the mountains. Dick Carroll, a surveyor, played by Jack Connolly, comes to her rescue. Following a series of the usual setbacks familiar to this genre, the young couple escape from the gang leader who accidentally drinks some poison.

Organized crime and its major racket of bootlegging continued to permeate the popular western. Ted Wells portrays the sheriff of a town plagued by the influx of bootleg whiskey in Ray Taylor's fast-paced action drama, *The Border Wildcat* (1928), set during the Prohibition years of the 1920s. He raids a gambling house but fails to find any of the bootleg alcohol being served. The sheriff is engaged to Mary Bell, played by Kathryn McGuire, whose father kills saloon owner Joe Kern in self-defense. Before the man dies, he absolves his killer. The sheriff pursues his fiancée's father, who is being hunted by Kern's henchmen, and saves him just in time. The lawman then proceeds to rid his community of the criminal element.

Bootleggers battle revenue agents and each other in Jack Conway's popular drama, *Twelve Miles Out* (1927), based on the play by William Anthony McGuire. John Gilbert and Ernest Torrence, two bootleggers, are friendly enemies who are not above stealing each other's illegal cargo. In one incident in which Gilbert is fleeing from revenue agents, he kidnaps an innocent couple, whom he later takes aboard his yacht. When he discovers they are not married, he becomes interested in romancing the attractive young woman (Joan Crawford). But he soon learns she's straight, and the two fall in love with each other. Suddenly, he sees another vessel bearing down on him, with men in white caps. Thinking it's a government boat, he orders his men to throw all guns overboard. But when the ship approaches and gets the drop on Gilbert and his crew, he realizes the attackers are Torrence and his men. When Torrence discovers Crawford below, his eyes light up. "Lay off," Gilbert warns him. "She's different." But Torrence doesn't listen to his rival. Eventually, a fist fight breaks out on deck between the two men. The fight ends with both men shooting it out, Gilbert shot in both arms, and Torrence mortally wounded. Both men then renew their old friendship. Revenue officers finally board the vessel, inquiring who owns the vessel loaded with bootlegged liquor. "It's mine," Gilbert announces. "He's a cockeyed liar," Torrence interrupts, "it's mine," he continues and then dies.

A mysterious ring provides the impetus for the limited suspense in Charles Hines's bland drama, *Chinatown Charlie* (1928), set chiefly in Chinatown. The coveted ring, whose inscription impels Chinese to obey it, is desired by a gang leader who sees the ring as a way to gain power. Its owner, played by Louise Lorraine, entrusts it to Chinatown Charlie and is then kidnapped and turned over to a Mandarin who plans to sell her into white slavery. A small-time thief gets the otherwise reluctant police to follow him into the quarters where all these plots are being concocted, and the young woman is rescued.

Wealthy adolescent Sue Carroll, the adolescent, in seeking thrills, finds herself enmeshed in a bootleggers' feud in Lewis Seiler's part-silent cautionary tale, *Girls Gone Wild* (1929). Carroll is bored with her conventional lifestyle. Her boyfriend, Nick Stuart, is the son of a motorcycle cop. She shuns him when she learns that his father is the officer who had once taken her to court for speeding. Later, at an outdoor dance, she and Stuart are kidnapped by gangsters who had just killed a bootlegger. After Stuart is thrown out of the car, he gives chase and rescues his girlfriend. The plot device about a bored member of the upper class mingling with notorious characters for thrills was quite familiar to audiences.

Burglary

I. The Comical and Sentimental Burglar

Several famous pioneer film directors turned out burglary films during their careers, including Edwin S. Porter, who made *A Burglar Cupid* in 1909 for Edison. Porter worked for Edison for many years and directed the historically important and famous *The Great Train Robbery* (1903), which introduced many of the film and editing techniques still used today. The master director of the early silent era, D. W. Griffith, contributed to the burglar cycle as well. J. Stuart Blackton was another popular producer-director during the early silent period. He directed and wrote the script for *The Burglar on the Roof* (1898), a Vitagraph short comedy. Burglary was a popular choice of criminal activity for those bent toward a life of transgression during the early years of the movies. Socially, this was a period before the rise of organized crime, so the early film studios were limited in their choice of illegal professions from which to choose. The burglar offered a range of plots, from tragedy to comedy. In fact, the one- or two-reel film was the standard length for both comedies and dramas during the early years of the century, with a high preference toward the former. Therefore, a preponderance of films about burglars were comedies, as anyone can gather from many of the titles. Others, like *The Burglar on the Roof* (1898) and *The Burglar and the Bundle* (1903), leaned toward comedy drama. Still others, like D. W. Griffith's *The Christmas Burglars* (1908), were sentimental dramas. Surprisingly, the burglar was often portrayed sympathetically, as in *Brother Man* (1910), regardless of the potential fear, danger or loss of property he represented. Allowing for an occasional exception, such as Griffith's *A Burglar's Mistake* (1909) in which a burglar is shot to death, the earliest crime films focused chiefly on bloodless crimes, including those associated with burglary, petty theft and prison escape, with the burglar dominating the world of the screen criminal. Within the next several years a string of burglary films filled the nation's screens. Most of them were rather short, usually one or two reels. Representative titles include *The Actor Burglar* (1909), *An Absent-minded Burglar (1912), At the Burglar's Command* (1912) with Gwendolyn Pate, *Billy's Burglar* (1912) and *Billy Turns Burglar* (1913).

The Burglar (1898), released by Edison, was one of the earliest crime stories to be put on film. The simple plot, set in a nondescript office, involves a thief's attempt to rob a safe. The masked burglar enters the office prepared to use his tools to crack the safe but soon hears someone coming. Another man enters, opens the safe, takes out all the cash and departs, leaving the empty safe open for the hapless crook.

That same year, in Edison's comedy drama, *The Burglar in the Bed Chamber*, a masked man enters the bedroom of a married couple and begins searching everywhere for valuables. Awakened by the noise, the wife gets up, steals out of the room and returns with a policeman who arrests the intruder. The husband awakens and, startled by the disturbance, hides behind the bed.

The Burglar on the Roof (1898), another example of a very early crime film to treat the subject lightly, depicts an intruder climbing through a roof skylight. As he reaches for his bag of tools, several women begin to attack him with brooms. Two men come to their aid and subdue the bruised burglar.

Many of these early burglar films treated the offense lightly. Biograph's simplistic *The Burglar and the Bundle* (1903) describes how a masked man, carrying a small tote bag, uses a bench as he tries to climb into the second-floor window of a building. But he slips and comes crashing down.

Sometimes special effects were added, as in *The Burglar-Proof Bed* 1902). When a masked burglar enters a man's bedroom he gets an unexpected surprise in this early comedy drama. As the gentleman prepares to go to sleep in his Murphy bed, the door to his bedroom slowly opens and a burglar enters, pointing a gun at the surprised victim. The captive suddenly releases a switch which allows the bed to fold up; he then discharges explosions through apertures in the bottom of the bed. The stunned intruder is finally subdued.

The Burglar (1903) was another early, crude depiction of a failed burglary. This short film, set in the bedroom of a married couple's home, shows a burglar entering through a window and hiding. The wife, awakened by the noise, alerts her husband. She arms herself with a gun and searches cautiously for the intruder while the husband calls the police. After the burglar is arrested, the wife faints.

The unusual film, *Sherlock Holmes Baffled* (1903), depends chiefly on trick photography to baffle a home owner who catches a burglar at work. As the burglar is busily engaged in filling his crude bag with stolen items, the owner approaches quietly and taps the intruder on the shoulder. Suddenly, the burglar disappears. The dazed owner sits down, lights a cigar and begins contemplating what he has seen. Suddenly, the burglar reappears in the cigar smoke. This occurs several times until the last shot, which pictures the thief outside the house.

Two girls dressed in pajamas and in their bedroom think they hear a noise outside their room in the one-reel comedy drama, *The Girls and the Burglar*

(1904). When they discover they cannot lock the door, they put together a dummy, place it in their bed, and hide under it. Soon, a burglar enters and begins to search the room. When he reaches the bed and sees the dummy, he bolts out of the room in fright.

In *The Athletic Girl and the Burglar* (1905), an energetic young woman engaged in calisthenics in a room resembling a gymnasium is startled when a burglar enters the premises. She halts her workout and attacks the intruder, beating him senseless. She then returns to her exercises. The film is an early example of the aggressive, self-sufficient screen heroine, a familiar icon in early silents and soon to be made extraordinarily popular by such stars as Pearl White and Ruth Roland.

The Burglar's Slide for Life (1905), an early Edwin S. Porter entry in the cycle of films about burglars, depicts the trials and tribulations of that discredited profession. Two women enter an apartment and surprise a burglar at work. He leaps out of a window and clings to a maze of clotheslines for support. Meanwhile, a bulldog pursues him and hangs onto him with its teeth. When the intruder lands on the ground, the tenacious bulldog holds on to the seat of the man's pants. Several women arrive with their brooms and begin thrashing the luckless thief.

D. W. Griffith offers *The Christmas Burglars* (1908) as his Yuletide entry in the cycle of early burglary films. A desperate woman, seeking to pawn her shawl, accidentally drops a note from her little daughter. After the curious pawnbroker reads the note, he gathers several cronies who later that night steal into the woman's apartment, decorate her Christmas tree, place food and presents under it and leave. The next morning, when the child awakens, she finds the presents she had asked for.

Griffith's early drama, *A Burglar's Mistake* (1909), marked a sharp turn for burglar films. The cycle demonstrated a proclivity toward a more violent tone with this entry, as Griffith explored the limits of a blackmail victim's patience. A burglar, under the guise of "protection," blackmails a married man with a large family. When the man refuses to make any further payments, the thief burglarizes his victim's home. The man catches him in the act and deliberately shoots him, after which he calls the police. By 1912 Griffith was busy directing dozens of films each year, including *The Burglar's Dilemma* (1912), for Biograph. This one-reel melodrama was based on a story by Lionel Barrymore.

A young woman uses her intellect instead of her brawn in Thomas Ricketts's drama, *A Woman's Wit* (1909). She enters her bedroom and discovers an intruder behind the curtain. She goes about her chores nonchalantly and steps out of the room for a moment, at which time she telephones the police. She returns to her bedroom where the burglar finally confronts her. She calmly stalls him, keeping him engaged in conversation. Finally, he begins to strangle her. He then heads for the window, but the police enter and capture him.

Some burglars are more fortunate. They may meet up with a pretty reformer, as does the amateur thief of the title, *Three Fingered Jack* (1910), who encounters a strong-headed Salvation Army volunteer. She meets Jack in a lowly dive and notices his middle finger is missing. Later, Jack enters a home through an open window, steals a roll of money from a desk drawer he forces open and leaves. The young woman happens to visit the same house to ask the owner for a donation. He invites her in, leaves her alone in his library while he attends to personal matters and then returns. When he opens the drawer and reaches for his money, he is surprised to find the roll of bills gone. He calls the police who suspect the young visitor. Meanwhile, she notices a hand print on the desk blotter that shows the impression of a hand with a missing middle finger. When the police release her for lack of evidence, she returns to the dive, finds Jack, and forces him to confess. She then leads him back to the homeowner so that Jack can return the money. The Salvation Army worker then persuades the grateful man to give Jack a job.

Other burglars may not be lucky, but they have something more important – a sense of humanity. A kindly and friendly burglar in the drama, *The Telephone Call* (1909), befriends a little girl in the park. The mother removes the child and frowns upon the stranger. The burglar is in collusion with the butler of a local mansion, both planning to rob the home that evening. When the burglar later enters the mansion, he discovers he is in the home of his little friend, the girl he had met earlier in the park. Refusing to rob the home, he turns on his companion. Meanwhile, the mother, who has been on the phone with her husband, hears the commotion and tells her husband to rush home. A thrilling car ride follows, and when the husband arrives, he finds the burglar fighting with the butler.

Another unlucky but humane burglar appears in D. W. Griffith's drama, *His Last Burglary* (1910). An impoverished couple, unable to afford milk for their baby, decide to abandon their child in a mansion, thereby giving their dear little one a head start in life. The father, by way of an open window, enters such a home and deposits the tot in a soft chair and then leaves. Meanwhile, a burglar and his wife have just lost their child to illness. The husband, thinking they have been punished because of his sinful life, says he is going on his last burglary. He enters the same house and starts to look around for valuables. He sees the abandoned child holding a note. He reads the message and promptly takes the baby home to his wife. The poor father later receives a letter with a check. He has sold one of his inventions. He and his wife rush to the mansion to reclaim their baby but discover the child is gone. The mother goes into hysterics and shock. The burglar, who has given up his trade, and is now employed as chauffeur to the doctor treating the hysterical mother, hears about her illness and promptly returns the baby to its rightful parents.

A gentleman has an unusual experience with a burglar in the short drama, *Brother Man* (1910). While playing cards at his club, the gentleman receives word that his wife has given birth. He hurries home to see the infant, but the nurse cautions him not to wake the baby. Instead, he falls asleep and is soon visited by a burglar who relieves him of his watch and money. Before he leaves, the burglar notices the baby and is touched by the sight of the infant. He then proceeds to return the watch and money and leaves ten dollars as a present for the newborn. A policeman catches the escaping thief, but the father shows the officer the ten dollars, saying the visitor was a brother at heart.

A burglar, recently released from prison, is lucky enough to receive some money from a passerby, a sympathetic young woman who feels sorry for the man in tattered clothes, in the short drama, *Thieves* (1913). Later that evening, the burglar resorts to his former trade. He enters a stately home where an elderly man is dying. Downstairs, he overhears two relatives plotting to cut a niece out of her inheritance. They open a safe and discover two wills, one disinheriting them and the second making the young woman the heiress. They switch envelopes and place the wills back in the same. Then the woman comes downstairs, and the burglar recognizes her as the same person who earlier had given him some money. When the threesome leave the room, the uninvited visitor quietly opens the safe and switches the wills, thereby restoring the inheritance to the rightful beneficiary.

Another reformed burglar tale, the one-reel drama *Mongrel and Master* (1914) stars Francis Bushnell and offers nothing to distinguish itself from its many hackneyed predecessors. The frail plot calls for a young woman to hand a rose to the burglar who, later seeing her picture in the house he is burglarizing, decides – then and there – to reform from his life of crime.

Ford Sterling's two-reel Keystone comedy *Baffles, Gentleman Burglar* (1914), offered this obvious parody of Hornung's popular fictional character, Raffles, the gentleman thief. The cast included well-known veteran comic players Sterling, Chester Conklin and Alice Davenport.

The appeal of the Raffles character in cinema fiction is once again illustrated in *The Burglar and the Lady* (1914), starring Jim Corbett as the gentleman cracksman. The story centers upon two brothers – one, the elder, raised by the father in luxury; the other poverty-stricken, forced to steal to care for his mother, becomes Danvers, the daring cracksman, pursued by his detective nemesis throughout the film. The obligatory reformation occurs when Danvers has a change of heart and decides to go straight. He marries the daughter of one of his victims. Corbett, the heavyweight boxing champion of the world, made his screen debut in this film. Other films followed, including *The Bank Burglar's Fate* (1914), *Beating the Burglar* (1914) and *A Bold, Bad Burglar* (1915).

Director Paul Powell's comedy, *Betsy's Burglar* (1917), with Constance Talmadge, Kenneth Harlan and Elmo Lincoln, portrays Talmadge as a boarding housekeeper's daughter who becomes entangled in a jewel theft. A romantic triangle includes Oscar, the delivery boy who aspires to become a detective, and Harry Brent, a man-about-town who boards at the house. Brent is actually after a strongbox containing the family jewels and a will naming him beneficiary. Jasper Dunn, it seems, was once a crooked lawyer and had hidden the items in his room at the boarding house. Brent convinces Talmadge of his good faith and persuades her to help him obtain the items which are rightfully his.

In director Harley Knoles's drama, *The Burglar* (1917), Carlyle Blackwell is haunted by an incident from his college days in this blackmail and robbery drama. Sid Burns (Harry LaMont) finds Blackwell years later and threatens to expose his involvement in an old college shooting unless he agrees to participate in Burns's planned bank robbery. Both are captured and imprisoned, but Blackwell escapes and is reported dead. His wife, believing herself a widow, remarries, further complicating his life.

Dick Rosson portrays the title character, a dying derelict, in Arthur Rosson's drama, *Cassidy* (1917), based on the short story by Larry Evans. Cassidy honors an early act of kindness. Though the district attorney at the time catches Cassidy burglarizing his home, he forgives him when he hears the sad story of Cassidy's life. He even provides money to pay for Cassidy's trip back to New York from San Francisco. The district attorney's kindness is repaid when upon learning that his benefactor's daughter has been kidnapped, Cassidy rescues her, returns her to her father and dies.

William Desmond, as an acrobatic young athlete and former Yale track star, joins a detective agency in Frank Borzage's action mystery, *Flying Colors* (1917). After graduating from college, he has had little success in earning a living or finding the proper career – all leading to his being cast out by his wealthy relatives. He is finally hired to investigate a raft of mysterious jewel thefts in Poughkeepsie, New York, perpetrated by an elusive burglar. Desmond's track skills as a pole vaulter help him to apprehend the thief and end the burglaries.

Another light comedy, E. Mason Hopper's *Boston Blackie's Little Pal* (1918), with Bert Lytell as Blackie, was not very well received critically. It suffered from predictability. The plot brings Jack Boyle's fictional crook-turned-sleuth Boston Blackie to the home of a small boy (Joey Jacobs) who shows no fear. Instead, he trusts and befriends the burglar. Blackie, impressed by the child, prevents a family breakup by scaring off the mother's lover and confiscating their hoard of jewels. This was the first screen version of Boyle's congenial crook character who was, throughout the twenties, played by a variety of actors. The Blackie character remained inactive during the first decade of talking pictures, reappearing on screen in 1941 in a long and popular series featuring Chester Morris as the popular reformed thief.

James Cruze's romantic drama, *The Love Burglar* (1919), based on the play, *One of Us*, by Jack Lait, concerns slumming author Anna Q. Nilsson who, while seeking local color, gets mixed up with the underworld and her future husband. Wealthy Wallace Reid, mistaken for a local tough by Wallace Beery, as Coast-to-Coast Taylor, meets Nilsson, who is working as a cabaret singer. Much of the film deals with the romantic angle between the two leads and Beery's jealousy, which almost destroys the romance. Reid finally learns that the woman he loves is a writer.

II. The Dark World of the Violent Burglar

By the 1920s, plots about burglaries and burglars began to become more complex and sophisticated, as in *Beating the Game* (1921). An occasional entry even dealt with a peripheral topic, such as drugs, as in *Face to Face* (1922). Others, like *Mark of the Beast* (1923), tried a psychological approach. A touch of comedy invaded some of these films, as in *Ladyfingers* (1921) and *Seven Sinners* (1925). Several entries employed women burglars, usually for romantic or comic reasons, as in *Silk Stocking Sal* (1924), *The Brass Bowl* (1924) and *Seven Sinners* (1925). Generally, the screen persona of the burglar was not treated seriously as a major character. With the introduction of Prohibition in 1920, the nation reeled from the swell of organized crime, and following in its wake an upsurge in violence. Smuggling and gang warfare replaced more conventional criminal activities. The lonely and often sympathetic screen burglar became a relic of a gentler past, an anomaly in the more violent world of the twenties.

In Victor Schertzinger's drama, *Beating the Game* (1921), Tom Moore portrays a burglar caught by a fellow crook who makes Moore an unusual proposal. He offers him $1,000 if he will go to a certain town and establish himself as an honest citizen. Later, his benefactor will arrive so that both can "score" greatly as a result of Moore's knowledge of the community. Moore agrees and becomes so popular that the townspeople want him to run for mayor. He has also fallen in love – a situation which compels him to reform. When his accomplice arrives, Moore learns that the man is a state senator and amateur criminologist who has been using Moore to test one of his favorite theories – honest living is its own reward.

A young burglar and his wealthy grandmother who refused to acknowledge him years earlier are reunited in Bayard Veiller's comedy drama, *Ladyfingers* (1921), based on the 1920 novel by Jackson Gregory. At first, a scheming lawyer who recognizes the burglar as the rightful heir to his client's estate, brings them together, hoping to discredit the thief. The young man falls in love with an attractive young woman, surrenders to the police and serves time in prison. When he is released, he marries his sweetheart with the blessings of his grandmother.

In the best tradition of Greek tragedy, a brilliant attorney is hired by the girlfriend of a burglar falsely accused of murder, in Jack Nelson's drama, *I Am Guilty* (1921). The attorney searches for a missing woman who was at the scene of the crime. Unknown to him, the missing witness is his own wife. There is dramatic irony in the specter of the attorney contributing to his own possible tragedy as he seeks out the witness. During a sensational trial scene in which the burglar is found guilty, the lawyer's wife reveals that she is the missing suspect. However, the murdered man's mistress then confesses to the crime, thereby exonerating both the lawyer's wife and the burglar. This *deus ex machina* saves the attorney from an Oedipus-like tragic fate.

Harry Grossman's low-budget suspense mystery, *Face to Face* (1922), boasts two offbeat elements: the amateur detective is an eighteen-year-old schoolgirl, and the chief suspect is a drug addict. The suspect, caught burglarizing a wealthy home and having fired a shot in fear, is accused of murdering the master of the household. His young schoolgirl sister arrives with a classmate (Marguerite Marsh), the latter doing the sleuthing and proving, at the burglar's trial, that he did not kill the victim. Instead, the victim's brother-in-law produces a letter that the dead man had committed suicide.

A burglar triggers a psychological disturbance in one of his victims in Thomas Dixon's low-budget, inferior drama, *Mark of the Beast* (1923). Doctor Robert Ellis's fiancée, Madelyn Clare, finds it difficult to resist a second-story burglar who happens to resemble her dead father. Ellis, researching this type of mental behavior, decides to follow his fiancée when she elopes with the burglar. Fortunately, the physician is present when the brutish groom begins to manhandle his bride. Ellis intervenes, rescues Clare and subdues the newly married burglar. The analysis of the human mind and its reactions to the subconscious leaves much to be desired in this film.

Anticipating the screwball comedies of the thirties, Maurice Campbell's zany comedy drama, *The Exciters* (1923), based on the play by Martin Brown, concerns a thrill-seeking socialite. Bebe Daniels thinks she is married to a burglar. Instead, her husband, Antonio Moreno, turns out to be a young man seeking to expose a gang of thieves who have harmed a close friend of Moreno's.

A young businessman is falsely accused of murdering his partner and is given the death penalty in Tod Browning's familiar but suspenseful drama, *Silk Stocking Sal* (1924). Evelyn Brent portrays the title character, a young woman burglar who helps Robert Ellis, the condemned man. Ellis had earlier caught Brent applying her trade and had given her a chance to reform. When his partner is found murdered and Ellis is arrested, Brent determines to find the guilty party. Suspecting a local gangster, she plants a microphone in his apartment. She then tricks him into boasting about the murder, a confession overheard by the district attorney, who then rescues Ellis from the electric chair. Director Tod Browning made another, more successful, drama about burglars the following year, titled *The Unholy Three* (1925), starring Lon Chaney.

In Jerome Storm's *The Brass Bowl* (1924), a minor mystery based on the 1907 novel by Louis Joseph Vance, Edmund Lowe portrays a wealthy estate owner who resembles a notorious crook. Arriving home unexpectedly one evening, he catches Claire Adams ostensibly burglarizing his safe and, as a lark, he turns over the jewels to her. Later the real burglar arrives, leading to a series of complications and mix-ups. The female thief finally admits she was searching for papers to help clear her father of criminal charges. Author Louis Joseph Vance was the creator of the popular romantic character known as the Lone Wolf, a mysterious fictional figure who often worked as a private detective in a long series of crime films.

Charles Hutchison is tricked into committing a burglary for a pretty female member of a gang in James Chapin's fast-paced action drama, *After Dark* (1924). The woman asks that he retrieve some personal letters. Instead, he steals valuable bonds. However, the daughter of the owner catches him and holds him at gun point while she calls the police. In the interim, she believes his story and tells the police Hutchison is her husband. Later, he discovers the thieves have taken off with the bonds. He pursues them in a wild car ride involving a motorboat and, following a fight on a cliff, he finally retrieves the stolen bonds.

A young man who desires to become a police officer fails the examination in William K. Howard's weak drama, *East of Broadway* (1924), set chiefly on New York's Lower East Side. Owen Moore has dreamed of becoming a cop for a long time, so that when he fails the civil service test, he sinks into despondency. However, he gets another chance after he captures two burglars. Unfortunately, little is shown or developed about the teeming tenement section of the city.

An old acquaintance of a noted inventor returns from the past and wreaks havoc on the latter's domestic home life in B. C. Rule's mystery thriller, *One Hour Past Midnight* (1924). Brent, the inventor, struggles with a burglar after midnight, and the next morning his daughter discovers that her father has disappeared. Following several mysterious incidents, including the return of the intruder, the police ascertain that Brent had been kidnapped by an old friend who had come to rob the inventor. After kidnapping Brent, the interloper returned to find the combination of the victim's safe.

A wedding is almost ruined by the actions of a careless groom in Frank S. Mattison's drama, *Flying Fool* (1925), based on the story, "The Ace and the Queen," by Putnam Hoover. When Dick Grace is late for his own wedding, his annoyed bride, Wanda Hawley, rushes home, accompanied by best man Gaston Glass. Her mother places the valuable jewels back in the safe, while the groom is refused entry to the house. He decides to enter through a bedroom window, but he is seen by a policeman who, thinking the intruder is a burglar, knocks Grace unconscious. Meanwhile, Glass, the best man, steals the jewels from the safe and plants them on Grace, who is then arrested. Glass persuades Hawley to elope with him by flying to San Diego. Grace is bailed out of jail and upon learning of the flight of his intended bride and Glass, begins to pursue them. He rescues Hawley and is eventually exonerated of all charges. The couple are finally married.

Complications arise in Lewis Milestone's crime comedy, *Seven Sinners* (1925), when newspaper stories announce that the private police force of an exclusive community has gone on strike. The news brings a horde of burglars and safecrackers to the wealthy homes, including female thief Marie Prevost and dapper Clive Brook. Brook interrupts her and her assistant trying to break into a safe. The man escapes, but Brook, posing as a guard, forces her to open the safe and then lets her escape. As he places the jewels in his pocket, she returns and gets the drop on him. The remainder of the film concerns a series of mix-ups as various crooks arrive on the scene, many of them posing as legitimate citizens.

Lon Chaney portrays the leader of perhaps one of the most bizarre gangs in the history of crime movies in Tod Browning's *The Unholy Three* (1925). He plays a ventriloquist who disguises himself as an elderly woman and owner of a pet shop. By "throwing" his voice, he tricks his customers into believing his parrots can talk. Later, when he is summoned to their homes to check on the "dumb" creatures, he "cases the joint." He then returns with his accomplices – the other members of the "unholy three" – a carnival strong-man to bend such obstacles as window bars, and a midget posing as a baby, who slips easily through the window opening to steal any valuable contents. Mae Busch, as Chaney's gun-moll girlfriend, falls in love with innocent pet-store clerk Matt Moore, a romance that presents problems for the trio. Chaney and midget Harry Earles repeated their roles as store owner and his accomplice in the 1930 sound remake, directed by Jack Conway. Chaney, at the height of his career, died shortly after completing the remake. Director Tod Browning, although a competent director of conventional films, became better known for his offbeat films, including the cult favorite, *Freaks* (1932).

Wealthy Conrad Nagel stumbles upon several burglars who are in the process of removing some jewelry from his mother's Florida houseboat in Howard Bretherton's comedy drama, *Caught in the Fog* (1928). First, he comes across May McAvoy and her male accomplice, who think Nagel is a fellow burglar. A fight ensues, but is quickly broken up by an elderly couple, also burglars posing as guests. Keeping his own identity secret, Nagel poses as the butler. McAvoy and her partner explain they are the maid and cook, respectively. A pair of highly incompetent detectives suddenly show up, accompanied by a heavy fog. Following a night of frightening sights, gun battles and other disturbances, the detectives remove all the thieves except for McAvoy, who has captured Nagel's heart as well as his jewels.

Arthur Lake, as the kid brother of two husky police officers in Nat Ross's farce, *Stop That Man* (1928), poses in one of their uniforms – with unexpected results. He unknowingly helps a burglar break into a home, but he later captures the thief and delivers him to the police precinct. Arthur Lake gained greater recognition in the sound era playing the confused husband and father, Dagwood Bumstead, in the long-running "Blondie" film series, costarring Penny Singleton as his wife, Blondie.

Capital Punishment

I. The "Disgrace to Civilization"

Albert Camus once argued, "What will be left of the power of example if it is proved that capital punishment has another power, and a very real one, which degrades men to the point of shame, madness, and murder?" By 1823, Britain abolished the death penalty for more than one hundred crimes previously listed as capital offenses. But in 1890, New York introduced the electric chair for use in capital punishment cases. Conventional wisdom at the time considered the apparatus more "modern" and humane than hanging. Early American silent films that condemned capital punishment may not have carried their arguments to Camus's extremes, but they did present several cogent reasons for its abolition. The Stielow case, in which a condemned man found guilty of murder was about to be electrocuted but was reprieved only minutes before when the actual killer confessed, spurred a bitter remark by former President Taft. "The administration of criminal law in this country," he commented, "is a disgrace to civilization." Some of these films were overly melodramatic, others farfetched, and more than a handful proved to be poignant and important. What remains striking to today's audiences is how early in the century and how fervently pioneering movie studios approached the subject. By 1915, only six states had abolished capital punishment. There are three major objections to capital punishment: (1) women are rarely sentenced to death and executed, even though 20 percent of all homicides in recent years have been committed by women; (2) a disproportionate number of nonwhites are sentenced to death and executed; and (3), poor and friendless defendants are most likely to be sentenced to death and executed. However, those who defend the death penalty insist that the laws of capital punishment do not refer to sexist, racist, or class bias in its execution. Presently, they argue, public opinion in the U.S. supports the death penalty for murder by a more than two-to-one margin. They add that no satisfactory deterrent to life imprisonment is effective for those currently serving a life term who commit murder while incarcerated. In addition, revolutionaries, terrorists, traitors, and spies who have not yet been caught would only be liable to a life term if arrested.

A Career of Crime, No. 5 (1902), Biograph's crude but effective depiction of a convicted criminal dying in the electric chair, realistically captures the condemned man's last moments. Prison guards, witnesses and a priest gather to take part in the execution. The subject is placed in the electric chair where he is tied hand and foot. After a blindfold is placed over his eyes, he is seen struggling as if bolts of current are racing through his body. This stark and disturbing film may well be one of the earliest cautionary dramas, or perhaps an intentional social commentary on the horrors of capital punishment.

The drama, *At the Eleventh Hour* (1910), concerns the struggle of the State Governor to adhere to the tenets of justice in the face of great personal loss. The plot also questions some of the weaknesses of capital punishment. A man is sentenced to die at 11:00 p.m. It is reported to be the Governor's estranged son, whom he has not seen in five years. To pardon him is a great temptation, but without proper grounds it would be a miscarriage of justice. The Governor's strength and rectitude are rewarded when he makes the right decision, and it turns out that the culprit is not his son after all.

In Rollin S. Sturgeon's sentimental western, *The Little Angel of Canyon Creek* (1914), based on the book by Reverend Cyrus Townsend Brady, Little Olaf, a New York immigrant orphan, has been sent to the West by a child welfare service. He ends up in a Colorado mining camp after several adventures with miners and Indians. Dead Shot Jackson, after cheating some Indians and then shooting them, returns to the mining camp with the ten-year-old orphan boy and one Indian lad who is about to be lynched for the killings. But Little Olaf, who has witnessed the murders, talks the mob out of the hanging, much to the chagrin of Jackson, who flees the scene. Somehow, the orphan influences several miners and others into reforming. Later, when the camp splits into two factions, one religious and another against the influential Sunday school, Jackson leads the latter group against the orphan boy and the leader of the religious movement. He shoots and wounds the boy, thereby transforming his followers against him and who want to hang him. But once again, the boy stops them from carrying out a lynching. Virtually everyone then joins the Sunday school movement, including the Indian, whose life the boy had saved earlier.

Honest Laura Sawyer saves the life of her flighty sister, Betty Harte, who is accused of killing her own baby, in J. Searle Dawley's drama, *A Woman's Triumph* (1914), based on the novel, *The Heart of Midlothian*, by Sir Walter Scott. Harte's wild boyfriend, Hal Clarendon, is arrested for smuggling just before his marriage. Harte, now pregnant, flees to Edinburgh, where she has her child that is soon stolen from her. She is accused of killing the baby and is imprisoned. Clarendon, who has escaped, asks Sawyer to lie so that her sister, sentenced to death, can be freed. But Sawyer refuses. Instead, she walks barefooted to London, where she asks the queen to pardon her sister. The queen, impressed by the sister's noble nature, grants the pardon.

Joseph Levering's *Capital Punishment* (1915), a tale of murder and the subsequent trial, depends a great deal on the willing suspension of disbelief. The plot is fairly simple and calls for a fight in a hotel room between a politician and Lenora Ulrich. After shooting the man in the arm, Ulrich falls to the floor. He thinks she is dead. (Why he would think this remains unexplained.) To avoid detection, he climbs out of a window and falls to his death. The woman's boy friend, to protect her, claims he threw the man out the window, and when it is determined that the bullet did not kill the politician, the boy friend (Sidney Mason) is tried and sentenced to hang. At the last moment, a missing witness appears to exonerate Mason. The film was adapted from a story by Clarence J. Harris.

Drunken Allen J. Holubar, who had earlier become involved in a bar fight with an elderly man and the inventor William Bailey, is later accused of killing Bailey, in Stuart Paton's forceful social drama, *Conscience* (1915). Later that fateful night, he goes to apologize to Bailey, and during their discussion, Bailey falls down dead. A gun is found and the police arrest Holubar, who is convicted of murder and electrocuted. Curtis Benton, a criminologist, discusses the case with the warden, who is delighted that capital punishment has finally been abolished in the state and admits that he believed Holubar was innocent. The criminologist investigates further and learns that Bailey's partner, William Welsh, who is conscious-driven and nervous, finally confesses to murdering his partner. He is sentenced to prison instead of going to the dreaded electric chair. Some of the scenes were filmed at New York's Sing Sing Prison.

Having recently been hired as a farm worker, John Doe is accused of murder when his employers are found dead, in Lois Weber's drama, *The People Vs. John Doe* (1916), an attack on capital punishment in cases of circumstantial evidence. An over-eager detective bullies Doe into a confession, and the suspect is sentenced to death. However, at the trial, attorney Leah Baird is convinced of Doe's innocence, and she sets out to prove it. The big-mouthed detective is only too willing to brag about his coercion of Doe, and the attorney uses this revelation to obtain a new trial. With the further discovery of a passing peddler's guilt, John Doe is exonerated and released. The film was based chiefly on the celebrated Stielow case of the period. A man convicted of murder and who was sentenced to die in the electric chair is reprieved only minutes before the sentence was to be carried out – after the actual killer had confessed.

Barbara Tennant tries desperately to help her brother, who has been wrongly accused of murder, in Maurice Tourneur's suspenseful drama, *The Closed Road* (1916). Lionel Adams, her brother, a doctor who is trying to find a cure for cancer, goes to an acquaintance's apartment to claim some money owed to him. When the man is found dead with Adams's gun at his side, the doctor is arrested. His sister, meanwhile, learns that a young playboy, House Peters, who has but a few months to live, plans to commit suicide. She persuades him to put his death to some useful purpose by confessing to the murder. He agrees, and the doctor is exonerated. House is sentenced to die in the electric chair.

Suddenly, the actual killer, the doctor's mentally disturbed uncle, confesses, and House, too, is freed. Scenes of the electric chair, the Tombs in Manhattan, and other visuals, as well as plot elements, offer strong arguments against capital punishment.

An innocent man is found guilty of killing a governor in William V. Mong's anti-capital punishment drama, *The Girl and the Crisis* (1917). The lieutenant governor finally decides to commute the man's death sentence, but he is too late. The condemned man has died of a stroke.

Burton King's social drama, *The Public Defender* (1917), based on the 1917 book by Mayer C. Goldman, supported and paved the way for acceptance of the office of Public Defender, an attempt to counterbalance the power of the prosecuting attorney. Robert Edeson, as the Public Defender, saves the life of a bank clerk on the eve of the clerk's execution. The Public Defender discovers proof of the clerk's innocence in the nick of time. The film also emerged as an indictment of capital punishment.

Greedy factory owner Ralph Lewis' actions of reducing his workers' pay while simultaneously raising the price of their food at the company store, leads to a strike in Richard Stanton's drama, *Cheating the Public* (1918). When the strike brings on results, Enid Markey goes to Lewis to speak for the workers' cause. Recalling that her mother had once rejected his offer of marriage, Lewis vindictively begins to molest the daughter. During the scuffle, Lewis is shot to death and Markey is arrested and convicted of murder. Before she goes to her death, factory foreman Tom Wilson confesses that he shot Lewis during the struggle. Lewis's son, Bertram Grassby, who has been instituting the much-needed reforms in the plant, speeds to the governor and wins a pardon for the innocent young woman. As a result, Markey and Grassby are married.

The title of Theodore Marston's mystery, *The Black Gate* (1919), refers to the door of the death chamber awaiting victims of capital punishment. The plot reveals a simple story of a rape committed by the lecherous Allen Bowen, and the subsequent murder of Bowen. Presumably an outraged friend of the rape victim, Vera Hampton, committed the crime as an act of retaliation. Wade DeForrest is accused. At this point, Earle Williams conspires with the mother of the accused to buy his freedom by means of a false confession. He agrees to confess to the crime only if Mrs. DeForrest deposits $100,000 to the account of his brother on the day he passes through the black gate to perdition. At the last moment, Williams reneges on the deal, and DeForrest confesses to the killing.

II. "Cruel and Unusual Punishment"

The death penalty in the United States fell into disrepute after World War II, and in 1972 the U.S. Supreme Court voided all federal and state laws advocating the death penalty. The Court ruled that condemned persons were being subjected to "cruel and unusual punishment," in violation of the eighth amendment to the Constitution. The Court allowed for the possibility of new, constitutional laws, and since then the nation and most states have enacted measures imposing the penalty in specific murder cases. By 1976, the Court reversed itself. Capital punishment does not constitute "cruel and unusual punishment," the U.S. Supreme Court ruled in a 7 to 2 decision handed down on July 2. The Court held in 1972 that the death penalty was unconstitutional, with Justice Thurgood Marshall citing evidence that the death penalty did not deter crime. However, The court allowed room for the possibility of new, constitutional laws, and since then the U.S. and most states have enacted measures imposing the penalty in specified kinds of murder cases. Indeed, Congress and most states have drafted new death penalty laws for murderers, and the Court has upheld such laws in Georgia, Florida and Texas. Several films during the twenties continued focus on the topic. For example, James Hogan's *Capital Punishment* (1925) continued to assail the death sentence, pointing out the cruelty and injustice of capital punishment. Others, like Sidney Olcott's *The Right of Way* (1921), approached the topic from the viewpoint of prison reform. At least one drama, Norman Dawn's *Five Days to Live* (1922), borrowed from a Dickens classic by having its hero, Chinese sculptor Sessue Hayakawa volunteer to substitute himself for a condemned bandit in exchange for enough money and several days of grace so that he may buy his beloved's freedom. Meanwhile, *Found Guilty* (1923) presented a series of graphic and disturbing sequences depicting the horrors of capital punishment – all no doubt meant to shake up its audiences. Some plots, like that of *The Social Code* (1923), *The Man in the Shadow* (1926) and *Faithful Wives* (1927), simply repeated the usual clichés – the familiar story of the last-minute rescue, the innocent suspect sentenced to death, the grieving mother waiting for her son's return. Other dramas had the faithful girlfriend or wife rescue the condemned man, as in *The Bright Lights of Broadway* (1923). Still others, such as William Parke's weird drama, *Legally Dead* (1923), offered some degree of originality. Using elements of science fiction, or at least the supernatural, it describes a reporter who is unfairly sentenced to death, executed, and then is brought back to life by a sympathetic physician!

Sidney Olcott's social drama, *The Right Way* (1921), contrasts the older and more brutal methods of prison treatment with those of the Mutual Welfare League, that advocates the honor system as one of their reforms. The plot deals with two youths, one wealthy, Joseph Marquis, and the other, Sidney D'Albrook, raised in the slums. The poor boy goes to a reformatory for a minor offense, and is turned into a professional thief. He is later sent back and faces the brutality of the old prison system. The rich boy is sent to the same prison for forging his father's name. They both befriend fellow prisoner Tammany Young, who is unfairly sentenced to die in the electric chair for killing a stool pigeon. The two pals escape – breaking the honor system – and find proof of Young's innocence. But they are too late to save their friend. The innocent pay is electrocuted. However, because they were sincere, the rich youth and the poor youth are paroled, to the delight of their girlfriends. The film was originally produced in 1920 in a longer version under the title *The Gray Brother*. The present version has been heavily edited. Later, it was reissued in 1927 under still another title, *Within Prison Walls*.

Norman Dawn's strange, slow-paced drama, *Five Days to Live* (1922), tells the story about Chinese sculptor Sessue Hayakawa, who loves the adopted daughter of greedy Goro Kino. The father, however, has other plans for the young woman. He orders her to marry a wealthy mandarin, but when she refuses, Kino locks her up. Meanwhile, in an incident reminiscent of Dickens's novel, *A Tale of Two Cities*, the sculptor negotiates with a wealthy bandit who has been condemned to death. Hayakawa, like Sidney Carton from the novel, will take the bandit's place at the time of the execution in exchange for a large sum of money. He then uses the money to buy the young woman he loves. The pair are married and spend the next five fateful days in bliss. At the predetermined time, the honorable Hayakawa starts out to meet his obligation, only to learn the bandit has died of cholera. He rushes back to his wife, who is near death from taking poison. She was scheduled to be turned over to the mandarin. Her husband revives her in time.

The drama, *Found Guilty* (1922), makes a strong case against capital punishment by depicting a series of unsavory scenes of hangings, beheading, and other assorted means of taking the lives of transgressors. Other sequences show a young woman living with a man who eventually abandons her to marry another woman. Finally, a sequence in which another young woman kills her sister, and an innocent man is tried for the murder. He is sentenced to die in the electric chair. Detailed scenes are subsequently revealed leading up to the condemned man's execution. Tom Santschi, an actor in numerous low-budget action films, is the only performer listed in the scanty credits of this offbeat feature.

Reporter Milton Sills, who believes that most victims of capital punishment are wrongfully sentenced to death, is himself executed for murder in William Parke's strange drama, *Legally Dead* (1923). Sills witnesses the murder of a detective. He picks up the gun and pursues the killer, who escapes. The reporter is arrested, tried and convicted of the crime. After he is executed, a sympathetic doctor brings him back to life by using adrenaline. The film is saved from the commonplace by introducing elements of science fiction and a concern for victims of capital punishment.

Oscar Apfel's melodrama, *The Social Code* (1923), based on the 1922 story, "To Whom It May Concern," by Rita Weiman, follows the timeworn plot about an innocent young man who is saved from the electric chair in the nick of time. The present version has the condemned man's girlfriend, Viola Dana, as the instrument of his rescue. To add to her glory, she simultaneously frees her older sister from an embarrassing complication. As with other similarly plotted films, this entry suggests the weaknesses of capital punishment.

A young man who is framed for murder faces the death sentence in Webster Campbell's familiar drama, *The Bright Lights of Broadway* (1923). The lights of the title attract country girl Doris Kenyon to New York, where she marries villainous Lowell Sherman before she is aware of what she is getting herself into. Her sweetheart, Harrison Ford, follows her to the city in an attempt to rescue her, but Sherman frames the youth for a murder that Sherman has committed. The remainder of the plot concerns Kenyon's efforts to save Ford by wrangling a confession from her husband. The last sequences hold enough suspense and thrills to overcome the otherwise threadbare plot. The flimsy circumstantial evidence that convicts Ford suggests the weaknesses of the arguments for capital punishment, for the youth barely escapes with his life.

Another youth unjustly faces the death sentence in Kenneth Webb's absorbing drama, *The Daring Years* (1923). Charles Emmett Mack, the only son of widowed Mary Carr, falls under the spell of cabaret entertainer Mildred Harris. The affair comes crashing down on Mack when Harris virtually is responsible for sending the youth to the electric chair. The plot includes the obligatory scene of an exciting car chase to the governor's mansion to get a pardon for Mack – in the proverbial nick of time. This is followed by another familiar scene in which Mack returns home to his anxious mother and forgiving girlfriend. Character player Mary Carr excelled in sympathetic and sentimental mother roles for two decades.

Edward Sloman's convoluted drama, *The Last Hour* (1923), suggests more than the usual crime story. Milton Sills portrays a safecracker who returns from South America only to be accused of a bank robbery his older brother has committed. The brothers meet in Carmel Myers's apartment. She and her father are both forgers. The police suddenly barge in and the older brother is gunned down in a fight. Meanwhile, Sills helps the father and daughter to escape. After serving in World War I, Sills returns in time once again to rescue Myers and her father, after the latter shoot a politician who has tried to seduce the daughter. Sills confesses to the killing and is sentenced to hang. But a pardon arrives just minutes before he is to be executed. The film contains more than the familiar plot about the last-minute rescue of an innocent man or the usual condemnation of capital punishment. Several critics commented about the brutality in the scene where the detective who earlier had killed the older brother did so in cold blood as fellow officers looked on. The detective and the others were never officially censured or disciplined for their actions.

Shannon Fife's familiar drama, *The Great Diamond Mystery* (1924), is just another crime tale in which the falsely accused hero, played by Buster Collier, is saved from execution at the last moment. The film offers little that is new or fresh. The plot involves the usual stolen diamonds, murders, red-herring butlers, false clues and an unctuous villain played by Philo McCullough, who was well known for this type of role.

Similar ingredients – the innocent youth sentenced to death, the grieving mother and the last-minute reprieve – are mixed together in George Melford's routine drama, *Going Crooked* (1926), based on the play by Winchell Smith. Leslie Fenton, the driver of an armored car, is falsely accused of killing the armed guard during a robbery and is sentenced to death. The real murderer, the head of a gang of jewel thieves who is masquerading as an antique dealer, is finally tricked into confessing. Bessie Love, as a former gang member forced to participate in the gang's activities, turns heroine by helping the prosecutor get the necessary confession from the leader. Because she helped save the young man, she is pardoned for her former criminal activities. The tension of Fenton's fate is carried to an extreme in this film by seeing him being strapped into the electric chair – leaving the audience to wonder if he will ever be saved in time.

James B. Hogan's blatantly anti-capital punishment drama, *Capital Punishment* (1925), depicts how easily an innocent person can receive the death sentence for a crime he did not commit. Wealthy criminologist Elliott Dexter, after failing to save an innocent man from execution, arranges with a friend, George Hackathorne, to be accused of murder, but at the last moment, the frame will be exposed and the reputation of capital punishment will be tarnished. Dexter arranges for his friend, Robert Ellis, to go on an extended sea voyage, while setting up the circumstances which will indict Hackathorne for Ellis's murder. The criminologist puts his plan into motion, Hackathorne is arrested, tried and sentenced to death. Meanwhile, Ellis returns from his trip and, in a confrontation with Dexter, the latter accidentally kills his friend. When Hackathorne protests his innocence, Dexter says he knows nothing about the defendant's charges. Finally, just before the death sentence is to be carried out, Hackathorne's girlfriend reveals all to the police.

Mary E. Hamilton, a New York police captain involved in the rehabilitation of young women offenders, plays herself in Joseph Levering's social drama, *Lilies of the Streets* (1925). Virginia Lee Corbin portrays a reckless young woman who accepts a ride home from hoodlum Wheeler Oakman, whose car accidentally struck her. Oakman, who specializes in blackmailing women, later takes her to a dance hall where he gets into a brawl. As a result, Corbin is arrested, along with Irma Harrison, Oakman's mistress, who encourages Corbin to plead guilty. She is now charged with prostitution. Oakman then uses her record to blackmail her mother. When he is killed mysteriously, Corbin, thinking her mother committed the murder, confesses to the crime. She is tried, convicted and sentenced to be executed. Harrison, the dead man's mistress, is finally persuaded by Mrs. Hamilton to confess to the killing, thereby exonerating the innocent Corbin.

Gayne Whitman, a crusading governor, battles a gang leader and a corrupt politician who heads an "invisible government" of crime, in Frank O'Connor's drama, *Exclusive Rights* (1926), based on the story, "Invisible Government," by Jerome N. Wilson. Charles Hill Mailes, the crooked political boss, plots to ruin Whitman, the new governor and former war hero. After a gang member is sentenced to death, Mailes secretly arranges to influences the governor to sign a bill abolishing capital punishment. But even when Whitman learns that Raymond McKee, his World War I buddy, has been falsely accused of murder, he refuses to sign it and allows the law to take its course. Mailes has deliberately framed McKee. Following several complications, Whitman tricks the gang leader into a confession in which he also implicates the politician and the falsely accused prisoner is freed. The richly detailed film includes well-staged nightclub sequences, the use of a silencer to kill a victim, and another brutal scene in which the big boss orders another thug to assassinate the killer, while he is taking a bath. As in *Are They Born or Made?* (1915) and other earlier crime films, this drama depicts the close ties between gangsters and politicians.

A valuable South American mine becomes the object of greed and murder in Walter Lang's complicated mystery, *The Golden Web* (1926), based on the 1910 novel by Edward Phillips Oppenheim. One of three original mine owners steals the deed and is later found murdered. Huntly Gordon, as the present owner, marries Lillian Rich, the daughter of the remaining partner, whose father has been accuses of murder. A long, drawn-out courtroom sequence finds the father guilty of murder, much of the case based on circumstantial evidence. Later, another man confesses to the crime, and Gordon prevents his wife from committing suicide over her anguish for her innocent father.

An innocent bank employee whom a gambler dupes into losing a large sum of money is falsely accused of murder in David Hartford's familiar drama, *The Man in the Shadow* (1926). Joseph Bennett, the clerk, after losing the bank's money, is then approached to give the gambler-blackmailer a floor plan of the bank in return for his debt cancellation. Meanwhile, another victim of the blackmailer kills his tormentor and Bennett, who is blamed for the murder, is convicted and sentenced to death. His girlfriend, Mary McAllister, arrives in the nick of time with the dying confession of the real killer.

The old story about an innocent youth about to go to his death while his suffering widowed mother grieves for him is resurrected in Norbert Myles's strained drama, *Faithful Wives* (1927), based on the story, "The Faithful Sex." Wallace MacDonald portrays the young man suspected of murder, with Edythe Chapman as his poor mother. Myrda Dadmarna plays MacDonald's wife. Niles Welch, the only man who can save the condemned youth, is thrown off a train during a fight and ends up on a hospital cot. But he appears in the nick of time to save the lad. This is just another film to illustrate the weakness of capital punishment – although the plot does not emphasize this theme.

Another one of those tales about a man falsely accused and convicted of a crime, this time Edward Laemmle's drama, *Held by the Law* (1927), tells of the heroine's elderly father who is tried for murdering his companion. It is not until the poor soul is within sight of the electric chair that he is exonerated. It seems that the murdered man's nephew committed the crime. Realistic scenes of Sing Sing Prison and its death house heighten the tension and add a chilling note to the film.

Once again, an innocent youth is accused of murder, in Noel Madison Smith's familiar drama, *The Night Patrol* (1926). Acrobatic Richard Talmadge portrays a brave cop who arrests Gardner James, the young brother of Rose Blossom, the officer's girlfriend. James is then charged with murder. Not completely satisfied with the evidence, Talmadge disguises himself as a notorious crook, infiltrates the gang he suspects of the crime and ferrets out the real killer. The overly familiar plot has appeared in numerous films, including the suspiciously similar 1925 Columbia release titled *The Fearless Lover*, with William Fairbanks in the role of the arresting officer.

An innocent man, sentenced to life imprisonment based on circumstantial evidence, is released because he is not expected to live, in E. H. Griffith's offbeat drama, *The Price of Honor* (1927). William V. Mong, the convict who has served fifteen years, wants to visit his niece, Dorothy Revier, who believes he is dead. He remains unseen, and learns that Malcolm McGregor, the son of the judge who sentenced Mong, has proposed to his niece, but the judge forbids his son to marry Revier. Mong then commits suicide after framing the judge's son for the alleged murder. He sends a note to the judge telling of the plot. McGregor is arrested and charged with murder. Although the judge loses the note of confession, Revier finds a copy, and her boyfriend is exonerated.

To get military secrets from the French troops, Jetta Goudal, a spy for the Sultan of Morocco, marries Victor Varconi, a French colonel, in Paul L. Stein's spy drama, *The Forbidden Woman* (1927), based on the story, "Brothers," by Elmer Harris. The marriage allows Goudal to gather valuable information which she sends back through her maid. She then journeys to Paris to meet her husband, but meets famous violinist Joseph Schildkraut, with whom she falls in love. She then discovers that the violinist is her husband's younger brother. When the colonel catches the lovers in a compromising position, he sends his brother to Morocco. Goudal, now desperate, frames her lover as a spy, hoping to keep him in Paris. Instead, she is forced to confess her treachery. The brothers reconcile their differences as they witness Goudal's execution as a spy.

A former gun moll tries to reform her gangster lover in William Wellman's underworld drama, *Ladies of the Mob* (1928). The film was adapted from Ernest Booth's hard-hitting true story about women who fall in love with mobsters and the wretched lives they lead. Clara Bow, as the embittered daughter of a murderer who died in the electric chair, is the girlfriend of tough guy Richard Arlen. After firing upon the police, both are captured and sentenced to long prison terms. Bow resigns herself to her fate, promising to reform upon release. After they serve their time, she saves Arlen from participating in a fatal bank robbery. Much of the power of the film derives from the compelling opening sequence. It symbolically and poignantly describes a convict being electrocuted while his wife and child (young Clara Bow) suffer in an adjoining room, watching the light grow dim. The wife's outbursts, condemning society, reinforce the film's anti-capital punishment theme. Author Booth wrote a similar story that Paramount later made into another successful drama, *Ladies of the Big House* (1931), starring Sylvia Sidney.

Capital vs. Labor

I. "We Do Not Deal with Labor Unions"

Because of the general lack of organized industry in the American colonies, strikes were rare. The earliest recorded strike occurred among the bakers in New York City in 1741, followed by the shoemakers in Philadelphia in 1792. Early social legislation in the United States was designed to improve working conditions, while labor organizing was restrained by the federal doctrine of conspiracy. This was superseded by state laws, beginning in 1842. Strikes became the major weapon of the labor movement. In 1897 U.S. Steel, by employing lockouts and a corps of informers and armed private detectives, broke the union. The battle cry of the steel industry became, "We do not deal with labor unions." U.S. iron and steel workers later ended a strike on January 13, 1914, at East Youngstown, Ohio, after receiving a ten percent wage hike. There were 2,000 other strikes by American workers in the first seven months of 1914. Over the years, changes in labor legislation included laws prohibiting night work and work in hazardous occupations for women and children; laws establishing minimum wages in certain occupations; and laws regulating interstate commerce to discourage sweatshop labor and child labor. Congress, in 1916, exempted unions from the antitrust laws. Legislation favorable to trade unions was achieved in the Wagner Act of 1935, which established the right of workers to organize and required employers to accept collective bargaining. But laws protecting children came under fire by the Supreme Court, which ruled, in the case of *Hammer v. Dagenhart*, that the Owen-Keating Child Labor Law of 1916 "is an unconstitutional encroachment on states' rights." Numerous capital-labor dramas were released in the first two decades of the century. Most were like *The Mill Girl – a Story of Factory Life* (1907), about an employer who covets a female employee, offering crude plots and generally second-rate acting. Perhaps because of the huge number of workers among the audiences and the humble backgrounds of the producers, these films were largely pro-labor. However, some were openly anti-labor, including *The Molly Maguires, or the Labor Wars in the Coal Mines* (1908), about an alleged secret band of terrorist workers who killed their bosses and incited strikes. Several addressed various social issues of the period. Ashley Miller's *Children Who Labor* (1912), *The Cry of the Children* (1913) and Henry MacRae's *The Blood of the Children* (1915) not only exposed the miserable working conditions to which children were subjected but pointed out how employers cut their costs by hiring children instead of their parents. During World War I, the War Labor Board prohibited yellow dog contracts, which forced workers not to join unions. But by 1919 the infamous practice returned. The year, the most strikebound in U.S. history, witnessed more than 3,000 strikes, with about four million strikers.

The drama, *The Power of Labor* (1908), begins with two burglars fighting over their ill-gotten gains, one slashing his accomplice, then fleeing, leaving the other for dead. Fifteen years later, the younger of the burglars, now a superintendent in a mill and wearing a beard, cuts the wages of the men to make up his personal losses in the stock market. He fails to tell the bosses, who are traveling in Europe. The workers are grumbling about these sudden cuts, when the son of one of the owners reports for work. He is in love with the daughter of a foreman. The son, learning of the workers' discontent, pleads with the unscrupulous superintendent, who hires some toughs to drug the son and put him in one of the coal cars on the way to the furnace. The young woman throws the switch and saves the young man's life. The superintendent, unaware of the rescue, cables the father that his son has been murdered. The father returns, learns the truth about conditions from his son, and the superintendent faces the same end he had planned for the son. The employers and the laborers reconcile their differences at a cordial meeting.

A telegraph operator who has been involved in a labor strike loses his job in an early, simplistic drama, *The Heart of a Race Tout* (1909). His wife is ill, the landlady wants to evict the couple, and he has no money for medicine. He works out a scam in which he goes to a public park carrying a noose and threatens to hang himself. He draws a sympathetic crowd, many of whom contribute enough money for him to purchase the needed medicine.

Van Dyke Brooke's optimistic drama, *Capital vs. Labor* (1910), tells about the daughter of an industrialist who is courted by a militia officer and a clergyman. When workers strike her father's factory and attack her home with threats upon her father's life, the minister dashes in and quiets the strikers. He gains from the industrialist all the workers' demands, thereby winning the father's respect, the trust of labor and the love of the daughter.

When one of three owners of an industrial conglomerate gives too many lavish parties, the business is suddenly threatened with a strike, in George Terwilliger's social drama, *The Daughters of Men* (1914), based on the 1906 play by George Klein. Arthur Matthews, the party-giving partner, marries an actress and begins to take more of an interest in his social life than in the business, which he shares with two brothers, Percy Winter and Gaston Bell. An outspoken orator, a German immigrant, and the latter's spirited daughter (Ethel Clayton) are the strike leaders. Labor lawyer George S. Spencer tries to moderate the labor dispute, and wins the admiration of Lilie Leslie, the brothers' sister. She assembles all the interested parties to the lawyer's apartment, where the strike is finally settled amicably.

A strike takes its usual toll on the workers and their families in the drama, *The Valley of the Moon* (1914), based on the story by Jack London. One young couple in particular suffer through a string of adversities before they find their "valley of the moon." Jack Conway, a boxer, promises to look for another line of work after he marries Myrtle Stedman. He is finally hired as a teamster, but when his wages are cut, the union calls a strike. Conway finds himself without money, gets beaten up in street fights with scabs hired by the company, goes to jail after brawling with a boarder, and starts drinking heavily. Following these adversities, he and his wife decide to begin a new life in the country. After searching for a farm they could somehow afford, the only opportunity left for them is his entering the ring to challenge a fighter – with a $300 prize to the winner. He wins the match and the desperate couple find their "valley of the moon."

Prizefighter Holbrook Blinn takes his prize money from his latest fight and buys a saloon and a freight-handling business, two steps on his ladder of success, in Emile Chautard's social drama, *The Boss* (1914), based on the 1911 play by Edward Sheldon. After persuading his men to work for half their wages, he gains grain-shipping contracts formerly held by his rival, Charles F. Abbe, now facing bankruptcy. He courts and then marries Alice Brady, Abbe's sister, but she remains his wife in name only. When Abbe's embittered son instigates a strike among Blinn's men, Blinn's pal, Bert Starkey, hits the troublemaker with a brick. Blinn, accused of initiating the fray, is sent to prison, where he releases his wife from their marriage. But she has grown to love him. When Blinn is released, the couple resolve their differences.

Hardworking, idealistic factory foreman H. B. Warner, who loves Catherine Carter, the boss's daughter, finally sides with the workers who strike against their dishonest employer, in J. Searle Dawley's social drama, *The Lost Paradise* (1914). The boss had earlier stolen Warner's labor-saving invention and made millions of dollars from it, with the foreman completely unaware of the entire venture. When the workers strike against the generally intolerable working conditions, Warner speaks out for their cause. He learns of the boss's treachery and confronts him with the proof. The owner's daughter breaks off her engagement to another and joins Warner at his side. Once married, the couple, now half owners in the plant, begin to make radical changes that benefit the workers. Finally, the boss yields to his workers' demands and peace is restored. Sequences show the sufferings of the strikers and their families, and mob scenes which threaten violence and destruction.

The workers at a plant owned by millionaire manufacturer Robert Broderick are forced to call a strike when Broderick refuses to give them a raise in the social drama, *The Better Man* (1914). As the strike grows uglier, Broderick, who has hired strikebreakers, is forced to call in the militia to keep the two factions apart when fights break out. Some of the strikebreakers start fires and instigate other acts of destruction, which they blame on the workers. They capture the millionaire's daughter, Alice Claire Elliott, and lock her in a burning building, which is set to explode. William Courtleigh, a minister of a poor parish who loves Elliott, rushes to her rescue in the nick of time.

Another hard-boiled boss plays a central role in the crude drama, *The Man With the Iron Heart* (1915). Al Filson portrays the title character, a tough company president who fires a worker arriving ten minutes late. The man had to attend to his sick wife before starting out to his job. Filson's workers, frustrated by his pettiness and insensitivity, go on strike, and one incensed striker, wearing a false beard, shoots and wounds the owner. Delirious while recovering from the gunshot, Filson is haunted by his conscience to the point that he finally yields to the strikers' demands. He even rehires the man he had fired earlier, bestowing upon him twice his previous salary.

Herbert Fortier, another hardhearted industrialist and self-made man, would rather see his workers strike than agree to their demands for a pay raise in Edgar Lewis's social drama, *Those Who Toil* (1916). His son, Victor Sutherland, on the other hand, prefers to personally investigate the working conditions of his family business. Finding intolerable conditions, impoverished family life and hungry children among the employees, he is ready to confront his smug, insensitive father. While among the workers, he meets Nance O'Neil, who is suffering from the same inferior lifestyle forced upon her and her fellow workers by the company's harsh policies. The owner's son soon falls in love with her. Not until the outraged and frustrated employees are forced to strike and turn into a mob that sets fire to the oil works does the capitalist finally yield. Nance O'Neil experienced adversity of a different kind one year earlier in the drama, *A Woman's Past*, in which she was seduced, betrayed and finally accused of infidelity and murder.

Thomas Meighan, the manager of a canning plant in Florida, also faces a callous factory owner in the drama, *Out of Darkness* (1915). He struggles to improve working conditions for the employees, mainly women and children – but with few results. A trip to the New York office and an attempt to meet with the owner, Charlotte Walker, both fail. While vacationing in Florida at a nearby plant, the owner suffers a blow to her head as the result of a boat wreck, and she is brought to Meighan's plant. Not recognizing her, he gives her a job, where she works along with the other women, while he slowly falls in love with her. The workers strike and make an attempt on Meighan's life, but Walker, regaining her memory, rescues him. The young couple resolve the problems of the workers and their personal differences.

Perhaps one of the worst screen bosses is the manager of a factory in John W. Noble's social drama, *The High Road* (1915), based on the 1912 play by

Edward Sheldon. He locks the women workers in to force them to work overtime, resulting in several of their deaths due to their being trapped in a fire. Earlier in the film, Virginia Valli, one of the workers, organizes the women to strike because of a wage cut. The owner hires hoodlums to cause trouble for the workers. When Valli protests to the mayor, C. H. Brenon, one of her former suitors, the workers' former wages are restored to them. After the tragic fire, the employer threatens to expose Valli's past – her living with a writer as his mistress. She leaves her job, with the mayor in pursuit. When he finds her, the couple marry. The fire incident and others were drawn from the real-life 1911 Triangle shirtwaist factory fire in New York City, resulting in the deaths of many workers.

Strife between mill workers and the president of a trust leads to violence and the death of the labor leader before peace is restored in Herbert Blaché's social drama, *The Song of the Wage Slave* (1915), based on the poem by Robert W. Service. Edmund Breese, a former mill worker, returns to the plant after an extended absence, and becomes the spokesman for the workers. Fraunie Fraunholz, as head of the paper trust, opposes the demands of the laborers. When Breese learns that a fanatical worker has planted a bomb in the boss's home, he rushes there to prevent the explosion. But while handling the device, it goes off and kills Breese. The head of the trust, grateful for the sacrifice of the labor leader, accedes to the demands of the workers.

Food speculator George Fawcett's cornering of the food market effects the closing of a local cannery in Walter Edwards's capital vs. labor drama, *The Corner* (1915). Willard Mack, a worker at the plant, loses his savings when a run takes place at the bank. When he sees his wife, Clara Williams, and their children going hungry, Mack begins to steal food and gets sentenced to thirty days in jail. A rent collector demands his money and forces Mack's wife to compromise herself in lieu of the bill. Mack is finally released and returns home, only to discover his wife working at a cheap dance hall, where she is frolicking with other men. When she arrives home, she cries, "I could not bear to see the children starve." Mack avenges himself by attacking Fawcett, the speculator.

Viola Dana in John H. Collins's social drama, *Children of Eve* (1915), experiences similar deplorable conditions in a factory that hires children and is owned by Robert Conness, a wealthy man uninterested in the physical plant of his establishment. Dana, from the slums, is caught stealing by Robert Walker, the owner's nephew, who is a settlement worker. He persuades her to come to his school, and they become good friends. Later, while she is working in the sweat shop, which has no fire escape and one staircase, a fire breaks out and she is trapped. She is taken out, close to death. The owner visits her and notices her mother's picture. He then realizes the dying girl is his daughter. Conness now resolves to reform and fight to abolish child labor exploitation and safe working conditions.

The tragic Ludlow massacre of April 20, 1914, provided material for several films. The struggle concerned Colorado coal miners seeking recognition of their United Mine Workers union. One battle with state militia ended with twenty-one dead, including two women and eleven children caught in tents that had been set ablaze. Angry strikers took possession of the Colorado coal fields, and they did not yield until federal troops arrived on June 1. The confrontation served as background for the romantic drama, *Hesper of the Mountains* (1916). Lillian Walker caters to the whim of her sickly brother, who wants to visit the West. They stay at the ranch of a family friend, where Walker meets Evart Overton, the shy foreman, who soon falls in love with her. The trio head for the mountains where the mining camp is situated. Conditions at the camp are so atrocious that the miners go on strike. Fist fights break out, the miners arm themselves, and the mine guards descend upon them. Finally, the state militia arrives in time to prevent a more serious confrontation from exploding.

Another fictionalized account of some of the incidents of The Ludlow Massacre and the oppression of miners was Cecil B. DeMille's social drama, *The Blacklist* (1916), in which the real malefactors are the superintendents who purposely do not inform the owner about conditions in the coal mines. When a guard kills a miner, resulting in unrest among the other workers, Blanche Sweet, a local teacher, writes to Charles Clary, the president of the company. When he refuses to yield to their demands, the men strike. Against Clary's orders, the guards use a rapid-firing gun that kills several strikers. Following the slaughter, the teacher is selected to assassinate Clary, the president. Several previous meetings between the pair have led to each falling in love with the other. Once in his office, she fires her pistol and slightly wounds Clary. He then grants the strikers' demands. Clary and Sweet then agree to supervise mine conditions jointly.

Idealistic Mary Pickford, one of three impoverished sisters, helps to correct unsatisfactory conditions in a typical sweatshop in John B. O'Brien's familiar drama, *The Eternal Grind* (1916). One sister (Lorette Blake), tired of life's struggle and poverty, trades in her virtue for a fashionable apartment and an easy life. The other sister (Dorothy West) suffers from consumption. The owner has two sons. John Bokers is decent, caring and hardworking, while Robert Cain is an idler and ladies' man. Cain supports Blake, Pickford's sister, and Bokers, working in the shop under a pseudonym, falls in love with Pickford, but his father objects to their marrying. Pickford forces Cain at gun point to marry her sister, whom he has abandoned. Later, when a floor collapses in the shop, Bokers is hurt and taken home to recover. In a delirious state, he cries out for Pickford. The doctor tells the young man's father to summon the girl to his son's side to help him recover. The owner goes to Pickford's quarters and pleads with her to help Bokers. She reminds her boss that when she needed help for her sister, he turned her down. She then makes him promise to raise the workers' wages, improve working conditions in the sweat shop and redress other wrongs. When he agrees to these terms, Pickford returns with him to his son's bedside. When Bokers regains his strength, the couple marry.

Franklin Ritchie, a young author researching factory conditions, discovers wretched surroundings in a factory owned by the father of his girlfriend, Winifred Greenwood, in Edward Sloman's social drama, *Dust* (1916). To protest his discovery, with the hope that the conditions will be redressed, he breaks off his relations with his girlfriend. When he is elected to the state senate, he introduces a law designed to improve factory conditions. As a result, Greenwood's father makes a personal inspection of his factories so that he can find ways to cut costs while meeting the minimal standards of the new law. When one of his properties bursts into flames, he becomes trapped in the conflagration and perishes. His daughter, finally realizing what Ritchie was battling against, understands that those who profit from the labor of others must take responsibility for them and their environment. She devotes herself to several charities and reconciles her differences with her boyfriend.

Mary Anderson, owner of the Blue Goose Mine, quells a fight between the striking miners and the sheriff's deputies in William Wolbert's social drama, *By Right of Possession* (1917). The owner resolves the workers' grievances by raising their pay and reducing their rent. Meanwhile, Antonio Moreno, the sheriff, is infatuated with the owner. They go below to examine mine conditions when suddenly a cave-in cuts the pair off from the entrance. Anderson manages to extricate the sheriff, who is temporarily trapped by debris. They finally effect their freedom from the mine. Later, the two compete for the job of sheriff, and the mine owner wins the position. Following several complications, a local villain dynamites a dam, with the flooding waters causing a cattle stampede. Anderson falls off her horse while trying to avoid the onrushing cattle and is rescued by Moreno. She finally yields to the former sheriff's charms. Suddenly, a whistle blast from the mine warns of danger.

A young woman ends a labor dispute in Ben Turbett's social drama, *The Royal Pauper* (1917), based on the story "The Princess from the Poorhouse," by Henry Albert Phillips. Francine Larrimore, an orphan adopted as a child by a wealthy woman, meets Richard Tucker, her boyhood Prince Charming, who has invented a loom and is now leading a strike of mill workers against a harsh owner, Larrimore's adoptive father. Following several complications, young Lattimore effects a reconciliation among all the concerned parties. Tucker gets his invention approved and becomes the mill manager. The young couple then marry.

Workers at a lumber camp threaten to go on strike when the payroll fails to arrive in Donald Crisp's outdoor drama, *Jules of the Strong Heart* (1918). The boss tries to assure the men that the storm is holding up the arrival of the payroll. But a local bully incites the men to strike. George Beban, a hot-headed Canuck, volunteers to fight the storm and bring back the money. The boss gives him a note that permits him to pick up the money. The bully, seeing an opportunity to flee with the payroll, says he will accompany the French-Canadian. Instead, he overpowers Beban and tortures him to hand over the note. Meanwhile, a companion of Beban's visits the camp and asks for the

Canuck. The owner's daughter, Helen Eddy, who loves Beban, explains the situation and both start out to find him. They rescue Beban from the bully, pick up the payroll at the railroad depot, and return to the camp in time to prevent the men from lynching the boss. The owner's daughter then proposes to Beban.

A rough, brawling longshoreman, following a string of adversities, rises to become president of the Lumber Workmen's Union, in Paul Scardon's drama, *The Golden Goal* (1918). Harry Morey, as the longshoreman, after fighting with a fellow worker in a waterfront dive, oversleeps on the docks and misses his ride back up the river to his job. Broke and desperate, he is hired by Florence Deshon, who is attracted by him, to manage her father's estate. After some time, he is let go because of his lack of education. Vowing to win Deshon's love, he has a stenographer educate him. He finally becomes head of the lumbermen's union. When Deshon's father wants to buy a lumber company, he invites Morey to his home and bribes him to lead a strike, thereby forcing the company into bankruptcy and an easy target for takeover. Morey agrees, but later confesses all to the union members, who want to kill him for his treachery. But the quick-thinking stenographer comes to his rescue and pacifies the angry men. Morey embraces his rescuer and realizes she is his true love.

Government agent Tom Mix is assigned to investigate turmoil at a tungsten mine in Lynn Reynolds's combination World War I drama and western, *Mr. Logan, U.S.A.* (1918). He discovers that German agents have gained control of key positions in the running of the mines and have manipulated the workers into calling a strike. Since tungsten is important to the war effort, Mix ends the strike and rounds up the enemy conspirators with lightning speed, although he is blocked by several obstacles before he can accomplish these feats. Our hero performs some of his usual stunting as he rides his horse up and down staircases, uses his lasso with expertise and chases after an automobile in which the chief villain has taken flight with the heroine. Kathleen Connors portrays the daughter of a mine foreman.

Pretty socialite Emmy Wehlen, as the title character in S. Rankin Drew's social drama, *The Belle of the Season* (1919), based on a poem by Ela Wheeler Wilcox, takes control of the family business and introduces changes that benefit the downtrodden workers. The former executors, she learns, had been exploiting the workers. She meets and falls in love with the young, idealistic S. Rankin Drew, whose wealthy father owns a newspaper. He rescues her from bully Louis Wolheim, who later incites striking laborers to attack Wehlen's executor. But Drew again comes to the rescue. Against his father's wishes, Drew donates $10,000 toward a much-needed settlement house in one of the poorest districts of the city. He suddenly disappears from sight when he reads a newspaper story about Wehlen, but he later reconciles his differences with her and the couple are married.

II. The Uneasy Marriage of Capital and Labor

Although unions grew in strength and strikes remained their right arm, capital-labor films diminished in number and significance during the twenties. The Amalgamated Clothing Workers Union in 1918 began striking against open shops, sweat shops, and piece-work pay. By 1919, labor unrest once again struck the United States. The Amalgamated Union staged at least 534 strikes in the next six years and claimed victory in 333. Four million workers struck or were locked out. Work stoppages in North America occurred as early as colonial times, but the first nationwide strike (by railroad workers) occurred in 1877. Strikes became more frequent in the late nineteenth century, with the rise of powerful labor organizations such as the Knights of Labor. Employers began to use armed guards or police, either to harass pickets or to protect strikebreakers, acts that often resulted in violence. In 1922, a thirteen percent wage cut announced by the Railroad Labor Board May 28 affected 400,000 U.S. railway workers. They struck from July 1 through the summer. One of the earliest films of the twenties to deal with conflicts between capital and labor exploited the theme of the evils of Bolshevism to bring the two ancient enemies together. One such film that attributes the struggles between capital and labor to the Bolsheviks is Frank Urson's *The Stranger's Banquet* (1922). The deeper bitterness and resentment between the two sides eventually softened – strikes were either avoided or settled quickly and amicably, as in such dramas as *Gossip* (1923). Films of the twenties reflected these changes by turning these conflicts into a string of popular comedies, including Joseph De Grasse's *The Tailor Made Man* (1922) and Clarence Badger's *Potash and Perlmutter* (1923).

Guy Hedlund's pro-labor drama, *The Contrast* (1921), produced by the Labor Film Service and which dealt with a controversial coal strike raging at the time, was plagued by censorship problems. The Kansas Board of Censors prevented its release. The film's original purpose was to contrast the life of the poor and the rich of the nation. It depicted a starving girl stealing garbage that a well-fed dog has rejected. In addition, the drama showed allegedly poignant sequences of cave-ins resulting from the negligence of the owners. By the time the courts permitted the showing of the film, the strike had passed into history.

Ollie Sellers's uninspiring pro-labor drama, *The New Disciple* (1921), which first suggests the strained relations between capital and labor, proceeds to advocate President Woodrow Wilson's "New Freedom" as a possible springboard for both sides to consider. Wilson's "New Freedom" referred to his domestic program, a generally progressive list of accomplishments which included the Federal Reserve System (1913), the Federal Trade Commission (1914) and the Clayton Antitrust Act (1914). Alfred Allen portrays an industrialist who grew wealthy during World War I. He continues to amass wealth by exploiting his employees. He tries to cut the cost of his work force, but suffers when his laborers strike. He cannot fulfill a major contract within the time limit, and finds himself facing bankruptcy. His rivals, meanwhile, try to buy up his mill at an auction. The united farmers intervene and, joined by the factory workers, outbid the competitors. The business, now a cooperative, continues to function.

A major shipyard faces labor unrest and violence when the workers are incited by a fanatical Bolshevik in Marshall Neilan and Frank Urson's social drama, *The Stranger's Banquet* (1922). Hobart Bosworth, the owner of the shipyard, leaves his daughter, Claire Windsor, in charge of the business when he dies. His adopted son, Rockliffe Fellowes, is general manager and in love with Windsor, but is too shy to express his feelings to her. Another son, Nigel Barrie, is a weakling. Thomas Holding, the fanatic, begins spreading his red propaganda after Bosworth's death, and the men take him seriously. Following several complications, Fellowes quits after claiming Windsor is too lenient in her handling of the tensions, but he returns when a strike seems imminent. The pair persuade Holding to address the workers, explaining the strike is bad for both factions. Meanwhile, a disgruntled follower of Holding's, in an attempt to assassinate Fellowes, shoots the agitator instead. But Holding was able to avert the strike before losing consciousness. With the settling of the labor problem, Windsor proposes to Fellowes.

A shipyard again plays a minor role in Joseph De Grasse's comedy drama, *The Tailor Made Man* (1922), based on the play by Harry James Smith. Charles Ray, as a tailor's assistant, tries to enter society by wearing the clothes of some of his more wealthy customers. He succeeds, until he realizes he is a phony, that his real self is the tailor's assistant back in the shop. This is where he belongs, with his unaffected girlfriend, Ethel Grandin, not with the superficial crowd he has met when he stepped out in society. After becoming involved in a labor dispute at the shipyard, he speeds through the streets to avert a strike at the yard. Meanwhile, he has to fight off those who are trying to prevent him from reaching his destination.

Ramsey Wallace, the third generation to control the major factory in town, faces labor problems in King Baggot's routine capital-vs.-labor drama, *Gossip* (1923). When his father and grandfather ran the factory, the workers looked up to their employers and the plant ran smoothly. But Wallace has failed to learn how to communicate with the workers and their leaders. In fact, he refuses to even meet with them to discuss their grievances. Meanwhile, Gladys Walton, an orphan, arrives in town and asks to meet with Wallace. Her aunt had been the fiancée of Wallace's father, but their two families broke up the romance. The young stranger is at first rejected by Wallace, but after his secretary meets with her, the factory owner and the visitor finally meet. Her charm, personality and good looks win over the hardened bachelor, who finds himself falling in love with her. In addition, he softens his position concerning his disgruntled workers, whom he decides to meet with, and a strike ends amicably. Wallace then proposes marriage to the young woman who has entered his home and heart.

A labor agitator invades another comedy in Clarence Badger's *Potash and Perlmutter* (1923), based on the play by Montague Glass and Charles Klein.

Two Jewish Americans, Abe Potash (Barney Bernard) and Morris Perlmutter (Alexander Carr), are partners in the clothing business. They hire Ben Lyon, an impoverished Russian violinist, as a fitter. When Lyon falls in love with Bernard's sister, Hope Sutherland, the brother is disappointed. He had hoped she would marry a well-to-do lawyer. A shooting occurs on the premise, involving a labor agitator, and Lyon is arrested as the chief suspect. But the agitator recovers, and Lyon is released. His marriage to Sutherland is accepted by all.

Tom Meighan, who wants to marry Lila Lee, the mine president's daughter, is turned down from his expected promotion, which is awarded to the president's nephew, in Edward Sutherland's drama, *Coming Through* (1925), based on the 1924 novel, *Bed Rock*, by Jack Bethea. However the couple are still married, against the wishes of her father, who then appoints his son-in-law as superintendent of the toughest mining camp, hoping that he will fail at the job. The couple leave for the camp, where they meet Wallace Beery, the assistant foreman, who is in collusion with the local saloon owner. Beery stirs up trouble among the labors, and a strike breaks out. When a drunken engineer almost kills some of the workers, Meighan wrecks the saloon. He next accuses Beery of using crooked scales to cheat the miners out of their pay. In a hand-to-hand struggle between the two antagonists, Meighan ends up killing the corrupt Beery and bringing peace the mining camp.

Red agitators plague a steel mill in George Archainbaud's brawny drama, *Men of Steel* (1926), based on "United States Flavor," a short story by R. G. Kirk. Milton Sills, as a fugitive wanted for a murder he did not commit, gets an important position using an alias in a steel mill after studying nights and working days as a laborer. The owner, Frank Currier, takes a liking to Sills, who is hurt as the result of an accident caused by agitators. He is taken to Currier's home, where he meets Mae Allison, the owner's daughter. Later, they become engaged, but Sills's former girlfriend, Doris Kenyon, shows up. Currier happens to be her father. When someone at the mill accuses Sills of being a murderer, he rushes off to tangle with his accuser. The man confesses that he is the real killer, thereby exonerating Sills, who then marries Kenyon.

Charles Delaney, an ironworker on a skyscraper who is studying engineering in the evenings, informs James Hogan, his foreman, that many of the steel beams have been incorrectly drilled, advice that Hogan ignores, in James Hogan's drama, *Mountains of Manhattan* (1927). When the contractor gets wind of the incident, he dismisses the foreman, who then instigates a strike among the workers. Delaney, who is promoted to foreman, is forced to battle Hogan on the steel girders, until the ex-foreman admits to his complicity in the approval of the faulty beams. Delaney then marries Dorothy Devore, the contractor's daughter.

Childbirth

I. The Miracle of Life and the Twilight Sleep

The topic of childbirth encompasses several potentially controversial issues, including, among others, abortion, birth control, women's rights, and overpopulation. Abortion has long been a means of birth control until the Roman Catholic Church exerted pressure and changing public opinion resulted in strict antiabortion laws in the nineteenth century. However, attitudes once again swung around to a more liberal belief in the twentieth century. Margaret Sanger (1883-1966) was a leader in the American birth-control movement in the early part of this century. Concerned about the poverty facing many American families, she believed offering these families alternatives was an important step in their social progress. Her efforts to promote birth control among the poor brought down upon her indictments and arrests. Eventually, she gained public and court support and went on in 1923 and 1925 to organize the first American and international birth-control conferences. She helped to establish clinics around the world. All these topics received at least some attention in a handful of early silent films. Some were luridly sensational or exploitative, as was *What the World Should Know* (1916). Others, like the imaginative drama, *The Miracle of Life* (1915), proved interesting. A lesser number, such as *The Twilight Sleep* (1915), which was filmed in a semidocumentary style, were simply serious and educational in a generally colorless way.

The two-reel documentary, *The Twilight Sleep* (1915), describes the different methods of childbirth, especially natural childbirth and that which employs the "twilight sleep." Various intimate views are shown concerning the operation. Although the production may have been staged for the most part, this did not diminish the overall effect or educational value of the project. One of the alleged advantages of the latter approach is its safety, but this has been challenged in some quarters. The procedure involves an injection of a drug given by a hypodermic needle near the time of birth to dull the sensibilities of the mother during the birth.

Margarita Fischer portrays a young, pregnant wife who worries that having a child will stifle her social life in the anti-abortion drama, *The Miracle of Life* (1915). She decides to end the pregnancy. A friend who wants to help suggests she take a certain drug for this purpose. The wife falls asleep with the bottle in her hand. The remainder of the film depicts her taking the drug and its consequences. Her husband, Joseph E. Singleton, condemns her act, leaves her and marries someone else. Years later she is shown as old and gray and all alone. She sees a vision of a child that claims she was the child that might have been. Other images show a woman dishonored by the Church, a group of babies waiting to be born, a house with children playing on the doorstep, and the young wife's ex-husband with his present spouse enjoying the expectation of a baby. She finally awakes from her disturbing dream, empties the drug out the window and informs her husband that she has decided to have the baby. The happy couple then embrace.

The anti-birth control social drama, *What the World Should Know* (1916), describes four families. In the first, the father believes in large families. In the second, the father hires a phony doctor to deliver their only child, with the wife dying in childbirth. The father of the third family raises his son to be selfish and a brute, with the boy later, in a state of drunkenness, killing his own father. Finally, the fourth father, a confirmed alcoholic, is rehabilitated by his patient and loving son. Meanwhile, the sons of the first father are all killed fighting for their country. An apparition of Uncle Sam appears to comfort the grieving family.

Disappointed when his wife gives birth to a girl, mountain man Frank Keenan tries to raise her as if he had a son, in Reginald Barker's comedy drama, *Jim Grimsby's Boy* (1916). When the mountaineer's wife dies after childbirth, he names the baby "Bill" and plans to raise her as a boy. But as the years pass, she steadily resists his efforts. She has inherited her father's strong will. "Bill" meets the local sheriff, Robert McKim, and soon falls in love with him. A clash between "Bill" and her determined father ends with his equally strong-headed daughter the winner.

Lois Weber's drama, *Where Are My Children?* (1916), which deals with the controversial topic of birth control, may be interesting, but it is not controversial. The first half starts off favoring birth control, but later the film shifts gears and takes a stand against abortion. A married district attorney (Tyrone Power), fond of children, has a wife whose social schedule is so busy that she has no time to consider having a child. Her brother returns from school and moves in with the childless couple. He takes an interest in the housekeeper's pretty daughter, who soon finds herself carrying the young man's child. He pleads with his sister to find a way out for the careless youngsters. She informs him about a local doctor who has been known to perform illegal abortions. The girl goes to the physician and dies as a result of a botched procedure. Power, the district attorney, learns of the incident and gets a conviction, which sentences the doctor to fifteen years behind bars. Before he is led off to prison, the condemned doctor tosses open his account book and advises the attorney to start cleaning his own house. Power, seeing his wife's name and those of many of her friends listed among the doctor's patients, realizes why his and other families are still childless. When he arrives home, where his wife is entertaining a group of her friends at tea, he asks them all to leave, announcing, "I should bring you to trial for manslaughter." He then turns to his wife and asks, "Where are my children?" Lois Weber co-directed another drama about birth control the following year, titled *The Hand That Rocks the Cradle*.

A young man from the city takes advantage of a young woman from the country in the overly familiar drama, *The Unborn* (1916). He abandons her and marries a member of his own group while she, now carrying his child, leaves home to work in a New York factory. The man, now happily married, does not know he has a son. The girl he wronged dies, leaving their son to fend for himself as a newsboy. The man, yearning for a child, meets the boy and adopts him, not knowing the alleged orphan is his own son. The father accidentally discovers the truth about the boy's identity. "You are my son," he says to the boy. "So you are the man who wrecked my mother's life," the youth replies. He leaves the home and returns to selling newspapers. Awkwardly interspersed into the film are scenes of a doctor who performs illegal abortions. When the police finally track him down, the doctor shoots wildly. The boy, noticing that his father happens to be in the path of the bullets, runs forward crying, "Daddy!" The youth, fatally wounded, forgives his father and dies.

Married couple Mildred Gregory and Howard Hall drift apart over the issue of children in Richard Garrick's domestic drama, *According to Law* (1916). The wife, who is socially active, does not want children, while her husband prefers to have a complete family. When Gregory learns that Hall is unfaithful to her, she files for divorce and moves to their vacation home. Her husband learns that a former boyfriend is visiting her and he begins to have second thoughts about their separation. During a storm, he observes the couple through the window, and she sees him. She has a flash of guilt and resists her visitor's lovemaking. The couple, realizing they still love each other, reconcile their differences, and she gives birth to a daughter. But in the process, she dies. Twenty years later, when their daughter, Helen Marten, is ready for marriage, it is revealed that she is illegitimate since her parents never remarried. In addition, she is not the legal heir to her father's fortune. However, the judge and father of her lover discovers that since the court fees were never paid for the original divorce, the couple remained married and their daughter is legitimate. Marten then marries Albert Macklin, the judge's son.

Directors and costars Phillips Smalley and Lois Weber based their pro-abortion social drama, *The Hand That Rocks the Cradle* (1917), on a contemporary newspaper story concerning birth control advocate Margaret Sanger, who opened the first birth control clinic in the United States in 1916. Lois Weber, as a physician's wife, tries to teach the women of the slums about birth control – information they cannot afford to get from doctors – the same facts readily available to wealthy women. For her trouble Weber is arrested and jailed, where she goes on a hunger strike. She is finally released and returns to her husband and children.

The documentary, *Birth Control* (1917), pleads the case of propagandist Margaret Sanger, the outspoken advocate of birth control. This unsensational film presents a dramatic, but not suggestive, story of a representative woman who benefits from Ms. Sanger's plan to control additional, unwanted births to a family already overburdened emotionally, financially and socially. What is unexpected and surprising is the number of scenes in which Ms. Sanger appears portraying herself. It is difficult to believe that the serene and knowledgeable woman seen on the screen is the same strong-willed crusader who incited audiences and defied authorities until she landed herself in jail and even after her release. To calm nervous exhibitors, the film was released with two sets of posters and titles – one set titled *Birth Control* and another titled *The New World* – each depending on the particular audience. In addition, the film was advertised to prospective exhibitors as: "Five reels of stirring, varied and picturesque expositions of the vital and dramatic phases of the crusade that sent its martyr heroine to a prison from which she has just been freed." Sanger herself commented: "This is the only picture on birth control in which I shall appear. Part of the profits go to extending our cause." However, the day before the film was to open in New York, the city license commissioner labeled the film "immoral, indecent, and directly contrary to public welfare." Sanger held a special showing for the press and hundreds of others interested in social welfare. A judge ruled in favor of its showing, but his decision was overturned by a state court and the film was only shown at private lectures – until the Supreme Court overturned the ruling in 1965, stating it was no longer a crime to spread information about birth control. But by this time, the film had deteriorated.

In the domestic drama, *Maternity* (1917), Alice Brady, as a young wife, finally marries a young man she sincerely loves. The well-bred wife is intelligent, sociable and well-liked by all, but harbors a deep fear of childbearing. She is afraid of giving her attentive husband that which he strongly yearns for – a child. It seems in her family that women somehow sacrifice their own lives whenever they attempt to give birth to children. Brady's wrenching problem is never satisfactorily resolved despite an exciting fire scene and her sensitive portrayal of the emotionally tormented wife.

Richard Travers has always desired to be a father, but his wife, Gretchen Hartman, after their twelve years of marriage, has deliberately never fulfilled her husband's dream, in Samuel R. Brodsky's domestic drama, *The House Without Children* (1919), based on the 1917 play by Robert McLaughlin. When a child is born to Travers's sister, Helen Weer, the result of a careless escapade, Gretchen recommends an abortion, but Weer rejects this. Gretchen then decides to claim the child as her own, thereby protecting Weer and satisfying Travers's longtime desire for a child. When Travers, her husband, returns from a trip abroad, he is pleasantly surprised, as is his traveling companion, Henry G. Sell, the real father of the child. Following a series of complications, the truth is finally revealed and the situation is resolved after Travers forgives his wife for the deception, especially when he observes that she has a genuine gift for caring for children.

Olive Thomas portrays a dual role in the drama, *Toton* (1919), first as a young mother, and later as her own daughter. The story opens with Thomas, as the title character, falling in love with an artist, whose father forces the couple to end their relationship. A child is born, with the mother dying during childbirth. Years later, the artist's ward comes to Paris and meets a young man, a clever pickpocket, whom he engages as his guide. In reality, the youth is a young woman – the daughter of the artist. Following a series of complications, she delivers her own father into the clutches of a gang of thieves and learns that stories about her father's abandoning her mother were not true. The ward and the father educate the former pickpocket, who then falls in love with the ward and they are married. Since the film was made near the end of World War I, a period overflowing with patriotism, the young man ends up in uniform while his wife becomes a Red Cross nurse.

II. The Intolerant Fears of Childbirth

Childbirth films changed dramatically during the twenties. No longer were they the heavy-handed semi-documentaries or cautionary tales warning prospective mothers and fathers about the evils of abortion, abandonment or avoidance of giving birth. Instead, the films reverted to the simple dramatic tale more popular with the audiences of the twenties. For example, a child is raised without her mother, who has died in childbirth, in Griffith's *One Exciting Night* (1922). In another, titled *On the Threshold* (1925), an embittered father forbids a child to marry. And in still another, *Wages of Conscience* (1927), a child is burdened with a father who has prevented his wife from marrying her true love.

Gail Kane portrays a young woman who, because her mother died in childbirth, resolves not to have children, in Frank Reicher's domestic drama, *Empty Arms* (1920). She agrees to marry Thurston Hall with the stipulation that they never consummate their marriage. Hall believed that after some time she would change her mind, but when she doesn't, he decides to leave her. Now all alone, she begins to dwell about her empty life and grows jealous of other mothers who receive pleasure from their children. Braced by her change of heart, she visits her husband. But on the way, her train is derailed and she is rescued by J. Herbert Frank. Hall learns about the wreck and finds his wife just as her rescuer starts to make advances toward her. The happy couple are reunited and plan to raise a family together.

A child, whose mother dies in Africa during an expedition, is adopted and raised by another woman in D. W. Griffith's heavy-handed drama, *One Exciting Night* (1922). Years later, the foundling, Carol Dempster, falls in love with Henry Hull. However, her adoptive mother, who is being blackmailed by Morgan Wallace, wants her to marry Wallace. Dempster joins Hull at a party being held at his unused country estate. Meanwhile, the house is being used by a gang of bootleggers whose leader is murdered by a mysterious figure just before the couple and their friends arrive. The killer has hidden a large sum of money somewhere in the empty house. A Scotland Yard inspector who lives nearby investigates matters and suspects Hull of murder. Later, when a close friend of Hull's is murdered, Hull again is suspected. Following several complications, including much searching for the hidden loot and an exciting chase through a terrible storm, the murderer is unmasked as Morgan Wallace, the man who has been blackmailing Dempster's adoptive mother. Dempster also learns her true identity, including the knowledge that she is the heiress of a large fortune belonging to her real mother. Griffith uses many of the gimmicks employed in the "old dark house" tales – strange sounds, masked characters, sliding panels, trap doors, clutching hands – all familiar to movie audiences. Unfortunately, he also uses the stereotyped African-American character's fear of the dark and ghosts for comedy relief. The character is played by Porter Strong, a white man using blackface.

When Henry B. Walthall's wife dies while giving birth, he vows that his daughter will never suffer the same fate as her mother, in Renaud Hoffman's domestic drama, *On the Threshold* (1925), based on the story by Wilbur Hall. He plans to forbid her from ever marrying. Eighteen years later, his child, Gladys Hulette, is still in love with her childhood boyfriend, Robert Gordon. Walthall, suspecting their love is serious, disallows them to continue seeing each other. They respect his wishes, and Gordon rises to the position of manager of a large ranch. He summons up enough courage to visit his girlfriend and asks her to marry him. Walthall enters suddenly, and upon seeing the lovers in each other's arms, he collapses to the floor. His worthless brother connives with an unscrupulous judge to make a will that will disinherit Walthall's daughter. When Walthall finally awakens, he refuses to sign the contrived will. Instead, he makes out a new one, leaving all to his daughter. Before he dies, he gives the young couple his blessing, permitting them to marry.

Although wealthy Allan Forrest falls in love with Patsy Ruth Miller, a young woman beneath his station, he does not marry her out of fear of his strict mother, in the society drama, *Rose of the World* (1925), based on the novel by Kathleen Norris. Miller, the title character of the film, later marries Rockliffe Fellowes, a scheming charlatan who has learned that she will someday inherit an ironworks. However, suspecting her husband's intentions, she ignores the generous will. Meanwhile, Forrest marries a seductress who dies in childbirth. After Miller's crazed grandfather kills her husband, she and Forrest renew their old love and find happiness together. An earlier film, *The Rose of the World* (1918), has an entirely different plot and is based on a different source.

Lon Chaney, an ex-sea captain and present unsavory owner of a dive, is known as "Singapore Joe" after his wife dies in childbirth, in Tod Browning's drama, *The Road to Mandalay* (1926), set chiefly in Mandalay. He struggles to keep his daughter, Lois Moran, from marrying Owen Moore, a suspicious character who has been living with a priest, Chaney's brother, and is not aware that Moran is Chaney's daughter. The priest receives money from his brother, which is used to support the young woman. Chaney, to prevent the marriage, has Moore shanghaied. When Moran enters Chaney's squalid brothel, she is set upon by a lewd customer. Chaney tries to protect his daughter and is stabbed. Moore enters in time to rescue Moran, and the young couple escape aboard a ship.

The conscience of a treacherous man haunts him for years in John Ince's cautionary drama, *Wages of Conscience* (1927). Jealous of Herbert Rawlinson, his rival for the love of Grace Darmand, John Ince frames him, and the innocent soul is convicted and sent to prison for life. Ince gets to marry Darmand. However, he gains little happiness from his treachery. His wife dies in childbirth, and he is forever haunted by his conscience. Twenty years later, the child (again played by Darmand) has grown into a beautiful woman who reminds the father of her mother. Meanwhile, Rawlinson escapes from prison and vows to avenge himself upon Ince, who is now broken in spirit and conscience-driven. Rawlinson witnesses the living hell that is consuming Ince. The fugitive falls dead before he has a chance to take his revenge.

The domestic drama, *Motherhood: Life's Greatest Miracle* (1928), tells the story of two families, one wealthy and the other poor. Both wives soon learn that they will become mothers at the same time. Their husbands, of course, are happy at the news. The women, however, react differently. The wealthy woman thinks the baby will interfere with her social life, and she asks her doctor for an abortion. The second prospective mother accepts the news and carefully follows the doctor's advice about preparing for the birth. The wealthy mother realizes she was wrong in her decision and is happy she never followed through, for she would never have given birth to her beautiful and loving daughter.

Circumstantial Evidence

I. "Who Shall Take My Life?"

At least one dictionary defines circumstantial evidence as evidence that does not support exactly the fact in question but suggests other circumstances which may permit a judge or jury to conclude the fact in contention. One of the most famous trials involving circumstantial evidence concerned the Sacco-Venzetti case, in which Nicola Sacco and Bartolomeo Vanzetti, two alleged anarchists, were charged with the murder of a Massachusetts paymaster and his guard in 1921. Despite circumstantial evidence and worldwide sympathy, both defendants were found guilty and executed in 1927, after the state supreme court and a governor's commission upheld the court's decision. The case continues to spark debates about the fairness of the trial. Circumstantial evidence as a theme in films appeared very early on the silent screen, usually in dramas and especially in the crime genre. In addition, it was often associated with a related topic – capital punishment. These film lent themselves to developing, or at least suggesting such social issues as prison reform, a re-examination of capital punishment as a solution to the crime problem, and the discrepancy between the sentences meted out to the poor and the wealthy. The films in this cycle developed their own set of conventions. For instance, in the short drama, *Circumstantial Evidence* (1912), a famous figure is introduced (in this case, Warden Thomas J. Tynan) to add authenticity to the film. Several films, including *And the Law Says* (1916), adopted the dramatic ploy of having a judge or a prosecutor confront his or her own son as defendant. *The Wheel of the Law* (1916) and *A Game With Fate* (1918) both use the device of purposely setting up an innocent person who is then accused of a crime based solely on circumstantial evidence – and then proving the defendant's innocence. Finally, *The People Vs. John Doe* (1916) was based on an actual murder case.

Circumstantial Evidence (1911), a one-reel drama, was one of the earliest films to tackle this subject. The following year, director Otis B. Thayer's *Cir-*

cumstantial Evidence (1912), a one-reeler based on Hapsburg Liebe's "The Little Good" and featuring William Duncan, expanded the titular theme by promoting the idea of the "honor system" in prisons. Perhaps this was the influence of real-life prison warden Thomas J. Tynan, who, for purposes of authenticity, appeared on screen. Duncan was a popular and successful stage actor who had a long and distinguished career on both the stage, silent screen and in sound features.

Richard Bennett, a respected judge and strong advocate of capital punishment, unknowingly sentences his own son to die in the electric chair based only on circumstantial evidence, in the farfetched anti-capital punishment social drama, *And the Law Says* (1916). Years earlier, when Bennett was a law student, he abandoned a doctor's daughter who later gave birth to his child. The boy is now a defendant in Bennett's courtroom. Before his execution, the youth's identity is made known to the shocked Bennett, who relents on the death sentence. But his plea is ignored, and his son is electrocuted. However, his former girlfriend's father, a doctor and opponent of the death penalty, revives the young man and sends him home to his mother.

George Baker's murder mystery, *The Wheel of the Law* (1916), focused on a young district attorney (Edwin Holt) with a penchant for prosecuting cases based on circumstantial evidence. He and his wife (Emily Stevens), a famous actress, differ on some important issues, namely concerning capital punishment and the reliance on circumstantial evidence in capital cases. When the wife's brother is falsely accused of murder, she sets out to prove her case to her husband. She concocts a bogus scenario whereby her husband would be accused of an attempted murder – all on manufactured, tainted proof, damning but highly circumstantial. The attorney is shaken when the hoax is revealed. In addition, he is further enlightened on the topic when he is informed that the actual murderer, in the case of the brother-in-law, has been apprehended.

A young man is wrongly convicted of a crime based solely on circumstantial evidence in the social drama, *In the Hands of the Law* (1917), based on a novel by William O. H. Hurst. An old man saves the accused's reputation by telling of his own similar experience. He had once believed that his own son was guilty of a bank robbery – also based only on circumstantial evidence. The young man's career suffered, and he served a long prison term. Finally, the son died ashamed, alone and miserable.

Circumstantial evidence entraps Scotland Yard detective J. Barney Fury and sends him to prison in Harry Harvey's mystery drama, *Feet of Clay* (1917),based on the story by William Morton. Fury was in the process of trying to extricate his nephew from the powerful control of a gang of crooks. The detective ends up behind bars with the gang. Betrayed by three former associates, he vows vengeance. He escapes from prison and tracks the trio to San Francisco, where he discovers one man has been murdered and Margaret Landis, the daughter of another, has been kidnapped. He then learns that Landis is his nephew's daughter. Following several complications, Fury is ready for a quiet life when another Scotland Yard detective finds him. Landis persuades the detective to return to England alone, leaving Fury to begin a new life in America.

June Elvidge, who is in love with a young lawyer, is forced to marry a middle-aged man when she learns her bankrupt father faces disgrace, in George Kelson's drama, *The Tenth Case* (1917). Her husband, George McQuarrie, is burdened with Gladden James, a knavish nephew who keeps asking for money. Meanwhile, a child is born. When the nephew returns for more money, McQuarrie finally cuts him off. The young man then turns to McQuarrie's wife, who gives him money one time, but then refuses all further demands. James, now desperate, steals into her bedroom to find her checkbook but is forced to hide when she enters. Unable to leave, he is caught when the husband enters and suspects the worst between the youth and his wife. He sues for divorce, and the judge grants it on the grounds of circumstantial evidence. The wife then frames the judge in a similar circumstance. The nephew, critically hurt in a car accident, confesses the truth about the wife's innocence before he dies, thereby exonerating Elvidge. The husband forgives her and takes her back. Although her former boyfriend, the lawyer, has stood by her through her entire ordeal, the young wife chooses to return to her husband and child.

Colin Campbell's didactic drama, *Who Shall Take My Life?* (1917), opens with a plea for life imprisonment instead of the death sentence, and goes on to cite many nations that have abandoned capital punishment. Fritzi Brunette, as a young woman who frequents local dance halls and dives, meets a young man with a criminal background. They fall in love, and she suggests that they both go straight. He reforms and gets an honest job. Later, as she plans to marry him, he meets someone else and leaves the woman who helped to rehabilitate him. Although completely innocent, the young man is accused of murder, the case based purely on circumstantial evidence. He is tried and sentenced to death. He is electrocuted at midnight, with proof of his innocence arriving one hour too late to save him. The drama presents a strong argument against cases based solely on circumstantial evidence and against capital punishment in general. Contemporary organizations opposed to capital punishment endorsed the film at the time of its release.

Paul Scardon's high-society thriller, *A Game With Fate* (1918), involves a foolish wager by Robert Harwell (Harry Morey) that he can have himself convicted of murder on fraudulent, concocted evidence. He succeeds only too well – until the man he is supposed to have murdered is lost at sea when his ship sinks. Later, a rival for his girlfriend Elaine Huntington (Betty Blythe) burns the remaining evidence, which was intended to clear him. The suspense continues until the last moment when all the complications are resolved.

Famous escape artist Harry Houdini portrays a newspaper reporter who is suspected of killing his tightfisted uncle in Irvin Willat's routine action drama, *The Grim Game* (1919). At first, upon the man's disappearance, Houdini accepts responsibility for the missing relative, believing this will help his newspaper. But when the uncle is found murdered by a group of the reporter's alleged pals, circumstantial evidence point to the nephew. Houdini decides to clear up the mystery. The master magician carries out his usual mystifying stunts, including escaping from handcuffs, scrambling out of chains, diving from a tall building while bound in a straitjacket, and, most spectacular of all, hanging from an airplane in pursuit of another plane, which he intends to drop down on – when, suddenly, the two aircraft collide in midair. This last shocking effect was not part of the script, but was the result of an accident, which the director decided to continue to film and which was included in the finished production. Ann Forrest, as the unfortunate uncle's attractive ward, provides the romance for Houdini. American magician Harry Houdini (1874-1926), world famous for his escapes, appeared on stage, in public, and in several silent action adventures before his untimely death. He was also noted for his fervor in exposing phony spiritualists.

An incorruptible police lieutenant and strong believer in the law demands the arrest of Mary MacLaren, his own daughter, in Thomas Ricketts's slow-paced domestic drama, *Secret Marriage* (1919). At her father's party to celebrate his promotion, innocent Mary sips too much punch, which another guest has furtively spiked. From this point on, her actions get her into situations which, in terms of circumstantial evidence, condemn her socially and legally. In one major incident, when her lieutenant-father, Fred Vroom, and several other policemen are set to raid a gambling ring in a hotel room, they accidentally crash into the wrong room – and find Vroom's daughter in a bedroom with a man. Because of her age and the suspicious circumstances, the father orders her arrest. Embarrassed by the public exposure, Mary heads for the docks, where she tries to end her life, but she is rescued. The film, told in flashbacks by Mary to a judge, supposedly is based on a true story. MacLaren uses her real name in the film, suggesting this was her own story. The title establishes that the man caught in the room with her was actually her secret husband.

II. Justice and the Lady From Hell

Films whose plots and characters evolved around circumstantial evidence remained popular during the twenties, perhaps for several reasons. Courtroom dramas grew in popularity. Crime films catered to a wider than usual audience, especially when they contained cabaret sequences with dancing choruses scantily dressed, backstage scenes of these young women preparing for the next show, and the lifestyles of high society intermingling with the underworld. All of these elements usually unfolded after dark under the bright lights of a major city. Somehow, the writers managed to set many of their circumstantial evidence plots against these frenetic and exciting backgrounds, accentuated by fashionable evening clothes, fast chauffeur-driven limousines and plenty of guns. All the timeworn plot gimmicks became well-known to audiences. The popular deathbed confession appeared in several films, including *Circumstantial Evidence* (1920) and *Love's Battle* (1920). The rescue in the nick of time appeared in *Hate* (1922), with a written confession presented in the nick of time to save a condemned man. *Dark Stairways* (1924) used the old device of a man wrongly arrested who escapes from jail to prove his innocence. Later in the decade, these dramas introduced several technological developments, such as the Dictaphone, which played an important role in *The Blind Goddess* (1926) and *Back to Liberty* (1928). All of these conventions, including the car chase to the governor for the obligatory pardon and the bleak scenes of the Death House, may have been gimmicky, but nevertheless they were effective in contributing to the action and suspense.

Famous detective Glenn White describes the story of how he became involved in the crime business in Tom Collins's mystery drama, *Circumstantial Evidence* (1920). While visiting David Wall, an old friend, a fight erupts between his friend and his butler. That night, Wall is murdered. The next morning, Wall's wife finds the body and a knife lying next to her husband. When she picks it up as if to kill herself, White takes it from her and tosses it out the window. The police misinterpret White's actions and arrest him, after which he is sentenced to prison. When a fire breaks out in the cell blocks, White rescues the warden's wife and child and wins a pardon. He returns home determined to solve the murder of his friend. Deciding the butler is innocent, he goes to the widow's deathbed and hears her confess to the murder. He then resolves to devote his life to saving innocent persons convicted only on circumstantial evidence.

Joe Moore, a young hobo, wins the admiration of local cowboys in a small western town, in William J. Craft's comedy drama, *Love's Battle* (1920). He soon wins the affection of Eileen Sedgwick, whom he rescues from a runaway horse. But he makes a foe of a suspicious character who frames Moore for a robbery and a murder. When Moore is sentenced to hang, his girlfriend pleads with the governor to pardon him, based on the flimsy circumstantial evidence presented at the trial. The governor refuses her request, forcing Sedgwick to tear her dress and scream for help. The incident convinces the governor's wife and others that he tried to attack the young woman. Sedgwick finally admits the deception, thereby persuading the governor of the fallacy of basing the death sentence solely on circumstantial evidence. He agrees to pardon Moore. Finally, the real killer confesses on his deathbed.

A woman judge, recently elected governor, is forced to choose between love and duty when her husband faces a death sentence for murder in Willis Robards's routine drama, *Every Woman's Problem* (1921). Falsely accused of killing a newspaper editor, the governor's husband is found guilty and sentenced to death. His wife, played by Dorothy Davenport, can pardon him but chooses not to. Fortunately, a confession by the actual murderer exonerates the husband in the nick of time.

Hobart Bosworth suspects his partner, Wade Boteler, of having an affair with his wife in Rowland V. Lee's domestic drama, *Blind Hearts* (1921). The two men are longtime partners in a Yukon gold mine, whose wives give birth around the same time. When Bosworth discovers that a birthmark on his daughter's shoulder is similar to the one on Boteler's shoulder, he suspects infidelity. Unknown to both families, the nurse had switched the babies so that each father would get his choice (Bosworth wanted a girl, while Boteler wanted a son). Years later, when the children grow up and fall in love, Bosworth, filled with hate toward his partner, does not allow the couple to marry. Bosworth then leaves the States and returns to the Yukon. Meanwhile, Boteler's son is accused of murdering Bosworth, who all believed perished in a fire aboard his yacht. Bosworth reads about the trial and rushes back to the States, helps to exonerate his partner's son, and finally agrees to the marriage.

Maxwell Karger's tense drama, *Hate* (1922), about a gambler who is falsely accused of murder and sentenced to die in the electric chair, is chiefly meant as a suspenseful bit of entertainment. However, it also suggests a plea against capital punishment. A gambler, knowing he has but a few weeks to live as the result of an illness, decides to make his suicide look like a murder committed by a rival gambler. The innocent man is brought to trial, sentenced to death and is led to the deadly electric chair, still claiming his innocence. Luckily, a written confession by the deceased, presented in the nick of time, has the warden rushing in to save the condemned man. Scenes of the assistant district attorney anguishing over whether he has sent an innocent man to his death; the victim walking into the chamber of death; and the haunting silhouette of the dreaded electric chair cast upon a stone wall; make one think twice about the wisdom of the death penalty.

An otherwise typical murder mystery, Frank Lloyd's *A Voice in the Dark* (1921) added a note of interest by exploring the problems of depending too heavily upon circumstantial evidence by way of several witnesses. They included a deaf woman and a blind man. The film was based on Ralph Dyar's melodrama of the same name. This was followed by Edmund Mortimer's *The Exiles* (1923), set chiefly in Algiers. Innocent Betty Bouton is convicted of murder on circumstantial evidence. John Gilbert, as a district attorney, searches for the alleged murderess and eventually effects Bouton's release.

George Chesebro is forced to flee when he is falsely accused of murder in Milburne Morante's routine outdoor drama, *Blind Circumstances* (1922), set in a Canadian seacoast town and later in the snow country. Chesebro gets into an altercation with a stranger on a dock and knocks him unconscious. When he is later charged with murdering the man, he takes off for the snow country, leaving behind his girlfriend, Vivian Rich. Several years later, he rescues a man who has lost his way along the snow trail. The victim turns out to be a member of the Royal Mounted Police who has temporarily lost his sight. In addition, the officer has been assigned to bring the fugitive in. He also happens to be the same man Chesebro was supposedly to have murdered. The stranger finally reveals he is a Mountie and arrests Chesebro. Following a series of complications, the officer regains his sight. Also, he had suffered from amnesia after his fight on the dock. Chesebro is finally exonerated and rejoins his girlfriend.

A bank cashier, falsely accused of stealing a valuable necklace and sent to prison for the crime, escapes so that he can prove his innocence in Robert F. Hill's familiar drama, *Dark Stairways* (1924). Herbert Rawlinson, as the cashier, and a fellow inmate make a daring escape from prison by means of a dirigible hovering over the institution. He then proceeds to clear himself and is reunited with Ruth Dwyer, his girlfriend, who never stopped believing in his innocence.

The lawyer-daughter of a man falsely accused of taking a bribe tries to extricate her father of criminal charges in Burton King's drama, *Counsel for the Defense* (1925), based on the 1912 novel by Leroy Scott. Betty Compson, as a neophyte attorney, takes the case but, overwhelmed by a mass of circumstantial evidence, loses. Later, she joins forces with a reporter to prove that a prominent lawyer-banker framed her father to gain control of a municipal water works.

Damaging circumstantial evidence almost convicts an otherwise successful lawyer in Frank Crane's drama, *Fair Play* (1925). Lou Tellegen, an obscure and struggling attorney, rises to prominence, thanks to the efforts of his loyal and hardworking secretary, Edith Thornton. But Tellegen is so busy trying to succeed that he pays little attention to his secretary. In fact, he falls in love and marries Betty Francisco, a conniving gold-digger. When his wife is killed accidentally, Tellegen falls under suspicion and is arrested and tried for murder, based only on circumstantial evidence. His faithful secretary, meanwhile, explores various haunts of the underworld, searching for information or clues that could help Tellegen. She finally uncovers enough evidence to free her boss, after which the grateful attorney offers her his undying love.

A lawyer defends his fiancée's mother, who is charged with murdering her wealthy husband, a politically powerful contractor, in Victor Fleming's society drama, *The Blind Goddess* (1926). Ernest Torrence, the contractor, has raised his daughter, Esther Ralston, to believe her mother, Louise Dresser, is dead. In reality, Dresser, a former prima donna, is now a broken-down entertainer at cheap theaters. She wants to visit her daughter in New York. But Torrence, her ex-husband, refuses to let her see Ralston. She carries a gun to the home, planning to take her own life if she cannot see her child. But when Torrence proves to her that their daughter will only be harmed if she is exposed to the truth about her mother's life, she puts the gun down and leaves. Torrence's crooked partner enters and wants the contractor to collaborate on some illegal scheme. When Torrence refuses, the man shoots him with Dresser's gun and flees. The police build a strong case of circumstantial evidence against the mother who, to protect her daughter, does not reveal her true identity. Jack Holt, a prosecuting attorney, believes she is innocent. He resigns his office and decides to defend her in court. As the jury is about to render its verdict, a Dictaphone recording proves Dresser is not guilty and that the real murderer is the victim's partner. With the defendant's release, the mother and daughter are finally reunited.

Roy Stewart portrays a Scotch lord who, while working on an American ranch in the West, is arrested for a murder, in Stuart Paton's romantic drama,

The Lady From Hell (1926). Stewart, a cowboy, returns to Scotland with a few fellow cowpunchers and kidnaps Lady Margaret (Blanche Sweet), who is about to marry another man. Instead, she and Stewart are married. Suddenly, the festivities are interrupted when Stewart is accused of murder, a charge based solely on circumstantial evidence. Just before he is to be hanged, a boy dashes to the scaffold and confesses that he shot the victim, his own father, because he was beating the boy's mother with a bull whip. Sweet, his recent wife, never loses faith in her husband's innocence, regardless of her family's suspicions about her husband, whom they look upon unfavorably. The title stems from the Scotch soldiers' kilts that the Germans, during World War I, had to face in battle. Surprised at the fighting spirit of their enemy, they described the Scotch soldiers as "the ladies from hell."

A drummer-composer and friend of a gangster is tried for murder in Luther Reed's farfetched society drama, *New York* (1927). The drummer, played by Ricardo Cortez, is accused of killing an ex-girlfriend who has come to his apartment to congratulate him on his success as a songwriter. Although he is convicted, he is later found not guilty and released. A third friend, his arranger, gets the gangster, who had committed the crime out of a sense of jealousy, to confess. Lois Wilson, as the daughter of a millionaire, is in love with Cortez and the two are reunited. The film was shot on location in Manhattan.

George Walsh portrays a criminal who wants to reform, but faces several obstacles, in Bernard McEveety's action drama, *Back to Liberty* (1928). He falls in love with the daughter (Dorothy Hall) of a big-time jewel thief, who is also a member of society. Her father, who has sent her to a private boarding school to keep her from learning about his illegal activities, tries to discourage the romance, even though Walsh has promised to go straight. Meanwhile, Walsh's partner continues his life of crime, and Walsh is falsely accused of murder. His girlfriend, using a Dictaphone, traps the actual murderer into a confession, thereby exonerating Walsh.

Betrayal, forgery and murder dominate Wilfred Noy's minor drama, *Circumstantial Evidence* (1929), about a ladies' man who took on one too many women in his romantic escapades. He is murdered by a former girlfriend whom he had abandoned. Meanwhile, an innocent secretary whom the victim had taken an interest in is accused of the crime based on circumstantial evidence. However, as in several similar films, including *The Bellamy Trial*, released the same year, the truth emerges during the trial.

Circus

I. Dreams Along the Sawdust Trail

The modern circus dates from the late eighteenth century and originated in acts of equestrian feats centered in a horse ring. Wild and trained animals, acrobats, freaks and clowns were all featured usually in a tent setting or outdoors. James A. Bailey introduced the first three-ring circus, and in 1919 he joined with showman P. T. Barnum and the Ringling Brothers to present the most famous American show, The Ringling Brothers' Barnum and Bailey Show & Circus. The famous traveling circus, featured in numerous silent films, declined in the 1950s, but by the 1980s thirty circuses were once again touring the U. S. and Canada. Several of the early silent circus films were adapted from novels (*Mrs. Wiggs of the Cabbage Patch, The Rose in the Ring*) or stage dramas (*Polly of the Circus*). Sometimes the studios shot segments of actual circuses for background interest or to cut production costs, as in *The Flying Twins* (1915). These excerpts gave audiences a chance to see professional artists perform their acts and preserved on film a piece of Americana for future generations to study and enjoy. Aside from the familiar plots and stereotyped characters, many of these films involved bareback riders and aerialists as sympathetic principal characters, with circus owners and managers often portrayed as villains, as in *The Rainbow Princess* (1916). One may well speculate about the social or political ramifications of these portrayals.

Jode Mullally hides out in a circus playing a clown after he is falsely accused of killing his grandfather in Oscar Apfel's drama, *The Circus Man* (1914), based on the 1910 novel, *The Rose in the Ring*, by George Barr McCutcheon. The circus owner and her daughter, Florence Dagmar, grow fond of him. Raymond Hatton, a jealous hunchback who loves the daughter, informs the police about Mullally. The hunchback's brother, Frank Hickman, however, replaces Mullally as the clown and later discovers that the fugitive's uncle committed the murder. Now cleared of all charges, Mullally proposes marriage to Dagmar, but her mother believes they are too young, and suggests they wait five years. Following several complications, the couple are finally reunited.

Andrew Robson, as Hiram Wiggs, leaves his wife and five children after he is fired from his plant job and joins a circus, in H. Entwhistle's drama, *Mrs. Wiggs of the Cabbage Path* (1914), based on the 1901 novel by Alice Hegan Rice and her 1903 novel *Lovey Mary*. He marries a bareback rider and they have a son, Tommy. Beatriz Michelena, as Lovey Mary, inherits a wealthy colonel's estate, the unscrupulous circus owner substitutes his own daughter as the heiress, and Mary flees with Tommy. They eventually seek shelter with Mrs. Wiggs. After the circus owner finds Mary and kidnaps her, Mrs. Wiggs discovers her locket with a picture of the colonel, proving Mary is the rightful heiress. Wiggs returns to his first wife after the death of his second wife, and Mary adopts Tommy and promises to keep Wiggs's bigamy a secret.

Madeline and Marion Fairbanks, twin sisters, are persuaded by a friendly couple to join a traveling circus in the drama, *The Flying Twins* (1915). They are billed as "The Flying Twins," but soon grow tired of their life with the circus and yearn to go home. Their father had sent them to live with an aunt when they took off on the sawdust trail. Meanwhile, detectives have been hired to locate them but have no luck. Following several complications, including a wild car chase, the twins gladly return home. Several of the actors who appeared in the film were actual circus performers.

Victor Moore portrays a "hick" circus clown with a good heart who helps out a young woman in trouble in William C. de Mille's poignant drama, *The Clown* (1916). Florence Dagmar, who believes her fiancé is dead, marries Moore to protect her prospective child. Later, she discovers the man she really loves, Thomas Meighan, is alive, and the couple are reunited. Moore, broken-hearted but glad that he was able to help the woman in her time of need, returns to the circus. The film offers several very touching and human sequences, including those depicting the ordinary home life of families while Moore, with his itinerant life, realizes how much of an outsider he really is. The film portrays circus life realistically, instead of the more conventional idealized depiction.

Ann Pennington, a dancer with a traveling circus, unknowingly becomes part of a scam to swindle an elderly gentleman, in J. Searle Dawley's suspenseful drama, *The Rainbow Princess* (1916). Her unscrupulous employer, the circus owner, devises a scheme to pass her off as the granddaughter of a wealthy man, who accepts the dancer, known as "The Rainbow Princess," as part of his family. Following a series of complications and disappointments, she learns the truth. She then decides to leave, having caused enough harm to the gentleman and other members of his family. But the man's adopted son, who has fallen in love with her, persuades her to return, and the young couple are married. The traveling circus sequences include side show freaks, the rise of a hot air balloon and the performance of a hula dance performed by a bevy of dancers led by Pennington.

Muriel Ostriche, a dancer with a carnival show, learns the truth about her father, whom she thought had died years earlier, in Charles M. Seay's simplistic drama, *A Circus Romance* (1916). George Larkin, a daredevil with the same carnival, loves the dancer, whose mother is also part of the troupe and handles the fortune telling. Before she dies, the mother reveals her past to her daughter. When her husband went off to war, her father evicted her, thinking she had gone wrong. When the husband returned, she explains, he could not find her and thought she had died. He then married another woman and became very wealthy. Ostriche then makes a point of finding her father, but when she does, she doesn't want to create a problem for him and his wife by exposing the story of his bigamous action at the time of his second marriage. The truth finally comes out, and the couple adopt Ostriche as their daughter. When she decides to marry Larkin, her father presents her with a large check as a wedding present that allows the young lovers to buy their own home. The superior circus atmosphere enhances the entire production, especially the external sequences concerning the tent show.

Lew Field, a professor involved in a plot by anarchists to assassinate a prince, is banished from his home country and comes to America, where he finds work as a circus barker, in J. A. Richmond's drama, *The Barker* (1917). Years earlier, the professor had grown despondent after learning that his little daughter has allegedly drowned. The father becomes friends with an aerialist who, unknown to him, in reality is his long-lost daughter. James Harris, the ringmaster, forces the young woman to support him financially. He tries to force her to marry the circus manager, but she refuses. Later, Harris is killed in an accident arranged by the manager. Before he dies, Harris reveals the aerialist's true identity. Father and daughter are now reunited, and the young woman marries Pat O'Malley, the circus owner.

Violet Mersereau plays a dual role of both mother and daughter in Rex Ingram's comedy drama, *The Little Terror* (1917). As the daughter, she portrays a brash and reckless juvenile who has been brought up on the back lots of circuses. When her father dies as the result of an accident, she is relegated to the home of her wealthy grandfather. Much of the comedy of the film derives from her youthful antics while living with her grandfather.

Two youths, Bessie Love and Harold Goodwin, run away from home and become circus performers, in Paul Powell's entertaining drama, *The Sawdust Ring* (1917). Love's mother, whose absentee husband is a circus ringmaster, discourages the girl from visiting circuses, fearing the youngster will form an attachment for that life. The pig-tailed young woman often dreamed about becoming a circus rider, and her boyfriend, Goodwin, encouraged her. When the mother becomes ill and is hospitalized, the two youngsters take off to find her father. By luck, they join a traveling circus whose owner is the girl's father. He takes an interest in the two runaways, who help him locate his wife. The girl's parents reconcile their differences and decide to rekindle their former love. The mother's health improves and she returns to her family.

Mae Marsh, as the title character, promises her fellow performers that she will do a double somersault on her horse during her next show – a promise that brings unexpected results – in Charles T. Horan and Edwin L. Hollywood's drama, *Polly of the Circus* (1917), based on the 1907 play by Margaret Mayo. Polly tries it and falls. The seriously injured rider is taken to the home of Vernon Steele, a local minister. Her sympathetic friends buy her horse, Bingo, and place it in the minister's yard. Charles Eldridge, a clown and good friend of Dolly's, had loved her mother, but the woman, an aerialist, was killed in the same ring years earlier. Now he is broke and desperate for money. Wellington Playter, another member of the troupe, writes Polly a letter, telling of the clown's plight. Polly decides to enter her horse in a local race that offers a prize of 500 dollars. Meanwhile, she and the minister have fallen in love. A local deacon extracts a promise from Polly that if she enters the race, she will never see Steele again. She agrees, enters the race and wins the money for her friend, Toby the clown. She returns to the circus and her world of friends. When the circus revisits the same town, the tent catches fire during one performance. The reverend's love for Polly is rekindled when he fears for her life, and he hurries to her rescue. The couple are then reunited.

A circus plays a minor role in Ernest C. Warde's slow-paced drama, *The Woman and the Beast* (1917). Marie Shotwell, as a widow living in an Italian colony outside of New York City, is being courted by Alphonse Ethier, who desires her. However, a handsome, musically inclined stranger wins her heart and she marries the latter. Ethier, however, is determined to win her back somehow. Meanwhile, a lion escapes from a traveling circus, and the police begin to pursue the beast. Ethier, who has stabbed a circus worker, flees and thinks the police are after him. Shotwell's husband also is determined to hunt down the escaped animal. Ethier sees Shotwell, who is searching for her husband, wandering in the woods and tries to assault her. But the pursuing police scare him off. He sees a powder shed and decides to hide there, unaware that the lion has sought the same place. The husband, knowing the lion is inside, drops a boulder into it, causing a tremendous explosion that kills both the lion and Ethier.

A family gets a short lesson in tolerance in Jerome Storm's simplistic drama, *The Biggest Show on Earth* (1918). Enid Bennett has been raised by her father on the back lot of a circus and has become a skilled lion tamer. Now seventeen years old, her father sends her to boarding school. While visiting the home of a fellow student, she falls in love with her friend's brother. When the young man's proud family learn of her circus background, they become alarmed. Finally, the father of the snobbish family grows impatient and announces that he is a half owner in the circus and partners with the girl's father. He also informs his family that they have been enjoying all the benefits that the circus money has brought to them. Enlightened by their annoyed father, the other family members drop their supercilious airs and openly accept their guest as part of the family.

Mabel Normand, who does odd jobs around a circus lot, is known as "The Jinx" among the troupe because she continually fouls things up in Victor L. Schertzinger's delightful comedy, *Jinx* (1919). At times, the circus owner would like to strangle her for all the trouble she causes. When his girlfriend, Florence Carpenter, runs off, Normand decides to get into her serpentine costume of silks and perform in her place. Once on stage, she fouls things up by getting entangled in all the silks. This causes a commotion that sends the audience fleeing from the show. When the owner tries to get his hands on her, the "Wild Man" of the show, Cullen Landis, comes to her rescue by beating up her attacker. Normand flees the chaotic scene and hides out at an orphanage where the children, because of her costume, mistake her for a fairy. The circus owner, meanwhile, has lost his girlfriend and is on the verge of losing his show. He finds Normand and tries to beat out of her the whereabouts of Carpenter. In his rage, he sets fire to the orphanage. Once again, Landis comes to the rescue and again thrashes the owner. Normand cannot resist falling in love with her hero, who also loves her. The circus sequences are quite entertaining, as are the antics of Normand, who proves her worth as a major comedienne.

Two circus men plan to pacify an irate reporter who has been refused a good seat at a performance of "The Savage," a popular side show act, in Paul Powell's comedy drama, *The Little White Savage* (1919). They tell the newsman how they and another person were shipwrecked on an island, where they met a tribe that spoke old English. Beautiful Carmel Myers escaped from the tribe and mistook the visitors for gods. One of the castaways, seeking animals for the circus, left with Myers. Later, back in the States, she appeared as The Savage with the circus. Harry Hilliard, a minister and one of the men telling the story, reveals how she entered his home and shocked his church members by her scanty clothes. Although dismissed from his religious post because of his association with The Savage, he realized he was in love with her and joined the circus so that he could be with her. The startled reporter later questions Myers and discovers the entire story is untrue.

II. Nostalgia in the Center Ring

The traveling circus in the United States reached its peak between 1880 and 1920. But Hollywood in the twenties showed no signs of any loss of public interest in the popularity of circuses or circus films. Perhaps this form of entertainment offered filmmakers a world of rich material – circus films were very visual, with acts that were thrilling and exciting, and sometimes dangerous; they presented a wide array of characters; they often expanded the film from the typical stage-bound set to the outdoors; and they catered to a wide audience of children and adults of both sexes. In addition, they furnished plots for a variety of genres, e.g., dramas (*The Fortune Teller*), romantic tales (*The Man Tamer*), comedies (Chaplin's *The Circus*), westerns (*Circus Cowboy*) and, at times, crime dramas (*The Devil's Circus*). Some more "arty" films even bordered on tragedy, such as *He Who Gets Slapped*. Finally, several reviewers continually pointed out the fascination of the circus dramas. They touched a nostalgic nerve in many of us by reminding us of our youth. Because audiences found them entertaining, circus films continued to be released throughout the twenties.

Shirley Mason, the daughter of a missionary who died in Africa, is assigned to be taken to a particular bishop in Scott Dunlap's drama, *Her Elephant Man* (1920). However, the circus troupe who finds her makes more of an impression on her than the prospective bishop, and she elects to stay with its members. She becomes a horseback rider and grows fond of Albert Roscoe, the caretaker of the elephants. The man has a mysterious past that still troubles him. He had been married years earlier when he discovered his bride only chose him for his money. To avoid any entanglement with Mason, he leaves the circus. He then discovers that his wife has divorced him. Relieved of his past problems, he rushes back to the circus and Mason. Meanwhile, a villain with the troupe tries to seduce her, but she resists. A storm finally brings Roscoe and Mason together.

Gladys Walton, a high-wire performer with a traveling circus, longs for a peaceful country life, in Reeves Eason's disappointing drama, *Pink Tights* (1920). Forced to stay in a small town while laid up with an injury, Walton is spurned by the conservative townspeople. Jack Perrin, the local parson, befriends the circus troupe, especially Walton. But he, too, opens himself to criticism from his flock, who protest his closeness with the show people. Eventually, Walton's boyfriend arrives and the pair become closer. The parson fades from the scene as a possible mate for Walton, who ends up winning the hearts of the townspeople. Walton made several circus dramas.

Gladys Walton returned to the circus background, where she tamed both a lion and an undisciplined young man, in Harry B. Harris's romantic drama, *The Man Tamer* (1922). When her father, a lion tamer, becomes incapacitated, his daughter, Walton, decides to take over his act. William Welsh, the circus owner, is romantically attracted to his new star, as is Roscoe Karns, the rich and spoiled son of a millionaire. She chooses neither one, but when Karns's father pleads with her to tame his son the way she handles her lions, she accepts the challenge. During her assignment, she begins to realize she is falling in love with her subject. Meanwhile, Welsh, the owner, begins to make unsavory advances toward her, although she has earlier rejected him. This leads Karns to forcefully rescue her from the lecherous owner.

Gladys Walton, in her third circus film, portrays a circus performer who grows tired of circus life and agrees to pose as the long-lost daughter of a wealthy couple, in Jack Conway's drama, *Sawdust* (1923). The elderly couple believe that their daughter has been kidnapped by show people. The corrupt ticket seller of the circus dreams up the scheme of having Walton pose as their lost child. Meanwhile, Walton, who has been substituting for a drunken clown, meets Niles Welch, a local lawyer. She temporarily brings joy to the lonely couple, who accept her as their lost daughter. The ring master, Frank Brownlee, who is Walton's brutal foster father since her parents died in an earlier circus accident, searches for her. Rather than return with him to the circus, she confesses to the couple the truth and then, suffering from pangs of guilt, tries to commit suicide. But Welch, the lawyer, rescues her. Brownlee is forced to leave without her, and the young couple plan their future together. Walton appeared in two earlier circus dramas, *Pink Tights* (1920) and *The Man Tamer* (1922).

Marjorie Rambeau's husband divorces her and takes custody of her child in Albert Capellani's drama, *The Fortune Teller* (1920), based on the 1919 play by Leighton Osmun. After he accuses her of having an affair with a circus manager, she takes a job as circus fortune teller. She begins to deteriorate morally as the result of her heavy drinking. Two decades later, Raymond McKee, her son, now down on his luck, comes to her to have his fortune read. Without revealing her identity, she inspires him to carry on. The young man leaves and becomes a successful political candidate. In addition, his fiancée is the governor's daughter. Motivated by her son's good fortune, his mother reforms and straightens out her own life. The mother and son are then reunited.

Several westerns and cowboy stars during the twenties began to use circus backgrounds for their outdoor adventures. Tom Mix, the most popular screen cowboy during this decade, made several westerns with circus backgrounds. Buck Jones, the second most famous cowboy after Mix, also tried his hand at a circus film. A young woman's hasty marriage to the wrong man affects several lives in William Wellman's action drama, *Circus Cowboy* (1924), set chiefly in a western town. Buck Jones's sweetheart marries the town's wealthiest citizen while Jones is away. When Jones returns, the young wife meets him and confesses her love for him. But Jones rejects her advances. Her stepson, who overhears the conversation, threatens her, forcing Jones to throw him through a store window. Later, her husband, thinking Jones is entering his house, shoots his own son. Jones is accused of the shooting and narrowly escapes capture by a posse. He joins a circus, where he meets Bird Taylor (Marian Nixon), falls in love and marries her. Silent westerns rarely offer as much plot detail as this action drama contains.

Hoot Gibson was another popular cowboy star who turned to the circus film for variety. His style of humor particularly fitted the comedy drama. East meets West once again in Edward Sedgwick's romantic comedy, *The Sawdust Trail* (1924), which is reminiscent of Shakespeare's *The Taming of the Shrew*. Gibson, as an effete college student, clashes with an emotional western rodeo star, played by Josie Sedgwick. Gibson poses as a weakling. His frustrated father gets him a job with a western circus and rodeo that has come to the East to perform in the college town. Gibson sets out to break the wild and independent spirit of the man-hating rodeo queen. She has humbled all other prospective romeos who have tried to conquer her. He succeeds, and she ends up falling in love with him. This is another example in which Gibson, playing a buffoon while accomplishing his goal, has succeeded in presenting a fresh, entertaining approach to an otherwise ordinary western.

Art Acord joined fellow screen cowboys Tom Mix, Hoot Gibson and others in setting one of his westerns in a circus background. He portrays a cowpuncher who helps a circus clown falsely accused of a bank robbery in Al Rogell's action drama, *The Circus Cyclone* (1925). In love with the daughter of the clown, Acord intercedes in the accused's behalf and rides like thunder after the real thieves and the loot. He returns in time to save the clown from a lynching. The introduction of a circus clown adds some freshness to an otherwise familiar plot. Long thought to have been a lost film, a copy of this western was found in 1991 in Australia.

Tom Mix blends action in the open spaces with that of the urban landscape in John G. Blystone's exciting action drama, *My Own Pal* (1926). As a cowboy who hankers for a look at the big city, Mix quits his ranch job and starts out for the tall buildings and bright lights. Mix and his horse Tony come across a small circus where he saves an eight-year-old girl from a brutal father. The dying mother begs Tom to take the child away. After a short chase by some of the circus people and the child's father, Tom, holding the tot securely and guiding Tony, the horse leaps into the baggage car of a moving train. Once in the city, he gets a job as a police officer and, using a motorcycle and his lariat, captures a jewel thief making a getaway by car. Later, he rounds up the entire gang and rescues the heroine (Olive Borden), the police chief's daughter, who has been kidnapped by the crooks.

Tom Mix successfully used a circus background in several of his films, including Ben Stoloff's entertaining western, *The Circus Ace* (1927), in which Mix rescues the heroine from a small-town political boss. Mix portrays a cowboy who rides and ropes well and likes a pretty circus entertainer, played by Natalie Joyce. At one point, he rescues her from a runaway elephant by lassoing her with his lariat. Most of the film is taken up with various circus acts worked into the thin romantic plot, with Mix and Joyce displaying their different attributes. Some villainy occurs when a lecherous politician from a small town in Arizona desires the heroine and threatens the small circus troupe with a mortgage payment. He is willing to forget the payment if she agrees to marry him. Tom Mix intercedes to the satisfaction of all.

Ken Maynard saves a traveling circus from sabotage by a rival owner in Harry J. Brown's routine drama, *The Wagon Show* (1928). Maynard, as Bob Mason, works for the reputable owner and fills in for the star rider who quits to join the competing outfit. Mason also retrieves some stolen wagons so that the show can go on. Marian Douglas provides the romantic element. The plot is designed to highlight the expert riding abilities of the star.

Madge Bellamy, the stepdaughter of Bert Sprotte, the cruel and miserly owner of a circus, is forced to portray the "Wild Woman from Borneo' and is locked in her cage by Sprotte, in John Griffith Wray's drama, *The Soul of the Beast* (1923). During a storm, the big top catches fire, and Bellamy, trapped in her cage, calls upon Oscar, an elephant, to help her. The creature moves her cage to safety. Later, she meets Cullen Landis, a frail young man who enjoys the violin. A lecherous Noah Beery, who desires Bellamy, pursues her and Landis after she escapes from the circus. Finally, the two men clash in a fight to the finish, with the elephant coming to the couple's rescue once again by dousing Beery with torrents of water – until Bellamy calls Oscar off. The couple marry, have a child, and Landis is cured of his lameness. This film and Conway's *Sawdust* are similar in several respects, including the introduction of a cruel stepfather.

Scientist Lon Chaney loses both his latest invention and his wife to Marc McDermott, a baron, in Victor Seastrom's drama, *He Who Gets Slapped* (1924), based on the 1921 play by Leonid Andreyev. This was supposed to be the evening of his great success. To forget his disappointments, he decides to lose himself in the life of a clown, a life that soon brings him much fame in France. When Chaney confides his love for bareback rider Norma Shearer, she laughs at him. She is in love with her partner, John Gilbert. When he discovers that Shearer's father, a count, has arranged for her to marry MacDermott, the man who stole Chaney's wife, he releases a lion that kills the pair of plotters. But the clown has been fatally stabbed by McDermott and falters around the circus ring to the enjoyment of the audience that thinks this is part of his act. He finally dies in the arms of the woman he loves, who is now free to marry Gilbert.

Ernest Torrence portrays a clown in a French circus when World War I breaks out in Herbert Brenon's drama, *The Side Show of Life* (1924). He enlists to fight with the British and soon rises to the rank of colonel. During a battle he saves the life of a captain who invites the former clown to stay at his home during his leave. He receives news that he has been made a brigadier general. As he is about to celebrate his new promotion, an armistice is declared. All that is left for the clown is to return to his former work. He locates his former partner, a young woman, and together they perform their old act. But his heart is not in it, and the audience shows its disapproval with catcalls and other derogatory exclamations. His partner returns from his dressing room and holds up his Legion of Honor Cross, announcing the last rank he had held. The audience applauds while the clown apologizes for his poor performance. A fellow soldier offers him an opportunity to start life over with a new career in Australia.

Norma Shearer works with an aerial act after her boyfriend, pickpocket Charles Emmett Mack, is arrested and sent to prison, in Benjamin Christensen's drama, *The Devil's Circus* (1926). The crude lion tamer, John Miljan, infatuated with Shearer, makes a play for her, an act that infuriates his jealous mistress. She tampers with Shearer's trapeze, resulting in the innocent young woman's fall and injury. After several years, Mack, now out of prison and working as a shoemaker, finds Shearer and the couple are married. When he discovers the truth about Miljan's treatment toward Shearer, he seeks revenge. But when Mack learns that the lion tamer has been wounded in the Great War and is now a blind beggar, his vindictiveness turns to pity.

A woman discovers that the man she had once eloped with has now been hired to prevent her daughter's marriage in Michael Curtiz's routine drama, *The Third Degree* (1926), based on a play by Charles Klein. Louise Dresser is the mother of Dolores Costello, a young circus aerialist. Dresser was the wife of Tom Santschi, a tightrope walker and knife thrower, who had been killed in an accident years earlier when she was planning to elope with a ringmaster. Her daughter, all these years, had been raised by others. When Costello is about to marry wealthy Jason Robards, his father objects and hires a detective to prevent the union. The detective, who had been the ringmaster the girl's mother was to have eloped with fifteen years earlier, threatens to expose the mother's past. To prevent him, Costello shoots him. Robards is arrested, but the mother confesses.

Marion Nixon portrays the title character, a world-famous circus bareback rider, who is torn between the love of two men, in Frank O'Connor's routine romantic drama, *Spangles* (1927), based on the book by Nellie Revell. Hobart Bosworth, the pleasant circus owner, is in love with Spangles and wants her for his wife. But he occasionally beats the elephant Sultana, who, like others of its species, never forgets a kindness or forgives an injury, as the lore of the circus goes. On the other hand, Pat O'Malley, on the run from the law, joins the circus and also falls in love with the champion bareback rider. Later, Bosworth is killed by the elephant he had been cruel to, and O'Malley, who is exonerated of a murder charge, gets to marry Spangles.

Charlie Chaplin portrays a tramp who, being pursued by cops, blunders into a failing traveling circus performance and accidentally wins the applause of an otherwise bored audience in Chaplin's last comedy during the silent era, *The Circus* (1928). When Chaplin leaves the scene, the professional clowns continue their performances, only to be met by boos from the irate audience, who cry for "the funny man." Charlie, unaware of his success, is hired by the circus owner to play a clown, and he soon becomes the star of the show. Throughout the film, he becomes involved in clever and funny bits, including a high-wire routine that ends with his exiting the circus and entering a drug store. Another bit involves his being ordered to blow a pill through a tube down a horse's throat. Instead, Chaplin accidentally swallows the pill, claiming the horse blew first. Chaplin introduces a note of pathos when he falls in love with bareback rider Merna Kennedy, the owner's abused daughter. But the clown loses her to the handsome new wire walker. To win her love and compete with his rival, Charlie takes up wire walking. When the circus prepares to close and move on, Chaplin is seen in the empty lot as the caravan of wagons departs. The tramp then turns his back and plods off in the opposite direction to face the world alone.

City vs. Country

I. The Cruel and Passionate City

Jean Baudrillard, the French semiologist, once wrote about New York: "It is a world completely rotten with wealth, power, senility, indifference, Puritanism and mental hygiene, poverty and waste, technological futility and aimless violence...." The Frenchman's observations may well fit many major cities. To temper this morbid description, we can add writer Thomas Wolfe's thoughts, written in 1939: "It was a cruel city, but it was a lovely one, a savage city, yet it had such tenderness.... It was so sweetly and so delicately pulsed, as full of warmth, of passion, and of love, as it was full of hate." The fears and anxieties conjured up by parents who saw their sons and daughters wandering into these terrible places contrasted sharply to the images their children had. To these restless innocents, the city held out a world of opportunity, a promising future and a life of excitement. The early silent films echoed these dreams as well as the fears of the parents, offering numerous cautionary dramas that warned the young of a multitude of pitfalls awaiting them – and always lurking in the shadows were the dual images – the cleanliness of the country versus the corruption of the city.

Wealthy Owen Moore, vacationing in the Adirondacks, accidentally shoots mountain girl Mary Pickford in the arm and ends up marrying her in J. Searle Dawley's comedy drama, *Caprice* (1913), based on the 1884 play by Howard P. Taylor. The untutored Pickford fails to learn the social amenities demanded of her as the wife of her cultured husband. Moore admits to his father, who had opposed the marriage, that he made a mistake. Pickford returns to her home in the mountains and attends a boarding school, where she meets Moore's sister. Following several complications, Pickford impresses his husband and his family with her refinements and the couple are reunited.

Consuelo Bailey and R. Riley portray a sister and brother from the country who move to New York City and become involved with gang leader H. B.

Walthall in James Kirkwood's chiefly unconvincing crime drama, *The Gangsters* (1914). The young brother eventually is convicted of murder based on circumstantial evidence and sentenced to prison. Walthall joins him when he is convicted of complicity in the same crime. Although Bailey, the boy's sister, knows Walthall's entire criminal background, she still loves him and, one year after his release and his reformation, they are both pictured journeying along a country road, where they hope to start a new life together. The drama touches upon several topics, including capital punishment, circumstantial evidence, and the corrosive influence of urban life. Several gun fights break out between rival gangs, all suggesting the sharp contrast between rural and city life. Details describe John Dillon, the murderer, going to the electric chair. They include his slow walk from his cell to the dreaded electric chair, a priest carrying a crucifix, the apparatus used to strap Dillon to the death seat, and the warden's signal to proceed with the execution by his dropping the handkerchief. The deliberate, slow pace of these scenes, along with the iconography, underscore the anti-capital punishment theme. Some critics thought the implausible love segment may have marred the film, which is sometimes listed as *The Gangsters of New York*.

Emmy Wehlen in the drama, *When a Woman Loves* (1915), portrays a poor, virtuous country girl who lives on the family chicken farm with a sickly mother. She likes a wealthy neighbor who persuades her to elope with him. She packs her one suitcase and waits for him at the wrong railroad station. He tires of waiting for her and drives back to his estate. Wehlen decides to take the train to the big city to visit her sister Nell, who is in collusion with a gambler. The pair see in the newcomer an attractive young woman who can lure rich men into their crooked card games. Unaware of their scheme, Wehlen succeeds in meeting men and directing them toward the games, where they invariably lose their money. One day, when Wehlen's wealthy neighbor falls victim to the gambler, she exclaims her disapproval when she realizes what he is doing to the neighbor. Just as the card sharp is about to attack the innocent player, Wehlen shoots him. A sympathetic detective lets her off, and the young couple return to the country, where they are married. To depict the city in an even worse light, the film, in its early sequences, shows the country girl becoming involved in a pool hall raid as she searches for her sister. The pool hall was an early icon of temptation and corruption.

Ruth Findlay, who lives at Lost Mountain with her grandmother, longs to visit the city in Arthur Donaldson's drama, *The Salamander* (1915), based on the novel by Owen Johnson. But her grandmother tells her terrible tales of the wicked city and how it destroyed Findlay's parents. Later, the villain responsible for leading the girl's parents to ruin, cheats the grandmother of her deed and the old woman dies. Findlay, now all alone, travels to the city to find the scoundrel. Meanwhile, she experiences a series of horrible encounters in the city. She finally wreaks vengeance on the villain while meeting and marrying the son of a millionaire.

A city gangster while on vacation in a small fishing village rescues a young woman who falls in love with him, in Lawrence McGill's simplistic drama, *Are They Born or Made?* (1915). The film emphasizes both the influence of environment on a gangster's life and the close bond between politics and crime. The couple marry without the bride knowing anything about her husband's business. They arrive in New York where she learns he is a gang leader and owner of a saloon. The gangster has close ties with a political boss who uses the gangster and his hoodlums to help during the primaries, while the rival party is in collusion with another gang who operate in a similar manner. The gangster recounts how he had a happy childhood on a farm, but after the death of his father, he was forced to move to the city slums. Realizing that he is a victim of his environment, his wife takes her husband back to her father's farm, where they carve out a new and happier life together. The film was based on a story by Jack Rose, a notorious gambler who was implicated in the sensational 1912 murder of Herman Rosenthal, a fellow gambler. Rose had appeared as himself in *The Wages of Sin* (1913), an exploitation drama depicting the events in the Rosenthal murder.

Marshall Neilan portrays the title character in Frederick Thomson's overly familiar drama, *The Country Boy* (1915), based on the 1910 play by Edgar Selwyn. Neilan is a naïve young man who comes to the big city after leaving behind his girlfriend, Florence Dagmar. The young woman's father, a local judge, will not allow Neilan to marry his daughter until Neilan can prove that he can support her. Once in the city, he immediately makes a fool of himself over a chorus girl. Dorothy Green, as the street-wise entertainer, at first takes a liking to Neilan, but the country boy, who cannot hold his liquor and spends too much on wining and dining her, ends up losing all his money. He finally learns that the city is no place for him, and that his girlfriend back home is the one he really loves. With a city pal, he returns to his home town to start a local newspaper. When the business succeeds, Dagmar, his girlfriend, forgives him and the couple are reunited.

Florence Reed, a simple country girl, makes the trek to the big city in search of success in Allan Dwan's drama, *The Dancing Girl* (1915), based on the 1891 play by Henry Arthur Jones. Surprisingly, despite a series of obstacles, she returns home after winning out against all the temptations that have defeated those who were seduced by the bright lights of the big city. A duke who wishes to win her love follows her to her small town and finally wins her promise to marry him. Reed's father, on the other hand, believing her to be an incorrigible daughter, places a curse upon her. Meanwhile, her local boyfriend ends up marrying her sister. But all is forgiven when she returns successfully from the proverbial wicked city.

Viola Dana, a small-town minister's daughter, would like to emulate the career success of her older sister in John H. Collins's threadbare drama, *On Dangerous Paths* (1915). Dana reads a newspaper story telling about her sister, reporting that she is one of the most successful business women in New York.

She returns home to find her minister father in financial difficulties. She writes a check for several hundred dollars so that the family could pay off its debts. When Dana observes her sister's independence, she decides to try her luck. She starts out for the big city, leaving behind her childhood beau, Pat O'Malley. The inexperienced young woman finds work as a nurse in a city hospital, where a doctor takes a liking to her. The feeling is mutual. Meanwhile, O'Malley, who has bought an engagement ring for Dana, journeys to New York to rescue her from the city's dangers. However, he ends up getting drunk. The doctor who likes Dana meets O'Malley and takes him back to the hospital. The country boy realizes he faces stiff competition in the doctor. He meets a young woman who takes the visitor to a fancy Times Square restaurant, where he sees Dana and the doctor enter a private dining room. O'Malley exchanges places with the doctor and wins back his girlfriend.

Giles R. Warren's political western comedy, *A Texas Steer* (1915), based on the play by Charles A. Hoyt, features Tyrone Power as Maverick Brander, a Texan who reluctantly enters politics to protect his ranch interests and those of his neighbors. He moves to Washington with his family, whose misadventures in the capital provide the basis for much of the comedy. The conflict between the ranchers and the railroad remains in the background, as it does in the 1927 remake, directed by Richard Wallace and starring Will Rogers.

June Caprice, the daughter of a mountaineer, falls in love with Harry Hilliard, a man from the city, in John G. Adolfi's romantic drama, *Caprice of the Mountains* (1916). When her father discovers the romance, he grows suspicious of the visitor and forces him to marry his daughter. The couple marry and settle in the big city, but the young bride soon grows disillusioned with urban life and the superficiality of her husband's friends. She returns to her beloved mountains, where she intends to raise her child. Her husband, at first annoyed by the forced marriage, begins to realize he really loves his wife and follows her, hoping to reconcile their differences. He meets his child and explains his feels to his wife. Overcome by the restorative powers of nature, he states his love for her and promises her they need never have to leave the mountains again.

George Beban, a simple Normandy farmer, and Doris Kenyon, his pretty peasant wife, get a bitter taste of Parisian life in Maurice Tourneur's romantic drama, *The Pawn of Fate* (1916). A visiting Parisian artist, John Davidson, is attracted to the farmer's wife, and tells Beban he has artistic talent. When he invites the couple to stay in his Paris home while Beban develops his latent talents, they foolishly agree. Meanwhile, Davidson tries to woo the wife. Beban paints a large canvas of his native sheep farm, and the artist arranges an unveiling for guests and art critics. With everyone drinking heavily at the affair, Beban doesn't realize the guests are laughing at the painting. Simultaneously, Davidson is trying to seduce Kenyon. Beban enters the room, sends his wife away, and announces only one man will leave the room alive. However, the differences are reconciled amicably and the peasant couple, who have had enough of the artifices of Paris life, leave for their farm.

When Ella Hall's mother dies, the poor country girl is sent to live with her aunt and female cousin in the city, in Robert Z. Leonard's familiar drama, *The Love Girl* (1916). Hall likes a wealthy young neighbor while her cousin, Betty Schade, is in love with a decent but poor young man. Her mother, meanwhile, disapproves of the match and hires a crooked swami to discourage the romance. The swami hypnotizes the daughter and arranges for her kidnapping while extorting money from the mother for her daughter's return. Hall and her wealthy neighbor friend foil the swami's plan, and Schade is reunited with her boyfriend. The grateful aunt embraces her heroic and resourceful niece.

Country girl Frances Nelson comes to New York after the death of her father to stay with her aunt in George W. Lederer's slight drama, *The Decoy* (1916), based on the short story, "The Country Girl," by Herbert Hall Winslow. The only problem is that her aunt is involved with a ring of gamblers who think the young girl's good looks could lure wealthy young men into the gambling den where they could be cheated. The country girl takes a liking to one of the victims and warns him about the crooks. Complications follow in which the head of the gang is killed and the young man held as the chief suspect. But he is soon exonerated and marries the young Nelson, who has warned him.

Alma Hanlon, the product of a small town, marries a New Yorker who is struggling to become a lawyer in Richard Ridgely's drama, *Pride and the Devil* (1917). The couple move to the city where he neglects his wife. Meanwhile, she misses her social gatherings she was used to in her home town. Because her husband never takes her into society, she finds a group of bohemian friends, two of whom are attracted to her. One is the son of her husband's boss, and the other an elderly roué. When her husband, who disapproves of her friends and her bizarre social life, divorces her, she marries the young man, thinking he will introduce her into society and the exciting night life of the city. But the young husband begins to gamble and drink heavily after his father cuts off his funds. Following a series of complications, including the murder of the wife's elderly suitor by her second husband, she is reunited with her ex-husband, who is now a lawyer. As the attorney for her husband, he saves the young man from going to jail.

Robert Harron, as the title character in Lloyd Ingraham's drama, *An Old Fashioned Young Man* (1917), is a country boy raised with old-fashioned values who finds himself caught in a web of urban corruption. The young man journeys to the city and, with a letter of introduction from his father to a senator, obtains a job with some crooked politicians. They are plotting to discredit Loyola O'Connor, a woman candidate for mayor associated with a rival party. When Harron learns of their intent to smear the woman's reputation and that of her daughter, he switches sides and sets out to prove the legitimacy of O'Connor's daughter, Colleen Moore. Visiting several cities to gather the necessary evidence, despite the interference of a gang of hoodlums hired by one of the unscrupulous politicians, Harron succeeds in his mission. For his reward, he wins the love of the daughter. Her mother wins the election and the crooked political cartel is exposed.

Frank Glendon, a prominent city lawyer who has been raised on a humble farm where his parents still live, is embarrassed to take his genteel wife, Agnes Ayre, to meet his parents, in Thomas R. Mills's domestic drama, *The Defeat of the City* (1917), based on the story by O. Henry. Although he fears she will be repulsed at the rural crudities she will be exposed to, he reluctantly agrees. After spending a tiring day around the farm, Glendon approaches his wife cautiously about her experience here and is astonished to learn that she is overjoyed. She tells him how proud she feels that her husband has sprung from such a worthy background and such hardworking parents.

Joseph Levering's timeworn drama, *The Road Between* (1917), tells about an unsophisticated rural family getting fleeced in the big city. Marian Swayne's stepmother always yearned for a life in the city, so when her husband comes into a small fortune, the family moves from their humble country home to the bright lights. They are soon overwhelmed by a pack of wolves in the form of crooked lawyers, shifty investment consultants, a sultry adventuress interested in the couple's son, and a dapper fortune hunter after their daughter, Swayne. In a few days, they lose their money and their new acquaintances. They return to their country home, where they soon discover a valuable coal deposit in their meadow. Once again they find themselves wealthy. Meanwhile, Swayne is reunited with her country boyfriend whom she had earlier left behind.

Charles Hutchison, content with his happy life in a small town, where he lives with his wife, Alma Hanlon, and little daughter, slowly becomes corrupted by greed in the drama, *The Golden God* (1917). When Al Stearn, a New York millionaire, offers Hutchison a job as his chauffeur, he accepts and soon discovers that most city people are obsessed with getting rich. When he finds his employer's wallet filled with money, he keeps it to speculate in the stock market. Attaining some financial success, he continues to speculate until he accumulates great wealth, all the while neglecting his family. His wife realizes what is happening to him and notices that he is not really happy. She persuades him to understand that true happiness does not stem from the accumulation of wealth alone, but from simpler, everyday pleasures.

J. Warren Kerrigan portrays the title character, a young man who has been doing what he wants – until his frustrated father finally abandons him, in Ernest C. Warde's interesting comedy drama, *Three X Gordon* (1918). Kerrigan and a pal end up on a farm, where they help to gather the hay. By the time the haying season is over, they have both changed as a result of the hard work and the responsibility. Kerrigan gets the idea for a business – using this experience of working close to the land in the great outdoors – to reform other rich sons who have been spoiled by city life, providing their parents are willing to pay for the conversion. His scheme succeeds, for he transforms several young men who "graduate" from his rural school – a happier and tougher lot. He even succeeds with the pampered and self-centered brother of Doris Wilson, his girlfriend. The youth at first refuses to participate in the experiment, so he has to be kidnapped. But in the end, even he comes around. The young men return to their surprised and delighted parents, who have all but given up on their wayward offspring.

A wife unexpectedly destroys her marriage when she makes the ultimate sacrifice for her husband in Kenean Buel's domestic drama, *Woman, Woman* (1919), based on the 1915 novel, *On Desert Altars*, by Norma Lorimer. Evelyn Nesbit, as the unfortunate wife, leaves her New England home and village for New York, where she rejects one suitor who believes only in "free love," for Clifford Bruce, a hard-working engineer. She next has to deal with her husband's employer, a millionaire, who propositions Nesbit, but she rejects his generous offer. The boss sends Bruce to the tropics, where he is stricken with fever. To raise money for his health, Nesbit goes to her husband's employer, sacrifices her honor and gets the necessary funds. Later, a child is born and the boss suspects it is his. When her husband sees the way his employer holds the child, he discovers the truth and turns his wife and the child out. He believes that nothing justifies a woman's sacrifice of her virtue. She returns with her child to New England, but the conservative citizens shun the divorced woman. Her husband, meanwhile, has second thoughts and visits her to reconcile their differences. "I made for you the greatest sacrifice a woman can make for a man," she reminds him, rejecting his offer, "and you failed to appreciate it." The millionaire proposes marriage, but she also refuses him.

II. Bright Lights in a Dark and Lonely City

Films of the twenties that contrasted country life with that of the city varied little in plot and theme from those of the earlier decades. The twenties were famous for the flappers, Prohibition, the rise of organized crime and a nation on a binge. Perhaps author Henry Miller's 1941 view of the city expresses that of the flappers' when he writes: "In New York I have always felt lonely, the loneliness of the caged animal, which brings on crime, sex, alcohol and other madnesses." To some extent, several films of the decade suggest Miller's depiction of city life. *Bright Lights* (1925) attacks the phony, flashy urban type for the sincerity of the country image. An innocent young woman is led astray in *Padlocked* (1926) by two typical city types, a lecherous reprobate and a seductress. The naïve sister of a streetwise "Follies" girl is seduced in *The Kid Sister* (1927). City vice and corruption prove too much for New Englander Pauline Starke in *Dance Magic* (1927). Conversely, Viola Dana opts for the love of her club manager and the city lights in *The Lure of the Nightclub* (1927), while rejecting her husband's traditional small-town values. Simultaneously, the twenties witnessed savage satirical attacks upon the ugliness and cultural barrenness of small town life by intellectual writers, including social critic H. L. Mencken and writer Sinclair Lewis in his novels *Main Street* (1920) and *Babbitt* (1922). Unfortunately, Hollywood produced two disappointing films of

Lewis's works. Harry Beaumont's *Main Street* (1923), about a country doctor who brings his city-bred bride to his hometown where she fails to effect changes among the indifferent inhabitants, proved tedious. Beaumont's second attempt in *Babbitt* (1924), about a successful small-town realtor and go-getter who grows bored with his family life, proved even more disastrous when it failed to capture the essence of its title character and the narrow-mindedness of the community.

Cabaret girl Pauline Starke returns to her New Jersey farm to help her mother and meets the refreshingly innocent Charles Ray in Robert Z. Leonard's charming romantic drama, *Bright Lights* (1925), based on a story by Richard Connell. Starke has finally met a young man she does not have to fear. Unfortunately, a misunderstanding sends her back to the bright lights of Broadway, with Ray following. Thinking she doesn't like his rural persona, he appears in the city overly dressed as a city slicker. This only annoys Starke more. When her friend tells him to be himself, the farm boy gets the hint and the couple are reunited.

Two cultures clash when cosmopolitan Pola Negri meets suspicious district attorney Holmes Herbert in Malcolm St. Clair's weak sophisticated drama, *A Woman of the World* (1925), based on the novel by Carl Van Vechten. Following a disastrous love affair abroad, countess Negri decides to visit her relatives in a small American Midwestern town. The local civic-minded citizens are in the midst of cleansing the community of its element of vice that has infiltrated the community. Herbert is leading this campaign. On her first night in town, the countess has an unpleasant confrontation with the district attorney, and she vows to win him over. After several confrontations between these two antagonists, the couple finally fall in love with each other. Meanwhile, the inhabitants look askance at their visitor's liberal lifestyle and attitudes, which contrast sharply with their own, more sedate and conservative ways.

An ambitious country girl leaves an unhappy home to journey to the big city to become a dancer in a cabaret in Allan Dwan's trite drama, *Padlocked* (1926), based on the story by Rex Beach. Lois Moran, the aspiring dancer, is the daughter of Noah Beery, an unsavory minister. The innocent young woman soon becomes the target of lascivious Charles Lane and procuress Louise Dresser, both of whom plot her moral ruin. Moran, not cognizant of the perils and temptations of a city, rushes headlong to her moral downfall before she is rescued in the nick of time by her boyfriend, Richard Arlen.

Marguerite De La Motte, a strong-willed "Follies" girl, bends slightly when her naïve younger sister gets into trouble in Ralph Graves's sexually oriented drama, *The Kid Sister* (1927), based on the story, "The Lost House," by Dorothy Howell. La Motte's kid sister arrives in the big city from her small town hoping to have a good time. She gets involved with a scheming young man who wants to seduce her. He takes her to a road house and, during a brawl, he begins to attack her. Meanwhile, the chorus girl discovers that her boyfriend, Malcolm MacGregor, a wealthy playboy, is posing as a theatrical stagehand to be closer to the young woman he loves. Annoyed at the deception, she breaks up with him. But when she learns her sister, Ann Christy, needs $5,000 for bail, she returns to MacGregor and takes him back if he will lend her the money. He agrees, and she bails out her sister, who has awakened to some of the realities of city life. MacGregor later takes La Motte to his home, leads her up a staircase to a bedroom – and introduces her to his mother.

Pauline Starke leaves her religious New England community and her stern father, who has forbidden her to dance, for a career in New York in Victor Halperin's social drama, *Dance Magic* (1927), based on the novel by Clarence Budington Kelland. Seeking a stage career, she meets a theatrical producer and Ben Lyon, a theatrical angel, who soon falls in love with her. The producer drops his mistress so that he can seduce Starke, whom he invites to his apartment. She finds him murdered and thinks Lyon did it. Lyon, thinking Starke committed the murder, confesses to the crime to protect the woman he loves. But the victim's mistress confesses to the crime and Lyon is released. Starke, meanwhile, disillusioned with city life, returns to her home in New England and her bigoted father. Lyon follows and asks her to marry him.

Successful Broadway entertainer Viola Dana gets time off to visit the scenes of her childhood and where she rekindles an old love in Thomas Buckingham's romantic drama, *The Lure of the Nightclub* (1927). During her visit, she meets Jack Daugherty, her former boyfriend. To Dana, he represents the older, traditional values she has missed during her stage career and agrees to marry him. Her club manager, Robert Ellis, releases her from her contract. She retires to Daugherty's farm, which is destroyed by a storm. Her manager, during a visit, agrees to rehire her temporarily so the couple could raise some money. But her husband, suspicious that his wife is carrying on an affair with Ellis, follows them to New York. Piqued by her husband's behavior, Dana decides to remain in the city, while her manager tries to reconcile the couple. Finally, Dana discovers that Ellis is the more deserving of the two men in her life.

A simple farmer is lured into a steamy romance by a visitor from the city in F. W. Murnau's powerful romantic drama, *Sunrise* (1927), based on the 1917 work by Hermann Sudermann. Margaret Livingston, the city-bred visitor, is attracted to George O'Brien, the hardworking farmer, who is married to Janet Gaynor. He soon finds himself mesmerized by the adventuress. She persuades him to kill his wife, sell his property and join her in the city. Unable to kill his wife, he rides into the city with her. Love suppresses her fears, and the couple rekindle their love for each other in a church. After spending a happy day together in an amusement park, the couple start for home. They are confronted by a terrible storm and are separated. Fishermen who were searching for her give up without success. O'Brien finds the temptress and begins to strangle her when news reaches him that his wife is safe. Returning at her bedside and caring for her, he watches the sunrise with uncommon joy.

Class Distinction

I. The Haves and Have-Nots: Two Worlds

More than one hundred years ago, English statesman Benjamin Disraeli compared the worlds of wealth and poverty: "Two nations between whom there is no intercourse, who are as ignorant of each other's habits, thoughts, and feelings, as if they were dwellers in different zones, or inhabitants of different planets. . . . The rich and the poor." Disraeli's insightful observation was especially true of the economic conditions in early twentieth century America. The nation's films of the first two decades reflected this contrast between the two classes. Society dramas and comedies emphasized the exclusive word of the wealthy, symbolized by opulent mansions, lush hotels and luxurious restaurants. Members of society could be distinguished by their fashionable attire. Conversely, social dramas about the poor usually depicted slum neighborhoods, dilapidated living quarters and poorly dressed children. Disraeli's comparison of the two distinct classes was certainly true of early twentieth century America, but the nation's films often suggested the possibility of a classless society with plots about individuals of one class becoming involved with those of another. The rich can sometimes treat those of a lower status very poorly, as the aunt demonstrates in *The Opened Shutters* (1914). On the other hand, they can also display gratitude, as Catherine Calhoon does to fisherman's daughter Muriel Ostriche in *A Daughter of the Sea* (1915), after the latter rescues Calhoon from the sea. Perhaps the quintessential blending of the classes occurs in *Sally in Our Alley* (1916), in which hardworking factory girl Muriel Ostriche wins the love of wealthy Carlyle Blackwell. Nothing is an impediment, Hollywood suggests – differences in education, resources and cultures mean very little when it comes to interests of the heart.

Anna Little, the orphaned daughter of a poor artist, has been ignored by her snobbish Boston relatives in Otis Turner's drama, *The Opened Shutters* (1914), based on the novel by Clara Louise Burnham. During a visit to Boston, she overhears her aunt complaining to young lawyer Herbert Rawlinson about the burden she is faced with because of her niece. Injured by the remark, Little refuses any assistance from these relatives. But the lawyer, Rawlinson, persuades her to accept help from a kindly judge. Later, a friend of her late mother invites her to spend the summer in Portland, where she meets socialite Betty Schade, Rawlinson's former fiancée. After some resentment against the wealthy Schade, the two young women become good friends. A reconciliation between Little and her relatives leads to their building a studio for Little to use for her art, and Schade volunteers to give her lessons.

Members of each of these classes get a chance to mingle as the result of a freak accident in Charles Seay's drama, *A Daughter of the Sea* (1915). Muriel Ostriche, as the coquettish title character, is the unrestrained daughter of a New England fisherman. She rescues Catherine Calhoon, a society woman, from a motorboat accident and, as a reward, is invited to spend some time in the grateful woman's home. Calhoon takes it upon herself to educate the girl, who soon falls in love with Clifford Gray, the hostess's son. His mother, always conscious of society's class distinctions, frowns upon the romance. When Clara Whipple, her daughter, becomes involved with a married man, who is later murdered, Ostriche confesses to the crime to save the daughter. Following several complications, all is resolved satisfactorily, and the mother, appreciative of her guest's sacrifice, grows fond of Ostriche.

Fay Wallace, a skeptical socialite who is disappointed in the men she has met in her social circle, bets that she can convert any man into a socially acceptable member of her set, in Theodore Marston's society comedy, *The Cave Man* (1915), based on the 1911 play by Gelett Burgess. Robert Edeson, a rugged coal laborer, is randomly selected as her guinea pig. Following a trip to a barber and a tailor, Edeson is tutored by Wallace in the social amenities, after which he is introduced to her acquaintances as a sociologist. Under her supervision, he soon emerges as a well-known figure. When one of her friends falls in love with him, Edeson realizes Wallace is just trifling with his affections. He also realizes he has fallen in love with Wallace. Inspired to prove his own worth, he invents a tool that brings him great wealth. Feeling he is now equal to the socialite, he holds her in his arms and the couple elope.

Roy Applegate's farfetched comedy drama, *All for a Girl* (1915), based on the 1908 play by Rupert Hughes, offers another film in which an honorable son is forced to take over his father's debts. Edward G. Longman is forced to quit college after his father is swindled in a stock deal and dies broke. When a friend, a married woman, suggests that Longman meet and date her wealthy niece, Renee Kelly, he agrees. But on second thought, the proud Longman feels the ploy is not honest and changes his mind. He then meets the young woman, whom he mistakes for Kelly's maid, and begins to enjoy her company. Later, he rescues her from an onrushing train. He gets a job paying twenty-five dollars a week, and proposes marriage. She accepts and then reveals her real identity and tells him about the wealth at her disposal. But he insists that they live on his salary. He soon becomes involved in a railroad transaction that makes him wealthy. Now he and his wife can live in luxury.

The mingling of members of two diverse classes turns to rivalry in Travers Vale's social drama, *Sally in Our Alley* (1916). A simple factory worker has to compete with a pretty socialite for the affections of a wealthy young man, when the worker's employer invites young Muriel Ostriche to her country estate to look after a group of slum children. The factory worker accepts and, once in the country, takes a romantic interest in wealthy Carlyle Blackwell, who is one of the house guests. However, another guest, the hostess's niece, angles aggressively to win the attention of Carlyle, a member of her social set. The desirable young man, who finds Ostriche attractive, ends up falling in love with the unpretentious factory worker.

Class differences can ignite hatred, especially when one party is overly contemptuous of the other, as in John W. Noble's social drama, *The Wall Between* (1916), based on the novel by Ralph D. Paine. John Davidson, an arrogant and snobbish army lieutenant, treats Francis X. Bushman, a sergeant, with disdain. The son of a banker who failed, Bushman, a college graduate, is forced to enlist in the army. He meets Beverly Bayne, the colonel's ward, and they both fall in love. Meanwhile, the lieutenant also harbors feelings for the young woman and resents Bushman's attentions toward her. The unit is sent to a Central American country to suppress a political uprising. During the fighting, class distinctions blur when Davidson proves he is a coward, while the sergeant, who saves the day and is awarded for his bravery, exhibits unusual heroism.

Members of the lower class meet and clash and reconcile their differences with those of the upper class in Edward Dillon's social drama, *A Daughter of the Poor* (1917). Bessie Love runs a little shop while her uncle, Max Davidson, works in the factory of Carl Stockdale, a noted publisher. Love accidentally meets Roy Stewart, Stockdale's son, while he is fixing his car. She assumes the young man, disheveled and dressed in overalls, is a worker. He, in turn, takes more than a casual interest in her and soon begins dating her. This relationship arouses the enmity of George Beranger, a radical worker and writer who also loves young Bessie. Following several incidents, Love meets the publisher, who befriends her and invites her to his home. Beranger, who mistrusts the intentions of the rich, arms himself and goes to the rich publisher's home to protect the woman he loves. But he finds nothing amiss. Instead, he learns that Stockdale has published his radical treatise and a check is waiting for him. The fanatical Beranger changes his opinion of the rich.

Kitty Gordon, as a mercenary young woman, forsakes the man she loves, and instead marries for money, in George Archainbaud's absurd romantic drama, *Diamonds and Pearls* (1917). Milton Sills, a young southerner who, after quarreling with his wealthy father, decides to make his own way in life. He meets Kitty Gordon, whose father is burdened with heavy debts. When he dies, his daughter, now penniless, refuses Sills's offer of marriage because he is poor. She travels north, meets a wealthy young man and marries him. Following several complications, Sills's parents also journey north and meet the young married couple, who are now in debt, partly because of the wife's extravagant lifestyle. Sills's parents decide to help her out financially. Soon, Sills is invited to his former girlfriend's home, where she realizes Sills is not of poor stock but rather from a wealthy family. Sills's father, meanwhile, has taken an unusual interest in the young wife, whose husband catches the elderly man making improper advances. A struggle ensues, and when Sills comes between the combatants, he is shot in the arm. Sills's father commits suicide. Sills and his widowed mother then leave the unhappy home.

William P. S. Earle's absorbing social drama, *His Own People* (1918), demonstrates that tensions between economic classes are universal. The film is set in Ireland and concerns the clashes between the gentry and shanty classes. Harry Morey, a rugged blacksmith, has loved Gladys Leslie since they were both young. William Dunn, the lord of a nearby estate, has invoked the anger of some of the local inhabitants because of his war against poachers. Betty Blythe, a wealthy woman visiting the lord, notices Morey and is physically attracted to him. She invites him to the lord's home. Meanwhile, young Leslie follows and looks through the window. Dunn, the lord, now drunk, sees her and drags her inside. When one of Dunn's servants shoots a poacher, the men in the vicinity rise up in anger. They storm the lord's estate, seeking revenge. Morey intervenes and holds the mob off, promising to turn over the guilty party to the law. He then turns to the lord and, finding Leslie in his room, proceeds to strangle Dunn. But she explains the situation to the irate blacksmith, who then takes her in his arms. Realizing they are in a strange world in which both do not belong, they leave the lord's splendid estate and return to their own world.

The clash between wealth and poverty is explored in E. Mason Hopper's slow-paced social drama, *The Answer* (1918). Joe King, who has been influenced politically by his socialist father, and Francis McDonald, his pal, settle in San Francisco, where they organize a refuge for workers. Claire Anderson, the daughter of one of the laborers, works as secretary for the refuge and falls in love with King. Later, socialite Alma Rubens takes an interest in the refuge's cause and volunteers her time to help out. King is suddenly called to England after his mother's death to settle the family estate. Once there, he learns why his parents split up. His father ended up resenting King's wealthy mother and her family, so he took his son and emigrated to America. But King, still loyal to helping his fellow men, decides to take his inheritance and pour it into the refuge. He sends for Anderson and they are married in the estate chapel. But his wife, in spite of her humble life and her now deceased father, begins to change and accepts her aristocratic status as mistress of the estate and ridicules her husband's idealistic views. As he starts back for the States, his friend, McDonald, arrives, observes the change in King's wife, and remains behind. Once King leaves, his friend kills King's wife and takes his own life. Back in San Francisco, King continues to run the refuge for the needy workers and falls in love with Rubens, the volunteer socialite.

A "golden wall" of money stands between wealthy Evelyn Greeley and impoverished marquis Carlyle Blackwell in Dell Henderson's romantic drama, *The Golden Wall* (1918). Blackwell leaves France for America, where he is hired by Greeley's father to oversee his estate. A wealthy young man courts Greeley and she accepts his offer of marriage, since she believes he is not after her money. Meanwhile, a drunken servant accidentally locks Greeley and Blackwell in an isolated tower, and she berates Blackwell, thinking he is behind the incident. He tells her he will never marry her unless she is as poor as he is or he as wealthy as she. Following several complications, Blackwell finds an opportunity to accumulate great wealth by speculating in oil fields and returns to the estate. He learn that Greeley's beau has been caught in a maid's bedroom and has been dismissed. She then becomes engaged to wealthy Blackwell.

A young woman, whose father has suddenly come into money, and her boyfriend from her old neighborhood, feel the sting of snobbery when they are rebuffed by upper society in J. W. McLaughlin's social drama, *Hell's End* (1918). Josie Sedgwick, thanks to her wealthy father, sheds her impoverished past once she is accepted by her new acquaintances, members of society. But unable to find an eligible young man of her liking among this set, she returns to her old haunts, where she renews her friendship with William Desmond. She helps him get a job at her father's factory and then wastes little time in introducing him to her new friends. But they reject Desmond and eventually shun young Sedgwick as well. Desmond soon begins to earn the respect of others, and he and Sedgwick fall in love. The couple, repudiating the same society that had earlier rejected them, decide instead to devote their spare time to helping out the less fortunate inhabitants of their old neighborhood.

Alice Joyce, a milliner who shares a New York tenement apartment with May Hopkins, meets millionaire's son Walter McGrail, and both overcome their social prejudices during their dating, in Tom Terriss's pleasant romantic drama, *Everybody's Girl* (1918), based on a story by O. Henry. The two milliners meet their prospective dates in parks and other public places. Joyce and McGrail meet by chance and go on boat rides from Manhattan to Coney Island. Although they have different views about poverty and wealth, they basically agree with each other on most issues. Eventually, he proposes and she accepts. The film offers a variety of interesting scenes of contemporary New York, especially of Brooklyn's Coney Island and beach.

Wealthy Edward J. Peel is infatuated with working girl Mildred Harris, but he is too shy to talk to her – until an incident at a beach brings them together, in Lois Weber and Phillips Smalley's bland social drama, *Borrowed Clothes* (1918). Harris was swimming with her date when the bathhouse catches fire. While her date looks for something to wear, Peel, who has followed her, offers Harris his car coat and a drive home. Instead, he takes her to his lush home, where she is in awe of his wealth and the food delicacies he offers her. Suddenly, his mistress, Helen Rosson, enters and immediately becomes jealous.

Peel sends her away, but before she leaves she warns Harris that he will do the same to her someday. He then drives Harris to her humble family home, leaving her to ponder over his wealth, his lifestyle and her decision to never marry poor. On their second date, he takes her to his place, where he subtly suggests that she become his mistress. At first she rejects his offer, but later accepts. Meanwhile, his mistress learns about Harris's presence and she notifies the police. While Harris tries on some of Rosson's gowns, she has second thoughts about Peel's offer and decides to leave through a window – just as the police enter. They find nothing and leave, and Harris returns to her own home, broken in spirit and disillusioned about romance. Peel telephones his mistress and admits that he has turned into a despicable scoundrel. Harris's father berates her for her actions, and her younger sister teasingly announces that Harris's boorish boyfriend has proposed to her. The passage of time heals feelings on both sides, and the apologetic Peel calls on Harris to make amends for the way he behaved.

Elsie Ferguson, as a wealthy young Englishwoman determined to find true love, takes up the life of a wandering gypsy, in Emile Chautard's romantic comedy, *Under the Greenwood Tree* (1918), based on the play by H. V. Esmond. Traveling only by a simple wagon, she is followed into the woods by several penniless suitors. When she puts them to work at various chores, they soon tire of this and leave. She decides to go swimming in a private lake, where she meets handsome Eugene O'Brien, whom she immediately likes. His feelings are mutual, and he jumps into the lake to join her. Love strikes both of them as they embrace. Later, some gypsies rob her valuables from her wagon and tie her up. O'Brien comes to her rescue, but he is knocked unconscious. After he recovers, she learns that the lake in on his estate. She decides to return to civilized life and marry O'Brien. The poor in this film, symbolized by the thieving or lazy gypsies, do not fare as well as the noble, heroic and generally naïve members of the wealthy class, represented by the two leads.

Upper-class snobbery almost ruins patrolman Tom Moore's happiness in Harry Beaumont's slow-paced drama, *One of the Finest* (1919). As a traffic cop, Moore meets Seena Owen, the daughter of a millionaire, and begins dating her. Her father frowns upon the relationship because of the officer's lower social standing, but when he learns that Moore has been studying nights to pass his law examination, his attitude quickly changes and the policeman is accepted as part of the family. Meanwhile, a weak plot concerning a convict who is seeking to kill Moore for a past incident slowly unfolds.

To survive in a hostile environment, shipwrecked aristocrats are forced to take orders from their more knowledgeable butler, in Cecil B. DeMille's social comedy, *Male and Female* (1919), based on the play, *The Admirable Crichton*, by J. M. Barrie. The men and women, masters and mistresses in their own world of upper-class society, are completely inept at surviving on a primitive island, so they reluctantly yield to their butler, Crichton, played by Thomas Meighan. Once they are rescued, they all revert to their original social positions. DeMille has tampered with Barrie's play by changing the title with more sex appeal; adding an all-star cast (Gloria Swanson, Lila Lee, Theodore Roberts, Raymond Hatton, Bebe Daniels); inserting a sequence concerning a king and slave girl in ancient Babylon, with the latter being tossed into an arena filled with lions; and Gloria Swanson in a suggestively sensational bathing scene. The Babylon sequence is introduced when Meighan, as the butler, quotes to wealthy Swanson from Henley's poem: "I was a king in Babylon and you were a Christian slave." Thanks to DeMille's flare for the spectacular and his erotic visions, the quirky film became the biggest box-office hit of the year.

A young woman who yearns to be a member of high society learns a hard lesson after getting her wish in W. Christy Cabanne's social drama, *The Triflers* (1919). Edith Roberts portrays the woman who finally enters the "fast set," but pays a terrible price for admission. After spending an entire weekend at a house party filled with socialites, playboys and other members of this frivolous group, she decides to return to her own social class. Although she comes from more humble origins than her new acquaintances, she is convinced that her own kind are more honest and generally live within their own means.

Bessie Barriscale, the adopted daughter of a Canadian farmer, is sent to boarding school, where she meets and marries Niles Welch, the son of a wealthy businessman, in Howard Hickman's drama, *Beckoning Roads* (1919), based on the 1919 novel, *The Call to Life*, by Jeanne Judson. After being treated as a servant by her in-laws, the young wife leaves her husband's family home and returns to her farm. Here she learns that her stepfather has committed suicide after losing all his money in a fraudulent stock deal manipulated by Hickman's father. Barriscale leaves for New York, where she works as secretary to Joseph J. Dowling, who together with Hickman's father, swindled her stepfather. She manages to bring the two men to financial ruin. When her husband disavows his father, the couple reconcile their differences.

II. The Myth of Classlessness

American journalist H. L. Mencken wrote in 1920 that "one may no more live in the world without picking up the moral prejudices of the world than one will be able to go to hell without perspiring." Mencken, known for his acerbic wit, knew the 1920s well and frequently commented on the class distinctions of the decade. Some of the films of the period broke through their escapist mold that tried to sell the myth that America was a classless society. They offered their own perceptive insights about class prejudices. In *Slaves of Pride* (1920), for example, a rich man is obsessed with his wealth, and in *The Loves of Letty*, released the same year, a young woman finds flaws in her suitors, regardless of their social backgrounds. Driven by her social prejudices, a wealthy mother-in-law in *Marriage License* (1926) cannot accept her son's marriage to commoner Alma Rubens, even when the latter presents her with a grandchild. Several of these films treated their themes very lightly, as in *Rich Men's Sons* (1927).

Ralph Graves, the idle son of a railroad magnate, blackmails his father with a photograph of the latter with a sexy blonde – a ploy Graves uses to avoid working on the railroad. Invariably, all the major characters in these films are forced to come to terms with their own moral class prejudices. *The Prince of Avenue A* (1920) points out the awkwardness of a relationship between a wealthy young socialite and a rough prizefighter, the son of a ward boss, played by real-life fighter James J. Corbett. Even at a social gathering in honor or the girl's father, Corbett gets into a fight with another man who is annoying the socialite. On the other hand, films that tried to surmount class differences often appeared contrived and artificial, as in *Forbidden Fruit* (1921), in which humble seamstress Agnes Ayres, tied to a drunken lout of a husband, meets and falls in love with millionaire Forrest Stanley, who takes her out of her misery. Hollywood continues to make these fantasies, regardless of cultural critics like Benjamin DeMott, whose 1990 book, *The Imperial Middle: Why Americans Can't Think Straight About Class*, tries to expose the American "myth of classlessness."

An ambitious young social climber snares a wealthy young man for herself, but her marriage suffers because he heedlessly takes his wealth and social standing too seriously in George W. Terwilliger's flawed social drama, *Slaves of Pride* (1920). Alice Joyce, as the young wife, sees her husband, Percy Marmont, falling under the malevolent influence of his general manager, who taunts Joyce, causes friction between the couple and then tries to steal the wife for his own licentious purposes. She tries to awaken her husband to what is happening, but he ignores her. Finally, only when he loses all his money does his distraught wife return to him.

Pauline Frederick, a young woman who must earn her own living, meets a wealthy young man and falls in love with him in Frank Lloyd's social drama, *The Loves of Letty* (1920), based on the play by Arthur Wing Pinero. But it happens the young man, John Bower, has a wife who will not divorce him. Her boss, wealthy but coarse and common, takes a romantic interest in her and proposes. Since he is from the same social class, she agrees, but on the day of the wedding, she cops out and runs off with another suitor. However, another concerned gentleman who is rather shy, and who really loves her, decides to bring her back.

Famous prizefighter James J. Corbett portrays the son of a ward boss who falls in love with the daughter of a mayoral candidate in John Ford's political comedy, *The Prince of Avenue A* (1920). When the wealthy candidate invite Corbett's father, who is supporting him, to a party, he brings his son. Corbett meets Cora Drew, the host's pretty daughter, but they don't get along too well. Corbett's rough ways, including dancing with a maid he knows from his old neighborhood, gets him evicted from the festivities. To make amends for his son, the ward boss arranges another party for the candidate and asks him to bring his daughter, who will lead the grand political march, along with his son. At this affair, Corbett apologizes to her and they become friends. Later, when a tough bully from the first party starts annoying Drew, Corbett steps in and an all-out fight ensues between the two men, with the bully getting beaten up.

Agnes Ayres, a humble seamstress in a wealthy home, is chosen by her mistress to be the dinner partner of a wealthy oil millionaire, an incident that introduces her to the temptations of luxury, in Cecil B. DeMille's social drama, *Forbidden Fruit* (1921), based on the play by Jeanie Macpherson. Ayres, burdened with Clarence Burton, her worthless husband, accepts the invitation and meets oil magnate Forrest Stanley, who is attracted to the seamstress. But she rejects his advances and returns to her rundown apartment and her drunken husband, who relieves her of her salary. Her employer, Kathlyn Williams, invites her for the weekend to keep the millionaire company. That night, a crooked butler in collusion with Burton, Ayres's husband, plots to rob the jewels of one of the guests. The husband is caught by Stanley, who disarms him. When the hostess discovers Burton's relationship to Ayres, she dismisses her and sends her home. The two crooks then plot to blackmail the millionaire by luring him to Ayres's apartment, where the husband demands $10,000 to keep quiet. Stanley pays him and leaves, announcing he will return to take the wife away. A fight ensues between the butler and Burton, with the former killing the husband. Stanley returns, overpowers the butler and rescues Ayres from her nightmarish existence.

Broadway dancer Anna Q. Nilsson turns down her dancing partner Earle Foxe's proposal and marries wealthy Freeman Wood instead, in Edward J. Le Saint's social drama, *Innocence* (1923), based on the story, "Circumstances Alter Divorce Case," by Lewis Allen Browne. However, Wood's conservative family, who resent having a "theater person" in the family, are against the marriage. After the honeymoon, Wood displays a semblance of jealousy when he sees his wife dancing with Foxe at a nightclub party for the newly wed couple. Later that evening, Foxe is arrested for stealing a diamond necklace. He is found guilty and sent to prison. Nilsson believes he is innocent and offers to help him, thereby raising more suspicion in her husband. Foxe escapes and seeks refuge in Nilsson's bedroom, where Wood finds him. Although he still loves his wife, he decides to divorce her. But she soon proves Foxe's innocence as well as her own, and the couple are reunited.

Priscilla Dean and her cruel father, both laborers in the English coal mines of the 1870s, clash with supervisor Robert Ellis, in Hobart Henley's drama, *The Flame of Life* (1923), based on the 1877 novel, *That Lass o' Lowrie's*. The idealistic and sympathetic Ellis tries to improve working conditions for the miners. Dean's father (Wallace Beery) is fired when Ellis catches him smoking in the mine. Beery, angry at Ellis, starts a fight with him but loses to the supervisor. Defiantly, he again begins to smoke in the tunnel, but this time an explosion occurs. Dean rescues Ellis, resulting in a romance between the two, regardless of class differences.

Gloria Swanson portrays a French music hall soubrette who falls in love with a diplomat in Allan Dwan's romantic drama, *Zaza* (1923), based on the play by

Pierre Francois, Samuel Berton and Charles Simon. At first, she believes he is not married, but when she learns the truth about H. B. Warner, the French diplomat, from Mary Thurman, a jealous fellow entertainer, she releases Warner from his obligations, although he promises to divorce his wife. Years later, the lovers are reunited after his wife dies.

Pilot Conrad Nagel, while seeking shelter during a storm, meets Alma Rubens in Canada before returning home to the States, in Albert Parker's society drama, *The Rejected Woman* (1924). On his return, Nagel learns that his father has died. Meanwhile, Rubens arrives in New York and begins to see Nagel socially, but his friends are critical of her unsophisticated clothing and manners. Nagel's business manager, Wyndham Standing, offers the young Canadian financial help, which she readily accepts. When her father intercedes, Nagel marries Rubens. But when he learns about her arrangement with Standing, he renounces her willingness to accept his offer. However, the couple soon reconcile their differences.

Walter McGrail, the high-born heir to a British title, returns home with Alma Rubens, his lower-class bride, to his strong-willed and race-proud mother, in Frank Borzage's dignified domestic drama, *Marriage License* (1926), based on the play, *The Pelican*, by F. Tennyson Jessie. Although the young wife is about to present her mother-in-law with a grandchild, this does not deter McGrail's resentful and socially prejudiced mother from her efforts to break up the marriage. She successfully manipulates a divorce based on contrived evidence to disown the young son. Years later, the boy has matured in France, where Rubens, his suffering mother, falls in love with another man. Just as she is about to find her long-deserved happiness with a new mate, her former husband arrives in an effort to convince her and their son to return with him to their stately home. Torn between her love for her son and his future and her own love for the man she is about to marry, she opts to return to England, where her son can claim his noble name and title.

Ralph Graves's slow-paced drama, *Rich Men's Sons* (1927), portrays several wealthy youngsters as lazy and manipulative of their parents, but nevertheless capable of succeeding on their own. Ralph Graves, as one of these idlers, angers his father, a railroad magnate, who wants his son to work in the family's railroad business. His son rejects his father's demands and finally proves his individual worth. Graves meets Shirley Mason, the daughter of an ironworks owner who becomes ill. His daughter takes over the operations of the business and hires the willing Graves to help out. He wins a contract from his father and gets to romance his pretty boss. The plot, filled with familiar stereotypes, has an exciting race between a car driven by the hero and a speeding express train.

Courtroom

I. Order in the Court

Early courtroom films seemed to flout more laws than those committed by the defendants portrayed in these films. A judge at a murder trial justifies the killing of his own son in *Fires of Conscience* (1916). A jury disregards all evidence and is swayed by the pleas of the defendant's mother in *The Old Folks at Home* (1916). A district attorney prosecutes his own son for murder in *The Weaker Sex* (1916). And in *The Last Sentence* (1917), a judge presides over the trial of his own daughter, who is accused of murdering her baby. With such contrived and implausible scenarios, it is surprising that courtroom dramas survived and reached such heights of popularity during the silent era and beyond. Their successes could probably be attributed to several factors. The films required low production costs, since most of the sequences were shot on studio sets. Another reason for their popularity was the familiarity of their original sources. *The Old Folks at Home* (1916) was based on the story by Robert Hughes. *The Last Sentence* (1917) was adapted from the novel by Maxwell Gray. *The Caillaux Case* (1918), set during World War I, was based on an actual contemporary trial. These films already carried with them a large, built-in potential movie audience. A third factor for their success was the tremendous drawing power of such screen stars as Blanche Sweet, Mae Murray, Dorothy Gish, Charles Ray, William Farnum and Belle Bennett. In addition, audiences found in these films a certain morbid, fascinating and voyeuristic interest that allowed them to enter the dark, private, often romantic, sometimes sleazy, worlds of innocent and guilty men and women caught in a web of evil not always of their own making.

D. W. Griffith portrays a court officer in *Falsely Accused* (1908), one of the earliest courtroom dramas. Several sources credit legendary cameraman G. W. Bitzer, who had worked with Griffith for years as his cameraman, as the director. Griffith was certainly ahead of his time in showing how technology can be used in courtroom cases. For example, in one courtroom sequence, a sheet is placed on the wall and used as a movie screen so that evidence concerning a murder trial can be shown to the judge and jury.

An incident in a young stenographer's life returns to haunt her years later in the domestic drama, *The Only Way Out* (1915). A man induces the young woman to accompany him to a hotel where he expects a minister to arrive to marry them. When she gets there, she realizes his true intentions and escapes. Years later she marries a wealthy businessman. The man who had earlier tried to ruin her appears and threatens to tell her husband about the past, so she introduces him as a former acquaintance. Her husband offers him a job, but the man turns out to be dishonest. He is later found dead in his apartment. The husband is suspected of foul play, and in a dramatic courtroom scene, he admits to killing the interloper. The dead man, he explains, had been threatening his wife and causing her anguish.

Allegedly based on a celebrated 1915 courtroom case, Frank Reicher's murder drama, *Public Opinion* (1916) exposes the evils of yellow journalism, whose practitioners sometimes condemn a defendant before he or she is tried. Blanche Sweet, the principal player, became a popular screen personality during this period. Reicher, the director, continued in films into the early sound era, during which time he appeared as a character actor in such films as *King Kong* (1933).

William Farnum portrays a husband who shoots and kills a man whom he finds visiting his wife in Oscar Apfel's slow-paced domestic drama, *Fires of Conscience* (1916). The deceased's father is a judge and friend of Farnum's father. Farnum, instead of going to trial, flees to the West, where he meets Gladys Brockwell, who persuades him to return and stand trial. The presiding judge is the victim's father. He announces that he was a witness to the tragedy and orders an acquittal based on the "unwritten law" of custom and public opinion. Farnum, now free, returns to Brockwell, the young woman he had met on his journey west. The major flaw in the film, of course, concerns the judge. Normally, he would have excused himself from serving in a case in which he was so personally involved.

A state senator tries to protect his undisciplined son, accused of murder, from the death sentence, in Chester Withey's absorbing drama, *The Old Folks at Home* (1916), based on the story by Robert Hughes. For the sake of the boy's mother, the father, Sir Herbert Beerbohm Tree, tries to shield his son, Elmer Clifton, from facing the electric chair. The young man, after associating with a group of disreputable acquaintances, kills his mistress's lover after the man strikes the youth. At the trial, the damaging evidence and the hostile witnesses virtually condemn the defendant. The mother, Josephine Crowell, rises from the stand and simply pleads to the jury, "I want my boy." The jury returns with a "not guilty" verdict. A final title explains that the verdict may not be legal, but who can refuse the simple tears and pleas of an aged mother? Famous English actor-manager Sir Herbert Beerbohm Tree (1853-1917), scheduled to appear in three American films for Triangle, walked out on the movie studio after completing this film. He made his English stage debut in 1876. Clifton, who portrayed the defendant, became a prolific film director, particularly of action dramas, during the silent era.

A feud between two families erupts when Dorothy Gish, the daughter of one clan, refuses to marry someone chosen for her, in Joseph Henabery's routine rural drama, *Children of the Feud* (1916). Instead, she loves Sam De Grasse, a local doctor and the son of a judge. The rejected suitor, determined to shoot the doctor, instead kills the sheriff by mistake. A murderer is arrested and tried for his crime. The sheriff happened to be a member of a rival clan, so when the defendant's clan arrives at the courthouse, a small war breaks out between the rival clans, with plenty of gunfire and smoke. The doctor finally recaptures the killer. In most cases, feuds occur in isolated areas, where legal means of redress of grievances are either not available or are deemed inadequate by the affected groups. Family feuds are, however, still known in such areas as the mountain regions of the southeastern U.S. The long-standing and bloody feud that broke out in the latter part of the 19th century between the Hatfield and McCoy families of Kentucky and West Virginia is famous in American history and folklore and became the subject of several films, including one released during the sound era.

Criminal lawyer Frank Keenan, who is busy leading a reckless life of womanizing and drinking, is called upon to defend a young stenographer who has killed a lecherous boss after he tried to attack her, in Walter Edwards's forceful courtroom drama, *The Sin Ye Do* (1916). Years earlier, Keenan's wife left him when he proved unfaithful. She then gave birth to a girl, but never told the father. Now Keenan, whose friend was the victim of the shooting, offers the prosecutor his assistance, believing strongly that such young women as the stenographer often provoke their bosses. He suddenly gets a phone call from his wife, asking him to defend the girl, revealing she is his own daughter. Meanwhile, Keenan has been having an affair with a married woman whose husband catches him in the act. When he threatens to kill the lawyer, Keenan makes a deal with the irate husband. After he defends his daughter, he will return for his punishment. The man agrees. In the courtroom, Keenan discloses his entire life, including how he wronged his wife and daughter, and concludes defending the latter's killing of such evil men as her employer. His daughter is acquitted, and his wife forgives him. He then reports to the husband whom he has wronged. "Three people have a claim on your life," the man says, "your wife, your daughter and myself. They win. Go home."

Dorothy Dalton portrays a famous lawyer who marries the district attorney, Charles K. French, who soon has to prosecute his own son for murder, in Raymond B. West's poignant drama, *The Weaker Sex* (1916). The unruly son, Charles Ray, becomes romantically involved with Louise Glaum, a cabaret queen and Oriental dancer, who loves Ray. When he tries to end the affair, she says she'd rather see him dead than in the arms of another woman. Her "protector" enters the room, and in the darkness, shots ring out. Glaum is dead, and Ray is arrested and tried for murder. Facing a death sentence, Ray is being prosecuted by his own father. But his stepmother, Dalton, finally proves that the victim's protector is the murderer, and Ray is set free.

Dorothy Donnelly portrays Jacqueline Floriot, wife of a famous French attorney, in George Marion's drama, *Madam X* (1916), based on the play by Alexandre Bisson, and one of the earliest of many productions under this title. The story opens with Louis Floriot who, after suspecting his wife of infidelity, drives her to a life of degradation in the streets. After twenty years of prostitution and drunken global wandering, she returns to France in a sorry state, a victim of drugs and desperation. When she is recognized by the blackmailer Edwin Fosberg, she rightfully fears he will expose her to her son, now a promising young attorney. To protect her son, she murders Fosberg and is arraigned as Madam X when she refuses to reveal her identity. In an ironic twist of fate, her lost son defends her in court and wins an acquittal – all the time unaware of his relationship to her. Fittingly, the drama ends with the mother's dying reconciliation with her family. The film was remade in 1920, 1929, and again in 1966.

A man who marries beneath his class soon abandons his wife and child, leaving his family to be brought up in humble circumstances, in Ben Turbett's threadbare drama, *The Last Sentence* (1917), based on the novel by Maxwell Gray. The child, when grown to young womanhood, works as a domestic servant. Her master's son sexually attacks her and a child is born. She is then charged with killing the child, based on circumstantial evidence. Once in court, she is brought before the judge – her own father – and found guilty. Shortly afterward, the baby is located and the mother is saved from the electric chair. She is cleared of all charges and marries the man who had ruined her.

A judge, who has not seen or lived with his wife for many years, is called upon to sentence his own son, in Harley Knoles's fast-paced western drama, *The Price of Pride* (1917). However, he sentences the wrong son – David, instead of the outlaw William. After suspending the sentence, he learns that the crime was committed by his younger son and a woman he had had an affair with but had never married. A subplot explains how the judge's wife had left him and their child to marry a gambler out west. She later meets her son William, now grown up and in the role of a train robber. Carlyle Blackwell plays the dual role, that of two brothers – William, a worthless outlaw, and David, who is mistaken for William and is arrested. William is accidentally mortally wounded, and on his deathbed he exonerates his brother David. David and his parents are finally reunited.

Mellbourne McDowell, a stern judge who administers the law without sentiment, argues with his younger brother and, during an altercation, strikes him with a decanter, in Jack Conway's chiefly implausible drama, *The Bond of Fear* (1917). Thinking he killed his brother, the judge flees to the West. While he and his guide, Roy Stewart, are crossing a desert, they find Belle Bennett, an exhausted woman, whom they take to an abandoned prospector's cabin until her health returns. When the judge is overcome by the heat, she helps him to recover. After he regains his health, he asks her if he has revealed anything while he was ill. She tells him she knows everything, and then admits that she, too, is a fugitive from the law. When they arrive in a small town and prepare to get married, he reads an old paper that says his brother is still alive. Now that he is no longer a wanted man, he marches off to Bennett and says it is his duty to turn her over to the sheriff, since she is a fugitive. But the guide helps her to escape into the desert. She then confesses to Stewart she only made up the story about her past to comfort the judge. Back in town, the judge learns that in a more up-to-date paper that his brother had died from the judge's blow. Once again a fugitive, the judge wanders off and is killed in a landslide. Bennett ends up in Stewart's arms.

Wealthy artist Antonio Moreno is on trial for murder in Paul Scardon's conventional drama, *Her Right to Live* (1917). Peggy Hyland and her brother and sisters are treated badly by their uncle, a corrupt politician. After living with him for a while following their mother's death, they decide to flee to a poor house and then to a cabin in the woods, owned by Antonio Moreno. His father is running for mayor against their uncle. The mayor murders a ward boss using Moreno's cane, thereby framing the son of his rival. Moreno is arrested and charged with the crime. Just as all the evidence points to Moreno's guilt, Hyland, who has escaped capture by climbing out of a window, dashes into the courtroom. She gives dramatic evidence that frees Moreno and eventually leads to the arrest of the guilty mayor.

Jean Sothern, a young country girl, to protect her father, confesses to a murder in George Terwilliger's hackneyed drama, *Her Good Name* (1917), another film that invokes the "unwritten law," that which is based on custom or tradition. Sothern meets a young artist from the city and immediately becomes infatuated with him. Meanwhile, a young local country boy takes her for a drive in the country and tries to kiss her. After keeping her out all night, he finally drives her home. Her irate father, William H. Turner, who had been drinking rather heavily, concludes that the country lad had ruined his daughter and shoots him. To save her father's life, the daughter takes the stand and maintains she had told her father the boy had raped her. The defendant intervenes, refusing to allow his daughter to perjure herself and confesses to the shooting. He then collapses and dies of a weak heart. His daughter then weds the young artist.

Mae Murray, fresh from the country, comes to the city to work, and is arrested by an overly eager detective on some vague charge, in Robert Z. Leonard's convoluted drama, *On Record* (1917). She escapes his custody, but she leaves behind a photograph and her fingerprints. Later, while she is engaged to Tom Forman, an inventor, his rival, Charles Ogle, makes trouble for the inventor. Following a series of complications, the couple, Ogle, and the latter's lawyer go to night court, where Ogle raises the issue of Murray's criminal record to the judge. The judge listens to the entire story and ends up destroying the set of fingerprints and the photographs, and orders Ogle and his lawyer out of his court. Murray is relieved that she no longer has to be burdened by the phony criminal record that had been haunting her.

Based on an actual sensational contemporary French trial involving spies and traitors, Richard Stanton's drama, *The Caillaux Case* (1918), is set during World War I and presents the incidents and courtroom scenes in semi-documentary style. Joseph Caillaux, the French minister of finance, and Henriette, marry after both get divorces from their spouses. Caillaux advances to premier and plots a conspiracy with Bolo Pasha to have the French and Germans join forces. An editor discovers the plot but is killed by the premier's wife before he can print the story. Henriette is acquitted. But when new evidence comes to light, Pasha is executed and the premier is charged with treason and imprisoned. At the time of the film's release, the French courts had already sentenced some of the traitors, while others were awaiting final judgment. Newspaper accounts of the trial described the rage of the French public toward the defendants. At the end of the war, when passions had cooled, Caillaux was pardoned, has his rights restored and was elected to the Senate.

II. Adaptations and Flashbacks

Courtroom dramas of the twenties relied heavily on adaptations of stories and plays. For instance, *The Woman God Changed* and *The Girl on the* Stairs were based on published stories. *The Witching Hour* was based on an old play by Augustus Thomas, and *The Woman on Trial* also came from a stage play. There were fewer overly sentimental, old-fashioned dramas. These were replaced by more complex psychological stories. Many were developed by way of flashbacks, with the defendant taking the stand, as in *The Woman on Trial*, where the defendant relates her heart-rending tale of misfortune to a sympathetic jury (and audience). Several dramas continued the ploy of the last-minute rescue by a witness. For example, in *The Miracle of Manhattan*, a witness, bedridden for a length of time, finally learns about a trial and rushes into the courtroom to testify in behalf of the defendant. Also, several dramas reverted to the innocent suspect falsely accused of murder, as in *A Million for Love*. The courtroom drama even ventured into other popular genres, such as the crime drama (*The City Gone Wild*) and the western (*Cyclone Kelly*). Headlines of sensational murder trials during the twenties, such as the Reverend Hall-Mrs. Eleanor Mills case (1922) and the Albert Snyder-Judd Gray trial (1926), no doubt inspired many melodramatic scripts. Reverend Hall and Mrs. Mills were found murdered outside New Brunswick, New Jersey, and a grand jury had made no indictment. But four years later a tabloid newspaper had the case reopened. Mrs. Hall and her two brothers were quickly arrested. In the second case, art editor Albert Snyder was murdered by his wife and her corset-salesman lover, Judd Gray. Both stories received exceptional coverage by the press. But whatever the shape, structure or source, these films often proved suspenseful, exciting and, most of all, entertaining.

Russian dancer Mae Murray flirts with David Powell, a millionaire's secretary, and marries him in George Fitzmaurice's romantic drama, *On With the Dance* (1920), based on the 1917 play by Michael Morton. Unfortunately, the flirtation interferes with Powell's true romance, leading to confusion among the individuals, comprising two couples. Following a string of complications, including some torrid lovemaking and Powell's murder of his wife's lover, the shooting ends in a trial. The dancer, to save her husband from a charge of murder, confesses openly to her own shameless actions which resulted in the accidental shooting. Her husband is exonerated and free to marry Alma Tell, while Murray marries an old friend of her husband – to the satisfaction of all the participants.

John Bowers, who is sent on a lengthy business trip by his boss, Robert McKim, suspects his motives after noticing his attentions to Bowers' wife, in Frank Lloyd's mystery, *The Woman in Room 13* (1920), based on the 1919 play by Samuel Shipman, Max Marcin and Percival Wilde. Bowers, who has hired a detective to keep an eye on his wife, Pauline Frederick, returns suddenly and goes to McKim's home, where a dinner party is going on. Using a Dictaphone, he overhears an amorous conversation in Room 13. Thinking the voice is that of his wife, he races upstairs and shoots his boss. On trial for killing McKim, Bowers is saved by his wife's testimony. She states that her husband was protecting her from McKim, who was about to attack her. Later, another woman, a former lover of McKim, reveals to Bowers that she was the woman in Room 13. The married couple now reconcile their differences.

Young socialite Elaine Hammerstein tries to prove her independence but ends up entangled in a killing in George Archainbaud's drama, *The Miracle of Manhattan* (1921). After failing at several jobs, she succeeds as a café singer, where she meets and falls in love with former gangster Matt Moore. However, a jealous rival assails her physically, and Moore, to protect the life of the innocent young woman, is forced to shoot the attacker. Hammerstein, emotionally shaken by the incident, escapes to her home and falls ill. When she recovers slightly and learns that Moore is on trial for his life, she rushes to the courtroom in time to exonerate him.

Robert G. Vignola's courtroom murder drama, *The Woman God Changed* (1921), based on the story, "Changeling," by Brian Oswald Donn-Byrne, unfolds chiefly in flashback. Seena Owen is on trial for murdering a playboy who had taken advantage of her and then abandoned her for another woman. Several witnesses testify, but the most important testimony is that of detective E. K. Lincoln, who tracks down the escaping murderess in Tahiti. A successful professional dancer before she met the playboy, Owen is seen performing in a Tahiti dance hall. The detective captures her and, while bringing her back to the States to stand trial, the ship is sunk. The pair become castaways of a desert island, where they undergo a series of adventures that end in Owen's regeneration. The peace and contentment she finds on the island influence her spiritually. Meanwhile, the couple fall in love. The jury, moved by the detective's tale, asks for mercy, and the court decrees that the detective marry her. This drama of redemption was remade as *Her Captive Woman* in 1929, with Milton Sills and Dorothy Mackaill in the principal roles. The later version exploited the more relaxed morality of the period and included a scene in which Mackaill apparently disrobes in front of Sills before she goes swimming.

Ed Sutherland, a neurotic young man who is ridiculed to the point of delirium, kills the man who has been taunting him in William Desmond Taylor's drama, *The Witching Hour* (1921), based on the 1907 play by Augustus Thomas. The incident took place at a party for Elliott Dexter, a gambling house operator. The young man is tried and sentenced to death. Dexter, an expert at mental telepathy, proves during a second trial that Sutherland, at the time of the shooting, was under the influence of menacing lawyer Robert Cain. The lawyer tries to shoot the gambler during the trial, but the latter's sheer psychic power prevents Cain's trigger finger from firing the gun. The defendant is finally acquitted. Several film versions of the play were made, one in 1916, with C. Aubrey Smith, and a sound version in 1934. Sutherland, the actor, later became a successful comedy director at Paramount. One year later, director Taylor's own shocking murder became the subject of national newspaper stories.

Patsy Ruth Miller portrays an innocent young woman accused of murdering a philandering husband in William Worthington's mystery drama, *The Girl on the Stairs* (1924), based on the story by Winston Bouve. Having earlier had an affair with the deceased before she learns about his marital status, she begs to have her love letters returned. The wife, after discovering her husband's body, reveals this meeting to the police. Meanwhile, a lawyer friend of the accused remembers that Miller has a sleep-walking affliction. In court, a doctor hypnotizes her and she describes the murder, including the presence of a South American who, after finding his wife with the philanderer, kills him. The foreigner who is in the courtroom confesses to the crime.

The courtroom drama occasionally adapted to other genres, such as in Alvin J. Neitz's western, *Cyclone Kelly* (1924). Another in a long line of westerns about the hero falsely accused of murder, this entry, which conforms to the familiar pattern, features Buddy Roosevelt, who must prove his innocence. He escapes from the courtroom, captures the outlaw gang trying to drive his boss out of the cattle business and brings its leader to justice.

Victor Varconi portrays a cigar-stand owner whose wife, Phyllis Haver, is accused of murdering her secret lover, an automobile salesman, in Frank Urson's routine drama, *Chicago* (1927), based on the 1927 play by Maurine Watkins. To help pay the high fee for her defense, Varconi steals a large sum of money from his unscrupulous lawyer, Robert Edeson. The lawyer had promised the desperate husband that for the right amount of money, he could get Haver acquitted. After she is freed following a highly publicized trial, the couple return home only to find two detectives waiting for them. They accuse him of stealing money from the lawyer's safe, but his maid, Virginia Bradford, had earlier removed the cash. When they fail to retrieve the stolen money they leave. Varconi then declares he is through with his unfaithful wife, who is enjoying the notorious publicity she has been receiving from reporters as a result of her trial. He evicts her from the house after demonstrating a terrible rage against her. He finally settles down and finds peace with his loyal maid.

Edward Laemmle's drama, *The Thirteenth Juror* (1927), is based on the play, *Counsel for the Defense,* by Henry Irving Dodge. Veteran actor Francis X. Bushman, as an unscrupulous lawyer, is informed that Quinn, a messenger sent by the district attorney, who is seeking to destroy Bushman, has accused him of having an affair with the wife of his best friend, Marsden. Bushman kills Quinn, and his friend is blamed. Hoping to win Marsden's wife, whom he secretly loves, Bushman refuses to defend him. But when Marsden is found guilty, the lawyer finally confesses and is released after he pleads self-defense. Dodge's play has been filmed several times.

Suspiciously similar in its crime elements – especially gang wars – to the highly successful *Underworld*, released earlier the same year, James Cruze's drama, *The City Gone Wild* (1927), focuses on Thomas Meighan, a clever criminal lawyer. Using legal trickery, he is able to get his crooked clientele off. Early in the film, some of his clients are involved in a violent gang war, and Meighan manages to effect a truce between the rival factions. His friend is Wyndham Standing, the district attorney, although both are rivals in the courtroom. They also compete for the affection of pretty heroine Marietta Millner. She is aware that her father, a powerful businessman, happens to be the mastermind behind the major crime ring in the city. When Standing discovers the leader's identity and other facts about the gangs, he is murdered. His friend, Meighan, decides to avenge his death and takes over his title. The concept of the lawyer being in collusion with gangsters, a familiar ploy in silent and sound films, was used effectively in *The Thirteenth Juror*, released the same year.

Pola Negri portrays the title character, a woman being tried for murdering a man who was paid to compromise her, in Mauritz Stiller's sentimental drama, *The Woman on Trial* (1927), based on the play, *Confession*, by Ernest Vajda. The film opens in a courtroom, then fades to a flashback of Negri's testimony. In Paris, she loves a poor artist, Einar Hanson, whose ill health demands that he leave Paris. Negri marries millionaire Arnold Kent to raise money for her lover. She buys his paintings without his knowledge and, after several years, has a son, Paul. Notified that he is dying, she goes to visit him, with her jealous husband following. Meeting the artist, the husband decides to sue for divorce. Although Negri gains control of the child, Kent plots to get the child by bribing an old artist to compromise Negri, thereby proving she is not a fit mother. The plot succeeds, and in retaliation she kills her betrayer. The jury finds her not guilty. The last scene shows her on a beach with her child and her artist lover, who has fully recovered.

Robert F. Hill's familiar drama, *A Million for Love* (1928), concerns the well-known story about an innocent young man falsely accused of murder. The film opens in a courtroom where Reed Howes is on trial for killing a gangster. He remains silent, refusing to defend himself, until the daughter of the district attorney testifies. In a lengthy flashback, she describes the fistfight between Howes and the gangster and how the defendant then escorted her out of the premises. It is then proved that another gang member finished off the unconscious victim with a knife. Howes is finally cleared of all charges against him. Howes was a popular silent screen player who usually was featured in action features.

A mother, to protect her son's marriage, remains silent at her own murder trial in Wallace Worsley's domestic drama, *The Power of Silence* (1928). Belle Bennett, the beleaguered mother, knows the actual murderer is her daughter-in-law, but says nothing during her own trial for the crime. But when her diary is introduced as evidence, she is finally acquitted. The film provides several flashbacks to establish her innocence and move the events out of the courtroom into the lives of the participants. Following the trial, the son invites his mother to stay in his home. Conflict then arises between the mother and her daughter-in-law, who demands that the older woman leave the premises. When they are alone, the mother reveals that she knows that the wife, who was invited to the dead man's apartment, was responsible for the death of the victim in the trial. The wife finally realizes the sacrifice her mother-in-law made for the couple and agrees to join her to bury the past, thereby protecting the man they both love from further grief.

The wife of a district attorney risks both their reputations when she appears as a surprise witness at the murder trial of her lover in Erle C. Kenton's domestic drama, *Name the Woman* (1928), based on the story, "Bridge," by Erle C. Kenton. Anita Stewart portrays the wayward wife of Huntly Gordon, the attorney, to support the alibi of defendant Gaston Glass. She testifies that she was with Glass during Mardi Gras festivities – the night of the murder. Glass is acquitted and Gordon, realizing he has neglected his wife, resigns from his position.

Cross Dressing

I. Clothes Make the Man (Woman)

Cross dressing in films has a long history, beginning in early silent comedies, with some of the most popular screen personalities of the period. Roscoe "Fatty" Arbuckle, for example, dressed himself as a female in several films, including *Seaside Lovers*, in which he falls from an airplane. Mabel Normand, one of the great early screen comediennes, posed as a male in *Mabel's Stratagem* (1913) to get a job as a secretary when the suspicious wife of an employer does not trust her husband with female employees. The wife, upon seeing the handsome "male" (Normand), begins to flirt with "him." In *Behind the Screen* (1916), Charlie Chaplin's leading lady, Edna Purviance, poses as Charlie's assistant – a male stagehand at a movie studio. A fellow worker, seeing them embracing – and assuming they are two males – suspects Charlie's manliness. Chaplin, perhaps the greatest screen comic, occasionally donned female clothes. Charlie appeared in *A Busy Day* (1914) as a tough wife who catches her husband flirting with another woman. In *The Masquerader* (1914), Charlie plays an actor who dresses up as a woman.

An ambitious laundry worker, who thinks she is a private detective, dresses in male attire and hunts down a group of dangerous anarchists in Mack Sennett's comedy, *Katchem Kate* (1912). Mabel Normand, as the worker, answers a newspaper advertisement on how to become a detective. Then thinking she has the power to arrest people, she becomes entangled in a series of misadventures. Finally, she suspects a gang of plotters who intend to blow up a barn. Disguising herself as a man, she succeeds in capturing the culprits.

The first reel of Joseph A. Golden's overly long detective drama, *The Eye of a God* (1913), shows a successful forger, Mr. Brockway, dressed in drag, being chased and captured as he tries to escape from the police. Much of the remainder of the film involves blackmail, theft, prison escape and wild chase scenes across Manhattan. Pathos arises when the daughter of the convicted Mr. Brockway is blackmailed by her father's erstwhile cell-mate, who threatens to expose her father's past to her wealthy husband.

Director-actor Francis Ford's two-reel Civil War drama, *In the Fall of '64* (1914), features Grace Cunard as Ford's sweetheart, a Southern belle whose estate is captured by Northern troops. When Ford, a Confederate captain, is arrested for spying behind Union lines, Cunard poses as a slow-witted boy to gain access to Union quarters where Ford is being held. She manages to extinguish a candle, allowing her lover to escape in the ensuing darkness. She later steals the enemy's battle plans and crosses into Confederate territory. The information permits Ford and his troops to score a victory over the Union. The melodramatics of the plot are no doubt fictitious, but a similar incident actually occurred during the conflict in Nashville. Ann Patterson, daughter of a Southern physician whose family members were all spies for the Confederacy, helped to free Thomas Joplin after his capture by Union troops. Joplin was a guerrilla spy in Coleman's Scouts, a force of about fifty agents operating in Tennessee.

Mary Pickford, known as "America's Sweetheart" to her fans, and handsome and dashing American hero Owen Moore appeared as leads in James Kirkwood's drama, *Mistress Nell* (1915), based on George Cochrane Hazelton's successful 1900 historical play about French political court intrigue. The plot concerns the love affair between flower girl Nell Gwyne and England's Charles II, with young Nell's discovery of a plot by the treacherous Duchess of Portsmouth and the Duke of Buckingham to sell out King Charles and England to France. Gwyne (Pickford) disguises herself as a young man so that she can spy on the two traitors. She gathers the necessary evidence against the duchess and hands it over to the king. Mary was so beloved by her fans that whatever she played in was widely accepted – except when she played mature women.

When Lillian Walker's father, an earl, is arrested for conspiracy, she dresses in male clothing and a mustache and goatee in an effort to save him, in Wilfred North's historical drama, *Hearts and the Highway* (1915), based on the 1911 novel by Cyrus Townsend and set in England. Her pleas in court having failed, she tries a more desperate approach. Still dressed in her male disguise, she intercepts Darwin Karr, the king's messenger, who is bearing her father's death warrant. After some heavy drinking at an inn, both Walker and Karr are forced to share the same room. Unable to remove the papers from him during the night, she waits for him on the road and grazes him with a bullet. She takes the warrant but faints from a sword wound inflicted by Karr, who awakens and discovers his foe is a young woman. Having fallen in love with her, he reports to his superiors that the papers have been stolen. But he is not believed and is subsequently arrested. Walker, again in disguise, approaches the king and offers him ten thousand pounds for the release of her father and Karr. The king agrees, but when he discovers her true identity, he abducts her for himself. Karr, now free, rescues her and they both sail away to freedom.

After Henry Woodruff is rejected by Rhea Mitchell, he leaves for India as a deputy commissioner, where he takes an interest in Tsuru Aoki, the daughter of an Indian nobleman, in Charles Swickard's romantic drama, *The Beckoning Flame* (1916). Her father, who wants her to marry a prince, whom she hates because of his depravity, has Woodruff transferred. On his wedding night, the prince is stricken with a seizure and dies, and his wife, according to custom, must die with him on a funeral pyre. Woodruff rescues her and she lives with him at his new station, disguised as a boy servant. She soon falls in love with him. When Woodruff's former girlfriend, Mitchell, arrives, the couple exchange love vows with each other. Aoki overhears them and decides to end her life in a fire to protect Woodruff.

Violet Mersereau, the daughter of a wealthy widower and horse owner, is raised as a boy by her father in Edwin Stevens's delightful comedy, *The Boy Girl* (1917). He dresses her in boys' garments, treating her as a male friend instead of a sweet daughter. She spends much of her time around a race track – until her father dies, and she goes to live with her two aunts in Washington Square. The two women grow upset with their tomboy niece, who soon decides to change her ways. She obtains a job as a stenographer, where she saves the company from going bankrupt by exposing a company spy. In addition, she rescues her employer's daughter from falling into a compromising position. Her reward for all this is her marriage to the boss's son.

Carmel Myers portrays a fortune teller determined to fulfill the dreams of others in Elsie Jane Wilson's comedy, *The Dream Lady* (1918). Her first challenge is to transform a young woman into a man. After dressing a young woman in male attire, the subject dupes a young man into becoming her friend. Later, the man discovers the deception and the couple become engaged. Myers later involves a male friend in a disastrous financial scheme, but the incident ends satisfactorily when the pair decide to marry. The marriage ends the ambitious Myers's fortune-telling career.

A young man who has turned to crime dresses in women's clothing to fool his victims and confuse the law, in H. D'Elba's offbeat drama, *Alias Mary Brown* (1918). After being cheated out of his inheritance by unscrupulous men, Casson Ferguson joins a gang of thieves who encourage him to retrieve what is rightfully his. He meets Pauline Starke, an associate of the gang, and falls in love with her. After they become engaged, he begins dressing up as an attractive young woman and gaining entrance into the homes of the men who have cheated him. The couple plan to go west and reform, but he is determined to pull off one last job. His victim happens to be Starke's uncle. But he is warned in time by a friend that an enemy of his has set up a trap. Ferguson's foe goes instead and when caught, kills the uncle. The police then arrest him for murder. Ferguson, in female attire, and Starke elude the police and drive to a farm, where they use her uncle's inheritance to begin a new life together.

Anita King, the daughter of a smuggler, dresses as a boy and leads a rather reckless life, in Robert Ensminger's western, *Whatever the Cost* (1918). When she finds her father shot and mortally wounded, she swears vengeance upon the person who shot him. She later works as a dancer in a saloon, where she hopes to find the killer, and meets Patrick Calhoon, an unsavory character, and Stanley Pembroke, who in reality is a revenue officer tracking down smugglers. Pembroke had seen King earlier, but dressed as a boy, so he doesn't recognize her. Unknown to her, Calhoon is the murderer of her father. Following several complications, including Calhoon's attempted rape of King and her rescue by Pembroke, the two men engage in a deadly battle that ends in the ocean. King rescues both, after which the dying Calhoon confesses to killing her father. King and Pembroke decide to stay together.

Mae Murray, a ragamuffin who dresses in boys' clothing, hops a freight train after the arrest of Jack Mulhall, her gang leader, in Robert Leonard's comedy drama, *Danger – Go Slow* (1918). In a small village, she becomes friends with Lydia Knott, a woman whom she later discovers is Mulhall's mother. When a local judge threatens to foreclose on the woman's property, since he holds the mortgage to the property, Murray decides to blackmail him if he carries out his foreclosure. The rapacious judge withdraws his threat. Next, she sells part of Knott's property for much more than it is worth, giving her hostess a substantial profit. She then persuades Mulhall to return to his mother and give up his life of crime.

Gail Kane, as Roberta Carruthers, whose father was killed in France during the World War, comes to the States to live with her uncle, in Francis Grandon's drama, *The Daredevil* (1918), based on the novel by Maria Thompson Daviess. Since her uncle expects a nephew, the orphan dresses in male attire and adopts the name "Bob." She is readily accepted by her uncle and soon finds a position as translator for the governor (Norman Trevor), who had met her years earlier. She is then instrumental in capturing a handful of German spies and finally reveals her true identity. The governor who had earlier fallen in love with her, offers to marry her and she accepts.

Evelyn Greeley, a motherless young woman raised by a poor but learned father – a Greek scholar – enjoys the bucolic life while dressing as a boy, in Oscar Apfel's drama, *Phil-For-Short* (1919). When her father dies and she becomes the ward of an elderly, bigoted man who wants her for his wife, she dresses up as a boy and takes to the open road with an older companion. She meets a wealthy young man whose recent experiences with women were so disastrous, that he has become a resolute woman-hater. The remainder of the film deals with how she gets him to fall in love with her, even to the point of first making him jealous of another, a foreign fiddler. His jealousy becomes so strong that he considers killing his supposed rival. "I always knew," she confides to him, "I could make you love me – if I could make you mad enough."

Julian Eltinge, a hard-riding ranch owner, disguises himself as a widow so that he may effect the rescue of his fellow ranchers, in William C. de Mille's outdoor comedy drama, *The Widow's Might* 1918). An unscrupulous and ruthless landowner has taken the other ranchers prisoner to force them to sell their land to him, although he was already independently wealthy. Eltinge, attractively dressed as an alluring woman, succeeded in his mission. Florence Vidor portrays the sweet and innocent ingenue. The star, Eltinge, was the most popular female impersonator of the period when the film was released. In fact, his name appeared in lights on Broadway in three different theaters at this time – at the Palace, where he was headlining in person, at the Rialto where this film was playing, and at the Eltinge theater, which was featuring another of his films.

In Wilfred Lucas's Civil War drama, *Morgan's Raiders* (1918), a young Southern belle falls in love with a Union captain. With the outbreak of the war, the girl's father joins John Morgan and his Confederate raiders. When a messenger is shot and killed, Morgan asks for a volunteer to take the dead soldier's place. The girl volunteers and, dressed in men's clothing, carries the message across Union lines. Later in the film she is captured and eventually rescued by Morgan's raiders. At the end of the drama she is reunited with her lover from the North, another of several films that created this romantic image of the bonding of both sections of the country to form one nation.

To protect herself, Viola Dana, who sells newspapers on the streets of New York's tough Chinatown, dresses as a boy in Henry Otto's *The Microbe* (1919), based on the story by Henry Attimus. During a street fight, she rushes toward Kenneth Harlan, a writer, for protection. He takes her home, where he discovers the boy is really a young woman. He then decides to help her out and let her live there. Harlan, who has been indulging in drugs, finds his new roommate a pleasant diversion and a distraction from his addiction. Friends enter the scene and evict Dana. But her letters to the writer rekindle his interest in her and encourage him to return to his writing. Eventually, he produces a best seller and manages to track her down. They then renew their relationship.

William Desmond portrays the title character in J. J. Franz's western drama, *Bare-Fisted Gallagher* (1919). He arrives in a valley to look for a mine his uncle has left him and is attracted to Agnes Vernon, a young woman dressed in male clothing, who shoots off his hat. Frank Lanning, the owner of the local general store, grows jealous of the newcomer. Later, Gallagher rescues Vernon from Lanning, who tries to sexually attack her. Gallagher has set a trap for a bandit and, to his surprise, he catches Vernon. The real bandit shows up and is shot by Gallagher's agent. It is Lanning, the store owner, who wanted to commit the robbery and fix the blame on Gallagher.

II. Tampering with the Classics

Several silent films, especially during the twenties, substituted popular female screen personalities for male characters in classic or popular works. The practice started quite early, with petite Marie Doro playing the title role in *Oliver Twist* (1916). She had successfully played Dickens's Oliver on Broadway in 1912. Mary Pickford portrayed the lead in *Little Lord Fauntleroy* (1921), whereas in the sound era, Hollywood reverted to casting a young boy, Freddie

Bartholomew, in the 1936 version. Similarly, Shirley Mason portrayed Jim Hawkins in Robert Louis Stevenson's classic tale, *Treasure Island*, in the 1920 silent screen version, but for the 1934 sound remake, popular child actor Jackie Cooper played the role. And again in 1950, the producers used a boy, Bobby Driscoll, for the Hawkins character. Betty Bronson was chosen by playwright J. M. Barrie himself to play the lead role in the 1924 screen version of his play, *Peter Pan*. One may well wonder if silent screen audiences were more tolerant in the tampering of their favorite novels and plays, or simply, that the studios wanted headline performers to draw larger audience. Another question arises as to the reasons for the sound versions adhering strictly to boys playing boys' roles. Were these later audiences more demanding in the casting or the studios more concerned about presenting these classics more realistically? In general, movie audiences during the twenties witnessed more comedies and farces – and fewer dramas – concerned with cross dressing, both female (*Charley's Aunt*) and male impersonations (*Finders, Keepers*), compared with the preceding two decades.

Maurice Tourneur endowed his production of the adventure drama, *Treasure Island* (1920), based on Robert Louis Stevenson's popular novel, with two qualities. The work contains pictorial beauty in several settings, and he selected a female star, Shirley Mason, to play the role of young Jim Hawkins. The director stayed rather close to the original story about piracy, murder and the search for hidden treasure, but he never failed to capture the close affection between the pirate Long John Silver (Charles Ogle) and Jim, an warmth upon which the climax depends. He also omitted scenes concerned with the hiring of the villainous crew.

Idealistic Raymond McKee criticizes his newspaper-publisher father for exploiting the poor and intends to prove his point in Howard M. Mitchell's drama, *The Little Wanderer* (1920). In the slums, McKee meets Shirley Mason, who is dressed in male clothing. Thinking she is an unfortunate male slum dweller, he intends to reform "him." He finds Mason a job in a restaurant. Once he discovers that Mason is a young woman, he falls in love with her. But his father meets her and recognizes her as the daughter of his former partner who had once swindled him, so he forbids the marriage. Later, the truth comes out when Mason's father charges McKee's father with perpetrating the theft. The publisher admits this, and his son takes over the paper to introduce the needed reforms. The couple, of course, now marry.

Pearl White, known as "the girl in pants," has been raised as a boy by her father, in Charles Giblyn's drama, *The Mountain Woman* (1921), based on the 1919 novel, *A Pagan of the Hills*, by Charles Neville Buck. When her father is wounded in a gunfight, his daughter struggles to get his logs to market by hiring a crew from the lumber camp. Several suitors compete for her affections, including roughnecks and a wealthy man from the East. Following several complications, she succeeds in delivering the logs. When she returns home, she accepts Corliss Giles, a young Irishman, for her lifetime mate.

Edith Roberts plays a dual role in Norman Dawn's routine adventure drama, *Thunder Island* (1921). She portrays both a young Mexican woman and her twin brother. Jack O'Brien, the American captain of a sailing vessel, rescues her after her brother is killed by a villain's underlings. Thinking she is married to the villain while she was on her deathbed, she resists falling deeply in love with the captain. But the lovers finally get together in the last reel.

When her stepfather is killed by the villainous Earl Metcalfe, Eleanor Boardman dresses in male clothing as she searches for his killer in Chester Franklin's weak drama, *The Silent Accuser* (1924). Boardman, while planning to elope with Raymond McKee, is attacked by Metcalfe, a boarder in her home. Her stepfather intervenes and is pushed down a flight of stairs to his death. When McKee enters, the police accuse him of the crime and he is sent to prison. Meanwhile, impersonating a male, Boardman tracks Metcalfe to a Mexican tavern, where Edna Tichenor is attracted to the stranger. She begins to flirt with Boardman and sits in her lap. Later, McKee's dog has followed him to prison and helps him to escape. Man and animal join Boardman in trapping the killer and forcing a confession from him.

Norma Shearer, a young woman living in the Maine woods, which some people considered dangerous, dresses as a young man during the day and returns to her feminine attire at night when she is safe at her home, in Oscar Apfel's romantic drama, *Trail of the Law* (1924). Year earlier, her mother had been murdered by a local resident whom the woman's father has sworn to kill. Wilfred Lytell, a young man from the city, meets Shearer, who is dressed as a boy, and later falls in love with her. When her father catches up with the man who had murdered his wife, he almost kills him. But Lytell intercedes, thereby saving the father from a possible death sentence or long prison term.

Sydney Chaplin portrays one of three Oxford University youths who need an aunt to chaperon a party, and Chaplin is pressed into playing the aunt, in Scott Sidney's comedy, *Charley's Aunt* (1925), based on the old stage play by Brandon Thomas. Chaplin, dressed as the eccentric elderly woman, impresses ingenue Ethel Shannon, who believes Chaplin's characterization. David James and Jimmie Harrison, as Chaplin's two college pals, are able to party with their girlfriends, Mary Akin and Priscilla Bonner, because of their friend's sacrifice. The play was adapted for the screen about seven times, and always managed to draw laughs. Charles Ruggles portrayed the title character in the first 1930 sound version, and Jack Benny assayed the role in 1941.

Sydney Chaplin repeated his female impersonation in Charles Reisner's farcical comedy, *The Man on the Box* (1925), based on the novel and play by Harold McGrath. Chaplin, as the son of a wealthy father, backs an inventor's gadget for airplanes while attempting to woo the man's pretty wife. Meanwhile, a foreign count is trying to steal the inventor's plans for his own country. Chaplin, who is caught in the wife's bedroom by her husband, poses as a parlor maid and is chased by police. The disappointing film, a remake of a 1914 version of the story, resembles *Charley's Aunt*, released earlier the same year, but the present work leaves much to be desired in the world of comedy.

A young woman, falsely accused of a crime, helps to reform several thieves, in Frank O'Connor's offbeat crime drama, *Lawful Cheaters* (1925). Clara Bow, as the innocent caught in a police roundup of suspects, persuades prison authorities that her two brothers and her boyfriend can be saved from a life of crime with her help. She is permitted to return to the city, where she disguises herself as a boy and manipulates events that lead to her brothers' going straight. She then recovers stolen bonds that led to her arrest, and the thief is caught. She is now free to marry her boyfriend. Her male impersonation impressed several critics.

Lionel Belmore, the uncle of David Jones, is suing his nephew's landlord, but the case has been postponed until a missing witness is found, in Scott Sidney's farce, *Madame Behave* (1925), based on a play by Jean Arlette. Following a series of complications, Jones's roommate, Julian Eltinge, is mistaken for a burglar. To avoid arrest, he dresses up as a woman. The disguise is so successful that Jones persuades him to pose as the missing woman. The landlord and the uncle reconcile their differences, thanks to Eltinge, and the two young men marry their fiancées. Julian Eltinge was the most famous female impersonator during the twenties and appeared in several films.

Dorothy Drew helps to rescue her boyfriend, Gaston Glass, an assistant district attorney who has been abducted by a gang of murderers, in Dell Henderson's action drama, *Pursued* (1925). After locating the gang's hideout, Drew poses as the notorious female gangster, Chicago Ann, who always dresses in male clothing. The gang leader is drawn to Drew, much to the annoyance of his gun moll, who soon exposes the impersonation. Drew is captured and held prisoner. But she soon escapes through the aid of a sympathetic gang member and notifies the police. The place is raided and Glass is rescued.

Two card players flee from the police and make their escape in a unique way in William Seiter's comedy, *What Happened to Jones* (1926), based on the play by George Broadhurst. Reginald Denny, who has been talked into the card game on his wedding night by his older crony, Otis Harlan, joins his pal in sneaking into a woman's beauty shop to avoid the police. They then make their escape by dressing in women's attire. They go to Harlan's home, where his wife is expecting him to bring back his reverend brother. Harlan, to justify his friend's presence, dresses Denny in church garb. Meanwhile, the police find Denny's wallet and proceed to his fiancée's home. The remainder of the film develops these farcical situations, with the police still looking for the pair and the real reverend making an entrance. The film ends with the reverend marrying the couple in a speeding car, with the police in pursuit. Several of the situations are not unlike those in the famous stage play about female impersonation, *Charley's Aunt*, and the screen version that appeared one year earlier.

Press agent Owen Moore, struggling to succeed in business, is hired to promote a failing pleasure island venture – with unpredictable results – in Archie

Mayo's flawed comedy, *Money Talks* (1926). Trying to turn the place into a health resort, Moore has trouble when the ship transporting his patients is hijacked. The captain, Ned Sparks, is actually a rumrunner. In one sequence, Moore is forced to dress in female clothing. Following other complications, he succeeds in making the venture a hit, gets hired at a salary of $50,000 per year, and wins back Claire Windsor, his estranged wife.

David Butler, who would like to get his hands on some of his wealthy aunt's money, hires prize fight promoter Little Billy, a midget, to pose as his daughter, and reporter Madge Kennedy to pose as his wife, in Harley Knoles's comedy, *Oh, Baby!* (1926). Supposedly only for a few hours, the impersonations last overnight when the aunt, Flora Finch, is so taken by the ersatz wife and daughter, that she insists they stay the night. To make matters worse, she wants Kennedy to put her "daughter" to sleep with the aunt. Much to Little Billy's annoyance, he reluctantly agrees, but he plans to sneak away, since he is managing his fighter that night for a major bout at Madison Square Garden. However, everything works out satisfactorily, even though the aunt walks in on their celebration the next day and learns the truth about her nephew's deception.

When the heir to the throne of Graustark is hurt, his American cousin, Marion Davies, decides to impersonate him – clothes and all – in Sidney Franklin's familiar comedy, *Beverly of Graustark* (1926). The film, about intrigue and romance in a mythical kingdom, was adapted from the novel by George Barr McCutcheon. The heir's presence is absolutely essential to foil the plot of a sinister general who is seeking the title of king for himself. Davies passes as the prince until he recovers from his illness. Meanwhile, the impostor manages to win herself a handsome bodyguard (Creighton Hale), with whom she soon falls in love. One particularly humorous situation occurs when he finds feminine garments in her luggage. "What kind of boy are you?" he asks, puzzled by the contents of the suitcase. But later, when Davies dresses as herself, he falls madly in love with her. The real prince finally arrives and discovers he is being impersonated, but all this is explained away for a pleasant ending.

Greedy Gaston Glass tries to cheat his innocent and naïve cousin, Glenn Hunter, out of his inheritance in Tom Terriss's routine drama, *The Romance of a Million Dollars* (1926). Their wealthy uncle has willed each of the young men $500,000, but if either one disgraces the family name, the other would inherit both sums. The well-groomed and villainous Glass plots to frame Hunter several times, including hiding stolen items in Hunter's room. His schemes culminate in the theft of a guest's valuable necklace. When the uncle offers to reimburse the irritated guest for her loss, she insists on the return of the necklace, for sentimental reasons. Glass, dressing up and posing as a Russian woman, offers to return the stolen necklace in exchange for $100,000. But Hunter's girlfriend, Alyce Mills, exposes Glass at the last moment.

A mixture of the Robinson Crusoe plot and a fascinating animal feature,

William G. Crosby's drama, *The Enchanted Island* (1927), tells the story of a father and daughter marooned for nine years on a South Sea island. Henry B. Walthall and his daughter, Charlotte Stevens, are the only inhabitants, and they soon befriend their only neighbors, a variety of peaceful animals. Suddenly, three castaways arrive, following a terrible storm at sea: Pat Hartigan, a boorish mate; Pierre Gendron, the ship owner's son; and the vessel's African-American cook. To protect his daughter from the strangers, the cautious father disguises his daughter as a boy. The rough mate discovers the truth and kills the father, who refuses to give his daughter to the villain. Meanwhile, the owner's son, unaware of the daughter's true sex, becomes friendly with her and soon learns her secret. When the mate threatens Gendron's life, the cook intercedes and, in a struggle, both men fall from a cliff into a stream of lava from an active volcano. The young couple escape on a raft and are rescued by a vessel that is conveniently passing.

Dorothy Devore, as a patient, falls in love with physician Bert Lytell, and in their romantic wake she leaves behind broken-hearted suitor Frederic KoVert, in Richard Thorpe's entertaining bedroom farce, *The First Night* (1927), based on the story by Frederica Sagor. Hoping to break up the romance, KoVort dresses as a woman and poses as the doctor's French wife. Through most of the remainder of the film, KoVort manages to fool house detective Harry Myers and the couple, who have eloped and are staying at the same hotel as the rejected suitor. Chases throughout the hotel, room mix-ups and the final exposure of the interloper wind matters up. KoVert gets attacked by Lytell and Myers when they catch him without his female wig.

A proud South American grandfather and ranch owner sends for his grandson to help him in a feud with another family, in Clarence Badger's comedy, *Senorita* (1927). The only problem is he never learned the truth – his grandson is Bebe Daniels, a pretty granddaughter. Not to disappoint him, Daniels dresses in male attire and promises to help him. She dresses in disguise (not unlike the fictional Zorro character) as she rides, duels and swings from chandeliers as she goes about protecting the old man's estate. Her chief opponent, James Hall, having just recently returned from Europe, is drawn into a fencing duel with Daniels, who is wounded in the arm. During the duel, her bandanna loosens and Hall discovers his foe is a beautiful young woman, so he begins to woo her. William Powell portrays a villainous foe trying to steal her grandfather's cattle that he plans to sell without the knowledge of Hall, his own cousin. Those who viewed the film as a send-up of swashbuckler films enjoyed the film even more.

Detectives

I. Early Private Eyes

Numerous early silent crime films, especially those emphasizing detectives, focused on the humorous aspects of crime. Parody and satire were not far behind. Films like Allan Dwan's *Calamity Anne, Detective* (1913), with Louise Lester, and *The Female Detective* (1913), with Mae Hotely, were straight farces. Several satirized the lawbreakers and the law enforcers, including such films as *The Amateur Detective* (1914), with Carey L. Hastings and Muriel Ostriche, and Arthur Hotaling's *Kate the Cop* (1913), again with Mae Hotely. Parodies included Edwin S. Porter's *Miss Sherlock Holmes* (1908), with Florence Turner; *Burstup Holmes, Detective* (1913); *Burstup Holmes' Murder Case* (1913); and *The Case of the Missing Girl* (1913), another entry in the "Burstup Holmes" adventure series; and Theodore Marston's *Miss Raffles* (1914), with Dorothy Kelly. Most of these comedies were one-reelers and were used to support longer dramatic features of three or more reels. Occasionally, a short film treated crime more seriously, such as pioneer director Edwin S. Porter's early semi-documentary attempt, *Getting Evidence, Showing the Trials and Tribulations of a Private Detective* (1906). *The Monogrammed Cigarette* (1910) was the first in a series of detective dramas by Yankee, an independent company. The film relates how a young woman follows in her father's footsteps after he, a well-known detective, is murdered. She solves the case. Future silent serial queen Pearl White starred in Phillip Smalley's crime drama, *Pearl As a Detective* (1913), part of a series of "Pearl" adventures for Crystal. She soon moved on to lengthier films. The short and extremely rare drama, *Exposure of the Land Swindlers* (1913), about political fraud, featured William J. Burns, who headed the National Detective Agency. He was considered by some to be "the greatest sleuth of all time." Alice Joyce provided the female interest.

Several early crime dramas experimented in filming on location, thereby introducing an early semi-documentary style. Biograph's short film, *The King of Detectives* (1902), depicts a shooting in broad daylight on a busy snow-covered street. After one man approaches and shoots another, the victim's female friend begins to rifle through his pockets and leaves. A crowd soon gathers.

Biograph released a later version of the film. *The King of Detectives* (1903) offered slightly more detail, such as a different opening in which a man shows a dagger to a woman companion and then leaves. When a well-dressed gentleman approaches the woman, the first man reappears and stabs the stranger. The woman removes something from the victim's pocket. A bearded man, hiding behind a store mannequin, comes forward and offers to help.

Cameraman Arthur Marvin continued this semi-documentary approach and shot the simplistic short drama, *Arrest of a Shoplifter* (1903), about a woman in a department store carefully placing items in her large bag and trying to walk out of the store with them. However, a store detective who has been observing her apprehends the shoplifter. This probably was the first silent film to deal with shoplifting, a rare screen topic in any case. What also made the film distinctive was having a woman as the criminal.

Straight crime dramas, about detectives or aspiring sleuths, combined the outdoor aspects of early films with more formal plots. A newsboy helps to capture two thieves in Wallace McCutcheon's early crime drama, *The Boy Detective* (1908). The youngster, Robert Harron, observes two suspicious-looking men following a woman whom they apparently intend to rob. Using his own unique detecting methods, the boy helps the police arrest the felons. McCutcheon directed several silent dramas during this period; meanwhile, young Harron continued his acting career. Although the film concerned a juvenile, the work was not listed or distributed as one appealing only for young audiences.

Barney Gilmore, as Detective Delaney, solves a kidnapping case by becoming a victim himself, in Herbert Blaché's intriguing drama, *The Fight for Millions* (1913), about an abduction. A millionaire banker and his daughter, Marian Swayne, are the targets of the gangster Sorenti (Joseph Levering), who not only is guilty of kidnapping but is able to frame an innocent person – that is, until Delaney steps in. Both director Blaché and his wife, Alice Blaché, turned out several interesting dramas during the early silent years. Soon, actor Joseph Levering turned to directing silent films as well.

D. W. Griffith's six-reel drama, *The Avenging Conscience* (1914), was adapted from Edgar Allan Poe's "The Telltale Heart," "Annabel Lee" and "The Pit and the Pendulum." Described by several critics as a "psychological drama," the adaptation contains a laudable sequence in which the half-crazed Henry B. Walthall, on the verge of madness resulting from his feelings of guilt, is being interrogated by a detective. Meanwhile, the camera explores a string of close-ups of Walthall's nervous hands on his knees, the detective's pencil tapping a desk, his foot tapping below the desk, a clock pendulum swinging to and fro. A title card reads: "Like the beating of a dead man's heart." Although this film appeared early in Griffith's career, he had just finished turning out two successful film series, one concerning dramas with Civil War backgrounds, and the other dealing with the sympathetic treatment of Native Americans.

A tour-de-force for Harry Carey, his action-detection drama, *The Master Cracksman* (1914), allows him to exercise his many talents, including staging, directing, and acting, along with some exciting acrobatic sequences. A contemporary critic suggested that Carey may have done some of the script-writing as well. The plot contains scenes of the theft of a valuable diamond, murder, suicide, and action footage galore, with Carey as Gentleman Joe, the cracksman, outwitting the captain of detectives and bringing the story to a neat conclusion. Fern Foster, as the romantic interest, and Herbert Russell, as the frustrated detective, support the star. However, several reviewers, sensitive to the feelings of minorities, felt that the character of the "fence" might offend Jewish viewers. The film was reissued in 1915 as *The Martin Mystery,* and again in 1920 as *The Square Shooter.*

Charles Ray portrays a detective who infiltrates a gang of crooks in Scott Sidney's early underworld drama, *The Gangsters and the Girl* (1914), adapted from a story by Richard V. Spencer. The chief's moll, Alma Rubens, falls in love with Ray, whose real identity is discovered by the gang after the police prematurely raid the gang's headquarters. Later, Ray is forced to kill the leader who accuses Rubens of squealing. The film ends with Rubens enrolled in a business college, with Ray continuing their romantic relationship. Although most early silent crime dramas were filmed in New York City, Sidney's little two-reel drama was shot in California, with Los Angeles and the commercial district of Venice used for backgrounds. Several film historians, impressed with the locations, especially the rooftop gun battle during which the gangsters take a policeman hostage, falsely concluded the drama was filmed in New York.

The somewhat overworked plot of Donald MacKenzie's drama, *Detective Craig's Coup* (1914), has Jack Staindley as the catalyst in the roundup and capture of a band of desperate and dangerous counterfeiters. Staindley, a high-living, fast-drinking man-about-town, is easy prey for the conniving Jim Dalton, who quickly involves him in his counterfeiting schemes. Of course, it is Staindley who goes to prison for four years while Dalton escapes. Pearl Sindelar corresponds with him, who upon his release marries her and plans to go straight. But Dalton, who wants his former partner back in his gang, tips off his employers about his past. Finally, Dalton persuades him to help rob his current employer, Gibson's Bank, but Staindley sends a letter to the banker revealing the plan. The letter, however, is intercepted by a Dalton cohort. Nevertheless, the gang does attempt to rob the bank and many of them are captured. The cohort who intercepted the letter was Detective Craig (Francis Carlyle), who is working under cover. An exciting chase ensues over land and water until the episode ends with the counterfeiters perishing after their boat explodes. The film was adapted from Charles Reade's story, "The Ticket-of-Leave Man."

The famous Romanoff diamonds serve as catalyst for theft, betrayal and murder in Daniel V. Arthur's drama, *The Great Diamond Robbery* (1914), based on a play by Edward M. Alfriend and A. C. Wheeler. Maria (Gail Kane), a South American adventuress, steals the diamonds, which are then taken by Plon, her former accomplice. Some time later he dies, and Maria, now married to a wealthy banker, retrieves the diamonds before a detective arrives on the scene. When her husband, suspecting her involvement, confronts her, she poisons him and blames it on an ex-employee. At an affair, she proudly wears the diamonds for all to see. When the detective challenges her, she consumes a poisoned drink and dies.

The drama, *The Other Half of the Note* (1914), about transatlantic skullduggery, offers a clever twist to the usual diamond-smuggling story. Richard Purden portrays Senator Monroe, and Edward Hoyt, the butler. The plot involves a ring of jewel thieves who hide the Senator's jewels inside the lining of a rare book. A message is sent to confederates aboard the ship describing the location of the hiding place. The detective discovers half of the note while the thieves have the other half. Tom Cole, the detective, is stymied. He decides to arrest the Senator's nephew to buy time and lull the real thieves into overconfidence. The nephew's sister, who is not privy to the scheme and who is engaged to Cole, returns his engagement ring in a fit of pique. Eventually, the case is solved.

Robert Warwick as Jimmy Valentine, is sentenced to ten years in prison when his pal Cotton informs on him, in Maurice Tourneur's drama, *Alias Jimmy Valentine* (1915), based on O'Henry's short story, "A Retrieved Reformation," and the play by Paul Armstrong. Rose Lane helps Jimmy, a.k.a. Lee Randall, to secure a pardon and to keep Detective Doyle at bay. Doyle is hounding Randall, suspecting that he is the notorious safecracker, still suspected of other crimes. Just when he has convinced Doyle of his innocent persona, Randall must jeopardize his freedom to save Rose Lane's kid sister who is locked in a vault. He does the right thing when he opens the vault and saves the child. Doyle is mollified, and Rose and Lee rejoice. Many of the scenes were shot in New York State's Sing Sing Prison, where the film was first shown in February 1915. Other screen versions of O. Henry's tale include one by Metro (1920) and another by MGM (1929).

John P. McGowan's entertaining screen adaptation of *Blackbirds* (1915), based on the 1913 detective-crook stage play by Harry James Smith, highlights U.S. Secret Service agents apprehending a band of smugglers known as the Blackbirds. A famous detective challenges his son (Raymond Hatton) to capture the smugglers. Following a series of complications, Hatton succeeds in capturing their leader. A romantic subplot involving two thieves (Laura Hope Crews and Thomas Meighan), who eventually reform, helps to sustain interest. Foreign scenes (Algeria) were shot in the studio and earned praise for their sets and costumes.

The first detective-mystery from Fox, W. S. Davis's drama, *The Family Stain* (1915), attempts to unravel a twenty-five-year-old puzzle that began when two babies were switched at birth. A series of events leads to the murder of the nurse involved in the deception, after which much of the film is given over to finding the killer. Detailed views of police "grilling" methods, commonly known as the "third degree," proved particularly interesting. The injection of a romantic entanglement does nothing to detract from the story, which was adapted from the 1866 novel, L'Affaire Lerouge, by Emile Gaboriau.

Unemployed screenwriter William Desmond steals onto a film studio lot, where he falls asleep and dreams that he is a detective called in to solve a shooting in Reginald Barker's comedy drama, *The Iced Bullet* (1917). A wealthy banker is shot after he rejects a suitor for his daughter. Desmond, a famous detective, is brought in and figures out how the weapon was fired unattended. It seems that the rejected suitor, before leaving, set the gun between logs so that the cold temperature would fire the bullet. Desmond then awakes and is chased off the studio property. Films with dream sequences were very popular during the silent period, often presenting the writer or director a facile way out of an otherwise complex plot development. Desmond had a long and distinguished career in silent films, often playing leads in social dramas. By the twenties, he shifted into serials and outdoor action dramas.

Frank Powell's mystery drama, *The Dazzling Miss Davison* (1917), based on the 1908 novel by Florence Warden, is notable for its early use of a female detective in a role usually reserved for men. Marjorie Rambeau is the sleuth who, posing as a designer, picks her friends' pockets for fun at parties. Actually, she is instrumental in capturing the socially prominent Van Santens and his accomplices, all part of a gang of international thieves who have targeted the wealthy. Following a long stage career, Rambeau became a distinguished character player in silent and sound films

Irene Castle portrays the title character in George Fitzmaurice's drama about robbery on the high seas, *Sylvia of the Secret Service* (1917). An American has been hired by an Amsterdam diamond merchant to carry the famous Kimberly diamond to London, where it will be set into the British Crown. However, he is not the only interested party to board the ship for England. Hemmings of Scotland Yard and Castle of the U.S. Secret Service also sail on the same vessel, unaware that another group of passengers includes a gang of jewel thieves who have targeted the coveted stone. When the gem is reported stolen, Hemmings accuses the American, but Castle, who is fond of the American suspect, will have none of it. Using various disguises, she outwits the crooks and clears the American of all charges.

Edward Le Saint's drama, *Her One Mistake* (1918), features Gladys Brockwell in a dual role. She plays two women in love with the same criminal. William Lewis enacts the part of the rotund but relentless Detective Scully. William Scott portrays Chicago Charlie. The themes of betrayal and revenge are played out in the predictable plot.

Robert Warwick stars as Asche Kayton in Ralph Ince's mystery, *The Argyle Case* (1919), adapted from the 1912 play by Harriet Ford and Harvey J. O'Higgins. The plot focuses on the murder of millionaire banker John Argyle (Frank McGlynn). Elaine Hammerstein, Argyle's adopted daughter, is suspected of the crime. However, Detective Kayton, using the latest scientific methods, uncovers a counterfeiting band that was responsible for the assassination. The gang members had been discovered by the banker, who intended to expose them. Hammerstein benefits doubly by inheriting her father's wealth and gaining Kayton's love.

II. The Rise of the Popular Sleuth

Detective comedies and dramas thrived throughout the twenties. Although many of these entries simply repeated the themes and plots of earlier films, there were some welcome innovations. For example, several showed the dark side of the otherwise heroic detective or crime fighter. *Partners of the Night* (1920), for instance, exposed police corruption. In *Alias the Night Wind* (1923), a corrupt detective stalks one of his victims. And a crooked detective agency blackmails criminals in *Before Midnight* (1925). But in most of these films the detective is sympathetic, as is the sleuth in *The City of Missing Men* (1921), in which he lets a rehabilitated criminal go free. *The Schemers* (1922), a rare film with an all-African-American cast, concerned a chemist whose daughter is kidnapped and then rescued by a detective. An African-American actor, Tom Wilson, had a major role in *His Darker Self* (1924). A handful of twenties films focused on famous fictional detectives who would later have their own film series, such as Sherlock Holmes, Boston Blackie, Charlie Chan and Philo Vance. In addition, a few detective films featured a woman sleuth, including *Beware of Blondes* (1928), with Dorothy Revier as a private detective. Even satire appeared in films like *Bachelor Brides* (1926), which poked fun at the mystery genre. Finally, films like *Cabaret* (1927) defined one of the democratic icons of the genre and the twenties – the cabaret, a microcosm of America, where politicians, criminals, high society, detectives, reporters, flappers and showgirls laughed, drank and danced away the roaring decade into the more solemn Depression years.

Based on false identities and false assumptions, Alfred Green's comedy, *The Web of Chance* (1920), features Peggy Hyland as a secretary who, while working at a detective agency, plays at being a detective. She blunders through one situation after another and with the aid of numerous disguises is able to shadow the man she suspects of stealing a million-dollar contract from her firm's client. Actually, she is trailing the client who, for his own reasons, is traveling incognito. When the plot is sorted out, the real criminal is captured and the heroine and the wealthy client are married.

Police corruption is the moving force behind Paul Scardon's drama, *Partners of the Night* (1920), that pits an honest cop against his boss. At stake is the philosophy that justice requires more than making arrests; it calls for helping lawbreakers to rehabilitate themselves. William Davidson plays Detective Clifford, the upright policeman and champion of the downtrodden. Pinna Nesbit, as the dynamic Mary Regan, is saved from a life of crime by the young detective.

A dedicated detective hunts down a vicious gang leader and falls in love with the man's wife in J. P. McGowan's routine melodrama, *Below the Deadline* (1921). H. B. Warner portrays the relentless sleuth, who wants Elliott (Bert Sprotte) for murdering a police officer. The killer uses his innocent wife as an alibi, but she is taken down to the local precinct and given facts about her husband's criminal activities. Later, while pursuing the gang during another of their crimes, the detective captures Elliott.

Jim, a country boy who, once in the big city, is framed by a gang of thieves, in Tom Forman's drama, *The City of Silent Men* (1921), adapted from the 1913 novel, *The Quarry,* by John A. Morosco. Accused of participating in a bank robbery and killing a guard, the young innocent is sent to prison. Here he meets a sympathetic convict who helps him to escape. Jim begins life anew in California and falls in love with his employer's daughter. A New York detective tracks him down and, impressed with Jim's rehabilitation, allows him to remain free. Jim is eventually exonerated.

Another rare silent drama featuring an African-American cast, *The Schemers* (1922) emulates the mainstream crime dramas about a coveted chemical formula, a kidnapping and a rescue of the heroine. An African-American chemist who has developed a substitute for gasoline is kidnapped by two hoodlums who think he has the formula with him. When the culprits fail to obtain the paper, they frame the chemist for theft. They then kidnap the chemist's girlfriend, but the chemist and a detective rescue her.

An early adaptation of William Gillette's play, based on A. Conan Doyle's popular detective, Albert Parker's *Sherlock Holmes* (1922) stars John Barrymore as the famous sleuth and Gustav von Seyffertitz as the arch-villain Professor Moriarty. Barrymore appears in a bizarre disguise as the sinister professor. Barrymore's brother, Lionel Barrymore, played Holmes in an earlier screen version of the same title. Both brothers continued as screen personalities well into the sound era. Hedda Hopper, who has a minor role in the film, later became a famous Hollywood columnist famous for her hats, and appeared occasionally in sound films in cameo roles. Another actor, Roland Young, played the lead in many sound films, including the popular "Topper" comedies.

A crooked detective stalks a fugitive whom he has framed for a bond theft in Joseph Franz's mystery drama, *Alias the Night Wind* (1923), based on the 1913 novel by Varick Vanardy. Donald MacDonald, as the corrupt sleuth, fails to capture his prey (William Russell) and is forced to turn over the case to detective Maude Wayne, who eventually proves MacDonald not only framed Russell but her own brother, who is currently serving time in prison.

Another tale in the Boston Blackie crime series created by Jack Boyle, Robert F. Hill's entry, *Crooked Alley* (1923), has the likable crook (Thomas Carrrigan) helping to reform a hard-nosed judge. When an elderly, dying convict pleads to be released so that he can spend his last moments with his friends and daughter, the judge refuses the request. Later, after the man dies, Blackie and the daughter seek revenge upon the judge. They try to lead his innocent son into a life of crime, but the young woman falls in love with him. Finally, the son persuades his stubborn father to change his ways. Carrigan had earlier portrayed Nick Carter, another fictional detective, in 1920 in a series of film shorts.

Unique detective Raymond Griffith is a sleuth who gathers vast amounts of information so that he can prevent a crime rather than solve one in Clarence Badger's drama, *Red Lights* (1923). An unscrupulous lawyer representing the president of a railroad schemes to marry his client's daughter (Marie Prevost), a young woman who had been kidnapped years earlier. As the father speeds by rail to be reunited with his long-lost daughter, the lawyer pushes his suit on the young woman who loves someone else. Griffith interferes in her behalf and exposes the villain.

Ethel Wales portrays an author of detective stories who investigates the mystery of her brother-in-law's death in William de Mille's suspenseful drama, *The Bedroom Window* (1924). She soon ends up both solving a murder and helping to establish the innocence of a young man falsely accused of the crime. Of course, heroine and victim fall in love.

When African-American servant Tom Wilson is falsely accused of murder, writer Lloyd Hamilton gets a chance to play detective in John W. Noble's satiric comedy, *His Darker Self* (1924). Disguising himself in blackface, Hamilton visits the haunts of a suspected gang of African-American smugglers responsible for the killing. Following several misadventures, he finally gets the necessary proof to establish Wilson's innocence.

William Russell, as a wealthy young man, is falsely suspected of smuggling a valuable emerald into the country in John Adolfi's crime drama, *Before Midnight* (1925). Barbara Bedford portrays the pretty heroine who helps Russell extricate himself from the familiar complications. The only interesting element in this otherwise routine film is a detective agency that blackmails criminals instead of bringing them to justice.

Grace Darmond portrays a detective who, along with an innocent bystander, is kidnapped by a jewel thief in John Ince's minor drama, *The Great Jewel Robbery* (1925). When she and her companion, Herbert Rawlinson, try to escape, they are thwarted by the thief whom she has been trying to capture. However, the couple are soon rescued by police officers.

As much a satire of the mystery genre as it is a comedy drama, William K. Howard's *Bachelor Brides* (1926), based on the 1925 play by Charles Horace Malcolm, is concerned with the theft of family pearls. Elinor Fair, as a young American, is about to marry English aristocrat Rod LaRocque when the theft occurs. The remainder of the film, set chiefly in the bridegroom's family home, deals with a comic butler, two blundering Scotland Yard detectives and three incompetent thieves.

Based on the 1926 play by Mary Roberts Rinehart and Avery Hopwood, Roland West's suspenseful mystery, *The Bat* (1926), offers atmosphere, fascinating characters and a surprise ending in which the real culprit has been masquerading as the detective. The story concerns a bank president's death, a young cashier's disappearance and the theft of $200,000. The title refers to a master thief whose disguise reminds victims of a bat. He announces in advance the theft of valuable jewels, but a rival pulls off the crime before him. Their trail ends at the bank president's estate, where The Bat is captured after killing and impersonating a detective. Although very popular at the time of its release, the film today seems very dated.

George Larkin, as a resourceful detective, poses as a jewel thief to protect a valuable set of diamonds in J. P. McGowan's routine drama, *Silver Fingers* (1926). In this guise, Larkin foils the attempt of a gang of crooks from carrying out their scheme and, in addition, romances Charlotte Morgan, the wealthy man's daughter.

The cabaret became the choice locale of crime dramas in the late twenties, especially following the highly successful 1926 stage play, *Broadway,* by Philip Dunning and George Abbott. In Robert G. Vignola's drama, *Cabaret* (1927), nightclub entertainer Gilda Gray, who has struggled to escape from New York's East Side ghetto, is coveted by detective Tom Moore and gangster Charles Byer. Gray's weak and ingenuous brother, Jack Egan, is mixed up with the gangster and, in self-defense, is forced to shoot Byer. The dead man's mistress, who has witnessed the shooting, claims the boy murdered Byer. Detective Moore, to help the woman he loves and to get to the truth of the crime, forces Byer's mistress to admit that the brother killed her man in self-defense.

Chinese detective Charlie Chan (K. Sojin) finds himself entangled in a kidnapping plot and jewel theft in Paul Leni's mystery, *The Chinese Parrot* (1927), based on the 1926 novel by Earl Derr Biggers. Florence Turner, as a previously wealthy woman who now needs money, offers her jewels for sale and hires Chan to handle the transaction. The purchaser, however, is kidnapped and a thief impersonates him. The jewels are then stolen several times until Chan unravels events. The Chinese detective first appeared on screen as a minor character in *The House Without a Key*, a 1926 serial. The present drama is his first appearance in a feature-length film.

Ben Lyon portrays a wealthy young man who dreams of becoming a detective in Howard Higgin's mystery comedy, *The Perfect Sap* (1927), based on the 1936 play, *Not Herbert, a Comedy of the Night in Four Acts,* by Howard Irving Young. As Lyon and his servant are practicing the art of burglary, they meet George and Polly, two real crooks, whom Lyon befriends and takes to his city apartment. Following several complications, including Polly's exposure of an infamous thief, she reveals that she is really a journalist.

Matt Moore portrays a jewelry firm secretary assigned to deliver a valuable emerald to Honolulu in George B. Seitz's mystery drama, *Beware of Blondes* (1928). On board the ship are Dorothy Revier, a private detective whom many mistake for "Blonde Mary," a notorious jewel thief, and Roy D'Arcy, another crook. Moore and Revier fall in love, although at first he suspects her of being "Mary." To trap D'Arcy and his gang of thieves and protect Moore from harm, Revier drugs her lover and steals the emerald from him. She then impersonates

"Blonde Mary" and, when the ship docks, she safely delivers the real emerald and substitutes a phony one to win the confidence of the gang. The police then round up the crooks.

The murder of a blackmailer conjures up many of his married clients as possible suspects in Duke Worne's conventional action-based murder mystery, *A Midnight Adventure* (1928). All the suspects, including a district attorney, are house guests of the deceased man. The female suspects had known him before they were married. The murderer, it turns out, is the detective investigating the case.

The vicious, spiteful former mistress of a wealthy widower has an affair with her ex-lover's son – and ends up dead in Frank Capra's drama, *Say It With Sables* (1928). A local detective arrives at the home of the former lover, now married, and accuses the son of the crime. The college student, thinking his father committed the deed, confesses. But the detective has found an earring that matches one belonging to the wife. When she explains that the shooting was accidental, the understanding sleuth registers the death as a suicide.

Acclaimed detective Philo Vance, played by William Powell, is called in by a district attorney to solve a murder, in Frank Tuttle's mystery drama, *The Greene Murder Case* (1929), based on the 1928 novel by S. S. Van Dine. The victim, an eccentric, was shot by a member of his own family, it seems, and before the sleuth wraps up the case, two more victims go to their deaths. The film was released in both a silent and sound version. Powell went on to play several detectives during the sound era, chiefly Nick Charles in the popular and highly successful "Thin Man" series.

Divorce

I. The Perils of Marriage and Divorce

Around the turn of the century, American author Ambrose Bierce (1842-1914) defined divorce as "a resumption of diplomatic relations and rectification of boundaries." Divorce was associated with disgrace in the early part of the twentieth century (it was virtually unknown a generation or two earlier). The film industry was soon to follow with a flood of comedies that focused on the topic of divorce. It depicted husbands who strayed, wives who flirted with other men and couples who abused each other – delighting their audiences with these crude films. By the end of 1910, one out of every ten marriages ended in divorce. Dramas, of course, treated the topic more seriously, and explored the various troubled marriages that ended either in court or abandonment. The causes for divorce were often laid to alcoholism, gambling or other vices. *Detected* (1903) portrayed a suspicious wife who hires a detective to spy on her husband. A husband in Cecil B. DeMille's *What's His Name* (1914) suddenly learns that his wife is divorcing him. In *Divorced* (1915), a wife and mother divorces her husband for her lover. The husband in *The Perils of Divorce* (1916) is lured away from his wife by his former girlfriend. The earlier films were crude in technique and simplistic in characterization, but they were the precursors to the more mature, sophisticated and witty films that showed up in the twenties.

One of the earliest dramas about divorce, *Detected* (1903), based on the play, *The Divorce*, depicts a wife becoming suspicious of her husband. She hires a detective, and both proceed to spy on the husband in a private dining room. When his wife sees him enjoying himself with another woman, she faints.

In Cecil B. DeMille's comedy, *What's His Name* (1914), the husband of a popular stage actress discovers he is being divorced. To his astonishment, he loses his home and all the furniture, which were in his wife's name. In addition, he finds that he has lost his daughter as well. In utter despair, he attempts to take his own life, but he fails when the gas is disconnected by the utility man. DeMille continued to make domestic dramas, often adding sexual sequences.

Hilda Spong portrays a mother with a young son who divorces her husband and becomes the mistress of another married man in Edward Warren's domestic drama, *Divorced* (1915). Although the married man promises to marry Spong as soon as he obtains a divorce from his wife, it never materializes. Years later, the son, Charles Hutchison, learns about the true relationship between his mother and the man she is living with and confronts him. The man tells Hutchison it was his money that put the son through school and supported both his mother and him all these years. Spong, in disgust, shoots the man. On trial for murder, she pleads temporary insanity and is acquitted by the jury. A wealthy young woman who loves Hutchison decides to marry him regardless of the scandal.

When flighty socialite Edna Wallace Hopper marries John Graham, many years her senior, no one in the social circle believed the match would last, in Edwin August's domestic drama, *The Perils of Divorce* (1916). But after several years of marriage, the happy couple are living in the country with their seven-year-old daughter. Alice Lorraine, Graham's former girlfriend, arrives on the scene and wants him back for his money. In addition, she seeks revenge upon Hopper, who stole him away from her. She succeeds, and after the couple are divorced, Lorraine marries Graham. Meanwhile, his ex-wife sinks to living in a slum and then becomes a society dancer. Lorraine finally abandons Graham and flees with another lover. She leaves behind a note revealing how she has tricked him. At the end, a reconciliation between Graham and Hopper is arranged by their daughter, and the family is reunited.

Lillian Gish and her younger sister, Violet Wilkie, are cared for by their nurse as they await the decision of the divorce court about who will have custody of the children in Lloyd Ingraham's domestic drama, *The Children Pay* (1916). Meanwhile, the neighbors and their children shun the two sisters. They are finally brought to court, where the younger is turned over to the mother and the older child is given to the father. The father has remarried and his wife is a young socialite who enjoys stepping out more than staying home. At her coming out party, Gish, who has a strong love bond with her sister, overhears gossip about her and her sister. She leaves the party, goes to her first home and escapes with her sister to their nurse. A court officer locates them and returns them to the court, where their parents wait outside. A young lawyer, recently out of law school, wins the confidence of Gish and her love. He proposes marriage and she accepts. The court then awards her custody of her sister. Although highly implausible, the film suggests a possible issue of the period and underscores the need for parents to place the interests of their children above their own concerns before they enter the divorce court.

A young woman watches her family disintegrate as her inexperienced father falls under the spell of a temptress in Frederick Sullivan's domestic drama, *Di-*

vorce and the Daughter (1916). Florence La Badie's father, an aspiring artist, inherits enough money to move his wife and daughter from the city to a country home, where he becomes involved with members of an artist's colony. He is particularly interested in an attractive woman who wagers with an acquaintance, a young man, that she can wreck the artist's family life. La Badie observes her father's neglect, while the young man meets her and tries to entice her into a life of free love. To strengthen his argument, he uses her parents' failed marriage as proof of the decline of marriage and the benefits of free love. He lures her to his apartment where a struggle ensues. She escapes, disillusioned about old-fashioned concepts of love and courtship, until she meets a sincere suitor who proposes conventional matrimony.

Thomas Meighan gives up his romance with married Veda McEvers when he falls in love with Blanche Sweet, McEvers's secretary, in Frank Reicher's domestic drama, *The Dupe* (1916). Sweet steals some money from her employer for a new dress, but her conscience forces her to confess. McEvers, who is seeking a divorce, threatens to prosecute her secretary unless she helps her get her divorce. The latter agrees to be seen having dinner in public with the husband. Meighan happens to see them in the restaurant and suspects the worst. The husband confides to Sweet that his wife wants the divorce so that she can marry Meighan. So Sweet rushes to her boyfriend and reveals the entire scheme. The couple reconcile their differences and arrange to get married.

Mary Anderson, while visiting Reno, Nevada, grows curious about the divorce colony and decides to impersonate a divorcée, in William Wolbert's comedy drama, *The Divorcée* (1917). Boston reverend Alfred Vosburgh, in Reno to discourage divorces, rescues Anderson from her runaway horse. Both pose as someone else, and their friendship leads to a romance. In town, she opposes the reverend's views on divorce in the local paper, each still not aware of the other's true identity. When she is ready to leave Reno, Anderson witnesses a hold-up and thinks Vosburgh is one of the bandits. She later warns him the sheriff is after him and both ride off together. He, in turn, thinks her husband is after her. The posse catches up to them and the sheriff reveals the reverend's true identity, while another rider tells the truth about Anderson. The couple decide to marry.

Factory owner John Sainpolis, in love with his secretary, wants a divorce from his wife, Pauline Frederick, whose religion does not permit such an act, in Hugh Ford's domestic drama, *Sleeping Fires* (1917). When she refuses, Sainpolis uses their son as a bargaining chip. If she gives the divorce, she can have her son. Following a separation, the wife returns home to claim her son and finds the secretary, Helen Dahl, installed as the mistress of Sainpolis's home. An argument ensues and the master is shot. Frederick is arrested and tried for the shooting. She is defended by a young lawyer she had met earlier. After she is exonerated, she and the lawyer begin to build a new life together.

A factory owner's son falls in love with Muriel Ostriche, a worker at a plant. He marries her against the wishes of his father, in Romaine Fielding's unconvincing comedy drama, *Moral Courage* (1917), based on the story, *The Wit of a Woman*, by Stanley Dark. The father, who believes his son, Arthur Ashley, has married beneath his standing, offers the wife $100,000 if she will divorce his son. She agrees, goes to Reno for the divorce and returns to collect the reward. She then turns around and remarries Ashley. The surprised father is impressed with her clever financial maneuver and accepts her as part of the family.

American heiress Alice Brady and her French husband, John Bowers, live far above their means in Travers Vale's farce, *The Divorce Game* (1917), based on the play, *Mlle. Fifi*, by Lee Dictrichstein, and set chiefly in France. Because of their extravagant lifestyle, the couple are haunted by creditors. Their efforts to raise funds to extricate themselves from their debts form the basis for much of the comedy.

Newspaper reporter Bessie Barriscale, strongly affected by a highly charged divorce trial she is assigned to cover, decides to break off her engagement to a fellow journalist in Charles Miller's simplistically resolved comedy drama, *The Hater of Men* (1917). Believing that all men will eventually behave in a detestable manner, as demonstrated by the husband in the case, she decides to return her fiancé's ring and live a singular and happy life. Her freedom brings her a host of men who fill her apartment, drink heavily, and eventually begin to tell off-color stories in her presence. As she begins to tire of this bohemian life, an old confidant persuades her to return to the man she loves. The friend arranges a meeting between the lovers, and the couple are soon reunited.

George A. Siegmann's provocative drama, *Should She Obey?* (1917), explores the problems of troubled marriages, wrong marriages, divorce and the mistreatment of wives in many cases. The stories of two married couples are portrayed, the Gordons and the Blakes. Both men, factory workers, marry and are blessed with children. Gordon grows rich, tires of his wife and becomes infatuated with an actress. Blake treats his wife badly and deserts her. Both wives end up in Reno and get divorces. The Blake daughter flees from her convent and wants a career in show business. She applies to her father, who doesn't recognize her, not having seen her since she was a child. He almost sends her to her destruction until he learns the truth. He then forces her into an unhappy marriage with a "bald-headed vulture." The young wife's mother and brother finally rescue her from the horrid marriage. Earlier, the film shows important political figures and state officials from the states of Nevada and Illinois. They comment upon such issues as the rising divorce rate and "poisoned marriages." The latter refers to cruel or unthinking husbands who misapply the word "obey" in how they treat their wives. Many state how they are trying to curb the number of divorces in their states. A crisp climate, legalized gambling, resort facilities, plenty of entertainment, and quick divorce laws have made Reno famous.

Josephine Whittell threatens to ruin an innocent woman's reputation if her husband, Wallace Worsley, doesn't give her a divorce, in Emmett J. Flynn's domestic drama, *Alimony* (1917). Although he himself is innocent, her husband agrees to a large alimony settlement. Whittell hopes to marry George Fisher, a millionaire, with whom she has been flirting. But when Fisher admits he does not love her, she vows to destroy him. Fisher falls in love with Lois Wilson, who agrees to marry him. But their marriage faces problems because of the interference of Whittell, who suggests that Wilson sue for divorce. She refuses to divorce Fisher, whose lawyer discovers Whittell's underhanded intervention. When the couple are happily reunited, Whittell, defeated and frustrated, kills herself.

Pauline Frederick, as a young wife and a college graduate, is treated as a child by her neglectful husband, in Robert Vignola's drama, *The Hungry Heart* (1917), based on the novel by David Graham Phillips. When she asks if she could assist him in his chemical experiments, he just laughs at her. After she has a child, their married life grows more empty as they drift apart. When she has an affair with one of his assistants, the husband finally sues for divorce. Suddenly, he realizes how important she was in their life together. He confesses that he has neglected her and permits her to work along with him. Although her lover proposes marriage to her, she returns to her husband. In one of the more rare cases in early silent films, an unfaithful wife does not suffer death, suicide or public disgrace for her act of adultery.

Frank Lloyd's slow-paced drama, or sermon, *The Blindness of Divorce* (1918), is burdened with too many titles and too lengthy a film. Charles Clary, who is married to Bertha Mann, would rather spend time at his club with his friends than at home with his wife. Bertram Grassby, a young lawyer quick to grasp the situation of the neglectful husband, visits the wife and begins to become overly friendly to his unwilling hostess. Clary, returning home unexpectedly, sees the pair in an embrace and suspects the worst. Although his wife tries to explain, the husband sues for divorce and wins custody of their child. His ex-wife and mother suffers disgrace by a society that shuns her. Fifteen years later, Clary's daughter, Rhea Mitchell, marries a district attorney. A blackmailer threatens the daughter that he will expose the truth about her mother, who now runs a brothel and gambling den. Mitchell visits the place and is caught in a police raid. The district attorney, running for re-election, sues for divorce, but at the trial, the mother appears and reveals the entire story and concludes with a condemnation of "man-made" laws. The husband and wife decide to reconcile their differences.

A wife, neglected by her husband who is overly concerned about his business, finds one too many faults in him and finds a substitute, in Cecil B. DeMille's clever and intelligent domestic drama, *Don't Change Your Husband* (1919). Gloria Swanson, as the annoyed wife, arranges for an amicable divorce from Elliott Dexter, who still loves her. She then marries Lew Cody, a nondescript husband with whom Swanson finds even more faults than she did with her first husband. So she proceeds to dump him and remarry Dexter. Now comfortably ensconced in her home with her ex-husband, she notices that his idiosyncrasies, which used to annoy her, seem more acceptable. Men, she realizes, are terrible. The film supposedly was designed as a sequel to George Loane Tucker's *Virtuous Wives,* released several months earlier.

The son of a millionaire marries telephone operator Gladys Brockwell and is immediately cut off from all financial aid by his father in Frank Beal's drama, *The Divorce Trap* (1919). Penniless, the husband now depends solely on the earnings of his wife, who has returned to her job. Meanwhile, he falls in love with another young woman, and a pal of his, a shyster lawyer, arranges for a phony divorce. Brockwell is aided by a friend, a young lawyer, who helps her straighten matters out to her satisfaction. Some of the overacting produces unintentional laughter, although Brockwell if effective as the duped wife.

Ethel Barrymore's recent marriage to a lord (E. J. Ratcliffe) proves an unhappy one because of his public insults in Herbert Blaché's drama, *The Divorcée* (1919), based on the 1907 play, *Lady Frederick,* by *W. Somerset Maugham*. Ratcliffe began his harangues after he saw her with her former fiancé, the poverty-stricken H. E. Herbert. When Barrymore later sacrifices her reputation to salvage her indiscreet sister's marriage, her husband divorces her. Originally, she only married the lord to please her parents. Years later, now heavily in debt, she wins the attention of young Eugene Strong in Monte Carlo, much to the annoyance of his mother. Despite the insults of the young man's mother, she discourages any further relationship with Strong. The young man's wealthy uncle learns the truth about the divorcée and proposes marriage to her.

A woman who has been divorced in one state and then remarries in another state finds that her second marriage is not only illegal, but she is found guilt of bigamy, in Robert J. Thornby's provocative domestic problem drama, *Are You Legally Married?* (1919). The film is based on a United States Supreme Court decision. Upon completion of the film, one copy was sent to Congress, resulting in two measures designed to nationalize divorce laws and force all states to adhere to the standard divorce law.

II. Divorce as a Matter of Course

Films of the 1910s and 1920s were preoccupied with stories about marriage and divorce. By the mid-twenties, audiences found themselves saturated with society dramas, in which the principals surrounded themselves in lavish settings, dressed in the latest fashions, indulged in cocktail parties, and suffered from unhappy marriages. Some divorce cases during the twenties became quite famous. For example, in 1927 Frances Heenan "Peaches" Browning, 16, sued New York real estate millionaire Edward W. "Daddy" Browning, 52, for divorce, after less than a year of marriage. The trial produced testimony that titillated newspaper readers. Divorces rose dramatically during the twenties. In 1914, for example, there were 100,000 divorces; by 1929, the number climbed to 205,000. Many of the later films about divorce treated the subject rather lightly. It seemed as though the studios were echoing the observations of journalist Helen Rowland, who as early as 1903, quipped: "Nowadays love is a matter of chance, matrimony a matter of money and divorce a matter of course." About two hundred films during the twenties dealt with the topic of divorce.

Spoiled Northern heiress Vivian Martin, while visiting Atlanta, meets and falls in love with Hugh Thompson, an impoverished Southerner from an aristocratic family, in Joseph Levering's society drama, *Husbands and Wives* (1920), based on the 1918 novel, *Making Her His Wife*, by Corra Harris. Thompson tries to have his wife follow the Southern customs and ideals of womanhood, but his efforts result only in disagreements between the newlyweds. The couple finally split up, but after a short separation, the pair reconcile their difference and rekindle their love for each other. Each agrees to find only virtue in the other, while overlooking any shortcoming.

The marriage of Mary MacLaren to Edward Pell, after several years and just as many children, is threatened by a newcomer in Phil Rosen's minor domestic drama, *The Road to Divorce* (1920). Pell begins to realize that his wife's work and attention to the children leave her little time for him, and he begins to resent this lack of attention. Bonnie Hill, a young intelligent Boston woman, pays the couple a visitor and Pell immediately is impressed by her. Their talks soon bring them closer together, resulting in his wife's growing upset with her husband's relationship with the visitor. Depressed by what she witnesses, the wife runs out into the stormy night. The husband suddenly is aroused by his wife's absence and bolts out to find her. He returns with his wife and decides to forget about his interest in the visitor.

The mother of a poor family decides to try her luck on the San Francisco stage, but gets involved in a divorce case instead, in James Cruze's weak domestic comedy. *Food for Scandal* (1920), based on the play, *Beverly's Balance*, by Paul Kester. Wanda Hawley, the aspiring actress, gets distracted by her former lover, who is practicing law – when he can find a client. They both meet a former college acquaintance, now wealthy, who is seeking a corespondent and a lawyer who will help him obtain a divorce. Hawley is hired as the corespondent, But she ends up bringing the couple together and having the unemployed lawyer hired as their business consultant for his college pal.

Herbert Blaché's bland comedy, *The New York Idea* (1920), based on the play by Langdon Mitchell, deals with the upper-class rich of New York and their attitudes about marriage as the first step to divorce, followed by alimony. Alice Brady and Lowell Sherman portray a newlywed couple who go through the entire experience of marriage, including the usual arguments and exchange of insults, but they find their true natures before it is too late. They finally reconcile their differences and are happily reunited, despite the cynicism of their crowd.

Katherine MacDonald, as the title character, has been named the corespondent in a well-known lawsuit, in James Young's drama, *The Notorious Miss Lisle* (1920), based on the 1911 novel by Baillie Reynolds. She accompanies her parents to a seacoast village in Brittany, where they hope to stay until the scandal diminishes. She meets Nigel Barry, and they fall in love. When she tries to tell him about the scandal, he refuses to listen. Encouraged by her parents, she marries Barry, who one day later learns about the scandal from a close friend. Embarrassed, she leaves him and goes to England. On board the vessel, she meets William Clifford, the man she has been linked with in the divorce case. She is hurt and Clifford cares for her. Her husband follows, convinced his wife is innocent of any charge – until he learns that Clifford is present. Following a series of complications, she is finally cleared of any insinuations and charges.

A grand opera prima donna devotes herself entirely to her career at the cost of neglecting her husband in Wallace Worsley's society comedy, *Enter Madame* (1922), based on the play by Frank Beresford. Waited on by an army of servants and catered to by as many domestic and foreign admirers, the singing star Clara Kimball Young thinks of her husband, Elliott Dexter, whom she loves, as sitting alone each evening. Instead, he has become fascinated with Louise Dresser, an attractive and seductive blonde. He is seriously thinking about divorcing his wife and marrying his new interest. When his wife learns about this, she rushes to his side and tries to make amends for her past neglect. At first, Dexter does not seem interested in these apologies, but Young proves persuasive, and the couple are finally reconciled.

Norma Shearer and John Gilbert portray schoolteachers who marry for love but soon separate because of Gilbert's obsession with wealth and social position in Monta Bell's domestic drama, *The Snob* (1924). Gilbert has attained much success and popularity formally speaking before various women's groups, an activity that leaves him yearning for more social exposure. Shearer, just out of a convent, receives news that her father has been killed in a scrape over another woman. She flees from the notoriety and her inheritance, leaving a note for Conrad Nagel, a wealthy friend who loves her. Several years later in a small Pennsylvania town where Shearer is teaching, she bids goodbye to the snobbish Gilbert, who is leaving for a university position. The two leads were paired as a romantic team for the first time in this film, and both became stars within a short time.

Helene Chadwick portrays a self-sacrificing older sister to Marie Prevost, who is prettier as well as silly, in Millard Webb's slow-paced drama, *The Dark Swan* (1924), based on the novel by Ernest Pascal. Chadwick's sacrifices are designed to shower upon her sister all the benefits of a successful social life. Finally, love, in the form of Monte Blue, enters Chadwick's life, but in a short time the more attractive and seductive Prevost steals Blue's love away and he marries her. Almost immediately after the wedding, the capricious Prevost begins flirting with a former lover. Her disillusioned husband leaves her and returns to the more mature and steady Chadwick, whom he has really loved all along.

Friction arises between businessman Monte Blue and his wife, Marie Prevost, in Ernst Lubitch's entertaining farce about the mechanics of romantic love,

Kiss Me Again (1925), based on the play, *Let's Get a Divorce*, by Victorien Sardou and Emile de Najac. The wife's fondness for music leads her into a romantic relationship with musician John Roche. The pianist, who becomes infatuated with the wife, begins to woo her, and she responds in kind. Blue, observing this flirtation, decides to step aside so that his wife, whom he loves, can enjoy her romance with Roche. He arranges for a divorce, which will give her full possession of the house and half of all his wealth. The terms delight the musician, who anticipates marriage with Prevost, followed by a comfortable and easy life. She, in reality, prefers Blue, whom she loves dearly, so she manipulates events that win back his affection. One very suggestive scene implies that the couple are disrobing, but this is all done cleverly by Lubitch, who has instilled his work with much wit and humor. *The New York Times* listed the film as one of the ten best of the year.

When bank teller Ben Lyon, distracted by his love for a restaurant worker, loses his job, he decides to work as an extra in movies, in Alfred Santell's *Bluebeard's Seven Wives* (1926), a broad satire of Hollywood and the film business. He scores a hit when he is asked to fill in for the leading actor who fails to appear. He is immediately signed up as the studio's latest discovery. Press agent Sam Hardy arrives and changes Lyon's name to Don Juan Hartez, a great Spanish lover. He sends the fledgling actor to sea and has him debark from the ocean liner in California. His new moustache and hair style make him the rage of young men around the country, all wanting to duplicate his romantic escapades with women. Agent Hardy then comes up with the idea of having him marry and divorce a parade of beauties, thereby keeping his name alive in print. However, this also causes a split between Lyon and his girlfriend, Lois Wilson, who loves him but believes all the romantic nonsense printed about him. The studio and his work prevent the couple from getting together, so Lyon decides to abandon the fame and money. He drives off with Wilson, and they settle down for a quiet rural life far from the frenetic and wild life of Hollywood. In addition to the press agent, the film pokes fun at several other aspects of the industry, including the director and his horde of yes men, the sheik-type of screen hero, the pretty leading lady, the screen temptress and the producers and businessmen.

Society debutante May McAvoy, while driving to her country home, accidentally hits careless hiker Ralph Graves, and insists on taking him to her home for treatment in Ralph Graves's romantic drama, *A Reno Divorce* (1927). Graves, the disinherited son of a steel magnate, tells his hostess that he is an impoverished artist struggling for acceptance. They soon become attracted to each other, and he wishes to stay around longer. So McAvoy hires him to paint a portrait of her dog. Meanwhile, divorced couple Robert Ober and Hedda Hopper come for a visit. The latter is romantically attracted to Graves, and Ober openly pursues the hostess, much to the dismay of the jealous artist, who denounces McAvoy as a flirt. Following several romantic complications, Graves and McAvoy resolve their differences.

Three young friends, children of inattentive, socially oriented parents, have grown up in luxury in Frank Lloyd's flawed society drama, *Children of Divorce* (1927), based on the novel by Owen Johnson. Clara Bow, selfish and mercenary, does not let lifelong friendships stand in the way of her romantic and financial desires. She lures Gary Cooper away from the more reserved and mature Esther Ralston, who is in love with Cooper. Ralston rebounds from the traumatic experience by marrying another man. Unfortunately, the affair ends in divorce. Later, Bow dies and Cooper returns to Ralston, his first real love. The reunited lovers finally find happiness with each other.

Florence Vidor portrays a lawyer who neglects her husband, Arnold Kent, in Luther Reed's sophisticated comedy, *The World at Her Feet* (1927). While the wife is busy furthering her career, her husband is devoting his time to romancing a philandering blonde, whose husband is seeking proof so that he can divorce her. When Vidor learns about the complication her husband is stepping into, she maneuvers events to save him from being implicated in a divorce scandal. The film brims with elegance and subtle humor. The plot, with its reversal of the neglected spouse, is not unlike that of *Enter Madame* (1922), in which opera singer Clara Kimball Young neglects her husband.

Owen Moore and Helene Costello, after six months of marriage, grow bored with each other and decide to get a divorce, in Henry Lehrman's humorous comedy drama about both marriage and divorce, *Husbands for Rent* (1927). Arthur Hoyt, as a snooping reporter for a society scandal sheet, is partially responsible for the couple's unhappiness. In addition, Costello thinks she still loves John Miljan, her former beau, while husband Moore thinks he still cares for his former fiancée, Kathryn Perry. Both are mistaken. Wealthy Englishman Claude Gillingwater, Costello's father, does not agree with the couple's decision for a divorce and tries to convince them they are truly in love with each other. Moore finally breaks their decision by confessing that he still loves Costello.

Drugs

I. The Devil's Needle

During the first two decades of the twentieth century, films about drug use focused chiefly on opium, cocaine and morphine. By the number of these films, one could assume the nation, or at least the major cities, were inundated with addicts, drug pushers and smugglers. Terms for the drug user, such as "pot-head," "snowbird" and "needle pusher," were widely used. Drug films focused on cities, especially areas like Chinatown or tenement sections, as breeding grounds for drugs. President Wilson, on May 2, 1916, signed into law the Harrison Drug Act, which required all persons licensed to sell narcotic drugs to file an inventory of their stocks with the Internal Revenue Service. The Supreme Court ruled on June 5 that users and sellers of opium are liable to prosecution. Movie studios wasted no time in exploiting the subject. The plots often depicted some element of crime, such as smuggling, as in *The Boundary Rider* (1914); or the underworld, in films like *A Romance of the Underworld* (1918); or a general degeneration of the drug addict, as in *The Devil's Needle* (1916). Some dramas were simply cautionary tales, as was *The Spirit of the Poppy* (1914); others, like *Black Fear* (1915), strongly suggested a more sensational approach to the topic.

One of the earliest films to deal with drugs was Selig's exciting one-reel drama, *The Smuggler's Game* (1910), whose subject was opium smuggling. The plot concerns a young woman who has two suitors. Forced to choose between the two, she selects the one who is an opium smuggler. She later discovers she has made the wrong choice. There are interesting scenes of a harbor, a tugboat hired to deliver the opium, drugged victims and an opium den. The cast included several Chinese, who lent a note of realism to the production.

The episodic crime drama, *Conscience* (1913), explores the haunts where opium, cocaine and morphine dominate the lives of some inhabitants of lower

New York City, especially Chinatown. These seekers of reckless pleasure are soon influenced by an image of Christ that forces them to search their consciences, after which they curb their appetites for their dangerous pastimes. The image is attired in the robes of the Messiah. In one sequence, a streetwalker captures the attention of a young man whose father is a money lender. The youth, desiring money to satisfy his craving for the woman, attacks his father. But he stops from going further when he sees the same image of the Savior. In another scene in the back room of a rundown saloon, a group of rough men and women select their next victim whom they intend to drug with the aid of opium, cocaine, etc. And once again, the image descends upon them and forces them to examine their consciences. Although chiefly crude in its production values, the film offers several effective moments and fascinating scenes of early New York.

The drama, *The Cocaine Traffic* (1914), tells the tragic story of a cocaine addict who marries the daughter of a cocaine dealer known as "The Cocaine King." The young husband then converts his wife into a steady user of the drug. The father finally rescues her, while the husband sinks to new lows by joining the white slave racket in which he entices innocent young women with drugs and then forces them into prostitution. Ironically, he has to rescue his own sister who has been brought to one of the white slave houses by another trader. Reduced to the life of a common vagrant, the young man returns to his father-in-law's house. The older man, about to escape to Europe, and the younger visitor become involved in a physical struggle. A fire breaks out and both men perish in the flames. Several contemporary critics, concerned about younger audiences, attacked the film for being more sensational than educational or informative.

Not all drug dealers were villainous characters or gang leaders. Sometimes they were conventional businessmen or storekeepers, familiar to their neighbors. A druggist sells illegal drugs to selected customers, including local youths, in the vice drama, *The Drug Traffic* (1914). Ironically, his own daughter becomes addicted and dies. The police eventually arrest the father.

Herman Lieb's revealing drama, *Dope* (1914), based on the 1909 play by Medill Patterson, dealt with the debilitating effects of drugs. The film had some stark sequences in it. In one such segment, Laura Nelson Hall, an addicted mother, leaves a comfortable home when she can no longer obtain cocaine to satisfy her habit and stoops to prostitution. She is arrested for soliciting and released when she promises to leave town with her son, Ernest Truex. Later, in New York, the son leads his father to the drug store that has been selling cocaine and where he sees his wife fall dead before the body of her brother, who has been shot by a crooked acquaintance. The husband realizes the death resulted from the drug habit. But the druggist shows him a bottle of cocaine, with the label carrying the name of the company the husband is associated with. The film suggests a direct connection between the retail and wholesale drug business.

One standard plot of drug-related films concerned smugglers. A gang of opium smugglers working in a wild wooded area have a smooth racket going – until a suspicious stenographer foils their operation in Leopold Wharton's action drama, *The Boundary Rider* (1914). Wild Bill and his gang ship the opium in hollowed-out logs down river where their conspirator, Maxwell, picks up the supply and sells it to some Chinese. Following several complications, Elsie, Maxwell's stenographer, secretly witnesses the whole operation and notifies the proper authorities, who take steps to capture the entire gang. In one sequence, Elsie dresses as a Chinese, goes to Wild Bill's camp, works for him and then escapes. Fights, gunplay and chases add to the excitement and suspense. The film seems more concerned with action than with opium and its effects.

A devious tea importer is smuggling more than tea into this country in the drama, *The Counter Intrigue* (1915). The importer schemes to seduce a friend's wife while arranging for the woman's husband to take the fall for a crime he did not commit. Though completely innocent, the husband goes to prison. The wife vows vengeance on the treacherous smuggler. Seeking the aid of a U.S. Secret Service agent, she elicits a confession from the importer after supplying him with enough liquor to loosen his tongue.

Frederick Thomson's capable cautionary drama, *The Spirit of the Poppy* (1914), explores the effects of drugs on innocent people. A very talented artist and his wife become addicted to drugs through the influence of others. The husband foolishly allows his deceitful female model to provide him with drugs she says will give him pleasure, while his wife's doctor gives her morphine to treat her minor nervous condition. They both soon descend morally, ending up in a slum and living abject lives.

A wife grows suspicious of her husband's assistant in Alexander F. Frank's contrived drama, *A Suspicious Wife* (1914), based on a Freeport, Long Island, murder case that achieved national newspaper coverage. The plot, which mixes crime, murder and drug addiction, begins with a young woman who jumps off a bridge. She is rescued by a sailor and a doctor, and finally becomes a drug addict, resulting from her stay in a hospital. She is arrested and convicted of attempted suicide, but the doctor's sympathetic wife tells the judge she will take the defendant home and help cure her of her addiction. The judge releases the woman to the married couple, with the doctor making the guest his assistant. Later, a village gossip warns the wife about a possible romantic affair going on between the husband and the assistant. The wife, overhearing the woman trying to seduce her husband, sends her away. The woman returns, seeking revenge and, mistaking a friend for the wife, shoots the stranger. Following several complications, the woman returns to her drug habit and is overheard admitting that she has committed the murder. She re-enacts the crime and loses her mind. The wife, who has been arrested for the murder, is released and reunited with her family. K. M. Turner, the inventor of the Dictaphone, appears as himself in the film.

Films about drug addicts allowed female costars to play the role of heroine and savior who rescue their loved ones from addiction. A pair of lovers narrowly escape an angry mob in John G. Adolfi's western drama about the misfortunes of a drug addict, *A Man and His Mate* (1915), based on the 1908 play by Harold Riggs Durant. Harry Woodruff becomes dependent on morphine after being treated with the drug for a football injury he suffered while in college. He is later helped by Gladys Brockwell, an old acquaintance. Sam De Grasse, a dishonest mine speculator, accidentally kills Brockwell's father. Everyone, including Brockwell, suspects Woodruff. When she discovers he is innocent, she helps him evade the pursuing mob. Her father's engineer kills De Grasse as the couple make their way to freedom.

An artist, induced by his scheming model to take an injection of morphine, begins to see his career and life spiral downward, in Chester Withey's familiar drama, *The Devil's Needle* (1916), about drug addiction and its terrible effects. Before the artist, Tully Marshall, descends all the way, he marries the daughter of a wealthy attorney. She had been engaged to a young lawyer in her father's office. After getting his wife to try drugs, Marshall returns to his model, Norma Talmadge, who by now has given up the habit. However, she purchases the drug for the artist, who is impoverished. But before he reaches the lowest depths, Talmadge, showing a change of heart, nurses him back to health. The power of love helps to rehabilitate both souls.

Louise Glaum portrays a gang moll who eventually straightens out her life after falling in love with a drug-addicted lawyer in Walter Edwards's romantic drama, *Love or Justice?* (1917). She even goes so far as to try to confess to a murder she did not commit to help her lover improve his conviction record. Despite the ambiguous title and the underworld setting, the film is as much a love story as it is a crime drama. Glaum was considered something of a cult heroine when playing underworld roles.

Country girl Gladys Hulette comes to New York City, opens a candy store and wins the hearts of two suitors in W. Eugene Moore's romantic drama, *The Candy Girl* (1917). One young man is a brawny musician, and the other, the son of a wealthy father, is addicted to morphine. She settles for the latter, and they are married. But her life with her addicted husband proves to be a struggle. She helps him through one crisis after another until her love and belief in him help to cure him of his addiction. At least one critic was disappointed that the country girl did not select the honest musician for her lifelong mate.

Broadway stage success Betty Brice, in Jack Pratt's romantic drama, *Loyalty* (1917), based on the novel by Ray Lewis, helps her drug-addicted husband conquer his habit. Raised in the West, Brice comes to the big city with a letter of introduction to one of the kings of the New York theater world. He immediately gives her a chance to perform when a leading lady walks out on him. Later, Brice meets the drug-addicted son of a wealthy widow who shuns the young singer when they meet at a posh restaurant. The son proposes marriage to Brice who, to spite the mother, accepts. Her jealous producer fires her the next day.

Following several complications, the mother offers Brice $5,000 to leave town. Brice, married by now, removes the wedding ring when her husband, in need of a drug fix, attacks her. She pawns the ring, collects the money from her mother-in-law and leaves for the West with her husband. It is there that they hope to begin a new life together and where she plans to help him kick his drug habit.

More rare in these films is the woman addict and her male rescuer. Phillips Smalley's semi-documentary, *Hop, the Devil's Brew* (1916), was adapted from a series of magazine articles by Rufus Steele. Supposedly based on actual files from the United States Customs Service, the film depicts the sordid aspects of addiction to opium in San Francisco. Lydia Jansen is one victim – the addicted wife of a customs official. Unaware of her problem, her husband smashes the drug ring that turns out to be controlled by the addict's father. Grief-stricken, the father takes his own life. The husband then nurses his wife back to health.

Undercover policeman Crane Wilbur, on the trail of a gang of thieves, poses as a drug fiend in Robert B. Broadwell's disappointing crime drama, *The Mystery of Carter Breene* (1915). The plethora of action, consisting chiefly of violence, murder and mayhem, is not enough to save this three-reeler. The comely heroine, who has fallen in love with the allegedly addicted detective, is left in the lurch at the end of the film. Crane Wilbur became a respected film director following his short career before the camera.

Many pre-World War I films, including drug dramas, had their leads play a dual role. William Farnum plays a dual role in Frederick Thomson's strange, implausible and misnamed drama, *The Wonderful Adventure* (1915), based on the play and novel by Captain Wilbur Lawson. Demarest, a businessman, falls under the spell of Dorothy Green, a mystic, who introduces him to drugs. He soon turns into an addict. Stanley, a construction engineer from the West, visits the East, and because he strongly resembles Demarest, is introduced to his look-alike by a mutual friend. The drug addict persuades Stanley to impersonate him, while he tries to recover from his addiction. Stanley agrees and takes over the man's wife and business. Following several complications, the mystic threatens to expose Stanley, who finally tells Mrs. Demarest the truth. An electrical storm kills Green, the blackmailing mystic, and Stanley and the wife find her husband in a dilapidated apartment. Demarest is dead, the result of his addiction. His widow, who has fallen in love with Stanley, pleads with him to stay with her, and he accepts her offer.

Hobart Henley plays a dual role in Charles Swickard's drama, *The Sign of the Poppy* (1916), about two brothers, one raised as Chinese, the other brought up as white. The evil, Chinese-reared brother hates his twin, as well as their father, and thinks nothing of drug dealing or committing murder. The drug-ridden son kills his father while the other brother is on his honeymoon. The remainder of the film deals with the unraveling of the circumstances surrounding the crime. Among the plot twists are the usual mistaken identity situations where one brother poses as the other. Reviewers gave unstinting praise to the cast and director for sustaining interest throughout – despite the unrealistic plot.

Drug addict Harmon McGregor maliciously makes trouble for his doctor brother by insinuating the latter's wife is unfaithful, in Edwin August's social drama, *Bondwomen* (1915). The trusting doctor, John Sainpolis, believes his addicted brother, and separates from his wife, Maude Fealy, and their child. At one point, the cocaine-addicted McGregor is assaulted by a drug-crazed young woman who tries to blind him with acid. Following several other complications between the doctor and his wife, they finally are reunited and the sick brother is cured of his drug addiction. The film depicts several realistic scenes of drug dens inhabited by those unfortunately addicted.

John W. Noble's drama, *Black Fear* (1915), alternates between sensationalism and exposé as it depicts how some unscrupulous Wall Street messenger services hand out drugs to their boys to keep them awake for their late shifts. Later, the companies are described as encouraging the youths to visit gambling joints and houses of ill repute. One such boy, whose father has died, goes to work for one of these companies to help support his two older sisters. He becomes a drug addict and dies from an overdose. The company boss lures the boy's younger sister to his apartment, drugs her and attempts to rape her. The older sister enters, intending to berate him for her brother's death, and a struggle ensues in which the man is shot to death. At the older sister's trial, the younger one testifies how the deceased tried to attack her. She removes her blouse to show the judge and jury her bruises as a result of her struggle. The defendant is freed and marries her lawyer, who describes in his summary to the court the immoral and illegal practices of the messenger services toward their young employees. The film opens with an allegory showing Satan listening intensely to Miss Cocaine, who offers to entice victims to sin using a novel approach.

Wilfred Lucas portrays an unfortunate bookkeeper who suffers because of another's drug problem in Paul Powell's murder drama, *Acquitted* (1916), adapted from Mary Robert Rinehart's 1907 short story. Lucas, a kindly family man, is accused of murdering a fellow employee, Spottiswoode Aitken, at a plant where they are both employed. The murder was actually committed by a watchman on drugs, stealing to feed his habit, and surprised in the act by the victim. Lucas is arrested and then released when the watchman confesses. However, the attendant notoriety was enough to cost Lucas his job, and he sinks into despair. When he finally reaches the point of contemplating suicide, his daughter arranges a reconciliation of sorts and his employer rehires him.

Some films focused on foreign settings and addicts from other lands. With the Indian Mutiny of 1857-1858 as background, Charles Swickard's drama, *The Beggar of Cawnpore* (1916), presents a series of intrigues between the rebellious sepoys and British troops. H. B. Warner portrays a physician in the employ of the British East India Service. During a cholera epidemic at a remote outpost, he takes morphine when he comes down with fever. He later discovers that he is addicted to the drug. Cashiered from the service, he becomes one of the numerous beggars of Cawnpore. When the sepoy rebellion erupts, he rescues his former girlfriend and conquers his addiction.

Widower William H. Thompson, the head of a real estate corporation, drains as much as he can from his tenants, cuts his workers' salaries and fails to attend his son's graduation from college, in Walter Edwards's domestic drama, *The Dividend* (1916). When his son, Charles Ray, comes home, he asks his father for a job, but the elder laughs at the lad and offers him three dollars a week to sweep the office. Finally, he hands his son money and tells him to go out and have a good time. Ray one evening visits an opium den and soon becomes an addict. The father finds out and evicts him from his home. "If you had been a real father to me," Ray exclaims, "I wouldn't have become a dope fiend!" The father, more obsessed than ever with his business, accumulates great wealth. He suddenly begins to miss his son, who is returned to him a physical and emotional wreck. Thompson helps his son to recover, and when Ray awakens from his unconscious state, he is happy to find his father embracing him.

Two cocaine addicts, a judge and his brother, serve as the focus of Allen Holubar's drama, *Fear Not* (1917). When the judge, Myles McCarthy, must hear charges against his brother (Murdock MacQuarrie), he resigns his office. He and his daughter and brother decide to leave the country, hoping another environment will help the brothers to beat their terrible habit of cocaine abuse. Instead of improving, their situation deteriorates when MacQuarrie kills a doctor who is trying to help them. The daughter is convicted of the crime, but she is later cleared of all charges. The film was originally titled *The Twisted Soul*.

Jack Standing saves several lives in Oscar Apfel's implausible cautionary crime drama, *The Price of Her Soul* (1917). First, he saves the life of the warden where he is imprisoned and wins a pardon. Next, he investigates the circumstances behind his brother's drug addiction and finds, to his dismay, that the dealer is a noted doctor, the father of the woman he loves. To drive a point home, Standing supplies the doctor's daughter with drugs. Horrified, the father renounces his past and joins Standing, his daughter and Standing's brother in the mountains. They all recover, and Standing and the doctor's daughter, who have fallen in love, are married.

Aristocratic Walt Whitman dreams about a marriage between his granddaughter and his son, although the young woman loves another, in E. Mason Hopper's domestic drama, *The Regenerates* (1917). She also rejects her cousin because of his addiction to drinking and drugs. The son has earlier had an affair with a housemaid, who gives birth to their baby and dies in childbirth. When a valet throws the profligate, drug-addicted son out of a window to his death, Whitman refuses to accept the baby as his grandson. Instead, his granddaughter and her husband take the child and raise it as their own. Years later, the couple bring the young boy to Whitman, who finally accepts his grandson, named after his dead father, as worthy of carrying on the proud family tradition.

When struggling doctor Edward Peil realizes he cannot support a wife, he loses Gail Kane to the wealthy William Conklin, in Rollin S. Sturgeon's drama, *The Serpent's Tooth* (1917). The couple marry, but the husband's social ambitions and interest in Jane Pascal cause a split in the marriage. The wife, to keep the marriage alive, presents her husband with a baby, but it soon dies. The despondent mother sinks into a deep depression, compelling Peil, the doctor, to give her morphine. Meanwhile, Conklin's mistress devises a plan in which the husband will force his wife to become an addict so that he can divorce her. But the plan backfires, and Conklin dies from an overdose of the drug. The doctor, who still loves Kane, then cures her of her addiction, and they plan their new life together.

Catherine Calvert portrays a young woman formerly from a convent, and now thrust among a gang of thieves and drug dealers headed by a scheming ward boss in James Kirkwood's social drama, *A Romance of the Underworld* (1918), based on the 1911 play by Paul Armstrong. To the desperate and miserable trapped in the poverty of New York's Lower East Side and products of an uncaring society, the underworld offers a romantic alternative. Calvert comes to live with her brother, who is part of the gang, but she remains naive about the crime and corruption that pervade the neighborhood. Here she finally learns about drugs, rape and death. Her brother kills the ward boss who tries to rape her. The police arrive and accuse her of the murder. However, she is exonerated at the trial. Like several other features of the period, the film strongly suggests that slums breed crime.

II. Drug Traffic and Its Human Wreckage

In 1915, Variety wrote during its review of *The Devil's Needle*, "The drug story has been so often sheeted there is nothing left for it, unless the plan is to keep on drilling against the evil effect of drugs." Many of the drug films of the twenties did indeed repeat the themes and plots of earlier films. For example, in *A Man and His Mate* (1915) and *The Devil's Needle* (1916), two earlier films in which a sympathetic woman helps a man overcome his drug problem, this basic idea was repeated in such dramas as *The Woman Gives* (1920). Films about smugglers reappeared in the twenties in several action dramas, including *Tearing Through* (1925). The crime genre provided additional features with drug related themes. The major change between the earlier and later films was the decline in the cautionary dramas. Instead, the entries released in the twenties showed the corrosive effects of drugs more subtly and developed their plots more through character development than through coincidence.

When artist John Halliday learns that his wife has been unfaithful, he resorts to opium as a way to forget his troubles, in R. William Neill's unconvincing drama, *The Woman Gives* (1920), based on the novel by Owen Johnson. Norma

Talmadge, who is in love with Edmund Lowe, is a close friend of Halliday's, and she decides to reclaim him from his life of degradation. She goes to the opium den that he frequents and takes him out of there. She then helps him to recover. Although he is still married, he proposes to her, but she turns him down. After he is cured, she returns to Lowe, her true lover.

Herbert Rawlinson, a doctor who is disillusioned by his girlfriend's infidelity, relies heavily on opium, in J. Stuart Blackton's drama of reformation, *Man and His Woman* (1920). After an abundance of drug use, the doctor ends up in a hospital. A fellow physician recognizes Rawlinson and takes him to his country home, where nurse May McAvoy helps him to recuperate and rekindles his will to live and finish his experiments. Before his drug habit, he had been working on a serum to cure tuberculosis. Meanwhile, the lecherous Warren Chandler, a rich importer who had seduced Rawlinson's girlfriend and then abandoned her, now takes an interest in nurse McAvoy. He tries to attack her, but she escapes unharmed. Following other complications, including Rawlinson's suspicions concerning the nurse, the patient and nurse are reunited.

Priscilla Dean, as a successful stage actress in Paris, discovers that a young American performer is impersonating her, in Stuart Paton's drama, *Reputation* (1921), based on the story, "False Colors," by Edwina Levin. Dean, now a drug addict, returns to the U.S., where she shoots a man and permits her imitator to take the blame. Dean then learns that the actress is her own daughter whom she had abandoned as a child. Her daughter was raised in an orphanage and had acquired her mother's talent for the stage. Dean then writes a confession and takes her own life.

A mix-up between U.S. Secret Service agents leads to comedy and romance in Bayard Veiller's entertaining film, *There Are No Villains* (1921), about the pursuit of drug smugglers. Viola Dana, as a government agent, suspects a young man of being in collusion with the head of an opium ring. However, her suspect, with whom she soon falls in love, turns out to be a fellow agent from another department.

A modern-day bluebeard hires a drug addict to hypnotize an innocent woman and bring her to him in the grim drama, *The Dungeon* (1922). When his hireling brings the woman, the bluebeard villain marries her while she is under a hypnotic spell and takes her to a house where he has killed eight other wives. He then locks her in a dungeon. The trapped victim is rescued by a former admirer, who then proceeds to kill the kidnapper and murderer. The crude and strange film was produced by Oscar Micheaux, who turned out a series of race films over several decades. Like his other works, this drama consists of an entirely African-American cast, probably the only unique characteristic of the production.

A successful surgeon becomes a drug addict in Irving Cummings's cautionary drama, *The Drug Traffic* (1923), about the deleterious effects of drugs. The surgeon at first uses drugs simply as a stimulant so that he can work all day and play all night. Slowly, he becomes addicted and is arrested. He escapes and breaks into the hospital where he has performed operations. He then realizes that he has destroyed his career and life. Although he plans to change his lifestyle, it is too late. He dies of an overdose.

Reformed burglar Betty Compson is persuaded to help an idealistic district attorney convict a gang of drug smugglers in Herbert Brenon's fast-paced drama, *The Woman With Four Faces* (1923), based on the play by Bayard Veiller. Richard Dix, as the attorney, resigns his office when a judge refuses to give him a search warrant necessary to gain evidence against the smugglers. Instead, he elicits the aid of Compson, who enjoys the adventure and is an expert at disguise. Together, they burglarize a safe that holds a key letter. The film has an interesting scene in which a convict in a prison yard escapes by means of an airplane equipped with a rope ladder.

John Griffith Wray's social drama, *Human Wreckage* (1923), attempted a serious examination of the traffic in drugs. A lawyer becomes addicted through his association with a doctor who is himself addicted to drugs. The lawyer's dependency and final struggle to kick the habit is graphically depicted is a series of surrealistic scenes. He is finally cured when his wife tricks him into thinking that she, too, has become dependent on morphine. As the attorney for the narcotics squad, he smashes the local drug ring. Mrs. Wallace Reid, whose husband in real life had died tragically as a drug addict years earlier, appeared in the film, along with other city, state and federal officials in the Los Angeles area. In addition, Mrs. Reid addressed the movie audience about the growing drug problem when the film opened in New York.

A young woman endangers her life when she tries to free an innocent man falsely accused of murder in D. W. Griffith's underworld drama, *That Royle Girl* (1925), based on the 1925 novel by Edwin Balmer. Carol Dempster, as the heroine burdened with an alcoholic father and a drug-dependent mother, falls in love with a married band leader who is soon arrested for murdering his wife. He is convicted and given the death penalty, but Dempster fights to save him. When she learns that a local gangster is the real killer, she befriends him and gains a confession. But she is captured and later found by a district attorney. The band leader is freed, and Dempster opts for the attorney. Several stories by science- and mystery-fiction writer Edwin Balmer were adapted for the screen. Comedian W. C. Fields, who would gain fame in sound films during the next decade, played Dempster's alcoholic father.

Idealistic assistant district attorney Richard Talmadge helps to smash a drug-smuggling ring centered in Chinatown in Arthur Rosson's routine action drama, *Tearing Through* (1925). When his boss is unable to capture the gang, Talmadge decides to investigate on his own. He learns that his girlfriend's brother is hooked on drugs and tries to help the youth kick the habit. Together, they discover that the brother's romantic rival owns the opium den and is holding the brother's girlfriend there against her will. Talmadge rescues the captive and proves that the district attorney has been receiving payoffs from the gang.

Robert Frazer, as the politically ambitious son of a reformed criminal, faces a blackmailer in William Neill's drama, *The City* (1926), based on the 1915 play by Clyde Fitch. With his mother overindulging herself in climbing the social ladder, and his sister tricked into marrying a drug addict, mayoral candidate Frazer decides to confront the blackmailer, who then commits suicide. To escape the urban temptations and corruption, the family leaves the city behind and returns home to a simpler village life.

Jack Holt, as the chief of British Intelligence in China, is working under cover to expose an opium-smuggling ring in George B. Seitz's action drama, *The Warning* (1927). Posing as a secretive, enigmatic captain of a tramp steamer used for smuggling, Holt is able to gain the confidence of smugglers who soon capture a female government agent. Holt helps her to escape, explaining to the gang that she got the drop on him. She is betrayed by her partner, who in reality is a smuggler, and she is recaptured. But Holt, with the help of a machine-gun and grenades, again rescues her while fighting off the gang members.

Internal Revenue agent Leo Maloney and policewoman Greta Yoltz join forces to round up a gang of heroin smugglers working the Canadian border in Leo Maloney's routine action drama, *Yellow Contraband* (1928). Maloney, who resembles a notorious Chicago gangster, impersonates the hoodlum in an attempt to intercept a drug shipment, but fails. However, with the help of the policewoman, also in disguise, both bring the culprits to justice.

Country boy Owen Gorin journeys to the big city to find his sister, Florence Dudley, who seems to have disappeared, in Norton S. Parker's drama, *The Pace That Kills* (1928). Once in the city, Gorin finds a job in a department store, where he meets Virginia Roye. An experienced "city girl," she quickly introduces him to narcotics, and he soon becomes dependent on drugs. His life begins to deteriorate, and he is dismissed from his job. A tormented addict and derelict relegated to wandering the streets, he comes across his lost sister, Florence, who also is a drug addict. To support her habit, she has become a prostitute. When she is jailed, Gorin enters a hospital, and after months of agony, he is cured of his dependence on drugs. Officials permit him to return home. He is welcomed by his parents and his childhood girlfriend.

Gladys Brockwell, as the ex-wife of a husband believed to be dead, is accused of murder in Edward Laemmle's convoluted drama, *The Drake Case* (1929). Brockwell is a servant in the home of Mrs. Drake, the victim. Following several complications and twists, the plot is resolved when all learn that the husband, still alive and under another identity, committed the murder. He was the secret lover of Mrs. Drake, both plotting to make her daughter a drug addict so they could claim her inheritance. Brockwell is found not guilty. The film was released in both a silent and sound version.

Eugenics

I. A Solution to the "Pitiable Waste of Life"

The study of improving inherited human characteristics suggested to some that reproduction should be discouraged by those whom society considers unfit, while encouraging those judged fit to reproduce. Extreme applications were practiced during the early part of the twentieth century, ranging from government intervention with its laws of miscegenation, enforced sterilization of the mentally incompetent in the United States, to Nazi Germany's Holocaust. In more recent times, China has restricted marriages embracing those with certain disabilities and importance. Early American films dealing with eugenics basically avoided political and social controversies while reflecting the values and attitudes of contemporary society. These films may be divided conveniently into two general areas. The first dealt with myths, fairy tales and fantasies, which occasionally embodied allegories, as in *Neptune's Daughter* (1914). The second concerned social dramas, chiefly about the lower economic classes, such as *The Escape* (1914). Several early silent fantasy films unfolded tales of love between mortals and others. These fairy tales gave their producers and directors a chance to have their heroines and other female players dressed with very little. However, these short scenes, which probably delighted many in the audience, were discreetly filmed. Other features, such as *The Sin Woman* (1917), employed allegory to help illustrate the theme of eugenics. Probably because of the controversial issue of alcohol abuse and the advent of Prohibition, several films about heredity, including *Blue Blood* (1918), *A Heart in Pawn* (1919) and *The Fear Woman* (1919), dealt with alcoholism as an inherited trait to be feared and watched carefully.

D. W. Griffith's drama, *The Escape* (1914), based on the play by Paul Armstrong, deals with an impoverished family – a father, two daughters, and a son – trying to survive in a New York tenement. Sympathetic doctor Owen Moore, who loves Blanche Sweet, one of the daughters, treats the son, Robert

Harron, who suffers from a venereal disease. Mae Marsh, the other daughter, marries tough, brutal Donald Crisp, who uses his hands freely on his wife. The doctor advises Sweet to move out of her depressing tenement. She moves uptown to a fashionable apartment where she becomes the mistress of a wealthy man. The drunken Crisp injures his newly born baby, resulting in its death. He slaps his wife who is holding the dead child. The doctor operates on Harron, curing him of his disease and his sadistic tendencies (he is seen earlier strangling a harmless cat). A contemporary review in the *New York Dramatic Mirror* took this social drama seriously. "Until our slums are peopled with eugenic husbands and wives," the periodical stated, "we must expect such a pitiable waste of life as is found here."

Herbert Brenon's fairy tale-like drama, *Neptune's Daughter* (1914), concerns the daughter of Neptune, the god of the ocean. Played by Annette Kellerman, a famous swimming star of the period, she is occasionally seen covered only by her long hair – always discreetly filmed. An undersea witch transforms her into a mortal. Her little five-year-old sister is found dead on the beach after being trapped in a fisherman's net and dragged to land, where she suffocated from lack of water. Kellerman swears to avenge the child's death by finding the one who supplied the net. This happens to be the King of the land, who is in the middle of a revolution. Following a series of complications, including Kellerman's falling in love with the King, she escapes an assassination attempt and helps to rescue the King, who is fighting off a handful of traitors. Brenon had a long and distinguished career in early films.

The appeal of the Raffles character in cinema fiction is once again demonstrated in Herbert Blaché's drama, *The Burglar and the Lady* (1914), starring Jim Corbett as the gentleman cracksman. The story, which touches upon the theme of eugenics, centers upon two brothers, each brought up in different surroundings and circumstances. One, the elder, is raised in luxury by the father. The other, Danvers, is poverty-stricken and forced to steal to care for his mother. Danvers, the daring cracksman, is pursued by his detective nemesis throughout the film. The obligatory reformation occurs when Danvers reconsiders and decides to go straight. As if to redeem himself, he marries the daughter of one of his victims. Corbett, the heavyweight boxing champion of the world, made his screen debut in this film.

Anne Lehr, the daughter of a wealthy mother well entrenched in society, has developed her own theory about the influence of heredity, and sets about testing it on her acquaintance, Ella Hall, in Robert Leonard's social drama, *Heritage* (1915). Hall, who has been adopted and raised by her tenement neighbors, the McMahons, works in a factory to help support her foster parents. Later, she meets Lehr, who invites her to stay at her posh home. Robert Leonard, Hall's stepbrother, is disappointed, especially when he learns she has married Lehr's brother, Allan Forrest. When Forrest begins to neglect his wife, she hurls things at him and returns to her foster parents. Her stepbrother, who has gotten over his jealousy, advises Forrest to treat her roughly to win her back. The advice works and she returns to her husband. She then attends boarding school, where she excels in her studies and acquires the necessary social and cultural amenities of her new class.

An early screen attempt to show the effects of environment on individual character, the action drama, *Environment* (1915), loses most of its intent by dwelling too much upon plot. The story opens with four-year-old Jack wandering away from his family who, while crossing the desert, are attacked by Indians. The only survivors are his mother and brother Robert. Jack is found by outlaws who adopt him. Twenty years later, Jack becomes the outlaw leader. Following a gun battle in which most of his band are killed, Jack wanders into Mexico and meets his brother, who has become a monk at a monastery. Upon learning of the bandit leader's life of crime, the brother upbraids Jack, who then decides to reform.

Henry Otto's enchanting fairy tale, *Undine* (1916), tells the story of Undine, a clever water nymph, who leads the other nymphs with her water skills. On land, she meets a mortal, Jack Nelson, and falls in love. They marry, and she gives up her life in the sea. One day, her husband enters the enchanted forest and shoots a sacred deer. The ruler of the forest slays the mortal, and Undine dies of grief. Her child has been cursed to dwell only on land – until a pure love atones for her mother's sin. Years later, Undine's daughter, raised by a fisherman's family as a mortal, captures the interest of a knight, Douglas Gerrard. He has been chosen by a sea spirit to fall in love with the young woman and marry her. The knight then takes his bride to his castle. This accomplished, the spirit sends Undine's daughter back to the sea where she belongs. Because of the lack of clothes worn by the star, one critic suggested the title should have been changed from *Undine* to *Undressed*.

A young man who deeply loves a young woman promises to remain pure in this exploitation drama, *The Garden of Knowledge* (1917). The remainder of this frank film focuses on the youth's temptations by various women. The producers explained that their work was intended to bring out that the eugenic theory has its mental and its physical perspectives, and when conflicts between the two arise, grief results.

Leopold Wharton's semi-scientific and thought-provoking drama, *The Black Stork* (1917), champions the cause of producing only healthy offspring – through the enactment of national eugenic laws. Much of the film is based on a contemporary incident in which Dr. Harry J. Haiselden of Chicago refused to save the life of a defective baby. Using a series of well-known contemporary personalities, several statistics, and dramatic examples, the film illustrates its point of view. For instance, it points out that the government allots millions of dollars for the healthy propagation of livestock and nothing for the birth of healthy children.

Marie Shotwell almost ruins the marriage of her son and daughter-in-law in Edmund Lawrence's domestic drama, *Married in Name Only* (1917). The mother announces that she and her parents are insane, and since her son's genes are tainted, the disease will probably be passed on to his children. Because of this news, the bridegroom, Milton Sills, avoids his wife, Gretchen Hartman, locking the door between their bedrooms. Although he loves her very much, he treats her kindly and respectfully – but more like a sister than a wife. After contemplating suicide, he is saved and his marriage restored when he discovers that he was adopted.

Following a series of introductory allegories depicting evil-doers as victims of heredity, George W. Lederer's drama, *The Sin Woman* (1917), tells of a modern day "vampire" in New York who lures men to their ruin. Irene Fenwick, as the seductress, flees to the mountains to elude the law and sets up a small hotel. She meets a well-built man who is happily married. He takes her to a cabin where they are forced to remain during a storm. She is infatuated with him, but he keeps his distance. She later meets Clifford Bruce, who decides to elope with her. Before leaving with her, he tells his wife that he is leaving with Fenwick. Determined to fight for her husband, his wife goes to Fenwick to plead to her. The first victim tells his mother about his experience, and she alerts the townspeople about the evil woman in their midst. A posse is formed. They strip the vampire to her waist and tar and feather her. The film ends with the question: "What will her future be?"

A decent young couple, raised properly by equally respectable families, are haunted by their past, in William Wolbert's drama, *The Wild Strain* (1918). By coincidence, each of the pair has a wild streak that can be traced back several generations to their ancestors. However, this is not revealed until the end of the film. The lovers are engaged to be married, but their proud parents worry about the background of the prospective in-laws. The parents of Nell Shipman, the prospective bride, call on the parents of Alfred Whitman, the young man, to check up on the family. Following several humorous complications, including both sides revealing their family skeletons, the couple marry. They both learn that on the bride's side there was a wild brigand, and in the groom's past there was a prizefighter.

A wealthy doctor's adopted son, whose father was a convict, almost suffers because of his father's past, in John S. Robertson's implausible drama, *The Menace* (1918). The young man is in love with Norinne Griffith, the daughter of a neighbor. The young woman's family learns about the man's father, and they assume that the son has inherited the blood and other characteristics of his father. However, when the young man finally asserts his own, noble, honest and virtuous nature, Griffith and her family accept him. In addition, the ex-convict father confesses that the boy is actually the doctor's real son. The contrived ending resolves little about the issue of heredity as an important factor in subsequent generations.

A member of an old aristocratic family, Howard Hickman, who is addicted to drink, hopes to marry a wealthy woman in Eliot Howe's domestic drama, *Blue Blood* (1918). The prospective bride's mother, interested in promoting her social standing, encourages the arrangement, regardless of his weakness. The mother, meanwhile, has been discouraging another suitor, George Fisher, a local doctor who loves her daughter. The doctor is reluctant to tell the young woman that Hickman's problem is the result of heredity. But the marriage proceeds as scheduled. The wife learns too late about the seriousness of her husband's defect. A child is born defective and dies. But she is unaware that a normal, healthy baby has been substituted. For the next five years, the mother believes the child is hers, and she would like to destroy it. Simultaneously, Hickman's mind manifests signs of deterioration, the result of his various orgies he carries out in his home. The mother, locked away in an apartment, escapes and is hurt during her flight. She awakens to the sight of her foster child standing over her. She takes him home to find her husband toppled over and dead from his excesses. The doctor has remained loyal to her all these years and shows up to comfort her in her grief.

Another film suggesting that the curse of whiskey is hereditary, Hugh Ford's *The Danger Mark* (1918) adapted from Robert William Chambers's 1909 novel, stars Elsie Ferguson as a socialite who has inherited a fortune. Unfortunately, she has also inherited a weakness for the bottle, which comes to the fore at her coming-out party. The villainous Crauford Kent, aware of her family skeleton, encourages her first few cocktails, and from there, it is downhill. Shortly afterward, she passes out and falls down a flight of stairs. When she regains consciousness, she realizes what has happened and declares that she will struggle with her desire for drink until she conquers it. Following a string of complications, including her refusal to marry the man she loves until she is cured, and the recurrence of Kent, who continually tempts her to return to the bottle, she is finally rehabilitated.

Sessue Hayakawa, as a young Japanese who has inherited from his ancestors a drinking problem, travels to the United States to study medicine, in William Worthington's drama, *A Heart in Pawn* (1919). In addition, he hopes to find a cure for his affliction. His studies with a famous bacteriologist prove successful. Before leaving Japan, he had married a young woman who had lent him the money for his journey and education. She said the money came from her grandfather, but in reality, she had sold herself as a Geisha girl. Her husband, meanwhile, has forgotten her and marries Vola Vale, the bacteriologist's daughter, who is part Japanese. He returns to Japan, where his wife is in prison for killing a banker who had attempted to raped her. A child had been born to her during his absence and, unknown to him, he and his second wife had adopted the child. He later finds out he adopted his own daughter. His Japanese wife escapes from prison, but as the guards approach, she drowns herself to protect her husband.

A strict aunt who is raising her niece reveals to her that the young woman's mother had led a very promiscuous life, in Robert Z. Leonard's drama, *The Scarlet Shadow* (1919). For this reason, the aunt is determined to keep a close watch over her niece, Mae Murray, who is not permitted to leave her home without a chaperone. However, Murray meets Frank Elliott, who accidentally keeps her out very late. He helps her to climb back into her bedroom, where the aunt catches them both. The older woman convinced now that the "scarlet shadow" of the girl's mother has descended upon the daughter, forces Elliott to propose marriage. But the young man's uncle intervenes in time, and the aunt evicts her niece. The uncle allows her to live in his spacious home. She next becomes engaged to a millionaire, whom she eventually rejects. She and Elliott are finally reunited, and the lovers are married, despite the dire predictions of her obsessed aunt.

Philanthropist Frank Whitson disagrees with his friend, who claims that only breeding can make a lady, and sets about to prove it in Howard Hickman's society drama, *Hearts Asleep* (1919). Bessie Barriscale, a poor waif, is drawn into a scheme to help a safecracker and his pals rob a home. But she deserts the crooks, who are caught, with the leader getting a five-year sentence. Barriscale meets Whitson and pleads with him to help her. He agrees and begins to make a "lady" out of her. Acting as her uncle, he sends her to a proper boarding school, where she quickly absorbs the proper culture and refinement. Following several complications, including the return of the safecracker and his eventual death while escaping from the law, Barriscale finally marries the gentle philanthropist. He has proven his case – that it is possible by culture and environment to produce a young woman of quality.

When Pauline Frederick learns from her father that alcoholism has plagued him and his family's past for several generations, she breaks off her engagement to attorney Milton Sills, in John A. Barry's domestic drama, *The Fear Woman* (1919). She fears, if the family curse is true, the disease may be passed down to her children. After sacrificing her reputation to help an adulterous friend, she leaves for a resort, where she meets Walter Hiers. But his mother wants to break up her son's affair with such a disreputable woman, so she hires lawyer Sills. At a party, Frederick acts drunk to test Sills's love. Following several complications, he protects her from verbal abuse and she admits that she was only drinking ginger ale. The couple then reconcile their differences.

II. The Fears of Tainted Blood

By 1900, modern genetics was transformed into an institutionalized movement known as the eugenics movement, which was especially strong in England, the U.S., and Germany between 1910 and 1940. It was closely associated with a belief in white Anglo-Saxon superiority. In the U.S., it exerted influence upon some state and federal legislation. Between 1911 and 1930, 24 states passed sterilization laws aimed at various social "misfits" – the mentally retarded, criminals, and the insane. Laws were also passed restricting marriages between races. Noted psychologists William C. McDougall and Carl C. Brigham, in their 1923 work, *A Study of American Intelligence*, based on crude and flawed intelligence tests administered to World War I draftees, concluded, "The intellectual superiority of our Nordic group over the Alpine, Mediterranean and Negro groups has been demonstrated." *The New York Times* (February 20, 1921) suggested that the nation was becoming "mongrelized." In 1924, many eugenicists and some big-business interests pushed through the Johnson Act, which limited immigration into the U.S. from eastern European and Mediterranean countries. Eugenicists charged that these immigrants were inferior and were polluting "pure" America. By 1925, eugenicists were attacked for their overt racial bias and their lack of scientific rigor. Fewer serious films about eugenics appeared during the twenties. Gone were the pseudo-educational dramatic tracts. But there was a handful of feeble attempts to raise the issue within the framework of mostly contrived plots. In general, movie studios exploited the eugenics theme by developing their plots around crime or fear. *The Silver Lining* (1921) offered a superficial look at whether environment or heredity plays a role in the life of a criminal. Similarly, *Rustlin' for Cupid* (1926), a routine western, tried to step off the range, at least temporarily, by having a cattle-rustling father justify his criminal behavior to his son by blaming it on heredity. In other entries, parents were concerned about producing mentally and physically superior offspring. For example, in comedies like *The Very Idea* (1920), a friend to a childless couple casually suggests they seek out a superior couple to produce a child for them. And in *The Devil's Trademark* (1928), which blends the themes of crime and fear, two thieves who marry and reform live in fear that their children may inherit their tainted blood. At any rate, the topic of eugenics is still prevalent in the world outside of movies. For instance, a "Eugenic Protection" law was enacted in occupied Japan, authorizing abortion on demand. That nation's population was nearly 80 million, up from more than 64 million in 1930. Today, however, eugenics is in disrepute.

The marriage of a maid and chauffeur is encouraged by a wealthy and childless couple for the purposes of producing a superior baby in the slight comedy, *The Very Idea* (1920), based on the play by William Le Baron. When the couple, Taylor Holmes and Virginia Valli, set out to adopt a child from an orphan asylum, a friend and firm believer in the theory of eugenics suggests they use their help to provide them with a superior offspring. They offer to set up the two young employees in a garage business if they will turn over their first child to their employers. They agree to these terms. After a suitable amount of time, they return to find the mother will not give up the child. Valli tries to persuade the mother to adopt a child from the orphanage. Finally, the disappointed wife whispers to her husband, suggesting that she is pregnant. The film was remade in 1929 as a sound feature, with a slightly different ending.

Roland West's inventive drama, *The Silver Lining* (1921), raises the familiar argument as to whether criminality is the result of heredity or environment. A narrator, a secret service agent, narrates the story of two orphans to a pair of his acquaintances who have taken opposite positions on the question. Jewel

Carmen, as an obedient, good-natured child, was abused by the bullying, malicious Virginia Valli. Both are eventually adopted. A pair of thieves adopt Carmen, and a wealthy couple, at the suggestion of a teacher, select Valli. Years later, Carmen reluctantly is forced to engage in petty crimes to placate her dishonest parents. Valli, on the other hand, has been raised as a pampered debutante. She is engaged to Leslie Austin, an aspiring writer. Following a string of complications, including Austin's breaking up with Valli when he finds her kissing someone else, his meeting and falling in love with Carmen, and Carmen's denunciation of her past, Austin and Carmen are married.

George O'Brien, as the son of a rancher, is more than surprised to discover that a local rustler turns out to be his own father in Irving Cummings's familiar but entertaining outdoor action drama, *Rustlin' for Cupid* (1926). O'Brien, who is busy courting Anita Stewart, the local schoolteacher, and fighting off a gang of outlaws, is confused when his father, who is caught red-handed, justifies his lawlessness by confessing to his son that outlawry is in the father's blood. This has O'Brien, his son, believing, at least temporarily, that his own blood may be tainted. However, his father's wrongdoing and his false explanation only harm the father's own hardworking and devoted wife and his honest son.

Robert F. Hill's generally weak rehabilitation drama, *Life's Mockery* (1928), raises the familiar controversy about whether crime stems from environment or heredity. A judge tries to settle this question by experimenting with a gang leader's daughter, who is found unconscious after trying to escape from the police. When she regains her senses, he tries to erase her past criminal life from her thoughts and dreams. The drama is one of many dealing with rehabilitation, including Lon Chaney's *The Penalty* (1920).

Two thieves, now married, reform when they have their first child, in Leo Meehan's drama, *The Devil's Trademark* (1928). Always fearful that their tainted blood may manifest itself in their child, the husband continuously studies the infant for such signs. His wife promises that if these signs do occur, the husband can return to his life of crime. Years later, with two children to observe, the father is eager for at least one to go wrong so that he can return to his past life. Meanwhile, his daughter falls in love with an employer of a foundry. The son, however, presents another problem when his mother catches him stealing.

A white man's affair with a young Indian woman results in near tragedy for all concerned in William Nigh's tasteless drama, *Her Debt of Honor* (1926). A child, the result of the romance between a white man and the Indian woman, has grown into a complete degenerate. The young man (William Nigh) is a repulsive character whose illnesses are irreversible, the result of his dissolute life. He tries to rape Virginia Valli, a young woman who is trying to help him. Her boyfriend, William Davidson, arrives in time to save her. Nigh returns to his reservation to die, and the couple, free of Nigh's threatening presence, make plans to marry.

Gangs and Gangsters

I. The Rise of the Gang

Organized crime was not introduced into the United States until the Prohibition years (1919-1933), although Geoffrey Perrett in *America in the Twenties* claims that modern organized crime began in 1909. Earlier criminals played a minor part in national crimes and their statistics. The average criminal usually "worked" independently and was known by his professional title: pickpocket, burglar, stick-up man, safecracker, etc. His trade rarely entailed violence. Occasionally, some big-time thief would organize a few fellow crooks to help him execute a complex job that required more than one person. Early silent films reflected these unlawful activities, which soon advanced to larger, more colorful and potentially more violent crimes, such as kidnapping, counterfeiting, smuggling and murder. *Chelsea 7750* (1913), for example, dealt with counterfeiting. Street gangs emerged as early as 1912, in such films as *The Musketeers of Pig Alley* and *The Rat*, released two years later. By 1914, films like *The County Seat War* began to depict the close links between politics and crime. However crude these films seem today, they helped to establish the patterns of the popular crime drama for the next several decades and introduced to audiences the singularly fascinating and mythical character – the American gangster.

The main character in all the short scenes of G. M. Anderson's crude drama, *Raffles, the Amateur Cracksman* (1905), is a well-dressed, elderly gentleman performing criminal acts. This is the first film version of E. W. Hornung's popular fictional character from his 1899 novel *The Amateur Cracksman*. The scenes show Raffles, played by J. Barney Sherry, as a respectable member of society who leads a secret life as a thief and gang leader. The film is also unique in its early depiction of a criminal who is never caught. Director Anderson became the first authentic western film hero portraying the good bad man, Bronco Billy, in hundreds of one-reelers during the next decade. Several versions of Hornung's work have appeared on screen, including a 1925 sequel titled, *Raffles, the Amateur Cracksman*.

The early caper drama, *The Great Jewel Mystery* (1905), was based on the actual theft of $100,000 in jewels stolen aboard a train between New York and Newport. Jewel thieves position one of their gang inside a coffin which is placed in the same railroad car carrying a jewel box. The man stealthily exits from his coffin, knocks a guard unconscious and takes the jewels into the coffin with him. When the train stops, the coffin is placed into a hearse that rides off. In the next scene the jewel thieves are celebrating their success, when suddenly a door comes crashing down and police enter. The gang is then rounded up.

A similar situation occurs when thieves place a gang member in a nailed crate that is then stored next to a Wells Fargo strong box in Wallace McCutcheon's early silent drama, *The Man in the Box* (1908). Later, the thief overpowers the shipping-company guard and admits his accomplices into the office, where they proceed to rob the place. The guard, however, manages to send a telegraph message to the authorities, who arrive in time to battle and subdue the gang. This short film had an interesting cast, which included the future director D. W. Griffith and the future king of comedy, producer Mack Sennett.

A young woman, kidnapped by bandits from a coach, uses her wits to escape from the gang in D. W. Griffith's short drama, *The Bandit's Waterloo* (1908). Florence Lawrence, as the victim, is taken from a coach that is being robbed and brought to the chief's hideout where he ties her up. He then takes her to town where he plans to ransom her. She exchanges clothes with a servant girl, tricks both her guard and the bandit chief, and escapes with the gang's loot.

One of New York's finest single-handedly takes on a gang of hoodlums in the one-reel comedy drama, *Clancy* (1910). He emerges badly beaten but undaunted, and recovers in time to spend the holidays at home. This sentimental film was released during the Christmas holiday season.

A gangster becomes infatuated with a young married woman in D. W. Griffith's remarkable drama, *The Musketeers of Pig Alley* (1912). Lillian Gish, as the young wife who finds herself entangled in the world of crime, gives one of her best performances. Elmer Booth plays the Cagney-like gangster in a sympathetic role. The setting (actually shot on and around New York's West Twelfth Street) is the vice- and crime-ridden streets of the Lower East Side, where Gish and her sensitive violin-playing husband live. The drama ends in a furious gun battle. The film has been singled out by film critics and historians for its camera work, realism and characterization. Critic Richard Schickel lists the work as "one of the masterpieces of the Biograph period." Film historian William K. Everson describes the film as "the first genre-oriented gangster film." Here Griffith gives us the gangster as a social evil, the significance of turf to the urban gangs, and examples of early police corruption.

Every action device imaginable is packed into J. Searle Dawley's run-of-the-mill counterfeiting drama, *Chelsea 7750* (1913). Henry Dixey's acting enhances the film, especially in the scenes where he becomes paralyzed and sets fire to his own home. Gunfire, explosions, clever disguises and trickery all tend to sustain audience interest. The title, a telephone exchange, figures in the clever strategy of the detective's daughter, who ultimately outwits a band of counterfeiters. A sequel to the film was released later in 1913 under the title *An Hour Before Dawn.*

Several early gangster or crime-oriented films suggest a special relationship between social workers and neighborhood culprits. The thin drama, *The Rat* (1914), is an early depiction of street gangs operating in America's urban areas. Belle Bennett, a millionaire's daughter who is also a slum worker, befriends Charles Strong, "The Rat," when he is wounded in a street fight. In gratitude, The Rat provides a whistle for the Good Samaritan so that, when in these dangerous streets, she can give three blasts to summon aid from his gang members. As fate would have it, she is eventually kidnapped by Handsome Bob's gang and, remembering the whistle, uses it to summon help. The movie addresses some of the dangers of urban life, especially the proliferation of street gangs. In this sense, the director and screenwriter may have been influenced by the urban paintings of George Bellows, especially his "Cliff Dwellers" (1913), which depicted the slums of the Lower East Side and the gangs of impoverished children who roamed its streets.

An apparent remake of *Little Gray Lady*, Bertram Harrison and William J. Burns's drama, *$5,000,000 Counterfeiting Plot* (1914), includes a scene with Sir Arthur Conan Doyle, whose Sherlock Holmes would seem to be the inspiration for William Burns's performance. Though he is proclaimed infallible by the Secret Service, Burns, who was a detective in real life, runs into difficulties when he is forced to solve a case twice. After a gang of counterfeiters are caught and convicted, they continue their operations from within prison walls. Burns is finally able to solve the crime – based on one of Burns's actual famous cases – the Philadelphia-Lancaster counterfeiting mystery.

Rockliffe Fellowes portrays a young hoodlum in Raoul Walsh's absorbing drama, *The Regeneration* (1915), based on Owen Kildare's autobiographical story, "My Mamie Rose," and a successful play by Kildare and Walter Hackett based on Kildare's autobiography about a local gang leader and a social worker. Anna Q. Nilsson, while doing social work in the slums, is attracted to Fellowes and convinces him to abandon his old life of crime. She then teaches him how to read and write. Carl Harbaugh, a young district attorney, wants Nilsson for himself and persuades the young tough to desert her. Thinking he has returned to his old gang, Nilsson goes to the hideout and is trapped by "Skinny the Rat." Fellowes comes to her rescue when he learns what has happened, but Nilsson is killed in the ensuing fracas. In real life, the social worker died from a cold one month before she was to marry Kildare, the former Bowery tough, bouncer and gang leader. Walsh's location shooting on the Bowery added to the realism of the film. A bland remake, *Fools' Highway,* appeared in 1924, with Pat O'Malley as the rehabilitated Kildare finally joining the police force and Mary Philbin as his sweetheart, now transformed from a social worker into a seamstress.

An early drama depicting a close link between corrupt politicians and the underworld, J. P. McGowan's *The County Seat War* (1914), concerns a "boss" who sends his gangsters to attack a court house. They confiscate the incriminating records and set fire to the building. The film also suggests the wanton destruction of government property. Included in the cast of this two-reel drama is Helen Holmes, who gained fame as one of the queens of silent serials.

The plot of the drama, *The Secret Seven* (1915), focuses on detective Paul Sleuth's retrieval of a diamond necklace, stolen by the Secret Seven. The ensuing abduction of Lady Evelyn complicates matters and draws Sleuth into a dramatic air chase that finds the pursuer leaping from an airplane into the basket of a gas balloon. Critics commented that the climactic scene in the balloon was underdeveloped. Early silents often used a crime plot only as a means to introduce the real purposes of the film – the chase and action.

Actor W. J. Ferguson reprises the role of Pop Clark that he created in the original stage production of James Young's light-hearted drama, *The Deep Purple* (1915), based on Paul Armstrong and Wilson Mizner's play. The plot concerns crooks engaged in the old badger game. William Lake, the hero, rescues a minister's daughter from the gang, led by Harry Leland, while the minister, who has paid for a non-existent organ, is saved from a terrible embarrassment when Lake offers to purchase an organ for the congregation.

Howard Estabrook portrays "The Tidewater Clam," a society thief and illegitimate son of a rich merchant, in Edward José's drama, *The Closing Net* (1915), an adaptation of Henry Rowlan's 1912 magazine serial. The Clam is involved in a series of escapades with a gang of thieves who refuse to allow him to reform from his life of crime. There is a strong love interest in this well-plotted tale of a man twice saved by women – once when his victim's wife recognizes the Clam's birthmark (which identifies him as her husband's half-brother), and again when a young woman fires a shot that saves his life.

J. P. McGowan's suspense thriller, *The Diamond Runners* (1916), with Helen Holmes (of serial fame) as a member of a gang of diamond smugglers, offers action and excitement as its main ingredients. The plot introduces the usual U.S. Secret Service agent (Leo Maloney) who is engaged in tracking down the smugglers. But in a bizarre turn of events, the female smuggler (Holmes) falls in love with the agent and decides to return the loot and go straight. Maloney was soon to become a popular screen cowboy who starred in numerous westerns.

Pretending to be deaf and dumb, Jack Pickford, as Barney Cook, employs "signing," or the hand language of the deaf, to great advantage in Francis Grandon's drama, *The Dummy* (1917). Cook, who has recently joined the detective force, pretends to be a deaf mute, son of a wealthy man and target of a band of kidnappers. The gang has already made off with the daughter of another rich family. When taken to the gang's hideout, Cook manages to contact Babbings, chief of detectives, who comes to the hideout disguised as a western gambler. As luck would have it, Mrs. Meredith, who has come to free her daughter, ostensibly by paying ransom, recognizes Babbings and gives him away. Babbings is trussed up, and the gang, along with Cook, escapes. With the help of a local sheriff, Cook engineers the capture of the gang, and the pretty captive is freed. Then Cook outwits the greedy sheriff who covets the reward for himself.

Jack Devereaux proves to be a formidable adversary in Arthur Rosson's drama, *Grafters* (1917), about blackmail gone awry. Mrs. Ames, "Laughing Louie," and "The Menace" comprise a gang of con artists who have been hired by Devereaux's uncle to teach him a lesson about life and money. Anna Lehr compromises the youth and then blackmails him. However, she falls in love with him and rejects the scheme when she realizes it is not just a lesson – the gang means business. Devereaux, on the other hand, proves infinitely wiser than any of them, for he has hired his own detectives to round up the grafters. The lovers end up together, and the uncle is convinced of his nephew's perspicacity.

Paul Scardon's drama, *All Man* (1918), about a gang of safecrackers, features Harry Morey as a foreman turned safecracker, and Betty Blythe as his lover. Morey allows himself to be captured after one crime so that his lover will not be suspicious of him. He serves five years and returns to her and pays back the $15,000 she has saved for him. He vows to buy a farm and go straight with her beside him, but she is not receptive.

Women often were an important influence in helping otherwise hard-core criminals to reform in several early films. Dell Henderson's drama, *Hitting the Trail* (1918), adapted from a story by Roy Sommerville, deals with the reformation of Kid Kelly (Carlyle Blackwell), a self-sacrificing gangster. He turns himself in so that Evelyn Greeley, a mission worker, will not do the time for his crime. The specter of jealousy rears its head when The Kid's former flame engineers the downfall of her rival and sets the stage for a series of plot twists. The Kid, however, falls under the stronger moral influence of the mission worker and reforms.

William Parke's drama, *Convict 993* (1918), based on a story by Wallace C. Clifton, stars Irene Castle as Roslyn Ayre, Convict 993, ostensibly a jewel thief and convict. Actually, she is an undercover U.S. Secret Service operative who turns the tables on her old cellmate Helene Chadwick and rounds up a gang of thieves.

Boston Blackie (Bert Lytell) decides to go straight and follow the path to the altar in John Ince's crime drama, *Blackie's Redemption* (1919). This was the latest entry in the film series built around the popular fictional crook-turned-sleuth created by writer Jack Boyle. Blackie's plans, though, are thwarted by "Fred the Count," who slips incriminating evidence into Blackie's pocket. Blackie, sentenced to twenty years in prison, escapes to gain his revenge on

Fred. He successfully engineers a reversal of their fates and is last seen heading for parts unknown with his girlfriend. The film blends material from two stories by author Boyle: "Blackie's Mary" and "Fred the Count."

Two bands of crooks, one of the upscale, society kind, and the other a group of hard-core gangster types, compete for the big payoff in Allan Dwan's comedy, *Cheating Cheaters* (1919). There are many surprises in store for both groups, providing laughs and excitement for the audience. The work of the cast drew attention from reviewers, who compared the film favorably with Max Marcin's original stage production. It remade in 1927 and again in 1934.

A band of counterfeiters prey upon Newport's society members in George Fitzmaurice's drama, *Counterfeit* (1919). Frisky Elsie Ferguson sets out to resolve this problem. Adventurer Vincent Charles Gerrard passes counterfeit bills to Mrs. Palmer under suspicious circumstances and under the watchful eye of our heroine. David Powell is in love with her but is perplexed after seeing her removing the bogus bills from the safe and then embracing Gerrard. She knows what she is doing though and engineers the capture of the gang. All is explained in the last reel, and she and Powell are reconciled.

Set against the backdrop of the New Orleans Mardi Gras festival, Reginald Barker's drama, *The Crimson Gardenia* (1919), presents Owen Moore as Roland Van Dam, a bored tourist seeking excitement. He finds more than he expected when he is mistaken for a U. S. Secret Service agent, and counterfeiters make him a target for revenge. Hedda Nova, as an unwitting tool of the counterfeiters, works to undermine Van Dam with whom she has fallen in love. The film was adapted from the short story by Rex Beach.

II. Gang Wars

Screen gangsters flourished during the twenties. Prohibition, nightclubs, jazz, vaudeville, movies, fast cars and the bright lights of the big city all suggested an edginess to urban life and contributed to the frenetic pace of modern America. In real life, Al "Scarface" Capone, an American gangster who ruthlessly ruled the Chicago underworld in the twenties, was finally imprisoned in 1931 for tax evasion. He was loosely portrayed in *The Racket* (1928), which some consider the most important silent gangster film. The term "organized crime" was first used during the twenties, with the rise of Prohibition, when local gang leaders created criminal organizations from their bootlegging profits. Later, they expanded into gambling, labor racketeering, narcotics trafficking, and other illegal activities. But by the end of the decade, the gangster fell out of favor. The decade, appropriately known as the Roaring Twenties, brought forth the rise of gangs and lavish gangsters' funerals, whose pallbearers often included judges, senators, congressmen and other notables (as in the case of Big Jim Colosimo, who was gunned down in 1920 and mourned by 5,000 people). The Chicago *Tribune* estimated that gang wars resulted in 1,291 murders between 1926 and 1929.

Wallace Worsley's drama, *The Penalty* (1920), is a cross between *Beauty and the Beast* and the Frankenstein themes. Crippled as a child by Dr. Ferris, Blizzard (Lon Chaney) conspires to avenge himself, using his powerful position in the underworld. Ethel Grey Terry, the doctor's daughter, in a bizarre turn of events, falls in love with the deformed Blizzard. He, in the meantime, forces Dr. Ferris, on pain of his daughter's death, to graft the legs of Terry's fiancé onto his (Blizzard's) misshapen body. Dr. Ferris, however, performs what amounts to a lobotomy that leaves Blizzard benevolent and loving. With his penchant for evil gone, Blizzard and Terry are married. The film provides the obligatory obeisance to morality when Blizzard is murdered a short time later by a member of his old gang. Portions of the plot and certain themes are similar to those in *The Brand of Satan* (1917).

Lon Chaney returned to the crime genre with his portrayal of a cripple who works for underworld queen Christine Mayo in Lambert Hillyer's drama, *The Shock* (1923), set in San Francisco. Mayo, seeking revenge upon a particular banker, assigns Chaney to the task. But he falls in love with his intended victim's pretty daughter, Virginia Valli, and fails to carry out his assignment. Mayo plots to kidnap the daughter and ruin her by luring her to San Francisco's dives. But the San Francisco earthquake and fire interfere with her plans. The crippled Chaney rescues Valli, but he remains trapped in the ruin of a building. When he recovers, he is somehow (miraculously) made whole again, as if he were rewarded for his heroic act.

Wesley Barry portrays a youth caught up in a kidnapping and blackmail plot in William Beaudine's drama, *Heroes of the Street* (1922). He wishes to follow in his policeman-father's footsteps. Suddenly, on Christmas Eve, his father is killed by the notorious "Shadow," a mysterious criminal. To help support his family, Barry gets a job as a property boy at a theater. The "angel," who in reality is the Shadow, plans to kidnap the star as part of a blackmailing plot. Barry grows suspicious and follows him. A struggle ensues and the villain is shot and killed accidentally by his own gang.

In *Purple Dawn* (1923), Charles R. Seeling's action drama, also about kidnapping, William E. Aldrich, as a young messenger, is virtually a slave aboard Bert Sprotte's ship. It is in this capacity that he is knocked unconscious twice by members of a Chinese gang – when he is driven into the country and dumped out of a car, and when he is again captured, tortured and almost strangled before the law rescues him in the nick of time. Meanwhile, the Chinese chief's daughter, Bessie Love, falls in love with Aldrich and, realizing he can never love her, helps him to rejoin Priscilla Bonner, his true love.

Early rural dramas continually painted the city as wicked and corrupt. Urban dramas needed to add little to this image. A young man who thinks his small town is too confining soon learns a bitter lesson in W. S. Van Dyke's cautionary drama, *The Little Girl Next Door* (1923). James Morrison, as the naive youth, loses his small bankroll in the city and unknowingly joins a gang of smugglers. When he realizes his mistake and tries to extricate himself from them, they will not let him quit. His girlfriend arrives and, following a series of harrowing incidents, Morrison develops some backbone and the couple survives. The film is sometimes listed as *You Are in Danger*.

The reformed criminal, already depicted often in earlier films, became a cliché by the twenties. A gangster, trying to reform to gain custody of his pal's seven-year-old son, finally proves he is worthy of the role of guardian in Allan Dwan's sentimental drama, *Big Brother* (1923), based on the story by Rex Beach. Tom Moore, as the former mobster, recovers a payroll heisted by some of his ex-cronies, thereby winning the confidence of the law. Contemporary critics praised the film for its accurate portrayal of New York's criminals and its authentic look (it was shot on location in Manhattan). At least one other critic cynically suggested it was propaganda for the Big Brother movement.

William Fairbanks portrays a wealthy criminologist who joins forces with U. S. Secret Service operative Carl Stockdale to smash a gang of waterfront crooks in W. S. Van Dyke's action drama, *The Beautiful Sinner* (1924). Fairbanks gains possession of the gang's loot, but is captured. A female member of the gang, whom he had met earlier, frees him, and he prevents the thieves from robbing a wealthy home. The gang leader is killed when his car careens off a cliff. Fairbanks then learns that his rescuer has been working under cover to expose the gang.

A handful of gangster dramas dealt with bored members of society who were fascinated with the lifestyle of the underworld. Wealthy and dissolute Richard Dix finds adventure and love in R. H. Burnside's implausible drama, *Manhattan* (1924), set chiefly in New York's tough Hell's Kitchen. Young Dix portrays the last of a famous line of Manhattanites who squanders away his life among other socialites. He meets a safecracker trying to rob him and who, thinking Dix a fellow thief, introduces him to his sister, Jacqueline Logan, an inhabitant of Hell's Kitchen. Following several fights, Dix defeats the villainous gang leader of the district, who is also Dix's romantic rival.

John Gilbert portrays another bored playboy – until he meets Marian Nixon, a struggling, unemployed actress who gets mixed up with a gang of counterfeiters in William Fox's drama, *Just off Broadway* (1924). Rescued by the girlfriend of a local gangster, Nixon becomes an acquaintance of the gang, including Gilbert, a millionaire and amateur sleuth who is posing as a member of the group. She falls in love with Gilbert, who eventually helps to bring the culprits to justice and reveals his true identity.

Sophisticated Raffles, the gentleman safecracker, is another playboy who is fascinated with crime. King Baggot's sequel, *Raffles, the Amateur Cracksman* (1925), was the third screen version of Ernest William Hornung's popular rogue hero. The film was adapted from Hornung's 1901 novel, *Raffles: Further Adventures of the Amateur Cracksman,* and the 1903 play by Eugene Wiley Presbrey. Aboard a ship bound for England, Raffles warns the owner of a valuable necklace to be cautious. The necklace is stolen and mysteriously returned. After the boat docks, Raffles is invited to a house party, where a famous criminologist guarantees that a valuable string of pearls cannot be stolen. Raffles succeeds but almost falls into a trap. A woman warns him and he escapes, after which he returns the necklace and reforms.

Dorothy Dalton, as the daughter of a thief, abandons her life of crime after she falls in love with a young criminologist in Ralph Ince's tale of redemption, *The Moral Sinner* (1924). Intimidated by her father's crooked gang, young Dalton lives in a world of crime until James Rennie, as the criminologist, rescues her from a burning building. Following several complications, including the theft of Rennie's jewelry, Dalton returns the items and goes among the poor to repent. Rennie finds her and the couple are married.

Film director and writer J. P. McGowan, as the leader of a gang of counterfeiters, escapes custody and swears revenge upon his nemesis, treasury agent William Desmond, in McGowan's action drama, *Outwitted* (1925). After being sentenced to twenty years, McGowan escapes the law on his way to prison and later kidnaps Helen Holmes, the daughter of the Assistant Secretary of the Treasury. Desmond discovers a yacht being used by the gang as a hideout and effects the young woman's rescue and the roundup of the counterfeiters.

Hard-working, honest Richard Barthelmess, who is constantly compared with his crooked brother, Frank Puglia, takes the rap for him when Puglia breaks the law, in Kenneth Webb's drama, *The Beautiful City* (1925). When Barthelmess is released, he tries to end a gangster's influence over his brother. During a fight, the hoodlum, who accidentally shoots Barthelmess's mother, is killed while attempting to escape. The mother recovers, and Barthelmess finds happiness with his girlfriend, Dorothy Gish, in the city he has grown to love.

An elderly grandmother outsmarts a gang of thieves planning to rob her in Roy Del Ruth's comedy, *The Little Irish Girl* (1926), based on C. D. Lancaster's story, "The Grifters." The crooks, using the young woman Dolores Costello as their lure, entrap men and rob them. Forced to leave town in a hurry, the grifters head for a small hotel run by Gertrude Claire, the grandmother of one of their victims. They then scheme to rob her, but she is wise to them and turns the tables on the gang. Sensing that the young woman has fallen in love with her grandson and wants to go straight, Granny gives the young couple some of the gang's money to start life anew.

A woman's love converts a society thief into a sleuth in Ralph Ince's drama, *The Lone Wolf Returns* (1926), based on Louis Joseph Vance's 1923 novel. Bert Lytell, as the romantic hero-crook "The Lone Wolf," seeks to recover his girlfriend's jewels that have been stolen by a rival gang. Following several suspenseful and exciting incidents involving the Lone Wolf and the thieves, Lytell succeeds in his mission and decides to walk the straight and narrow. Vance's romantic character was played by various actors during the silent and sound eras.

An innocent young socialite, seeking independence, inadvertently joins a gang of thieves in Walter Lang's drama, *The Ladybird* (1927), set chiefly in New Orleans. Betty Compson, as the adventurous heroine, is exposed to both danger and romance in her escapades. Finally, she is forced to subdue the chief villain, who is then arrested by the police. This drama is typical of many crime films of the period in which women played formidable roles usually reserved for men.

The plot of William James Craft's drama, *Birds of Prey* (1927), is similar to that of Tod Browning's 1925 film, *The Unholy Three*, starring Lon Chaney – especially the ploy of having a midget impersonating a child. The perennial master criminal, Gustav von Seyffertitz, heads a gang of crooks in this weak production. They are all killed while robbing a bank, the result of a convenient earthquake. Happily, the hero and heroine are rescued. Seyffertitz later played the kindly Dr. von Helsing in the classic 1931 version of *Dracula*, starring Bela Lugosi.

Joseph von Sternberg's seminal crime drama, *Underworld* (1927), focuses on gang rivalry and gun battles between the law and the lawless. The gang rivalry aspect was a familiar theme, introduced earlier in Griffith's 1912 classic gangster yarn, *The Musketeers of Pig Alley*. In Sternberg's brilliant film, George Bancroft, as the gangster, rescues the alcoholic lawyer Clive Brook from his dissolute life. Meanwhile, Bancroft's sweetheart (Evelyn Brent) falls in love with Brook, who tries to remain loyal to his benefactor. After a series of gun battles with a rival gang, Bancroft is caught, tried and sentenced to death. Brook tries to free him, but the scheme fails. Thinking he has been betrayed by Brent and Brook, Bancroft makes his way back to the hideout. During a furious fire fight with the surrounding police, Bancroft realizes that the young couple were loyal to him. Finding his situation hopeless, he surrenders to the authorities while Brook is mortally wounded. Several film historians list *Underworld* as the first modern gangster drama and Bancroft the first gangster star.

A series of films reverted to the old ploy about an innocent person wrongly accused of a crime. When a young man is falsely accused of murder, his sister determines to rescue him in Ray Enright's drama, *The Girl From Chicago* (1927). Myrna Loy, as the brave sister, infiltrates a gang of mobsters. She meets Conrad Nagel, who is part of the gang but in reality is an undercover cop. After a furious machine-gun battle between police and the gang, the dying gang lord confesses to the murder, thereby freeing the brother. Loy, who had a distinguished screen career during the sound era playing sophisticated roles, occasionally portrayed women involved with hoodlums, as in *Penthouse* (1933), in which she played a call girl.

Another young person – a nightclub entertainer – becomes involved with gangsters and murder in Fred Windermere's drama, *Broadway After Midnight* (1927). Priscilla Bonner portrays the unfortunate sister of a weak brother. To protect him, she is forced to marry gangster Matthew Betz. Later, Betz persuades her to impersonate a socialite who is then murdered. The police arrest Bonner, but at her trial her maid gives evidence that proves her innocence.

Barbara Bedford, another young woman with a weak brother, is determined to extricate her naive brother from the influence of gangsters in Burton King's minor drama, *Manhattan Knights* (1928). When she learns that he owes a large sum of money to the crooks, she decides to retrieve the postdated check. Along with her new-found boyfriend, Walter Miller, she finds her brother, who has been held captive, but they, too, are caught. They escape from a burning warehouse and manage to bring the chief villain to justice. Character player Noble Johnson, a much underrated African-American actor, had a long screen career that spanned both the silent and sound eras.

Two jazz-age youths become entangled with gangsters in Rupert Julian's drama, *Walking Back* (1928), based on the 1927 story, "A Ride in the Country," by George Kibbe Turner. Sue Carol and Richard Walling take their wrecked car, which he had borrowed from a neighbor, to a garage, only to discover that it is run by a gang dealing in stolen vehicles. The crooks force the young couple to drive them to a bank, which the gang proceeds to rob. During a shooting, Walling's father is wounded and young Walling engages on a wild ride that ends at a police station, where the gang is rounded up and he is rewarded.

Ralph Ince's drama, *Chicago After Midnight* (1928), a conglomeration of crime film plots and characters, including bootleggers, hijackers, informers, cops and show girls, focuses more on action and gunplay than on originality. Gangster Ralph Ince, released from prison, seeks out a rival crook who had double-crossed him. He kills the man and frames a nightclub band leader who is in love with the club's dancer. She joins Ince's gang to try to prove her lover's innocence, but the gang learns of her connections to the police and begins to torture her. Ince, learning that she is his daughter, rescues her but is mortally wounded by a fellow member. Before he dies, he exonerates the band leader from the murder. The film is faintly reminiscent of the immensely popular 1926 stage play *Broadway*, and tries to exploit its elements.

A gangster is regenerated while serving out his prison sentence in William Nigh's underworld drama, *Four Walls* (1928), based on the 1927 play by Dana Burnet and George Abbott. John Gilbert plays Benny Horowitz, a product of New York's East Side slum ghetto. As a gang leader, he killed a rival gangster during a gun battle and was arrested. On a prison farm where he is growing vegetables he concludes: "That's the first thing I ever touched that went straight." Released from prison, he returns home determined to go straight, but his ex-gun moll, Joan Crawford, tries to lure him back into his former life. Escaping from another rival gang war and a personal fight in which his opponent falls to his death, Gilbert, completely innocent of the evening's illegal activities, rushes home to establish an alibi. A suspicious detective interrogates him about the death and, convinced of his innocence after overhearing certain conversations, informs him that he is not under any suspicion.

The pursuit of a coveted diamond brings only tragedy to those who try to possess it in John P. McCarthy's drama, *Diamond Handcuffs* (1928), based on the

1921 story, "Pin Money," by Henry C. Vance. The film begins in South Africa, where a mine worker who has stolen the diamond is killed. Before he dies, he gives the precious stone to Lena Malena, a local woman. The diamond then appears in New York City, where gangsters steal it. Following incidents of greed and jealousy, their leader is killed in a police raid.

A despondent young woman and former gang member is saved from committing suicide by a young doctor in Dallas Fitzgerald's bleak drama, *The Lookout Girl* (1928). Jacqueline Logan, as the title character, had worked as the lookout for a gang of thieves before deciding to end her life. After being rescued, she marries Ian Keith, the doctor who restores her faith in living and gives her a new life. His friend, a member of the U. S. Secret Service, recognizes her and elicits her help in capturing the gang.

Raoul Walsh's didactic drama, *Me, Gangster* (1928), based on Charles Francis Coe's 1927 novel, reveals in diary style the story of a youth gone wrong. Don Terry portrays the young man who progresses from street-corner loafer to small-time thief and finally to a participant in a murder. Jailed on a robbery charge, he decides the missing $50,000 belongs to him since he is serving the two-year term for it. However, the death of his mother and the influence of girlfriend June Collyer persuade Terry, now paroled, to return the money. But his former cronies scheme to take the money for themselves. A fight ensues between Terry and the hijackers, while Collyer is held captive. The morality play ends with the anonymous principal character (on whom this story is based) writing that he hopes others, having learned that they cannot beat the law, will be deterred from following in his path. Don Terry later was featured in several sound serials. The film is sometimes listed under the title *The Diary of Me, Gangster*.

Lewis Milestone's hard-hitting underworld drama, *The Racket* (1928), based on the successful 1928 play by Bartlett Cormack, exposes the dangerously close ties between racketeers and politicians. The principal conflict is between honest cop Thomas Meighan and brutal bootlegger king Louis Wolheim, who seems to hold a tight grip on the city by way of its politicians. When Wolheim realizes he cannot bribe Meighan, he has him transferred to a remote area. Wolheim's kid brother is held on a hit-and-run charge and, in the process of avenging the boy, the bootlegger is himself arrested. A district attorney in league with Wolheim double-crosses him and has him shot while trying to escape. Author Cormack based his play (which featured Edward G. Robinson as the bootlegger) on his newspaper background in Chicago. His strong hints at political corruption and the ties of organized crime with the police and politicians made the film a significant social drama but also led to its being banned in Chicago and other locations. Particularly damaging was the film's thinly disguised references to Big Bill Thompson, Chicago's corrupt mayor. The gangster, Nick Scarsi (Wolheim), whose influence spreads throughout both the criminal world and many legitimate businesses, was allegedly based on the career of the notorious mobster Al Capone.

Greenwich Village

1. New York's Bohemia

New York City's Greenwich Village is a region in lower Manhattan's West Side. Early in its history, persons such as Thomas Paine, Edgar Allan Poe, Mark Twain and Walt Whitman resided nearby. By the early 1900s, an influx of artists and freethinkers had established the Village's reputation for bohemianism. The area reached its greatest fame during the early decades of the twentieth century, when writers, artists, journalists, actors, revolutionaries and other bohemians joined the Italians, Irish, African Americans and other residents of the area. The development and fame of the Village occurred at approximately the same time as the growth and popularity of the film industry. Several of these early films set their plots in picturesque and fascinating Greenwich Village – a world of idealism and disillusionment, occupied with offbeat characters whose bright hopes often ended in broken dreams.

Ida May Park's *Bondage* (1917) suggests a clash between two opposing lifestyles – that of the values of conventional married life, and that of the more modern type of casual relationship. Dorothy Phillips, a small-town young woman, gets a job as a reporter in Manhattan. She shares an apartment in Greenwich Village with Gretchen Lederer and soon falls into the fast night life of the community. She meets William Stowell, a lawyer originally from her home town who reproaches her for her loose way of living. She vindictively writes a satire about his restrictive moral principles and sells it to a magazine editor who finds her attractive. He joins her wild crowd and, although they are supposedly engaged, he elopes with one of her friends. She meets Stowell the lawyer again and marries him. After one year she grows restless, missing her old pals. She joins them at one of their haunts, where she sees the editor and learns that his wife is dead. She decides to leave her husband and go off with the widower. Stowell later meets her again in the street where she appears impoverished. He takes her home and goes off to beat up the editor whom he holds responsible for his wife's condition and for breaking up Stowell's happiness.

Lured by the stage and the bohemian life of Greenwich Village, Nell Craig leaves home for New York City in Fred E. Wright's sociological problem play, *The Trufflers* (1917), based on the novel by Samuel Merwin. While acting in Ernest Maupain's theater, she meets playwright Sydney Ainsworth and critic Richard C. Travers. Both men fall in love with her, but she rejects Ainsworth. The jealous playwright plots revenge by reporting to the press that the actress's father has stolen money from the church. The disgraced father, unable to cope with the exposé, takes his own life. His distraught daughter becomes aware of the hypocrisy of many of the people in her circle. Disillusioned, she abandons her stage career and turns to the critic, whom she finds to be honest and sincere.

Theda Bara publicly confesses her sordid life in J. Gordon Edwards's drama of redemption, *The Forbidden Path* (1918). Agreeing to pose as a Madonna for Greenwich Village artist Sidney Mason, Bara meets his wealthy friend, Hugh Thompson, and the pair soon become lovers. But once her baby is born, he sends her away. The baby grows ill and dies. Years later, the artist finds Bara living in impoverished conditions and offers her a modeling position for his portrait, "End of the Forbidden Path." Meanwhile, she forces Thompson to give her money and marry her or she will publicly disgrace him. At the altar, Bara faces the congregation and emotionally reveals the entire story of her sordid relationship with Thompson, including the death of their child.

Irene Castle, as the title character in Lawrence B. McGill's drama, *The Girl From Bohemia* (1918), settles in Greenwich Village to forsake the conventional life and embrace an artist's existence and its promised freedom. Following her participation in several orgies and a failed attempt at modeling, she agrees to join her maiden aunt in her country home. The woman promises Castle a steady income. Castle arrives at her new address, with all of her "modern" ideas. At a dinner party in her honor, for example, she wears an outrageous gown and casually smokes cigarettes. After redecorating the home in modern fashion, she becomes the talk of the local inhabitants. Shipyard owner Canton Leigh falls in love with her, but is turned off by her bizarre behavior. Later, when Castle saves a child from drowning and suppresses a strike by climbing on a roof, the townspeople accept her as one of their own. She and Leigh then embrace.

Harry Mestayer, a popular New York author in search of his ideal woman, meets New Englander Jean Calhoun at a Greenwich Village bohemian café, in Gilbert Hamilton's romantic drama, *High Tide* (1918). She has come to New York to meet the author, with whom she has been corresponding, and to ask his advice about her own literary aspirations. After dining with her, he thinks he has fallen in love with her and advises that she return home. Several months later, Mestayer, who has a girlfriend, actress Yvonne Pavis, visits Calhoun in

New England and proposes to her. She accepts, but he doesn't marry her. He realizes he is unworthy of her because he is afflicted with tuberculosis. Instead, he returns to the city and, in an act of self-sacrifice, he marries his actress girlfriend, who has lured Calhoun's young and innocent brother into a romantic entanglement.

Peggy Hyland arrives in New York City to further her art education in Albert Parker's drama, *The Other Woman* (1918), based on the 1910 play by Frederic Arnold Kummer. She meets Milton Sills, a broker, and the two become friends. After she reaches a degree of success as an artist in Greenwich Village, she asks Sills for financial advice. Bored with his wife, Sills becomes infatuated with the personable artist and the couple become lovers. When his wife, Anna Lehr, learns that her husband is having an affair with Hyland, she denounces the artist. In turn, Hyland criticizes the wife for not attending to Sills's needs. Lehr determines to improve her role as wife, and Hyland returns to her boyfriend in her home town.

Jack Livingston, a Greenwich Village poet of German descent, is the leader of an artistic circle, in Thomas N. Heffron's psychological study, *The Price of Applause* (1918), based on the story by Nina Wilcox Putnam and Norman Jacobson. Always seeking recognition, he announces that he is a German sympathizer when World War I erupts. With the sinking of the Lusitania, the poet, again seeking recognition, announces that he will join the Legion of France. A companion accompanies him. Before leaving, Livingston marries Claire Anderson, who is oblivious to his posturing. In France, Livingston suffers from cowardice when his unit is assigned to go over the top. Once in the open, he passes out, and when he awakens, he finds himself in the middle of No Man's Land. Stunned by the slaughter around him, he exchanges clothes and identification with a dead German soldier, whose head has been blown away. He crawls off as his friend discovers the body with Livingston's tags. The poet is taken as prisoner, and his friend sails home and reports the poet's heroic death. Livingston, meanwhile, is shown a book of poems supposedly written by a soldier who has died in battle. They are his that he had given to his friend. Seeking applause for his own work, he escapes and returns to the States, where he finds his wife is remarried. She rejects him as a fraud, preferring to hold on to her fond memories of the man she had once admired. He meets a German friend who introduces him to a band of German saboteurs. When the leader asks for a volunteer to set off a time bomb at a factory, Livingston, who has awakened to the political realities of the time, volunteers. He denounces Germany and tosses the bomb into the center of the group, killing all its members. The film, made during America's entry into the war, served as one of numerous patriotic dramas.

When young Alice Brady is driven from her village, she heads for New York, in George Archainbaud's romantic drama, *The Trap* (1918), based on a story by Robert F. Hill. Once in the city, she begins work as a waitress and soon meets Crauford Kent, her former lover. He allows her to stay at his Greenwich Village studio, while he finds other accommodations. He then gets her a job posing as a model for a baking powder advertisement. Curtis Cooksey, a young cattleman from the West who has fallen in love with her poster image, arrives in the city, finds her and proposes marriage. She refuses, but invites him to remain a friend. Kent grows jealous of the cattleman's relationship with Brady and when she announces she intends to marry the Westerner, Brady arranges a party for her. The celebration turns into an orgy, as Kent anticipated, and early in the morning he calls the Westerner to say Brady needs her. Cooksey rushes over, sees the orgy and denounces her. She accuses Kent of arranging the entire incident, and prepares to leave for Boston. Cooksey has overheard the argument and realizes Brady is innocent. He joins her on the train, where they are married.

A movie producer plucks Edna Goodrich, a sewing machine operator, from a factory and transforms her into a film star in Dell Henderson's routine romantic drama, *Who Loves Him Best?* (1918), set chiefly in Greenwich Village. Although the producer has trained her and helped her to succeed in films and finally offers to marry her, Goodrich, who has fallen in love with a sculptor, rejects the producer's proposal. She gives up her screen career to pose for her lover. A complication arises when a wealthy widow desires the sculptor for her second husband. The former film star battles the widow for the man she loves and, in the end, succeeds. Some of the sequences were supposedly filmed on location somewhere along West 12th Street, off Fifth Avenue.

Young, impoverished Gladys Leslie lives in Greenwich Village with her stepfather, who runs a gambling operation in the area, in William P. S. Earle's domestic drama, *Little Miss No-Account* (1918). Leslie, who dreams of a life of love, kindness and happiness, captures the interest of the district attorney. He plans to clean up the Village of its vice. A raid rounds up a variety of low characters, including Leslie, who was deliberately sent to the premises with a promise of a job. She spends time in a cell, just like many of the local miscreants. Following several complications, the district attorney falls in love with Leslie. In addition, he restores any property in her name that others were trying to steal from her. The impoverished young woman's wishes seemed to come true.

When ambitious sculptress Enid Bennett's guardian, criminal lawyer Andrew Robson, suffers the death of his mother, he invites the sculptress to move in with him in Fred Niblo's drama, *The Law of Men* (1919). However, she refuses to give up her Greenwich Village studio. Robson then marries a socialite who becomes the lover of lecherous architect Donald MacDonald, who quickly shifts his amorous appetite toward Bennett. The sculptress agrees to accompany him to a small town, where he promises her a lucrative assignment to decorate a public library. As he tries to rape Bennett in a roadhouse room, Niles Welch, her fiancé, rushes into MacDonald's room and is evicted by hotel detectives. Bennett and Welch marry the following day. Suddenly, Welch is arrested for the murder of the architect. Bennett elicits her guardian's help and arrives in time to prevent his suicide. He confesses in court that he killed MacDonald, whom he claims had corrupted his wife. He then ends his own life by taking poison.

A young couple, separated by their individual careers, finally are reunited in William P. S. Earle's romantic drama, *The Broken Melody* (1919). Eugene O'Brien aspires to be an artist, and Lucy Cotton, his girlfriend, who lives in the same Greenwich Village apartment house, hopes for a singing career. When she finally wins a role in a Broadway production, the couple celebrate in a Village café, where they meet Corinne Barker, a wealthy patron, who offers to help O'Brien's art career by sending him to Paris to study. He rejects the generous offer, and instead proposes to Cotton. But she refuses, not wanting to stand in the way of Barker's offer. Once in Paris, O'Brien discreetly avoids his sponsor's amorous overtures. His portrait of his girlfriend brings him accolades. Meanwhile, Cotton gains recognition on stage, but she collapses during a performance. O'Brien, hearing about this, speeds back to New York, where the lovers are reunited.

When struggling Greenwich Village artist Creighton Hale fails to meet a prospective buyer at a fashionable hotel, he mistakenly takes the wrong coat that contains an invitation to a party for June Caprice, in George Archainbaud's comedy drama, *The Love Cheat* (1919), based on a 1919 play by Tristan Bernard. Feeling rather hungry and curious about the woman being honored on the invitation, he goes to the coming-out party and quickly falls in love with the guest of honor. Aware of the differences in their social and economic backgrounds, he begins to leave. But he meets a fellow classmate, Charles Coleman, who lends the artist money and introduces him to Caprice as a successful manager. The relations between Caprice and Hale grow serious until it is time to announce their engagement. Guilt prevents Hale from continuing the charade. He writes a letter confessing he is an impostor. Caprice becomes engaged to another whom her father has chosen for her, and later, meets Hale, who is a clerk in an antique shop. He tells her the truth about his love for her, and the couple reconcile their differences. For the sake of his daughter's happiness, her father consents to their marriage.

Successful novelist Tom Moore, whose wild lifestyle in Greenwich Village has affected his writing, is warned by his publisher that there will be no more advances until he changes his environment, in Harry Beaumont's comedy, *Toby's Bow* (1919), based on the 1919 play by John Tainter Foote. A friend suggests that he stay with an aristocratic Southern family, especially Doris Pawn, an aspiring writer who admires Moore's work. He agrees and reports to the home under an assumed name. Moore then proceeds to help Pawn edit her own work, which is turned into a successful novel. The money from the book helps her to pay off the mortgage on the estate. When she learn Moore's true identity, she angrily announces she wants none of his charity. She visits Greenwich Village and falls in love with it before returning home. She later returns to the Village, forgives Moore and marries him.

II. Bright Lights and Broken Dreams

Many of the inhabitants of Greenwich Village flouted conventional clothing and mores. By the late twenties, the Village became a refuge more for the pretentious than for the artists. Generally, the Village lumbered through the twenties characterized by two images – the epitome of urban sophistication, and a reputation for its all-night parties, its discussions of "free love," its theaters, cafés and art galleries – all fascinating attractions for its steady stream of curious tourists. The Wall Street crash of 1929 swept away the fortunes of many famous personalities, such as Jack Dempsey, the first millionaire athlete, and other wealthy magnates, including Greenwich Village's famous millionaire bohemian, Robert Clairmont. As the cultural life of the Village waned, so did the lure of the area fade as a unique background for Hollywood films during the late silent era. The scant number of releases were burdened by inane plots, with the Village itself relegated to a minor role – an unfitting end for such a rich and diverse community.

A popular Hindu fiction writer uses his real-life romantic escapades with a young woman who loves him as inspiration for his stories in Charles Swickard's absorbing drama, *The Devil's Claim* (1920), set in Greenwich Village. Sociologist Rhea Mitchell, aware of Sessue Hayakawa's cavalier attitude toward his girlfriend, Colleen Moore, is determined to convert him to a more earnest and caring lover. She conjures up a romantic tale that he eventually translates into a highly successful popular magazine serial. Meanwhile, Hayakawa is unaware that the story is a parable of the author's own superficial romantic life and attitudes about love. By the last installment – and the last reel of the film – the writer is left without an ending when he runs out of inspiration. But both plots, the serial and the film, are resolved when the sociologist and girlfriend appear to show the writer the true and proper meaning of love.

Anita Stewart portrays the title character, a naïve young woman who is duped into a "mock marriage" by Ward Crane, a young rake, in Bertram Bracken's problem drama, *Harriet and the Piper* (1920), based on the 1920 novel by Kathleen Norris. Crane takes his "bride" to his Greenwich Village apartment, where she soon discovers the truth about him, but by this time it is too late, and she resolves herself to her fate. Later, the scene shifts to the country home of Charles Richman, where Stewart is employed as secretary to Richman's wife. Soon after, the wife runs off with her lover and both are killed in a car accident. Suddenly Crane, Stewart's false lover, returns from India, posing as an occult reader. He is interested in Richman's daughter, Margaret Landis. When Stewart warns him to leave, Crane threatens to expose her to her employer. She marries Richman, who then considers Crane as a possible son-in-law. When Stewart confesses the story about her mock marriage, her husband rejects Landis's request and sends him away with a check for $20,000. But the daughter insists on eloping with him. As the couple are about to enter his car, an old avenging Hindu appears and stabs Crane, who has betrayed a sacred virgin in India. The film is loosely based on the legend of *The Pied Piper of Hamelin*, suggesting that if one dances to the piper, one must pay the price.

The more wild side of some Greenwich Village inhabitants clashes with members of society in Hugo Ballin's society comedy, *Help Yourself* (1920), based on the novel, *Trimmed With Red*, by Wallace Irwin. Department store clerk Madge Kennedy and her wealthy aunt attend a party, where a distinguished radical lectures the guests and then leads them to his Greenwich Village haunts to meet his friends. Kennedy, impressed with the odd group, invites the professor and his comrades to her home, where the guests consume too much vodka and begin behaving disruptively. Joseph Striker, a young man who is romantically attracted to the store clerk but is rejected by her aunt as a fortune hunter, arrives in time to take control of the situation and eject the rowdy revelers. The young couple eventually marry.

The daughter of an elderly and dying prisoner promises to repay those who have broken her father's spirit in Martin Justine's revenge drama, *They Shall Pay* (1921). Lottie Pickford, as the avenging daughter, learns that two of her father's three former business partners are still living; she then decides to add the son of the third partner to her list. Using disguise and deception, she ruins the careers of the two living partners and then aims at the young son, Allan Forrest, a Greenwich Village architect. However, she soon falls in love with him and casts aside her vindictiveness.

Carmel Myers, a waitress at a popular Greenwich Village restaurant, likes one of the customers, a certain artist, but this provokes the jealousy of her suitor, George Rigas, in Marcel De Sano's drama, *The Dangerous Moment* (1921). Rigas warns Myers to stay away from the artist. Later, when Rigas is found murdered, the police suspect the waitress. They find her hiding in the artist's studio. When the real murderer confesses, Myers is exonerated and the couple fall in love.

The lure of Greenwich Village comes between a happily married couple in Irvin V. Willat's, domestic drama, *Face of the World* (1921), based on a novel by Johan Bojer. Edward Hearn and his wife, Barbara Bedford, come to New York, where he studies surgery and she, searching for self-expression, joins a wild group of bohemians in Greenwich Village. She soon falls victim to sculptor Lloyd Whitlock, who persuades her to leave her husband because of his neglectful attitude. The couple separate, with the doctor emerging as chief of the hospital, and his wife spending a year as guest in the home of Whitlock's aunt. Whitlock, deciding to ask the husband to divorce his wife, is hurt in a car accident. The doctor saves the sculptor and returns to his wife's country home where she joins him. The couple, who truly love each other, reconcile their differences.

Artist's model Audrey Munson, after fleeing from a Greenwich Village painter who has tried to attack her, later meets a sculptor who wants her to pose in the nude for him, in Robert Z. Leonard's drama, *Heedless Moths* (1921), based on Munson's autobiographical magazine articles. The sculptor's wife, jealous of the model, befriends a painter. The artist's model, whom he had earlier seduced, seeking retaliation, tells the sculptor about his wife's affair with the painter. Following several complications, Munson brings about a reconciliation between the sculptor and his wife. The film had the reputation of containing several risqué scenes – bordering on nudity.

Greenwich Village artist Truman Van Dyke, having grown tired of a flock of women chasing him, ends up proposing that his young housekeeper, Carmel Myers, marry him, in Rollin Sturgeon's inane drama, *The Mad Marriage* (1921). They marry the very night he proposes. He feels content and safe with his bride, whom he continues to treat as his servant. And she plays her role well, cleaning and darning his socks, and presenting him with a son. However, unknown to him, she has written a play in collaboration with Arthur Carewe, whom she had met earlier. The play has proved to be a large success. After she leaves him to strike out on her own, he finally realizes how important she was to his very existence. He offers her a divorce, but the illness of their child reunites the couple.

Greenwich Village bachelor Douglas Fairbanks loves his neighbor Marguerite De La Motte, who believes that poor children can learn much by being exposed to the homes of the wealthy, in Theodore Reed's society comedy, *The Nut* (1921). To get closer to her, he entertains wealthy patrons, who become indignant when fireworks explode prematurely. Following a series of complications, Fairbanks rescues his neighbor from a rival and the lovers marry.

Country boy and chief cook for a Maine lumber camp David Butler, and snobbish socialite Leatrice Joy take control of a Greenwich Village restaurant in Fred J. Butler's comedy drama, *Smiling All the Way* (1921), based on a story by Henry Payson Dowd. Although they have made a success of the Purple Guinea Pig, their restaurant, Joy's aunt, Frances Raymond, prefers that she marry a rich suitor. She has her niece kidnapped aboard the prospective suitor's yacht, but Butler rescues his partner and the couple return to Greenwich Village – after visiting a minister.

Gloria Swanson portrays a liberated daughter in constant conflict with her more staid millionaire father, Theodore Roberts, in Sam Wood's silly comedy drama, *Prodigal Daughters* (1923), based on the novel by Joseph Hooking. At one point, she decides to set herself up in a Greenwich Village bohemian studio to prove her independence, much to the chagrin of her father. The film tries to suggest the wider theme about the clash between the modern younger generation and its parents, but ends up treating the youths as flippant and the grownups as either foolish or uncertain in their actions. One particular conflict arises when Swanson decides one Sunday morning to dress up outlandishly for a spin around the local golf course instead of attending church with her father.

A husband's slight, insincere affair with a Greenwich Village temptress leads to a divorce action by his loving wife in Whitman Bennett's familiar domestic drama, *Love of Women* (1924). The film suggests that couples deeply in love can often be torn apart by external pressures or short-lived misunderstandings. Lawford Davidson and Helene Chadwick love each other, and had eloped years earlier. Now they have a baby as one of their responsibilities. When the wife learns of his momentary affair with Mary Thurman in her studio, she is willing to forgive him, but her relatives interfere and persuade her to file for a divorce. Just then, their baby becomes ill. Their concern for their child takes precedence and ultimately brings the couple back together.

A wealthy father hires Donald Keith to look after his incorrigible daughter, Clara Bow, who has joined other bohemians in Greenwich Village, in Dallas M. Fitzgerald's society drama, *My Lady of Whims* (1925), based on the story, "Protecting Prue," by Edgar Franklin. Keith rents a room in the same building where the wayward daughter lives, and the two soon become good friends. However, when she discovers that her father has hired him to spy on her, she breaks off her relationship with Keith and announces her engagement to ladies' man Francis McDonald. When Keith learns that the wedding is to take place aboard McDonald's yacht, he stops the affair and carries off his loved one, despite all her protests.

Ralph Lewis, who owns several hotels, disapproves of the lifestyle of his son, Charles Rogers, who spends his time playing the ukulele in a Greenwich Village studio in Sam Wood's romantic drama, *Fascinating Youth* (1926). Lewis insists that Rogers manage one of the father's hotels at a winter resort and promises the youth that if he succeeds, he can marry the young woman of his choice. Ivy Harris, his girlfriend, works as an artist for a film studio. Rogers decides to promote the hotel's winter sports by using film stars in his advertising campaign. Complications set in, but his girlfriend takes over and helps him succeed in making the hotel a huge success.

Two young people, Lois Wilson and George K. Arthur, leave their small town for New York, she to promote her popular baked cookies and he to pose as a model for Myrta Bonillas, a Greenwich Village artist, in David Kirkland's comedy drama, *The Gingham Girl* (1927), based on the story by Daniel Kussell. A misunderstanding between the couple separates them. Sometime later, Arthur gets a job in a cookie factory, owned by his former girlfriend and her partner, Jerry Miley. The lovers are reunited, and her partner retires from the business.

Jungle

I. Heroism and Romanticism Among the Trees

The history of jungle films parallels America's history of jungle warfare. The earliest silent jungle films were set chiefly in the Philippines, particularly during the Spanish-American War or the Philippine Insurrection. The U.S. experience in jungle warfare emerged with its engagements in the Philippines, with the arrival of its troops in 1898. Dressed in heavy khaki, they quickly suffered from the heat, dysentery, malaria, cholera and fever. By the end of the campaign, thousands of men had come down with these illnesses. Frequent revolutions in Nicaragua led to American troops landing there several times by 1910 "to protect American lives and property." Few films of the period focused on these issues. Instead, heroism and romanticism, not disease and imperialism, monopolized these early films about the Philippines and other areas in which American troops encountered jungle perils. Occasionally, a feature or documentary used Hawaii for its background. But it was not until the films were set on the Dark Continent, or the jungles of Central and South America, that audiences witnessed a full-fledged string of jungle pictures. Many of the earliest entries are either lost or unavailable, such as D. W. Griffith's *The Zulu's Heart* (1908); Wallace Carleson's *Lost in the Jungle* (1911), with Tom Mix; Colin Campbell's *Alone in the Jungle* (1913) and *Thor, Lord of the Jungle* (1913); and *Hearts of the Jungle* (1915), again with Tom Mix. These films helped to establish the familiar obligatory devices – hostile natives, primitive rituals, references to the slave trade, exploitation of the continent, traders, hunters and the romance of the jungle. "A savage land," the narrator of a Tarzan film intoned about Africa, "where the struggle for survival is a never-ending drama." The jungle film, from its inception, promised the moviegoer several unique features – a glimpse at strange customs and creatures; the lure of adventure, danger and romance; and a chance to escape to an exotic land.

One of the earliest romantic tales to be set in the jungles of the Philippines, the two-reel drama, *The Capture of Aguinaldo* (1913), focuses more on a romance than the capture of the guerrilla leader of the Filipinos listed in the title. The film studio boasted of superior battle sequences and included scenes of local headhunters and a generally savage land. The Philippines were used for decades as the location for numerous action and war dramas following World War II.

The next film continued to feature jungle drama set in the Philippines. Wrongly disgraced army officer J. Warren Kerrigan journeys to Manila and, using an alias, enlists as a private, in Lorimer Johnson's one-reel drama, *For the Flag* (1913), set during the Philippine Insurrection. His former regiment arrives and, during a battle with the Filipino forces, Kerrigan gets a chance to perform some choice heroics. These include rescuing the governor and his daughter from the insurrectionists. Following his reinstatement in his old outfit, he wins the love of the young woman he had saved. The American Film Company that produced this standard drama was better known for it numerous westerns. The familiar plot of *For the Flag* demonstrates how easily a studio was able to shift from one setting, and genre, to another.

The Philippine jungle continued to serve as background for romantic adventures. William Wolbert's domestic drama, *The Last Man* (1916), set on a remote army post in Montana and in the Philippines, centers on an army major's failed marriage and newfound love. William Duncan returns from the Philippines after the Spanish-American War and discovers that his wife, Mary Anderson, is having an affair with a young lieutenant. Following the couple's divorce, she marries her lover. The major meets and falls in love with Corinne Griffith, a local young woman of the mountains. When he is reassigned to the Philippines, he takes Griffith along as a nurse. The lieutenant also is ordered to the islands and takes his wife along. The remainder of the film deals with intriguing jungle battles during the Moro War and the former wife's fruitless efforts to win Duncan, her ex-husband back. Friction between the two officers soon arises.

One of the themes of jungle films deals with the intrusion of outsiders. Lorraine Otto lives with her father in the wilds of South Africa, where she is engaged to a neighbor, Harry T. De Vere, in the weak drama, *The Vengeance of the Wilds* (1915). One day, Charles Wheelock, a hunter and small-time museum owner, appears and falls in love with Otto, despite warnings by her father. His daughter elopes with the stranger, who takes her to a big city, where a mock marriage is performed. Wheelock soon grows tired of Otto, who feels neglected. When he takes her to a sleazy dance hall, she begins to realize his true character. Her attempt at suicide fails. Meanwhile, her jungle fiancé tracks Wheelock to his small-time museum and zoo. The two men engage in a terrible fist fight, ending only when Wheelock flees from De Vere. He hides in a lions' cage, where the animals claw him to death. As the victor is about to leave, his fiancée enters and the couple embrace.

The outsider again intrudes upon a peaceful family raised close to nature in Africa. A scientist who hates civilization makes a home for himself in a jungle where he raises two children whose parents were killed in a native attack in the drama, *The Jungle Lovers* (1915). Years later, the children have grown up and have fallen in love with each other. The young woman, Bessie Eyton, plays with the wild animals. An ivory hunter arrives and falls in love with Eyton. He offers to marry her, but the scientist says she is engaged to the young man living with him. The hunter says he will take her by force if the scientist does not give his permission. The youth enters and knocks down the hunter. Following a series of complications, including the youth's capture by the hunter's entourage and an attack by a tribe of natives upon the hunter's party, led by Eyton, the captured youth is freed. Finally, the native chief, after a hand-to-hand combat with the hunter, throws the white man off a cliff to his death. The scientist then performs a marriage ceremony uniting the young lovers, with the friendly natives attending the festivities.

The clash of cultures is another theme prevalent in jungle dramas. Lou Tellegen, an English explorer, is about to leave for the wilds of Africa, in George Melford's outdoor drama, *The Explorer* (1915), based on the 1909 novel by W. Somerset Maugham. Dorothy Davenport, the woman he loves, pleads with him to take her brother, Tom Forman, along. Forman, a worthless idler, is spoiled and lazy, and she thinks the journey will teach him responsibility. Tellegen agrees, and the group sails for the African jungle. Tellegen and his fellow whites establish peace treaties with the various tribes of natives – until Forman, after drinking heavily, tries to attack a young native woman. When another native intervenes, Forman shoots him in the back. The tribal chief declares war on the visitors, who build a stockade for defense. Greatly outnumbered, the Europeans decide to withdraw at night, while one volunteer will remain behind to trick the natives. Forman is elected to stay. The party leaves, but a furious battle takes place in a stream where the natives overtake the whites. The spears are no match for the guns, and the natives fall back. Meanwhile, Forman puts up a valiant fight, but is struck down by a spear. Back in England, Tellegen is treated as a hero, but his girlfriend is piqued about his abandoning her brother. When she hears the entire story from the others in Tellegen's party, she understands more fully the circumstances of the incident and accepts his love.

Problems arise in the outdoor drama, *The Leopard's Bride* (1916), set at an army post in the jungles of India, when the colonel and one of his officers fall in love with the same woman. The object of the romance favors the subordinate officer. In retaliation, the colonel assigns his rival to a remote part of the jungle and stops all his letters from reaching her. During his journey, the young officer rescues a woman about to be sacrificed. The grateful native becomes the officer's servant and quickly falls in love with him. Later, the colonel, the young woman from the outpost and others trek through the jungle, where the woman gets lost. The servant girl rescues her and leads her to the second officer, who is now ill. The two lovers are reunited, and the missing letters are finally explained to the satisfaction of both. The servant girl, realizing her present romantic status, goes out into the jungle where she is killed by a leopard.

Sometimes the line between civilization and primitivism blurs, especially when a supposedly civilized individual acts otherwise. American heiress Kathlyn Williams, drunken engineer Guy Oliver and valet Harry Lonsdale, who is posing as a titled gentleman, all survivors of a shipwreck, are swept ashore on the African coast in T. N. Heffron's low-budget drama, *Into the Primitive* (1916), based on the 1908 novel by Robert Ames Bennet. Rather than trusting the alcoholic, Williams relies on Sir Lonsdale, who is really a valet posing as a gentleman of society. She soon learns that she has made the wrong choice, for Oliver ends up saving her from lascivious Lonsdale's sexual attack upon her. Lonsdale is killed before the remaining couple are finally rescued. The film was cheaply made and unimpressive.

When divinity student Boyd Marshall learns that the young woman he loves cares for another, he journeys to Africa to forget his failed romance, in Ernest Warde's drama, *Hidden Valley* (1916). He accidentally penetrates Hidden Valley, where a beautiful young white woman is about to be sacrificed to the natives' god. By posing as a god who has descended from the heavens, he is able to rescue her from the natives. The freed captive and Marshall leave the valley and return to civilization.

Duncan McRae's absorbing jungle tale, *Man and Beast* (1917) is set in the South Africa veldt during a great drought and concerns two families. One family's land contains a spring of free-running freshwater that the owner, who has a son and a daughter, uses only for his needs, but not for his stock. He also allows his neighbor, who has one son, to take water back for their needs. This man's son and the neighbor's daughter are in love, and when their fathers argue over water rights, the lovers continue their romance and eventually marry. The couple suffer several hardships, and their child becomes the catalyst for the two families reconciling their differences. The child wanders into the jungle and is befriended by a chimp. But an elephant rescues the infant and returns it to its parents.

Lord Greystoke in 1897 is assigned to investigate the sudden unrest in South Africa over the slave trade in Scott Sidney's unique but generally disappointing drama, *Tarzan of the Apes* (1918), based on the 1914 novel by Edgar Rice Burroughs. Following a mutiny and other incidents aboard his vessel, Greystoke and his wife end up abandoned somewhere in a jungle with their newborn son. The parents die, and the child is adopted and raised by an ape that has lost her infant. Gordon Griffith, as the ten-year-old jungle boy, Tarzan, dominates the next segment of the story. Elmo Lincoln then portrays the adult Tarzan. Meanwhile, back in England, rumors hint that a Greystoke heir still lives somewhere in Africa, and an expedition is sent to find the lost son. A young woman, Enid Markey, who is to marry the heir, accompanies the group that eventually finds Tarzan. The man of the jungle rescues Markey, and the two become friends. A romance develops between them.

Wilfred Lucas's sequel, *The Romance of Tarzan* (1918), followed *Tarzan of the Apes*, released earlier in the year, and is also derived from the stories by Edgar Rice Burroughs, especially the last few chapters of *Tarzan of the Apes*. Once again, Elmo Lincoln appears as the Ape Man, attired only in a breech cloth and knife. This time around, Tarzan follows Jane (Enid Markey) back to California – specifically, a modern ranch – where he tangles with bandits who have captured Jane, and Cleo Madison, a temptress hired by Colin Kelly, and who clashes with Jane, the ape man's true love. Jane, thinking Tarzan has been unfaithful, breaks up with him, and he returns to Africa. But she follows him when she learns of Kelly's treachery. The best parts of this disappointing drama occur only when Tarzan is back in his natural habitat – the African jungle. Other silent films about the fictional Tarzan include *The Return of Tarzan* (1920), *The Adventures of Tarzan* (1920), *The Son of Tarzan* (1920), *Tarzan and the Golden Lion* (1927), *Tarzan the Mighty* (1928) and *Tarzan the Tiger* (1928).

Jack Holt, a philanderer, is forced by his wealthy family to work as an ivory hunter in Africa or lose his inheritance, in James Young's pretentious adventure, *The White Man's Law* (1918). Holt and Sessue Hayakawa, an Oxford graduate and son of an Arab chief, become partners. Hayakawa is courting Florence Vidor, a French-Sudanese young woman. Holt takes her riding where she loses her innocence to him. When his partner sees them returning and questions her, she admits she is secretly engaged to marry Holt. Disappointed, he shakes Holt's hand and congratulates him. They both leave with their crew for the interior to carry out their ivory trading. Hayakawa finds a letter from Holt's wife and a fight ensues in the water. Holt returns alone, thinking his partner has drowned. The Arab survives, returns to the base camp and gives Holt a revolver to take his own life. Later, when Holt's widow arrives, she is told her husband's death was an accident. The last sequence shows the Arab chief's son riding toward his tribe with Vidor at his side. The title refers to a local unwritten law which states that those who break the "white man's law" (as Holt did) become social outcasts.

Kitty Gordon, the daughter of a university trustee, scientist Irving Cummings, and several others journey to Africa in search of relics of an ancient Greek race, in Frank Crane's adventure, *The Unveiling Hand* (1919). Gordon has married Cummings, not out of love but purely for the interests of science. George MacQuarrie, who loves Gordon, goes along as Cummings's business manager. During the journey Cummings shows his true character, one that is repulsive, selfish and mean-spirited – resulting in his wife's loathing him. When she contracts fever, her alcoholic husband drinks the last bottle of brandy that she needs for medicinal purposes. It is MacQuarrie, and not her husband, who helps her to recover. A native guide announces that Cummings has died in a cave-in. When they return to the university campus and prepare a memorial for Cummings, the scientist shows up alive, drunk and smelling of drugs. He begins accusing his wife and MacQuarrie of plotting his death. The Arab guide, who has returned as the doctor's valet, stabs Cummings to death. His widow in now free to marry MacQuarrie, the man she really loves.

William Farnum undergoes a series of unusual hardships when the treacherous Lyster Chambers, his rival, sends him on a false journey to Africa, in Richard Stanton's adventure, *The Jungle Trail* (1919). While both men desire Anna Luther, Chambers plots to get rid of his competition by sending Farnum on this wild goose chase and paying two guides to kill him. Once in Africa, Farnum becomes aware of the treachery. After swimming across a great lake, he comes across a native village, whose people are cultured and wealthy. However, their superstition places the white man in danger, so he wins their respect by displaying his superior strength. But he is faced with a new problem when the lover of a native woman who helped save Farnum challenges the stranger to a fight. Before the entire village the two men battle, until Farnum tosses his foe into a river. When the man returns at night, Farnum topples over a statue which crushes the lover, allowing Farnum and the native to escape. Later, when he returns to civilization, he sets himself up as a mystic, forces a confession from Chambers and wins back the love of Luther.

Madlaine Traverse accompanies her father to South Africa to investigate diamond mines in which he has invested, in Edmund Lawrence's routine drama, *Lost Money* (1919), set both in England and Africa. Father and daughter are members of a well-to-do English family. Several scenes depict some of the problems the daughter encounters, including her terrifying experience on the veldt, where both she and her lover, "Ox" Lanyon, are on the edge of madness because of the lack of water. Other jungle scenes are rather tame for this type of jungle film, which ends with plenty of shooting and a large conflagration.

Not all jungle films were set in the Philippines or Africa. An Indian woman finds a Spanish child whose family had perished in the South American jungle and raises her as her own, in Walter Edwards's fascinating drama, *The Jungle Child* (1916). The child grows up possessing tremendous physical strength. Her foster mother holds papers proving the young woman (Dorothy Dalton) is heir to great riches. Howard Hickman, an explorer who has left his party after stealing their supplies, shows up and reads the native woman's papers. Planning to claim the fortune for himself, he marries Dalton and takes her to New York. Once he gets the money, he celebrates with a party. When the jungle-raised Dalton hears him boasting how he tricked her to get her wealth, she dresses in her native costume and strangles her deceitful husband.

II. The Dark Continent and Other Lost Worlds

Jungle films of the twenties were chiefly set in Africa; however, there were exceptions, such as the fantasy *The Lost World* (1925) and the drama *From Headquarters* (1929), both set in South America, and *The Showdown* (1928), which uses Mexico for its background. There were light-hearted comedies like *Hold That Lion* (1926) and fascinating semi-documentaries like *Chang* (1927), as well as traditional dramas. Gone were the films set in the Philippines. In their place came romantic tales of Hawaii, some concerned, albeit obliquely, with the problem of miscegenation. But entertainment predominated, with heroes and heroines reenacting mankind's universal struggles: surviving in the jungle against predatory beasts, other tribes and aggressive foreign states. The primary focus, however, remained on Africa. Perhaps the aging doctor (Henry Travers) in *Stanley and Livingstone* (1939) stated it best when he romanticized his experiences in Africa to newspaperman Henry Stanley (Spencer Tracy). "Nothing could match it," he began. "Evenings in camp, the breeze cool off the plateau, the tropical rivers gleaming like silver in the moonlight, and the feeling of life around you everywhere. And more than anything, the knowledge that you're thousands of miles from civilization – close to nature as God made it."

Gene Pollar portrays the King of the Jungle in Harry Revier's adventure drama, *The Return of Tarzan* (1920), set chiefly in Africa and based on the novel by Edgar Rice Burroughs. This entry contains more action than the previous entries in the series. Tarzan battles lions, fights off a horde of hoodlums, gets tied to a tree in the jungle, is thrown overboard from a vessel, and has to contend with Ormond Cortez, a formidable foe whom Tarzan had earlier caught cheating at cards. Recognized by Cortez aboard a vessel, Tarzan is thrown overboard and reaches a jungle coast. Later, a yacht with his girlfriend Jane aboard, is shipwrecked. When a lion attacks Jane, Tarzan comes to her rescue. The couple rekindle their love for each other. Endowing the hero with superhuman strength (obviously, from leading a good life among the apes), strains credibility at times, but at least the film moves.

A search for treasure in Africa leads to betrayal and death in Sam Warner's adventure drama, *A Dangerous Adventure* (1922), based on the story by Frances Guihan. Two sisters (Grace Darmond and Derelys Perdue) and their uncle search for a treasure chest left by their uncle somewhere in East Africa. The unscrupulous uncle, however, agrees to turn over Darmond to a tribal chief in exchange for a caravan. Following several complications, Philo McCullough, who loves Darmond, along with a friend, rescues her. During a terrible storm, the natives flee the caravan, and the treacherous uncle perishes.

Not all jungle perils stem from the wild beasts or hostile savages. Vernon Steele, an officer in the British service in East Africa, is assigned to another post, in Paul Scardon's familiar domestic drama, *A Wonderful Wife* (1922). Accompanied by his wife, he reports to the post, run by Landers Stevens, reportedly a cold-hearted commissioner. Stevens, upon meeting the wife, decides he wants her for his own. To this end, he devises a scheme to send Steele into the interior, a venture during which he will certainly be killed – although the official order listed a different assignment for Steele. The wife, learning about Stevens's unscrupulous plot, realizes she was jeopardizing her marriage by allowing the commissioner to flirt with her. She then upsets Stevens's plot and rescues her husband.

The wilds of the African jungle provide the background for John Harvey's drama, *The Woman Who Believed* (1922), about the building of a railroad through the jungle. Walter Miller and Ann Luther, who soon become part of a romantic triangle, are members of a small group of explorers. They witness the dangers from wild beasts and from their own shortcomings. One of the highlights of the film, which also deals with the problems resulting from a jealous mind, is the dynamiting of a huge bridge.

Charles Vogt, a fugitive from the law, and Claire Lotto are shipwrecked and land in an African jungle in Nathan Hirsh's drama, *The Master of Beasts* (1922). Vogt and Lotto manage to survive the dangers of the jungle, including savage beasts and hostile natives. When they are brought back to civilization, they both join a circus, Vogt as an animal tamer and Lotto as a trapeze artist. Vogt, meanwhile, is exonerated of the murder charge brought against him and which caused him to flee from the law.

American engineer Maurice Flynn, who has been working in Africa, returns to America and marries Mary Miles Minter, only to be reassigned to his old job among the natives, in Charles Maigne's drama, *Drums of Fate* (1923). Since he will be gone for only a few months, he journeys alone, leaving his wife behind. In the jungle, his small band is attacked by a hostile tribe and he is taken prisoner. Somehow, news gets back to the States that he has been killed in the attack. His wife, pressured by her guardian who always preferred that she marry an accomplished musician, remarries. Meanwhile, Flynn escapes and returns to America, where he learns about Minter's remarriage. Believing she loves her second husband, he resigns himself to these circumstances and returns once again to Africa. News finally reaches Minter and her husband. The report shocks the musician, who dies. Minter is determined to find Flynn, whom she really loves, and sets sail for Africa. Once in the jungle, her small party is attacked by natives and she is captured. Taken to the tribal king, a friend of Flynn's, the couple are soon reunited.

Stowaways, a burning ship, a forced landing on a desert island and the danger of cannibals – all these elements cannot save Jack Dawn's old-fashioned, weak drama, *A Desperate Moment* (1926), from a disaster worse than that suffered by the vessel. Wanda Hawley, on a yachting trip with her father, falls in love with Thodore von Eltz, the captain of the vessel. Crooks, who have stowed away aboard the yacht, take control and set the crew and Hawley's father adrift in a small boat. They hold the captain and Hawley hostage. The vessel catches fire, and all abandon the yacht. On an island, the leader of the crooks, after inciting the natives to attack the others, is killed. A passing ship finally rescues the others in this pedestrian and forgettable film.

Douglas MacLean, thinking he has met the young woman of his dreams (Constance Howard), follows her as far as South Africa and continually misses meeting her, in William Beaudine's comedy, *Hold That Lion* (1926). Office worker MacLean, upon learning Howard is about to leave on a trip with her father, begins to follow her throughout Europe – and always fails to meet her. Following an embarrassing predicament in a hotel in South Africa when he is caught in the hall without pants, MacLean decides to join a group of tourists the next day who are attending a lion hunt. However, they refer to the activity as a "cat hunt," which MacLean misinterprets. He proudly bets a fellow hunter $10,000 that he will bring in the first "cat." By sheer accident, he wins the bet – although the sequence shows the lion chasing MacLean.

Tarzan (James Pierce), at his African estate, goes out to meet his wife and a party of visitors, in J. P. McGowan's jungle adventure, *Tarzan and the Golden Lion* (1927), based on the 1923 novel by Edgar Rice Burroughs. A native tells Tarzan he has escaped from a city of diamonds. When the party is safe at his estate, Tarzan goes on a hunting trip. Meanwhile, Frederic Peters, a treacherous trader, attacks the estate and captures Edna Murphy, Jane's niece. Tarzan follows them, accompanied by his pet lion. The high priest of the Palace of Diamonds prepares the woman captive for a human sacrifice to the lion god. Tarzan enters the city through a secret passage, kills the lion god and rescues Murphy. The sinister trader is killed by Tarzan's lion. The people of the city laud Tarzan as their new god.

Gladys Hulette and Mahlon Hamilton, the only survivors of a shipwreck, are swept ashore on the coast of Africa, in Edgar Lewis's routine adventure, *Life's Crossroads* (1928). Early scenes reflect the couple's lack of fondness for each other, but they are forced to cooperate for the sake of survival in this primitive environment. A white man eventually rescues them and leads them to his ranch on the edge of the jungle. Supposedly friendly, he plots to take the young woman for himself and kill Hamilton. As the latter is recuperating in his sick bed, his rescuer hovers over Hamilton and is about to slay him. But Hulette shoots the stranger, thereby saving Hamilton's life. The two survivors now feel differently toward each other and embrace.

The remainder of jungle films are set in areas other than Africa, with several earning a unique place in film history – including *The Lost World*, for its special effects, and *Chang*, for its poetic and memorable animal sequences. Lloyd Hughes portrays Ed Malone, a budding reporter who helps Professor Challenger (Wallace Beery) prove that dinosaurs are alive and well and living in the Amazon in Harry O. Hoyt's intriguing fantasy, *The Lost World* (1925), based on the novel by Sir Arthur Conan Doyle. The managing editor of a London newspaper, threatened with a lawsuit by the professor, assigns the awkward reporter to cover Challenger's lecture that same evening. "I believe Professor Challenger is insane," the editor remarks to a colleague. "He nearly killed three reporters I sent to interview him today." He turns to Malone and, referring to the lecture hall, warns: "Reporters are barred – but get in." Following two confrontations with the easily excitable professor, Malone is finally accepted as a member of the expedition, especially after promising to get his paper to sponsor a rescue mission to find the father of Paula White (Bessie

Love). The famous explorer Sir John Boxton (Lewis Stone), who has befriended Malone, also volunteers for the journey to South America. Scientists mock Challenger's belief that dinosaurs still exist and consider him a fraud. The remainder of the film is a tribute to the special effects persons who have created a world that may have existed millions of years ago – a strange place where ferocious creatures prowl the terrain and struggle to survive. Members of the small expedition undergo a series of dangers and witness a dinosaur, pterodactyl and brontosaurus, before they return to London. They bring with them a brontosaurus they had captured. But the great creature breaks loose from its confinement and, in several remarkably filmed scenes, wreaks havoc upon the city and its terrified inhabitants. Finally, it smashes through London Bridge and disappears down the Thames River to the open sea. The film anticipates the classic adventure film *King Kong* (1933). Willis O'Brien created the animals and sets for both films.

Impoverished poet Syd Chaplin, following a series of mishaps, finds himself aboard a ship, where he is saved from the angry crew by English lord Crauford Kent, in Charles Reisner's comedy, *The Missing Link* (1927). Kent, an explorer and scientist who is timid in front of women, switches roles with Chaplin, his valet, both of whom accompany their host, Tom McGuire, and his daughter, Ruth Hiatt, on their journey from London to Africa. The remainder of the film is concerned with Chaplin's antics as a scared explorer trying to escape from various lions, gorillas and other creatures in the Hollywood-made jungle. The star is not as funny as his half-brother, Charlie, but he works hard at his routines, which are usually good for a few laughs.

Chang (1927), produced by Merian C. Cooper and Ernest B. Schoedsack, is often cited as one of the best wild animal pictures ever made. Shot chiefly in Siam, the film includes scenes of a herd of almost 100 wild elephants tramping through the jungle, in addition to shots of virtually every other kind of animal. In one fascinating sequence, a baby elephant is captured and chained to a hut – until the mother appears and wrecks the hut. In another scene, which underscores the dangers of jungle life, a native is high up in a tree while a tiger below tries to climb up the same tree. The film also depicts, in melodramatic terms, native life in the jungle, focusing in particular on one small family trying to build a home for themselves. But leopards steal their food while tigers lurk nearby, all frightening or driving away the family.

Officer Monte Blue leads a command of U.S. Marines in Central America in a search for a group of lost sightseers stranded in the jungle in Howard Bretherton's bloated and implausible drama, *From Headquarters* (1929). When the men finally reach their goal, only two have survived the awful ordeal. In addition, all members of the party have perished – except for a baby girl. The marines must now help transport the infant to safety – suffering through storms, fever, jungle heat and other such hardships. The derelict captain, Blue, is assisted by Guinn Williams, a hard-boiled marine sergeant. The film was released as a part-talking and part-silent feature.

Mythical Kingdoms

I. The Splendors of the Royal Court and the Royal Bed

Early silent romantic adventures about life, love and intrigue in mythical kingdoms chiefly resembled the plots of popular novels and plays, such as *Graustark, The Prisoner of Zenda* and *Rupert of Henzau*. George Barr McCutcheon, a city editor of a Lafayette, Indiana, newspaper, in 1901 wrote the popular novel *Graustark*, whose title soon came to symbolize any romantic fictional kingdom. The same conventions that won over audiences of the original works spilled over to the screen – romance, court intrigue, danger, exotic lands and customs, heroism and villainy. But what films added were the visual splendors of courtly ceremonies and swordplay, garish costumes and uniforms, seductive boudoirs, and rebellious mobs. Unfortunately, many of these treats soon became the subject of ridicule by repetitive plots, tiresome characters engaged in familiar treachery, and anticipated endings. In addition to these external conventions, the films suggested at least two distinct political threads running through them. One hinted at the promise of democracy, such as in *A Son of the Immortals* (1916) and *The Gilded Cage* (1916). Some of these films depicted revolutionaries ready to rise up against their abusive rulers. Other films, like *His Majesty, the American* (1919), struggled to contain the status quo. These portrayed their heroes as the protectors of the established regimes. Although these two elements seem contradictory, they both actually promoted the American agenda – if there was one. In the first, the films suggest, democracy takes precedence over any other system. In the second, stability (the status quo) is preferred over disruptive revolution. American film studios were able to play their cards either way without offending its government or its citizens.

Royal marriages at times became a problem for at least one of the partners in a handful of these films. A young prince and heir to the throne of a European nation, formally betrothed to a princess of a neighboring country, decides to reject the marriage and flees to America in Leon D. Kent's familiar drama, *The Red Virgin* (1915). He falls in love with a young American woman in a small New England village and secretly marries her. Because of his behavior back home, his country is threatened with war. His father's agents and his prospective fiancée call on the prince. To give his country time to prevent any hostilities, he agrees to marry the princess. His wife suddenly enters the room and sees her husband embracing the stranger. She flees, leaves a note for him and throws herself from a cliff. The husband reads the note and thinks she is dead. Meanwhile, she survives the fall, is taken to her home by a woman, where she gives birth to a baby girl before she dies. The saddened husband returns home, marries the princess and is blessed with a son. Twenty years later, the daughter grows up hating all men and becomes an actress. The prince has become king, but his country is in turmoil, tottering on revolution. He flees with his son to America, where the son meets the father's daughter. She tries to ruin the young man, especially when she learns that his father abandoned her mother. Following several complications, all problems are reconciled, with the king and his two children returning to his now peaceful country.

Another royally decreed marriage poses a problem for the prospective bride in Hal Clarendon's routine romantic drama, *One Day* (1916), based on the 1909 novel by Elinor Glyn. John W. Dillon, after usurping the throne of a mythical European state, arranges for a marriage between his daughter and a prince, to help solidify his position as ruler. Although his daughter, Jeanne Iver, agrees, she travels to England, where she meets Victor Sutherland, the legitimate ruler of her father's country. Since she promised her father that she would marry the man of his choice, she gives up her love for Sutherland. Revolutionaries assassinate her father and install Sutherland to the throne. He returns to his native land to reclaim his title and marries Iver. The film is a sequel to the drama, *Three Weeks* (1914), based on the 1907 novel by Glyn.

At other times, the royal wedding is threatened by political forces. The king of Ostrau (Howard Hall) decides that his son (Maurice Costello) will marry the princess of a neighboring principality in Van Dyke Brooke's romantic drama, *The Crown Prince's Double* (1916). The prince agrees, but the country is threatened by a revolution, which occurs just before the ceremony. So the king and his son flee to London. Costello is sent to America, where he falls in love with Anna Laughlin, his friend's sister, and the lovers elope. Anders Randolf, a baron from the prince's country, arrives in America to tell Costello he must have the marriage annulled and return to his land, which is now politically quiet. The couple flee to New York, where the prince's friend finds a double for Costello. Desperate for money, the look-alike agrees to impersonate the prince for $1,000. Detectives locate him and mistake him for the real prince.

Once again, an arranged marriage presents trouble between two states. Both principalities are pledged to have a marriage between their two royal families in Ben Turbett's romantic drama, *When Love Is King* (1916). Richard Tucker, the king of one land, is to marry Vivian Perry, the princess of the neighboring country. But she loves Harold Meltzer, the king's cousin. Tucker flees to America to avoid the marriage, and Meltzer, now appointed regent, sends a Japanese bandit to prevent the king from returning. On a walking tour across America, the king and his traveling companion come across the estate of a millionaire who is hosting a party. A butler in need of additional servants hires the two strangers. At the reception, the ambassador of Tucker's country recognizes his king, who requests that he remain unidentified. He meets Carroll McComas, the host's daughter, and they become friends. Following several complications, including an attempt on the king's life, he decides to return to his native land to protect it from the usurper. He renounces his love for the host's daughter and plans to marry the princess. But the millionaire buys a large estate belonging to the princess's family and declares his own daughter a princess so that the king can marry her.

John Barrymore plays a dual role – as a crown prince scheduled to marry the princess of a neighboring country, and as an actor, in Fred Thomson's familiar romantic drama, *Nearly a King* (1916). The princess is presently attending an American school. The prince loves a dancer and refuses to obey his father's request. Barrymore's secretary has an actor friend who resembles the prince and, if sent for, would be willing to impersonate him. The ploy would give the prince a chance to flee to London, where he could marry the dancer. Meanwhile, the princess is requested to return home. The American actor and the princess meet aboard the same vessel and fall in love. Following a series of complications in which the two lovers are married, the princess defends her actor-husband and, using her supreme power, decrees that he is her lawful husband. The film unfolds within a frame that opens with a valet presenting his employer, an actor, with a manuscript he has written. As the actor begins to read his valet's script, the drama comes alive on the screen. The scenes set in London were filmed in New York and its suburbs.

Court intrigue is used to ensnare a prince but backfires on its practitioner in Scott Sidney's inappropriately titled romantic drama, *Bullets and Brown Eyes* (1916). With two neighboring European states at war with each other, the countess of one lures the prince of the other into a trap. William Desmond, as the prince, falls in love with Bessie Barriscale, who is assigned by her scheming brother, Wyndham Standing, a count, to ensnare their foe. Desmond is tried and sentenced to face a firing squad at nightfall. But his temptress, who has fallen in love with the prince, rescues him and hides him in her boudoir. Her brother rushes in and a duel ensues between the two men, with the prince wounding the brother in the arm. The prince escapes and joins his troops, who, in a large battle sequence, rescue the woman he loves. The lovers, now reunited, ride off into the night, kissing each other.

According to virtually all American films about mythical kingdoms, the people of these lands yearn for democracy and freedom. J. Warren Kerrigan portrays a prince of a mythical European principality in Otis Turner's bland drama, *A Son of the Immortals* (1916), a weak imitation of the *Graustark* class of dramas. When Harry Carter, a strongman general takes control of the state, he appoints Kerrigan, a prince, as titular ruler. But the young man surprises all by instituting a string of democratic reforms. However, he cannot marry Lois Wilson, the woman he loves, because she is an American. But when he discovers his mother was born in the U. S., he abdicates and marries Wilson, and his father takes over the reigns of power, pledging to continue the democratic reforms of his son.

The dream of democracy burned bright among some members of the royalty as well as the peasants, albeit obliquely, in several of these films. A young queen has her love reciprocated by a young prince, but neither knows the identity of the other, in Harley Knoles's romantic drama, *The Gilded Cage* (1916), set in a mythical European country. Alice Brady portrays the queen, who has disguised herself as a peasant so that she could learn about her people, and Alec B. Francis, the prince, has renounced his title to join his people. Montagu Love, a villainous and powerful baron, has the prince arrested when he seems to be gaining power. In addition, he jails the disguised queen. She escapes, but is powerless to save the prince, who is sentenced to death. But an uprising erupts suddenly and the revolutionaries rescue the prince and kill the baron. The prince is made ruler, with Brady at his side as his queen. Splendid palace sets, including a moat, dungeon and other comparable backgrounds, enhance the entire production.

Henry Otto's overly dramatic adventure, *The Great Romance* (1919), is an interesting and innocuous blend of the specter of democracy and the fairy-tale aspect of these films. When Columbia University student Harold Lockwood is first informed by mysterious foreigners that he is of royal blood and a citizen of a mythical kingdom, he laughs it off – until his girlfriend is kidnapped. The young woman, whose father is an American millionaire, is to marry the nephew of the king of the impoverished state of Rugaria, Lockwood's alleged native land. Lockwood immediately sets out to rescue his girlfriend. He meets with the revolutionaries and makes an impassioned speech about democracy and freedom. Following a series of exciting action sequences, including Lockwood's dueling with a host of guardsmen, he is finally subdued and faces a firing squad. A countess comes forth and announces to the dying king that Lockwood is his own son, who had been sent to America to learn about democracy. Lockwood, now king, publicly renounces his throne and calls upon his fellow citizens to form a new democratic government. He is then elected the first president of the new republic, with his rescued girlfriend as his wife. The film offers several lavish interior and exterior settings.

Olga Petrova, as a runaway princess of a small European country, is seen as an organ grinder's helper, in Burton L. King's drama, *The Eternal Question* (1916). Meanwhile, Mahlon Hamilton and Warner Oland bet $25,000 that the latter can convert a peasant woman into a successful socialite in three months. They select Petrova as their subject. Hamilton falls in love with the young woman, who is soon transformed into a popular member of the social class. But the young man is unable to pay the wager to his friend. The social success then reveals that she is the daughter of a king, and that she ran off to avoid marrying a man she did not love. Oland, angry at losing the wager, kidnaps the young woman and delivers her to the duke who was to marry her. Hamilton comes to her rescue and the lovers are quickly married, thereby preventing the duke from making any further claims on Petrova.

A lonely and love-starved prince of a Balkan country dreams of romance and escape in Charles Giblyn's implausible romantic drama, *The Vagabond Prince* (1916). H. B. Warner, the prince, befriends an itinerant artist from San Francisco and decides to go there for a visit and to search for true romance. Traveling as a common sailor, he reaches his goal and enters a cabaret with his fellow seamen. When Dorothy Dalton, a singer, is accosted by some roughnecks, Warner intercedes and a brawl ensues. Warner is arrested for disorderly conduct, and Dalton helps to bail him out with money from his artist friend. The couple are invited to celebrate with the artist's bohemian friends without revealing to the singer the prince's true identity. Hours later, the group decides that the couple should be married, but before the ceremony begins, agents from the prince's homeland arrive. They inform him that he is now the king of his native land and he must return – he must choose between his country and Dalton, who begins to leave, thinking he was just an ordinary sailor. But the revelers kidnap her and hold her for Warner, who chooses love over patriotic duty.

Fred E. Wright's romantic drama, *The Prince of Graustark* (1916), is emblematic of the fairy-tale quality of several of these entries. Bryant Washburn, as the title character, sails to America in search of a loan and, privately, a bride. He meets Marguerite Clayton, a young woman he believes is the daughter of the millionaire who is providing the loan. They meet again aboard the vessel sailing for Europe as he journeys home. His advisers tell him he must marry a certain princess when he returns, although his heart is not in the prearranged love match. Finally, it turns out the young traveling companion happens to be the very princess he is to marry – much to his delight. The film was meant as a sequel to *Graustark,* a novel by George Barr McCutcheon.

Jack Pickford, the son of an American millionaire, decides to visit a foreign country for adventure and romance, and he finds both, in Lou Tellegen's romantic comedy drama, *What Money Can't Buy* (1917), based on the play by George Broadhurst. Pickford meets Louise Huff, a princess, and the two fall in love. Meanwhile, his father is negotiating for the rights to build a railroad through the mythical kingdom. Following several complications, including Pickford's incarceration in prison on false charges and his father's arranging the kidnapping of the princess and her small brother, all the conflicts are resolved. In addition, it seems Pickford's grandfather, a citizen of the country, holds a royal title, thereby permitting the young man to marry the princess.

Jack Mulhall and a fellow cowboy, who have recently struck pay dirt in their mine, travel to Europe and become entangled in a mythical kingdom's conflict with one of its neighbors, in Raymond Wells's action drama, *Fighting for Love* (1917). Ruth Stonehouse provides the romantic interest for Mulhall. This became an occasional plot device for several silent westerns throughout the following decade, including one starring Tom Mix.

An unexceptional tale of intrigue and spying during a fictitious Balkan war, Frank Reicher's drama, *Sacrifice* (1917), casts former stage actress Margaret Illington in a dual role. She portrays both Vesta, the illegitimate daughter of a warlord, and her half-sister Mary, the legitimate daughter. Vesta is a spy who steals strategic military plans from a neighboring country. At the border she persuades her sister, Mary, to exchange passports. Mary is then arrested as a spy and sentenced to face a firing squad. Vesta delivers the vital information to the proper sources and returns to take her place before the firing squad. Mary is reunited with her beau, Jack Holt, a captain in her country's army.

To prevent war between two neighboring European states, the leaders of both plan a marriage between J. Frank Glendon, the Iron Duke of one, and Gladys Leslie, the princess of the other, in William P. S. Earle's familiar romantic drama, *The Wooing of Princess Pat* (1918). When she first meets the duke accidentally, the princess is enamored of him, but when she later is introduced to him formally, she rejects him. However, to avoid a war, she consents to the marriage. At first, she reacts coldly toward her husband, and almost stumbles into an affair with William Dunn, an evil count. Finally, she begins to appreciate her husband's worthy qualities and displays her love toward him.

A World War I drama set in a mythical European kingdom, George Irving's *Daughter of Destiny* (1918) concerns the romantic affairs of an American ambassador's daughter. Olga Petrova, as the title character and daughter, believes her husband, a German spy posing as an artist, has been killed in battle. She accompanies her father to Belmark, where she falls in love with that nation's crown prince. The remainder of the complex plot deals with several themes: her giving up her lover so that he may marry a princess, America's entering the war against Germany, and a German agent trying to keep the kingdom from declaring war against his country. Released during the war, the film is blatantly anti-German. One agent, in an attempt to disrupt a patriotic rally, throws a bomb during a crowd scene when he thinks the leaders of Belmark are about to side with America against Germany. The drama even proposes that all the German leaders should be executed.

Ethel Clayton portrays the title character in William C. de Mille's contrived drama, *The Mystery Girl* (1919), based on the story, "Green Fancy," by George Barr McCutcheon. Clayton, an ambulance driver for the Allies during World War I, receives a message by carrier pigeon from her uncle, the reigning prince of a small kingdom. She returns the message, stating she has the crown jewels and state papers, and she will meet him in America. But a master crook intercepts the message and notifies a treacherous prince who covets the uncle's throne. A wounded American soldier accompanies her to Vermont, where the rendezvous is to take place. Following a string of complications, the uncle succeeds in holding on to his throne, despite threats resulting from his decision not to join Germany in the world conflict. The crook, meanwhile, disappears with the valuable jewels, and the young couple return to the front, where the traitorous prince is brought in, wounded in battle, after having enlisted to atone for his crimes.

Conspirators plot the overthrow of a small European country in Joseph Henabery's romantic comedy drama, *His Majesty, the American* (1919), starring Douglas Fairbanks in the title role. The acrobatic Fairbanks portrays a New York *bon vivant* who receives large sums from an unidentified source to journey to the mythical kingdom. He arrives in the nick of time to foil the band of plotters from usurping the rightful dynasty that includes Fairbanks as the heir to the throne. Marjorie Daw, as a local countess, provides the romance in this rather lavish production well suited to the energetic talents of the star.

II. Romance, Intrigue and Comedy in Exotic Lands

Comedies and dramas about mythical kingdoms remained popular throughout the twenties and even continued into the next decade – especially with the advent of sound, in such satires as *Duck Soup* (1934), with the Marx Brothers. But for the most part, romance (*A Dark Lantern*), adventure (*A Fool and His Money*), intrigue (*Sink or Swim*) and comedy (*The Thrill Hunter*) dominated these films of the twenties. Some of the entries even shifted from Europe to South America and Central America, as in *Hutch of the U.S.A.* and *Cowboy Cavalier*, while others adhered to the conventional settings, as did *Graustark*, which referred back to McCutcheon's 1901 novel for its inspiration. Surprisingly, several popular cowboy heroes of the period set an occasional plot in a mythical kingdom and, for the most part, got away with the transmogrification. Tom Mix starred in *The Rough Diamond* and Ken Maynard made *The Royal Rider*. But the shifting away from Europe and the blending of western themes could not destroy the resiliency of the fabric of the mythical kingdom. The intrinsic value and popularity of these films remain embedded in all of us, for who is there who doesn't enjoy a good fairy tale?

Robert Warwick portrays the hero in James Cruze's bland romantic drama, *An Adventure in Hearts* (1920), based on the 1900 novel, *Captain Dieppe*, by Anthony Hope, and the 1903 play by Hope and Harrison Garfield Rhodes. When Warwick, an American agent, refuses to reveal confidential information until they pay him, secret service agents pursue him in Northern Italy. Meanwhile, a countess persuades her cousin to impersonate her as she goes to Rome to raise money for her gambling debt. Warwick falls in love with the cousin, Helene Chadwick, another countess, thinking she is the real countess. He fights for her and steals the evidence of her debts and arranges for a reconciliation between her and her husband, although that means giving up his love for her. Finally, he discovers the truth, and the real couple are reunited, as are the young lovers.

James L. Crane, a doctor who believes that most women are hypochondriacs and not to be trusted, finds himself falling in love with Alice Brady, in John S. Robertson's slow-paced romantic drama, *A Dark Lantern* (1920). Because of his attitude, he shuns Brady when he first meets her. Meanwhile, she is being romanced by Reginald Denny, a prince of a mythical kingdom somewhere near Tyrol. Although engaged to marry a princess for state reasons, he tries to persuade Brady to have an affair with him while he seeks to break the promised marital alliance. He vows that he would be willing to renounce his title so that he could marry Brady. The doctor, however, has other plans for her. He decides to put her through a severe test to see whether she could meet his standards for a lifetime mate. To his delight, she passes the test splendidly. Brady discovers that she loves the doctor and decides to break off her relationship with the prince.

Court intrigue in a mythical country ensnares a young American in Richard Stanton's satirical comedy adventure, *Sink or Swim* (1920). George Walsh portrays the young hero whose carefree life in the States compels his wealthy father to send him to Lithoonia on family business. Meanwhile, that country is about to erupt in a revolution instigated by the traitorous prime minister. Walsh intercedes in behalf of Enid Markey, the beautiful princess, who is about to lose her throne. He succeeds almost single-handedly in defeating the chief villain and his henchmen and preserving the title for the heroine.

Tom Mix stars in Edward Sedgwick's *The Rough Diamond* (1921), a satirical film about mythical kingdoms, revolutions and gallant heroes. The leader of a Latin-American country, threatened by an insurrection, hires Mix, a rodeo cowboy. Attracted to the President's pretty daughter and anxious to show his mettle, Mix accepts the challenge and leads the army to victory, thereby saving the throne for the girl's father. This was a digression for the famous cowboy star, who usually played his roles straight. The threat of a Latin-American insurrection was a current topic in the newspapers of the period. Several countries could have served as inspiration for the plot. A revolution threatened Nicaragua in 1912. The U.S. Navy in 1914 intervened in the Dominican Republic's revolution by establishing a neutral zone. Panama (1918-1920), Honduras (1919) and Guatemala (1920) also were torn by threats of revolution.

Victor Fleming's farce, *Red Hot Romance* (1922), involves an unusual will and the mythical principality of Bunkonia. The story concerns young Basil Sydney, who will inherit his father's fortune only after he has proved himself by working as an insurance salesman for one year. His sweetheart, Mae Collins, is taken by her father to Bunkonia, where he has been appointed the American ambassador. Sydney decides to sell insurance in that country so that he can be near Collins. He arrives in the midst of a revolution that he helps to crush with the aid of a battalion of U. S. Marines. For a simple comedy employing broad burlesque, the film offers several unusual scenes. The troops are made up of black soldiers for no apparent reason. This was rather controversial for the period, especially since the soldiers use their rifles to control the unruly white crowds. In a courtroom scene a black bailiff addresses the spectators as "miscolored white trash."

Young Jackie Coogan, as the crown prince of a mythical kingdom, yearns to be like other boys, so he runs away with an American friend, in Victor Schertzinger's juvenile adventure, *Long Live the King* (1923), based on the 1917 novel by Mary Roberts Rinehart. When the king suddenly dies and the young prince does not show up, the masses begin to revolt. Finally, the prince hears the death knoll for his father and rushes back to the palace. But he is intercepted by the revolutionaries, who hold him captive, until he is rescued by an American lieutenant, Allan Forrest, whom the boy had earlier befriended. The prince arrives at the palace and restores order to his land.

American correspondent Edward Burns finds himself steeped in foreign intrigue in Robert Z. Leonard's minor drama, *Jazzmania* (1923). He persuades Mae Murray, the queen of mythical Jazzmania, to abdicate and flee her country that is in the midst of a revolution. The trouble arises after the queen rejects Prince Otto, who has been chosen for her husband. In return, Otto incites the revolution. Once in Monte Carlo, Murray meets Rod LaRocque, another American. She returns to her restive native land to quash the turmoil and establish a republic. With calm restored to the country, she is ready to marry LaRocque.

The problem of citizens of a democracy helping to protect the throne of kings, no matter how benevolent, never seemed to disturb those who turned out the numerous silent westerns. Cowboys in Francis Ford's action drama, *The Cowboy Prince* (1924), set both in the West and in the mythical South American country of San Gordio, help to restore a nobleman to his rightful throne in this minor drama.

Charles Hutchison, as the stereotypical American hero, becomes entangled in a South American revolution in James Chapin's minor action drama, *Hutch of the U.S.A.* (1924). Hutch, a journalist, is sent to investigate events in mythical Guadala, where he falls in love with the ward of General Moreno. The general is planning to overthrow the president and make himself dictator. Hutch decides to join the revolution, which ultimately fails. But Hutch gets the girl. Several battles occur, with plenty of fighting on Hutch's part as he straightens matters out almost single-handedly. There is some comic relief from character player Ernest Adams. The continuous instability of countries south of the border gave impetus to a series of adventure dramas and satires during the 1910s and 1920s concerning revolution and general unrest, but only a handful involved reporters.

An American falls in love with the princess of a mythical European country in Dimitri Buchowetski's familiar romantic drama, *Graustark* (1925), based on the 1901 novel by George Barr McCutcheon. When Eugene O'Brien sees Norma Talmadge, a princess, sitting in a dining car in an opposite train, the American immediately switches trains. During the transcontinental trip, they become acquainted, although he is not aware of her regal status. However, he knows that in his heart he loves her. And she holds the same feelings toward him. Suddenly, she is called home to fulfill a marital agreement as a matter of state. O'Brien, still unaware of her title, tracks her down to her country, where he gets the American ambassador to help him in his search. Finally, at a ball he is startled to see her in her royal robes as she descends a grand staircase with her father, the king. Together, the young lovers outmaneuver the villainous prospective bridegroom. The high production values and competent directing add to the overall entertainment values of the film.

An American writer buys a castle in Europe and becomes embroiled in a domestic dispute in Erle Kenton's fast-paced romantic adventure, *A Fool and His Money* (1925), based on the novel by George Barr McCutcheon. William Haines is the fortunate heir who buys the old castle and soon discovers a young woman, Madge Bellamy, hiding in a secret room from her wicked husband. Following a series of complications, Haines plans her escape by airplane, but he remains behind to ward off their pursuers in a bold sword fight in which he is slightly wounded. Bellamy gets away to the States, while her American hero loses his property and returns home broke. "A fool and his money," he begins to mumbled to himself. Fortunately, his servant, who had been trapped in the basement during the escapade, discovered a treasure chest containing a fortune in jewels. The man returns with the chest, and Haines is back on his feet and reunited with Bellamy in a tale that stretches credibility.

Western conventions are transported to a mythical Central American country in Albert Rogell's comedy drama, *Cyclone Cavalier* (1925), with Reed Howes as an American who helps – cowboy style – to crush a revolution. Howes portrays an adventurous dynamo of energy sent to Costa Blanca on his father's business. Overhearing plans by the secretary of President Gonzales to overthrow the government, he warns the president of the plot. He then helps to defend the palace against the attackers until troops arrive. Carmelita Geraghty provides the romantic interest for Howes. Several silent films released during this period placed cowboys in mythical or foreign countries, including, among others, *The Cowboy Prince* (1924), *The Yankee Señor* (1926) and *The Royal Rider* (1929).

An agent of the U.S. Secret Service becomes involved in the intrigues of a fictitious Central American republic in Jack Nelson's inept drama, *Modern Youth* (1926). Geno Corrado, as an ex-French army captain who has seen action in World War I, yearns to travel, relax and put the violence behind him. However, he soon discovers that the leisurely life is not for him. He volunteers to work for the U.S. as a special agent. Assigned to the mythical republic of Centralia, he soon uncovers a plot to overthrow the current president. Corrado also effects the rescue of the heroine who is being held captive by the plotters.

Emigrant Pola Negri arrives in America and works as servant in a theatrical boarding house, where she begins to imitate the various poses of the boarders, in Dimitri Buchowetski's farfetched romantic drama, *The Crown of Lies* (1926), based on a story by Ernest Vajda. Another boarder, car salesman Robert Ames, befriends her. Suddenly, a servant approaches her and says that she looks exactly like the missing queen of a mythical kingdom, and he takes her to his master, Noah Beery, a count, who persuades her to impersonate the queen, to help restore order, and to force the present ruler to restore the fortunes of other nobles. When she arrives in the kingdom, accompanied by Ames, she begins to act regally, thanks to her earlier emulations.of the actors. The people soon accept her as their queen and demand the resignation of the present ruler. When Ames says he is leaving for the States, she begs him to take her with him, regardless of the titles, wealth and popularity she has achieved in her adopted land.

Writer William Haines is mistaken for the king of a mythical kingdom somewhere in Europe in Eugene De Rue's romantic comedy, *The Thrill Hunter* (1926). He is kidnapped and forced to marry Alma Bennett, a princess. He eludes his guards, and the leaders of the backward state blow themselves up. Haines then marries Kathryn McGuire, the daughter of his publisher, in this madcap adventure. Haines, a popular leading player in romantic comedies, starred in a similar film one year earlier, titled *A Fool and His Money*. Child actor Frankie Darro, who has a minor role, was to become a popular film personality during the next two decades.

The prince of a Balkan state falls in love with the niece of an innkeeper in Ernst Lubitsch's slow-paced romantic drama, *The Student Prince* (1927), based on the 1902 novel, *Karl Heinrich,* by Wilhelm Meyer-Forster, and the popular 1924 operetta by Dorothy Donnelly and Sigmund Romberg. Ramön Navarro, as the love-struck prince, and Norma Shearer, as the woman of his dreams, received expert direction and were surrounded by a lavish production in the bittersweet romance set in Old Heidelberg. In the end, Navarro, the heir to the throne, is forced to give up his love for Shearer because of his loyalty to his country. Instead, he marries the princess, according to his dead uncle's request. An earlier screen version of the novel, titled *Old Heidelberg*, was released in 1915, covering the same plot, with Wallace Reid and Dorothy Gish playing the leads.

Ronald Colman, a clown with a traveling circus, closely resembles the villainous prince of a small European country in Henry King's pleasant and sophomoric romantic drama, *The Magic Flame* (1927), based on the novel and play, *King Harlequin,* by Rudolph Lothar. Colman ends up killing his look-alike in his castle during a personal fight in which the former is attempting to rescue Vilma Banky, a trapeze performer. The clown then replaces the dead man and becomes king over the land that he then rules fairly and justly. He marries Banky, the woman he loves. Colman practically made a career of playing dual roles. His other dual roles during the sound era include *The Masquerader, The Prisoner of Zenda* and *A Double Life*.

Norma Talmadge portrays the title character, an alluring dancer desired by Noah Beery, the ruthless ruler of a fictitious Mediterranean country, in Roland West's passable romantic drama, *The Dove* (1928), based on the play by Willard Mack. However, "The Dove" rejects the ruler's advances, expressing instead her love for gambler Gilbert Roland. The jealous Beery, in retaliation, has Gilbert face a firing squad. But when the dancer mockingly challenges the ruler's virility, he responds boastfully by freeing Roland, thereby allowing the lovers to be reunited. Art director William Cameron Menzies was the first in his field to win an Oscar for his creative sets and exotic atmosphere.

Patriotism

I. "For the Honor of Old Glory"

Patriotism was a popular topic throughout the silent era. Producers discovered early that any scenes or shots of Old Glory, servicemen or military hardware such as American warships, whether in newsreels or feature films, were invariably greeted with loud applause from movie audiences. The height of patriotic fervor was reached both before and during World War I and the Second World War. In the years surrounding the former, the conflict saw the rise of two distinct film cycles. One advocated pacifism, with such antiwar films as *War O' Dreams* (1915) and Thomas Ince's epic, *Civilization* (1916). Following close on its heels, such dramas and cautionary tales as Stuart Blackton's *The Battle Cry of Peace* (1915) and Bartley Cushing's *The Fall of a Nation* (1916), called for preparedness and a buildup of arms and men. Of course, the latter won out as the war in Europe grew more intense and hinted at engulfing America. Films that attacked slackers, incited audiences against the brutal Huns, and praised those on the home front who kept the war materiel flowing, all served to feed the propaganda machine. Those who evaded the draft drew the wrath of public opinion, thanks to such films as *The Slacker* (1917) and *Draft 258* (1918). Perhaps the cycle reached its peak with *A Little Patriot* (1917), in which the child star, Baby Peggy, chides other children to spit on those suspected of being slackers. The excesses of patriotism spilled over to 1919, after the Armistice. For instance, during a Victory Loan rally in Washington, a uniformed sailor fired three shots into the back of a spectator who refused to stand up during the singing of the national anthem. The crowd applauded the serviceman.

J. Stuart Blackton's landmark film, *Tearing Down the Spanish Flag* (1898), a short re-creation of the fighting in Cuba during the Spanish-American War, is probably the first American war movie ever made. It is also considered by screen historians as America's first propaganda film. Blackton, a former Englishman with a background in journalism and cartooning, produced the patriotic work on the roof of the Morse Building located on Nassau Street in New York City. He plays a stalwart soldier who removes the Spanish colors and hoists the American flag. That is virtually all there is to the film, which lasts but a few short minutes. However, it captured the attention of the public. Contemporary audiences, impressed with the work, believed it was actually made in Cuba during combat.

Young aviator Earle Williams, of an unnamed European nation, falls in love with Edith Storey, a young American who also attracts the attention of a nobleman, another flier, in Frederick A. Thomson's romantic drama, *Warfare in the Skies* (1914). When a revolution threatens the nation, both rivals enlist on the side of the Loyalists, but the nobleman switches allegiances to the rebels and proceeds to drop bombs from his airplane. The young patriot takes his plane aloft and crashes into the traitor's airship. The wounded hero is captured by the revolutionary forces and hospitalized. When his girlfriend, Storey, is captured as a spy and is faced with a firing squad, our young hero once again takes to the air and rescues her. This was one of the earliest films about air warfare to be released during World War I although the story did not deal with that conflict.

A Mexican spy manipulates his way into the good graces of an American colonel in the unrealistic Mexican War drama, *For the Honor of Old Glory* (1914). The spy becomes a second lieutenant in the colonel's cavalry regiment. The remainder of the film relates how the spy leads the colonel, his family and the regiment into a trap in Mexico. The colonel's pretty daughter is kidnapped, while battles break out between the American troops and Mexican soldiers. The original title was the more lengthy *For the Honor of Old Glory or Carrying the Stars and Stripes into Mexico*.

When local villager James Cruze in an unnamed European country marries Marguerite Snow, a rival suitor harbors feelings of jealousy and revenge, in the World War I drama, *The Patriot and the Spy* (1915). At first, the remote village seems out of danger of the war, but the conflict soon spreads. Cruze, hurt by a speeding car while rescuing one of his children, is unable to serve in the army. Later, his former rival, Alphonse Ethier, now a spy and traitor, tricks the hero into blowing up a bridge. The husband, desperately seeking a way to serve his country, is captured by the invading troops but escapes in time to find his wife, who is being threatened by the spy. A fight ensues with predictable results. The war, like the country, goes unnamed in this drama, but the setting, characters' names, battle sequences and weaponry seen on the screen, strongly suggest World War I.

Set during World War I, George Fitzmaurice's drama, *Via Wireless* (1915), concerns a U.S. Navy lieutenant and an architect, rivals in the invention of a big gun that the War Department is interested in for coastal defense. The architect sabotages the officer's gun so that it fires with disastrous results. Following several melodramatic incidents, the villain is exposed. The film was not without its propaganda value at a time when the American public was in the midst of a heated debate between advocates of pacifism and those who cried out for preparedness. President Wilson appears briefly in an early portion of the film as an advocate of appropriate coastal defenses.

A veteran of the Spanish-American War prospects for gold on his New Mexico homestead in William S. Hart's drama, *The Patriot* (1916). An unscrupulous land agent, realizing the value of the land, forces the veteran (Hart) to move. Hart pleads his case in Washington but fails to regain his land. Upon his return, he finds his motherless son has died. Bitter at the turn of events, he joins Mexican guerrillas who raid American towns. On one of these incursions he comes across a child the same age as his dead son and comprehends the errors of his actions. Several exciting battle scenes follow. As the film concludes, Hart walks off with his newly adopted son to begin life anew. The background of the Mexican raids was no doubt inspired by the activities of Pancho Villa during the Mexican Revolution. When the U.S. intervened on the side of President Carranza, whom Villa opposed, the revolutionary responded by raiding American border towns and killing several U.S. citizens. This resulted in a punitive expedition by General "Black Jack" Pershing in 1916 against Villa.

During World War I, both the government and private studios supplied a series of films showing how those at home could serve the war effort. The subject matter gave actresses an opportunity to play the leading characters. Mary Miles Minter, a popular screen personality of the period, portrays a patriotic young woman in *Her Country's Call* (1917). She sets out to prove that women can replace men in war plants and shipyards, thereby releasing the workers for military service.

In James Young's World War I drama about the home front, *Her Country First* (1918), Vivian Martin, anxious to do her share for the war effort, organizes a girls' aviation auxiliary. When German agents break into her home, she and her troop help to capture the spies. The film, adapted from a novel by popular writer Mary Roberts Rinehart, not only exemplifies the patriotic spirit of the period. It was one of many features released during the conflict to draw the female population into the war effort by paying tribute to the role of women on the home front.

Walter Miller portrays the title character in Christy Cabanne's strongly patriotic drama, *The Slacker* (1917), one of the earliest films to use the term "slacker." Miller's sweetheart (Emily Stevens) persuades the idler to do his share, and before long he is off to France along with thousands of others. Historical images are conjured up, showing scenes of America's glorious past and its famous heroes. These include Paul Revere's famous ride, Nathan Hale's death and General Lee's surrender at Appomattox. The term "slacker," as applied to healthy young men who shirked their duty to their country when the "call to arms" went out, was very common during World War I. One of the initial goals of the government's newly formed Committee on Public Information, with its voice of propaganda in the film industry, was to instigate the public to come down hard on those who evaded the draft. Patriotic fervor was at its peak when the film was released, and *The Slacker* certainly contributed its share.

Hobart Henley's minor World War I drama, *Mrs. Slacker* (1918), concerns a cowardly young man who rushes into marriage with his fiancée, a local laundress, to keep out of the draft when war erupts. When the wife (Gladys Hulette) learns of her husband's real reason for the hasty marriage, she insists that she will not be known as "Mrs. Slacker." She is determined to set an example for her spineless husband (Creighton Hale). An opportunity presents itself when German agents plot to destroy a nearby reservoir. "Mrs. Slacker" foils their plans, and in the process, embarrasses her husband, who finally enlists in the army.

The slacker played a major role in Christy Cabanne's overly patriotic drama, *Draft 258* (1918). Mabel Taliaferro has two brothers. Walter Miller, the older, speaks out against the draft and has ties with a group of German spies. When he is called upon to address a meeting of pacifists and others, his sister intervenes and reminds the audience of the nation's glorious history and of those heroes who sacrificed their lives for their country. Later, a troop of cavalry arrests the conspirators who are plotting sabotage. The older brother is finally made to see his errors, and he marches off to war with his younger brother, to the approval of their sister.

Wallace Reid, as a fortune-hunting slacker in James Cruze's World War I drama, *Alias Mike Moran* (1919), is called to serve in the army. He exchanges places with an ex-convict, Mike Moran (Emory Johnson), who is eager to fight, but is rejected because of his past. When Moran dies a hero's death in France, Reid, now posing as Moran and working at a shipyard, has a change of attitude. He enlists in the Canadian army and is sent overseas where he, too, becomes a hero. Ann Little, who provides the romantic interest, finds him when he returns home and professes her love for the belated hero. Although released after the war, this patriotic tale reflected the national resentment toward slackers during the conflict. Reid took a chance with his career by agreeing to portray such an unsympathetic character for the first half of the film.

Marguerite Clark portrays a patriotic young woman determined to help her country by increasing food production in John S. Robertson's World War I comedy, *Little Miss Hoover* (1918). She persuades her grandfather, with whom she is living, to help her start up a chicken farm. Many of the farm workers are less than enthusiastic until Clark instills in them a spark of patriotism. Wounded veteran Eugene O'Brien is assigned by the government to visit farmers and encourage them to produce more. He establishes himself near the Clark poultry farm. Appearing out of uniform, he is mistaken for a slacker and is almost lynched by the community. Released only weeks after the armistice, the film may have lost some of its immediacy in terms of its original purpose. However, war-ravaged Europe found itself with a critical food shortage when hostilities ceased. The film, therefore, may well have served as a stimulus for American farmers to produce more.

The war provided the film studios with material for comedy as well as propaganda, sometimes successfully blending the two. Charlie Chaplin's one-reel propaganda short, *The Bond* (1918), based on a political cartoon and released during World War I, stars Chaplin as a patriotic citizen who turns over a bag of money to Uncle Sam. The money passes to Industry who in turn hands a soldier a rifle. Charlie proceeds to pummel the Kaiser with an oversized mallet. He then places one foot on the flattened Kaiser and addresses the audience to buy Liberty Bonds. Chaplin was criticized by some during the war for not enlisting in the armed forces. Those at home thought that Chaplin, a native and citizen of Britain, should have set an example for his fellow Englishmen by joining up. However, he made a short propaganda film for Britain and toured the U.S. for several months with other famous screen stars selling Liberty Bonds. His supporters felt that he did more for Allied propaganda by making comedies that cheered up both those at the front and those at home.

John Emerson's World War I comedy, *Come On In* (1918), starring Ernest Truex, tells about a patriotic young man's abortive attempts to enlist in the army. It seems that he is a half-inch too short. Strolling in a park, he becomes involved in a fight with a German who smashes a bottle on his head. Ernest feels his head and dashes to the nearest draft board. He passes the height requirement because of the bump on his head. Once in the service he continually moves up in rank due to a series of humorous misadventures in which he is able to display his peculiar style of bravery. The concept that military service can change a man for the better was a prevalent one in early silent films, especially those made during World War I, when patriotism and propaganda were major forces on the screen. The theme spilled over into the 1920s and showed up in comedies, dramas and westerns in which some of the most popular male stars portrayed cowards, weaklings or slackers – until they donned their nation's uniforms.

Hobart Henley's patriotic World War I comedy, *Too Fat to Fight* (1918), based on a story by Rex Beach, concerns a patriotic young American who is rejected by his draft board because of his obesity. Frank McIntyre portrays the principal character who is desperate to do his share but cannot get into uniform until he pulls some political strings. "I'm too fat too fight and too immoral for the Y.M.C.A.," he muses, "but I'd give a leg to be with the boys over there." He is finally sent overseas, where he distinguishes himself in battle although he is wounded. Florence Dixon portrays his sweetheart. The film was released immediately after the armistice, so the propaganda sequences, as well as scenes of American troops landing in Europe, seemed unimportant to the story or the audience. Americans quickly grew tired of this type of film that promoted enlistment and falsified the ease with which one could achieve medals in the trenches.

A group of twelve-year-old boys, hungry for excitement and adventure, uncover a plot by German spies to stir up dissent among miners in William Taylor's drama, *The Spirit of '17* (1918), set during World War I. The goal of the enemy agents is to have the mine put out of commission, thereby crippling American war production. Young Jack Pickford (Mary's brother) plays the leader of the youngsters. He calls upon the residents of a veterans' home to help him capture the alien agents. Based on a story by Judge Willis Brown of the Chicago Juvenile Court, the film proudly proclaimed itself as a "red, white and blue story . . . vibrant with patriotism."

Wesley Ruggles's World War I drama, *For France* (1917), concerns the fighting at the front. A lone American displays his heroism as he advances to a machine gun in the heat of battle and holds numerous German soldiers at bay. There are several battle scenes and much sniper fire and killing until the last scene that shows the French and American flags flying side by side. The film is not without its share of propaganda. As with similar war movies of the period, it portrays the Huns as brutal and bestial, who specialize in taking advantage of defenseless women. One young Frenchwoman is rescued at the last moment from a lascivious German by a brave American. But a peasant mother does not fare so well. A Prussian officer and his aide attack her. However, an American pilot eventually avenges her death. The German aide is played by Erich von Stroheim, who specialized in this type of role during and after the war.

Released only a few weeks after the Armistice, Frank Crane's World War I drama, *Wanted for Murder* (1918), was already dated in its anti-German propaganda and its patriotic fervor. The film emphasizes the alleged atrocities committed by the Germans upon civilian populations. The French heroine (Elaine Hammerstein), in love with an American soldier, barely escapes the clutches of an enemy soldier before she is brought to America by her doughboy hero. Another scene shows the Kaiser questioning Hindenberg as to why the German armies have not taken Paris. "We did not know America had a Pershing," he explains. There are several well-staged battle sequences. The film continued the trend – begun even before America entered the war – of placing the entire blame for the conflict on Kaiser Wilhelm and portraying him as a bestial creature and war criminal. In a dream sequence the hero envisions himself inundating Berlin with posters of the Kaiser, charging him with murder. Hollywood during the postwar period allowed Wilhelm, who had abdicated, to slip into obscurity.

Clara Kimball Young portrays a young French patriot who saves her village and its people in Edmund Mortimer's World War I drama, *The Road Through the Dark* (1918). To protect her village from being destroyed and her neighbors from being slaughtered by the advancing German army, she elects to become the mistress of a German aristocrat. Meanwhile, for the remainder of the war, she acts as a spy for the Allies as she gathers information about enemy troops and strategy. Some critics, disturbed by the heroine's loss of innocence, questioned the moral tone of the film.

Earl Schenck portrays the Kaiser's illegitimate son who was raised in the U.S. in John Joseph Harvey's World War I drama, *The Kaiser's Finish* (1918). Schenck, who can easily be mistaken for the Kaiser, turns agent and journeys to

Germany to assassinate the Crown Prince and his son. The film cleverly blends its scenes with actual newsreel inserts of the Kaiser inspecting the front lines. At times, it is difficult to discern which portions are fictitious and which are real. The film added fuel to America's hatred of the Kaiser, a feeling brought about four years earlier by Germany's show of militancy as reflected by a series of international confrontations. One particular scene suggests that he be lynched in Times Square. This was one of Warner Brothers' first entries into the burgeoning film industry and helped launch the studio into its eventual success.

A large-scale production based on the sinking of the Lusitania and its aftermath, Leonce Perret's unabashed propaganda drama, *Lest We Forget* (1918), cries out for revenge. The film stars Rita Jolivet, one of the actual survivors. Scenes include the salon of the vessel, with the passengers dressed in evening clothes; the inside of a submarine with a view of a torpedo speeding toward the ill-fated ship; people rushing to the decks, others jumping overboard, and children swimming helplessly. The film later shows scenes in the trenches, where an American joins a Canadian unit fighting against the Germans so that he can avenge the one he loves. Released during World War I, the production contains an abundance of patriotic elements, including much flag-waving. A doughboy, for instance, salutes the flag while in the trenches as another fatally wounded soldier embraces Old Glory in his arms. Concluding with a cry for revenge, it evokes images of the Statue of Liberty and the spirit of Edith Cavell, the English nurse who was executed by the Germans. The propaganda element was so persuasive that during one of Rita Jolivet's appearances in Connecticut, she was able to raise more than $250,000 in sales of Liberty Bonds. After the armistice, the German consul in Geneva, Switzerland, objected so strongly to the film being shown there that several scenes had to be cut from the production.

Wallace Worsley's World War I drama, *An Alien Enemy* (1918), concerns a young woman of German heritage who marries an important American involved in military matters. A German agent threatens the couple unless they turn over to him secret documents. The film contains patriotic scenes of American troops liberating French villages and sequences of a prisoner-of-war camp where Germans try to escape. Louise Glaum, the star of the film, plays a dual role, that of a mother and her daughter.

Director Francis Ford, brother of John Ford, portrays an American flier employed by the U.S. Secret Service in this routine World War spy drama, *Berlin via America* (1918). Posing as a traitor to his country, he gains the confidence of Prussian spies and is transported to Germany, where he joins Baron von Richthofen's Flying Circus. He soon emerges as one of their leading aces while secretly dropping messages to the Allies concerning imminent enemy advances. Eventually, he escapes to America where he exposes a German spy. The patriotic fervor of the period permitted a character who used stealth and deception for the Allied cause to be considered a hero. However, when a foe used similar tactics to aid his country's cause, he was branded as vile and treacherous. To emphasize the morality of the actions even more strongly, film studios used their most popular leading men in the former role, while utilizing their traditional "heavies" in the latter role.

A dramatic, large-scale spectacle, John W. Noble's drama, *The Birth of a Race* (1919), covers a variety of historical events to develop its multiple themes. Included are highlights from the arrival of Adam and Eve, the story of Noah, the latter part of Christ's life, the signing of the Declaration of Independence, Lincoln's Gettysburg Address and the beginning of World War I. The modern story concerns two sons of a German-American family, one who goes to Germany to fight for the Kaiser and the other who enlists in the American army. They later meet at a hospital where the American brother is recovering from his battle wounds. Meanwhile, the father has fired patriotic Americans from his munitions factory and replaced them with those loyal to Germany, a decision that causes a riot to break out. The film suggests that the power of love is stronger than that of hate; that all wars should be abolished; and that America, to survive, must be united in its struggles against those forces that would seek to destroy it. Released in the wake of World War I, the film also attempts to address some of the international causes that led to the conflict by showing the destructive forces of excessive nationalism.

A patriotic young woman "adopts" an American soldier fighting in France as a pen pal in Leonce Perret's World War I romantic drama, *The Unknown Love* (1919). Treating the correspondence lightly, the doughboy sends a photograph of a fellow soldier to her. When she learns that he has been wounded, she persuades an American naval officer who is in love with her to hide her aboard his vessel that is embarked for Europe. At sea the ship is attacked by a German submarine and the officer is mortally wounded. When she finally arrives at the hospital where the wounded soldier is recuperating, he confesses to her that he sent another's picture. But she explains she has grown fond of the inner person who wrote the letters, not the outward appearance. Some action sequences include actual newsreel shots that add realism to the fighting.

World War I serves as background for D. W. Griffith's romantic drama, *The Girl Who Stayed at Home* (1919), about two young brothers who, as doughboys, are shipped to France during the conflict. Clarine Seymour portrays the title character who is in love with one of the brothers (Robert Harron). Meanwhile, Richard Barthelmess, the other brother, falls in love with Carol Dempster, a French wife whose husband is away at the front. Dempster, who is harassed by the ruthless Germans and whose husband is killed in action, is rescued by Barthelmess. Each American ends up with the woman he loves. Released immediately after the war, the film, which contains some actual shots of airplanes in battle, failed to cash in on its subject matter. Its topics of patriotism and anti-German propaganda became dated too quickly, despite director D. W. Griffith's last-minute revisions that showed a German soldier killing a fellow German who is about to violate the pretty French wife. It joined the list of dozens of other similar features in the storage vaults. Also, the critics were disappointed in the plot, with one labeling the latest work by the master director as "muddled."

II. The Price of Glory After the Great War

During the silent era, patriotism was defined in terms of World War I, and the films of the period reinforced this delineation. The plots, out of necessity and conviction, focused on romanticism and idealism. The literature that emerged following the conflict concentrated on the condemnation of war as mindless cruelty and the disillusionment with uncontrolled militarism. Except for a handful of postwar films that excoriated war – *The Big Parade* (1925), *What Price Glory?* (1926) – the majority of war films of the twenties generally continued to support wartime idealism and war as an adventure. Sometimes the spirit of patriotism was disguised through different settings, such as South America in *Fortune's Mask* (1922) or early California in *A California Romance* (1923). Other films used comedy to promote patriotism, as in *Friendly Enemies* (1925) and Harry Langdon's *Heart Trouble* (1928). But the major literary themes to come out of the death, destruction and general horror of the Great War – endorsement of wartime idealism, disillusionment, antimilitarism and isolation – were all but forgotten by Hollywood. Instead, the commercially driven studios highlighted the adventurous and romantic elements of war films during the twenties, while generally avoiding those aspects that would unnerve their audiences. Meanwhile, the patriotic aspects, which the public often greeted with applause, were suggested by individual acts of heroism, large battle scenes that emphasized a sense of duty and glory, and popular screen personalities whose roles reflected honor, duty and heroism. America during the postwar decade grew tired of images that repeatedly fueled the patriotic impulse and supported recollections of victory. The country during the twenties began to turn its sights to the future and a world of prosperity and plenty, and wished to forget the past, with its "war to end all wars" and its self-sacrifice. The war film, with its symbols of patriotism, honor and duty, fell out of favor with both the critics and the public.

A strong antiwar drama and advocate of President Wilson's League of Nations, George A. Beranger's *Uncle Sam of Freedom Ridge* (1920) tells the story of a West Virginia mountain man and true patriot who sends his son to answer his nation's call to arms when World War I erupts. Convinced that his boy is fighting for Wilson's cause – to make the world safe for democracy – the father accepts the news of his son's death with a sense of comfort and resignation. Later, when he realizes the cause has been betrayed by those who are resisting the movement to abolish all wars through the League of Nations, the father sacrifices his own life. He wraps himself in his cherished flag that has always flown over his cabin and shoots himself in protest.

A tale of South American revolution and political intrigue, Robert Ensminger's drama, *Fortune's Mask* (1922), based on the story, "Cabbages and

Kings," by O. Henry, stars Earle Williams as the son of a murdered president. Williams had been sent to the U.S. for his schooling and is now ready to right the wrongs against the corrupt regime in his native country and avenge his father. He rekindles the flame of patriotism in enough of his fellow countrymen to overthrow the present regime. Enough political unrest was going on south of the border at the time to make the story timely. Several Latin-American countries were plagued with possible insurrections, including, among others, Panama (1918-1920), Honduras (1919), and Guatemala (1920). American audiences may also have been attracted to this type of film since American troops were often involved in these conflicts. The U.S., for example, intervened in all three of these countries either to protect Americans or its legation, to maintain order or to secure a neutral zone during an anticipated revolution.

A satirical comedy about the early days of California, Jerome Storm's romantic tale, *A California Romance* (1923), stars John Gilbert as a Spaniard who is rejected by his girlfriend, Estelle Taylor, also of Spanish heritage. It seems he is reluctant to take up arms against the Americans who are invading the Spanish territory. George Siegmann, a smooth-talking stranger, arrives and persuades the natives to join him in the battle against the Americans. Meanwhile, he is planning after the battle to scoop up the land grants for himself, kill the rich owners and capture their women. The U.S. Cavalry rides to the rescue and saves the people from this self-appointed leader and his band of outlaws.

Social worker Cornelius Keefe and Leslie Stowe, an elderly American Civil War colonel, help to straighten out Charles Brook and his son in the drama, *The Fifth Horseman* (1924). The colonel helps to teach the son about the meaning of patriotism, while emphasizing the home, God and country. Keefe, meanwhile, disentangles Brook from a gang of bootleggers and his involvement in crooked city politics. Keefe also helps Brook's daughter to find a cure for her lameness, an affliction that has been with her since her birth.

George Melford's comedy drama, *Friendly Enemies* (1925), set during World War I, was the first full-length feature that the famous vaudeville and stage comedians, Weber and Fields, appeared in. They both portray German-Americans. Fields, a loyal patriot of his adopted country, is proud of his son who is in the army and about to be shipped to France to fight against Germany. His friend, Weber, however, remains loyal to the Fatherland and donates money to a German organization he hopes will bring an early end to the war. He later learns that his money was used to sink a troopship of American soldiers. Fortunately, Fields's son was not aboard at the time. Aside from its humor and love interest, the film, released years after the war, emphasizes the duties and responsibilities of foreign-born Americans and their offspring toward their new homeland. This was a real-life dilemma for many German-American citizens when the original play by Samuel Shipman and Aaron Hoffman first appeared in 1918 during World War I. A 1942 remake updated the original story to World War II. Charles Winninger and Charles Ruggles portrayed the bickering German-American tycoons who differ in their loyalties to the U.S. and Germany. Winninger, who is sympathetic to Germany, is deceived into contributing to enemy saboteurs and learns too late that he has helped sink an American troop ship that was transporting his own son.

One of the major war films of the 1920s, King Vidor's *The Big Parade* (1925) brought back the genre to movie houses across the country. Prior to its release, Hollywood producers were hesitant about turning out films whose subject matter was devoted so thoroughly to gritty details of World War I. They believed the public was tired of all the war movies released at the time of the conflict and did not want to be reminded of the struggle. But this film and another film stripped of the usual patriotic images, *What Price Glory?*, released the following year, proved them wrong. *The Big Parade* tells the story of three young men who meet as recruits and stay together through most of the war. John Gilbert, as the son of a wealthy mill owner, enlists not out of any particular ideological commitment, but because he is caught up with the spirit of war. Karl Dane, as a former ironworker, contributes much of the comic relief, including the uncanny ability to put out a candle flame with a well-directed mouthful of tobacco juice. Tom O'Brien, as a bartender in civilian life, makes up the third member of the trio. Once in France, Gilbert falls in love with a French peasant, played by Renée Adorée, but they are soon separated in a touching scene when Gilbert and his unit are ordered to the front lines. In the harrowing battles that follow, Gilbert's two close buddies are killed. He returns home after the armistice – minus one leg, but he is alive. Growing restless and impatient with those around him who do not understand him or what he has been through, he returns to France and the girl with whom he had fallen in love. Vidor, the director, utilizes the images of men moving in unison, whether it was the "big parade" of the Yanks filled with fighting spirit at the beginning of the film as they embarked for France, the soldiers marching to the front, or the men moving silently and cautiously through the enemy-infested Argonne forest during battle. The numerous battle scenes are realistic, especially the American advance through the woods, the hand-to-hand combat and the deadly accuracy of the machine guns. The film was a commercial and artistic success although the British were critical. They objected to its depicting the Americans as the predominant force in winning the war.

Richard Barthelmess portrays a slacker and professed coward who undergoes a redemption in Alfred Santell's sometimes tasteless World War I drama, *The Patent Leather Kid* (1927). Meeting with some success as a prizefighter but disliked by the public because of his egotism, he finally loses a major bout by means of a setup. Barthelmess is drafted into the army, where he boasts of his cowardice through much of his military service. Molly O'Day, his girlfriend, volunteers as a nurse and follows him to France, eventually effecting a change in him. He performs a series of heroic acts that result in the paralysis of his hands and feet. While hospitalized, he struggles to rise up in an effort to salute the American flag as troops march by and the band plays "The Star-Spangled Banner." He accomplishes this feat after much effort. Although a silent film, the accompanying music in this scene was scored so the National Anthem was displayed at that moment. Some critics found the film excessively patriotic and in bad taste. One reviewer singled out the ludicrous scene in which the hero undergoes an operation without an anesthetic, while his girlfriend-nurse assists the surgeon. Critic Pare Lorentz described this scene as "the most sickening exhibition of bad taste I have ever witnessed."

Harry Langdon, one of the four major screen comedians during the silent period (along with Chaplin, Buster Keaton and Harold Lloyd), had problems with his screen career near the end of the twenties, and his last silent feature, *Heart Trouble* (1928), which he directed, has become a lost film. The sad, moon-faced comic, during World War I, portrays a German-American who tries desperately to enlist in the U.S. army. His main reason is to prove his patriotism to his girlfriend, Doris Dawson. He fails to get into uniform, on several grounds – he is several inches too short, underweight, flatfooted and nearsighted. He also has a bad case of dandruff. But fate provides the opportunity for Langdon to prove that he is a true American. He accidentally stumbles across a hidden base, where spies are supplying German submarines. Unknown to him, he has helped rescue an American officer and is the cause of the destruction of the base and the capture of the enemy agents. His town turns out to honor its local hero, but Langdon is too occupied with wooing Dawson to notice. There are fewer comic routines in this film compared with his others, but some are very clever.

An immigrant's faith in America never wavers as he undergoes one adversity after another in William K. Howard's World War I drama, *A Ship Comes In* (1928). Rudolph Schildkraut portrays the Hungarian immigrant who happily works as a janitor in a government building. An anarchist cousin tries to influence him, but he will have none of this chatter against the land that he has adopted. When his time comes to receive his citizenship papers, he is so overjoyed that he has his wife bake the judge a cake. However, his villainous cousin conceals a bomb in the cake. After it explodes and wounds the judge, Schildkraut is arrested and jailed. Meanwhile, the unfortunate victim loses his son in the war. He is soon released and returns to his janitorial duties. The use of European immigrants as main screen characters was carried over from the previous decade when such films as Charlie Chaplin's *The Immigrant* were popular, especially in the cities which housed large populations of foreigners.

A World War I comedy drama emphasizing the woman's role during the conflict, Henry King's part-sound and part-silent *She Goes to War* (1929) stars Eleanor Boardman as a spoiled socialite who journeys to France in search of excitement. She finds work in a service canteen. Meanwhile, her cowardly fiancé, Edmund Burns, another member of the idle rich, shirks his responsibilities as a soldier. When the time comes for his outfit to move up, he avoids going. Boardman, wishing to learn about the war first-hand, disguises herself and goes in his place.

Political Corruption

I. The Rogues of Politics

America witnessed a string of progressive reforms during the first two decades of the twentieth century, including legislation to improve safety in the mines and on the railroads, establishment of a Children's Bureau, provision for employer liability in work done under government contracts, increased power over railroads, and legalization of income taxes. However, much legislation under President Wilson's first term was more symbolic than practical. Minorities, most organized labor, and the urban poor were continually exempted from government assistance. Many early silent films during this period, especially those that focused on politics and political corruption, often touched upon some of these shortcomings. However, rarely would a film attack an actual company or famous politician, except in rare instances, such as *The Governor's Boss* (1915), about real-life impeached ex-Governor Sulzer of New York State, or films that closely resembled the actual Triangle Shirtwaist Fire tragedy. Although not as explosive in their exposés as the muckrakers of the press, many early social dramas played a fairly competent role in exposing various social and political ills – child labor abuse in *The White Terror* (1915), corrupt lobbyists in *The Man From Oregon* (1915), voting fraud in *The Human Orchid* (1916) and police corruption in *A Son of Erin* (1916). In addition, several features reminded the public about the close ties between politics and the underworld.

Political films emerged from the studios quite early during the silent period. The short drama, *Exposure of the Land Swindlers* (1913), about political fraud, featured William J. Burns, who headed the National Detective Agency. Burns was considered by some to be "the greatest sleuth of all time."

"Big Boss" politician George Siegmann offers to award an aqueduct contract to financially desperate A. Balfour – only if the man's daughter, Muriel Ostriche, agrees to marry Siegmann – in Frederick Sullivan's drama, *The Big*

Boss (1913), about political graft and corruption. Ostriche, however, is promised to reporter Irving Cummings, who has been assigned to expose the prevalence of corruption that has gripped the city. The young couple use a Dictaphone to gain evidence of Siegmann's duplicity. But the crooked politician discovers the device and pummels the reporter. Balfour comes to Cummings's rescue and persuades Siegmann to reform and allow the contract to go to the lowest bidder.

Impeached Democrat Governor William Sulzer of New York portrays himself in the semi-documentary drama, *The Governor's Boss* (1915), based on the 1914 novel by James S. Barcus. The film allegedly is an exposé of the story behind the former New York State governor's downfall. Rape, blackmail, ballot-box fraud, bribery of political officials and forgery all play a part in this political drama. Also part of the story which claims that the governor was framed is the introduction of relatively modern devices, such as the Dictaphone and the motion picture camera.

Pat O'Malley, a high-wire walker and law student, rescues reporter Gladys Hulette and a state senator in Ashley Miller's routine drama, *The King of the Wire* (1915). The reporter is assigned to interview the senator, who is fighting for a bill to prevent child labor abuses. Meanwhile, a corrupt political leader and a hired thug are intent on stopping him. The journalist maneuvers her way into the senator's home, where the politician and his hired man are holding the senator at bay with a pistol. She dashes into another room to call for help, while the two interlopers pursue her. O'Malley, interested in seeing Hulette again after meeting her in her home town, learns from her newspaper office about her predicament. He climbs up a telephone, scales the wires to her room and rescues her. He then returns to battle the thug on the wire. The man falls to his death, while the senator holds the politician for the police. He then hires O'Malley, who plans to marry the reporter.

George Boulle Spencer, with the help of Charles Brandt, his father-in-law who heads the local political machine, is elected District Attorney in Barry O'Neil's drama, *The District Attorney* (1915), based on the 1895 play by Charles Klein and Harrison Grey Fiske. Brandt, a wealthy contractor, is responsible for forging city treasury vouchers and bribes a city clerk to plead guilty to the crime. He promises the clerk an early release from prison and gives him 50,000 dollars. But Brandt cannot convince Spencer to cancel a grand jury investigation. Following several complications, Brandt has a nervous breakdown and confesses. The imprisoned clerk is released, and Brandt's own daughter refuses her father's request for mercy.

When Howard Hickman, as a recently elected senator from Oregon, proves too incorruptible, certain lobbyists hire Clara Williams to compromise him in Reginald Barker's drama, *The Man From Oregon* (1915). Instead, she falls in love with the senator and decides to protect him from the schemers who are seeking to ruin him. They plan to photograph him in the midst of attacking Williams, thereby forcing him to vote for their controversial land bill. The plot proceeds, but when the bill is debated, Hickman fights against it. Williams, now driven by her conscience, goes to the corrupt lobbyist's office to recover the damaging photo but is unsuccessful. When she leaves, the lobbyist changes the combination of the safe. She returns later that night to try to get the picture. Following some complications, she gets the plate, but the lobbyist returns and grabs it from her. She finds a gun and shoots the plate, thereby destroying the evidence. She then sends the pieces to Hickman, who in return invites her to have tea with him and his mother.

The corrupt political ring of a town makes the mistake of manipulating honest George Fawcett into the mayor's seat in Otis Turner's familiar drama, *The Frame-Up* (1915). The politicians are compelled to try several means to force the new mayor to sign a bill beneficial to their financial and political interests, but he refuses. Meanwhile, the chief political boss, who has a penchant for luring young women into illicit acts, is shot to death by the brother of one of his victims. When the mayor is charged with the murder, his wife takes the stand in his defense and proves his innocence. The real killer is then caught. However, he, too, is exonerated since he was only avenging his sister's ruination at the hands of the lecherous politician.

Wealthy Hobart Henley buys a newspaper and, in fine muckraking tradition, attacks quack medicine practitioners, uncaring factory owners and crooked politicians, in Stuart Paton's social drama, *The White Terror* (1915). He is in love with Frances Nelson, the daughter of a wealthy plant owner, but she shuns him until he can prove his sense of social responsibility. Meanwhile, her father employs child labor and ignores health regulations. He also controls a chemical company that produces harmful patent medicines. When his daughter becomes ill and his own medicine is discarded by her doctor, the father finally is made aware of his blundering beliefs, including the intolerable working conditions of his employees, and decides to improve them. Henley's romantic rival, the villainous William Welsh, a crooked politician and the plant owner's general manager, has continually deceived his employer about the deteriorating plant conditions. He is killed trying to blow up the newspaper office. Other social issues raised in the film include child labor abuses, inadequate housing for the poor and the "excesses of the idle rich."

Crooked politician Lionel Barrymore ruins a young Gypsy woman in Lawrence Marston's drama, *The Woman in Black* (1915), based on the 1897 play by H. Grattan Donnelly. The politician, while visiting the South, comes upon a Gypsy caravan and is attracted to the daughter of a Gypsy woman. He lures her into a nearby abandoned barn where he proceeds to rape her. She exits the barn crying, while another member of the group witnesses the scene. When the victim and her fiancé are married, the witness reveals all to the priest and the husband, and the marriage is annulled. Seeking revenge, the mother of the victim takes her daughter in search of the politician, who has blackmailed the daughter of a contractor into marrying him. At the wedding ceremony, the Gypsy mother substitutes her daughter, now heavily veiled, for the prospective bride. When the ceremony is completed and the bride lifts her veil, the shocked politician looks on with amazement. The Gypsy mother then thrusts a dagger into the politician's back.

Lust also dominates another corrupt politician in C. C. Field's drama, *The Human Orchid* (1916), that is plagued by too many coincidences. A saloon owner and politician desires Irva Ross, a young woman who, as an orphan, has been raised by a poor woman and her drunken husband. The husband wants to sell Ross to the politician. The orphan's mother had been loved by a certain doctor who has been searching for young Ross for several years. The young woman flees from the clutches of the saloon keeper and in her haste, takes refuge in a passing limousine. The owner, a rich politician, takes her to his home and clothes and educates the unfortunate Ross. She works as the man's secretary and witnesses a political arrangement in which the saloon owner will deliver the votes of a district to the wealthy politician for the sum of ten thousand dollars. The deal is set down in writing and paid by check. When the wealthy man tries to sexually abuse his ward, she again flees after striking him with a candlestick. In desperation, she confides in a young district attorney who is willing to make a dishonest deal with the others. Following a string of complications, she finally meets the doctor who has been searching for her and falls in love with him.

A governor assigns George Marlo, his secretary, to investigate complaints made by Mignon Anderson, a local health inspector, against a mayor, in W. Eugene Moore's flawed drama, *The Woman in Politics* (1916). When the health inspector discovered a case of smallpox at a certain address, she reported it to her supervisor who ordered her to withdraw her report. It seems the mayor owns that property. When she refuses, the mayor has her fired. She decides to write to the governor, stating all the facts. The governor's secretary arrives, investigates matters, and rescues Anderson from the clutches of the corrupt officials. At one point, the villains capture her and lock her up in a sanitarium, but Marlo eventually helps her to escape. The inspector later is brought into the courtroom to testify against the mayor at his trial, and he is stripped of his office by the governor. One wonders whether the governor has the power to remove an elected official from office.

A civic-minded married man who exposes a mayoral candidate is faced with a frame-up in Ralph Ince's uninteresting drama, *The Destroyers* (1916), based on the novel, *Peter God*, by James Oliver Curwood. After the exposé, the candidate plots revenge against the innocent young man. He sets up his mistress, Virginia Norden, to be found with the man in a compromising position. Later, the man follows Norden back to the politician's office and a struggle takes place for possession of a gun. In the fight, the mistress and her lover are shot. The framed man flees, unaware that the mortally wounded man has confessed all. Thinking he will be charged with a double murder, the man journeys to the Canadian woods, where Leslie Lee Stewart, his wife, finally finds him and tells him what had happened after the shooting.

Crooked politicians force the resignation of New York City night court judge Thomas Meighan, who is seeking to expose a local crime syndicate leader, in William C. de Mille's absorbing drama, *Common Ground* (1916). His early retirement is arranged by corrupt politician Theodore Roberts, who is one of those who wish to silence Meighan. He frames the judge on a phony charge. Meanwhile, the judge's fiancée, Mary Mersch, who is the daughter of the leader, ends their engagement. Instead, Meighan marries Marie Doro, a factory worker whom he befriends and falls in love with. The film resorts to the familiar device of having the hero in love with the daughter of the villain.

Gail Kane, as the wife of an inventor, accompanies him to Washington D.C., but both find it difficult to promote his invention without the proper influence, in Maurice Tourneur's drama, *The Velvet Paw* (1916). Kane obtains a letter of introduction to Ned Burton, a senator who heads a ring of crooked politicians. Burton promises to help her. When she returns home, she discovers her despondent husband has taken his life. The senator then befriends the widow and hires her to help him convince other politicians to vote in favor of the senator's bills. The chief legislation concerns strict child labor laws that would prevent the exploitation of the young. Following a string of conquests of some of her victims, she finds satisfaction in her new role – until she meets House Peters, a congressman with whom she falls in love. She finally realizes she is defending an unworthy cause and switches allegiance. She encourages Peters to fight for the legislation, which results in its passage. One of her ruined former lovers returns and shoots her, but the bullet only wounds her. The film ends with Kane and Peters embracing.

Dustin Farnum, a poor Irish lad who believes he can get a job as a New York policeman, leaves Ireland for America in the hopes of fulfilling his dream, in Julia Ivers's implausible drama, *A Son of Erin* (1916). Although it takes him longer than he had planned, he finally gets a job as a police officer, but is soon dismissed when he gets caught collecting graft money for his superior. Following other adversities, Farnum is later reinstated on the police force and eventually is promoted to captain. Now secure in his future, he sends to Ireland for Winifred Kingston, his girlfriend, who has been patiently waiting to join him.

The press comes in for some deserving criticism in Henry Otto's early political drama, *Half a Rogue* (1916), based on the 1906 novel by Harold McGrath. New York playwright King Baggot, upon returning to his home town, is nominated as mayor. The opposing party, desperate to discredit the popular Baggot, discovers that an actress has spent the night in the playwright's apartment. In reality, she had fainted and Baggot had given her shelter. A newspaper favoring his opponent and opposed to the popular mayoral candidate tries to involve him in a scandal. The paper exaggerates the incident. After he explains the situation to the husband of the actress, Baggot pummels the person who printed the story.

To protect her innocent husband, a wife is forced to steal, in Robert Vignola's unconvincing drama, *Double Crossed* (1917). Pauline Frederick overhears a corrupt detective trying to convince her husband to steal some evidence from a wealthy reformer's home. It seems the man gained possession of a receipt that would incriminate a powerful political boss's involvement in an illegal deal. The boss hires the crooked private detective to recover the paper. But when Frederick's husband refuses to steal the receipt, the detective, who holds a confession, threatens to expose him as a former thief. Later, the wife makes a deal to retrieve the paper in exchange for her husband's confession. She gets into the wealthy man's home, steals the receipt from his desk and returns to the detective. Following a series of complications, including the treacherous detective's attempt to sexually attack her and her escape, she returns the paper to the man's desk and hands the confession to her husband. The couple then embrace.

Elmer Clifton's crime drama, *The Man Trap* (1917), incorporates a number of sure-fire themes, including police corruption, wrongful imprisonment, and delayed revenge. These are among the important motifs that are blended together with an interesting twist on the usual love triangle. Herbert Rawlinson, the reporter hero, is framed by police inspector Frank MacQuarrie and his managing editor Mark Fenton to cover up their own corrupt deals. Rawlinson eventually escapes from prison, determined to avenge himself on those who framed him. He finally outwits the crooked police chief who confesses to MacQuarrie's murder. The reporter then outmaneuvers his pursuers and wraps up the case, despite sustaining a bullet wound to the wrist. The confession exonerates Rawlinson, who is now free to marry his girlfriend, Sally Starr.

Henry Walthall, as a sleazy lawyer in Rex Ingram's drama, *His Robe of Honor* (1918), is hired to defend Clifford Nordhoff by Boss Nordhoff (Noah Beery). The charge is murder and the reward for Walthall is a judgeship if he clears Clifford. Using dishonest tactics, he wins the case and becomes a judge, but once on the bench, he begins to change. His falling in love with Lois Wilson coincides with his desire to reform his ways. Standing up to the political bosses, he wins the young woman's love and his battle for justice on the bench.

Italian immigrant George Beban gets a lesson in the dark side of American politics – until he is helped by a dedicated reporter in William C. de Mille's social drama, *One More American* (1918). Beban's popularity among his fellow aliens invokes the anger of a local political hack who would like to control the popularity of the personable immigrant. Beban, who is both emotional and pathetic at times, is anticipating the arrival of his wife and daughter, but the influential politician is able to prevent their entrance into the United States. He threatens Beban that his family will be sent back to Italy unless he submits to the politician's power in the community. While the immigrant refuses, an inquisitive reporter learns about the family's predicament and the political corruption involved in preventing the innocent wife and child from joining Beban. He exposes the crooked ward healer, who is sent to jail, and the family is reunited. Beban specialized in portraying immigrants during this period.

II. The Rise of the Political Boss

Whether we describe the twenties as the "Roaring Twenties," "the aspirin age" or the "era of excess," the decade was a period that embraced all that was "modern." Simultaneously, it discarded the horrors and sacrifices of World War I, it rushed headlong into the Depression, collecting along the way the benefits of the new technology, a booming stock market and the excesses of a hedonistic spirit. This "modern" decade witnessed the rise of organized crime, the middle class, bureaucracies and suburbia – elements that would influence future generations socially, politically, economically and personally. While the second wave of films echoed this vivacity and depicted political corruption that touched upon some of the social and political ills of the previous decades, the twenties witnessed political corruption among high government officials. The Teapot Dome scandal of 1921 that rocked the Harding administration began when Navy Secretary Edwin Denby transferred control of naval oil reserves to the Department of the Interior. Albert Fall, secretary of the Interior, secretly leased Teapot Dome to private oil operators Harry Sinclair, who gave Fall $100,000, as an interest-free "loan," and Edward Doheny, who handed Fall more than $300,000 in cash and bonds. Both operators lost their leases after a congressional investigation in 1923. They were finally acquitted of bribery charges in 1928. Meanwhile Fall, who had resigned in 1923, served one year in prison and was fined $100,000 for accepting a bribe. Political corruption appeared in several films. *The Flash* (1923) tells of a lone police chief who battles corruption is a crime-infested town. Lust rules two corrupt politicians – Lionel Barrymore in *I Am a Man* (1924) and Dustin Farnum in *My Man*, released the same year. Reformer Robert Frazer in *Traffic in Hearts* (1924) wants better housing for the poor, despite opposing politicians. Close ties between gangsters and politicians are again emphasized in *Exclusive Rights* (1926). Finally, corrupt politicians are held responsible for the deaths of several firefighters in *The Fire Brigade* (1926).

Ex-convict Robert Colton returns home to his small town and daughter to find a local political boss steeped in corruption in Carlyle Ellis's low-budget drama, *Home-Keeping Hearts* (1921), based on the story, "Chains," by Charles W. Barrell. Colton finds that his daughter has been raised by the greedy politician who gives the father a job in his creamery. When other farmers in the community protest the politician's monopoly of his creamery, he ignores them. But when they threaten to start their own cooperative to compete with his, he then bribes health inspectors to condemn the rival farmers' stock. In addition, the politician has been appropriating funds from the school board. Finally, he loses all political control when he fails to win re-election. Colton, who has served a ten-year sentence based only upon circumstantial evidence, has been able to put his past behind him after meeting and befriending a local schoolteacher.

Jack Conway's implausible drama, *Don't Shoot* (1922), mixes crime and politics when a crooked politician forces a married, reformed safecracker to commit another crime. Herbert Rawlinson, as the ex-thief, is blackmailed by the politician into framing his rival, an honest alderman. Rawlinson refuses and has to battle a gang of crooks. But with the reform alderman on his side, he succeeds and wins the trust of society. The incredulous events begin in the opening scenes when the safecracker is caught applying his trade by the owner of a wealthy home. He mistakes the intruder for his daughter's lover and forces the young couple to marry. The groom then decides to go straight.

Impoverished inventor John Gilbert makes a strange bargain – all in the name of love – in Howard Mitchell's unusual drama, *The Lone Chance* (1924). To win the woman he loves, Gilbert agrees to plead guilty to a murder he didn't commit in return for a one-year sentence and $20,000. When he is betrayed, he escapes from jail. Seeking justice, he confronts the governor whose daughter had shot the victim in self-defense. Learning that the daughter, whom Gilbert loves, is being forced to marry a corrupt politician, he rescues her, and she, in turn, exonerates him from the crime. She is absolved of all charges, and the couple are reunited.

Political power clashes with religious faith in R. William Neill's awkward religious drama, *By Divine Right* (1924). Political big city boss Anders Randolf tries to wield his power by forcing the preacher of a slum mission to release Mildred Harris, a young woman who is seeking sanctuary under his roof. When Elliott Dexter, the religious leader, refuses, Randolf orders his minions to set fire to the building. The preacher is then accused of starting the fire and sentenced to seven years' imprisonment. However, the prison train is wrecked, and Dexter escapes. Later, Dexter, now changed in appearance, is hired as the politician's social secretary. When the doctors announce that the political boss's little daughter will remain crippled all her life, Dexter intervenes. His prayers bring about a miraculous healing. He also helps the boss and his wife reconcile their personal differences. The political leader, now a firm believer in religion, changes his corrupt ways.

Some plots focused on influential politicians who use their power to satisfy their lust. Powerful political boss Lionel Barrymore, who covets Seena Owen, the daughter of a rival politician, ruins the man so that he can marry his daughter, in Ivan Abramson's weak drama, *I Am a Man* (1924). Barrymore and his equally villainous brother (M. J. Faust) have come from the West and changed their name so that they can enter big city politics. First, Barrymore frames the father, who is sentenced to ten years in prison, then he steps forward as the man's savior, promising to drop the sentence if the daughter will marry him. Later, he grows suspicious of his wife and a young lawyer whom he has appointed as district attorney. He assigns his brother to spy on the couple. Instead, the brother tries to make love to his sister-in-law. Barrymore kills his brother and frames a chorus girl for the murder. When he discovers that the defendant is his own daughter, he confesses everything and takes his own life.

Cigar-puffing political boss Dustin Farnum loves a rich man's daughter who doesn't care for him in David Smith's weak romantic drama, *My Man* (1924), which, by the way, has nothing to do with the popular song. Farnum is prepared to smash all obstacles that stand in the way of his goal toward winning Patsy Ruth Miller, including her father, who loses an important traction deal because of the politician. Meanwhile, the young woman thinks she loves Niles Welch, a gold-digging suitor who is able to charm Miller away from others. But Farnum finally wins her love when he proves to her that her phony suitor is only interested in her money. He then helps her father win back the lost contract, thereby gaining the admiration and respect of both the father and daughter.

Political reformer Robert Frazer is determined to build modern housing for the poor, while smashing a corrupt band of graft-takers, in Scott Dunlap's overly familiar social drama, *Traffic in Hearts* (1924). However, the reformer has to overcome several hurdles, including his ongoing battle against the leader of the crooked ring – and who happens to be the father of Mildred Harris, Frazer's girlfriend. Several scenes are overly sentimental, such as the one in which a stereotyped Irish policeman, after running off some thugs who have disrupted a prayer meeting, pledges to support the reformer. Another involves Dan Marion, a boy of the streets who wins Frazer's affection. It is this mixture of sentiment and politics that weakens the effectiveness of the production.

A family of firefighters suffers tragedy when at least one son dies in a fire resulting from corruption in William Nigh's exciting drama, *The Fire Brigade* (1926). Charles Ray is a rookie firefighter whose two brothers are firefighters and whose father, another fireman, was killed earlier fighting a blaze. When fire chief DeWitt Jennings discovers that the fire that has recently taken the life of one of Ray's brothers is attributed to the inferior construction of a building, signs point to a political boss of the town who struts about as a generous philanthropist. In reality, he is the silent partner of the contractor who has been carrying out all these constructions while the politician has been approving all the possible violations. Meanwhile Ray, who has fallen in love with May McAvoy, the political boss's daughter, is appointed to investigate an orphanage for fire violations. Ray finds evidence that his girlfriend's father is the murderer of several firefighters, whose deaths are attributed to inferior structures. When McAvoy discovers the truth, she leaves home. Suddenly, a large conflagration erupts in town, including the orphanage. Ray's unit is called into action and he ends up a hero after saving several children while endangering his own life.

Tom Santschi, the political boss of a small town, promises Gladys Brockwell, a bright lawyer, that he will reform, in Scott Pembroke's drama, *The Law and the Man* (1928). To impress Brockwell and win her love, he evicts the grafting officials he had originally hired and asks her to run for district attorney. He pledges to support her in prosecuting the criminal element. Meanwhile, she begins to fall in love with architect Robert Ellis, much to the dismay of

Santschi, who was about to propose to her at a party – until he sees her walk across the ballroom to kiss her fiancé. Although Ellis turns out to be a forger, the politician, out of his affection for Brockwell, decides to protect him. When Brockwell is impeached, Santschi testifies that he committed the crime the district attorney has been accused of, thereby saving her fiancé, the crooked architect.

Exuberant cub reporter George O'Hara gains possession of important incriminating papers from a corrupt politician's safe in the mild comedy drama, *Is That Nice?* (1926). At first, the owner of the newspaper and his managing editor are delighted – until they learn that O'Hara has no proof of the suspect's acts of corruption. His story, it seems, borders chiefly on being libelous. Following several complications, the neophyte newspaperman, with the help of girlfriend Doris Hill, collects the evidence needed to bring down the politician. Laughs depend chiefly on disguises and thrill sequences, such as those outside skyscraper windows, car chases and clever title cards.

Hollywood reporter Frank Merrill gets his editor out of a tight spot in Bruce Mitchell's routine action drama, *The Hollywood Reporter* (1926). Merrill is in love with Peggy Montgomery, editor Charles K. French's daughter. Shady political boss Jack Richardson, seeking the mayor's job, threatens to blackmail French, who had earlier served a prison term. Richardson wants French to help him win the election. Reporter Merrill agrees to help French by trying to find something on the politician. When he discovers that Richardson is running a gambling concession from his home, the reporter floods the front page with the story and accompanies it with an incriminating photograph of the establishment taken by his assistant. Meanwhile, his editor proves that his own earlier conviction was a frame-up, leading to a full exoneration of all charges.

Star newspaper reporter Gaston Glass discloses a cover-up of a dead mayoral candidate, but the story is never printed, in Burton King's offbeat drama, *Broken Barriers* (1928). A cowardly mayoral candidate, faced with exposure, opts not to run. But political boss Joseph Girard threatens the timid soul at the point of a gun. The candidate suddenly dies of a heart attack. Girard makes it appear that the man died as the result of a car accident. Glass discovers the deception, but his editor quashes the story as a present to the reporter who is about to marry Helene Costello, the daughter of the political boss.

George Melford's mystery drama, *Freedom of the Press* (1928), deals with family honor and political corruption. The son of a crusading newspaperman takes over the family paper after his father is brutally murdered. Malcolm McGregor, as the idealistic son who is following in his father's footsteps, battles to expose corrupt politician Lewis Stone. The crooked Stone intends to run for mayor. The fighting journalist succeeds in bringing to justice the politician, who also happens to be the leader of the local underworld. The plot was based on the real-life murder of Canton, Ohio, newspaper publisher Don Mellett. The film was originally released for review under the title *Graft*, which is not related to a 1931 sound drama with the same title.

Prejudice

I. "The Fate of the Helpless"

American author Ambrose Bierce around the turn of the century once defined prejudice as "a vagrant opinion without visible means of support." Like the intolerance, prejudices and racism of society in the early twentieth century, the movie industry displayed the same attitudes in their films. But it wasn't long before a handful of studios began to take up the cause of the victims. The Native American, the half-breed and the Mexican became easy targets and were often portrayed as villains at first. Intermarriage between Indian and white was explored in such dramas as *The Kentuckian* (1908) and *Comata, the Sioux* (1909). Other early films began attacking the injustice toward the Native American, including *A True Indian Brave* (1910) and D. W. Griffith's *A Romance of the Western Hills* (1910). Tom Mix helped to dispel hatred toward Mexicans with his sympathetic treatment of an innocent, hardworking Mexican in *The Mexican* (1914). Sporadically, films began to examine the problems of other minorities. In 1912, Congress, in a surprising decision, passed a law prohibiting the interstate transportation of films showing prizefights. This simply was a blatant attempt to suppress knowledge about the skills of Jack Johnson, the first African-American heavyweight boxing champion of the world who had a white wife. Although this and other legislation may have set the tone for numerous racist films that followed, there were occasional breakthroughs. In *The Sleeping Lion* (1919), for example, an ignorant bully terrorizes an Italian immigrant who has bought a ranch. However, the return of the Ku Klux Klan in the early decades of the twentieth century brought back the horrible lynchings and floggings that plagued many Southern communities during the days of Reconstruction. The Klan, under the guise of preserving "Americanism" and law and order, spread its tentacles of hate against blacks, foreigners, Jews and Catholics to major Western and Northern cities, including Detroit, Pittsburgh, Dayton, Indianapolis, Denver and Chicago. In Oklahoma alone in 1922 the Klan was responsible for 2,500 floggings.

The Justice of the Redskin (1908) was one of several early silent dramas portraying the Native American as a sympathetic character. An Indian, falsely accused of killing a white girl, is forced to set out to prove his innocence. He eventually tracks down the real killer and locates the body of his victim. The Indian then tosses the guilty man off a cliff. By having the white community summarily assume the guilt of the Indian, the film suggests the inherent bigotry that prevails among whites.

D. W. Griffith's drama, *The Redman's View* (1909), depicts the encroachment of the white man onto Indian land, thereby suggesting some of the harsh injustices thrust upon Native Americans. Whites, by force of arms, callously evict Kiowas from their land. Minnewanna, the chief's attractive daughter, and her noble and handsome lover, Silver Eagle, are permitted to visit the grave of her father before they, too, are driven off the land. Director Griffith's socially provocative drama, part of his outstanding cycle of early Indian films of this period, precipitated a contemporary critic of the New York Dramatic Mirror to view it as ". . . symbolical of the fate of the helpless Indian race as it has been forced to recede before the advancing white. . . ."

An unusual western for its time, *His Last Game* (1909) is set in Oklahoma and centers around a baseball game. An Indian, pitching for the favorite of two teams, becomes the focal point of gamblers, who scheme to poison him so that they can score big on their bets. Another Indian, aware of their plans, warns the pitcher. A fight ensues between one of the gamblers and the Indian and the former is killed. The Indian is removed and about to be shot for murder when the sheriff gives the condemned man a reprieve to finish the game. The Indian hits a home run and his team wins. He is then taken back to the site of the execution where the sentence is carried out. This may be the first baseball western, although some purists may not consider it a western at all. But the western characters, the harshness of western justice and the cruel treatment of the Indian justify it as a legitimate entry in the genre.

One of the earliest films to portray vividly the bigotry of some whites toward the Indian, D. W. Griffith's drama, *A Mohawk's Way* (1910), deals with a white doctor who refuses to treat an Indian child. When a member of a nearby tribe entreats the physician to come to the camp, the doctor not only refuses, but hits the Indian. However, the doctor's wife, showing more compassion, secretly journeys to the encampment, treats the child and restores the infant to health. Except for sporadic forays into this theme, it was not until 1950, with the release of *Broken Arrow*, that Hollywood issued forth a cycle of social westerns dealing with prejudice.

Another early drama showing white injustice toward the Indian, *A True Indian Brave* (1910) deals with a Native-American maiden and her lover who are almost lynched after he comes to her defense. Earlier in the film, some white settlers insult the maiden, causing the brave to intercede in her behalf. The whites consider the Indians interlopers who do not deserve to live – in this crude early drama.

A Romance of the Western Hills (1910) is another D. W. Griffith film that underscores the injustice suffered by Indians at the hands of intolerant whites. A white family adopts Mary Pickford, a young Indian maiden, who is treated cruelly by a white man with whom she has fallen in love. With the help of a former lover (Arthur Johnson), an Indian brave, she seeks revenge upon her oppressor.

The first of four screen versions of Helen Hunt Jackson's 1884 novel, D. W. Griffith's drama, *Ramona* (1910), deals with anti-Indian discrimination in the West. The film features Mary Pickford in the title role. Perhaps another "first" for the film was the fact that Biograph paid the publishers $100 for the motion picture rights – an unheard of practice during this period. Director Griffith in his trouping days played the part of Alessandro in a stage version that toured California in 1905. The director was quite at home with the subject matter, since the ill treatment of the Indian was one of his favorite themes during the early silent period. The film is subtitled "A Story of the White Man's Injustice to the Indian."

An American lieutenant falls in love with an attractive Filipina in the romantic drama, *A Rose of the Philippines* (1910), set during the Spanish-American War. Although the young man's parents and his commanding officer try to persuade him to end the romance, the lieutenant opts for the islander rather than his fiancée in the States. This was one of the earliest South Sea island films to touch upon a racial theme.

The first half of Tom Mix's otherwise routine drama, *The Mexican* (1914), about a Mexican who helps to save the life of a baby, suggests the innate prejudice of some whites toward all Mexicans and may be considered an early example of a social problem film. Tom Mix portrays a Mexican who, to help his hungry family, seeks a job at a nearby ranch. However, he is taunted and persecuted by the other hands until he threatens the life of the foreman. The owner fires him and chases him off the property. In a moment of rage, he plots to burn down the ranch house. After the men leave for their chores, he is about to carry out his plan when the owner's wife cries out for help after her baby is bitten by a rattlesnake. The Mexican forgets his hatred and rides for a doctor. The foreman, seeing him at a distance, thinks the Mexican has stolen a horse and shoots at him. The Mexican returns with the doctor, thereby saving the baby. In return, the hero is rehired and able to help his own family.

American schoolteacher Wallace Reid opts to work in the Philippines, where he falls under the influence of a lovely native in Donald Crisp's drama of lust, greed and racism, *At Dawn* (1914), based on a story by Frederick Moore. Reid's girlfriend back home grows tired of his unfulfilled promise to send for her. After inheriting a fortune, she sets sail to meet her lover. Reid, now more interested in the inheritance money than his current romance, poisons his island lover when she refuses to leave. A U.S. Army sergeant who had earlier seen Reid trying to dispose of the young woman's body, brings in the teacher for questioning and arranges for his girlfriend to leave for Manila. Reid betrays his blatant racism with his indifferent remark to several American soldiers about his victim: "What's another Filipino, more or less?"

Dorothy Donnelly, a Native American, leaves her valley to find a physician for her sick mother, in Lawrence B. McGill's drama, *Sealed Valley* (1915), based on the 1914 novel by Hulbert Footner. The doctor, J. W. Johnson, agrees to make the long journey to the Indian settlement. On the way, he begins to fall in love with the young woman, but she rejects his love and eventual proposal, fearing the consequences of a mixed marriage for them and their future children. Later, the doctor is rescued from a river by the daughter of a miner. Donnelly, who accidentally meets Johnson, whom she secretly loves, encourages him to marry the woman who saved him from drowning, while she returns to her settlement and her own people in the Sealed Valley.

Donald Crisp's version of the drama, *Ramona* (1916), set in California in the late 1840s, focuses on Ramona, a half-Indian and half-Scotch young woman (Ada Gleason), who elopes with Alessandro, a full-blooded Native American (Monroe Salisbury). Driven from place to place by bigoted whites who continue to encroach upon Indian land, the couple struggle on until their land is stolen and Alessandro is murdered in cold blood by whites. The hour-long film recounts enough detailed incidents from the original work to underscore the author's plea for social justice for the Indians. Helen Hunt Jackson's popular 1884 novel about the white man's brutal treatment toward the Indian had appeared on screen in one earlier version in 1910 and two later adaptations, one in 1928, and a sound version in 1936.

Douglas Fairbanks portrays Lo Dorman, the title character, in Allan Dwan's social drama, *The Half Breed* (1916), about the mistreatment of those born as a result of mixed marriages. Lo's Native American mother had been sexually attacked by a white man. After Lo was born, his mother committed suicide and the child was raised by an old native. Lo makes his home in the redwood forests of California. When he journeys to a nearby town, he is rejected by the white inhabitants. He soon finds happiness with Teresa, the former mistress of a traveling showman. The film was adapted from the 1883 Bret Harte novel, *In the Carquinez Woods*. Director Allan Dwan, as a lark, included famous lawman Wyatt Earp in a crowd scene in the film. Earp, 67 at the time, had been visiting the set during shooting. Dwan had a productive career in directing sound features.

Sometimes differences in social backgrounds can be bridged by way of love, as demonstrated in Perry N. Vekroff's social drama, *Should a Baby Die?* (1916). A wealthy young man, while working as a laborer, meets the daughter of a Jewish pawnbroker and falls in love with her. When he proposes marriage, her father, Arthur Donaldson, objects, basing his decision on religious differences, while the young man's friends discourage the union because of social and religious differences. The girl was taken in by the Jewish couple after her parents died in a car accident. The doctors at that time gave the child only a short time to live and suggested the couple allow the baby to die. But the pawnbroker's wife rejected their advice and decided to nurture the child and care for her until she recovered her health. Meanwhile, the narrow-mindedness of both the pawnbroker and some of the friends and family members of the sincere young man almost broke up the love affair of the young couple.

Perhaps the most significant release during 1916 was that of D. W. Griffith's spectacle, *Intolerance*. A much more complicated and ambitious drama than the director's masterpiece, *Birth of a Nation* (1915), the film consisted of four stories on the theme of intolerance and "love's struggle throughout the ages." The four parts included Christ's conflict with Rome and the intolerance of the Pharisees; the massacre of St. Bartholomew and the persecution of the Catholics in 16th century France; the moral fall of ancient Babylon; and the struggle between capitalists and workers and injustice in contemporary America. Using crosscutting through the entire film, Griffith scrupulously worked his effects to have them all come to a climax at the same time. The work never enjoyed the acclaim he had hoped for, but it remains an awesome spectacle of Griffith's vision of cruelty and prejudice throughout the ages. More than 16,000 extras appear simultaneously on screen in the Nebuchadnezzar sequences, for instance. Several years later, he released one segment, *The Fall of Babylon*, as a separate film.

A Native American is forced to choose between two cultures in Bertram Bracken's romantic drama, *The Primitive Call* (1917). Brain Elkhorn, an Eastern-educated Indian, played by Fritz Leiber, is duped by Betty (Gladys Coburn), a white woman, into turning over tribal lands to her and her father. When the tribe banishes him, he abducts Betty and takes her to live with him in the mountains where he returns to the customs of his people. Shedding her racial prejudice, she soon falls in love with him. But he rejects her for a young Indian woman. Betty then returns to civilization.

An American member of the diplomatic service stationed in China falls in love with the daughter of a Chinese mandarin and secretly marries her in Sidney A. Franklin's drama, *The Forbidden City* (1918). Thomas Meighan, the husband, is assigned to Shanghai, and the father takes his daughter to the emperor, hoping she will be chosen as one of his favorites. The husband returns and, unable to find his wife, leaves, thinking her father had her killed for having an affair with a foreigner. When the daughter, Norma Talmadge, is brought before the emperor, she is nursing her baby. The irate emperor sentences her to death for not saving herself for her royal lover. He then recants. He takes her child away and allows her to join her American. As she is led from the palace, several assassins attack her with knives and kill her. "The half-American child shall live," the emperor decrees, "to be a warning that East and West can be no twain." The women of his court raise her as a whim. When she reaches 18, she escapes to the U. S. embassy, where she finds work as a nurse in Manila at a military hospital. Reed Hamilton, an American lieutenant, falls in love with her and they become betrothed. He takes her to his guardian, who happens to be her father and who condemns the engagement. About to commit suicide, she is summoned to Meighan, who is very ill. Delirious with fever, he calls out his wife's name. Talmadge realizes her relationship to Meighan and dresses up as her mother. Her father is restored to his normal health, and the young couple are happily married.

Monroe Salisbury portrays Kut-Le, an educated Native American, who falls in love with a white woman in Wilfred Lucas's romantic drama, *The Red Red Heart* (1918), set in recent times somewhere on the edge of a Southwest desert. Ruth Clifford, as the object of Kut-Le's heart, has come to the desert to help her recover from her melancholia. The couple first meet when he rescues her from a tarantula. A friendship develops and he offers to cure her of her illness by taking her into the desert. But her racial prejudice forces her to reject him, and she informs him that they are never to see each other again. Kut-Le kidnaps her, takes her into the hills and cures her. Meanwhile, a posse is formed to find her. The film, based on the 1913 novel, *The Heart of the Desert*, by Honore Morrow, ends with her cure and her marriage to the Native American. The theme of interracial romance and marriage, although still rather startling for the pre-1920s screen, was not entirely new to movie audiences. G. M. Anderson's *Broncho Billy's Indian Romance* and Cecil B. DeMille's *The Squaw Man*, both released in 1914, had already been seen and their interracial romances accepted by American audiences.

Petite Marguerite Clark portrays both the angelic Little Eva and her naughty playmate Topsy in J. Searle Dawley's gripping drama, *Uncle Tom's Cabin* (1918), based on the famous 1852 novel about slavery by Harriet Beecher Stowe. Slaves Uncle Tom (Frank Losee) and Eliza (Florence Carpenter) are sold by their master. Eliza escapes with her child across the frozen Ohio River. Tom is taken South, where he saves the life of Little Eva. Her parents buy Tom, who remains content for a time, until Eva and her father die. Tom is next sold to cruel Simon Legree, who physically tortures the slave to death. Ruby Hoffman, a much abused slave girl, kills Legree. About seven other film versions of the novel have appeared over the years.

Mitchell Lewis portrays Wolf, an Indian who treats the flirtations of Yvette Mitchell, a white woman, seriously, in Robert N. Bradbury's drama, *The Last of His People* (1919), about social and racial prejudices. He falls in love with Yvette, whose father raised Wolf.

George Irving's drama, *As a Man Thinks* (1919), based on Augustus Thomas's 1911 play, concerns the problem of intermarriage between a Jew and Gentile. When Leah Baird learns that her husband, Henry Clive, has had an affair with another woman, she begins to flirt with a former boyfriend, Warburton Gamble, whom her father had once rejected because Gamble was of the Jewish faith. Clive learns of this past relationship and questions his wife about the paternity of his son. Peeved by his insinuation, Baird returns to Gamble, and both seek refuge with a Jewish physician. The doctor learns that

Gamble had been in jail for two years before Baird's marriage. He informs Clive of this, and the married couple reconcile their differences.

Madge Kennedy's love for John Bowers, a Christian, is threatened by her Orthodox Jewish father in Clarence Badger's poignant drama, *Daughter of Mine* (1919). Bowers suddenly disappears. Kennedy, working for a publisher, conceives finding him by submitting one of his manuscripts to her employer who will then advertise for the author. Her boss, Arthur Carewe, has fallen in love with Kennedy. He invites her to his home to read the manuscript, provides her with dinner and tries to make love to her. While she reads the story, set in medieval times, it is reenacted on the screen. Carewe then advertises for an ending to the unfinished story. The best ending is submitted by Bowers, the writer, who truly loves Kennedy. The couple are then reunited.

Evelyn Nesbit, portraying Hawaiian princess Laone, a composer, is the victim of racism during her visit with a California society matron in Kenean Buel's lavishly produced social drama, *The Fallen Idol* (1919). At first, the beautiful and personable Laone is socially successful, but when Sidney Mason, the nephew of her hostess, falls in love with her, attitudes toward the Hawaiian visitor change. Her hostess tries to persuade her to break off the romance because of the differences in their races. Meanwhile, Mason's friends are determined to prevent his marriage to "the little brown thing." When Mason leaves for New York to visit his ailing father, his aunt tells the princess that he has abandoned her. Disillusioned, she leaves for Hawaii with Lyster Chambers, an unsavory character. Mason, upon learning of her flight, follows. In Hawaii, she rejects him out of a sense of guilt and betrayal. She had been forced to have sex with Chambers aboard his yacht. He had threatened to turn her over to his crew. Following several complications, including Mason's false arrest for stealing a necklace and Nesbit's ability to prove Chambers the thief and smuggler, the couple are reunited. Several earlier dramas have used Hawaii for their settings, but this was one of the earliest to offer extensive picturesque views of Hawaii.

An Italian immigrant from New York's East Side decides to make a new home for himself in the West, where he faces unexpected problems, in Rupert Julian's drama, *The Sleeping Lion* (1919). Monroe Salisbury, as Tony, the Italian, loves the land, so he buys a little ranch for himself and a little orphan boy he has adopted. He soon gets into an altercation with Durant, the local bully, played by Herschel Mayall. Tony, to prepare for the next confrontation, begins to practice how to use a six-shooter. But in the end he beats Durant in a fistfight. The major conflict between the two men is their romantic interest in Kate Billings, played by Rhea Mitchell.

II. The Struggle Against Bigotry

Despite the attempts of private and public organizations, including those associated with the Hollywood community, to break down some of the barriers of bigotry and racism toward minorities, the nation was still plagued with its hate-mongers and groups such as the Ku Klux Klan. As early as 1906, American Jews founded the American Jewish Committee to protect the civil and religious rights of Jews and to fight prejudice. The years of World War I intensified racial tensions. Blacks who migrated from the South, lured by economic boom, alarmed Northerners, who responded with intimidation and imposed residential requirements upon the newcomers. Mobs attacked blacks who dared to venture out of their neighborhoods. Riots erupted in twenty-six cities in 1917, including East St. Louis, Omaha and Houston. Racial conflicts continued after the war, when returning black soldiers resented further discrimination. Four days of rioting in Chicago in 1919 only ended after troops stepped into the fray. Other groups faced intolerance, including radicals and antiwar socialists. Leaders of the radical I.W.W. union were arrested during the war years and sentenced to prison terms of up to twenty-five years. In 1926, Father Coughlin, a Detroit priest, began broadcasting over radio, spewing his sermons of racial bigotry and right-wing views. And by 1928, the National Conference of Christians and Jews was founded to fight bigotry, following the defeat of Catholic presidential candidate Alfred E. Smith. Meanwhile, throughout the twenties, American silent films occasionally touched upon the theme of prejudice, ranging in genres from romance to the western. The films dealt with intolerance in the U.S. in such dramas as *Symbol of the Unconquered* (1921), about a young African-American woman with a mining claim, and *Welcome Stranger* (1924). *Put 'Em Up* and *The Rawhide Kid*, both released in 1928, dealt with anti-Semitism in the West. Other productions were set in various parts of the globe, including India in *Without Benefit of Clergy* (1921), the South Seas in *Where the Pavement Ends* (1923), and Russia in *Prejudice* (1922).

Thomas Holding, an English engineer in India, falls in love with Virginia Brown Faire, a native, and marries her in a native ceremony, in James Young's drama, *Without Benefit of Clergy* (1921), based on the story by Rudyard Kipling. The young woman's fear of losing her lover to a woman of his own race is lessened when she presents him with a son. The child binds them even more closely. But her basic fear of losing Holden still lingers in her heart and mind. However, it remains for external forces to take their toll on the happy and loving couple. Cholera claims the boy and his pathetic mother, and rain destroys the couple's love nest, as fragile as their short-lived marriage.

One of the rare westerns with major black characters, the drama, *Symbol of the Unconquered* (1921), deals with a young black woman who journeys to the West to take possession of her mining claim. After she is evicted from the only hotel in the frontier town, she finds refuge with a prospector. She later repays his kindness by saving his life. Oscar Micheaux, the producer, turned out a series of silent and sound non-western dramas, known as "race" films, designed for black audiences and featuring an all-black cast. Leigh Whipper, a minor player in the film, became an established character actor and appeared in several films.

Wheeler Oakman portrays the title character, an educated Native American, in Charles Taylor's revenge drama, *The Half Breed* (1922), set in the Southwest. He seeks revenge on a racist judge who evicted the Native American's mother from her land and interfered in Oakman's love for a young white woman. When his attempts at kidnapping the judge's children are foiled by the local sheriff and his posse, Oakman rides off to start a new life elsewhere. The film was adapted from the play, *Half Breed: A Tale of Indian Country*, by H. D. Cottrel and Oliver Morosco.

A Jewish community leader in Russia is falsely arrested for the murder of Sascha's little sister in Joseph Belmont's social drama, *Prejudice* (1922). Sascha, a Gentile and childhood friend of the leader's daughter, is sympathetic to the plight of the Jewish people. Against his inner feelings, he is forced to point an accusing finger at the defendant. He tries to reverse his accusation by saving the leader's family and stopping the physical attack by a mob that began when the leader was first arrested. The alleged victim suddenly appears – alive and well, but the mob gains access to the prison and stones the accused man to death. Sascha admits to the victim's daughter that he was prejudiced and begs her to forgive him.

Ramön Navarro, a dark-skinned South Seas islander, and Alice Terry, the daughter of a European missionary, fall in love – a forbidden act acknowledged by both races – in Rex Ingram's romantic tragic drama, *Where the Pavement Ends* (1923), based on the story, "The Passion Vine," by John Russell. Although she accepts his love through most of the film, Terry eventually rejects Navarro because of the racial barrier between them. He then takes his own life, giving the film a disappointing downbeat ending. The production is enhanced by picturesque settings and poetic photography, which include an undersea pearl diving sequence in which a shark threatens the hero. Another notable sequence depicting a fight between the handsome Navarro and a crude, burly, intoxicated seaman underscores the contrast between the innocent and beautiful spirit of the islanders and the harsh and potentially malevolent Europeans. The racial theme is unusual for South Sea island movies, which were designed chiefly as escapist fare, although it showed up sporadically, as in John Ford's *The Hurricane*, released in 1937.

Dore Davidson portrays a Jew who manages to infiltrate a New England town where those of the Jewish faith are normally restricted in James Young's social drama, *Welcome Stranger* (1924), based on the play by Aaron Hoffman. Davidson, by his sheer stubbornness, survives and soon, he and his daughter, Virginia Brown Faire, overcome the local prejudice. In addition, he becomes the community's hero by bringing to the town electric lights and trolley cars. Lloyd Hughes, the banker's son, joins Davidson as his partner in the power company. Florence Vidor, a stenographer, provides the romantic interest for Hughes.

A young and idealistic African-American Harvard College graduate settles in a small Southern town in Oscar Micheaux's social drama, *Birthright* (1924). J.

Homer Tutt, as the optimistic graduate, has to suffer the bigotry and cruelty of both races as he struggles to survive in the hostile environment. Micheaux produced a series of "race" dramas, comedies and musicals during the twenties and thirties, films of limited budgets designed chiefly for black audiences and theaters.

One of the best films about racial injustice involving Native Americans, is George B. Seitz's drama, *The Vanishing American* (1925), based on Zane Grey's novel. It features Richard Dix as Nophaie, a World War I veteran, who is killed in a battle between the Navajo and the whites. The film opens with a long prologue depicting the history of the American Indian from the defeat of the cave dwellers to the arrival of the Spanish Conquistadors. The film then shifts to World War I, when Nophaie, the leader of his clan of Navajos, encourages his young braves to follow him into the U. S. Army. Nophaie serves in the trenches in France and returns a hero. But he finds a corrupt Indian agent has taken over and has confiscated his tribe's land and driven its members onto barren soil, where many are dying. When his tribe rises up, Nophaie warns the whites who take refuge in a blockhouse. He goes out to talk to his tribe but is killed by a crazed warrior. Before he dies, a white schoolteacher whom he loves announces that Washington has discharged the crooked agent. Although Nophaie's death underscores the tragedy and plight of the Indians, it conveniently serves to evade the issue of intermarriage. The film was plagued with some of the same weaknesses as *The Pony Express*, another western epic, released only months earlier. Both suffered from a trite, sentimental story.

Bebe Daniels, a young Frenchwoman, leaves a convent to join her father on the island of Martinique in William K. Howard's social drama, *Volcano* (1926), based on the 1922 play, *Martinique*, by Laurence Eyre. She discovers her father has died and his widow believes that Daniels is the product of a quadroon and the father. The widow sends her to live in the mulatto quarter, where Ricardo Cortez becomes interested in her. He soon offers her his love, and she accepts. But his brother suggests that a mixed marriage would be disastrous for the family. The brother then persuades Daniels to end the affair. On the evening that Cortez is about to marry another young woman, a volcanic mountain erupts, and Cortez rescues Daniels. When the couple learn that both of her parents were French, they renew their love for each other.

William Desmond portrays a Native American who meets up with racial prejudice in Ernst Laemmle's social drama, *Red Clay* (1927). A veteran of World War I, a recognized scholar and a popular football star, Desmond upon his return to the States begins to date the daughter of a congressman who believes that Desmond is equal to and, in many ways, superior to the white man. However, the politician's more narrow-minded son resents the romantic relationship. The young man does not know that it was this same Native American who had saved his life when he was fighting in France. Later, the Indian is mortally wounded and dies in the arms of the prejudiced son who repents and tries to comfort his sister.

Two brothers enlist and are sent to France when the United States enters the European conflict in 1917 in John P. McCarthy's social drama, *His Foreign Wife* (1927). One son is killed in action, and the other, Wallace MacDonald, remains in Germany with the occupation forces. He meets, falls in love with and marries Greta von Rue, a young German woman, whom he brings back to his home town and family. To his consternation, MacDonald discovers that his own father is filled with hatred toward the Germans and is hostile toward his daughter-in-law. When his father, a town leader, is to pin a decoration of bravery on his son, Macdonald, before a large assembly, castigates his father's sense of phony patriotism and his failing to put aside the hatreds of the past. The father later realizes his shortcomings and forgives his son. The family is once again united.

Rosettal and Vivian Duncan portray the title characters in Del Lord's unsuccessful burlesque, *Topsy and Eva* (1927), based on the 1924 play by Catherine Chisholm Cushing. Topsy, a little African-American girl, is auctioned off on the Shelby estate by the cruel Simon Legree (Gibson Gowland). When no one bids for her, little Eva bids one nickel and gains possession of Topsy. In company with Uncle Tom (Noble Johnson) and other slaves, Topsy is given over to Aunt Opelia, who is to correct and clean the little imp. When the master cannot pay his debt to Legree, the latter demands his property to be returned. Topsy escapes while Legree and Shelby battle it out. Topsy heads for the river before Legree and his hunting dogs can track her, and reaches a graveyard used by other runaway slaves. When she learns that Eva is very sick, she prays for her to get well. Eva recovers and the two friends are happily brought together.

Fred Humes portrays a cowboy hero who rids a town of its thieves in Edgar Lewis's action drama, *Put 'Em Up* (1928). The chief villain and his underlings are so bold that they blatantly kidnap the heroine and plan to force her to marry the chief. But our hero rescues her in the nick of time. One incident shows the gang trying to intimidate a Jewish merchant who befriends Humes and who is also responsible for saving the hero's life. A similar scene appears in *The Rawhide Kid*, starring Hoot Gibson, also released in 1928. Except for a handful of dramas dealing with Indian injustice, social problems such as anti-Semitism were virtually never explored in the action-oriented and escapist silent western.

A western with a unique feature for a change, Dell Andrews's action drama, *The Rawhide Kid* (1928), has cowboy hero Hoot Gibson defending a Jewish peddler and his daughter, who have left the Eastern ghettos for the vast opportunities of the West. Well into the film, the peddler, played by William H. Strauss, has succeeded to the point that he has expanded his business throughout the town, thereby igniting hatred in the chief villain, his competitor.

By the time Edwin Carewe's social drama, *Ramona* (1928), the third screen adaptation of Helen Hunt Jackson's novel, was released, the book had gone through more than 90 printings and the ballad "Ramona" was the season's hit song. This time around the alluring Dolores Del Rio portrays the title character, a half-Indian who defies her stern guardian and marries the Indian sheep shearer, Alessandro (Warner Baxter). Tragedy dominates the remainder of the film – bandits massacre the local natives, the couple lose their baby because a village doctor refuses to treat Indians, and Alessandro is brutally murdered after being accused of horse-stealing. Ramona lapses into a state of shock and is then reunited with her white foster-brother.

Richard Dix had already gained fame for his portrayal of a proud Navajo in George B. Seitz's drama, *The Vanishing American* (1925), before embarking on Victor Schertzinger's drama, *Redskin* (1929). As Wing Foot, an iconoclastic Native American, he faces rejection by both whites and his own people. Educated in the East where he encounters racial prejudice, he returns home only to become an outcast when he rejects his tribe's customs. He accidentally discovers oil in the desert after visiting his sweetheart in a rival Indian village. To prevent some greedy whites from gaining possession of the site, he rushes to file his claim. Later, when a clash flares up between the two tribes, he informs them of the ensuing boon to both groups. He then takes his sweetheart for his bride, symbolically linking the destinies of both tribes.

French farm girl Pola Negri falls in love with a German prisoner of war, causing anger among her neighbors, in Rowland V. Lee's drama about post-World War I prejudice, *Barbed Wire* (1927), based on the 1923 novel by Hall Caine. Negri has lost a brother in the war. Her once-happy community now has become the site of a prisoner-of-war camp, where she meets and falls in love with Clive Brook, a prisoner. When they decide to marry, the other villagers are shocked and enraged at her decision. After the war, her brother, who was thought to have been killed, returns home sightless. "I came home to my own people to find peace," he says. "Instead, I find bitter hatred in your heart – a hatred strong enough to start another war." His pleas to accept the German touch the community. The film was one of several made after the armistice that attempted to soften the image of the German from a bestial figure bent on rape and pillage to a sympathetic soul misled by power-hungry leaders. Brook, as the German prisoner, describes to the heroine how his people suffered almost as much as the French.

W. S. Van Dyke's lushly filmed romantic island drama, *The Pagan* (1929), based on the short story by John Russell, underscores the contrast between the simple and kindly half-caste native and the hypocritical brutality of the white trader. "When East meets West," a subtitle states, "the result is six barrooms and one bank." This suggests that civilized man's main purpose in the South Seas is to corrupt and exploit the idealistic islanders. Native Ramón Navarro falls in love with islander Dorothy Janis, whom the villainous captain Donald Crisp at one point holds captive aboard his ship. A final battle ensues between Navarro and Crisp. The film is part silent and part sound, the latter containing singing – most notably the popular "Pagan Love Song" – and sound effects, but no dialogue. Several film critics scoffed at leading man Navarro, a second-string romantic actor during the silent period, whom they thought looked ridiculous in the film, singing while on his back in the water.

Prostitution

I. Scarlet Women and the "Sporting Palaces"

The history of prostitution, both around the world and in the United States, is a tragic and sordid story. An epidemic of sexual diseases in 16th-century Europe led to efforts to control prostitution, and public health considerations motivated regulatory legislation. International cooperation to control the traffic in prostitutes began in 1899. By 1900, Storyville in New Orleans had more than two dozen ornate Basin Street "sporting palaces" or houses of prostitution in two blocks set aside three years earlier. Poorer prostitutes operated out of "cribs" behind these "palaces." James Robert Mann's White Slave Traffic Act of 1910 forbade interstate and international transportation of women for immoral purposes. By 1925, organized crime was deeply involved in a variety of vices, including prostitution. For example, Chicago gangster Al Capone soon controlled not only bootlegging but also gambling, prostitution, and the Chicago dance-hall business. Today, houses of prostitution are illegal in all states except Nevada. American silent films about prostitutes and prostitution appeared relatively early in the history of this media. Within a few years, movie studios were exploiting the topic – often playing it safe by turning their works into cautionary tales, emphasizing the destructive and debilitating effects of engaging in a life of sin, as in *The Libertine* (1916). Prostitutes, however, were rarely treated as parasites or evil women – except in some rare cases, as in *The Supreme Sacrifice* (1916). Films tended to treat them sympathetically, often suggesting external causes, such as economic, social or political failings, for their fall from grace. Films like *The Scarlet Woman* (1916) portrayed mothers or wives who felt they were forced to sacrifice themselves for their husbands or children. Some were naïve young women fresh from the farm and easily misled into the sinful life by deceitful and lecherous men who preyed on their innocence. Others voluntarily sacrificed themselves for the man they loved, as did the title character in *Camille* (1915), or, later, in *The Woman Disputed*

(1928), for their country. Finally, these early films, while often depicting prostitutes sympathetically, simultaneously painted society as cruel and heartless in treating these women as sinners and criminals. In addition, society tended to absolve the men who helped to create or support prostitution.

A prostitute in the very early drama, *How They Do Things on the Bowery* (1902), picks up a visitor to the big city and takes him into a saloon where she proceeds to drug his drink. She then robs him and leaves. The dupe, who is unable to pay, is tossed out with his suitcase by the waiter. This was the first time the Edison studio used a panning camera for a fiction film. This short, crudely made film probably was intended as a simple cautionary tale for tourists, travelers and other visitors to the big city.

Another early film, *The Girl That Went Astray* (1902), reverses the tables on the young prostitute, who is now the victim. A pimp assaults a young street walker just as her aged parents, who have apparently been out searching for her, finally locate their daughter. The father is thrown to the ground as the girl is dragged off by the pimp. The mother faints in horror, as a police officer nonchalantly swinging his nightstick passes by and is oblivious to the turmoil that has just transpired.

An artist, seeking a model for his next painting, visits night court, where he hires streetwalker Bessie Barriscale, who has been arrested for soliciting, to pose for him in Scott Sidney's realistic drama, *The Painted Soul* (1915). He has just finished a portrait titled "The Painted Soul" and wants the young woman for his next portrait, "The Fallen Woman." The first painting inspires her to reform, for even she admits to a fellow prostitute, "This is a hell of a life." When he completes the picture, the artist pays her, and they both suddenly realize they have fallen in love with each other. They embrace and kiss. But when his mother arrives, she explains this romance could never be. The young woman leaves while her lover grieves for her. The mother locates her and pleads for her son's happiness. "Marrying you," she states, "would make him a social outcast." The reformed Barriscale puts on her former clothes and deliberately reverts to her life on the street, where she unknowingly propositions a detective. After her arrest, she sends the artist a telegram. In the courtroom she pleads guilty in his presence. After he pays her fine, he shakes her hand for the last time, saying, "Goodbye." At night, she secretly visits the studio for a last look at her portrait of "The Fallen Woman."

Clara Kimball Young portrays the famous title character, a beautiful, consumptive courtesan, who has a stormy and compassionate love affair with a young lawyer, in Albert Capellani's competent romantic drama, *Camille* (1915), based on the popular drama by Alexandre Dumas. After leading a gay and carefree life with a variety of lovers, Camille falls seriously in love with Armand (Paul Capellani), whose father protests the relationship. He persuades her to leave his son, whose career and life would otherwise suffer. She agrees and returns to her former lover, a count. The young lawyer now believes Camille loves the count. When he learns the truth about his father's intervention, he rushes to Camille, who is now stricken with consumption. They embrace, pledging their love for each other, as she dies in his arms. Several foreign and American screen versions of Dumas's masterpiece have graced the screen over the years: in 1917 with Theda Bara, in 1921 with Nazimova, and in 1937 with Greta Garbo.

Nihilism, the Russian secret police, persecution and the massacre of Jewish people are all woven into Edwin August's stirring drama, *The Yellow Passport* (1916). The title refers to a Russian passport granted to prostitutes. Clara Kimball Young, a voice student and daughter of a wealthy Russian Jewish family, has John Sainpolis, a police spy posing as a valet, fired when he tries to rape her. The vindictive Sainpolis incites an anti-Semitic group to attack Young's house, resulting in the death of her parents. She is allowed to pursue her music studies only if she accepts a yellow passport, which labels her as a prostitute. Finally forced to leave the country, she and her uncle travel to America, where they meet a famous impresario and his son, Edwin August. The young couple eventually become engaged. Sainpolis also arrives in America and exposes Young as receiving the yellow passport under false pretenses. Her fiancé denounces her, but two of her Russian friends prove her innocence, and the couple are finally reunited.

Robert Warwick, as a struggling author, would rather go to jail than tarnish the reputation of a dead friend, in Harley Knoles's drama, *The Supreme Sacrifice* (1916). His close friend, reverend Vernon Steele, had had a mistress during his college days. The mistress, Christine Mayo, who has become a prostitute, later blackmails the reverend, a settlement house worker in the slums and now in charge of the institutional funds. To meet her demands, he borrows this money, intending to pay it back when he sells some stock. But the market crashes and his stocks prove worthless. The reverend suffers a heart attack and dies. Warwick, the executor of Steele's estate, covers up his friend's theft and is accused of stealing the money. Rather than taint his friend's memory, he says nothing and is sentenced to four years in prison. His experience behind bars proves invaluable toward his writing career, for he learns more about life by associating with his fellow inmates than he had ever known. After succeeding as a writer, he proposes to a young woman who has always believed in his innocence.

A hardworking and devoted wife, who because of circumstances forced upon her, turns to prostitution, in Edmund Lawrence's effective drama, *The Scarlet Woman* (1916). Olga Petrova, as the unfortunate wife, manages to rehabilitate herself and straighten out her life. She remarries a decent man and is leading a happy life, when suddenly her past returns to haunt her and threaten her second marriage. But this time, although forced out into the street, she does not resort to her past means of existence. Instead, she finds a job which, although hard, keeps her on a moral path. She is soon reconciled with her forgiving husband.

Alma Hanlon, a struggling working girl, has a choice between a hardworking man she really loves and a wealthy libertine, in Julius Steger and Joseph A.

Golden's familiar drama, *The Libertine* (1916). The young woman, who works in a cloak house, chooses to become the mistress of John Mason, the libertine. Following several complications, Hanlon, who expected a life of ease and luxury, faces a chain of adversities. Her ill fortunes lead to her taking her own life. However, the cop-out ending shows that the entire story was just a dream by the cloak worker who in reality has accepted the love of the working man as her mate for the rest of her life.

Courtesan Eugenie Forde arranges through an intermediary to support her lawyer son, Hal Cooley, who believes both his parents are dead, in Arthur Maude's domestic drama, *The Courtesan* (1916). The lawyer's father had abandoned the family years earlier. When a crooked politician wants his son, William Carroll, to run for district attorney, Cooley challenges him for the office. Carroll, who wants to discredit his opponent, learns about Cooley's mother's past and exposes the story. Cooley wins the election, but he loses his fiancée because of the resultant scandal. When the loser's father arranges for a recall, the intermediary learns that the political boss is really Cooley's father. His mother suffers a heart attack, the politician's career comes to an end, and Cooley's fiancée returns to him.

Newspaper reporter Stella Razeto and editor William Wister Jefferson threaten a political candidate with exposing his wife's hidden past unless he drops out of the race in William Desmond Taylor's early domestic drama, *Out of the Wreck* (1917). William Conklin, who is running for a senate seat, learns from his two visitors that his wife had earlier been involved in a murder case in another city. Kathlyn Williams, Conklin's wife, enters and explains her tale by way of a series of flashbacks. Left an orphan, she had been befriended by alcoholic William Clifford, whom she agreed to marry as a reward for his kindness. When his drinking problem resulted in their extreme poverty, he insisted she turn to prostitution to raise money. He threatened her with a pistol that she then uses to defend herself. Her trial resulted in her acquittal, after which she engaged in missionary work, where she met her present husband. Upon hearing her tragic tale, the two journalists decide not to publish the story.

Smalltime actress Clara Kimball Young falls for the life of ease and luxury when she indulges in a night of orgies in Albert Capellani's absorbing drama, *The Easiest Way* (1917), based on the play by Eugene Walter. She stays the night with wealthy Joseph Kilgour, and becomes his mistress. In Denver, as "a third-rate actress with a first-class man backing her," she meets Rockcliffe Fellowes and falls in love with him. Back in New York, she is once again drawn to her former wild crowd of partygoers. "Doll me up, Annie," she announces to her maid. "I'm going over to the Montmarte and to hell." She goes to the Montmarte, where she sees Fellowes, who leaves in disgust. He then sees her entering a taxi with an elderly lascivious escort who keeps trying to embrace her. She exits from the taxi and sits on a park bench, envisioning to herself her future as a streetwalker. She proceeds to a dock and jumps into the water. Fellowes is notified and arrives to read a farewell note she has left for him.

Unfortunately, he arrives too late. He kneels at her cot and watches her slip away from life.

S. Rankin Drew's hard-hitting social drama, *Who's Your Neighbor?* (1917), makes a plea for cities to segregate the prostitutes and other similar types from the morally straight and law-abiding citizens to their own sections. When a new law banning red light districts forces streetwalker Christine Mayo to seek shelter in a residential section, she befriends William Sherwood, a devoted churchgoer, who lends her his apartment. Later, when she invites a group to her apartment, including the churchman's son and daughter, the father suddenly appears and is shocked to find his children in such company. He now understands the error of the reformers in closing down the segregated districts.

A poor scrubwoman suffers a series of tragedies in Robert Vignola's drama of maternal love, *The Love That Lives* (1917). Her husband, a loafer and gambler, is shot to death in a dice game, and one of her children is run over by a car. Pauline Frederick is now left alone to raise her reckless son, who is turning into a carbon copy of his father. A successful broker whose office she cleans offers her a life of luxury and ease, but she rejects this – until she realizes what little chance her son Jimmy will have in life. So she accepts the man's proposition and sends her son off to a technical school. Years later, following an argument with the broker, she leaves him and begins frequenting different dives. Her son, meanwhile, becomes a firefighter and falls in love with a stenographer. His mother, realizing how low she is sinking, decides to start earning her own living once again. She is rehired as a scrubwoman. Her son has lost track of his mother. Meanwhile, his girlfriend is hired by the same man who had led the mother to ruin. When he tries to rape the young woman in his office, the mother comes to her rescue by stabbing the broker in the back. Suddenly, a fire breaks out and Jimmy enters to rescue his fiancée. The mother perishes in the flames. "I saved them both," she says. "It isn't much, but I owed it to Jimmy."

Wealthy American Irving Cummings persuades Spanish courtesan Kitty Gordon to return with him to the States, where he sets her up in her own Southern estate, in Frank Crane's hokey drama, *The Scar* (1919). As soon as she settles in to her new home, she begins an affair with Cummings's best friend, David Herbin. Cummings catches them together and, following a tempestuous scene, his mistress feigns that Cummings has shot her. He is imprisoned, while she moves in with Herbin. Soon growing tired of her new lover who has lost his fortune, she moves on to a string of different men. Upon his release, Cummings marries a respectable young woman whom he fails to tell about his past. Gordon, still seeking revenge, tries to break up the marriage but fails. She ends up losing her mind and is institutionalized.

II. The Scars of Immorality

Dramas about prostitution continued to be popular throughout the twenties, with some famous works, such as W. Someret Maugham's story "Rain" and

Eugene O'Neill's play *Anna Christie* serving as sources for several silent and sound versions. Most of these films simply were conventional romantic dramas that the Hollywood studios turned out with such efficiency and regularity. The familiar plot devices about a wife's sacrifice remained popular, as in *Burnt Wings* (1920). Also popular were domestic dramas, such as *Hoodman Blind* (1924), which showed how the daughter of a neglectful father could end up in the streets. As the films of the twenties improved generally in setting, camera techniques, photography and lighting, those dealing with the sleazy lives of prostitutes and their johns were particularly filmed more realistically. However, as in the dramas of the previous decade that dealt with streetwalkers, the image of women changed little, for they still bore the scars of immorality and crime associated with their profession, while the men who used them, chiefly for their own ends, were usually exonerated of any responsibility.

Struggling artist Frank Mayo marries Betty Blythe, his model, who soon foolishly commits an indiscretion, in J. Christy Cabanne's simple and familiar romantic drama of infidelity, *Burnt Wings* (1920). She has an affair with a rich man when her husband gets sick and they have no money for food. Eventually, Mayo succeeds as an artist and develops a reputation in social circles. Lois Wilson, the wealthy man's daughter, is attracted to the artist and begins to fall in love with him. To satisfy his daughter's desire, her father tries to entice the wife with a huge sum of money to leave her husband so that his daughter can marry him. But the artist intervenes in an attempt to save his marriage. "You have everything," Mayo says to the daughter. "She has only me." He then returns to his wife.

Blanche Sweet portrays the title character, a Chicago streetwalker who has earlier run away from her brutal farm life in Minnesota, in John Griffith Wray's absorbing drama, *Anna Christie* (1923), based on the 1922 play by Eugene O'Neill. Tired and disillusioned, she visits her father, an old skipper now living in New York City, who knows nothing of her past experiences in the Windy City. She longs for a little peace and some shelter. He invites her to stay with him on his coal barge. She meets William Russell, a sailor, and, to her father's regret, falls in love with him. He intended to keep her free of men who make their living at sea. The two men begin to argue about Anna's future, and she interrupts them, informing the two about her sordid past. The two men, wounded and upset by her confession, leave quietly, but they returns in a few days to reconcile their differences with her. Greta Garbo starred in a 1930 talking remake of O'Neill's work.

Gladys Hulette plays a dual role in John Ford's domestic drama, *Hoodman Blind* (1924), based on the play by H. A. Jones and Wilson Bartlett. She portrays two daughters of different mothers and the same father, Marc McDermott, a wanderer who ends up in South Africa. McDermott abandoned his wife and daughter, living in a small town, and traveled to the West, where he married, had a second daughter, and once more abandoned his family to journey to Africa. Years later, with his two wives dead and his second daughter now a prostitute, McDermott returns home. He discovers that the money he had sent a friend to support the second daughter was never given to her. Following a series of complications and hardships faced by both the father and his two children, he is finally reunited with his two daughters. Director John Ford was a popular filmmaker during the silent era, but gained his greatest reputation during the sound era, especially with his series of westerns, beginning with his classic, *Stagecoach* (1939), with John Wayne.

A husband's neglect of his wife forces her to seek attention elsewhere in Cecil B. DeMille's bland domestic drama, *The Fast Set* (1924), based on the play, *Spring Cleaning*, by Frederick Lonsdale. Betty Compson, as the neglected wife who is bored with her husband's inattentiveness, joins a group of fast-living, carefree acquaintances, including Adolphe Menjou, a professional womanizer. Menjou is attracted to Compson and hopes to conquer her. Her husband, Elliott Dexter, meanwhile, becomes aware of his wife's activities and personal interest in Menjou. Dexter, who personally despises the amorality of his wife's friends, deliberately invites them to a dinner party that includes streetwalker ZaSu Pitts, whose presence makes the other guests uneasy. "I never heard of an amateur billiard player," he announces sardonically to his uncomfortable dinner guests, "refusing to play with a professional." Later, Dexter and Menjou discuss the best way the former could win back his wife. Dexter finally accomplishes his goal, and the couple embrace.

When the parents of both Enid Bennett and Ramön Navarro refuse to allow them to marry, the young couple run away from home and go to Paris, in Fred Niblo's romantic drama, *The Red Lily* (1924), about lost and found love. Once in the city, the two lovers become separated. Navarro, the mayor's son, becomes a petty thief, and Bennett, to survive, turns into a woman of the streets. They meet again years later, but he is arrested and sent to prison. When he is released he returns to her and finds she is a changed person.

The trials and tribulations of a struggling young voice student in a big city are explored in Phil Rosen's conventional drama, *This Woman* (1924), based on the novel by Howard Rockey. Irene Rich, as the young student, visits a cheap cabaret with a fellow roommate of their boarding house. Her friend, a known streetwalker, has saved the impoverished student from committing suicide earlier in the evening. Following a police raid, the two innocent companions are arrested and serve thirty days in jail. After her release, the student joins an organ grinder, singing along with his music, until a music teacher hears her and, impressed with her singing, offers to give her voice lessons. Later, she meets a respectable young man, a member of society, and the couple fall in love. Curious about her past, the young man learns about her jail sentence and breaks off their relationship. Ironically, it was his wealthy brother who had given false testimony at her trial to protect his own presence at the cabaret. Disheartened, she returns to the music teacher and marries him.

Robert Agnew, a petty thief, and Viola Dana, a streetwalker, fall in love and vow to go straight in Marshall Neilan's low-budget routine drama, *Wild Oats*

Lane (1926). Dominating the film is the central figure of Father Kelly (John MacSweeney), a portly fatherly parish priest who is devoted to helping the fallen and downtrodden of the city. It is in his district that he meets and tries to help the young couple who depend on each other for support. In an early and especially realistic sequence, Agnew undergoes a terrible ordeal at the hands of the police, who give the thief the "third degree," with their victim sweating and squirming under a bright light as he tries to avoid their questions and accusations. Among the officers in a plainclothesman who keeps an eye on the young couple as they try to reform. Another absorbing sequence is a police raid on a prostitution camp.

Another unlikely pair of lost souls find sustenance in each other's company, but without the police ordeal, in Hugh Dierker's routine drama, *Camille of the Barbary Coast* (1925). When a young man knowingly serves a jail sentence because of a woman, his disappointed father disowns him. After serving several years, Owen Moore, the unfortunate young man, is finally freed and drifts into a Barbary Coast dive. Here he meets prostitute Mae Busch, who takes him in and helps to rehabilitate him. Moore, after undergoing a complete regeneration, gets a job, but he is dismissed when his prison record is revealed to his employer. By his next job, he reclaims his self-respect, and his father, noticing the change in him, invites him back to the family home – but without the presence of the woman who had helped him to reform. Moore opts to stay with Camille, who deeply loves him. Once the father realizes how the couple need and depend upon each other and how much they are in love, he relents and accepts both as part of his family.

A young woman is called upon by the U.S. Secret Service to uncover a spy in Joseph C. Boyle's World War I sea drama, *Convoy* (1927), based on the 1923 novel, *The Song of the Dragon,* by John Tainter Foote. It seems that someone, in league with foreign agents, is leaking transport departures to the enemy. Dorothy Mackaill is asked to stay with the suspected agent day and night. At one point, her brother and her fiancé find her in the spy's apartment, and naturally, they suspect the worst. Her fiancé, Lawrence Gray, immediately breaks off their engagement, and her family disowns her. The spy, Lowell Sherman, is finally arrested. When Mackaill goes to the Navy Yard to find her brother, she is arrested as a prostitute and sentenced to a year in jail. During the course of the war, her brother is killed in action. At his funeral, she meets her fiancé, and the couple are reunited after he discovers the truth about her affaire d'amour with Sherman.

Gloria Swanson, as the blowsy title character, tries to escape her shady past on an island in the South Seas in Raoul Walsh's pulsating drama, *Sadie Thompson* (1928), based on the short story by W. Somerset Maugham and the play by John Colton and Clemence Randolph. Stranded on the island of Pago Pago, she falls in love with Sergeant O'Hara (Raoul Walsh), a robust, virile U.S. Marine, but tyrannical reformer Alfred Atkinson (Lionel Barrymore) intervenes in the romance. Obsessed with the subject of immorality, the self-righteous Atkinson attacks her for her past life as a prostitute and threatens to expose her to the island authorities. "Don't resist," he orders, "I'm only trying to save your soul." Under pressure, she submits to Atkinson's strong will to repent. She reforms – only to be seduced by him. He finally commits suicide, and Sadie Thompson and her lover leave for Australia to begin a new life together. Other adaptations of the sin-sex-and-salvation story include the sound versions *Rain* (1932), with Joan Crawford, and *Miss Sadie Thompson* (1953), with Rita Hayworth in the starring role. *Dirty Gertie from Harlem, USA* (1946), a low-budget adaptation with an all-black cast, featuring Francine Everett in the title role, was loosely based on the original story.

Prostitute Marceline Day, after ditching a wealthy yacht owner, seeks refuge with alcoholic derelict Don Alvarado in Christy Cabanne's island drama, *Driftwood* (1928), based on the story by Richard Harding Davis. She leaves the yacht, intending to stay on an island that is largely owned by the man from whom she is fleeing. When she rejects the advances of the owner's aide, he threatens to have her deported on the basis of lacking any means of visible support. She then hastily marries Alvarado. Eventually, the couple fall in love – in spite of several complications. The film has elements of W. Somerset Maugham's popular short story "Rain."

Lon Chaney, a Limehouse magician who is paralyzed in both legs following a fight with ivory trader Lionel Barrymore, meets his foe again in Africa, in Tod Browning's thriller, *West of Zanzibar* (1928). Barrymore had stolen Chaney's wife (Jacqueline Gadsden) years earlier. Over the years, Chaney, now an ivory thief, took possession of Barrymore's daughter (Mary Nolan) and raised her in his jungle retreat, training her to become a prostitute. When the two enemies meet again in the jungles of Africa, Chaney has Barrymore killed by his voodoo-crazed natives. But before he dies, the trader reveals that the young blonde woman is really Chaney's own daughter. Later, as a sign of redemption, Chaney sacrifices his own life to allow his daughter to escape with Warner Baxter, an alcoholic doctor, whom the young woman has regenerated with her love.

George Bancroft, a stoker on a tramp steamer, saves Betty Compson's life, when she tries to commit suicide, in Josef von Sternberg's drama, *The Docks of New York* (1928). Compson, a waterfront hooker, grows weary of her sleazy life. Bancroft, on eight hours' leave, gets drunk and ends up marrying Compson, the ceremony performed by a local missionary worker. In the morning, he returns to his ship. When a fellow engineer tries to attack Compson, his wife kills him and Compson is charged with the murder. But the real killer confesses. Bancroft, once aboard the steamer as it is leaving the harbor, realizes he loves Compson. He jumps overboard and swims to shore. His wife, meanwhile, has been arrested for stealing some clothes that Bancroft had given her for the marriage ceremony. He admits to the theft and is sentenced to sixty days in jail. Before he leaves to serve his time, he promises his wife he will return to her.

Streetwalker Corinne Griffith, after being evicted from her San Francisco boarding house and left with only three dollars, meets the drunken socialite Edmund Lowe, in William A. Seiter's romantic drama, *Outcast* (1928), based on the 1914 play by Hubert Henry Davies. Lowe, who is suffering from a broken heart, finds Griffith charming and takes her to the church where his former fiancée, Kathryn Carver, is about to marry the rich Claude King. Growing fond of his new friend, Lowe rents her an apartment. She has quietly fallen in love with him. Suddenly, his former sweetheart returns to him and lures him back into a romance. Griffith resigns herself to returning to her life as a woman of the pavements, but can't bring herself to be with any other man since falling for Lowe. She then proves to the man she loves that Carver is interested only in his money. When Lowe realizes the truth, he embraces Griffith.

A stoker, a prostitute and a stowaway are the only three survivors of a shipwrecked tramp steamer in Fred Myton's low-budget drama, *The Singapore Mutiny* (1928). Ralph Ince, as the stoker in charge of the black gang aboard the steamer, dislikes Estelle Taylor, a Broadway hooker and the only woman aboard the vessel. He continually thrusts insults her way. She is seeking refuge on any South Pacific island – far away from her past life. When the ship hits a derelict and sinks, only these two and James Mason, a stowaway, manage to escape. Taylor and Mason, two of society's outcasts, find much in common and begin to fall in love. The trio soon run out of water. Ince, aware of the romantic complication and the desperate situation confronting them, purposely drowns himself so that the pair of lovers have a better chance of surviving.

A prostitute serves her country in Henry King and Sam Taylor's romantic drama, *The Woman Disputed* (1928), based on the novel by Denison Clift. The film is set in Austria chiefly during World War I. Norma Talmadge portrays a woman of the streets whom an Austrian and a Russian officer decide to salvage. They set her up as a respectable woman, both eventually falling in love with her. She chooses the Austrian officer (Gilbert Roland). The Russian (Arnold Kent) is left only with hatred for Roland. Kent then leads a Russian invasion of the Austrian town and captures a spy masquerading as a priest. Kent promises to release the priest if Talmadge willingly gives herself to him. When she refuses, the spy convinces her that his escape will help deliver vital information to the Austrians. She reluctantly surrenders herself to Kent. After the Austrians retake the town, Roland learns about her affair with Kent and treats her with contempt. But when he discovers the truth from the dying Kent about her patriotic sacrifice, he forgives her.

Red Scare

I. The Bolsheviks and the Palmer Raids

The advent of the Communist Revolution in Russia in 1917 stirred up an international wave of fear in Western capitalist countries. To the general public in the United States, anarchists and Communists were linked together as violent, anti-American bomb throwers. A number of bombs were thrown during the course of some fierce strikes in the post-World War I years. As a result, public opinion was ready to support anti-Red legislation. Chief of Staff General Leonard Wood asserted that Bolsheviks be deported in "ships of stone with sails of lead, with the wrath of God for a breeze and with hell for their first port." Attorney General A. Mitchell Palmer led a national drive to incarcerate Communist radicals. During the course of the campaign, Palmer's Washington home was bombed. In part, Palmer once described many of these radicals as follows: "Out of the sly and crafty eyes of many of them leap cupidity, cruelty, insanity, and crime; from their lopsided faces, sloping brows, and misshapen features may be recognized the unmistakable criminal type." Eventually, about 6,000 suspected Red agitators were arrested. Of these, 250 were deported to Russia. Various states joined the anti-Red crusade. Legislation was passed to prohibit the use of violence as a political weapon. The American film industry used the Red Scare of 1919-1920 for various plots, ranging from drama to comedy. Although most of these films were based on fiction, they served to reinforce in the moviegoer his or her own perceptions of the Communists. However, even before the Red Scare, American films about revolution and terrorism trickled out of the studios. Biograph's *The Nihilists* (1905) – filmed in New Jersey – told of members of an aristocratic family in Russian Poland who were enmeshed in political revolution. In Edwin S. Porter's *Russia, Land of Oppression* (1910), made chiefly on Staten Island, depicted a Cossack raid on a Jewish village. *The Girl Nihilist* (1908), set in Russia, was filmed on Ellis Island. Political intrigue and bomb throwing dominated *Lost in Siberia* (1908), a drama whose low production values were attacked by critics. The same fate fell upon *A Russian Heroine* (1910). These earlier films about nihilists who were generally portrayed sympathetically, differed chiefly in this respect from the later Red Scare releases.

Incidents of bomb throwing appeared on screen even earlier than the years of the Red Scare. In Edwin August's drama, *The Bomb Throwers* (1915), local Communists threaten the life and family of an honest district attorney. After one of their members, a dangerous terrorist, is jailed through the efforts of the attorney, the remainder of the gang seeks revenge. They convince a local Italian immigrant widower that the attorney was responsible for his wife's death. They hand him a bomb to be placed under the home of their victim. The man discovers in time that the terrorists have lied to him. He tosses the bomb at a shed where they are hiding, thereby killing the gang and saving the targeted family. The film gained unexpected publicity at the time of its release. Newspapers were carrying sensational stories of a Communist conspiracy to blow up St. Patrick's Cathedral in New York City. A live bomb was actually found inside the church. Several suspects were arrested and convicted.

Christy Cabanne's *Sold for Marriage* (1916) reveals a dark side of the low status of Russian civilized life. In prerevolutionary Russia, A. D. Sears and Pearl Elmore, the guardians of Lillian Gish, their niece, plan to sell her by marrying her off, but she resists them. When she is threatened by the police chief (Walter Long), who tries to molest her, she is forced to strike him to effect her escape. Thinking she has killed him, she and her family escape to America, with the Cossacks in full pursuit. Once in Los Angeles, her uncle again tries to make money by offering Gish for sale in the Russian colony, whose men are willing to pay a high price for young women. Her lover (Frank Bennett) from the old country, who has also journeyed to America, rescues her in the nick of time as she is about to be sold to an elderly admirer.

William C. de Mille's drama, *The Sowers* (1916), about revolutionaries in prerevolutionary Russia, was adapted from the 1895 novel by Henry Seton Merriman. Blanche Sweet and her boyfriend, Prince Paul (Thomas Meighan), belong to an illegal Russian league bent on improving the lot of the Russian peasants. When the czar orders the prince to marry Helena, he at first hesitates, then agrees – at the request of Sweet. She believes that their group may benefit from the alliance. Besides, she explains, they must be willing to make personal sacrifices for the cause. Following a series of intrigues, including the exposé of the prince as a revolutionary, Princess Helena dies and Sweet and Meighan flee Russia, after realizing the country is not prepared to accept social revolution. Raymond Hatton, a popular character actor in both silent and sound films, portrays a peddler.

The International Workers of the World figured in several films of the period. J. Stuart Blackton's patriotic World War I drama, *Safe for Democracy* (1917), describes a variety of slackers – Americans shirking their duty either as soldiers or workers in war-related jobs. It also presents a story filled with intrigue as members of the I.W.W., a radical union of the period, initiate a bomb plot. Blackton, who also produced the film, interjects newsreel footage between the fictional scenes, thereby adding a sense of authenticity to the production. In the end, the men realize their responsibilities to the war effort and join the fight. The theme of the film was suggested by a remark made by a contemporary military leader. "Work or fight!" General Crowder demanded of the citizenry. Blackton's attack on members of the I.W.W., whose leaders he equated with alien agents, casts the drama more in the form of an anti-union tract than as a patriotic tale. The film was retitled *Life's Greatest Problem*.

Robert Frazer, a young captain recently returned from France after World War I, meets and falls in love with Pinna Nesbit, a Socialist who influences his political thinking, in Harley Knoles's social drama, *Bolshevism on Trial* (1919), based on Thomas Dixon's 1909 novel, *Comrades*, a satire on Upton Sinclair's social experiment in New Jersey. They participate in an ideal colony in a summer hotel on a Florida island. A crowd joins them, but they soon reject their leader, who puts them to work. They replace him with Leslie Stowe, a man who declares a Bolshevist regime and announces his divorce from his wife. At a meeting, with a wall poster that reads: "The Lamp That Will Light the World: Socialism," Stowe pleads for funds to purchase the island. His plans for the colony include the abolition of religion and marriage. His romantic interest is now aimed at Nesbit, whom he pursues until Frazer and his chauffeur rescue her from Stowe's clutches. A U.S. warship arrives nearby and Stowe, along with the other plotting Bolsheviks, is taken into custody. An officer orders his men to take down the red flag, and Frazer's father replaces it with the American flag, inciting the sailor to cheer.

A controversial propaganda drama about a Communist conspiracy, George Irving's *The Volcano* (1919) concerns bomb plots, Red agitators and a New York schoolteacher-heroine who becomes embroiled with the conspirators. Leah Baird portrays the teacher who naïvely joins the Communist movement in hopes of bettering the lives of children on New York's Lower East Side. Suspended from her job by the superintendent, she is convinced by Jacob Kingsbury, one of the leaders of the agitators, to join the group. The U.S. Secret Service assigns Edward Langford, an army captain, to investigate the growing Communist threat in the area. He visits Baird's home to tell her that her brother, who had saved the captain's life during World War I, is returning. Meanwhile, he falls in love with her. The Communist leader, jealous of the blossoming romance, incites Baird against the captain, leading to a plot to assassinate him along with Governor Alfred E. Smith, Attorney General Palmer, and others. However, Baird's brother and a handful of other soldiers appear and disrupt the conspiracy. She realizes her mistake and marries the captain. The film was a timely one, since New York City had undergone a bomb scare that resulted in a sensational trial. Controversy plagued the production from the beginning. Local Jewish newspapers labeled it anti-Semitic. The studio was forced to alter some of the dialogue in the title cards and characters' names. The hero, a captain in the secret service, was given a more Jewish-sounding name – Nathan Levison. Alexis, a major villain, explains that he is not a Jew but a Bolshevik. Several important political figures who had previously endorsed the film withdrew their support, including Franklin Delano Roosevelt, then Assistant Secretary of the Navy, and Governor Smith. The latter, however, appeared in a cameo role in which he signed a bill prohibiting the display of the red flag.

Dorothy Phillips portrays a Russian spy who is sent to America to stir up industrial unrest in Allen Holubar's anti-Bolshevik drama, *The Right to Happiness* (1919). Raised as a revolutionary by a Russian peasant family, in reality she is the lost daughter of an American millionaire. During the turmoil of a pogrom years earlier, the American, residing near Petrograd at the time, was able to save only one of his daughters, thinking the other had perished in a fire. Phillips arrives in the States and begins instigating the workers of her own father's factory, unaware of her relationship to him. She is ultimately killed by a gunshot while protecting her sister from a frenzied mob.

Russian agents spread dissent and propaganda among Americans in the hope of eventually bringing about a world revolution in Wilfred North's anti-Communist drama, *The Undercurrent* (1919). Guy Empey portrays a returning World War I veteran who joins a group of Bolsheviks. He soon grows disillusioned with the organization and denounces its cause. Betty Blythe, a Russian agent who, upon learning that the authorities are about to arrest her, shoots a fellow provocateur and then turns the weapon upon herself. Before making his screen debut in this film, Empey, a real-life war veteran, had gained a certain degree of popularity with the publication of *Over the Top*, a book about his war experiences.

The Red Scare managed to penetrate several popular film genres usually devoid of political controversy. In Lloyd Ingraham's comedy, *The Amazing Impostor* (1919), young and innocent Mary Miles Minter brings upon herself a series of misadventures aboard a train, involving jewel thieves, Bolshevik spies and the search for romance. Minter, the whimsical daughter of a chewing-gum mogul, dreams of a more romantic life in an effort to escape the reality of her father's mundane business. She meets a Russian countess during a train journey and is impressed by the aristocratic woman. The countess, however, actually is a jewel thief. Minter allows herself to be taken in by the bogus aristocrat and exchanges identities with her. The result of the switch is that Minter is chased by other thieves who want the jewels and by two Bolshevik agents who think she is carrying important documents. Meanwhile, Allan Forrest, an amateur sleuth, is attracted to her and tries to help her out of some of her predicaments. The culprits are arrested, Minter reveals her true identity and the young couple profess their love for each other.

In another comedy, Frank P. Donovan's *Bullin' the Bullsheviki* (1919), a young American woman journeys to Russia to wipe out Bolshevism. Marguerite Clayton portrays Lotta Nerve, the determined Yankee Joan of Arc who, along with two spies masquerading as a horse, decides to save the world from the

Bolsheviks. Once in Russia, she encounters Billy Ruge, a Trotsky-like leader who takes the pretty American visitor to a hotel room and begins to undress her. She resists his advances and sends her two agents to summon an army. Meanwhile, she steals his military plans. Lotta then reports to the battlefield and sends an ultimatum to Ruge that he and his followers take a bath and seek employment. Following a battle that claims most of the Bolsheviks, Ruge and his key staff surrender. They are court-martialed and shot – to the cheers of the troops and Lotta.

A young maid saves the lives of two world leaders in Elmer Clifton's spy comedy, *Boots* (1919). Dorothy Gish, as a servant at an old English inn, reads romantic novels to brighten her dull and cheerless life. She likes Richard Barthelmess, a young student who is a boarder at the inn. Unknown to her, in reality he is a Scotland Yard detective who has another guest, a sculptress, under surveillance. When Gish sees the student and the sculptress together, she grows disillusioned with her private world of romance and decides to get rid of all her novels. She takes them to the cellar, where she discovers an underground passageway that connects the inn to the rooms where President Wilson meets with King George. Meanwhile, Bolsheviks devise a plot to kill the two world leaders. Gish accidentally stumbles across the conspiracy, led by the sculptress, who is a Bolshevik. Gish manages to foil the assassination attempt, after which she marries the Scotland Yard investigator who professes his love for her. The title refers to Gish's name. Following the Russian Revolution, the British considered the Bolsheviks a potential threat. Britain's Intelligence service considered the Soviets the chief danger to the empire.

J. Searle Dawley's social drama, *Everybody's Business* (1919), attempted to combat the growing concern with Bolshevism in America by promoting Americanism. While the film warned of the dangers posed by Bolshevism, melodramatic incidents and a love story (Charles Richman and Alice Calhoun) helped to make this didactic work palatable to general audiences. According to at least one studio official, virtually every governor, mayor and other major American politician endorsed the film, which was also recommended by the National Security League and the American Legion chapter in Detroit. Much information about the entire product remains lost. H. C. Witwer converted the screenplay into a novel, which appeared in serialized form as a Sunday supplement in newspapers across the nation. Louis Weslyn helped to promote the film when he was contracted to write a song that would tie in with the theme and plot.

Private secretary Inez Marcel, after learning that her company's foreman, a Bolshevik, plans to blow up a ship, foils the plot with the help of her brothers, in the anti-Bolshevik social drama, *The Burning Question* (1919). An activist against Bolshevism had been aboard the targeted vessel. After the war, Marcel's younger brother, a U.S. Secret Service agent posing as a Bolshevik, learns of the organization's plot to overthrow the government. Following a series of complications, including the discovery of the younger brother's real identity and the capture of the brother and sister, Marcel's older brother and his former army buddies come to their rescue. The Catholic Art Association produced and released the film.

The evils of Bolshevism were also depicted in films set in revolutionary Russia. Geraldine Farrar, the daughter of an American engineer working in Russia, has always aspired to marry Lou Tellegen, a prince whose father has employed Farrar's father, in Frank Lloyd's drama, *The World and Its Woman* (1919). However, the prince marries an unfaithful baroness, while Farrar emerges as a popular opera singer. Tellegen renews his friendship with Farrar, but World War I interrupts their relationship and the prince goes to the front. He returns after the birth of Bolshevism and learns that both his wife and her lover have been killed. A Bolshevik, W. Lawson Butt, who desires Farrar, captures her and tries to convert her politically. Tellegen arrives in time to help her outwit Butt, and the pair escape to America, where they begin their new life together. The film was originally titled *The Golden Song*. Farrar, a popular contemporary opera singer and stage personality, performs Jules Massenet's opera *Thais* in the opera sequence.

During the Russian Revolution, Reds invade a ball given to celebrate the engagement of Russian princess Norma Talmadge and prince Pedro de Cordoba, in Chester Withey's overly dramatic *The New Moon* (1919), based on the story by H. H. Van Loan. The prince battles the mob and manages to escape with his princess. Later, they are separated, with Talmadge posing as a shopkeeper in a small village and the prince desperately trying to locate her. He finally joins her and the couple make their way to freedom across the border. Meanwhile, Bolshevik villains Charles Gerrard and Stuart Holmes pursue them. Probably the most startling element in the film is the Bolsheviks' decree that "it would be unlawful for a man to possess his wife alone, but that she would become public property." When the Reds gained control of Russia, American newspapers reported such events – evidently stimulating the imagination of writer Van Loan, who remarked, "Such a story . . . had never been equaled in history."

E. K. Lincoln, who is hired as a lumberjack by lumber and shipbuilding magnate John P. Wade, eventually foils a plot by a band of Bolsheviks intent on sabotaging a government contract for the construction of a fleet of special ships, in Ralph Ince's anti-Bolshevik drama, *Virtuous Men* (1919). Superior in intelligence to his fellow workers, Lincoln soon wins the confidence of his superiors and moves up to a position of trust. In dealing with some of the more pugnacious troublemakers, he is forced to control them by means of hand-to-hand combat. But his major foe is the villainous Robert W. Cummings, an outspoken Bolshevik and instigator among the men. Lincoln eventually resolves all these difficulties and wins the love of Grace Darling, the owner's daughter.

II. An Assault on Civil Liberties

After a bomb was thrown in Wall Street in 1920 that killed 38 people and wounded hundreds more, additional anti-Red pressure was brought to bear in state legislatures and by the federal government. Members of the I.W.W. (International Workers of the World) were prosecuted solely because they belonged to that radical union. In Chicago that same year, dozens of defendants were prosecuted in a single trial on charges of Bolshevism. All were convicted after a Department of Justice undercover agent testified that one of the defendants used an American flag to cover his toilet floor. By the end of 1920, the fear of Bolshevism subsided in the U.S. and Europe, and many of those arrested were released. Americans ignored Attorney General Palmer's warnings of imminent revolution. The callous treatment of dissenters during this period revealed the most extensive assault on civil liberties in the country's history. Palmer's report to Congress on American radicals showed his total inability to understand the fundamental liberties of Americans under the Bill of Rights. Palmer's punitive attitudes no doubt helped to incite the public against the rights of dissenters. Several films of the period referred to enemy aliens, Bolsheviks and plotters determined to agitate workers, assassinate political and industrial leaders and generally cause national turmoil. Virtually all of these releases were blatantly anti-labor and portrayed workers as dupes of radicals, as in *Dangerous Hours* (1920). Films did not generally show any sympathy for or understanding of dissenters or their causes. The films most likely reflected the mood of the country and the attitudes of the film studio bosses. But with the ebbing of the Red Scare during the twenties, fewer anti-Bolshevik films appeared on the nation's screens. Capitalist America was more interested in trading than in bashing. Leading the shift in propaganda was Hollywood's influential Cecil B. DeMille, who directed *The Volga Boatman* in 1926. The film softened the violence of the Bolsheviks while it emphasized the abuses of the Czar's regime.

Set during the post-World War I years, Fred Niblo's anti-Bolshevik propaganda drama, *Dangerous Hours* (1920), concerns Russian agents sent to the U.S. to foment industrial unrest. Lloyd Hughes portrays an unsuspecting American shipyard worker who is duped by Communist agitators, including foreign born Claire Du Brey, who pretends to love him. He finds himself attracted to her. Barbara Castleton, the owner of the threatened shipyard that she inherited from her father, is in love with Hughes. To further their own destructive ends, the Reds exploit Hughes's popularity among his fellow workers. But Hughes eventually gets wise to their purpose and turns against the revolutionaries. "You are not interested in humanity – but murder!" he exclaims. "We in America do not fight that way and what you say shall not be. This is America!" At first, he is beaten down, but he rises for his final confrontation with the Bolsheviks. When they plan to set off a bomb, he tosses it at them. The film ends with a group of happy workers evicting the remaining tarred-and-feathered agitators out of town. The painted title backgrounds by artist Irvin Martin reveal glaring representations of death and destruction.

Labor and management, after a violent struggle, finally learn to compromise and come together in Harley Knoles's anti-Bolshevik propaganda drama, *The*

Great Shadow (1920). The film depicts how Russian agents operate to incite tensions between capital and labor. The focus of the agitators' attentions is an American shipyard, where they instigate a major strike by thousands of workers. Tyrone Power portrays a labor leader who, during the shipyard strike, agrees to come to terms with management. Before this stage is reached, sequences depict thousands of dock workers striking, additional mob scenes, and a runaway team of horses that knocks down a child. In addition, other scenes show repugnant-looking Russian aliens instigating trouble among the workers. Representatives of labor and capital, aware that they must join forces against this common evil, agree to a moratorium between both camps for a period of one year, while wages are increased to meet the rising cost of living, with leaders of both factions working out the details that are advantageous to each side.

The anti-Bolshevik film occasionally turned to comedy, as in David Kirkland's *The Perfect Woman* (1920), in which Constance Talmadge makes herself unattractive so that misogynist Charles Meredith will hire her. He is helping the government to round up Bolshevists, who one evening enter his home, bind and gag him, and plant a bomb under his chair. His secretary rids herself of her disguise and lures the trio of terrorists off their guards. She then knocks each one senseless with a brass statue, thereby saving Meredith's life. Her courage and quick wit encourage him to discard his contempt for attractive women, and he proposes marriage to his secretary.

On the lighter side of anti-Bolshevik films released during 1920, Hugo Ballin's comedy, *Help Yourself* (1920), based on the story, "Trimmed with Red," by Wallace Irwin, pokes fun at some of the wealthy pillars of society who support kookie cults and pseudo-religious groups. Madge Kennedy, who is labeled by her fiancé's wealthy mother as a "shop girl," wins over her prospective mother-in-law by exposing a phony group of religionists who in reality are Bolsheviks. The rich woman's daughter, Helen Greene, has been taken in by its members who have her convinced that they, the religionists, are a worthy cause, and she becomes their financial sponsor. Kennedy, engaged to Joseph Striker, Greene's brother, proves to her that their leader, Sydney Vautier, is simply and greedily exploiting the rich and foolish sponsors for his own benefit. The mother then consents to her son's marriage to the bright and clever "shop girl."

Bolshevik agents pursue the ex-princess of a European country to New York in George Fawcett's romantic drama, *Little Miss Rebellion* (1920). Dorothy Gish portrays the title character, whose principality has been overthrown during a revolution. Escaping with the crown jewels and a faithful servant, she journeys to the U.S. for safety. Rebel forces at home order her assassination and want the valuable stones returned. The alien agents track her down to her humble apartment and, during their search, take her prisoner when she returns and tie up her personal bodyguard. They then proceed to pressure her into revealing the whereabouts of the jewels. A former U.S. serviceman, Ralph Graves, who had met her while he was stationed overseas, learns her address and arrives at her apartment in time to rescue her. Following his victorious battle with the culprits, the police burst in and march off with the Bolsheviks in custody. The plot concerning royal jewels may have been inspired by several stories circulating in Europe about the sale of the czar's diamonds.

H. B. Warner, the spoiled son of a wealthy father, works as a plumber for his uncle when he father disowns him, in Henry King's drama, *Uncharted Channels* (1920). He joins the union and soon discovers that another laborer, Bolshevik Sam De Grasse, who pretends to be sympathetic to the workers' cause, in reality is creating labor agitation. Warner prevents De Grasse and his cronies from cheating heiress Kathryn Adams out of thousands of dollars and simultaneously wins her love. She offers Warner the check instead, and he uses it to buy the factory and give the workers a raise. He then evicts the troublesome radicals.

Anarchists plan to cleanse society and thereby improve the world by murdering off wealthy industrialists in Wallace Worsley's intriguing drama, *The Ace of Hearts* (1921). The cabal, after deciding upon its next victim, uses a deck of cards for the selection of the assassin. Whoever receives the ace of hearts must perform the killing. Two members, Henry and John, both love Lillith, another member of the group. John gets the fatal card and agrees to plant a bomb under the table of the victim who happens to frequent the restaurant where John is a waiter. When he arrives at his job and sees his intended prey, he prepares to carry out his assignment, but notices that a young couple at an adjoining table will also be killed by the explosion. Placing human life above the aims of his secret society, he declines to activate the bomb. When his fellow conspirators learn of his failure, they vote to kill him. Henry, meanwhile, also has second thoughts as the cards are being dealt out. Disillusioned with the group and its destructive aims, he decides to set off the bomb in the meeting place, thereby killing off the entire society. Lon Chaney portrays Henry. Leatrice Joy plays Lillith.

The Red Scare also touched the crime genre. Russian agents, the U.S. Secret Service, a reformed criminal-hero and a Grand Duchess all play a role in Alan Crosland's drama of mystery and intrigue, *The Face in the Fog* (1922). A blind beggar slips a packet into the pocket of Boston Blackie (Lionel Barrymore), a former thief who is now an amateur detective The beggar is then cold-bloodedly murdered. Once at home, Blackie discovers that the contents consist of valuable jewels. A U.S. Secret Service agent, on the trail of the jewel thieves, enters into the plot. It seems that the jewels belong to Russian Duchess Seena Owen, who plans to use them to finance a campaign to overthrow the present Russian government. Agents of her country are bent on opposing her. The unfortunate beggar was one of her servants. Eventually, the foreign spies are rounded up, and Blackie returns the valuables to their rightful owner. The basis of the plot may have stemmed from a post-World War I incident in England involving the czar's diamonds. Russian agents allegedly sold the diamonds to subsidize a pro-labor newspaper in England. British intelligence agencies, virtually all of whom were infected at the time with a fear of Bolshevik subversion, were quick to investigate every suspicious move on the part of Russians residing in England.

Harrison Ford, an Englishman working as a chauffeur for a Russian nobleman, escapes during the Russian Revolution with a diary he has found on a dead Russian officer, in Harold Shaw's drama, *A Fool's Awakening* (1924), based on a 1912 novel by William John Locke. Ford discovers that the diary gives a detailed accounting of the officer's exciting adventures among the Bolshevists. Ford returns to England and continues to work as a chauffeur. Meanwhile, he begins to take up writing. When his works are steadily rejected by various publishers, he decides to use the material in the diary. He suddenly attains fame. He next poses as the dead officer and marries heiress Enid Bennett. But when she discovers the truth about her husband, she abandons him. Later, they meet again and decide to rekindle their relationship.

The Red Scare even intruded upon films about mythical kingdoms, which are generally apolitical. A beautiful young princess is to marry a doddering old king – until a handsome young duke and a revolution intervene – in Jack Conway's romantic drama, *The Only Thing* (1925), set in a mythical kingdom somewhere in the Balkans. English duke Conrad Nagel falls in love with bride-to-be Eleanor Boardman, whose duty it is to marry Edward Connelly, the aged king. Endangering his own life, Nagel finally appeals to her on the night before the wedding to run off with him. Although she admits her love for the Englishman, she refuses, citing her duty to her country. The next day, a revolution suddenly erupts, with the Reds taking control of the government. The death of the king releases the princess from any marital vows, but the new tribunal cries out for her death as well. Following a series of complications, Nagel and Boardman escape the turmoil by swimming to Nagel's yacht after they are thrown into the sea, and the former princess admits her love for the duke.

Russian peasant Einar Hanson, after spending seven years in prison for insulting Corinne Griffith, a grand duchess, is released and joins the Bolsheviks, in Svend Grade's romantic drama, *Into Her Kingdom* (1926), based on the 1925 story by Ruth Comfort Mitchell. The Reds are plotting to assassinate the imperial family. Hanson's former tutor and friend persuades him to leave Russia with Griffith and go to America. Although Griffith dislikes Hanson because of his low birth, she accompanies him to the New World, where they both settle in New Jersey as husband and wife. She works as a clerk in a local store, where she regales the neighborhood children with stories about a princess, using her own personal experiences for background material. Recognizing their different social backgrounds, Hanson decides to take her back to Russia. He works for the diplomatic service, giving its members historical information on aristocratic families. The duchess, meanwhile, now a mother, renounces her former title and is reunited with Hanson, the child's father.

An informal conference of diplomatic powers brings together assorted people who are involved in love, intrigue and murder in Marshall Neilan's obtuse drama, *Diplomacy* (1926), based on the 1878 play by Victorien Sardou. Neil Hamilton portrays an American diplomat who has lost an important document. Blanche Sweet plays his attractive wife. Possession of the coveted document results in one act of torture, one shooting and two murders of members of the diplomatic service. Matt Moore, masquerading as a buffoon, turns out to be a U.S. Secret Service agent who salvages the conference. Earle Williams portrays a British diplomat. Arlette Marchal, as a countess, is involved in selling political secrets to a baron, a reputed agent of the Bolshevik government. The film ends with a tribute to all secret service agents who protect and defend the integrity of international law and diplomacy. An earlier screen version of Sardou's play appeared in 1916.

Orphan Shirley Mason, as the title character, and John Harron, another orphan, are raised by a Jewish couple who run an East Side artificial flower factory, in Phil Rosen's drama, *Rose of the Tenements* (1926), based on the 1923 novel, *The Stumbling Herd*, by John A. Morosco. When the elderly couple die, they leave their business to Mason and Harron, the latter falling under the influence of a Bolshevik agitator and his sister, Valentina Zimina. When the couple protest America's entry into World War I against Germany, a crowd attacks them. Harron prevents the sister from throwing a bomb. A politician helps exonerate Harron from the riot, and he enlists in the army.

Seduction and Abandonment

I. Lure of the Innocent

As in the abandoned spouse cycle, many films about seduction and abandonment deal with generally naïve country girls lured by young men from the city to leave home and elope with them, only to face ruin and desertion. *Life's Cycle* (1910), *Redemption* (1914) and *The Girl at the Lock* (1914) exemplify this plot line. Occasionally, as in *The Haunting Fear* (1915), a film describes how a young country girl is taken advantage of only after she reaches the city and meets a roguish young man. Other entries increase the ruined young woman's problems by leaving her stranded with the seducer's baby, as in *Up From the Depths* (1915). In virtually all of these dramas, it is the woman who is seduced, abandoned and faced with shame and ruin, often to end up in seedy dives or, worse, the streets. Meanwhile, seldom is the man held responsible for the woman's plight, and just as rarely does he ever suffer moral or legal retribution. At times, a film will delve into vengeance from the hands of the woman, as in *The Moth and the Flame* (1915). The ruined victim shows up just as her seducer is about to marry another, at which time she publicly denounces him. In other films, albeit more rare, the revenge turns violent, as in *The Haunting Fear* A seduced woman stabs the man who has attacked her and then plans to abandon her. Still other productions, such as *In Life's Cycle* (1910), inject a note of morality by having the seducer, who is about to die, marry the woman he has ruined and left with his child, thereby making an honest woman of her and giving the child a name. Several of these earlier entries tend to lean toward the cautionary drama, as in *The Girl Who Doesn't Know* (1916), or suggest the allegorical approach, as in *The Love Victorious* (1914).

A young man, after being rejected by an artist he loves, goes on a vacation and meets a shepherdess in D. W. Griffith's familiar drama, *A Summer Idyl* (1910). She secures him a job on her father's farm as one of the field hands engaged in the haying and threshing. One evening, after work, he makes love to the young woman. Back in the city, the young man's friends worry about him, while the artist who rejected him has second thoughts. She obtains his address and writes to him, begging him to return to the city. By her second letter, which includes one of her perfumed cigarettes, the man is lured back to the artist. The country girl, who did not even receive a goodbye from her lover, finds the second letter and resigns herself to her loss. She then seeks comfort in her affectionate grandfather.

A young woman who has taken the wrong turn in life finally returns home to her father and brother in D. W. Griffith's domestic drama, *In Life's Cycle* (1910). She had run off to live with her lover, a heavy drinker who, while in his favorite saloon, falls and strikes his head against a railing. The fall proves fatal, just as the young woman arrives to bear him home. Before he dies, he manages to marry the woman he has wronged. Filled with unhappy memories, loneliness and poverty, she decides to return home, where her brother faithfully has been visiting their mother's grave.

A young woman runs off with a young man who has been boarding with her family in their country home in D. W. Griffith's drama, *Sunshine Sue* (1910). The couple lived together in the city, with no prospect of marriage for Sue. In addition, she experiences only sorrow from the affair. She finally returns to her home and family, the only place she has known any happiness.

Cleo Madison portrays another young woman who strays from the decent path of life in Wilfred Lucas's dramatic allegory, *The Love Victorious* (1914). Although she finds True Love, she stumbles into a life of iniquity after falling for Vanity. She finds herself relegated to a sleazy dive where she has to beg for a drink of liquor. During her fall, she learns that her mother has died of a broken heart. However, she is touched by Hope, who suggests that she can be redeemed by Pure Love regardless of her defiled past.

Once again, a country girl falls for the charms of a young man from the city in Herbert Brenon's overly familiar drama, *Redemption* (1914). After some time and the birth of a child, the husband turns them out. She takes the little girl and returns to her former country boyfriend. A fight breaks out between the two men, ending with the death of the city man, the imprisonment of the country bumpkin, and the death of the country girl. The child grows up and meets a fellow from the city who takes advantage of her innocence. Meanwhile, her mother's former country boyfriend is released from prison and learns about the seduction. The ex-convict, thinking about what had happened earlier to the girl's mother, kills the man from the city.

A country girl from the lock country loves a young man from the area – until she meets a visiting artist who paints her portrait – in Edgar Jones's romantic drama, *The Girl at the Lock* (1914). But the impoverished artist, who has enchanted Louise Huff, the young girl, during his visit, is forced by economic circumstances to abandon her and marry a wealthy young woman. When the country girl journeys to the city to see her portrait, the artist she thought loved her informs her he is engaged to another. She dashes from the house and falls into the arms of her former boyfriend from the locks. Together, they make a joyous pair of lovers.

An employer takes advantage of his stenographer and sets her up in her own apartment in Harry Myers's drama, *The Hard Road* (1915). Rosemary Theby, the young woman, who has been living in humble circumstances with her mother and sister, delights in this new arrangement and comfortable life. After a few months, her lover, Harry Myers, grows tired of her and evicts her. Meanwhile, her sister is happily married. Theby begins to descend morally, and several years later ends up as a streetwalker. She meets her sister, who brings her to her home, but her husband informs her they cannot board the poorly dressed sister because of their children. Overhearing the conversation, the sister leaves voluntarily. Wandering the streets, she stops at a mission where she sees a derelict. It is Myers, the man who turned her out. They enter the mission together, their arms embraced.

When artist's model Olga Petrova is betrayed by her lover, the artist, for the daughter of a wealthy man, she begins to descend on the crimson path, in the drama, *The Heart of a Painted Woman* (1915). A millionaire's son meets her, and when he offers her money, she tears it up, much to his bewilderment. Explaining that money should be better spent, he sends her a large check. When next they meet, she takes him on a tour of an orphan asylum, which she now heads. Meanwhile, the artist who had abandoned her has had numerous confrontations with his father-in-law, who ends up killing the artist. Petrova's wealthy young friend is convicted of the murder. Petrova traps the real murderer into a confession, and he is arrested by the police. She then joins the freed young man, and both realize their love for and dependence upon each other.

Stewart Baird, a scoundrel and womanizer, wrongs a young maiden whom he quickly abandons and ends up paying a high price for his actions, in Sidney Olcott's drama, *The Moth and the Flame* (1915), based on the 1898 play by Clyde Fitch. Irene Howley, the young woman whom he had seduced, shows up just when Baird is about to marry Adele Rey, another young and unsuspecting woman. The wedding services are ruined by the uninvited visitor who responds to the minister's question about anyone present who objects to the union. She publicly exposes and denounces her stunned seducer. The prospective bride, Rey, returns the wedding gifts and marries someone else. Baird humbly returns to Howley and their child.

Foreign settings sometimes enhanced an otherwise threadbare plot. England was usually the preferred country. The mother of Mabel Trunnelle, a young Englishwoman in love with a soldier, has arranged for her daughter to marry a lord, in Richard Ridgely's old-fashioned drama, *Shadows of the Past* (1915). But the otherwise decent soldier has thoughtlessly made his girlfriend pregnant. To make matters worse, he struck another man in a local bar who had insulted his girlfriend. When others falsely tell him the man he hit has died, he ships out, leaving only a note for Trunnelle, who has been packing in preparation for their elopement. She then learns he has died at sea. After she gives birth, her mother tells her the baby was born dead. She then prods her daughter to marry the wealthy lord, which she does. Her husband, discovering the truth about her illegitimate child, sends her away. Fifteen years pass before the lord, now wiser and lonely, asks her to come home. She returns and is reunited with her husband.

In J. Gordon Edwards's *Her Double Life* (1916), also set in England, Theda Bara portrays a young orphan who runs away from her adopted father after he tries to seduce her. Her experience with the next man in her life, Stuart Holmes, proves even less rewarding. He ruins her before she is able to flee from him. She volunteers to serve as a nurse in France during World War I. Posing as a refined woman, she returns to England as the niece of a wealthy family. But the real niece shows up, with Holmes, now a correspondent. Bara, accepted by the wealthy family, has fallen in love with the son of the clan, who is a minister. The marriage plans have been set when Holmes suddenly discloses Bara's past indiscretions. But the kind and gentle minister forgives Bara, aware that he could not spending the rest of his life without his loved one at his side.

Betty Nansen portrays Katusha, a young woman who visits the home of a countess, where she is seduced and abandoned by Prince Dimitri (William J. Kelly), in J. Gordon Edwards's romantic drama set in Russia, *A Woman's Resurrection* (1915), based on the novel, *The Resurrection,* by Leo Tolstoy. Several months later, Katusha, now deserted and with a child, loses the baby and is forced into the sordid life of a streetwalker. Arrested and accused of poisoning a man, she is sentenced to Siberia. Dimitri, her seducer, has been a member of her jury, and publicly admits he was responsible for her condition, but the sentence stands. He and his servant journey to Siberia, hoping to aid her. Following a series of humiliating experiences, Katusha is saved from a lascivious commander by Dimitri and his servant, but in the scuffle, she is mortally shot while trying to save Dimitri. Her death represents her resurrection. A more somber screen version of Tolstoy's impassioned novel was released in 1927, titled *The Resurrection*, with Rod LaRocque and Dolores Del Rio in the main roles.

At times, films depicted their vulnerable heroines as recent arrivals in this country – and easy prey for the lecherous ready to pounce. Valeska Suratt, as a young Russian immigrant, arrives in America and falls into the hands of Theodore Roberts, a corrupt contractor, in George Melford's absorbing drama, *The Immigrant* (1915). Unable to escape her impoverished condition, she unwillingly becomes his mistress – after he sexually attacks her the first night that he ostensibly employed her as his housemaid. When she threatens to escape, he promises to marry her. Meanwhile, Thomas Meighan, an engineer whom Suratt had met earlier during her voyage to the States, beats Roberts out of a contract to build a bridge. Roberts, vowing to ruin his rival, dynamites the dam, but in doing so, is killed. Although financially ruined for the moment, Meighan is determined to begin over, with Suratt as his wife.

Adventuress Anna Q. Nilsson, while vacationing, invites a naïve country girl to visit with her in the big city, in Robert Vignola's familiar drama, *The Haunting Fear* (1915). While enjoying the various restaurants and hotels, the young visitor, Alice Hollister, is charmed by a dapper playboy who convinces her of his love. He ends up wronging her, and she finds out the truth about his deception too late. Seeking revenge on her seducer, she stabs him and, thinking she has killed him, flees to a convent. Later, the fear that has haunted her – that she had taken his life – is lifted from her heart and mind, although she spends the remainder of her life as a nun.

Itinerant preacher Courtenay Foote, who wears the clothes of a religious leader only for the potential financial gain it can bring, wrongs a young woman in one of the towns he visits, in Paul Powell's drama, *Up From the Depths* (1915), based on the play by Charles Battell Loomis and Robert Stodard. Following his revival meeting, he persuades Gladys Brockwell, the naïve woman, to elope with him. Once they arrive in the city, he abandons her as he searches out other prospects. After she gives birth to his child, she seeks out ways to support herself and her baby. She finds work as an entertainer in a sleazy dance hall. Meanwhile, Foote has become a noted social leader and reformer who leads a raid on the same dive where Brockwell is employed. He recognizes the woman he had seduced earlier and is about to hit her when a drunken admirer of the entertainer intervenes and shoots the reformer. A local mission priest who is familiar with Brockwell's background attends to mortally wounded Foote and forces him to marry Brockwell before he dies.

Some films described the hard times single women face in a world where they are treated either as prey for depraved men or chattel for prospective husbands. Blanche Sweet, an innocent young woman fresh from a convent, is ruined by Edward Mackay, the treacherous Duke of Cluny, in Frank Reicher's drama, *The Secret Orchard* (1915), based on the novel by Agnes and Egerton Castle, and the play by Channing Pollock. After leaving the convent, Sweet visits her friend, Cleo Ridgely, where she meets the duke. After several meetings with him on the beach and in the moonlight, he tells her he must leave and promises her nothing in return for all she has given him. She later meets Carlyle Blackwell, a lieutenant in the U.S. Navy, who falls in love with her. When she says she cannot accept his proposal of marriage, he demands to know why. Eventually, he learns how the duke took advantage of her and then abandoned her. In a confrontation with the betrayer, Blackwell slaps him and a duel is arranged. The officer kills the duke, but Sweet does not readily accept Blackwell's proposal, explaining that she will at least think about it.

Nance O'Neil is seduced, betrayed and finally accused of infidelity and murder in Frank Powell's drama, *A Woman's Past* (1915), based on the play by Captain John King. O'Neil, an aspiring writer, is seduced by magazine editor Alfred Hickman, who later abandons her. She then marries Clfford Bruce, a captain in the army, who is later sent to the Philippines. His wife lives alone with their little son. Hickman, her former lover, returns and tries unsuccessfully to renew their relationship. Her father-in-law sees them embracing and sends her away. He then notifies his son of her presumed adultery. The distraught Bruce exposes himself to leprosy and spends several years in confinement. Meanwhile, his wife is accused of murdering Hickman. Her son, now a lawyer, defends her in court but loses the case. Bruce suddenly appears and confesses to the murder.

The cautionary drama became popular in the late 1910s. In Charles E. Bartlett's *The Girl Who Doesn't Know* (1916), for example, the moralistic preaching is so strong that virtually no audience could miss the warning to decent parents to see to it that their innocent daughters don't stray from "the straight and narrow path." Captions throughout the film underscore this. "Ignorance is a young girl's weakness," says one, followed by "knowledge is her strength." Another caption warns, "Ninety percent fall through ignorance." Marie Empress leaves her slum home and surroundings and goes to work for casino owner Robyn Adair, who uses her to cheat his customers. Disillusioned with her job and her life, she plans to kill herself, but R. Henry Grey, a kindly minister, rescues her and puts her up in his home. The young couple soon fall in love. Adair finds her and, attracted by the reverend's sister, tries to seduce her. He then informs the reverend of Empress's sleazy past. But when Grey witnesses his girlfriend persuading the reverend's sister not to be taken in by the casino owner, he forgives her and plans to marry her.

Worldly Frank Mills, in George Archainbaud's drama, *As Man Made Her* (1917), seduces schoolgirl Gale Kane and then sets her up as his mistress. Years later, he abandons her. She then decides to marry Edward Langford, his younger brother, a decent young man. When she eventually tells her husband the truth, he embraces her. In contrast, Mills's wife, upon learning of his past, evicts him from her home.

Kitty Gordon, as a poor young woman, struggles to lead a decent life in George Cowl's drama, *Her Hour* (1917). Early in the film, she is fired from her department store job when she rejects the affections of a floorwalker. Her mother's death leaves her a small sum of money. Using the money for better clothes, she begins working for a lawyer. His generosity toward her sways her into an affair with him after he promises to marry her. But he soon tires of her and abandons her. He is unaware that she will have his child. In a park, she meets a widower with his little son. The pair become friends and are soon married. The lawyer appears on the scene, hoping to renew their relationship. The husband learns from her about her previous affair and divorces her. Following a series of further complications in her life, including her successful rise as a lobbyist, her daughter, now grown, kills a man who has tried to attack her. The young woman is to be tried by her own father, now a district attorney. Gordon tells her ex-lover he will be prosecuting his own daughter. When her former husband enters and is willing to help, Gordon, to protect her daughter from disgrace, states the girl is not hers, but the adopted daughter of friends. She then dies of heart failure in the district attorney's office.

Inexperienced Miriam Cooper in R. A. Walsh's hackneyed drama, *The Innocent Sinner* (1917), falls for city-bred Charles Clary. He takes her to the bright lights, uses her and then abandons her. The deserted young woman is left to fend for herself. In despair, the penniless and disillusioned Cooper almost ends up a street walker. However, Jack Standing, Clary's cousin, comes to her rescue. Virtually plucked from the streets, the resurrected former country girl now must choose between a young sailor who loves her and the wealthier Standing. She marries the latter.

In another cautionary tale, William Haddock's *The Girl Who Didn't Think* (1917), Gale Kane fails to heed her mother's warning about falling for a Wall Street playboy. She has an affair with a broker, whom she meets while delivering a gown to his mistress. When he provides Kane with a lavish apartment, she moves out of her parents' humble quarters. Meanwhile, her despondent mother places a burning lamp in the window each night, expecting her child's return. Kane refuses to listen to the pleas of the abandoned mistress who begs her to give up the broker. Instead, Kane is proud to be carrying his child. Suddenly, she finds she is equally betrayed when her lover tires of her and finds another woman. She leaves with her maid. Later, after giving birth and reading about the betrayer's upcoming wedding, she takes her child to the ceremony and publicly exposes him.

Zena Keefe portrays a young woman who, unfortunately, makes a fatal mistake one night, in Ivan Abramson's preachy *Enlighten Thy Daughter* (1917). Keefe goes driving with an ostensibly decent young man and, when a storm takes both by surprise, they spend the night together. The girl's mother, busily engaged in her gambling addiction, does not realize her daughter has been out all night. Months later, the same youth begins dating Ruby De Reimer, Keefe's cousin. They fall in love and prepare to marry. When Keefe, who is now pregnant, tells her mother about her past experience, the parent takes her to an illegal abortionist. The unfortunate daughter dies as a result of the procedure. The stunned cousin breaks off the engagement with the guilty young man.

Country girl Frances Nelson journeys to New York to study art in Emile Chautard's drama, *Love's Crucible* (1916), based on the play, *The Point of View*, by Jules Eckert Goodman. However, she is unaware that her boyfriend back home is paying for her education. She meets a young man living in an adjacent studio, who lures her into an affair. After taking advantage of her, he abandons her to become engaged to someone else. About to drown herself, the disillusioned Nelson is rescued by the young man's sister, who takes her home. When the lovers again meet, the young man, out of a sense of guilt, proposes marriage, but her revulsion toward him forces her to reject the offer. When her boyfriend arrives to take her home, she also rejects him, explaining she would prefer to have a successful career in the city first. Meanwhile, her false lover's fiancée, upon learning about his affair, breaks off their engagement.

Bessie Barriscale, in Raymond B. West's absorbing drama, *The Payment* (1916), portrays another young woman from a small town who wants to study art. To accomplish this, she heads for New York, where she soon begins working as a saleswoman while studying at night. She meets Charles Miller, a wealthy playboy who is married but is attracted to her. They have an affair, and he agrees to finance her trip abroad. Barriscale returns after several years, a successful artist who is recognized by society. She meets her former lover and his wife at a party. The woman later arranges for her brother, William Desmond, to meet the charming artist. A romance blossoms, but Miller, believing the artist is not good enough for his brother-in-law, wants her to break off the relationship. He threatens to confess the past affair to young Desmond unless she agrees. To avoid hurting Desmond, whom she loves deeply, she refuses to continue the romance.

Clara Kimball Young portrays the title character in Emile Chautard's drama, *Magda* (1917), based on the play by Hermann Sudermann. Banished from her home and community because of her rebelliousness, Magda decides to pursue a singing career in the city. But she is soon tricked by a lover (Edmund Fielding) into thinking they have been legally married. However, the only thing he gives her is a child. Reduced to singing in the street and in low-grade dance halls, she is eventually discovered by a former teacher, who promotes her into a major artist. Fielding, learning of her good fortune, comes to her and proposes marriage, but Magda, recalling all the pain and treachery he had brought her, rejects him. The screen version differs sharply from the original work in which Sudermann's Magda gives herself freely to the lover.

Walter Richard Stahl's drama, *Hate* (1917), explores the issue of illegitimacy and the resultant hate it can engender. Jack McLean, whose mother, Adelaide Holland, had been betrayed years earlier by Norman Acker, seeks vengeance upon the man who had ruined her and made the son an outcast. Acker had callously turned his back on the young woman he ruined when she desperately sought his help. Years later, he enters the life of his illegitimate son, who is now grown to manhood. McLean, consumed with hate, murders his father. Later, a jury exonerates the youth. After the trial, McLean's girlfriend, Mae McAvoy, whom he had earlier rescued from drowning, rejects him and marries an unworthy but wealthy man. A subplot depicts the bitter rivalry between the young lovers' fathers, McLean's foster father, who is a newspaper editor, and McAvoy's father, who is a powerful politician.

Alice Brady, another innocent country girl who has come to New York City and is ruined, discovers a novel release for her anger, in Robert G. Vignola's morbid and disarming drama of betrayal, *The Knife* (1918), based on the play by Eugene Walter. Brady is drugged by the villain so that he can take full advantage of the prospective bridegroom. When she realizes she has been betrayed, she vows to kill him, but her surgeon brother proposes an alternative. Why not use the reprobate for scientific experimentation so that humanity may benefit from the surgery? This idea came across much stronger in the original stage production, whereas the film version sanitized this prospect, thereby almost neutralizing the impact of the original.

In Frank Beal's *Broken Commandments* (1919), escaped convict William Scott violates Gladys Brockwell, in whose California home he seeks refuge from the law. He leaves the next day, but his conscience forces him to return and marry her. However, he is captured before he can fulfill his mission. Brockwell goes to the city and finds work as an author's secretary. They fall in love and he proposes marriage. At first reluctant because of the earlier incident, she consents for the sake of the child that is on its way. Several years later, her husband visits a prison to research one of his books and meets Scott, whom he invites to his home when he is released. Scott shows up and faces Brockwell. The trio now face the dilemma to decide who is the rightful husband. The ex-convict suggests they throw dice to settle the problem. The visitor, observing the happy family, uses his loaded dice and purposely loses to the author. He happily walks out into the night.

Writer-director Erich von Stroheim in *Blind Husbands* (1919) explores the sexual frustrations of American wife Francella Billington, who is vacationing with her physician husband in the Austrian mountains. The doctor, a decent fellow, takes his wife for granted. Here they meet Stroheim, an intelligent and cultured Austrian army officer. Observing the tenuous relationship between the married couple, the opportunistic officer eventually seduces the receptive wife, whom he has showered with his attention and gifts. This was Stroheim's first directorial attempt, which he soon followed with other similar dramas, *The Devil's Passkey* (1920) and *Foolish Wives* (1921), the latter a sort of extended sequel to *Blind Husbands*.

II. "Let Me Take You Away"

Films of seduction and abandonment remained relatively popular during the twenties, often featuring popular actors and actresses. The basic plots deviated little from earlier similar dramas. Rich women remained easy prey for the Lothario, as in *Foolish Wives* (1922) and *The Eternal Three* (1923), while young and innocent orphans were targets for otherwise decent young men, in such films as *The White Rose* (1923). In addition, films like *Port of Missing Girls* (1928) illustrated how women from the country continued to fall prey to the charms and stratagems of city sophisticates. In at least one instance, *Their Hour* (1928), we are privy to how a young woman, who is engaged to another man, delights in seducing a naïve young shipping clerk. Sometimes, as in *Time, the Comedian* (1925), the innocent young woman about to be ruined is saved by a caring mother who knows best.

Erich von Stroheim's third film, *Foolish Wives* (1922), presented a sophisticated tale of seduction, blackmail, suicide and murder, among other elements, all set in a magnificently reproduced set of Monte Carlo. Stroheim, as a lascivious Russian captain of the Hussars, uses his polished manners to pursue with equal vigor any female within sight, from chambermaid to the wife of an American diplomat. After he lures the wife to his tower, his seduction is interrupted when a maid whom he has betrayed jealously sets fire to the building. Later, the repulsive Stroheim, after caning to death a black cat, is himself killed by an old counterfeiter who catches the officer approaching the bedside of the man's half-witted sister.

Raymond Griffith, as a lecherous womanizer, schemes to impede his female victims with alcohol before he seduces them in Marshall Neilan and Frank Urson's drama, *The Eternal Three* (1923). His tactics prove successful with a young woman, Bessie Love, whom he soon abandons after having her. But during his attempt to conquer his next victim, he meets with the unexpected. After filling her with drink, they amble carelessly down a street where a truck hits Griffith. His foster father, Hobart Bosworth, an eminent surgeon, is called upon to perform a major operation. The doctor was suspicious of Griffith's attentions to Bosworth's wife before the accident, so when he learned of their tryst, thoughts ran through his mind about the impending operation. But the doctor's ethics win out and he successfully performs the surgery on his repulsive patient.

Mae Marsh, upon leaving an orphan asylum in good standing, secures a job at a Southern resort, where she meets theology student Ivor Novello, the son of an important aristocratic family, in D. W. Griffith's absorbing romantic drama, *The White Rose* (1923). Novello, traveling under a pseudonym, is engaged to Carol Dempster, a member of his social set. He has an affair with Marsh, whom he thinks has had former relationships, and abandons her to return to his studies. Marsh, meanwhile, has his child and loses her job and sleeping quarters. On her own now and destitute, she seeks work elsewhere. Ironically, she inquires at the home of her seducer's fiancée, but is unsuccessful in obtaining a position. However, an African-American servant helps Marsh and offers her shelter in a cabin belonging to Dempster's family. When she becomes severely ill, the servant notifies Novello, who is now an ordained minister. He visits Marsh and, after learning of her innocence before their affair, he reconciles his differences with her and they are married. His former fiancée marries another member of society.

Dorothy Devore deliberately enters into a loveless marriage with William Haines in David Kirkland's *Who Cares* (1925), based on a story by Cosmo Hamilton. Devore refuses to fall in love with her husband, claiming she is too young to make such a serious decision. At the home of a female acquaintance she meets the amoral but well-mannered Lloyd Whitlock, and the two become fast friends. One evening, on returning home with Whitlock, she is upset to see her husband with another woman, although the situation is far from compromising. Haines leaves for his private club while Devore remains at home with Whitlock. Whitlock then tries to seduce her, but Haines re-enters the apartment in time to rescue her. Devore then realizes she loves her husband and confides this to him.

Mae Busch portrays a mother who sacrifices her reputation to protect her daughter against a false lover in Robert Z. Leonard's weak drama, *Time, the Comedian* (1925), based on the novel by Kate Jordan. The plot relates how the lecherous Lew Cody abandons his love for Busch while plotting to seduce her daughter, Gertrude Olmstead. The mother, however, manipulates events so that when her daughter enters Cody's place, she will find her mother in his arms. Busch justifies her deception with the thought that she is saving her child from mistakenly putting her trust and faith in such a wretch as Cody.

Constance Talmadge plays a dual role in Sidney Franklin's farcical comedy, *Her Sister From Paris* (1925), set in Vienna. She portrays Helen, the conservative wife of prudish Ronald Colman, and Lola, her twin sister, an outgoing dancer, who arrives from Paris with an entourage of reporters, photographers and suitors. A fight erupts between the married couple, ending in Helen's leaving the apartment. She meets her sister at the railway station, where they plot to exchange personalities. Helen decides to teach her husband a lesson by changing her appearance so that she looks like the wilder sister. She then plans to seduce her own husband so that he will appreciate his more reserved wife. "Lola" enters the sedate life of Colman and drags him dancing, drinking and cavorting to all hours. She then lures the tired husband to the same hotel room where he had his honeymoon. By this time, he has had it with "Lola" and wishes for his former wife to return. Suddenly, the real Lola enters the room, leaving Colman in a state of shock and confusion. The film had problems with the censors in Ohio, resulting in several cuts relating to certain sexually explicit material.

Dorothy Mackaill, who has learned early in life not to trust men, purposely dresses and acts in a manly style to ward off advances, in John Francis Dillon's domestic drama, *The Crystal Cup* (1927), based on the story by Gertrude Atherton. Earlier, the wealthy young heiress had experienced a brutal seduction. Now, to avoid gossip about her affected mannerisms, she reluctantly consents to a platonic marriage with successful novelist Rockliffe Fellowes, whom she has met at a fashionable ball. He reluctantly agrees to the arrangement only to satisfy his secret desire to seduce her. Later, she finds honest love with her husband's friend, Jack Mulhall, a young surgeon, for whom she dons silk stockings and feminine attire. Her husband's yearning for his wife leads him into her bedroom one night, where his frightened wife accidentally shoots him. Mortally wounded, he realizes that his friend is the only one who can arouse the feminine characteristics in his wife.

Duke Martin, the tender of a river searchlight, covets the wife of Ralph Emerson, his assistant, in Al Raboch's routine romantic drama, *The Albany Night Boat* (1928). Both men take turns sweeping the Hudson River with the searchlight as the Albany night boat glides along carrying its lovers. While on duty, Emerson focuses on a yacht where Olive Borden, to avoid being seduced, dives into the river. Emerson jumps in and rescues her. Following a short courtship, the couple marry, with Martin befriending the couple and wishing them happiness. On another evening during which Emerson is tending the searchlight, the beam passes his apartment which overlooks the river. He sees silhouettes that indicate his wife is in trouble. Once again, he swims toward his dwelling, enters the apartment and finds his friend, Martin, in the act of assaulting his wife. A fight breaks out and the intruder is eventually subdued.

Unscrupulous ladies' man John Gilbert, a baron, abandons one of his women and plans to seduce innocent student Eva von Berne, the girlfriend of his best friend, in Victor Seastrom's romantic drama, *Masks of the Devil* (1928), based on the 1910 novel by Jacob Wassermann. To accomplish his scheme, he invites her to accompany him on a trip to Borneo. Meanwhile, countess Alma Rubens, an old flame of his who deeply loves the baron, jumps in front of a car and is seriously hurt. Her husband is shot while struggling with the baron for control of a pistol. Gilbert is also forced to take Berne's aunt along as chaperone. Reminiscent of Oscar Wilde's novel, *The Picture of Dorian Gray,* the film has Gilbert occasionally scrutinizing his own face in a mirror, where he sees the image only of a devil. By the end, the baron redeems his wicked nature when he falls in love with Berne and gives up his old libertine lifestyle.

A young bootlegger takes advantage of a district attorney's daughter and then rescues her from a depraved theatrical manager in Irving Cummings's unconvincing drama, *Port of Missing Girls* (1928). Barbara Bedford, the daughter, leaves home after a dispute with her mother, and decides to make her own way in the city. She meets charming bootlegger Malcolm McGregor, who ends up violating her. Meanwhile, wealthy theatrical manager Wyndham Standing has worked out a scheme in which he lures young women from dancing and acting schools interested in a stage career to his office on the pretense of promising them careers in show business. Bedford falls for Standing's line and soon finds herself in the manager's lair. However, McGregor, who by now realizes he has fallen in love with her, confesses his own feelings to the district attorney and directs the police to the lecherous manager's office. At times, the film seems to resemble an old-fashioned cautionary tale, warning parents and young women about acting and dancing school scams and lustful men ready to ensnare their young prey.

Wealthy, spoiled socialite Dorothy Sebastian seduces young, working lad John Harron in Al Raboch's sexy drama, *Their Hour* (1928). The pampered socialite decides to "borrow" Harron, the shipping-clerk boyfriend of her poorer and more reserved cousin, June Marlowe, for a weekend. Harron has been partying with the upper social class through Marlowe's contacts. At this particular affair, Sebastian, who owns her own airplane, takes Harron for a ride to a small village hundred of miles from the city, where they settle at a country inn. Although they have adjoining rooms, she makes a play for the nervous and naïve clerk and succeeds in her intent. When her fiancé arrives on the scene, Harron realizes that he has made a fool of himself. He leaves quickly and returns to his girlfriend, who forgives him for his escapade.

Young Helen Foster seeks to avenge the rape of her innocent sister in Scott Pembroke's routine drama, *Should a Girl Marry?* (1928). Her younger sister, who perhaps loves liquor too much, falls into the clutches of a lecherous rake who seduces her and then leaves her. Foster finds him and kills him. A courtroom drama follows after her arrest, with a judge giving a sermon about young women going wrong. Although Foster eventually is acquitted of the charge, she admits to her boyfriend that she committed the murder. The film, made during the transition period, was chiefly silent, except for some dialogue scenes, especially near the end, in which the judge's remarks and the counsel's summation are spoken.

Lillian Gish portrays city girl Letty, who arrives in a desolate Texas area, where the wind and sand are all-pervasive, in Victor Seastrom's powerful and grim drama, *The Wind* (1928), based on the novel by Dorothy Scarborough. The film explores the forces of nature and their effects on people. On the rebound, she marries a man who ultimately is repugnant to her. Her relentless battle against the wind and the sand is virtually useless. One day, when she is left alone, with only the howling wind and the encroaching sand for company, a smooth-talking salesman appears. "Let me take you away," he offers, "where the wind can never follow you." He then proceeds to rape her, regardless of her struggles. Gish is driven to kill her attacker, whom she then buries outside in the ever-shifting sand. Back inside the wind-battered house, the hysterical and pitiful Gish notices the sand of the temporary grave keeps blowing away, exposing the corpse. The film, with its primitive symbols, suggests a terrifying picture of how human beings are the victims of the elements, and that they are at the mercy of nature.

In John P. McCarthy's drama, *The Eternal Woman* (1929), Olive Borden returns home to Buenos Aires to learn that her father has been killed and her sister violated by an American guest at a local hotel. Following a series of complications, including the pursuit of the wrong man, Borden, who has sworn to avenge the wrongs done to her family, finally meets Ralph Graves, with whom she falls in love, but is unaware he is the man she is seeking. Before their wedding, she discovers the truth and plans to shoot him. But at the last moment, she discovers she is in error and the real killer is exposed.

John Barrymore, during a drunken revel, seduces Mona Rica, a village coquette, whom he is later forced to marry, in Ernst Lubitsch's romantic drama, *Eternal Love* (1929), set in the Tyrolean Alps during the Franco-Austrian conflict of 1812. Meanwhile, the young woman whom he really loves, Camilla Horn, reluctantly is compelled to marry Victor Varconi. When Varconi is found murdered, circumstantial evidence points to Barrymore, who is forced to escape with his true love, the widow. Meanwhile, the irate villagers form a posse to hunt for Barrymore. The pair of lovers climb the Alpine heights together to avoid capture. But they encounter a glacial avalanche. Unable to avoid their fate, they hold each other tightly as they find their "eternal love" in their impending doom. Made during the transitional years in Hollywood, the film contained sound effects and a musical background, but no spoken dialogue.

Slums

I. "How the Other Half Lives"

Urban slums existed in major cities for hundreds of years. The United States has had its share of slums spread out across the nation, with the same problems other countries have encountered. The major cities attacked the blight from various directions. *The New York Tribune* in 1881 took over the Fresh Air Fund for city slum children, an endowment initiated four years earlier. The newspaper appealed to it readers for donations to continue the program. Private organizations raised funds for community centers called "settlement houses." For example, the New York Educational Alliance, a settlement house organized in 1889 by German-Jewish groups, provided education and recreation for slum dwellers on the city's Lower East Side, most of whom were from eastern Europe. Meanwhile, Chicago's Hull House, opened around the same time, in 1889, in the South Halsted Street slums. The center was under the direction of social workers Jane Addams, 29, and Ellen Gates Starr. Their settlement house was also designed to help the poor of the city. Other major social milestones included the book, *How the Other Half Lives* (1890), written by New York Evening Sun police reporter Jacob August Riis, 51. He portrayed slum life and the conditions that breed crime, vice, and disease. "When the houses were filled," the journalist wrote, "the crowds overflowed into the yards. In winter [there were] tenants living in sheds built of old boards and roof tin, paying a dollar a week for herding with the rats." City planning commissions built projects for the poor, but the slums did not disappear. Neither did the problems. Early silent films touched upon some of the problems created by slums – with a strong focus on crime, poverty and despair. The crime theme was prevalent in such films as *The Bridge of Sighs* (1915) and *The Ragamuffin* (1916). Poverty dominated other films, including *A Prince in a Pawnshop* (1916), while *The Little Liar* (1916) emphasized despair. Another popular theme concerned an idealistic member of society contributing to the welfare of the poor. Wealthy Marguerite Snow in *A Corner in Cotton* (1916) volunteers to work in a settlement house. Defrocked minister William Desmond opens a mission for the poor in *The Waifs* (1916). Finally, an idealistic doctor elects to work only in a slum district in *Her Better Self* (1917).

Jeff Davis, known as the "King of the Hoboes," portrays himself in the drama, *The Bridge of Sighs* (1915). He prevents young hobo Bill Stevens from shooting a brakeman who ejected him from a train, and offers to help the lad. He warns him to avoid the thief Reardon, who will only lead him to the "Bridge of Sighs," a passageway leading from the courthouse to the Tombs of New York City. Stevens meets the impoverished Dorothy Welsh, who is seeking a job to raise money for her sickly mother. The devious Reardon tells her he is a detective and wants to hire her as his assistant. But Stevens eventually rescues her from the crook, who plans a robbery and intends to frame Stevens for the crime. Reardon is arrested, and Davis finds work for the couple on a farm out of town.

William Wadsworth portrays the title character, Abe Cohen, in John H. Collins's comedy drama, *Cohen's Luck* (1915), based on the play by Lee Arthur. Cohen, president of his union, is fired from his sweatshop job after he endorses a politician whom his boss opposes. Later, he has problems with his daughter, who claims she has married his former boss, now separated from his wife. Cohen suspects the legality of the marriage and evicts her from his home. The marriage is finally invalidated, and the young woman and her beau, John Walker, are reunited. Other complications include Cohen's outwitting a crook who has stolen half of his lottery ticket, and a flood from the apartment above his during the engagement party for his daughter and Walker.

Walker Whiteside, as a Russian immigrant violinist, supports himself by giving concerts in East Side concert halls, in James Vincent and Oliver D. Bailey's social drama, *The Melting Pot* (1915), based on the 1908 play by Israel Zangwill. Valentine Grant, a Russian baron's daughter who has also escaped from Russia, falls in love with the violinist. He convinces a German music master to promote his symphony representing the blending of races and religions in America's "melting pot." Meanwhile, the baron arrives in New York to condemn his daughter for her dissident actions in her homeland. Whiteside, who has seen his family slaughtered under the baron's orders, admits to the woman that a river of blood separates them. The baron acknowledges his guilt and offers his life. As the violinist is about to avenge his family at the baron's expense, a broken violin string reminds him of the theme of his symphony. The symphony is finally performed, with a giant crucible on stage which converts all people of various backgrounds into American citizens.

Slum dweller Violet Mersereau dances in the streets of New York's Lower East Side to the delight of passersby until she is struck by a passing limousine in Francis J. Grandon's drama, *The Narrow Path* (1916). The woman owner helps the impoverished victim get a job as a model. She eventually makes a successful Broadway debut as a dancer. When Niles Welch, a theatrical agent, shows more than a passing interest in the star, the jealous Clara Beyers sets out to ruin the dancer's reputation. At first her plot works, but the couple are finally reunited.

Blanche Sweet, raised in the slums, is coaxed by her foster father to help him and his friend burglarize a wealthy home in William C. de Mille's social drama, *The Ragamuffin* (1916). She reluctantly agrees and is sent in through a window to collect valuables, exit from the front and meet her two accomplices across the street. However, young Tom Forman, who was born in luxury, catches her in the act of robbing his home. Fascinated by the pretty burglar, he states, "A thief is the meanest thing there is." He then asks her why she is doing this and she replies that no one ever trusted her. "Give me your word and I'll trust you," he states. She does and he retires upstairs, leaving her alone. All she takes is his photograph and leaves him fifty cents. Later, she announces to her cronies that she is "going straight." Once again, she meets Forman, and this time she helps him by preventing him from robbing his elderly housekeeper. Following a string of other complications, the reformed couple enjoy each other's company, and Forman, now short of funds, gets a job paying twenty dollars per week.

Jewell Hunt, another child of the slums, is forced to assist her father, a petty thief, in his burglaries in C. Jay Williams's drama, *By Love Redeemed* (1916). When she protests during one of their capers that she prefers to go straight, he hits her over the head with his blackjack. The blow results in her insatiable desire to steal. Years later, Logan Paul, a young man who had earlier befriended Hunt, meets her at a cabaret, where she works as an entertainer. He dates her and notices that she has stolen the change the waiter had put on the table. Paul works for an artist who needs a model, and the young woman gets the job. Meanwhile, Paul takes Hunt to Anders Randolf, a doctor who has cured criminals through his operations. He operates on her and cures her of her criminal tendencies. She now works as a maid for the artist. One day, her father sees her in the street and follows her to the artist's home. That night, while the artist's wife and child are out, he plans to rob the safe. But the explosion he precipitates kills him. When Paul arrives with the police, they witness the scene, and the couple embrace.

Wealthy Marguerite Snow, who is interested in doing settlement work in the slums, is criticized for this by her equally wealthy fiancé in Fred J. Balshofer's slow-paced, chiefly unconvincing drama, *A Corner in Cotton* (1916). The independent-minded young woman decides to break off her engagement rather than give up her volunteer work. Later, she rescues a Southern businessman and his son from her own father's attempt to corner the cotton market. She journeys to the South to investigate the family's business and falls in love with the son, who proves to be honest and sincere. In fact, he comes to her aid when she is assaulted by a factory mill foreman.

At a reception celebrating William Desmond's being ordained by the bishop, the young man's drunken condition results in the bishop's defrocking Desmond, in Scott Sidney's drama, *The Waifs* (1916). Earlier during the ceremony, some prankster had spiked the punch. Desmond had been engaged to Carol Halloway, the bishop's daughter. After a bout with drinking, Desmond drifts into a slum district near a waterfront. He trades his crucifix for a final drink and heads for the water. Jane Gray, a piano player at a nearby dive, follows him and saves him from the river. She takes him to her quarters, where he sleeps in a different section. Soon, he redeems himself by opening a mission, and Gray works as his assistant. The bishop and his daughter learn of the good work Desmond is doing in the slums and visit the mission. The bishop invites Desmond back. Although Desmond proposes to Gray, she rejects him, realizing he still loves Halloway. The film ends with Desmond's presentation of his first real sermon. As he walks down the church aisle, near the back, hidden in the shadows, is the humble but proud figure of Gray, whose little hands barely reach out to touch the hem of his gown.

Idealistically inclined socialite Dorothy Gish decides to take up social work in a slum district, where she meets Owen Moore, in Paul Powell's romantic drama, *Susan Rocks the Boat* (1916). Moore, whose father is a local politician in the district, is liked by the poor residents, and the two soon fall in love. Moore rescues Gish from the lascivious designs of the villainous Fred J. Butler, a neighborhood tough, who ends up shooting Moore. But Gish nurses her hero's wounds as they embrace.

Mae Marsh, a young woman raised in the slums, depends heavily on her imagination – her great ability to lie – for her survival, in Lloyd Ingraham's slight drama, *The Little Liar* (1916). The only problem with her approach is that she continually gets into scrapes and finally ends up behind bars. But her mind refuses to remain idle, so she writes down her impressions of her experiences and the various persons she has encountered in her short but volatile life. The judge, reading her chronicle and favorably impressed, brings her writing talents to the attention of a newspaper editor. The two men rush to her cell to congratulate her, but to their shock they find that she has taken her life. What little recognition she received in her life of poverty and anonymity is compensated for by the elaborate funeral she receives after her suicide.

Marguerite Skirvin, the leader of a reform movement to improve the unsanitary conditions of tenements, succeeds in her efforts, but at the cost of ruining her landlord father, in Charles Horan's farfetched drama, *The Upheaval* (1916), based on the short story by Lawrence McCloskey. Throughout her struggle for social upheaval in the city, she clashes with young political leader Lionel Barrymore who, along with her father, defies her. But the reform legislation she and her movement have proposed passes, and several landlords are bankrupted by the improvements. In the end, when her father needs funds to tide him over, the politician lends him the money and marries his daughter, who eventually begins to fall in love with her former rival.

Barney Bernard portrays a sort of Jewish Robin Hood of the slums in Paul Scardon's entertaining drama, *A Prince in a Pawnshop* (1916). Part of each day, Bernard is a banker who extracts his fair share of interest from his rich clients. But during another part of the day, he runs a pawn shop in a tenement section of the city, where he lends the unfortunate slum dwellers various sums of money, taking in trade obviously worthless merchandise. Meanwhile, his son, who is secretly married, is approached by a vindictive man who reveals that the son's wife is his former mistress. The irate son abandons her. Several years later, the wife and her child, unknown to the husband, are living in poverty in a rundown tenement. Bernard accidentally discovers them during his charitable rounds and arranges a reconciliation.

When a slum dweller is falsely accused of murdering a member of high society, he delights in the recognition he is getting and welcomes a death sentence as an escape from poverty and the slums, in William Nigh's offbeat drama, *His Great Triumph* (1916). But before the condemned man, portrayed by Nigh, is about to be executed, socialite Marguerite Snow comes forward to risk her reputation by clearing Night of the charge. It seems while she was having an affair with a count, she witnesses the crime. She finally names the real murderer. Later, Nigh gains legitimate fame when he rescues Snow's father from a kidnapping attempt by a group of gangsters.

Vivian Martin, a child of the tenements, is informed by a doctor that her young brother will die if he is not moved to a different climate, preferably California, in E. Mason Hopper's inane and disappointing drama, *The Right Direction* (1916). Upon hearing this, Martin immediately packs up a baby carriage and with the little boy inside, begins to wheel the carriage toward the healthier climate. She meets up with a band of hoboes who care for the children and place them safely inside a freight car. Just as they begin to suffer from lack of food and water, they meet the son of a millionaire who is speeding in his limousine across country. He decides to take them with him to his wealthy estate, where he and his father care for the two homeless orphans.

Viola Dana and her brother live in a broken-down tenement and run a newsstand, which provides them with a meager living, in John H. Collins's bleak drama, *Rosie O'Grady* (1917). Dana meets a prizefighter who proposes to her and, after a phony marriage, takes her to Europe. But he returns without her and with another woman. Meanwhile, her brother learns about the abandonment and waits to confront the fighter. He kills him and is charged with murder. Dana returns in time to testify in his behalf, but the boy is found guilty. To relieve the audience of all the despondency and misery laid upon the brother and sister, the film suddenly reveals that the entire plot was only a dream. The film suffers as the result of its gimmicky and evasive ending.

A local reporter learns about Ella Hall, who had been an abandoned child left at a pawnshop by a widowed mother, in Jack Conway's drama, *A Jewel in Pawn* (1917), set in a city slum district. The reporter senses an appealing human interest story. It seems many years ago an impoverished widow left her little daughter with elderly Jewish pawnbroker Walter Belasco in exchange for enough funds to travel to her wealthy father. But during the journey she dies before she can reveal the fate of her daughter. Belasco raises the child as his own until the story is printed. The girl's grandfather comes to the rescue and sends Hall to a fine private school and plans to have her marry into wealth. But Hall returns to her boyfriend in the slums whom she marries in the old pawnshop amid her childhood friends and neighbors.

Socialite Pauline Frederick has a choice of two men, a wealthy titled gentleman and a hardworking, idealistic doctor who caters chiefly to the poor of a slum district, in Robert G. Vignola's *Her Better Self* (1917). She selects Thomas Meighan, the latter, chiefly because of his social awareness and dedication to the poor. But after their marriage, complications arise, especially concerning a young woman he rescues from night court and then treats. Frederick believes that her husband had earlier been responsible for ruining the woman. However, she later learns he is innocent. When the patient commits suicide, Meighan is accused of killing her and is tried for her death. His wife, who was present at the suicide, testifies at the trial, although her presence in court will publicly soil her reputation among her social class. Her testimony exonerates the doctor and they are reunited in their love that is now stronger then ever.

Young millionaire Charles Ray bets a club member that he can live on six dollars a week in Victor Schertzinger's absorbing drama, *The Millionaire Vagrant* (1917). The wager arises after a district attorney at his social club tells the story about his arrest of a young woman who stole sundry items, leading another member of the club to express sympathy for those who are trying to survive on six dollars a week. Immediately, Ray announces that he can, and the bet is arranged. He rents a room in a tenement boarding house, where he meets and befriends a petty thief, a young working woman and a woman of mystery. They soon all become very close. When the woman of mystery is arrested in the street for soliciting, Ray and the thief decide to try to raise enough money to gain her release. Ray decides to get the funds from the district attorney's home. When they go there, they discover that he is using his position to blackmail those unfortunates who are facing court charges. They are told that either they do what he desires or they will face stiff sentences. The next day in court they expose the crooked attorney. To help them, the woman of mystery identifies herself as an investigator from a women's settlement house, and she, too, offers evidence of the district attorney's corruption and shady dealings with various defendants. Ray and the woman decide to get married, and their two boarding house friends are hired as servants in the couple's home.

Writer Harrison Ford, to gain background material for a book about how the poor live, rents a room in a slum district next door to Lila Lee, in George Melford's sentimental romantic drama, *The Cruise of the Make-Believes* (1918), based on the 1907 novel by Tom Gallon. The young woman who lives with her lazy father and brother is constructing a yacht in her back yard, where she uses discarded scraps of wood and other sundry items for her project. Ford visits her world of fantasy and they both envision sailing to exotic lands aboard their imaginary yacht. He invites her and her family to his wealthy father's country estate, where her father and brother get drunk and act boorishly. Meanwhile, Lee has also invited some of the slum children, who enjoy the fresh air and open space. The young couple soon fall in love.

A young sweatshop worker's life undergoes a radical change when she unexpectedly inherits a fortune in Edward Dillon's sentimental and entertaining comedy, *The Embarrassment of Riches* (1918), based on the 1906 play by Louis K. Anspacher. Lillian Walker, as the sudden heiress who had earlier complained of her constant poverty and ached for wealth, finally gets her wish, which is not all she expected. After receiving her inheritance, she becomes overwhelmed with handling the money, the mail and other responsibilities. But of more importance to her, the idealistic settlement worker she loves rejects her because of her wealth. She has a difficult time trying to convince him that she is not a simple flighty socialite who is only slumming. However, she eventually wins him over following a series of comical complications.

New York's Lower East Side street urchin Madge Evans is hit by John Bowers's car in William P. S. Earle's drama, *Heredity* (1918). Bowers takes the slightly shaken but unhurt girl for a ride to the country to make up for running her down. Later, upon learning about the incident, Evans's cruel stepfather would like to swindle the wealthy young man, but his stepdaughter prevents him from doing so. Years later, the stepfather, in a drunken frenzy, kills Evans's mother and she is accused of the murder. Bowers reads of the case in a newspaper story and recognizes Evans by her ring. He comes to her defense. The stepfather is arrested for the crime, and Bowers marries the young woman who has always loved him since that fateful car ride in the country. The film is hindered by its misleading title.

Young artist Vincent Serrano meets model Dolores Cassinelli, a product of the slums, and marries her, in Albert Capellani's domestic drama, *The Virtuous Model* (1919). But the marriage does not progress smoothly. Another woman who is jealous of the virtuous wife stirs up trouble in the mind of the artist, resulting in the estrangement of the couple. However, following a series of romantic complications, Franklyn Farnum, a good friend of Serrano's, works out a reconciliation between the couple who finally resolve their differences.

II. Crime, Poverty and Despair

Silent films about slums and slum dwellers continued to appear throughout the twenties – chiefly dramas that focused on familiar plots and themes explored earlier. Films like *Fools' Highway* (1924) and *The Dawn of a Tomorrow* (1924) returned to the subject of crime. Poverty and despair marked such films as *The Swamp* (1921), which pictured a shattered slum family, with sickly Bessie Love, abandoned by her husband and trying to survive with her little son. Once again, a member of an upper class prefers helping the needy in *When Dawn Came* (1920), in which surgeon L. C. Shumway works in a slum neighborhood ministering to the poor. In *The Plaything of Broadway* (1921), doctor

Crauford Kent contributes his services to a settlement house. Occasionally, the setting shifted, as in *The Gift Supreme* (1920) and *Determination* (1922), both taking place in the slums of London. Most of these films suggested that unemployment, poverty and slums breed crime and disease. Some even hinted that regeneration is possible under the influence of a noble woman. But chiefly, these films lacked the necessary depth, or desire, to inspire new approaches to the debilitating consequences of slums. This was left to studios like Warner Bros., who took up this social cause in the following decade of 1930s.

Aspiring young writer Bernard Durning, wanting to gain worldly experience at first-hand, visits the London slums to gain background material for his book, in Ollie L. Sellers's familiar drama, *The Gift Supreme* (1920), based on the novel by George Allan England. He meets Seena Owen, a pretty mission singer, with whom he falls in love. When Durning's wealthy father learns of his son's romance, he frames the innocent young woman on charges of prostitution. Owen, embarrassed by the charge, disappears. But Durning remains in the slums, where he opens a restaurant for the poor. The local thug who framed Owen stabs the young man, who is rushed to the hospital. Following the sinister machinations of the father and the vindictive attempt on Durning's life, Owen, now a nurse at the same hospital, provides him with "the gift supreme" by donating her own blood to save his life. The couple are then reunited.

The young and ambitious surgeon, L. C. Shumway, who contributes his significant skills to the charity patients in a slum district, meets magazine writer Kathleen Kirkham, in Colin Campbell's strong drama, *When Dawn Came* (1920). The reporter is in the neighborhood gathering material for a story. Her vehicle has accidentally hit a boy, one of the doctor's patients. Learning about Shumway's skills and reputation, Kirkham introduces the surgeon to William Conklin, a famous doctor with an exclusive uptown clientele, who takes the young surgeon into partnership with other physicians. The new assignment brings only misfortune to Shumway, who begins drinking heavily and is unable to handle affluence. The final blow comes to him when he discovers that Kirkham, whom he loves, is having an affair with Conklin. After physically attacking both, the disillusioned Shumway sinks into a world of anonymity, ending as a common derelict. James O. Barrowes, the local slum priest, is now working in South America, where he takes an interest in Colleen Moore, a blind young woman. Shumway, a tramp and an atheist, drifts into this environment, where the priest rescues him and introduces him to Moore. The former surgeon regains his faith and confidence in himself and God through the love of the blind young woman. He operates on her and restores her sight. He, too, is now restored to his old self.

Jewish mother Vera Gordon, who has prayed that one of her sons should be an accomplished musician, has her prayers answered – with mixed results – in Frank Borzage's touching drama, *Humoresque* (1920), based on the story by Fannie Hurst. The son, Gaston Glass, another child of the ghetto, masters the violin and gains fame and wealth from his concerts. He is able to move his family out of the slums to a fashionable uptown apartment. He then proposes to his childhood sweetheart, Alma Rubens. But World War I interferes with his successful career. When he returns from France with a wounded arm, he informs his girlfriend that he is useless, that he will never again play the violin, and that he cannot marry. The young woman faints. When he tries to help her recover, he discovers that he can use his wounded arm. He reaches for his violin and begins playing again.

Newspaperwoman Clara Kimball Young contributes much of her time to helping slum children and still holds a spot in her heart for lawyer Lowell Sherman in Harry Garson's drama, *What No Man Knows* (1921). Sherman, whose wife is a kleptomaniac, tries to protect her by bribing a witness. He is caught and disbarred. The journalist, during one of her trips to the slums, meets the disheveled Sherman and takes him to her quarters. When she suggests he give his wife another chance, he agrees. But later, when he disapproves of her new friends and her loose lifestyle, he demands a divorce. Following several complications, she agrees. Meanwhile, Young is reported by her neighbors as not fit to associate with children after she brings a blind orphan to her apartment. She is exonerated of all charges and renews her relationship with the child, and Sherman returns to her.

Breezy Eason Jr., a good-natured orphan of the slums, is mistreated by his brutal stepfather, who forces the boy to steal for him, in Reeves Eason's routine drama, *The Big Adventure* (1921). The abused boy decides to run away. With his little dog, he hops a freight train to a neighboring town and is taken in by Molly Shafer, the sister of the town judge. Meanwhile, the stepfather, Lee Shumway, himself now a hobo, finds the boy and holds him and a local girl, Gertrude Olmstead, captive. Breezy escapes and reports the kidnapping. He then leads a posse to rescue the young woman and capture Shumway.

Deserted wife Bessie Love and Frankie Lee, her little son, living in New York's Lower East Side slum neighborhood, where they struggle to survive in Colin Campbell's sentimental and implausible drama, *The Swamp* (1921). The boy sells newspapers, with the help of his sick mother. His friend, Sessue Hayakawa, a Japanese youth, tries to help the family financially. Frankie's father, who is living with a socialite, hires Hayakawa for their engagement party to tell the couple's fortune. He purposely concocts a story that breaks up their engagement. Meanwhile, a boyhood admirer of Frankie's mother proposes to her and she happily accepts. Hayakawa plans to return to his native land to marry someone of his own culture. The title refers to the name given to this section of the city.

Broadway dancer Justine Johnstone, who is more than familiar with several wealthy members of an exclusive club for industrial giants, accepts a wager that she can make a certain doctor fall in love with her, in Jack Dillon's contrived drama, *The Plaything of Broadway* (1921), based on Wesley J. Putnam's "Emergency House." She poses as a helper to Crauford Kent, the doctor who does settlement work. Impressed by the charitable work he performs among the poor and needy, the Broadway dancer is herself transformed. She cashes in her bet and uses the funds to build a private hospital for Kent to continue his work. A friend of the doctor relates the sordid background of his assistant, including the incident of the wager. She is warned that her presence will hurt the doctor's career, so she agrees to walk out on him. She also decides to discourage his love by arranging for a wickedly wild party at her apartment. Following a series of sentimental complications, the couple are finally reunited when the doctor rescues the woman he loves from an angry mob.

Gladys Walton portrays a dual role in Harry B. Harris's society drama, *Rich Girl, Poor Girl* (1921). As Nora, a resident of a tenement, she visits a nearby estate of a wealthy family, where she meets Beatrice, the owner's daughter. They both discover that they look very much alike and decide to switch places temporarily just for a lark. Beatrice is soon taken captive by Nora's intoxicated and brutish father, who holds her for ransom. Meanwhile, Nora meets Harold Austin, Beatrice's admirer, and confesses the truth to him, including Beatrice's capture. Austin and the prisoner's father rescue Beatrice, and the kidnapper is arrested. The wealthy family then adopt Nora, who is now a grateful orphan with a loving adoptive family.

Socialite Shirley Mason, searching to do something meaningful with her life, is not ready to marry Alan Forrest, who is constantly proposing to her, in Joseph Franz's drama, *The New Teacher* (1922). The young couple, while flying in an airplane above New York City, are forced to land on the Lower East Side, in the heart of a slum district. It is here that Mason gets the inspiration to help the young children of the neighborhood by becoming a teacher. Forrest, who has again been turned down after proposing to her during the flight, plans to follow by joining the police department of the same district. Both work in their respective jobs for several months, each learning about the neighborhood and its residents. At times, the new teacher seems overwhelmed by a series of classroom scrapes and other escapades by her young charges. Finally, she realizes Forrest's worth and accepts him as her lifetime mate.

Alpheus Lincoln is a settlement worker in the slums of London who is unaware that he has a twin brother living a wild life in Paris, in Joseph Levering's drama, *Determination* (1922). Corinne Uzzell, the daughter of an American senator, takes an interest in Lincoln's work and begins to fall in love with the settlement worker. Walter Ringham, a noted lord and rival, informs the young woman that Lincoln is really his roguish Paris brother. Following a series of complications set in the back streets of Paris and London, Ringham is found to be the leader of a gang of thieves. Lincoln is reunited with his twin who promises to reform, and the pair of lovers plan for their future together.

A woman is again responsible for the regeneration of a questionable character in George Melford's romantic drama, *The Dawn of a Tomorrow* (1924), this time the seting is in a London slum. Jacqueline Logan and Raymond Griffith, a petty thief, are in love with each other, with the former trying to persuade her lawbreaking lover to reform. But he, like his fellow crooks, believes that the only way to survive is to feed off the better classes of citizens. When Griffith is implicated in a shooting by another criminal, David Torrence, a gentle and kindly lord, provides the necessary alibi that eventually exonerates Griffith from the killing. Griffith always thought that Torrence was a thief. Following this incident, and under the powers of his girlfriend, Griffith decides to give up his life of crime.

Rabbi and pushcart peddler Rudolph Schildkraut barely scratches out a living for his wife and two sons on the Lower East Side of New York in Edward Sloman's domestic drama, *His People* (1925). He favors Arthur Lubin, the older and more studious son, rather than George Lewis, who is more loyal and who sells newspapers to help his brother get through college. When the father learns that Lewis has become a common prizefighter, he forces him to leave the house. Lubin meanwhile becomes engaged to his boss's daughter but is ashamed of his parents. When the father arrives for the engagement party, Lubin refuses to acknowledge him as his father. Lewis, who has won the lightweight championship, condemns his arrogant brother for his behavior and forces him to face their father. Recognizing his faults, Lubin begs his father's forgiveness. The old man then expresses his gratitude to Lewis and blesses him and his Irish girlfriend.

Norma Shearer plays a dual role in Monta Bell's romantic drama, *Lady of the Night* (1925), that of Molly, a poor young woman from the slums and daughter of a convict, and her look-alike, Florence, the debutante daughter of a wealthy judge. Molly, recently released from reform school, returns to her slum neighborhood where she was raised. She renews her friendship with George K. Arthur, an old friend, and they go to a dancehall, where they meet Malcolm McGregor, a young inventor. He has recently perfected an instrument that can open any safe. Molly tries to convince him to sell it to the banking industry, while one of his pals suggests selling it the mob. "Don't give it to the bankers," his friend advises, "they'll rob you. Give it to the crooks, they'll treat you square." The inventor selects the banks, and meets with their representative, a judge. The man introduces tthe inventor to his daughter Florence. The couple soon fall in love, although at first she is reluctant to become involved with him. She believes Molly has a claim on the inventor. Much to her regret, Molly realizes McGregor loves Florence, so she sacrifices her love for McGregor's happiness.

Millionaire Harold Lloyd meets and falls in love with Jobyna Ralston, the daughter of a slum mission worker, in Sam Taylor's entertaining comedy, *For Heaven's Sake* (1926). To establish Lloyd's overwhelming wealth, we see him continually buying a new car each time he wrecks his present model. Minutes after an accident, he simply enters an auto showroom, hops into the seat of a new vehicle, signs a check for the car, and drives away – only to wreck that one as well. At one point, he accidentally destroys a coffee cart that Ralston's father uses to serve the needy. He gives the mission worker a check for one thousand dollars toward the repairs and drives away. The worker thinks the check is a donation for a new mission, resulting in the next day's headlines: "Millionaire Establishes Mission." This gives Lloyd a reason to revisit the mission worker's daughter. Following a series of comic situations involving gangsters, police, mobs and chases, Lloyd ends up helping to make a success of the mission and winning the love of Ralston.

Schoolgirl Dolores Costello goes to pieces when she learns that her mother, Louise Dresser, whom she believes is a woman of high society, in reality is a dancehall hostess in a seedy club, in Michael Curtiz's routine drama, *The Madonna of Avenue A* (1929). Costello, a student at a plush private school, meets bootlegger Grant Withers, who introduces her to some of his private scotch. A police raid results in her dismissal from school. Withers, meanwhile, is part of Dresser's gang. At this point in the plot, daughter meets mother and the former is shocked and disillusioned to learn the truth. Dresser had earlier tried to protect her daughter from how she earned her money. Costello decides to marry Withers, but Dresser, to protect her daughter from following in her footsteps, frames the bootlegger. When the mother finally realizes she made a mistake – that Withers is on the level – she takes her own life. The film is part silent and part talkie.

Ricardo Cortez, the son of a Jewish immigrant family living on the Lower East Side of New York City, becomes a successful antique dealer on Fifth Avenue, in Frank Capra's domestic drama, *The Younger Generation* (1929). He changes his name and moves his family to his lush apartment uptown. His father, Jean Hersholt, becomes ill and longs for the old neighborhood. His sister, Lina Basquette, marries her childhood sweetheart, who is soon sent to jail. Cortez then evicts his sister from his apartment. When his father dies, his mother returns to the Lower East Side to join her daughter, whose husband has been released from prison.

Vampires

I. Vampires and Their Seductive Powers

English novelist William Makepeace Thackery, in *Vanity Fair,* with his unscrupulous adventuress Becky Sharp, suggests that society puts a premium on hypocrisy, and that a person without money or influence must violate the ethical principles to which society pays lip service. Is he right in justifying the amoral road taken by temptresses and seductresses? Most early silent dramas about these vampires suggest otherwise. Audiences may have been infatuated by them, but at the same time they strongly condemned them. Male audiences were attracted to these women but recognized their inherent danger. Wives and sweethearts denounced them as home-breakers. But between 1914 and 1917, a flood of vampire films was unleashed on American theaters and did not recede until the mid-twenties. And Theda Bara led the parade of actresses.

Edward José, the "Fool" in Frank Powell's domestic drama, *A Fool There Was* (1914), based on the poem, "The Vampire," by Rudyard Kipling, is a happily married Wall Street lawyer – that is, until he meets the notorious Theda Bara, the "Vampire," during his voyage to Europe. Appointed as special diplomatic representative to England, José soon falls under the seductive powers of the Vampire, who has ruined a long line of men before she met her latest victim. After being slighted by the lawyer's wife, Bara is determined to ruin the husband. Only several months later, the Fool ends up but a shell of a man who has abandoned his family, become dependent on drink, and remains under Bara's influence, although she has abandoned him for another man. When his wife, Mabel Fenyer, comes to reclaim her broken husband, Bara once again comes between them, and the weak husband rejects his wife's offer. The Fool allows his life to deteriorate despite offers from his family and friends to help him recuperate. Bara's line from the film, "Kiss me, you fool," became her catch-phrase for the remainder of her short career. Within the next four or five years she starred in about forty dramas, often proudly listed as "Theda Bara Superproductions," and by 1920 her film career was virtually over. The sophistication of film dramas advanced to the point that her exotic pose as a vampire became laughable to her audiences.

Olga Petrova portrays the title character in Alice Blaché's often awkward drama, *The Vampire* (1915), about a young woman who uses her looks and charms to attract a variety of men. At a mountain resort, she is rescued from a car accident and attracts the attention of several male guests, especially a married doctor who falls in love with her. He leaves his wife and family and marries his former patient. However, he soon grows tired of her and returns to his wife. Petrova leaves for Europe, where she soon gains the reputation of "The Vampire" and is later referred to as "The Spider." Foreign agents soon hire her to learn the secret of important papers in the hands of an American in the diplomatic service. But she falls in love with him. She then discovers that he is the son of the doctor who earlier had married her and then abandoned her. She vindictively plots to ruin the young man's life, but finds that she cannot carry this out. Back in the States, she agrees to marry him. When spies break into his home to steal other important documents, she learns about this and tries to warn her lover. She arrives in time only to stop a bullet meant for the diplomat. Before she dies, she arranges for her lover to reconcile his differences with a young woman he had been engaged to earlier.

The selfish and sensuous desires of a strong-minded businessman almost ruins his life and the lives of his family in James A. Golden's domestic drama, *The Master of the House* (1915), based on the 1912 play by Edgar James. Julius Steger, the husband and father who earlier had ironically condemned his son who announced that he wanted to marry the father's secretary, followed the same path. He divorces his wife, Grace Reals, for the younger, more attractive secretary, Margot Williams, whom he then marries. Fortunately, his lawyer friend discovers that the new wife is an adventuress who is having an affair with a musician. So the businessman returns to the divorce court, where he secures his second divorce. The lawyer then arranges a meeting between his friend and his first wife. The husband admits that he was wrong and foolish to neglect his responsibilities in an effort to seek happiness away from his family.

Holbrook Blinn, as a regretful husband and father who has fallen for a wanton chorus girl, causes several problems for his family that he has neglected in Frank Crane's drama, *The Family Cupboard* (1915), based on the play by Owen Davis. The adventuress eventually marries her companion, a vaudeville entertainer, leaving Blinn to contemplate the trouble he has brought to his wife and son. Repentant about his past, Blinn soon learns that his own son has succumbed to the chorus girl's charms. Finally, the youth also sees the error of his ways and returns to his family, which is together once again .

Henry King falls in love with cabaret entertainer Lillian Lorraine and forgets about his obligations to his wife and young son in the drama, *Should a Wife Forgive?* (1915). The adventuress, who has Lew Cody, a wealthy companion, paying for her own home, manipulates her latest lover to finance her new play. To accomplish this and continue his affair with Lorraine, King is forced to use $10,000 of his wife's money. After the show flops, King unexpectedly meets Cody, his rival, and a fight ensues. Later, the vampire is found dead, and her two lovers are under suspicion of murder. A suicide note is eventually found in which Lorraine confesses she was tired of her life and wished to end it. Both men are exonerated, but when King tries to return to his wife, Mabel Van Buren, she rejects him. The film ends with the titled question: "Should a Wife Forgive?"

An inexperienced youth falls in love with an older woman, despite his father's warnings, in the cautionary drama, *His Crucible* (1915). The young man justifies his actions by blaming his father, who had promised his son after his wife's death that he would never remarry. After the father's remarriage, the son becomes disillusioned with his father and stepmother and begins to lead a reckless life. When the adventuress learns that the father has disinherited the son, she abandons him and leaves for Paris. Later, the son writes to her and she responds that she is returning and that he should meet her at the dock. When he does, she slips him her cigarette case containing a pearl necklace. A customs agent witnesses the transfer and arrests him. The stepmother arranges for his bail and persuades her husband to renew his relationship with his son. The young man now accepts his father's love and learns to appreciate his stepmother. In addition, he admits that the woman he thought he loved was only using him.

William Courtleigh Jr. was another youth who succumbed to the charms of an attractive woman. A weak youth who enjoys good times and nightclubs, he easily falls in love with an actress who treats the young man casually, in Henry King's familiar drama, *Souls in Pawn* (1915). Courtleigh neglects the young woman he is engaged to for the wiles of the vampire, Vivian Prescott. His friend, Ben Wilson, who also loves the neglected fiancée, tries to help him out of his difficulties, but his friend refuses his advice. Wilson then offers Prescott money to break off relations with his friend, and she accepts. Later, Courtleigh becomes involved in shooting another lover caught in the actress's apartment and escapes through a window. Wilson arrives and is arrested by the police for the shooting. Meanwhile, the fugitive hides out for several days in a Chinese opium den. He finally stumbles home, and before he dies, he confesses to the shooting. Wilson is exonerated and proposes to the young woman Courtleigh had abandoned. Unfortunately, the film suffered from stereotyped characters.

Vaudeville performer Valeska Suratt has captured the hearts of at least two men, one an elderly companion who showers her with money, and the other a young man who has fallen in love with her, in Herbert Brenon's contrived drama, *The Soul of Broadway* (1915). William E. Shay, the young man, witnesses the companion leaving Suratt's home. When Shay enters and finds a check for $1,200 that the man left for her, he angrily tears it up. A struggle ensues between him and Suratt, who reaches for a revolver. In the fracas, Shay shoots her and flees. He gives himself up to the police just as Suratt calls in for his arrest. He is tried and sentenced to five years, and is released after several months. He meets and marries Mabel Allen, who does not want to know anything of his past. Meanwhile, Suratt and her elderly companion go to Atlantic City, where she meets gambler Sheridan Block. She quickly abandons her companion and begins an affair with the gambler. When she learns that Shay and his wife are on the beach nearby, she decides to expose his past. At Block's gambling house, she meets the young wife and is about to tell her about her husband's sordid past when Suratt suddenly goes insane and begins acting irrationally. She falls down a flight of stairs and dies.

Eugene Pallette, the married son of a wealthy banker, becomes infatuated with cabaret entertainer Jewel Carmen, who is only interested in Pallette's money, in C. M. Franklin and Sidney A. Franklin's drama, *The Children in the House* (1916). When the adventuress demands more money from the husband, he asks his father but is refused. He then reluctantly goes along with Carmen's advice that he join her gang in robbing his father's bank. Meanwhile, his neglected wife, Norma Talmadge, asks her sister and detective brother-in-law, W. E. Lawrence, for advice. After the robbery, bank teller William Hinckley, a former beau of Talmadge's, is arrested. The gang is caught in their hideout, and in the shootout that ensues, all but one member perishes, including Pallette. Talmadge is left a widow and forced to raise her children alone. The film suggests that she and Hinckley will rekindle their old love. The title means very little to the film.

Malcolm Duncan, a hardworking bookkeeper and part-time inventor, inherits a large sum of money and immediately falls victim to New York's lively night life and a clever seductress in the drama, *The Scarlet Road* (1916). Duncan, who has been trying to promote his new airplane motor, confides to his girlfriend, Della Conner, and her mother that if he sells his invention they can marry. But when he inherits his father's $200,000, he forgets about his invention and Conner and falls for the charms of Anna Q. Nilsson, a dancer and temptress of the cabaret circuit. After spending all his inheritance on her, she quickly drops him. The down-and-out Duncan considers taking his own life and heads for the river. Just then, the daughter of a millionaire falls overboard and Duncan rescues her from drowning. The grateful daughter introduces Duncan to her father, who then backs him in his invention. When Nilsson, learning of his good fortune, she tries to rekindle their affair, but the successful and wiser inventor rejects her and returns to his girlfriend, whom he marries.

Seductress Kitty Gordon, who has many admirers, moves heartlessly from one lover to another, depending on their wealth, in Robert Thornby's weak drama, *Her Maternal Right* (1916). She is seen rejecting one lover who has gone bankrupt buying her gifts and who ends up taking his own life. Her next victim, a young cashier, has embezzled $12,000 from his bank to splurge on Gordon, who then rejects him to marry a millionaire. Later, the cashier meets a simple country girl and marries her. Just as he is about to become a father, inspectors begin to examine his books. Threatened with prison, he goes to Gordon to ask her to return the money to protect him and his family. She refuses his request just as his wife enters and threatens her with a gun. She forces Gordon to write a check upon the threat of killing her and her husband and then exposing the entire story.

Some early vampire dramas focused more on the element of greed than on lust, making the work more of a crime film. Villainous Renzi de Cordova plots with Southern adventuress Elaine Terriss to ruin a Northerner in Tom Terriss's romantic drama, *Flame of Passion* (1915), set chiefly on the island of Jamaica. Tom Terriss, the intended victim, has inherited an estate in Jamaica and journeys there to settle business matters. Cordova, who is next in line to inherit the property in the event of Terriss's death, want to see his rival's destruction. Terriss immediately falls for the charms of the adventuress. Meanwhile, his fiancée, Marguerite Hanley, hears about his affair and joins him in Jamaica to rescue him from the vampire's clutches. Cordova's scheme backfires when he becomes infatuated with the fiancée and kidnaps her for his own lust. His jealous lover intervenes and a struggle between them ends in the vampire's death. Terriss, now freed of the adventuress's hold on him, rescues his fiancée and they both leave for home to marry.

Billie Brockwell, as an adventuress from the city, journeys to the small village of Hicksville to seduce the cashier of a gold mine, in the two-reel burlesque, *A Village Vampire* (1916). Joseph Swickard, as the naïve cashier, is duped into stealing the nuggets in the safe and eloping with Brockwell. Somehow, on the way to the city where Swickard is to join his lover, the bags are switched. The woman's gang grabs the cashier and the bag, but then discover the mix-up. They return to Hicksville, clean out the mill of all the available gold and leave the cashier tied up. He manages to call the police and the big chase is on. At least three bridges are dynamited, a train is wrecked and a stamping mill is set afire before the final showdown – a gun battle between the gang and the police. With the restoration of law and order, a marriage is arranged between the station master's daughter and Swickard's son.

Wealthy playboy Robert Warwick has an affair with café dancer Leonore Harris, a mercenary adventuress who arranges for her gang to rob his house, in Emile Chautard's drama, *Human Driftwood* (1916). Warwick discovers the burglars and a fight ensues in which Harris's lover is killed. Warwick, emotionally moved by the experience, joins the city's reformers, and years later is sent to investigate vice in Alaska, where Harris runs a dancehall. But Warwick does not recognize her. Frances Nelson, one of Harris's major entertainers, keeps aloof of the ruffians who inhabit the place. Harris eventually arranges for the "sale" of Nelson, allegedly her niece, to Albert S. Hart, who has struck pay dirt. But when Warwick and the local priest enter, the arrangement is postponed. Nelson meets the reformer and both fall in love with each other. When Warwick goes to Harris to get her consent to the marriage, she reveals her true identity and says the young woman is the result of their earlier affair. That night Hart kidnaps Nelson, and in the shootout Harris is mortally wounded. Before she dies, she confesses that Nelson is not related to her. Warwick pursues Hart, throws him into the icy river and rescues the young woman he loves.

Ernest Maupin plays Python Grant, the heavy, in Lawrence Windom's ironic thriller, *The Discard* (1916). Opposite him is Virginia Hammond, as Alys Wynne, who must decide where her loyalties lie – the choice is between her husband and her daughter. The plot is complicated with mother and daughter separated over the years and the mother moving to America with her husband, also known as "The Python," a highly accomplished swindler. Hammond is enlisted by The Python to help entrap and fleece young Keith Bourne. What she doesn't know is that Bourne is her son-in-law, and in destroying him she is ruining her own daughter's life. When faced with deciding between her own daughter and her husband, she chooses to turn over The Python to the police. She then commits suicide.

Theda Bara, as secretary to H. Cooper Cliffe, a U.S. colonel, lures him into an affair which shortly bankrupts him, in James Vincent's drama, *Gold and the Woman* (1916). The colonel is ward to orphan Alma Hanlon, who has inherited her own estate. She is in love with Harry Hilliard, a Harvard student, who also succumbs to Bara's charms. When Hanlon sees Hilliard in the arms of the temptress, she breaks off relations with him. To save himself from complete bankruptcy, the colonel proposes marriage to Hanlon, who accepts after her disillusioning experience with Hilliard. Shortly after the wedding, Hanlon loses her sight. Bara then persuades the colonel to get his wife to sign over all her property to him, but the plan fails. The blind wife manages to discover her husband asleep with his secretary. As she is about to end her life by jumping from a wharf, Hilliard rescues her. Thinking his wife has died, the colonel marries Bara and dies as the result of his heavy drinking. The blind widow and Hilliard reconcile their differences and find happiness with each other.

An Eastern seductress plies her charms in the West, but eventually forfeits her life in Roland West's drama, *The Siren* (1917), set chiefly in a rowdy dancehall. Valeska Suratt, as the title character, learns that Clifford Bruce, a young prospector, has inherited a large fortune and sets her sights on him. She almost succeeds in marrying Bruce, but comes to an untimely end. Actress Theda Bara, the supreme screen vamp, set the tone for this type of lurid drama several years earlier. The western proved a flexible genre capable of embracing a variety of themes and characters, including that of the vamp.

Harry Carey, as "Sky High," a cowboy who inherits a fortune from an uncle, becomes the subject of a plot by a jealous cousin in George Marshall's comedy drama, *Love's Lariat* (1916). The inheritance hinges upon the cowpuncher's resettlement in the East. The cousin, in an attempt to distract the cowboy, hires Goldie, a young woman, to seduce him. The plan backfires when the cowboy and the seductress fall in love. Olive Fuller Golden, who played Goldie, was Carey's real-life wife and the mother of Harry Carey Jr.

The vampire drama proved flexible enough to fit various genres. One quite popular, especially during wartime, was the spy drama. English actress Kitty Gordon portrays a vicious adventuress in Frank H. Crane's drama, *As in a Looking Glass* (1916), based on the 1887 novel and play by Francis Charles Phillips. She leaves Europe for the U.S. to escape her oppressive lover and a string of wealthy men with whom she had had affairs. In Washington she meets government worker F. Lumsden Hare, whom she had met earlier during her journey across the Atlantic. A foreign agent familiar with some of her more seedy affairs in Europe blackmails her into stealing naval plans from the American with whom she has unintentionally fallen in love. Instead of betraying him, she elopes with him. Enemy agents find the couple, steal the plans and force her to accompany them to their leader. She manages to destroy the vital papers and is fatally shot. She lives long enough to telephone her husband and confess all.

Emile Chautard's romantic drama, *The Eternal Temptress* (1917), set in Italy during World War I, has as its theme the power of women over men. The internationally famous actress, Lina Cavalieri, portrays the beautiful temptress who enchants a young American, Elliott Dexter, with her feminine charms. Meanwhile, Austrian secret agents, bent on getting their hands on vital documents stored in the American embassy, plot to use the American, who is blinded by love, as their tool. So enthralled with Cavalieri is the young man that he is willing to steal the papers. The siren, however, who has fallen in love with Dexter, saves him from betraying his country. A preface introduces the theme of the drama by depicting various historical examples of victims ensnared passion.

A continental flavor enhanced some vampire films by the addition of foreign settings. Theda Bara portrays the daughter of Russian peasants in R. A. Walsh's drama, *The Serpent* (1916), set both in Russia and England. After Bara is raped by a duke, her boyfriend, who has rushed to the duke's castle to rescue her, is killed by the guards. The duke, when he is finished with her, hands her some money and tells her to leave the country. She settles in England, where she becomes a cold-hearted seductress and a popular stage personality. At one of her performances, the duke who had attacked her is in the audience. Unaware that she is the same peasant girl, he goes backstage to meet her. An affair takes place in which he admits that if anything should happen to his son, he would die. When Bara learns that his son has been wounded in battle, she volunteers as a nurse and gets assigned to the duke's son. She lures him into an affair and they are married. She then joins his father and arranges for the son to see his father embracing her. The disillusioned young man leaves and commits suicide. Bara then reveals her real identity, stating, "I swore to repay you and I've done it." Suddenly, she falls out of bed, and the film now makes known to the audience that the entire story was just a dream. The dream device in films seemed to be popular at this period, especially during 1914 and 1915, and was used in such films as *The Avenging Conscience, Thou Shalt Not Kill, The Chimes, The Ordeal, Alice in Wonderland, The Despoiler, The Dust of Egypt, The Hypocrites, The Magic Skin,* and *The Marble Heart.*

II. The Decline of the Temptresses

The leader of the early film vampires, Theda Bara, was out of work by 1920, and with her disappearance from films, the cycle she so ably enriched, promoted and dominated with her strange and bizarre persona both on and off screen for about half a dozen years began to diminish. In addition, the previous decade ended with *The Amateur Adventuress* (1919), a satire on vamps that served as a harbinger of hard times for the cycle. For the next several years, other actresses, including Kathlyn William in *The Tree of Knowledge* (1920) and Viola Dana in *Blackmail* (1920) and *Being Respectable* (1924), did a capable job in ruining bankers, lawyers, husbands and young men who were foolish enough to succumb to their sensual charms. But the cycle was sounding its death knell by the mid to late twenties, with Greta Garbo in *The Temptress* (1926) giving a languorous interpretation of a tired and worn vampire who had seen better days. Generally, vampire films provided popular entertainment and furnished their leading actresses with a chance to dominate the screen while they strutted their attributes. The film vampire promised sexual pleasure but ended up sucking the blood and life force from her male victims, added an interesting contrast to the popular image of the conventional heroine. Stars like Mary Pickford, Lillian Gish, and Blanche Sweet were terrific as kid sisters or the innocent girl next door or, as Pickford was called, "America's Sweetheart," but they were not exactly sex symbols. The exotic femme fatale, the immutably evil seductress who vamped her way across the screens of the 1910s, finally yielded to a more sexually liberated America, with its new female icon of the twenties, the exuberant flapper.

Film studios were quick to fill the vampire void created by Theda Bara's absence from the screen. Englishman Robert Warwick, living in Paris with adventuress Kathlyn Williams, finally proposes to her, but she rejects him for a wealthier titled European in William C. de Mille's romantic drama, *The Tree of Knowledge* (1920), based on the play by R. C. Carton. Warwick returns to England to manage the estate of his friend, Tom Forman, where he meets his friend's ward, who falls in love with Warwick. Forman, while in Paris, meets Williams and, thinking her innocent, marries the seductress. When the couple return to England, she meets Warwick, her ex-lover, but says nothing. Warwick, learning that she next intends to elope with another of her victims, prevents her latest betrayal, and the entire affair is brought into the open. The young ward then forgives him for his earlier romantic indiscretions.

Viola Dana, another popular actress of the period, portrays Flossie Golden, a seductive blackmailer, in Dallas Fitzgerald's comedy, *Blackmail* (1920), based on Lucia Chamberlain's story, "The Underside." After luring wealthy men into love trysts, Flossie extorts money from them. This continues until an attorney, hired by one of her victims, turns the tables on her. Flossie is so taken with the lawyer that they end up marrying. In a form of poetic justice, Flossie's marital joy is threatened by her old accomplices who want payoffs to buy their silence about her lurid past. The blackmailer-turned-victim, however, is an old hand at this game and refuses to comply. The police arrive to collar the extortionists and Flossie's husband reveals that he had already known about her past and had long forgiven her.

A superior remake of the 1914 Lasky-Paramount film (which starred Edmund Breese), Kenneth Webb's drama, *The Master Mind* (1920), features Lionel Barrymore as Henry Allen, the title character. Allen's brother was convicted, improperly it seems, by a ruthless district attorney Ralph Kellard. Allen's revenge calls for a blackmail attempt by a young woman with a criminal record seducing Kellard. When the district attorney marries her, the trap is sprung. But at the very moment that his revenge is within his grasp, "The Master Mind" relents and does not expose his role in the marriage. The film underscores the concept of forgiveness.

A selfish mother, to hold on to her son, plots to break up his relationship with a young woman he loves in Emile Chautard's uninteresting comedy drama, *Forsaking All Others* (1922). Cullen Landis is the unfortunate young man who is dragged off to a resort by his mother who wants to separate him from Colleen Moore, who loves him. But the overbearing mother is confronted with an unforeseen complication when Landis is lured into a romantic affair with a married adventuress staying at the same resort. Unable to save her naïve son from possible ruin, she calls upon his former girlfriend to help her save Landis. Moore agrees, and the man she loves finally returns to her arms. His mother finally relents and allows her son to marry Moore.

A cowboy is lured off the ranch by a city temptress, but saves himself in the nick of time, in Marcel Perez's drama, *The Better Man Wins* (1922), which once again extols the virtues of the West, while condemning the lurid and wicked ways of the East. Pete Morrison portrays the clean-cut cowboy who becomes infatuated with an actress staying at a nearby ranch. Rejected by Nell, played by Dorothy Wood, who has decided to run her family ranch without his help, Morrison falls prey to the seductive charms of the actress, while her lascivious manager tries to seduce Nell. Morrison returns from the city in time to save Nell from making a similar mistake.

A half-white, half-Chinese villain, seeking to avenge his jilted sister, stalks a prospector for years in the absurd drama, *Her Half Brother* (1922), set in Texas. The elderly prospector takes in a partner, who had earlier helped him fend off a group of outlaws, and the two men prosper. The villain then unleashes Nina, a young seductress, upon the two men. When they are alone, the half-breed explains why he wants to avenge his half-sister who was white and then reveals that Nina, the young woman, is the prospector's daughter.

Ricardo Cortez is virtually swallowed up by the sensual pitfalls of modern society, including the charms of temptress Lya de Putti, in D. W. Griffith's heavy-handed drama, *The Sorrows of Satan* (1926), based on the 1895 novel by Marie Corelli. Adolphe Menjou, as a Satan-like wealthy prince, contributes to Cortez's dissolute life. The film is based on the legend of Lucifer's banishment from heaven and his punishment as Satan, who is cursed to tempt mankind. For each soul who rejects him, he is rewarded with one hour at heaven's gates. The sorrow of Satan is that no one rejects him. This includes Cortez, an impoverished book critic, who meets Menjou when the former, in a fit of despair, renounces God during a raging storm, and Menjou suddenly appears. Under his influence and tutelage, Cortez lures the innocent Carol Dempster into his room and later abandons her on the day of their intended wedding. Instead, he marries de Putti, the temptress whose ulterior motive for the union with the critic is to be close to Menjou, with whom she is fascinated. When Cortez realizes the infidelity, Menjou reveals his true identity and threatens to take away all of the writer's wealth. The next morning finds Cortez in his attic, reunited with Dempster.

Greta Garbo, an amoral seductress, drives men to disgrace, murder and suicide – and, ironically, she herself ends up in the gutter – in Fred Niblo's disappointing, but sumptuously mounted, romantic drama, *The Temptress* (1926), based on the novel by Blasco Ibanez. In Paris, during a masquerade ball, unhappily married Greta Garbo meets engineer Antonio Moreno and they fall in love. When Moreno later learns that she is married and had earlier been the mistress to a wealthy banker whom she had driven to suicide, he returns to Argentina in disgust. She and her husband follow, and through her charms ruins the lives of several other admirers – except for Moreno, who resists her. "Men have gone to ruin for you," he says reproachfully. "Not for me," she replies, "for my body. Not for my happiness, but for their own." He then admits to his own fascination toward her. But she disappears, as if sparing him further pain. Years later, he returns to Paris with his fiancée, and sees Garbo relegated to a life of degradation as a drunkard and streetwalker, loitering, bleary-eyed.

Family man Emil Jannings is ruined by his own lust in Victor Fleming's domestic drama, *The Way of All Flesh* (1927). Assigned to carry bearer bonds from his Milwaukee bank to Chicago by train, Jannings, while on board, is seduced by Phyllis Haver. In a hotel room, she relieves him of the valuable bonds. When he awakes, he discovers the bonds are missing. He returns to the café where he had been with Haver. Following a confrontation with her lover, the man strikes a chair over Jannings's head. He is deposited near railroad tracks, where he awakens to someone robbing his personal belongings. He shoves his assailant into an oncoming train. Newspaper accounts list the dead man as Jannings, since the man had the cashier's belongings on his person. Years later, after spending time as a park attendant and selling chestnuts, he returns home. On Christmas Eve, he stands outside his home, broke and a derelict, observing his family from a distance. He finally fades into the distance up the street during a blizzard. This was Jannings's first Hollywood film.

White Slavery

I. The Traffic in Souls

By 1899, the control of traffic in prostitution became an international issue. In the U.S., interstate and international transportation of women for immoral purposes became illegal with the introduction of James Robert Mann's White Slave Traffic Act (1910), which became better known as the Mann Act. Today, houses of prostitution are illegal in all states but Nevada. The subject of prostitution was often cloaked in euphemisms. The section where prostitutes usually lived and worked was known as the "red light" district. They were labeled "women of easy virtue," "street walkers," "pros," and the establishment where they plied their trade was described as a "resort" or "house." But "white slavery" took on a more menacing tone, since it threatened decent young women who were caught in the vice web against their wishes. This practice affected all families and all classes. The white slave issue exploded in New York about 1913, about the same time the Rockefeller Commission report was released, concluding that police corruption was the most significant element in the white slave traffic. A congressional committee investigating immigration discovered that thousands of young immigrant women never reached their destination; instead, they were abducted into the white slave trade that often began in Europe, where the traffickers became engaged or married to the girls. The men would then leave for the States and send tickets for the women to follow. Once in New York, they were escorted to the various "houses," where they were put to work. Stripped of their money and clothes, they were trapped in these brothels and at the mercy of the traffickers. Many of these incidents were described in graphic detail in several dramas, such as *Traffic in Souls* (1913) and *White Slaver* (1914), while others in this cycle, such as *The Inside of the White Slave Traffic* (1913), bordered on blatant sensationalism. Even major directors turned familiar plot devices into the service of the explosive topic of white slave trafficking.

Villainous Chinese white slavers plot a horrible end for an undercover police officer in D. W. Griffith's gimmicky minor drama, *The Fatal Hour* (1908). The female officer, on the trail of the kidnappers, rescues a white woman from their clutches but is then herself captured. The slavers, in revenge, arrange for her death by wiring a gun to a clock. But the police arrive and rescue her before the fatal hour is struck. Griffith, the pioneer director, anticipated at least two popular subjects with this film – the burst of white slave dramas that would flood the market in the next few years, and using a woman as an undercover police officer.

Considered influential in the development of the feature film, George Loane Tucker's exploitation social drama about white slavery, *Traffic in Souls* (1913), relates how Ethel Grandin, an innocent young woman, is lured into a brothel. The man who ensnares his unwary victim is considered a nicely mannered gentleman. Meanwhile, her sister, Jane Gail, loses her job and is almost tricked into a life of prostitution by the leader of a gang of white slavers, while he poses as the head of a purity committee. Fortunately, she grows suspicious of her supposed benefactor and, together with her boyfriend, a police officer, she helps to expose the sordid racket. The drama, which was the first commercial success of the neophyte Universal studio, reportedly was inspired by the Rockefeller White Slavery Report. Film historian William K. Everson in his book, *American Silent Film,* labeled the drama an underworld film rather than a gangster film, though he acknowledged that the work illustrates the considerable influences of organized crime. The film was one of the earliest full-length American dramas, preceding Griffith's American Civil War spectacle, *Birth of a Nation* (1915), by two years.

Frank S. Beal's exploitation drama, *The Inside of the White Slave Traffic* (1913), was no doubt inspired by the success of *Traffic in Souls*, released earlier in the year. The latest work was just another steamy vice film, which the producers passed off as a cautionary drama. One sequence depicts a lone streetwalker in New York City entrapped by a fake fight over her, during which she is drugged and hurried to the procurer's den. She is kept overnight, then forced into a fake marriage, and finally sold to a New Orleans house of prostitution. She escapes, but when she tries to return to her solo trade, she is forbidden to work the streets. Defeated on all sides, she is forced to return to the group that had first tricked her. Producer and writer Samuel H. London led the Rockefeller commission's White Slavery Report and had directed the U.S. Secret Service. The film exceeded the box-office intake of its predecessor, *Traffic in Souls*.

When Lottie Pickford leaves her middle-class family with Armand F. Cortes, who has promised to marry her, she is unaware that he is a procurer for a brothel, in Pierce Kingsley's drama about white slavery, *The House of Bondage* (1914), based on the 1910 novel by Reginald Wright Kaufmann. Forced to work in a New York house of prostitution, Pickford manages to escape, only to discover all other avenues of employment are closed to her. When she returns home, her father evicts her, forcing her to go back to the brothel. But Sue

Willis, who runs the illegal operation, refuses to let her enter because of her deteriorated physical condition. She collapses on a street, where a kindly gentleman finds her.

Newspaperwoman Rose Austin and her detective boyfriend work out a scheme to expose a white slavery ring in the early social drama, *Trapped in the Great Metropolis* (1914). Posing as a South American interested in purchasing slaves, Austin worms her way into the confidence of the gang until she meets the leader, who is posing as a philanthropic lecturer. He escapes before the police arrive, and a chase ensues after the office manager who is soon shot. Meanwhile, the leader, although safe in his own home, dies from the excitement. No doubt the film was designed to capitalize on the highly successful and sensational drama, *Traffic in Souls*, also about white slavery, released one year earlier.

Tight direction and plotting help Allan Dwan's suspenseful drama, *The Conspiracy* (1914), based on the play by Robert B. Baker and John Emerson. A mystery writer (Emerson) decides to solve a murder. He discovers that the murdered man had been the head of a gang of white slavers and had been killed by the victim's secretary (Lois Meredith). It seems she took the job to gain evidence to convict the gang, but the leader caught her rifling his papers. To protect herself, she was forced to kill the chief. Emerson is instrumental in the capture of the gang and in exonerating Meredith of the murder.

An innocent young woman is decoyed and locked up in a "pleasure palace" belonging to her "buyer" in the flagrant exploitation drama, *White Slaver* (1914). A spotter for one of the gangs or organizations involved in the white slave trade notices her at a railway station. He picks her up and takes her to the house of prostitution, designed to look like a marble palace. Here she is beaten and exploited, while two rivals battle to possess her. Meanwhile, the young victim thinks she is going to meet her relatives. Jack Lester, a young man she had met earlier on a boat ride, finally comes to her rescue after a terrible hand-to-hand battle over rooftops with a white slaver.

A gang of white slavers sets up operations in a small town to ensnare unwary young women to work in the gang's immoral "houses," in the poorly produced drama, *Smashing the Vice Trust* (1914). The gang members then persuade their victims to accompany them to New York, where they are locked up in rooms until they agree to participate with the "Vice Trust." A police raid on the establishment finally rounds up the white slave traffickers and sets the young women free. Several scenes are reminiscent of those in *Traffic in Souls*, released one year earlier. To help authenticate the production, the film introduces New York's District Attorney Whitman, who offers a few words of advice concerning the social problem depicted on the screen. Several scenes, which were filmed in New York, take on further historical significance today.

U.S. Secret Service agent James O'Neill helps to smash a white slavery operation in the bland drama, *The Lure* (1914), based on the original 1913 stage production by George Scarborough. One of the reasons for the tameness of the production was the heavy censorship forced upon the original play by New York's police. For example, the physical setting of the bawdy house in the play was condemned, forcing the producers to curtail the set and its suggestiveness. The film version suffers from similar restrictions. The basic plot concerns the agent's pursuit of a slaver recruit and his political boss who runs the entire operation. The pair, after escaping to the country, return to the city to silence Fraunie Fraunholtz, one of their girls who knows too much about their entire operation. The agent learns of their plans and is present to arrest them when they return.

Yancsi Dolly, a young woman of the slums who is burdened with an alcoholic father, becomes entangled with white slavers before achieving success on stage as a dancer, in George L. Sargent's weak drama, *The Call of the Dance* (1915). A friend takes her to a dancehall, where a gang of white slavers have their headquarters. The gang leader is attracted to Dolly and wants her for his brothel. Her father enters and, in his attempt to take her home, becomes involved in a fight with some of the gang and is shot to death. The slavers take Dolly to one of their houses where they lock her up. An assistant district attorney later arrives to investigate the shooting. Dolly, in the next building, attracts his attention by flashing her pocket mirror. The gang leader is in another room with another man, who is the attorney's lascivious uncle. The elderly man, who covets young women, has been secretly dealing with the leader for some time, and is here to look over his latest acquisitions. The gang leader overhears the attorney in the cellar, goes below with his gun, and is knocked unconscious by the attorney, who then rescues the trapped woman. Meanwhile, the uncle escapes unnoticed. Following several complications, Dolly, now a successful dancer, is reunited with the assistant district attorney, who has captured the leader of the white slavers. Earlier, a musician, seeking to avenge his girlfriend whom the uncle has earlier ruined, kills the reprobate.

Violet Mersereau, as Mignon, is the target of a white slave trafficker in Rex Ingram's interesting action drama, *Broken Fetters* (1916), that spans two continents. The daughter of a murdered U.S. consul in Hong Kong, Mignon is raised by a Mandarin but longs to see America. She does, but not without trouble, as both a young American artist, Lawrence Demarest, and the white-slaver Foo Shai desire the young woman. Foo Shai is eventually killed by Mignon's friend Chang (Charles Fang), after which Demarest and Mignon plan their marriage. This was one of the earliest dramas about New York's Chinese gangsters.

An ill-tempered stepmother, a dallying husband and a vindictive female companion almost drive innocent young shop girl Frances Nelson to a life of shame in Barry O"Neil's drama, *The Revolt* (1916), based on the play about white slave conditions. The film explores the sad life of the main character, a mistreated wife who visits a brothel where her friend works. Once there, the innocent visitor is physically and sexually attacked by the white slavers who control the establishment. Whereas the stage production aimed at exposing the brutal conditions of the white slave traffic, the film version underlined the human suffering of the abused wife.

Another exposé of white slavery, Jacques Jaccard's drama, *Is Any Girl Safe?* (1916), was supervised by Rev. Dr. Charles Parkhurst, who gained fame in the 1890s for his inquiries into vice. The plot concerns two youths who make a living by soliciting young women for houses of prostitution. One of the young men persuades a factory worker to enter one of these houses, promising her a more lucrative salary. After selling her to a life of bondage, he visits his friend who is in the same business and discovers his own sister in the other's private room, about to become a recruit for the same work he has just turned over the factory worker to perform. He and his sister escape in time. The brother realizes the close call they had just had and the dangers they had undergone from participating in these activities. A unique feature of this exploitation film was the appearance of Yusha Botwin, a self-confessed practitioner of white slavery.

Produced as an exposé of the white slavery traffic in Chicago, Richard Foster Baker and M. Blair Coan's drama, *The Little Girl Next Door* (1916), ran into trouble in Illinois, where the politicians opposed its showing. Each attempt to censor the film brought columns of newsprint and free publicity, all of which finally resulted in making money for the producers. Supposedly dealing with the Crime Commission investigating vice in Chicago, this semi-documentary moves back and forth between the houses of sin and the panel room of the State Morals Committee. Public figures are seen interviewing other public figures and occasionally witnesses who have been under the yoke of the white slavers. Then the camera cuts to reenactments of what the young women had experienced. At least one critic pointed out that ironically the women who work in these houses seemed better dressed, better fed and of better disposition than the factory workers in the audience. Other scenes show some the houses of prostitution that have been boarded up after the reform wave got through with them.

Two innocent young women are kidnapped and eventually enticed to work in a brothel in Frank C. Griffin's farfetched drama, *Where Love Leads* (1916). Ormi Hawley is prodded by her parents into marrying the elderly lord, Charles Craig, although she is in love with a younger man. Seventeen years later, Hawley, now a neglected wife, decides to send her two daughters to America, away from the influence of their father. She unknowingly entrusts them to a white slaver, who makes plans for their capture. When the ship arrives in America, they are rescued by Rockliffe Fellowes, who happens to be their mother's former boyfriend. The two sisters then arrange for a reconciliation between their rescuer and their mother.

Slum children Mae Murray and her little brother are left to fend for themselves after their father is sent to jail in John B. O'Brien's predictable drama, *The Big Sister* (1916). The young woman barely escapes the clutches of a white slaver who covets her for one of his girls. Later, her brother is struck by a car belonging to Harry C. Browne, a wealthy man who, to make amends, takes both

Murray and her brother to his country estate, where Murray and her benefactor eventually fall in love. Murray's idyllic life is almost shattered when the white slaver appears and tries to blackmail her by threatening to expose her as one of his "girls." However, he is foiled in his plan, and the couple continue with their ideal relationship.

Persistent reporter Frank Mayo rescues Lois Meredith, the young woman he loves, in Sherwood MacDonald's farfetched suspenseful drama, *Sold at Auction* (1917), that touches upon the theme of white slavery. Placed in the care of a selfish woman by William Conklin, her father, when she was just a child, Meredith runs away when she grows up. The father, who has never visited his daughter, is unaware of the woman's bad treatment towards her charge. When Meredith falls in love with the reporter, the woman, afraid of losing the support money, tells her she has mulatto blood. At this point, the young woman flees and ends up seeking employment with a "matrimonial agency," which in reality is in business to sell sex. She is offered up for auction in front of a group of men – including her own father, who is unaware that she is his daughter. While he engages in bidding against the competition, Mayo arrives after tracking her down. He then reveals her identity to Conklin.

Mary Martin, who must choose between two suitors, one who is earnest and hardworking and the other an idler, marries the latter, Stuart Holmes, in Carl Harbaugh's drama, *The Derelict* (1917). After their marriage and the birth of a daughter, Holmes's wild life and reckless attitude toward his family force his wife to divorce him and marry the other suitor. Several years later, her daughter returns from finishing school and loses her pocketbook at the railway station. A well-dressed man approaches her and offers to help. He sends her to his home, where his wife will put her up for the night and send her safely on her way in the morning. He then follows her to his home, which in reality is a brothel. Meanwhile, a drifter at the station finds her pocketbook, which he shares with a fellow derelict, who turns out to be Holmes, the girl's father. He recognizes her name as that of his daughter and, finally tracking her down, comes to her rescue. In the scuffle, he kills the owner of the bawdy house. His daughter is accused of the killing, but her father confesses to the crime and dies of a heart attack at the police station.

Adapted from Elwyn Barron's novel *Marcel Leviget*, Donald Crisp's drama, *The House of Silence* (1918), was applauded as one of the finest mysteries of its day. The "house" is actually a den of ill repute, where an innocent young woman is lured to her imminent downfall. In an act of desperation she kills her attacker. This sets into motion a series of discoveries, clues and cover-ups. The film, with its tawdry scenes within the bawdy house, owes much to the more sensational white slavery drama, *Traffic in Souls* (1913).

Anna Luther's father sells pottery and young women for illicit purposes in Frank Beal's sprawling, farfetched drama about white slavery, *Why Blame Me?* (1918), which opens in Romania and ends in New York. Although she has a boyfriend who has gone to America, her father sells Luther as mistress to

Robert Brownlee, the owner of a gambling house. He keeps her for himself, and they travel together to Syria, China, and finally to a mining camp in America's West. Here she inadvertently meets William Garwood, her Romanian boyfriend, while Brownlee is carousing at a local gambling house. But she keeps her face covered so that Garwood does not recognize her. Later, when Brownlee staggers home drunk and passes out, she flees to New York, where she again meets Garwood in the street. But she is arrested for soliciting and taken to a women's reclamation center for interrogation. Garwood finally rescues her, and the couple marry. The film offers a variety of settings. One interesting sequence shows a volcanic eruption, whose lava flow engulfs Luther's repugnant father.

II. "Is Your Daughter Safe?"

Probably as the result of Prohibition and the spread of rum running, organized crime and other more lucrative illegal activities, films about white slavery lost their luster in the twenties. Prostitution as a popular social institution continued to flourish, but films about white slave traffickers diminished. Some studios released an occasional film on the subject, but these were chiefly low-production dramas heavily immersed in the crime or gangster genres. In *Crooked Streets* (1920), for instance, although the gang is involved in white slavery, their chief business is smuggling. *Idle Hands* (1921) focuses more on political corruption than on the white slave trade. The gang in *Ignorance* (1922) is more concerned with kidnapping and assassination than with white slavery. And *The Salvation Hunters* (1925) is more of a *bildungsroman* than an exposé of the white slave trade. Films that focused on the illicit trade added very little insight to the problem. *Red Kimono* (1926) featured an innocent heroine lured into a life of prostitution, and *Is Your Daughter Safe?* (1927) tried to resurrect the cautionary dramas of the preceding decade. Finally, mediocre films like the threadbare *Unguarded Girls* (1929), with its tired plot of the seedy roadhouse, the naïve young woman, the lecherous manager and the upstanding hero, brought the decade of white slavery films to an undistinguished end.

Political corruption and white slavery in the exotic setting of Chinatown provide the impetus for Frank Reicher's otherwise conventional drama, *Idle Hands* (1921). A naïve country girl who has come to New York seeking an acting career is held captive in a Chinatown dive. Her sister, who journeys to the city to find the aspiring actress, exposes the crooked chairman of the vice commission as the head of a prostitution ring. The film ends with the rescue of the kidnapped sister. Curiously, the producers featured the popular Ted Lewis dance band – despite the nature of this silent film.

The familiar ploy of a volcanic eruption serves as both a sexual symbol and a serendipitous dramatic climax to Frank Beal's ugly drama of white slavery, *Soul and Body* (1921). Set on a remote island, the film relates how heroine Ann

Luther finds herself mixed up with ruthless white slavers. A notorious slave market is finally brought down by nature when a volcano erupts and destroys everything in its path.

The underworld drama, *Ignorance* (1922), focuses on white slavery, a jewel theft, and other assorted crimes. A gang of thieves inhabit a sleazy dancehall, where they plan their criminal activities. They engage in kidnappings and an assassination attempt on the life of a district attorney. In one particular sequence, gang members lure a woman into a man's rooms and threaten her until she surrenders her jewels.

George K. Arthur, Georgia Hale, and a child (Bruce Guerin) find their search for a better life remains an elusive goal in Josef von Sternberg's drama, *The Salvation Hunters* (1925). They live aboard a steam dredge with a cruel dredge master who has lascivious designs on Hale. The trio, fed up with their waterfront environment and the villainous dredge owner, decide to strike out on their own. The journey to the city where they encounter a white slaver who tries to induce Hale to work for him. He even shows some romantic interest in her and tries to seduce her. Arthur, the youth, finally works up enough courage to challenge him and protect Hale. Once again, the three start out in their quest for happiness.

Part exposé of the white slave traffic and part exploitation, Walter Lang's social drama, *Red Kimono* (1926), is set in the red light district of New Orleans, circa 1917. Priscilla Bonner, an innocent young woman from a small town, is lured into prostitution by a local ladies' man who lives off her earnings. When she learns that her lover intends to marry another woman, she shoots him as he is buying a wedding ring. She is tried for the killing and acquitted. A publicity-crazed socialite takes Bonner in, who at this point in her life is broke. But the woman soon tires of her and evicts her. About to return to her old brothel in New Orleans, Bonner finds love with the woman's chauffeur, who is suddenly inducted into the military and sent overseas. Bonner is once again left alone to wait for her lover's return. Mrs. Wallace Reid, the producer, appeared on screen to plead for tolerance toward wayward girls.

A cautionary tale about white slavery, Louis King and Leon Lee's drama, *Is Your Daughter Safe?* (1927), depicts how those dealing in this traffic lure young women into houses of prostitution and the brutal treatment the victims suffer. Other scenes show the effects of venereal disease on children born from infected parents. The film is composed of a series of separate incidents, linked together by the themes of white slave traffic and venereal disease.

A Chinese secret service agent foils the plans of an arch-villain trafficking in drugs and white slavery in Frank S. Mattison's action drama, *The China Slaver* (1929), set on a remote island. Sojin portrays "The Cobra," a depraved ruler of an island whose inhabitants deal in illicit acts. The agent poses as a stowaway, reaches the remote base of The Cobra's operations and begins to gather information that will eventually lead to the nefarious leader's downfall.

Women's Rights

I. What Women Want

The women's rights movement, also known as feminism and women's liberation, arose in Europe in the late 18th century. The rise of feminism benefited by the Enlightenment, with its egalitarian political focus, and the Industrial Revolution, with its economic and social changes. In France during the Revolution, women's republican clubs pleaded unsuccessfully that the goals of liberty, equality, and fraternity should apply to both sexes. In England, Mary Wollstonecraft wrote *A Vindication of the Rights of Woman* (1792), the first major modern feminist work. But its revolutionary tone made it unacceptable at that time. The Industrial Revolution marked the beginning of women's independence. Machine-powered mass production meant that lower-class women could earn income in factories, regardless of the hazardous factory conditions and the lower pay they received compared to men. In rapidly industrializing Great Britain and the United States, feminism was more successful. The leaders were primarily educated, reform-minded women of the middle class. In 1848 more than 100 persons held the first women's rights convention at Seneca Falls, N.Y. Led by the abolitionist Lucretia Mott and the feminist Elizabeth Cady Stanton, they demanded equal rights, including the vote and an end to the double standard. Married women's property acts, passed at various times in the United States., gave women control over their property. Later, provisions were made for divorce, alimony, and child support. Labor legislation improved hours and wages for women. Suffrage, which became a major goal of American feminists, encountered substantial resistance, despite massive and sometimes violent campaigns. The right to vote was only granted after World War I, partly in recognition of women's contributions to the war effort. Advocates of birth control campaigned for decades before women's right to family planning was recognized. An Equal Rights Amendment to the U.S. Constitution to remove social and other restrictions on women, failed to gain acceptance after it was introduced into Congress in 1923. Hal Reid's drama, *Votes for Women* (1912), was the first significant film about women's suffrage. The film begins with suffrage workers visiting an impoverished family in a dilapidated tenement building owned by an arrogant senator. He refuses to listen to the women's group, who then turn to his fiancée. The woman finally persuades him to change his views on the suffrage issue. The film was quite successful and was used extensively as a propaganda vehicle by various organizations. Unfortunately, this historically important film has disappeared. Early silent films about suffragettes reflected a similar hard line, and they were treated comically, as in *Suffrage and the Man* (1912), *A Suffragette in Spite of Himself* (1912), The *Suffragette* (1913), The *Suffragette Minstrels* (1913) and *The Suffragette Battle of Nuttyville* (1914). Most of these films were just one or two reels in length.

The short imaginative comedy, *When Women Win* (1909), envisions a society in which women have risen to local and state supremacy and are employed as police officers, letter carriers, court officers and in other municipal roles. This early fantasy, aware of the women's suffrage movement, also pictures the new woman dressed in knee-length skirts, in contrast to the men who are still attired in long pants.

Will Lewis's drama, *Eighty Million Women Want* (1913), deals with the exposing of machine politics as well as women's suffrage – both told within the framework of a detective story. Ronald Everett, a young lawyer, considers Ethel Jewell, his fiancée, irresistible, but he disagrees with her politics. George Henry, a crooked political boss, hires Everett, who takes on an auto accident case involving a young man versus a district political leader. Everett convinces the young man he can win the case, but his boss pays off the judge and Everett loses. Later, Henry, the boss, denounces the Women's Political Union in the press, resulting in its leader, Harriot Stanton Blatch, excoriating him in person. Henry plans to give the names of absentee voters to his gangsters, who will then vote for his candidates. However, the women's group plants a spy in his office, and she learns the details of the plot. At least one observant critic pointed out the irony of one scene in which a well-dressed African American on the corrupt boss's payroll had the right to vote, while women did not. The title was later changed to *What Eighty Million Women Want*. Harriot Blatch (1856-1940) was a popular American women's suffrage leader who, in 1907, founded the Equality League of Self-Supporting Women.

Margaret Wycherley, as a daughter who inherits control of her father's bank, struggles against male opposition and prejudice when she decides to run for mayor, in George Lederer's drama, *The Fight* (1915), based on the play by Bayard Veiller. Her strongest opponents are Tim Cronin, the corrupt political leader, and John E. Kellard, who runs a large brothel in town and secretly controls the town's politics. Wycherley finally overcomes the numerous obstacles her adversaries have placed in her path and wins the election in a town noted for its suffrage sympathies. She then marries her lover, Albert Gran, a prominent doctor. The film suggests several women's rights issues, including those of male domination and gender intolerance.

Geraldine O'Brien portrays a young woman who faces a parade of adversities in a lifelong struggle to protect her honor and innocence in Herbert Blaché's social drama, *A Woman's Fight* (1916). She is fired from her factory job when she tries to protect an innocent girl from the lascivious boss. Later, as the mistress of a thief, she is sent to jail when the police find stolen goods in her room. She escapes from prison by drugging the warden whom she has lured off his guard. A young minister whom she tries to rob helps her to get an honest job at a day nursery. Later, they fall in love and marry. Just as she is about to bask in a little happiness after a life marked by hardship and despair, the thief with whom she had once lived shows up and tries to blackmail her. But he is mortally wounded trying to escape from the police.

Herbert Brenon's powerful drama, *War Brides* (1916), with its strong pacifist theme, takes place in a mythical country, where the king orders the women of the land to produce more children as future soldiers. The international star, Nazimova, portraying a factory worker, rebels against the senseless decree. "No more children for war!" she cries out and shoots herself in the presence of the king as a protest against his inhuman command. Other women rise up, vowing not to have any more births until war is outlawed. The star reportedly received $1,000 per day for one month for her performance in this loosely based adaptation of Aristophanes's *Lysistrata*. The handful of pacifist dramas that appeared during the early years of World War I were overwhelmed by those that advocated preparedness. Germany's sinking of the British liner, the Lusitania, in May 1915, with the loss of 128 American lives, did not help the pacifist cause. America's entry into the war in 1917 put an end to the pacifist film cycle. At least one contemporary critic saw the film more as women's suffrage propaganda. "It has as its basis," he wrote, "the demand of women for equal voting rights in national government whereby they can approve or veto the plunging of their country into war."

An inexperienced country girl is left under the guardianship of a libertine who takes advantage of her in Lucius Henderson's problem drama, *The Strength of the Weak* (1916), based on the play by Alice M. Smith and Charlotte Thompson. Mary Fuller, the young woman, later meets a decent young man and the couple fall in love. Fuller, a basically decent and honest person, reveals her terrible earlier ordeal to her boyfriend, who is willing to marry her regardless of her past, which was not her fault. Then her seducer enters, and he turns out to be the young lover's father. The film ends with Fuller and her boyfriend just staring into each other's eyes. Earlier in the drama the young man is shown having his own sexual affairs, liaisons designed to prove his manhood to his approving father. This is evidently intended to illustrate society's double standard in its treatment of men's and women's premarital sex life.

The double standard became the theme of several films released during the next few years. Rita Jolivet and Leah Baird portray the wives of James Morrison and Vincent Serrano in Ivan Abramson's domestic drama, *One Law for Both* (1917), about the discrepancy in treatment between men and women. With one couple, it is the woman who has been unfaithful, whereas with the second couple, it is the husband who has strayed. In the first case, the wife is condemned harshly. But ironically, with the unfaithful husband, he is exonerated.

The plot of Raymond B. West's familiar drama, *Within the Cup* (1918), once again raises the question of the inequality of the sexes when it comes to standards of behavior – where women are judged more harshly for their liberal approach to sex than their counterparts. Before returning to New York, Bessie Barriscale fails in her artistic efforts in Paris and where she is jilted by a son of royalty because of the differences in their backgrounds. She soon gains fame as a novelist, with stories exploring her sexual problems. In a Greenwich Village café, she has her fortune told to her by a popular local character. She will seek true love, the woman prophesies, but will never attain it. The author becomes enraged and forces the woman to leave the café. At a masked party, she meets artist George Fisher, who is searching for a model for his painting of Psyche. The couple soon become lovers, but he shuns marriage after learning about her past and her theories on love. Fisher goes through a period of despair while his mistress is tortured by his rejection of her. But their deep love for each other brings them back together.

Wilfred Lucas and Elda Millar, who have graduated from law school together, are longtime lovers, with the latter turning down the former's marriage proposals over the years, in Albert Parker's weak social drama, *Her Excellency, the Governor* (1917), with its dual issues of child labor and women's rights. Early in their legal careers, they are on opposite sides of a law case with opposing clients. Later, Lucas becomes governor of the state, but Millar notices that he has become a lackey of the political bosses and their machine politics. She decides to oppose him and run on the Suffragette ticket for the office of lieutenant governor. Her party wins, but Lucas is re-elected to the governor's seat. The political battles between the rivals and lovers end only when the political bosses are driven from their offices and the pair finally embrace.

Dorothy Phillips portrays Nora Helmer, a young and subservient wife who risks imprisonment to help restore the health of her young lawyer husband, William Stowell, in Joseph De Grasse's stagy and disappointing drama, *A Doll's House* (1917), based on the popular play by Nenrik Ibsen. She forges her dead father's name to a note that allows her to borrow money from unscrupulous moneylender Alex K. Shannon, which she uses to send her ailing husband abroad. Later, Stowell is appointed bank manager and fires Shannon, who had engaged in dishonest acts. Shannon retaliates by sending a note to Stowell about his wife's earlier forged note. Stowell repudiates his wife's act, although Shannon promises to keep the matter a secret. Phillips, now aware of her husband's selfishness, walks out on him. Another adaptation of Ibsen's play appeared the following year, with Maurice Tourneur as director, Else Ferguson as Nora and H. E. Herbert as her husband. New York Times columnist Frank Rich, in a praiseworthy review of a 1997 revival of the play, updates the theme by describing the story as that "of a young woman who makes a grave mistake – she lies on a legal document – and yet refuses to accept her excessive punishment quietly. By the end, . . . the heroine walks out on her home, husband and children rather than surrender her own idea of right and wrong. . . ."

Maurice Tourneur's artistic tribute to the opposite sex, *Woman* (1918), is an extravagant production worthy of its subject. The first half, about one hour, is devoted to showing the wickedness and treachery some women are known for and the ruin they, as seductresses and sirens, have inflicted on men down through the centuries. Just about when the audience feels there is too much degradation of women, the director unfolds the second half, extolling the virtues of women in peace and war, illustrating their contributions, especially during World War I, as members of the Red Cross and workers in industries.

Constance Talmadge portrays a young socialite torn between marrying Harrison Ford, a young lawyer, and joining the suffrage movement, in Robert G. Vignola's comedy drama, *Experimental Marriage* (1919), based on the play, *From Saturday to Monday*, by Winthrop Ames. Her ingenious compromise has the married couple spending weekends together, and the remainder of the week they are to go their own ways. In addition, the arrangement requires that neither is to question the activities of the other. All goes smoothly the first week until Talmadge discovers that Ford, her husband, is having an affair with another woman. She decides to retaliate, but her scheme fails. So by the end of the week she rushes into his arms and they call a halt to the experimental arrangement.

Actress-manager Ethel Clayton sets out to prove the theme of Robert G. Vignola's disappointing comedy drama, *More Deadly Than the Male* (1919), that in the constant struggle between the sexes, women must use cunning if they are to succeed. The film is set in a world of affluence, where Clayton flirts with wealthy adventurer Edward Hoxen, who is about to leave for the land of the Zulus. He believes there is more challenge in pursuing African women, who are protected by their burly men, than in going after "civilized" women. Once Clayton introduces him to her husband, she challenges the hunter to join her and her husband in her mountain camp. There she embraces him, but her husband, Herbert Heyes, intervenes. A duel results which leaves Heyes seriously wounded. Just as she tells Hoxen she loves him, a dam breaks and both try to repair it before the flood reaches a home for crippled children. Hoxen then kidnaps Clayton and takes her aboard his yacht. When police arrive, he dives overboard and bangs his head against a police patrol boat. He next awakens to discover that Heyes is unhurt and in reality is Clayton's brother. In addition, he becomes aware that she has lured him into falling in love with her – even though she is one of his "civilized" women.

II. "A Woman's Place Is in the Home"

American films during the twenties began to reflect some of the freedoms that women had fought for. Mary Alden in *A Woman's Woman* (1922) finally attains her own independence after she learns about her philandering husband's activities, but her strong sense of morality forces her to return to her family when they need her most. Fiercely independent Claire Windsor in *Grand Larceny* (1922) rejects two husbands who try to change her. On the other hand, audiences during later silent films occasionally displayed a general resentment toward the feminist movement. For example, in dramas like *The Temptress* (26), when a subtitle, meant to express a deep philosophical thought about women being the noblest work of God, the audience response came in the form of giggles. The feminist movement underwent a resurgence in the 1960s, however, as a result of changing demographic, economic, and social patterns. Lower infant mortality rates, soaring adult life expectancy, and the introduction of the birth-control pill (after 1960) gave women more freedom. These aspects, combined with inflation – and the rise of the two-income family and a growing divorce rate – propelled more women into the job market. In the late 1960s women represented about 40 percent of the work force in the U. S. By the mid-1980s, the figure rose to more than 50 percent. As working women encountered discrimination in many forms, the women's movement in the U.S. gained momentum. A presidential commission was established in 1960 to consider equal opportunities for women. Acts of Congress entitled them to equality in education, employment, and legal rights. In 1964 the Civil Rights Act, intended only for blacks, was extended to women. By 1970 most women throughout the world had gained many rights according to law. In 1972 the Supreme Court declared that abortion was legal, and the Equal Rights Amendment was passed by Congress and sent to the states for ratification.

The theme of intolerance in B. A. Rolfe's absorbing drama, *Madonnas and Men* (1920), is suggested in its final subtitle: "Remember, a nation with unrestricted moral standards cannot endure; and no civilization is permanent which is founded on the debasing of womanhood." The dual plot is set in two historical periods, ancient Rome and today's New York City. In Rome, Emperor Turnerius (Anders Randolf), accompanied by Evan-Burrows Fontaine at the Coliseum, watches the gruesome games in the arena. His son (Edmund Lowe) is asked by a magician to rescue a young Christian woman about to be fed to the lions, but Lowe refuses. The magician then prophesies the empire's fate by relating a story set in the future. In New York, a similar tale unfolds concerning a young man who is encouraged to prevent the disreputable plans of his father. Lowe is so affected by the anecdote that he rushes into the arena to save the young woman. His action causes his father, the emperor, to collapse and die in a fit of rage. The son is then proclaimed emperor.

In Charles Giblyn's domestic drama, *A Woman's Woman* (1922), Holmes Herbert takes up with another woman when his wife, Mary Alden, a mother-turned-housekeeper to her family, dresses slovenly. Two of their three children create further problems for the hardworking wife and mother. Louise Lee, their independent-minded older daughter, becomes a suffragette and leaves for Greenwich Village. The younger daughter, Dorothy Mackail, is seduced by a young man and ends up in a hospital after swallowing poison. Meanwhile, Alden discovers that her husband has a mistress. She decides to make herself over while developing an air of independence. She then enters politics and leaves for Washington, D.C. But when her youngest child, seventeen-year-old Albert Hackett, is shot trying to force the seducer to marry Hackett's sister, Alden returns home and resumes her role as housekeeper.

Claire Windsor, a flirtatious Southern belle, marries Northern corporation lawyer Elliott Dexter, who has a strict sense of justice, in Wallace Worsley's society drama, *Grand Larceny* (1922), based on the story by Albert Payson Terhune. Absorbed by his legal work, Dexter permits his wife to continue her social life only when escorted by one of his friends. Lowell Sherman, an architect and close friend of Dexter's, mistakes Windsor's flirtations for something more serious and begins to fall in love with her. When Dexter returns home suddenly, he finds the couple embracing. Without asking for an explanation, he divorces his wife, who then marries Sherman. All the while, Dexter claims that she has engaged in "grand larceny" by her actions with the architect. Her second marriage bings her unhappiness because of Sherman's jealousy of her continual acts of flirting. When the two men meet at a concert, an argument erupts. Windsor finally intervenes and explains she is rejecting both men, thereby establishing her independence.

Members of the working class were not the only victims of alcoholism. The affliction, of course, affected the highest pillars of society as well. At the prodding of her sister, Agnes Ayres marries millionaire and heavy drinker Jack Holt, in William C. de Mille's domestic drama, *Bought and Paid For* (1922), based on the 1916 play by George H. Broadhurst. After two years of successful married life, Holt begins to arrive home drunk. To add to this repulsive behavior, he insults his wife by claiming she is his property, "bought and paid for." Infuriated by his behavior and his master-slave mentality, Ayres leaves him and returns to her former life. Her sister's husband arranges for a reconciliation between Holt, who finally has stopped his drinking, and his estranged wife.

Anna Q. Nilsson, the attractive wife of an affluent husband, finds her role as housewife dull and yearns for freedom and women's rights, in Alfred E. Green's drama, *The Talker* (1925), based on the 1912 play by Marion Fairfax. Her preaching about women's freedom and rights annoys her husband, Lewis Stone, and delights his easily impressed sister, Shirley Mason. Stone's sister decides to follow her sister-in-law's exhortations and elopes with a married man. She soon leaves him when she discovers his criminal inclinations. Nilsson's husband blames her for Mason's troubles and leaves his wife. He then begins divorce proceedings. Mason returns and helps to reconcile the couple.

She eventually becomes romantically involved with a decent and honorable young man whom she had known earlier and who has always loved her.

Jacqueline Logan, influenced by the actions of her mother and her married sister, agrees to marry Creighton Hale as long as he turns over half his paycheck to her, in Frank Borzage's domestic comedy, *Wages for Wives* (1925), based on the 1924 play, *Chicken Feed; or Wages for Wives*, by Guy Bolton and Winchell Smith. But after the couple are married, Hale refuses to the terms, so Logan decides to strike. She encourages her mother and sister to join her, leaving the three abandoned husbands to face their lives without their spouses. But they stubbornly refuse to surrender to their wives' demands. Followings several complications, all three couples reconcile their differences by means of compromise.

Edward Sloman's romantic society comedy, *Butterflies in the Rain* (1926), based on the novel by Andrew Soutar and set chiefly in England, concerns the relationship between Laura La Plante, the daughter of an aristocratic family, and James Kirkwood, a wealthy commoner. The young woman meets Kirkwood, whom her family resents, and she invites him to dinner, where she intends to ridicule him for his old-fashioned lifestyle. But when he later saves her from a raid on a disreputable nightclub, she begins to fall in love with him. La Plante marries him as long as he agrees that she should have absolute freedom. During their holiday in Spain, she naïvely falls in with a group of unsavory bohemians, some of whom threaten her with blackmail. Although Kirkwood is personally suffering from financial difficulties, he protects his wife's reputation. The blackmailers are exposed as swindlers, while his wife proves her innocence. The couple reconcile their differences and continue their love for each other.

Independent Bebe Daniels, who believes in the equality of the sexes, makes a pact with James Hall, her fiancé, in Clarence Badger's slight comedy drama, *The Fifty-Fifty Girl* (1928). Hall will do the housekeeping, and Daniels will run the gold mine they jointly own. Furthermore, whoever requires help first will relinquish his or her share of the mine. Arriving at their mine, they discover that an unscrupulous neighbor has been working their claim. When the claim jumper fails to drive the couple off their claim, he orders his men to attack Daniels. She finally calls out for help, and Hall rushes to her rescue.

Kathryn Crawford, who wants to marry Charley Chase, but would like to continue as designer for an exclusive dressmaking concern, persuades her beau that they should keep separate apartments, in Arch Heath's comedy drama, *Modern Love* (1929). Although Chase holds conventional views, such as "a woman's place should be in the home," he agrees to his fiancée's terms. After their marriage, Crawford meets Jean Hersholt, the owner of the dress company, who likes more than just her work. He invites her to join him on a trip to Europe, where she can develop new dress designs. Meanwhile, her husband is forced to pose as a butler at a dinner party honoring Hersholt. The incident proves too much for Crawford, who agrees to resign from her job.

Bibliography

Allen, Frederic Lewis. *Only Yesterday: An Informal History of the 1920s*. New York: Harper & Row, 1931.
American Film Institute Catalogue of Motion Pictures Produced in the United States. New York: R. R. Bowker, 1971, 1976.
Brownlow, Kevin. *Behind the Mask of Innocence: Films of Social Conscience in the Silent Era*. New York: Knopf, 1990.
Carnes, Mark C., ed. *Past Imperfect: History According to the Movies*. New York: Henry Holt & Co., 1997.
Cook, David A. *A History of Narrative Film*. New York: W. W. Norton, 1981.
Dash, Joan. *We Shall Not Be Moved: The Women's Factory Strike of 1909*. New York: Scholastic, 1997.
DeMott, Benjamin, *The Imperial Middle: Why Americans Can't Think Straight About Class*. New Haven: Yale University Press, 1992.
DiCanio, Margaret. *Encyclopedia of Marriage, Divorce and the Family*. New York: Facts on File, 1989.
Edwards, P. K. *Strikes in the United States*. New York: St. Martin's, 1981.
Everson, William K. *American Silent Film*. New York: Oxford University Press, 1978.
Fadiman, Clifton, ed. *The Collected Writings of Ambrose Bierce*. New York: The Citadel Press, 1946.
Harries, Meirion, and Harries, Susan. *The Last Days of Innocence: America at War, 1917-1918*. New York: Random House, 1997.
Horowitz, Irving L., ed. *The Anarchists*. New York: Dell, 1964.
Hufton, Olwen. *The Prospects Before Her: A History of Women in Western Europe*. New York: Alfred A. Knopf, 1997.
Hughes, Laurence A., ed. *The Truth About the Movies*. Hollywood: Hollywood Publishers, 1924.
Isenberg, Michael T. *War on Film: The American Cinema and World War I*. East Brunswick, NJ: Associated University Presses, 1981.
Karpf, Steven. *The Gangster Film: Emergence, Variation, and Decay of a Genre*. New York: Arno Press, 1973.
Kennedy, Randall. *Race, Crime, and the Law*. New York: Pantheon Books, 1997.
Langman, Larry. *A Guide to Silent Westerns*. Westport, CT: Greenwood Press, 1992.
Lauritzen, Einar, and Lundquist, Gunnar. *American Film Index: 1908-1915*. Stockholm, Sweden: Film-Index, 1976.

Leavitt, Judith Wolzer. *Brought to Bed: Childbearing in America, 1750-1950.* New York: Oxford, 1986.
Miller, Henry. *The Colossus of Maroussi,* pt. 3. London: Heinemann, 1960.
O'Brien, Robert, and Cohen, Sidney. *The Encyclopedia of Drug Abuse.* New York: Facts on File, 1984.
O'Connor, John E., and Jackson, Martin A. *American History/American Film: Interpreting the Hollywood Image.* New York: Frederick Ungar Publishing Co., 1980.
Patterson, James T. *America in the Twentieth Century: A History.* New York: Harcourt Brace Jovanovich, 1983.
Perrett, Geoffrey. *America in the Twenties: A History.* New York: Simon and Schuster, 1982.
Porges, Irwin. *Edgar Rice Burroughs: The Man Who Created Tarzan.* New York: Ballantine Books, 1976.
Ramsaye, Terry. *A Million and One Nights: A History of the Motion Picture Through 1925.* New York: Touchstone, 1986. (Originally published by Simon and Schuster, 1926.)
Schickel, Richard. *D. W. Griffith, an American Life.* London: Pavilion Books, 1984.
Silverstein, Alvin, and Silverstein, Virginia B. *Alcoholism.* New York: Lippincott, 1975.
Spears, Jack. *Hollywood: The Golden Era.* New York: Castle Books, 1971.
Tobias, Sheila. *Faces of Feminism: An Activist's Reflections of the Women's Movement.* Boulder, CO: Westview Press, 1997.
Walker, Alexander. *The Shattered Silents.* London: Elm Tree Books, 1978.
Wenden, D. C. *The Birth of the Movies.* New York: E. P. Dutton, 1975.
White, David Manning, and Averson, Richard. *The Celluloid Weapon: Social Comment in the American Film.* Boston: Beacon Press, 1972.

Name Index

Abbott, George, 55, 187, 229
Abramson, Ivan, 3, 282, 325, 365
Acker, Norman, 326
Adair, Robyn, 324
Adams, Kathryn, 15, 315
Adams, Lionel, 93
Adolfi, John G., 69, 78, 142, 186, 201
Agnew, Robert, 78, 303
Ainsworth, Sydney, 232
Aitken, Spottiswoode, 77, 204
Alden, Mary, 9, 367, 368
Aldrich, William E., 225
Allen, Alfred, 109
Allen, Mabel, 347
Allen, Russell, 78
Allen, Winifred, 17
Anderson, G. M., 219, 290
Anderson, Mary, 107, 191, 242
Anderson, Mignon, 3, 278
Anderson, Robert, 21, 39
Apfel, Oscar, 20, 35, 96, 129, 160, 172, 175, 205
Applegate, Roy, 150
Archainbaud, George, 27, 111, 151, 165, 233, 235, 324
Arlen, Richard, 100, 146
Arliss, George, 70
Arnold, Marcella, 363
Arthur, Daniel V., 181
Arthur, George K., 239, 343, 362
Ashley, Arthur, 27, 58, 59, 60, 68, 191
August, Edwin, 190, 203, 299, 308
Austin, Albert, 62
Austin, Rose, 357

Ayres, Agnes, 156, 369
Badger, Clarence, 21, 109, 110, 178, 186, 290, 370
Baggot, King, 110, 226, 279
Bailey, Consuelo, 139
Bailey, Oliver D., 334
Baird, Leah, 93, 290, 309, 365
Baird, Stewart, 321
Baker, George, 36, 122
Baker, Richard Foster, 359
Balfour, A., 275
Ballin, Hugo, 236, 314
Balshofer, Fred J., 335
Bancroft, George, 19, 22, 228, 305
Banky, Vilma, 41
Bara, Theda, 4, 53, 232, 299, 322, 345, 350, 351, 352
Barker, Reginald, 45, 61, 114, 183, 224, 276
Barriscale, Bessie, 45, 48, 155, 192, 216, 253, 298, 325, 366
Barry, John A., 216
Barry, Nigel, 195
Barrymore, Ethel, 56, 75, 194
Barrymore, John, 26, 70, 72, 185, 253, 331
Barrymore, Lionel, 83, 185, 277, 281, 282, 304, 305, 315, 336, 352
Barthelmess, Richard, 38, 227, 270, 273, 311
Bartlett, Charles, E., 324
Baxter, Warner, 28, 30, 78, 295, 305
Bayne, Beverly, 151
Beal, Frank, 193, 326, 360, 361

Name Index

Beaudine, William, 225, 248
Beaumont, Harry, 9, 16, 20, 50, 145, 154, 235
Beban, George, 55, 75, 79, 107, 142, 280
Bedford, Barbara, 51, 62, 186, 228, 237, 330
Beery, Noah, 59, 61, 62, 136, 146, 260, 261, 280
Beery, Wallace, 62, 70, 86, 111, 157, 249
Belasco, Walter, 337
Bell, Gaston, 54, 102
Bell, Monta, 196, 343
Bellamy, Madge, 31, 136, 260
Belmont, Joseph, 293
Belmore, Lionel, 176
Bennet, Frank, 45, 308
Bennett, Alma, 261
Bennett, Belle, 10, 159, 162, 168, 221
Bennett, Chester, 39, 58
Bennett, Enid, 7, 132, 234, 303, 316
Bennett, Frank, 308
Bennett, Joseph, 99
Bennett, Richard, 122
Bennett, Whitman, 238
Beranger, George, 151
Bernard, Barney, 110, 336
Bernard, Dorothy, 35
Bertram, William, 14, 59, 79
Billington, Francella, 327
Blaché, Alice, 47, 346
Blaché, Herbert, 105, 180, 194, 195, 212, 364
Blackton, J. Stuart, 19, 81, 207, 263, 308
Blackwell, Carlyle, 24, 58, 85, 149, 151, 152, 162, 223, 323
Blake, Lorette, 106
Blinn, Holbrook, 15, 48, 103, 346
Blood, Adele, 25
Bloomer, Raymond, 30
Blue, Monte, 21, 37, 41, 78, 196, 250
Blystone, John G., 136
Blythe, Betty, 123, 152, 223, 302, 310
Boardman, Eleanor, 50, 175, 274, 316
Boggs, Frank, 64
Bokers, John, 106
Bonner, Priscilla, 175, 225, 228, 362
Booth, Elmer, 220
Borden, Olive, 80, 136, 329, 331

Borzage, Frank, 86, 158, 340, 370
Bosworth, Hobart, 12, 15, 40, 63, 64, 68, 109, 125, 138, 328
Bouton, Betty, 126
Bow, Clara, 8, 61, 100, 175, 197, 238
Bowen, Allen, 94
Bowers, John, 20, 47, 165, 192, 290, 339
Boyd, William, 306
Boyle, Joseph C., 304
Brabin, Charles J., 66
Bracken, Bertram, 236, 289
Bradbury, Robert N., 64, 71, 290
Bradford, Virginia, 166
Brady, Alice, 13, 27, 48, 67, 103, 116, 192, 195, 233, 254, 257, 326
Brady, Ed, 40
Brady, William A., 48
Breamer, Sylvia, 19, 28
Brenon, Herbert, 9, 31, 137, 207, 212, 320, 347, 365
Brent, Evelyn, 21, 22, 88, 228
Bretherton, Howard, 89, 250
Broadwell, Robert B., 203
Brockwell, Billie, 349
Brockwell, Gladys, 160, 183, 193, 201, 209, 283, 323, 326
Broderick, Robert, 103
Brodsky, Samuel R., 116
Bronson, Rose, 40
Brook, Clive, 89, 228, 296
Brooke, Van Dyke, 102, 252
Brown, Clarence, 9, 10
Brown, Halbert, 68
Brown, Harry J., 136
Browning, Tod, 5, 88, 89, 118, 227, 250, 305
Bruce, Clifford, 145, 214, 323, 350
Buchowetski, Dimitri, 259
Buckingham, Thomas, 147
Buel, Kenean, 144, 291
Burns, Edward, 259
Burns, William J., 179, 221, 275
Burnside, R. H., 226
Burton, Clarence, 157
Busch, Mae, 6, 10, 89, 304, 328
Bushman, Francis X., 4, 151, 167
Bushnell, Francis, 85
Butler, David, 5, 177, 238
Butler, Fred J., 238, 336
Butt, Lawson, 38, 72, 312

NAME INDEX 375

Byer, Charles, 187

Cabanne, William Christy, 44, 155, 265, 266, 302, 305, 308
Cain, Robert, 106, 166
Calhoon, Catherine, 149, 150
Calhoon, Patrick, 171
Calhoun, Alice, 311
Calvert, E. H., 14
Campbell, Colin, 37, 123, 241, 340, 341
Campbell, Maurice, 31, 87
Campbell, Webster, 96
Campeau, Frank, 38
Capellani, Albert, 17, 135, 298, 300, 339
Capellani, Paul, 298
Capra, Frank, 49, 52, 188, 344
Caprice, June, 235
Carewe, Arthur Edmund, 51, 238, 291
Carewe, Edwin, 35
Carey, Harry, 181, 350
Carleton, Lloyd, 38
Carmen, Jewel, 29, 67, 217, 348
Carpenter, Florence, 133, 290
Carr, Alexander, 110
Carr, Mary, 50, 97
Carrigan, Thomas, 185
Carroll, William, 300
Carter, Catherine, 103
Carter, Harry, 254
Castle, Irene, 183, 223, 232
Castleton, Barbara, 30, 47, 313
Chadwick, Helene, 196, 223, 238, 257
Chambers, Lyster, 245, 291
Chandlee, Harry, 4
Chandler, L. V., 18
Chaney, Lon, 47, 51, 88, 89, 118, 137, 218, 224, 225, 227, 250, 305, 315
Chapin, Benjamin, 67
Chapin, James, 78, 88, 259
Chaplin, Charlie, 62, 138, 169, 266, 274
Charleson, Mary, 16, 18
Chautard, Emile, 15, 67, 103, 154, 325, 326, 349, 351, 353
Chesebro, George, 126
Christensen, Benjamin, 137
Claire, Gertrude, 227
Clarendon, Hal, 92, 252
Clark, Marguerite, 266, 290

Clary, Charles, 106, 193, 324
Clayton, Ethel, 33, 57, 59, 102, 256, 361, 367
Clifford, Ruth, 290
Clifford, William H., 30
Clifton, Elmer, 13, 160, 280, 311
Clive, Henry, 290
Coan, M. Blair, 359
Coburn, Gladys, 289
Cody, Lew, 193, 328, 346
Cohan, George M., 18
Collier, Buster, 97
Collins, John H., 34, 105, 141, 334, 337
Collins, Tom, 125
Collyer, June, 61, 62, 230
Colman, Ronald, 41, 261, 329
Compson, Betty, 19, 20, 21, 127, 207, 227, 303, 305
Conklin, Chester, 85
Conklin, William, 29, 60, 205, 300, 340, 359
Connelly, Edward, 316
Connolly, Jack, 79
Conway, Jack, 14, 80, 89, 103, 134, 162, 281, 316, 337
Coogan, Jackie, 62, 258
Cooley, Hallam, 7, 300
Cooper, Gary, 197
Cooper, Merian C., 250
Cooper, Miriam, 324
Corbett, Jim, 85, 156, 212
Corbin, Virginia Lee, 9, 98
Corrado, Geno, 260
Cortez, Ormond, 247
Cortez, Ricardo, 128, 294, 344, 353
Costello, Dolores, 138, 227, 343
Costello, Helene, 9, 198, 284
Cotton, Lucy, 234
Courtleigh, William Jr., 104, 347
Cowl, George, 67, 324
Cox, George L., 7
Craft, William J., 125, 137, 227, 283
Crane, Frank, 13, 127, 245, 268, 301, 346
Crane, Ward, 236
Crawford, Joan, 80, 229, 305
Crews, Laura Hope, 182
Crisp, Donald, 107, 212, 288, 296, 360
Crosby, William G., 177
Crosland, Alan, 72, 79, 315

376 NAME INDEX

Crowell, Josephine, 160
Cruze, James, 21, 50, 59, 86, 167, 195, 257, 264, 266
Cummings, Irving, 207, 218, 245, 275, 301, 330
Cummings, Robert W., 312
Curley, Pauline, 17, 76
Curran, William, 363
Currier, Frank, 35, 111
Curtiz, Michael, 138, 344

Dagmar, Florence, 129, 130, 141
D'Albrook, Sidney, 95
Dalton, Dorothy, 37, 38, 49, 161, 226, 246, 255
Dana, Viola, 50, 96, 105, 141, 145, 147, 173, 207, 303, 337, 351, 352
Daniels, Bebe, 88, 154, 178, 294, 370
D'Arcy, Roy, 187
Darling, Ida, 8
Darmond, Grace, 17, 186, 247
D'Arrast, Harry, 41
Darro, Frankie, 261
Daugherty, Jack, 147
Davenport, Alice, 85
Davenport, Dorothy, 125, 243
Davidson, Dore, 50, 293
Davidson, John, 142, 151
Davidson, Max, 151
Davies, Marion, 36, 49, 177
Davis, Will S., 53, 182
Daw, Marjorie, 257
Dawley, J. Searle, 50, 92, 103, 130, 139, 220, 290, 311
Dawn, Norman, 96, 174
Dawson, Doris, 274
Day, Marceline, 72, 305
Daye, June, 54
De Cordova, Renzi, 348
De Grasse, Joseph, 16, 26, 46, 61, 109, 110, 366
De Grasse, Sam, 44, 161, 201, 315
De la Motte, Marguerite, 70
De Mille, William, 51, 186, 279, 280, 308, 335, 352
De Putti, Lya, 353
De Rue, Eugene, 261
De Sano, Marcel, 237
De Vere, Harry T., 242
Dean, Julia, 46
Dean, Louis, 19

Del Ruth, Roy, 41, 227
Delaney, Charles, 111
D'Elba, H., 171
DeForrest, Wade, 94
DeMille, Cecil B., 5, 44, 54, 68, 106, 154, 156, 189, 193, 290, 303, 313
Dempster, Carol, 117, 208, 270, 328, 354
Denny, Reginald, 70, 176, 257
Deshon, Florence, 107
Desmond, William, 16, 79, 86, 153, 166, 173, 183, 227, 253, 294, 300, 326, 334, 335
Devereaux, Jack, 223
Devore, Dorothy, 111, 328
Dexter, Elliott, 5, 8, 98, 166, 193, 196, 282, 303, 351, 369
Dierker, Hugh, 304
Dillon, Edward, 151, 338
Dillon, John (Jack), 29, 77, 140, 329
Dillon, Robert A., 24
Dixey, Henry, 221
Dixon, Thomas, 87
Donaldson, Arthur, 140, 288
Donnelly, Dorothy, 162, 261, 288
Donovan, Frank P., 310
Doro, Marie, 55
Dowling, Joseph J., 155
Dresser, Louise, 127, 138, 146, 343, 344
Drew, Cora, 156
Drew, S. Rankin, 108, 300
Dudley, Florence, 209
Duncan, Malcolm, 348
Duncan, William, 27, 122
Dunlap, Scott, 134, 283
Dunn, William, 152, 256
Durning, Bernard, 77, 340
Dwyer, Ruth, 127

Earle, William P. S., 5, 7, 57, 152, 234, 256, 339
Eason, Reeves, 134, 341
Eddy, Helen Holmes, 7
Edeson, Robert, 94, 150, 166
Edwards, J. Gordon, 4, 30, 34, 40, 70, 222, 332
Edwards, Walter, 16, 105, 161, 202, 204, 246
Elliott, Alice Claire, 104
Elliott, Frank, 215

NAME INDEX 377

Elliott, Robert, 77
Ellis, Carlyle, 281
Ellis, Paul, 41
Ellis, Robert, 87, 88, 98, 147, 157, 283
Elvidge, June, 58, 59, 60, 123
Emerson, John, 267, 357
Empey, Guy, 310
Enright, Ray, 228
Ensminger, Robert, 171, 271
Entwhistle, H., 130
Estabrook, Howard, 222
Evans, Madge, 339
Eyton, Bessie, 243

Fair, Elinor, 186
Fairbanks, Douglas, 70, 238, 257, 288
Fairbanks, William, 100, 226
Farnum, Dustin, 64, 66, 279, 281, 282
Farnum, Franklyn, 26
Farnum, William, 35, 67, 70, 159, 160, 203, 245
Farrar, Geraldine, 44, 61, 68, 312
Faversham, William, 25
Fawcett, George, 105, 277, 314
Fellowes, Rockliffe, 110, 118, 221, 300, 329, 359
Fenton, Leslie, 97
Fenton, Mark, 280
Fenwick, Irene, 214
Ferguson, Casson, 171
Ferguson, Elsie, 154, 215, 224
Field, C. C., 278
Fielding, Edmund, 326
Fielding, Romaine, 191
Fife, Shannon, 97
Fillmore, Clyde, 60
Filson, Al, 104
Finch, Flora, 177
Findlay, Ruth, 140
Fischer, David O., 18
Fischer, Margarita, 13, 114
Fischter, Walter, 13
Fisher, George, 192, 215, 366
Fitzgerald, Dallas M., 229, 239, 352
Fitzmaurice, George, 8, 41, 55, 164, 183, 224, 264
Fleming, Ethel, 6
Fleming, Victor, 127, 258, 354
Flood, James, 9
Foote, Courtenay, 323
Ford, Francis, 65, 170, 259, 269

Ford, Harrison, 315, 338
Ford, Hugh, 191, 215
Ford, John, 62, 156, 269, 293, 302, 350
Forde, Eugenie, 300
Forde, Hal, 4
Forman, Tom, 163, 185, 243, 335, 352
Forrest, Allan, 118, 212, 237, 259, 310
Forrest, Ann, 124
Fosberg, Edwin, 162
Foss, Darrel, 5
Foster, Helen, 330
Foxe, Earle, 157
Frank, Alexander F., 201
Frank, J. Herbert, 54, 117
Franklin, C. M., 348
Franklin, Chester, 175
Franklin, Sidney A., 60, 177, 289, 329, 348
Franz, Joseph, 173, 185, 342
Fraunholz, Fraunie, 105, 358
Frederick, Pauline, 7, 156, 165, 191, 193, 216, 279, 301, 338
French, Charles K., 64, 161, 284
Fury, J. Barney, 122

Gail, Jane, 356
Gamble, Warburton, 7, 290
Garbo, Greta, 9, 299, 302, 352, 354
Garrick, Richard, 115
Garson, Harry, 37, 341, 353
Garwood, William, 55, 360
Gaskill, Charles L., 44
George, Burton, 76
Gerrard, Charles, 58, 70, 224, 312
Giblyn, Charles, 174, 255, 368
Gibson, Hoot, 50, 135, 295
Gilbert, John, 7, 9, 10, 76, 77, 80, 126, 137, 196, 226, 229, 273, 282, 329
Gillingwater, Claude, 198
Gilpin, Charles, 20
Girard, Joseph, 58, 284
Gish, Dorothy, 39, 43, 45, 159, 161, , 227, 261, 311, 314, 336
Gish, Lillian, 44, 190, 220, 308, 331, 352
Glass, Gaston, 89, 168, 176, 177, 284, 340
Glaum, Louise, 161, 202, 269
Gleason, Ada, 288
Glennon, Bert, 80
Golden, Joseph A., 169, 299

Golden, Olive Fuller, 350
Goodrich, Edna, 234
Goodwin, Harold, 9, 60, 131
Gordon, Bruce, 78
Gordon, Huntly, 10, 40, 99, 168
Gordon, Kitty, 151, 245, 301, 324, 348, 350
Gordon, Robert, 19, 28, 118
Gordon, Vera, 340
Gorin, Owen, 209
Gorman, Jack, 56
Goudal, Jetta, 100, 306
Goulding, Edmund, 10
Grade, Svend, 316
Graham, Charles, 37
Graham, John, 190
Grandin, Ethel, 110, 356
Grandon, J. Francis, 172, 222
Grant, Valentine, 334
Grassby, Bertram, 94, 192, 193
Graves, Ralph, 146, 155, 158, 197, 314, 331
Gray, Clifford, 150
Gray, Gilda, 187
Gray, Lawrence, 304
Greeley, Evelyn, 77, 152, 172, 223
Green, Dorothy, 141, 203
Gregg, Paul, 10
Gribbon, Eddie, 80
Griffin, Frank C., 359
Griffith, Corinne, 49
Griffith, David W., 1, 12, 29, 34, 65, 67., 81, 83, 84, 117, 159, 180, 208, 211, 220, 270, 285, 286, 287, 289, 306, 319, 320, 328, 353, 355
Griffith, Edward, 49, 100
Griffith, Raymond, 186, 328, 342
Grossman, Harry, 87

Hackathorne, George, 31, 98
Haddock, William, 325
Haines, William, 260, 261, 328
Hale, Creighton, 177, 235, 266, 369
Hale, Georgia, 295, 362
Hall, Dorothy, 128
Hall, Ella, 142, 212, 337
Hall, Howard, 115, 252
Hall, James, 178, 370
Hall, Thurston, 77, 117
Halperin, Victor, 147
Hamilton, Gilbert, 232

Hamilton, Mahlon, 57, 249, 254
Hamilton, Neil, 316
Hammerstein, Elaine, 8, 165, 183, 268
Hammond, Virginia, 349
Hamper, Genevieve, 34
Hampton, Vera, 94
Handworth, Harry, 24
Hanlon, Alma, 44, 143, 144, 299, 350
Hansen, Juanita, 46
Hanson, Einar, 167, 316
Hanson, Gladys, 4
Harbaugh, Carl, 221, 360
Hardin, Neil, 6
Hare, Lumsden, 35, 350
Harlan, Kenneth, 85, 173
Harris, Harry B., 134, 342
Harris, Leonore, 349
Harris, Mildred, 97, 153, 282, 283
Harron, John, 31, 62, 178, 317, 330
Harron, Robert, 28, 143, 180, 211, 270
Hart, William S., 71, 265
Hartford, David, 99
Harvey, Harry, 122
Harvey, John Joseph, 247, 268
Hatch, Riley, 17, 57
Hatton, Raymond, 68, 129, 154, 182, 308
Haver, Phyllis, 166, 354
Hawley, Ormi, 359
Hawley, Wanda, 89, 195, 248
Hayakawa, Sessue, 35, 37, 54, 61, 76, 96, 215, 236, 245, 341
Hearn, Edward, 237
Hedlund, Guy, 109
Heffron, Thomas N., 233, 244
Henabery, Joseph, 161, 257
Henderson, Dell, 152, 176, 223, 234
Henley, Hobart, 15, 75, 157, 203, 265, 267, 277
Herbert, Holmes, 10, 146, 368
Hersholt, Jean, 344
Heyes, Herbert, 40
Hickman, Alfred, 323
Hickman, Howard, 48, 155, 214, 216, 246, 276
Hiers, Walter, 216
Higgin, Howard, 187
Hill, Doris, 284
Hill, Lee, 3
Hill, Robert F., 126, 167, 185, 218, 233
Hilliard, Harry, 133, 142, 350

Hillyer, Lambert, 78, 225
Hinckley, William, 348
Hines, Charles, 80, 362
Hirsh, Nathan, 248
Hoffman, Otto, 56
Hoffman, Renaud, 118
Hogan, James B., 98, 111
Hohl, Arthur, 40
Holding, Thomas, 110, 292
Hollister, Alice, 323
Holmes, Helen, 7, 35, 79, 222, 227
Holmes, Stuart, 4, 34, 54, 312, 322, 360
Holt, Edwin, 122
Holt, Jack, 51, 55, 127, 208, 245, 256, 361, 369
Holubar, Allen, 3, 205, 310
Hopkins, May, 153
Hopper, De Wolfe, 46
Hopper, E. Mason, 5, 86, 152, 205, 337
Hopper, Edna Wallace, 190
Hopper, Hedda, 185, 197
Hopwood, Avery, 50, 186
Horan, Charles T., 132, 336
Hotaling, Arthur, 71, 179
Houdini, Harry, 123
Howard, Constance, 248
Howard, William K., 88, 186, 274, 294
Howe, Eliot, 214
Howes, Reed, 167, 260
Howley, Irene, 321
Hoyt, Arthur, 3, 198
Hoyt, Edward, 182
Hoyt, Harry O., 20, 41, 249
Huff, Louise, 46, 59, 70, 255, 320
Hughes, Lloyd, 249, 250, 293, 313
Hughes, Rupert, 50, 150
Hulette, Gladys, 52, 118, 202, 249, 265, 276, 302
Humphrey, William, 45
Hunt, Jewell, 335
Hunter, Glenn, 50, 177
Hutchison, Charles, 78, 88, 144, 190, 259
Hyland, Peggy, 28, 163, 184, 233

Illington, Margaret, 256
Ince, John, 7, 27, 119, 186, 223
Ince, Ralph W., 26, 183, 226, 227, 229, 278, 306, 312
Ince, Thomas H., 65
Ingraham, Lloyd, 46, 72, 143, 190, 310

Ingram, Rex, 131, 280, 293, 358
Irving, George, 54, 256, 290, 309
Ivers, Julia, 279

Jaccard, Jacques, 358
James, David, 175
James, Gladden, 123
Janis, Doris, 296
Jannings, Emil, 354
Jefferson, William Wister, 300
Johnson, Arthur, 287
Johnson, Emory, 59, 266
Johnson, Lorimer, 242
Johnson, Noble, 228, 295
Johnstone, Justine, 341
Jolivet, Rita, 269
Jones, Edgar, 320
José, Edward, 58, 222, 345
Joy, Leatrice, 29, 238, 315
Joyce, Alice, 5, 9, 153, 156, 179
Joyner, Francis, 54
Julian, Rupert, 51, 68, 228, 291
Justine, Martin, 237

Kane, Gail, 67, 117, 172, 181, 205, 279
Karger, Maxwell, 126
Karns, Roscoe, 134
Kaufman, Joseph, 54
Keefe, Cornelius, 272
Keefe, Zena, 325
Keenan, Frank, 114, 161
Keith, Donald, 238
Keith, Ian, 52, 229
Kellard, Ralph, 352
Kelly, Renee, 150
Kelly, William J., 322
Kelson, George, 123
Kemble, Lillian, 36
Kennedy, Madge, 314
Kennedy, Merna, 138
Kent, Arnold, 167, 197, 306
Kent, Crauford, 215, 233, 250, 339, 341
Kenton, Erle C., 52, 168
Kenyon, Doris, 15, 47, 96, 111, 142
Kerrigan, J. Warren, 14, 144, 242, 253
Kibbee, Guy, 9
Kilgour, Joseph, 300
King, Anita, 171
King, Burton, 2, 40, 52, 94, 127, 228, 284

380 NAME INDEX

King, Henry, 38, 261, 274, 306, 315, 346, 347
King, Joe, 76, 152
King, Louis, 362
Kingsley, Pierce, 356
Kingston, Winifred, 66, 279
Kino, Goro, 96
Kirkham, Kathleen, 38, 340
Kirkland, David, 239, 314, 328
Kirkwood, James, 26, 43, 139, 170, 206, 370
Klein, Charles, 30, 110, 138, 276
Knoles, Harley, 25, 60, 85, 162, 177, 254, 299, 309, 313
Knott, Lydia, 172
Kolker, Henry, 16, 17, 70
KoVert, Frederic, 178

Laemmle, Edward, 99, 167, 209
Lake, Alice, 7, 29, 54
Lake, Arthur, 90
Lake, William, 222
Landis, Cullen, 64, 71, 133, 136, 353
Landis, Julia, 15
Landis, Margaret, 122, 236
Landowska, Lydia, 2
Lane, Charles, 146
Lane, Rose, 182
Lang, Walter, 99, 227, 362
Langdon, Harry, 273
Langford, Edward T., 57, 309, 324
Lanning, Frank, 173
Larkin, George, 131, 187, 283
LaRocque, Rod, 186, 259, 322
Larrimore, Francine, 107
Laughlin, Anna, 252
Lawrence, Edmund, 16, 18, 46, 213, 246, 299
Lawrence, Florence, 220
Le Saint, Edward J., 29, 157, 183
Lederer, George W., 143, 214
Lederer, Gretchen, 58, 231
Lee, Leon, 362
Lee, Lila, 8, 51, 78, 111, 154, 338
Lee, Rowland V., 125, 296
Lehr, Anne, 212
Lehrman, Henry, 198
Leiber, Fritz, 70, 289
Leigh, Canton, 232
Leni, Paul, 187

Leonard, Robert Z., 48, 142, 146, 163, 172, 212, 215, 237, 259, 328
Leslie, Gladys, 152, 234, 256
Levering, Joseph, 93, 98, 144, 180, 194, 342
Lewis, Edgar, 104, 249, 295
Lewis, Mitchell, 290
Lewis, Ralph, 94, 239
Lieb, Herman, 200
Lillie, Beatrice, 51
Lincoln, Alpheus, 342
Lincoln, Elmo, 85, 244
Livingston, Jack, 48, 233
Livingston, Margaret, 147
Lloyd, Frank, 66, 126, 156, 165, 193, 197, 312
Logan, Jacqueline, 226, 229, 342, 369
Long, Walter, 80, 308
Lord, Del, 295
Lorraine, Lillian, 346
Lorraine, Louise, 80, 362
Losee, Frank, 290
Louis, Willard, 9
Love, Bessie, 46, 47, 52, 98, 121, 151, 225, 249, 328, 341
Love, Montagu, 41, 57, 68, 254
Lowe, Edmund, 88, 206, 305, 368
Lowell, John, 20
Loy, Myrna, 41
Lubitsch, Ernst, 9, 261, 331
Lucas, Wilfred, 73, 173, 204, 244, 290, 320, 366
Luther, Ann(a), 245, 360
Lyon, Ben, 147, 187, 197
Lytell, Bert, 29, 86, 178, 223, 227

MacDonald, Donald, 185, 234
MacDonald, Sherwood, 359
MacDonald, Wallace, 31, 99, 294
Mack, Charles Emmett, 97, 137
Mackaill, Dorothy, 165, 304, 329
Mackay, Edward, 323
MacKenzie, Donald, 181
MacLaren, Mary, 5, 124, 195
MacLean, Douglas, 248
MacQuarrie, Frank, 280
MacQuarrie, Murdock, 2, 205
MacRae, Henry, 102
MacSweeney, John, 303
Macy, Carleton, 3

NAME INDEX

Madison, Cleo, 30, 245, 320
Maigne, Charles, 19, 248
Mailes, Charles Hill, 98
Maitland, Jack, 55
Maloney, Leo, 209, 222
Mamoulian, Rouben, 8
Mantell, Robert, 34
Marcel, Inez, 311
Marion, George, 162
Markey, Enid, 94, 244, 258
Marlo, George, 278
Marmont, Percy, 21, 156
Marsh, Mae, 132, 211, 328, 336
Marshall, George, 350
Marshall, Tully, 202
Marston, Theodore, 4, 94, 150, 179, 150
Martin, Vivian, 194, 265, 337
Marvin, Arthur, 180
Mason, John, 2, 299
Mason, Shirley, 76, 134, 158, 173, 174, 317, 342, 369
Mason, Sidney, 28, 93, 232, 291
Matthews, Arthur, 102
Mattison, Frank S., 71, 89, 362
Maude, Arthur, 45, 300
Mayall, Herschel, 291
Mayo, Christine, 225, 299, 301
Mayo, Frank, 302, 359
McAvoy, May, 89, 197, 206, 283
McCarthy, John P., 6, 229, 294, 331
McCarthy, Myles, 205
McCoy, Gertrude, 48
McCullough, Philo, 30, 48, 56, 59, 97, 247
McCutcheon, Wallace, 64, 74, 180, 220
McDermott, Marc, 137, 302
McDowell, Claire, 1
McDowell, Melbourne, 162
McEveety, Bernard, 128
McGill, Lawrence, 25, 140, 232, 288
McGlynn, Frank, 183
McGowan, J. P., 79, 182, 184, 187, 222, 227, 248
McGrail, Walter, 153, 158
McGregor, Harmon, 203
McGregor, Malcolm, 100, 284, 330, 343
McGuire, Kathryn, 79, 261
McKee, Raymond, 98, 135, 174, 175
McKim, Robert, 114, 165

McLaughlin, J. W., 153
McLean, Jack, 326
McQuarrie, George, 123
McRae, Duncan, 26, 48, 244
Meehan, Leo, 218
Meighan, Thomas, 28, 104, 111, 130, 154, 167, 191, 230, 278, 289, 308, 322, 338
Melford, George, 59, 97, 243, 272, 284, 322, 338, 342
Menjou, Adolphe, 41, 303, 353
Meredith, Charles, 314
Meredith, Lois, 357, 359
Merrill, Frank, 284
Mersereau, Violet, 131, 171, 334, 358
Mestayer, Harry, 232
Metcalfe, Earl, 49, 175
Micheaux, Oscar, 207, 292, 293
Michelena, Beatriz, 14, 130
Middleton, George E., 14
Milestone, Lewis, 89, 230
Miljan, John, 137, 198
Millarde, Harry, 28, 60
Miller, Ashley, 102, 276
Miller, Charles, 192, 325
Miller, Patsy Ruth, 118, 166, 282
Miller, Walter, 228, 247, 265, 266
Mills, Frank, 36
Mills, Thomas R., 143
Minter, Mary Miles, 248, 265, 310
Mitchell, Howard M., 174, 282
Mitchell, Rhea, 170, 193, 236, 291
Mitchell, Yvette, 290
Mix, Tom, 40, 108, 135, 136, 241, 255, 257, 258, 285, 287
Mizner, Wilson, 3, 222
Mong, William V., 94, 100, 137
Montgomery, Peggy, 284
Moon, Arthur, 5
Moore, Colleen, 143, 236, 340, 353
Moore, Matt, 8, 31, 89, 165, 187, 316
Moore, Owen, 88, 118, 139, 170, 176, 198, 211, 224, 304, 336
Moore, Tom, 20, 86, 154, 187, 226
Moore, Victor, 130
Moore, W. Eugene, 202, 278
Moran, Lois, 30, 118, 146
Morante, Milburne, 126
Moreno, Antonio, 88, 107, 163, 354
Morey, Harry T., 5, 17, 20, 108, 123, 152, 223

Morosco, Walter, 40
Morrisey, Edward, 45
Morrison, James, 225
Mortimer, Edmund, 268
Mulhall, Jack, 6, 7, 59, 172, 255, 329
Mullally, Jode, 129
Murray, Mae, 48, 159, 163, 164, 172, 215, 259, 359
Myers, Harry, 321
Myers, Carmel, 9, 97, 133, 171, 237
Myles, Norbert, 99
Myton, Fred, 306

Nagel, Conrad, 19, 39, 89, 157, 196, 228, 316
Naldi, Nita, 8
Nansen, Betty, 322
Navarro, Ramön, 261, 293, 296, 303
Negri, Pola, 55, 146, 167, 260, 296
Neilan, Marshall, 18, 39, 73, 109, 141, 303, 316, 328
Neill, R. William, 206, 208, 282
Neitz, Alvin J., 166
Nelson, Frances, 143, 277, 325, 349, 358
Nelson, Jack, 55, 75, 87, 213, 260
Nesbit, Evelyn, 144, 291
Nesbit, Pinna, 184, 309
Niblo, Fred, 7, 8, 234, 303, 313, 354
Nigh, William, 68, 218, 229, 283, 337
Nilsson, Anna Q., 20, 221, 322, 348, 353
Nixon, Marian, 135, 226
Noble, John W., 25, 56, 104, 151, 186, 204, 269
Nolan, Mary, 305
Norris, Kathleen, 118, 236
North, Wilfred, 170, 310
Novak, Jane, 15, 20, 29, 31, 35, 39
Noy, Wilfred, 128
Nye, Carroll, 10

Oakman, Wheeler, 292, 98
O'Brien, Eugene, 154, 234, 259, 266
O'Brien, George, 147
O'Brien, John B., 106, 359
O'Connor, Frank, 98, 138, 175
O'Connor, Loyola, 143
O'Day, Molly, 273
Ogle, Charles, 51, 163, 174
O'Hara, George, 284

Oland, Warner, 254
Olcott, Sidney, 95, 321
Oliver, Guy, 243
Olmstead, Gertrude, 328, 341
O'Malley, Pat, 30, 52, 76, 131, 138, 141, 221, 276
O'Neil, Barry, 15, 276
O'Neil, Nance, 104, 323
Ostriche, Muriel, 47, 131, 149, 150, 151, 179, 191, 275
Otto, Henry, 173, 213, 254, 279
Owen, Seena, 58, 59, 154, 165, , 282, 315, 340

Pallette, Eugene, 348
Park, Ida May, 46, 231
Parke, William, 7, 96, 223
Parker, Albert, 17, 157, 185, 233, 366
Paton, Stuart, 93, 127, 207, 277
Patrick, Jerome, 29
Pearson, Virginia, 18
Peil, Edward, 205
Pembroke, Scott, 283, 330
Pembroke, Stanley, 171
Perez, Marcel, 353
Perret, Leonce, 269, 270
Perry, Vivian, 252
Peters, House, 93, 279
Petrova, Olga, 57, 254, 256, 299, 321, 346
Philbin, Mary, 51, 221
Phillips, David Graham, 5, 193
Phillips, Dorothy, 16, 46, 231, 310, 366
Pickford, Jack, 51, 80, 222, 255, 267
Pickford, Lottie, 237, 356
Pickford, Mary, 43, 69, 76, 106, 139, 170, 173, 287, 352
Pierce, James, 248
Pitts, ZaSu, 303
Platt, George Foster, 69
Pollar, Gene, 247
Pollard, Harry, 13
Pollock, Channing, 52, 323
Porter, Edwn S., 81, 83, 179, 307
Powell, David, 164, 224
Powell, Frank, 73, 183, 323, 345
Powell, Paul, 4, 38, 85, 131, 133, 204, 323, 336, 361
Powell, William, 22, 178, 188
Power, Tyrone, 114, 142
Poynter, Beulah, 23

NAME INDEX 383

Pratt, Jack, 202
Prevost, Marie, 89, 186, 196
Puglia, Frank, 227
Purden, Richard, 182

Raboch, Al, 329, 330
Ralston, Esther, 127, 197
Rambeau, Marjorie, 183
Randolf, Anders, 36, 252, 282, 335
Rawlinson, Herbert, 119, 126, 149, 186, 206, 280, 281
Ray, Charles, 110, 146, 159, 161, 181, 204, 283, 338
Razeto, Stella, 300
Reed, Florence, 26, 141
Reed, Luther, 128, 197
Reed, Theodore, 238
Reicher, Frank, 45, 117, 160, 191, 256, 323, 361
Reid, Hal, 13, 363
Reid, Wallace, 45, 68, 86, 208, 261, 266, 287, 362
Reisner, Charles, 175, 250
Reticker, Hugh, 66
Revier, Dorothy, 100, 137, 184, 187
Revier, Harry, 69, 247
Reynolds, Lynn, 15
Rich, Irene, 6, 9, 21, 40, 303
Rich, Vivian, 126
Richardson, Jack, 284
Richman, Charles, 236, 311
Richmond, J. A., 131
Ricketts, Thomas, 33, 83, 124
Ridgely, Cleo, 45, 323
Rigas, George, 237
Ripley, Ray, 37
Ritchie, Franklin, 106
Robards, Jason, 138
Robards, Willis, 125
Roberts, Edith, 8, 155, 175
Roberts, Theodore, 44, 59, 68, 154, 238, 279, 322
Robertson, John S., 214, 257, 266
Robson, Andrew, 234
Rockwell, Florence, 54
Rogell, Al, 135 260
Roland, Gilbert, 261
Roland, Ruth, 73, 83
Ronald, Lucille, 55
Roosevelt, Buddy, 166
Roscoe, Albert, 7, 30, 134, 169

Rosen, Phil, 20, 31, 195, 303, 317
Ross, Irva, 278
Ross, Nat, 90
Rosson, Arthur, 85, 208, 223
Rubens, Alma, 8, 152, 155, 157, 158, 181, 274, 330, 340
Ruggles, Wesley, 8, 21, 178, 268
Rule, B. C., 88
Russell, William, 77, 185, 186, 302

Sainpolis, John, 191, 203, 299
Salisbury, Monroe, 18, 288, 290, 291
Santell, Alfred, 197, 273
Santschi, Tom, 25, 96, 138, 283
Sargent, George L., 358
Sawyer, Laura, 92
Scardon, Paul, 17, 108, 123, 163, 184, 223, 247, 336
Schade, Betty, 142, 150
Schertzinger, Victor, 86, 258, 296, 338
Schildkraut, Joseph, 100
Schildkraut, Rudolph, 274, 343
Schoedsack, Ernest B., 250
Sears, A. D., 58, 308
Seastrom, Victor, 137, 329, 331
Seay, Charles M., 131, 150
Sedgwick, Edward, 50, 135, 258
Seeling, Charles R., 225
Seiter, William A., 30, 176, 305
Sellers, Ollie, 109, 340
Sennett, Mack, 169, 220
Shannon, Ethel, 175
Shay, William E., 347
Shearer, Norma, 137, 175, 196, 261, 343
Sheridan, Frank, 27
Sherman, Lowell, 96, 195, 304, 341, 369
Sherrill, Jack, 14
Sherry, J. Barney, 15, 219
Shotwell, Marie, 132, 213
Shumway, L. C., 340, 341
Sidney, Scott, 175, 176, 181, 244, 253, 298, 335
Sidney, Sylvia, 100
Siegmann, George, 272, 275
Sills, Milton, 78, 96, 97, 111, 151, 165, 213, 216, 233
Singleton, Joseph E., 13, 114
Sloman, Edward, 29, 97, 106, 343, 370
Smalley, Phillips, 47, 115, 153, 202

Smith, Bessie, 20
Smith, Clifford, 71
Smith, David, 282
Smith, Noel Madison, 99
Snow, Marguerite, 264, 333, 335, 337
Sothern, Jean, 163
Spencer, George Boulle, 276
Spencer, George W., 103
Spong, Hilda, 190
Sprotte, Bert, 136, 185, 225
St. Clair, Malcolm, 146
Stahl, Walter Richard, 326
Staindley, Jack, 181
Standing, Jack, 205, 325
Standing, Wyndham, 57, 158, 167, 253
Stanley, Edmund, 3
Stanley, Forrest, 49, 156, 157
Stanton, Elizabeth Cady, 6, 53, 363
Stanton, Richard, 94, 163
Starke, Pauline, 145, 146, 171
Starkey, Bert, 103
Stedman, Myrtle, 37, 103
Steele, Vernon, 132, 247, 299
Steger, Julius, 3, 299, 346
Stein, Paul L., 100
Sterling, Ford, 85
Stevens, Charlotte, 178
Stevens, Edwin, 25, 171
Stevens, Emily, 17, 122, 265
Stewart, Anita, 26, 168, 218, 236
Stewart, Roy, 38, 71, 127, 151, 162
Stiller, Mauritz, 167
Stockdale, Carl, 46, 151, 226
Stoloff, Benjamin, 136
Stone, Lewis, 6, 8, 62, 249, 284, 369
Stone, Phil, 51
Stonehouse, Ruth, 40, 255, 284
Storey, Edith, 264
Storm, Jerome, 88, 132, 272
Stowe, Leslie, 272, 309
Stowell, Frederick, 62
Stowell, William, 16, 46, 231, 366
Strauss, William H., 295
Strong, Charles, 221
Strong, Eugene, 194
Sturgeon, Rollin S., 27, 92, 205, 237
Sullivan, Frederick, 190, 275
Suratt, Valeska, 322, 347, 350
Sutherland, Victor, 104, 252
Swanson, Gloria, 1, 3, 154, 157, 193, 238, 304

Swayne, Marian, 144, 180
Sweet, Blanche, 39, 106, 127, 159, 160, 191, 211, 302, 308, 316, 323, 335, 352
Swickard, Charles, 54, 58, 170, 203, 204, 236
Sydney, Basil, 258

Talmadge, Constance, 85, 314, 329, 367
Talmadge, Norma, 3, 58, 202, 206, 259, 261, 289, 306, 312, 348
Talmadge, Richard, 99, 208
Taylor, Charles, 292
Taylor, E. Forrest, 14
Taylor, Estelle, 250, 272, 306
Taylor, Ray, 79
Taylor, Sam, 51, 306, 343
Taylor, William D., 55, 66, 166, 267
Tearle, Conway, 9, 75
Tell, Alma, 165
Tellegen, Lou, 61, 127, 243, 255, 312
Tennant, Barbara, 93, 137
Terriss, Elaine, 348
Terriss, Tom, 39, 153, 177, 348
Terry, Alice, 293
Terry, Don, 230
Terwilliger, George W., 30, 102, 156, 163
Thayer, Otis B., 121
Theby, Rosemary, 29, 321
Thomas, Augustus, 75, 164, 166, 290
Thomas, Richard, 10
Thompson, Hugh, 18, 194, 232
Thomson, Fred, 72
Thomson, Frederick, 141, 201, 203, 264
Thornby, Robert, 37, 194, 348
Thornton, Edith, 78, 127
Thorpe, Richard, 178
Thurman, Mary, 157, 238
Tilden, William T., 30
Torrence, Ernest, 80, 127, 137
Torres, Raquel, 21
Tourneur, Maurice, 47, 57, 62, 77, 93, 142, 174, 182, 279, 366, 367
Travers, Richard, 37, 116
Trevor, Norman, 9, 172
Trimble, Larry, 35
Truex, Ernest, 200, 267
Trunnelle, Mabel, 44, 321

NAME INDEX 385

Tucker, George Loane, 193, 356
Tucker, Richard, 50, 107, 252
Turbett, Ben, 107, 162, 252
Turner, Otis, 15, 24, 149, 253, 277
Turner, William H., 163
Tutt, J. Homer, 293
Tuttle, Frank, 188

Ulrich, Lenora, 93
Urson, Frank, 109, 166, 328

Vale, Louise, 27
Vale, Travers, 27, 57, 67, 151, 192
Vale, Vola, 56, 215
Valli, Virginia, 52, 105, 217, 218, 225
Van Dyke, W. S., 21, 225, 226, 296
Varconi, Victor, 40, 100, 166, 331
Veiller, Bayard, 4, 87, 207, 364
Vekroff, Perry N., 47
Velez, Lupe, 250, 306
Vernon, Agnes, 173
Vidor, Florence, 5, 173, 197, 245, 293
Vignola, Robert G., 49, 59, 74, 165, 187, 193, 279, 301, 322, 326, 338, 367
Vincent, James, 334, 350
Von Berne, Eva, 329
Von Eltz, Theodore, 21, 248
Von Rue, Greta, 295
Von Seyffertitz, Gustav, 185, 227
Von Sternberg, Josef, 22, 228, 305, 362, 363
Von Stroheim, Erich, 327
Vosburgh, Alfred, 191
Vroom, Fred, 124

Wadsworth, William, 334
Wales, Ethel, 186
Walker, Johnny (Johnnie), 52, 137
Walker, Lillian, 106, 170, 339
Walker, Robert, 105
Wallace, Fay, 150
Wallace, Ramsey, 110
Walsh, George, 128, 258
Walsh, R. A., 67, 324., 351
Walsh, Raoul, 221, 230, 304
Walthall, Henry B., 6, 14, 16, 18, 66, 118, 177, 180, 280
Walton, Gladys, 110, 134, 342
Ward, Norman, 31
Warde, Ernest C., 132, 144, 244

Warner, H. B., 37, 41, 103, 157, 184, 204, 255, 315
Warner, Sam, 247
Warren, Edward, 190
Warren, Giles R., 142
Warwick, Robert, 15, 47, 67, 182, 183, 257, 299, 349, 352
Washburn, Bryant, 71, 255
Wayne, John, 303
Webb, Kenneth, 77, 97, 227, 352
Webb, Millard, 196
Weber, Lois, 16, 48, 93, 114, 115, 153
Webey, Chet, 70
Wehlen, Emmy, 108, 140
Welch, Niles, 40, 99, 134, 155, 234, 282, 334
Wellman, William A., 69, 100, 135
Wells, Raymond, 76, 255
Welsh, William, 93, 134, 277
Werker, Alfred L., 72
West, Dorothy, 106
West, Raymond B., 48, 49, 75, 76, 161, 325, 366
West, Roland, 29, 186, 217, 261, 350
Wharton, Leopold, 200, 213
Wharton, Theodore, 64
Wheelock, Charles, 242
Whipple, Clara, 2, 150
White, Pearl, 83, 174, 179
Whiteside, Walker, 334
Whitlock, Lloyd, 237, 328
Whitman, Alfred, 214
Whitman, Gayne, 51, 98
Whitman, Walt, 205
Whitson, Frank, 216
Whittell, Josephine, 192
Whitworth, Robert, 54
Willat, Irvin, 123, 237
Williams, C. Jay, 335
Williams, Clara, 105, 276
Williams, Earle, 94, 264, 271, 316
Williams, Guinn, 250
Williams, Kathlyn, 157, 243, 300, 352, 353
Williams, Margo, 346
Williams, Ted, 31
Willoughby, Lewis, 35
Wilson, Ben, 38, 347
Wilson, Elsie Jane, 171
Wilson, Lois, 14, 41, 79, 128, 192, 197, 239, 254, 280, 302

Wilson, Margery, 5, 16, 76
Wilson, Tom, 94, 184, 186
Windermere, Fred, 228
Windom, Lawrence, 349
Windsor, Claire, 109, 177, 368, 369
Withee, Mabel, 14
Withers, Grant, 344
Withey, Chester, 58, 160, 202, 312
Wolbert, William, 18, 107, 191, 214
Wolheim, Louis, 108, 230
Wood, Dorothy, 353
Wood, Freeman, 157
Wood, Sam, 238, 239
Woodruff, Henry, 170

Worne, Duke, 188
Worsley, Wallace, 168, 192, 196, 224, 269, 315, 369
Worthington, William, 76, 166, 215
Wray, John Griffith, 136, 208, 302
Wright, Fred E., 232, 255, 356

Young, Clara Kimball, 37, 4,3, 196, 198, 268, 298, 299, 300, 326, 341
Young, James, 28, 35, 55, 195, 222, 230, 245, 265, 292, 293
Young, Tammany, 95

Zimina, Valentina, 316

Title Index

Abraham Lincoln (1924), 67
Absent-minded Burglar, An (1912), 81
According to Law (1916), 115
Ace of Hearts, The (1921), 315
Acquitted (1916), 204
Actor Burglar, The (1909), 81
Adventure in Hearts, An (1920), 257
Adventures of Buffalo Bill, (1914), 64
Adventures of Tarzan, The (1920), 245
After Dark (1924), 88
After the Show (1925), 51
After the Storm (1928), 10
Age of Innocence, The (1924), 8
Alamo, The (1960), 67
Albany Night Boat, The (1928), 329
Alias Jimmy Valentine (1915), 182
Alias Mary Brown (1918), 171
Alias Mike Moran (1919), 266
Alias the Night Wind (1923), 185
Alien, The (1915), 75
Alien Enemy, An (1918), 269
Alimony (1917), 192
All for a Girl (1915), 150
All Man (1918), 223
Alone in the Jungle, 241
Amateur Detective, The (1914), 179
Amazing Impostor, The (1919), 310
And the Law Says (1916), 122
Anna Christie (1923), 302
Answer, The (1918), 152
Are They Born or Made? (1915), 140
Are They Born or Made? (1915), 99
Are You Legally Married? (1919), 194
Argyle Case, The (1919), 183

Arrest of a Shoplifter (1903), 180
As a Man Thinks (1919), 290
As in a Looking Glass (1916), 350
As Man Made Her (1917), 324
As Ye Sow (1914), 13
At Dawn (1914), 287
At the Burglar's Command (1912), 81
At the Eleventh Hour (1910), 92
Athletic Girl and the Burglar, The (1905), 83
Avenging Conscience, The (1914), 180

Babbitt (1924), 9
Bachelor Brides (1926), 186
Back to Liberty (1928), 128
Backstage (1927), 51
Baffles, Gentleman Burglar (1914), 85
Ballet Girl, The (1916), 48
Bandit's Waterloo, The (1908), 220
Bandolero, The (1924), 39
Bank Burglar's Fate, The (1914), 85
Barbed Wire (1927), 296
Bare-Fisted Gallagher (1919), 173
Barker, The (1917), 131
Barricade, The (1917), 35
Barriers of the Law (1925), 79
Bat, The (1926), 186
Beating the Burglar (1914), 85
Beating the Game (1921), 86
Beautiful City, The (1925), 227
Beautiful Sinner, The (1924), 226
Beckoning Flame, The (1916), 170
Beckoning Roads (1919), 155
Bedroom Window, The (1924), 186
Before Midnight (1925), 186

Beggar of Cawnpore, The (1916), 204
Behind the Scenes (1914), 43
Belle of the Season, The (1919), 108
Beloved Rogue (1927), 70, 72
Below the Deadline (1921), 184
Berlin via America (1918), 269
Betsy Ross (1917), 67
Betsy's Burglar (1917), 85
Better Man, The (1914), 103
Better Man Wins, The (1922), 353
Beverly of Graustark (1926), 177
Beware of Blondes (1928), 187
Beyond the Crossroads (1922), 38
Big Adventure, The (1921), 341
Big Boss, The (1913), 275
Big Brother (1923), 225
Big Parade, The (1925), 271, 272
Big Sister, The (1916), 359
Biggest Show on Earth (1918), 132
Billy Turns Burglar (1913), 81
Billy's Burglar (1912), 81
Birds of Prey (1927), 227
Birth Control (1917), 116
Birth of a Nation, The (1915), 289
Birth of a Race, The (1919), 269
Birthright (1924), 293
Bitter Apples (1927), 41
Black Fear (1915), 204
Black Gate, The (1919), 94
Black Hand, The (1906), 74
Black Roses (1921), 37
Blackbirds (1915), 182
Blackie's Redemption (1919), 223
Blacklist, The (1916), 106
Blackmail (1920), 352
Blessed Miracle, The (1915), 4
Blight of Sin, The (1909), 2
Blind Circumstances (1922), 126
Blind Goddess, The (1926), 127
Blind Hearts (1921), 125
Blind Husbands (1919), 327
Blindfold (1928), 30
Blindness of Divorce, The (1918), 193
Blood and Sand (1922), 8
Blood of the Children, The (1915), 102
Blood Ship, The (1927), 40
Blue Blood (1918), 214
Bluebeard's Seven Wives (1926), 197
Body and Soul (1915), 54
Bold, Bad Burglar, A (1915), 85
Bolshevism on Trial (1919), 309

Bomb Throwers, The (1915), 308
Bond, The (1918), 266
Bond of Fear, The (1917), 162
Bondage (1917), 231
Bonded Woman, The (1922), 20
Bondwomen (1915), 203
Bonnie Annie Laurie (1918), 28
Boots (1919), 311
Border Wildcat, The (1928), 79
Born Again (1914), 23
Borrowed Clothes (1918), 153
Boss, The (1914), 103
Boston Blackie's Little Pal (1918), 86
Bought and Paid For (1922), 369
Boundary Rider, The (1914), 199, 200
Bowery Cinderella, A (1927), 52
Boy Detective, The (1908), 180
Boy Girl, The (1917), 171
Brand of Lopez, The (1920), 61
Brand of Satan, The (1917), 225
Brass Bowl, The (1924), 88
Breaking Point, The (1924), 31
Bred in the Bone (1915), 4
Bridge of Sighs, The (1915), 334
Bright Lights (1925), 146
Bright Lights of Broadway (1923), 96
Broadway After Midnight (1927), 228
Broadway Broke (1923), 50
Broadway Lady (1925), 21
Broadway Love (1917), 46
Broken Barriers (1928), 284
Broken Commandments (1919), 326
Broken Fetters (1916), 358
Broken Melody, The (1919), 234
Broncho Billy's Indian Romance, 290
Brother Man (1910), 84
Buddy, the Little Guardian (1911), 12
Buffalo Bill on the U. P. Trail (1926), 71
Buffalo Bill's Indian Wars (1914), 71
Buffalo Bill's Last Fight (1927), 71
Bullets and Brown Eyes (1916), 253
Bullin' the Bullsheviki (1919), 310
Burglar, The (1898), 82
Burglar, The (1903), 82
Burglar, The (1917), 85
Burglar and the Bundle, The (1903), 82
Burglar and the Lady (1914), 85, 212
Burglar in the Bed Chamber (1898), 82
Burglar on the Roof (1898), 82
Burglar's Dilemma (1912), 83

TITLE INDEX 389

Burglar's Mistake, A (1909), 83
Burglar's Slide for Life (1905), 83
Burglar-Proof Bed (1902), 82
Buried Alive (1909), 34
Burning Question, The (1919), 311
Burning the Candle (1917), 16
Burnt Wings (1920), 302
Burstup Holmes, Detective (1913), 179
Burstup Holmes's Murder Case (1913), 179
Busy Day, A (1914), 169
By Divine Right (1924), 282
By Love Redeemed (1916), 335
By Right of Possession (1917), 107

Cabaret (1927), 187
Caillaux Case, The (1918), 163
Calamity Anne, Detective (1913), 179
California Romance, A (1923), 272
Call of the Dance, The (1915), 358
Called Back (1915), 24
Camille (1915), 298
Camille of the Barbary Coast (1925), 304
Candy Girl, The (1917), 202
Capital Punishment (1915), 93
Capital Punishment (1925), 98
Capital vs. Labor (1910), 102
Caprice (1913), 139
Caprice of the Mountains (1916), 142
Capture of Aguinaldo, The (1913), 241
Career of Crime, No. 5, A (1902), 92
Case at Law, A (1917), 17
Case of the Missing Girl (1913), 179
Cassidy (1917), 85
Cast-Off, The (1918), 48
Caught in the Fog (1928), 89
Cave Man, The (1915), 150
Chang (1927), 250
Charley's Aunt (1925), 175
Cheat, The (1915), 54
Cheating the Public (1918), 94
Chelsea 7750 (1913), 220
Chicago (1927), 166
Chicago After Midnight (1928), 229
Chicken Casey (1917), 49
Child of Mystery, A (1916), 75
Child of the Prairie, A (1925), 40
Children in the House, The (1916), 348
Children of Divorce (1927), 197
Children of Eve (1915), 105

Children of the Feud (1916), 161
Children of the Night (1921), 77
Children Pay, The (1916), 190
Children Who Labor (1912), 102
China Slaver, The (1929), 362
Chinatown Charlie (1928), 80, 362
Chinese Parrot, The (1927), 187
Chorus Lady, The (1915), 45
Christmas Burglars, The (1908), 83
Cinema Murder, The (1919), 36
Circumstantial Evidence (1911), 121
Circumstantial Evidence (1920), 125
Circumstantial Evidence (1929), 128
Circus, The (1928), 138
Circus Ace, The (1927), 136
Circus Cowboy (1924), 135
Circus Cyclone, The (1925), 135
Circus Man, The (1914), 129
Circus Romance, A (1916), 131
City, The (1926), 208
City Gone Wild, The (1927), 167
City of Illusion (1916), 3
City of Silent Men, The (1921), 185
Clancy (1910), 220
Closed Gate, The (1927), 31
Closed Road, The (1916), 93
Closing Net, The (1915), 222
Clown, The (1916), 130
Cocaine Traffic, The (1914), 200
Cohen's Luck (1915), 334
Come On In (1918), 267
Coming Through (1925), 111
Common Ground (1916), 279
Conqueror, The (1917), 67
Conquest (1929), 41
Conscience (1913), 199
Conscience (1915), 93
Conspiracy, The (1914), 357
Contraband (1925), 79
Contrast, The (1921), 109
Convict 993 (1918), 223
Convoy (1927), 304
Corner, The (1915), 105
Corner in Cotton, A (1916), 335
Corruption (1917), 56
Counsel for the Defense (1925), 127
Counter Intrigue, The (1915), 201
Counterfeit (1919), 224
Country Boy, The (1915), 141
County Seat War, The (1914), 222
Courage of Silence, The (1917), 5

Courtesan, The (1916), 300
Cowboy Prince, The (1924), 259, 260
Criminals, The (1913), 74
Crimson Challenge, The (1922), 38
Crimson Gardenia, The (1919), 224
Crisis, The (1916), 67
Crooked Alley (1923), 185
Crown of Lies, The (1926), 260
Crown Prince's Double (1916), 252
Cruise of the Make-Believes, The (1918), 338
Cry of the Children, The (1913), 102
Crystal Cup, The (1927), 329
Curse of Drink, The (1922), 20
Custer's Last Fight (1912), 65
Custer's Last Scout (1915), 65
Custer's Last Stand (1910), 65
Cyclone Cavalier (1925), 260
Cyclone Kelly (1924), 166
Cytherea (1924), 8

Dance Magic (1927), 147
Dancing Girl, The (1915), 141
Dancing Mothers (1926), 9
Danger – Go Slow (1918), 172
Danger Mark, The (1918, 215
Dangerous Adventure, A (1922), 247
Dangerous Hours (1920), 313
Dangerous Moment, The (1921), 237
Daniel Boone Thru the Wilderness (1926), 64
Daniel Boone's Bravery (1911), 64
Daredevil, The (1918), 172
Daring Years, The (1923), 97
Dark Lantern, A (1920), 257
Dark Stairways (1924), 126
Dark Swan, The (1924), 196
Daughter of Destiny (1918), 256
Daughter of Mine (1919), 291
Daughter of the Poor, A (1917), 151
Daughter of the Sea, A (1915), 150
Daughters of Men, The (1914), 102
David Garrick (1916), 66
Davy Crockett (1910), 64
Davy Crockett (1916), 64, 66
Davy Crockett at the Fall of the Alamo (1926), 64, 67
Davy Crockett in Hearts United (1909), 64
Dawn of a Tomorrow, The (1924), 342
Dawn of Revenge (1922), 37

Daybreak (1918), 17
Dazzling Miss Davison (1917), 183
Decoy, The (1916), 143
Deep Purple, The (1915), 222
Defeat of the City, The (1917), 143
Defense or Tribute? (1916), 67
Deliverance (1919), 69
Derelict, The (1917), 360
Desperate Moment, A (1926), 248
Destroyers, The (1916), 278
Destroying Angel, The (1915), 44
Destruction (1915), 53
Detected (1903), 189
Detective Craig's Coup (1914), 181
Detectives of the Italian Bureau, The (1909), 74
Determination (1922), 342
Devil's Circus, The (1926), 137
Devil's Claim, The (1920), 236
Devil's Needle, The (1916), 199
Devil's Needle, The (1916), 202
Devil's Passkey, The (1920), 327
Devil's Toy, The (1916), 25
Devil's Trademark, The (1928), 218
Diamond Handcuffs (1928), 229
Diamond Runners, The (1916), 222
Diamonds and Pearls (1917), 151
Diana of the Follies (1916), 44
Diane of Star Hollow (1921), 77
Diplomacy (1926), 316
Dirty Gertie From Harlem, USA (1946), 305
Discard, The (1916), 349
Disraeli (1921), 70
District Attorney, The (1915), 276
Dividend, The (1916), 204
Divorce and the Daughter (1916), 190
Divorce Game, The (1917), 192
Divorce Trap, The (1919), 193
Divorced (1915), 190
Divorcée, The (1917), 191
Divorcée, The (1919), 194
Docks of New York, The (1928), 305
Doll's House, A (1917), 366
Don't Change Your Husband (1919), 193
Don't Shoot (1922), 281
Dormant Power, The (1917, 57
Double Crossed (1917), 279
Dove, The (1928), 261
Draft 258 (1918), 266

TITLE INDEX 391

Drag Net, The (1928), 22
Drake Case, The (1929), 209
Dream Lady, The (1918), 171
Driftwood (1928), 305
Drug Traffic, The (1914), 200
Drug Traffic, The (1923), 207
Drums of Fate (1923), 248
Drunkard's Fate, The (1909), 12
Duck Soup (1934), 257
Dummy, The (1917), 222
Dungeon, The (1922), 207
Dupe, The (1916), 191
Dust (1916), 106

Easiest Way, The (1917), 300
East of Broadway (1924), 88
80 Million Women (1913), 364
Embarrassment of Riches (1918), 339
Empty Arms (1920), 117
Enchanted Island, The (1927), 177
Enchantment (1921), 49
Enlighten Thy Daughter (1917), 325
Enter Madame (1922), 196
Environment (1915), 213
Ermine and Rhinestones (1926), 40
Escape, The (1914), 211
Eternal Grind, The (1916), 106
Eternal Love (1929), 331
Eternal Question, The (1916), 254
Eternal Temptress, The (1917), 351
Eternal Three, The (1923), 328
Eternal Woman, The (1929), 331
Even As You and I (1917), 16
Every Woman's Problem (1921), 125
Everybody's Business (1919), 311
Everybody's Girl (1918), 153
Exciters, The (1923), 87
Exclusive Rights (1926), 98
Exile (1917), 57
Exit Smiling (1926), 51
Experimental Marriage (1919), 367
Explorer, The (1915), 243
Exposure of the Land Swindlers (1913), 179, 275
Eye of a God, The (1913), 169
Eye for an Eye, An (1909), 2

Face in the Fog, The (1922), 315
Face of the World (1921), 237
Face to Face (1922), 87
Fair Lady (1922), 77

Fair Play (1925), 127
Faithful Wives (1927), 99
Fallen Idol, The (1919), 291
False Colors (1914), 47
Falsely Accused (1908), 159
Family Cupboard, The (1915), 346
Family Stain, The (1915), 182
Fascinating Youth (1926), 239
Fast Set, The (1924), 303
Fatal Hour, The (1908), 356
Fear Not (1917), 205
Fear Woman, The (1919), 216
Fearless Lover (1925), 100
Feet of Clay (1917), 122
Felix O'Day (1920), 37
Female Detective, The (1913), 179
Fifth Horseman, The (1924), 272
Fifty-Fifty Girl, The (1928), 370
Fight, The (1915), 364
Fight for Millions, The (1913), 180
Fighting Chance (1920), 19
Fighting for Love (1917), 255
Final Curtain, The (1916), 44
Finders Keepers (1928), 178
Fire Brigade, The (1926), 283
Fires of Conscience (1916), 160
First Night, The (1927), 178
Five Days to Live (1922), 96
$5,000,000 Counterfeiting Plot (1914), 221
Flame of Life, The (1923), 157
Flame of Passion (1915), 348
Flash, The (1923), 283
Flesh and the Devil (1927), 9
Flying Colors (1917), 86
Flying Fool (1925), 89
Flying Twins, The (1915), 130
Food for Scandal (1920), 195
Fool and His Money, A (1925), 260
Fool There Was, A (1914), 345
Fool's Awakening, A (1924), 315
Foolish Wives (1921, 327
Footlights of Fate, The (1916), 45
For France (1917), 268
For Heaven's Sake (1926), 343
For the Flag (1913), 242
For the Honor of Old Glory (1914), 264
Forbidden City, The (1918), 289
Forbidden Fruit (1921), 156
Forbidden Path, The (1918), 232
Forbidden Woman, The (1927), 100

Forsaking All Others (1922), 353
Fortune Teller, The (1920), 135
Fortune's Mask (1922), 271
Forty-Horse Hawkins (1924), 50
Found Guilty (1922), 96
Four Walls (1928), 229
Frame-Up, The (1915), 277
Francis Marion, the Swamp Fox (1914), 65
Freaks (1932), 89
Freedom of the Press (1928), 284
Friendly Enemies (1925), 272
From Headquarters (1929), 250
Fury (1923), 38

Game With Fate, A (1918), 123
Gangsters, The (1914), 139
Gangsters and the Girl, The (1914), 181
Garden of Knowledge, The (1917), 213
Garter Girl, The (1920), 49
Gentleman of Paris, A (1927), 41
Getting Evidence ... (1906), 179
Ghost City (1921), 79
Gift Supreme, The (1920), 340
Gilded Cage, The (1916), 254
Gingham Girl, The (1927), 239
Girl and the Crisis, The (1917), 94
Girl at the Lock, The (1914), 320
Girl From Bohemia, The (1918), 232
Girl From Chicago, The (1927), 228
Girl Nihilist, The (1908), 307
Girl of the Sunny South, The (1913), 27
Girl on the Stairs, The (1924), 166
Girl That Went Astray, The (1902), 298
Girl Who Didn't Think, The (1917), 325
Girl Who Doesn't Know, The (1916), 324
Girl Who Stayed at Home, The (1919), 270
Girl's Folly, A (1917), 47
Girls and the Burglar, The (1904), 82
Girls Gone Wild (1929), 80
Gladiola (1915), 34
Going Crooked (1926), 97
Gold and the Woman (1916), 350
Gold Diggers, The (1923), 50
Golden Goal, The (1918), 108
Golden God, The (1917), 144
Golden Wall, The (1918), 153

Golden Web, The (1926), 99
Gossip (1923), 110
Governor's Boss, The (1915), 276
Grafters (1917), 223
Grand Larceny (1922), 369
Gratitude (1909), 53
Graustark (1925), 259
Great Accident, The (1920), 20
Great Adventure, The (1918), 47
Great Diamond Mystery (1924), 97
Great Diamond Robbery (1914), 181
Great Jewel Mystery, The (1905), 220
Great Romance, The (1919), 254
Great Shadow, The (1920), 313
Great Silence, The (1915), 4
Greene Murder Case, The (1929), 188
Grim Game, The (1919), 123

Half a Rogue (1916), 279
Half Breed, The (1916), 288
Half Breed, The (1922), 292
Hand at the Window, The (1918), 76
Hand That Rocks the Cradle, The (1917), 115
Hangman's House (1928), 62
Hard Road, The (1915), 321
Harriet and the Piper (1920), 236
Hate (1917), 326
Hate (1922), 126
Hater of Men, The (1917), 192
Haunting Fear, The (1915), 322
He Who Gets Slapped (1924), 137
Heart in Pawn, A (1919), 215
Heart of a Hero, The (1916), 67
Heart of a Painted Woman, The (1915), 321
Heart of a Race Tout, The (1909), 102
Heart of Lincoln, The (1915), 67
Heart of Maryland, The (1927), 67
Heart Strings (1916), 3
Heart Trouble (1928), 274
Heartaches (1915), 54
Hearts and the Highway (1915), 170
Hearts Asleep (1919), 216
Hearts of the Jungle (1915), 241
Heedless Moths (1921), 237
Held by the Law (1927), 99
Helena Ritchie (1916), 56
Hell Morgan's Girl (1917), 16
Hell's End (1918), 153
Help Yourself (1920), 236

Her Better Self (1917), 338
Her Captive Woman (1929), 165
Her Country's Call (1917), 265
Her Double Life (1916), 322
Her Elephant Man (1920), 134
Her Excellency, the Governor (1917), 366
Her Good Name (1917), 163
Her Half Brother (1922), 353
Her Hour (1917), 324
Her Husband's Friend (1918), 36
Her Maternal Right (1916), 348
Her One Mistake (1918), 183
Her Right to Live (1917), 163
Her Sister From Paris (1925), 329
Heredity (1918), 339
Heritage (1915), 212
Heroes of the Alamo (1938), 67
Heroes of the Street (1922), 225
Hesper of the Mountains (1916), 106
Hidden Valley (1916), 244
High Road, The (1915), 104
High Tide (1918), 232
His Crucible (1915), 347
His Darker Self (1924), 186
His Foreign Wife (1927), 294
His Forgotten Wife (1924), 30
His Great Triumph (1916), 337
His Last Burglary (1910), 84
His Last Game (1909), 286
His Lost Self (1916), 26
His Majesty, the American (1919), 257
His Own People (1918), 152
His People (1925), 343
His Robe of Honor (1918), 280
Hit-the-Trail Holliday (1918), 18
Hitting the Trail (1918), 223
Hold That Lion (1926), 248
Hollywood Reporter, The (1926), 284
Home, Sweet, Home (1914), 65
Home-Keeping Hearts (1921), 281
Honeymoon Express, The (1926), 9
Hoodman Blind (1924), 302
Hop, the Devil's Brew (1916), 202
Hour Before Dawn, An (1913), 221
House of Bondage, The (1914), 356
House of Silence, The (1918), 360
House Without Children, The (1919), 116
How They Do Things on the Bowery (1902), 298

Human Driftwood (1916), 349
Human Orchid, The (1916), 278
Human Wreckage (1923), 208
Humoresque (1920), 340
Hungry Heart, The (1917), 193
Hurricane, The (1937), 293
Husbands and Wives (1920), 194
Husbands for Rent (1927), 198
Hush (1921), 37
Hutch of the U.S.A. (1924), 259

I Am a Man (1924), 282
I Am Guilty (1921), 87
I Will Repay (1917), 57
Iced Bullet, The (1917), 183
Iconoclast, The (1910), 12
Idle Hands (1921), 361
Idol, The (1915), 14
If I Were King (1920), 70, 72
Imar the Servitor (1914), 55
Immigrant, The (1915), 322
In Life's Cycle (1910), 320
In the Fall of '64 (1914), 170
In the Hands of the Law (1917), 122
Infatuation (1915), 13
Innocence (1923), 157
Innocent Cheat, The (1921), 38
Innocent Sinner, The (1917), 324
Inside of the White Slave Traffic, The (1913), 356
Into Her Kingdom (1926), 316
Into the Primitive (1916), 244
Is Any Girl Safe? (1916), 358
Is That Nice? (1926), 284
Is Your Daughter Safe? (1927), 362
Island of Happiness, The (1916), 55
It Is the Law (1924), 40

Jazzmania (1923), 259
Jesse James (1927), 72
Jewel in Pawn, A (1917), 337
Jim Grimsby's Boy (1916), 114
Jinx (1919), 133
Joan the Woman (1916), 68
John Barleycorn (1914), 12
Jules of the Strong Heart (1918), 107
Jungle Child, The (1916), 246
Jungle Lovers, The (1915), 242
Jungle Trail, The (1919), 245
Just off Broadway (1924), 226
Justice of the Redskin, The (1908), 286

394 TITLE INDEX

Justified (1909), 33

Kaiser, the Beast of Berlin, The (1918), 68
Kaiser's Finish, The (1918), 268
Katchem Kate (1912), 169
Kate the Cop (1913), 179
Kentuckian, The (1908), 285
Key to Yesterday, The (1914), 24
Kid Sister, The (1927), 146
King Kong (1933), 160, 250
King of Detectives, The (1902), 180
King of Detectives, The (1903), 180
King of the Wire, The (1915), 276
Kiss Me Again (1925), 196
Kit Carson (1910), 63
Kit Carson (1928), 72
Kit Carson Over the Great Divide (1925), 71
Kit Carson's Wooing (1911), 63
Knife, The (1918), 326

Ladies of the Big House (1931), 100
Ladies of the Mob (1928), 100
Lady From Hell, The (1926), 127
Lady of the Night (1925), 343
Ladybird, The (1927), 227
Ladyfingers (1921), 87
Lair of the Wolf, The (1917), 58
Lash, The (1916), 55
Last Hour, The (1923), 97
Last Man, The (1916), 242
Last of His People, The (1919), 290
Last of the Ingrahams, The (1917), 16
Last Sentence, The (1917), 162
Law and the Man, The (1928), 283
Law of Compensation, The (1917), 3
Law of Men, The (1919), 234
Law of Nature, The (1919), 18
Law of the Land, The (1917), 57
Lawful Cheaters (1925), 175
Legally Dead (1923), 96
Leopard's Bride, The (1916), 243
Lest We Forget (1918), 269
Libertine, The (1916), 299
Life of Abraham Lincoln (1908), 65
Life of Big Tim Sullivan, The (1914), 66
Life's Crossroads (1928), 249
Life's Mockery (1928), 218
Light of Victory, The (1919), 18

Light Within, The (1918), 35
Light Woman, A (1920), 7
Lilies of the Streets (1925), 98
Lincoln Cycle, The (1917), 67
Little Angel of Canyon Creek, The (1914), 92
Little Brother of the Rich, A (1915), 15
Little Girl Next Door, The (1916), 359
Little Girl Next Door, The (1923), 225
Little Irish Girl, The (1926), 227
Little Liar, The (1916), 336
Little Miss Hoover (1918), 266
Little Miss No-Account (1918), 234
Little Miss Rebellion (1920), 314
Little Red Schoolhouse, The (1923), 78
Little Terror, The (1917), 131
Little Wanderer, The (1920), 174
Little White Savage, The (1919), 133
Lone Chance, The (1924), 282
Lone Wolf Returns, The (1926), 227
Long Lane's Turning, The (1919), 18
Long Live the King (1923), 258
Lookout Girl, The (1928), 229
Lost Bridegroom, The (1916), 26
Lost in the Jungle (1911), 241
Lost Money (1919), 246
Lost Paradise, The (1914), 103
Lost World, The (1925), 249
Love (1927), 10
Love Auction, The (1919), 18
Love Burglar, The (1919), 86
Love Cheat, The (1919), 235
Love Girl, The (1916), 142
Love of Women (1924), 239
Love or Justice? (1917), 202
Love That Lives, The (1917), 301
Love Victorious, The (1914), 320
Love's Battle (1920), 125
Love's Crucible (1916), 325
Love's Lariat (1916), 350
Loves of Letty, The (1920), 156
Loves of Ricardo, The (1926), 79
Loyalty (1917), 202
Lullaby, The (1924), 39
Lure, The (1914), 357
Lure of the Nightclub, The (1927), 147

Mabel's Stratagem (1913), 169
Mad Marriage, The (1921), 237
Madam X (1916), 162
Madame Behave (1925), 176

TITLE INDEX 395

Madonna of Avenue A, The (1929), 344
Madonnas and Men (1920), 368
Magda (1917), 326
Magic Flame, The (1927), 261
Maid of Belgium, A (1917), 27
Making of O'Malley, The (1925), 78
Male and Female (1919), 154
Man and Beast (1917), 244
Man and His Mate, A (1915), 206
Man Beneath, The (1919), 76
Man From Oregon, The (1915), 276
Man Hater, The (1917), 17
Man in the Box, The (1908), 220
Man in the Shadow, The (1926), 99
Man of Sorrow, A (1916), 35
Man on the Box, The (1925), 175
Man Tamer, The (1922), 134
Man Trap, The (1917), 280
Man Who Forgot, The (1917), 15
Man With the Iron Heart, The (1915), 104
Manhattan (1924), 226
Manhattan Knights (1928), 228
Mark of the Beast (1923), 87
Marriage License (1926), 158
Marriage Market, The (1917), 58
Married in Name Only (1917), 213
Martin Mystery, The (1915), 181
Masks of the Devil (1928), 329
Masquerader, The (1914), 169
Master Cracksman, The (1914), 181
Master Mind, The (1920), 352
Master of Beasts, The (1922), 247
Master of the House, The (1915), 346
Maternity (1917), 116
Matinee Idol, The (1928), 52
Me, Gangster (1928), 230
Melting Pot, The (1915), 334
Men of Steel (1926), 111
Menace, The (1918), 214
Merton of the Movies (1924), 50
Message of the Violin, The (1910), 12
Mexican, The (1914), 285
Mexican, The (1914), 287
Microbe, The (1919), 173
Midnight Adventure, A (1928), 188
Mill Girl – a Story of Factory Life, The (1907), 101
Million Bid, A (1914), 26
Million for Love, A (1928), 167

Millionaire Vagrant, The (1917), 338
Miracle of Life, The (1915), 114
Miracle of Manhattan, The (1921), 165
Miss Raffles (1914), 179
Miss Sadie Thompson (1953), 305
Miss Sherlock Holmes (1908), 179
Missing (1918), 28
Missing Link, The (1927), 250
Mistress Nell (1915), 170
Modern Cain, A (1925), 31
Modern Husbands (1919), 6
Modern Love (1918), 48
Modern Love (1929), 370
Modern Youth (1926), 260
Mohawk's Way, A (1910), 286
Molly Maguires, The ... (1908), 102
Money Talks (1926), 177
Mongrel and Master (1914), 85
Moonshine Trail, The (1919), 19
Moral Courage (1917), 191
Moral Sinner, The (1924), 226
More Deadlier Than the Male (1919), 367
More to Be Pitied Than Scorned (1922), 29
Morgan's Raiders (1918), 173
Moth, The (1917), 58
Moth and the Flame, The (1915), 321
Motherhood: Life's Greatest Miracle (1928), 119
Mountain Woman, The (1921), 174
Mountains of Manhattan (1927), 111
Mr. Logan, U.S.A. (1918), 108
Mrs. Slacker (1918), 265
Mrs. Wiggs of the Cabbage Path (1914), 130
Musketeers of Pig Alley, The (1912), 220
My Four Years in Germany (1918), 68
My Lady of Whims (1925), 239
My Man (1924), 282
My Own Pal (1926), 136
My Own United States (1918), 67
Mystery Girl, The (1919), 256
Mystery of Carter Breene, The (1915), 203

Name the Woman (1928), 168
Narrow Path, The (1916), 334
Nearly a King (1916), 253
Neptune's Daughter (1914), 212

396 TITLE INDEX

Net, The (1923), 30
New Disciple, The (1921), 109
New Moon, The (1919), 312
New Teacher, The (1922), 342
New York (1927), 128
New York Idea, The (1920), 195
Night of Love, The (1927), 41
Night Patrol, The (1926), 99
Nightingale, The (1914), 75
Nobody (1921), 29
Notorious Miss Lisle, The (1920), 195
Nut, The (1921), 238

Oh, Baby! (1926), 177
Old Fashioned Young Man, An (1917), 143
Old Folks at Home, The (1916), 160
Old Loves and New (1926), 62
Old Shoes (1925), 62
Old Wives for New (1918), 5
On Dangerous Paths (1915), 141
On Record (1917), 163
On the Threshold (1925), 118
On With the Dance (1920), 164
Once to Every Man (1918), 14
One Day (1916), 252
One Exciting Night (1922), 117
One Hour Past Midnight (1924), 88
One Law for Both (1917), 365
One More American (1918), 280
One of the Finest (1919), 154
Only Thing, The (1925), 316
Only Way Out, The (1915), 160
Opened Shutters, The (1914), 149
Organ Grinder, The (1909), 74
Other Half of the Note, The (1914), 182
Other Man, The (1918), 17
Other Woman, The (1918), 233
Other Woman, The (1921), 29
Out of Darkness (1915), 104
Out of the Dust (1920), 6
Out of the Wreck (1917), 300
Outcast (1928), 305
Outer Edge, The (1915), 14
Outwitted (1925), 227

Pace That Kills, The (1928), 209
Padlocked (1926), 146
Padrone's Ward, The (1914), 75
Pagan, The (1929), 296

Page Mystery, The (1917), 60
Painted Soul, The (1915), 298
Paliser Case, The (1920), 7
Partners of the Night (1920), 184
Pasquale (1916), 55
Patent Leather Kid, The (1927), 273
Patriot and the Spy, The (1915), 264
Patriot, The (1916), 265
Pawn of Fate, The (1916), 142
Payment, The (1916), 325
Pearl as a Detective (1913), 179
Penalty, The (1920), 224
Penthouse (1933), 228
People Vs. John Doe, The (1916), 93
Perfect Sap, The (1927), 187
Perfect Woman, The (1920), 314
Perils of Divorce, The (1916), 190
Phantom of the Opera, The (1925), 51
Phil-For-Short (1919), 172
Pink Tights (1920), 134, 135
Pioneer Peacemaker, 71
Planter's Wife, The (1908), 1
Plaything of Broadway, The (1921), 341
Poison (1924), 78
Polly of the Circus (1917), 132
Port of Missing Girls (1928), 330
Potash and Perlmutter (1923), 110
Power of Labor, The (1908), 102
Power of Silence, The (1928), 168
Prejudice (1922), 293
Price of Applause, The (1918), 233
Price of Fame, The (1910), 34
Price of Her Soul, The (1917), 205
Price of Honor, The (1927), 100
Price of Pride, The (1917), 162
Pride and the Devil (1917), 143
Primitive Call, The (1917), 289
Primrose Path, The (1915), 4
Prince in a Pawnshop, A (1916), 336
Prince of Avenue A, The (1920), 156
Prince of Graustark, The (1916), 255
Prodigal Daughters (1923), 238
Prodigal Wife, The (1918), 3
Prohibition (1915), 13
Public Defender, The (1917), 94
Public Opinion (1916), 160
Purple Dawn (1923), 225
Pursued (1925), 176
Put 'Em Up (1928), 295

TITLE INDEX 397

Racket, The (1928), 230
Raffles, the Amateur Cracksman (1905), 219
Raffles, the Amateur Cracksman (1925), 226
Ragamuffin, The (1916), 335
Rain (1932), 305
Rainbow Princess, The (1916), 130
Ramona (1910), 287
Ramona (1916), 288
Ramona (1928), 295
Ransom, The (1916), 46
Rasputin (1917), 68
Rat, The (1914), 221
Raven, The (1915), 66
Rawhide Kid, The (1928), 295
Reapers, The (1916), 2
Red Clay (1927), 294
Red Hot Romance (1922), 258
Red Kimono (1926), 362
Red Lights (1923), 186
Red Lily, (1924), 303
Red Red Heart, The (1918), 290
Red Virgin, The (1915), 251
Redemption (1914), 320
Redman's View, The (1909), 286
Redskin (1929), 296
Regenerates, The (1917), 205
Regeneration, The (1915), 221
Rejected Woman, The (1924), 158
Reno Divorce, A (1927), 197
Reputation (1921), 207
Resurrection, The (1927), 322
Return of Tarzan, The (1920), 245, 247
Revolt, The (1916), 358
Reward, The (1915), 45
Rich Girl, Poor Girl (1921), 342
Rich Men's Sons (1927), 158
Richard, the Lion-Hearted (1923), 70
Right Direction, The (1916), 337
Right of Way, The (1915), 25
Right of Way, The (1920), 29
Right Off the Bat (1915), 66
Right to Happiness, The (1919), 310
Right Way, The (1921), 95
Road Between, The (1917), 144
Road Through the Dark, The (1918), 268
Road to Divorce, The (1920), 195
Road to Mandalay, The (1926), 118
Robes of Sin (1924), 78

Robin Hood (1922), 70
Romance of a Million Dollars, The (1926), 177
Romance of Tarzan, The (1918), 244
Romance of the Air, A (1918), 69
Romance of the Underworld, A (1918), 199, 206
Romance of the Western Hills, A (1910), 285, 287
Rose of the Philippines, A (1910), 287
Rose of the Tenements (1926), 317
Rose of the World (1925), 118
Rough Diamond, The (1921), 258
Royal Pauper, The (1917), 107
Royal Rider, The (1929), 260
Russia, Land of Oppression (1910), 307
Rustlin' for Cupid (1926), 218

Sacrifice (1917), 256
Sacrifice of Jonathan Gray, The (1915), 2
Sadie Thompson (1928), 304
Safe for Democracy (1917), 308
Salamander, The (1914), 21
Salamander, The (1915), 140
Sally in Our Alley (1916), 151
Salvation Hunters, The (1925), 362
Salvation Nell (1915), 14
Sawdust (1923), 134
Sawdust Ring, The (1917), 131
Sawdust Trail, The (1924), 135
Say It With Sables (1928), 188
Scar, The (1919), 301
Scarlet Car, The (1917), 26
Scarlet Road, The (1916), 348
Scarlet Shadow, The (1919), 215
Scarlet Woman, The (1916), 299
Sealed Door, The (1909), 34
Sealed Valley (1915), 288
Searchers, The (1956), 350
Secret Marriage (1919), 124
Secret of Black Mountain (1917), 56
Secret Orchard, The (1915), 323
Secret Seven, The (1915), 222
Señorita (1927), 178
Serpent, The (1916), 351
Serpent's Tooth, The (1917), 205
Seven Sinners (1925), 89
Shadows of the Past (1915), 321
Shall We Forgive Her? (1917), 60

398 TITLE INDEX

She Goes to War (1929), 274
Sherlock Holmes (1922), 185
Sherlock Holmes Baffled (1903), 82
Ship Comes In, A (1928), 274
Shock, The (1923), 225
Should a Baby Die? (1916), 288
Should a Girl Marry? (1928), 330
Should a Wife Forgive? (1915), 346
Should a Woman Tell? (1920), 7
Should She Obey? (1917), 192
Side Show of Life, The (1924), 137
Sign of the Poppy, The (1916), 203
Silent Accuser, The (1924), 175
Silent Battle, The (1916), 14
Silk Stocking Sal (1924), 88
Silken Shackles (1926), 40
Silver Fingers (1926), 187
Silver Lining, The (1921), 217
Sin Woman, The (1917), 214
Sin Ye Do, The (1916), 161
Singapore Mutiny, The (1928), 306
Sink or Swim (1920), 258
Siren, The (1917), 350
Sitting Bull at the Spirit Lake Massacre (1927), 71
Sitting Bull - the Hostile Sioux Indian Chief (1914), 65
Slacker, The (1917), 265
Slaves of Pride (1920), 156
Sleeping Fires (1917), 191
Sleeping Lion, The (1919), 285, 291
Smashing the Vice Trust (1914), 357
Smiling All the Way (1921), 238
Smuggler's Game, The (1910), 199
Snob, The (1924), 196
Social Code, The (1923), 96
Sold at Auction (1917), 359
Sold for Marriage (1916), 308
Son of Erin, A (1916), 279
Son of Tarzan, The (1920), 245
Son of the Immortals, A (1916), 253
Song of the Wage Slave, The (1915), 105
Sorrows of Satan, The (1926), 353
Soul and Body (1921), 361
Soul of Broadway, The (1915), 347
Soul of the Beast, The (1923), 136
Souls for Sale (1923), 50
Souls in Bondage (1923), 30
Souls in Pawn (1915), 347
Sowers, The (1916), 308

Spangles (1927), 138
Spirit of '17, The (1918), 267
Spirit of the Poppy, The (1914), 199, 201
Sporting Age, The (1928), 10
Square Shooter, The (1920), 181
Squaw Man, The (1914), 290
Stagestruck (1917), 45
Stanley and Livingstone (1939), 246
Stop That Man (1928), 90
Stranded (1916), 46
Stranger's Banquet, The (1922), 109
Street of Illusion, The (1928), 52
Strength of the Weak (1916), 365
Struggle, The (1916), 27
Student Prince, The (1927), 261
Summer Idyl, A (1910), 319
Sunrise (1927), 147
Sunshine Sue (1910), 320
Supreme Sacrifice, The (1916), 299
Susan Rocks the Boat (1916), 336
Suspicious Wife, A (1914), 201
Swamp, The (1921), 341
Sylvia of the Secret Service (1917), 183
Symbol of the Unconquered (1921), 292

Tailor Made Man, The (1922), 110
Talker, The (1925), 369
Tarzan and the Golden Lion (1927), 245, 248
Tarzan of the Apes (1918), 244
Tarzan the Mighty (1928), 245
Tarzan the Tiger (1928), 245
Tearing Down the Spanish Flag (1898), 263
Tearing Through (1925), 208
Tears and Smiles (1917), 59
Telephone Call, The (1909), 84
Telltale Step, The (1917), 76
Temple of Dusk, The (1918), 35
Temptation (1915), 44
Temptress, The (1926), 354
Ten Nights in a Bar Room (1921), 20
Ten Nights in a Bar Room (1909), 12
Tenth Case, The (1917), 123
Tess of the d'Urbervilles (1924), 39
Texas Steer, A (1915), 142
That Royle Girl (1925), 208
Their Hour (1928), 330

There Are No Villains (1921), 207
They Shall Pay (1921), 237
Thieves (1913), 84
Third Degree, The (1926), 138
Thirteenth Juror, The (1927), 167
This Woman (1924), 303
Those Who Dance (1924), 78
Those Who Toil (1916), 104
Three Fingered Jack (1910), 83
Three X Gordon (1918), 144
Thrill Hunter, The (1926), 261
Through the Wall (1916), 27
Through Turbulent Waters (1915), 48
Thunder Island (1921), 174
Time, the Comedian (1925), 328
Toby's Bow (1919), 235
Too Fat to Fight (1918), 267
Topsy and Eva (1927), 295
Toton (1919), 117
Traffic in Hearts (1924), 283
Traffic in Souls (1913), 356
Trail of the Law (1924), 175
Trap, The (1918), 233
Trapped in the Great Metropolis (1914), 357
Treasure Island (1920), 174
Tree of Knowledge, The (1920), 352
Triflers, The (1919), 155
Triumph (1917), 46
Trouble (1922), 62
True Indian Brave, A (1910), 285, 286
Trufflers, The (1917), 232
Twelve Miles Out (1927), 80
Twilight Sleep, The (1915), 113
Two Natures Within Him, The (1915), 25, 27

Unborn, The (1916), 115
Uncharted Channels (1920), 315
Uncle Sam of Freedom Ridge (1920), 271
Uncle Tom's Cabin (1918), 290
Under the Black Robe (1914), 75
Under the Greenwood Tree (1918), 154
Undercurrent, The (1919), 310
Underneath the Paint (1915), 44
Underworld (1927), 167, 228
Undine (1916), 213
Unfaithful Wife, The (1915), 34
Unholy Three, The (1925), 88, 227
Unknown Love, The (1919), 270

Unpainted Woman, The (1919), 5
Unpardonable Sin, The (1916), 15
Unveiling Hand, The (1919), 245
Up From the Depths (1915), 323
Upheaval, The (1916), 336

Vagabond King, The (1930), 72
Vagabond Prince, The (1916), 255
Valley of the Moon, The (1914), 103
Vampire, The (1915), 346
Vanishing American, The (1925), 294, 296
Velvet Paw, The (1916), 279
Vengeance of the Wilds (1915), 242
Very Idea, The (1920), 217
Via Wireless (1915), 264
Village Vampire, A (1916), 349
Virtuous Men (1919), 312
Virtuous Model, The (1919), 339
Voice in the Dark, A (1921), 126
Volcano, The (1919), 309
Volcano (1926), 294
Volga Boatman in 1926), 313
Votes for Women (1912), 363

Wages for Wives (1925), 370
Wages of Conscience (1927), 119
Wagon Show, The (1928), 136
Waifs, The (1916), 335
Walking Back (1928), 228
Wall Between, The (1916), 151
Wandering Fires (1925), 31
Wanted for Murder (1918), 268
War Brides (1916), 365
Warfare in the Skies (1914), 264
Warning, The (1915), 16
Warning, The (1927), 208
Water, Water, Everywhere (1920), 21
Way of All Flesh, The (1927), 354
Weaker Sex, The (1916), 161
Web of Chance, The (1920), 184
Welcome Stranger (1924), 293
West of Zanzibar (1928), 305
What Happened to Jones (1926), 176
What Love Forgives (1919), 47
What Money Can't Buy (1917), 255
What No Man Knows (1921), 341
What Price Glory? (1926), 271, 273
What the World Should Know (1916), 114
Whatever the Cost (1918), 171

What's His Name (1914), 189
Wheel of the Law, The (1916), 122
When a Woman Loves (1915), 140
When Dawn Came (1920), 340
When Fate Decides (1919), 60
When Fate Leads Trump (1915), 24
When Love Is King (1916), 252
When Women Win (1909), 364
Where Are My Children? (1916), 114
Where Love Leads (1916), 359
Where the Pavement Ends (1923), 293
Whispers (1920), 7
White Circle, The (1920), 77
White Man's Law, The (1918), 245
White Rose, The (1923), 328
White Shadows in the South Seas (1928), 21
White Slaver (1914), 357
White Terror, The (1915), 277
Who Cares (1925), 328
Who Loves Him Best? (1918), 234
Who Shall Take My Life? (1917), 123
Who's Your Neighbor? (1917), 300
Why Blame Me? (1918), 360
Widow's Might 1918), 172
Wild Bill Hickok (1923), 71
Wild Oats Lane (1926), 303
Wild Strain, The (1918), 214
Wild Youth (1918), 59
Wind, The (1928), 331
Witching Hour, The (1921), 166
With Lee in Virginia (1913), 67
Within Prison Walls (1927), 95
Woman and the Beast, The (1917), 132
Within the Cup (1918), 366
Without Benefit of Clergy (1921), 292
Without Honor (1917), 5
Woman (1918), 367

Woman Gives, The (1920), 206
Woman God Changed, The (1921), 165
Woman in Black, The (1915), 277
Woman in Politics, The (1916), 278
Woman in Room 13, The (1920), 165
Woman in the Suitcase (1920), 7
Woman Next Door, The (1919), 59
Woman of the World, A (1925), 146
Woman on Trial, The (1927), 167
Woman the Germans Shot, The (1918), 69
Woman Who Believed, The (1922), 247
Woman With Four Faces, The (1923), 207
Woman, Woman (1919), 144
Woman's Awakening, A (1917), 58, 59
Woman's Fight, A (1916), 365
Woman's Law, The (1916), 26
Woman's Past, A (1915), 104, 323
Woman's Resurrection, A (1915), 322
Woman's Triumph, A (1914), 92
Woman's Wit, A (1909), 83
Woman's Woman, A (1922), 368
Wonderful Adventure, (1915), 203
Wonderful Wife, A (1922), 247
Wooing of Princess Pat (1918), 256
World and Its Woman, The (1919), 312
World at Her Feet, The (1927), 197

Yankee Señor, The (1926), 260
Yellow Contraband (1928), 209
Yellow Passport, The (1916), 299
Younger Generation, The (1929), 344

Zaza (1923), 157
Zeppelin's Last Raid, The (1917), 69
Zulu's Heart, The (1908), 241

About the Author

LARRY LANGMAN is a freelance writer who has taught the art and history of film for many years. He has written or coauthored several titles, including *A Guide to American Silent Crime Films* (Greenwood, 1994), *A Guide to American Crime Films of the Forties and Fifties* (Greenwood, 1995), *A Guide to Crime Films of the Thirties* (Greenwood, 1995), and *A Guide to Silent Westerns* (Greenwood, 1992).

PN 1995.75 .L37 1998
Langman, Larry.
American film cycles

DATE DU